# BATTLESHIP NEW JERSEY

**Below:** USS *New Jersey* during the mid-1950s.

# BATTLESHIP NEW JERSEY

## An Illustrated History

### Paul Stillwell

NAVAL INSTITUTE PRESS
Annapolis, Maryland

Published and distributed in the United States of America by the Naval Institute Press, Annapolis, Maryland 21402.

Second printing, 1989

This edition is authorized for sale only in the United States and its territories and possessions.

ISBN 0-87021-029-7
Library of Congress Catalog Card No. 86-62515

Line drawings by Alan B. Chesley.

Designed by David Gibbons; layout by Anthony A. Evans; typeset by Typesetters (Birmingham) Ltd., camerawork by Anglia Repro Ltd., Rayleigh.

Printed in the United States of America

**Above:** The *New Jersey* at Hawaii, September 1968. (U.S. Naval Institute Collection)

# CONTENTS

# Preface

To go to sea in the USS *New Jersey* in the 1980s is to have the sense that she has managed to transcend the normal limitations of time. This feeling probably becomes most evident at night as she glides through the dark sea, the water making a swishing sound as it travels from bow to stern and leaves a luminescent wake beneath the starlit sky. With the coming of night, the eyes no longer focus on the details which command attention during daytime. Instead, the imagination conjures thousands of nights past when this majestic giant has also moved beneath these same stars. The darkness obscures the changes which have been wrought in order to make her again a potent weapon, as she was when she first took to the sea two generations ago.

A look back from the *New Jersey*'s forecastle fills one with a certain knowledge of why battleships have inspired awe for so long. In the foreground loom six gun barrels, each longer than many warships are wide. Beyond them is her towering superstructure, climbing toward that night sky. And one can see also the ship's bridge, illuminated by a dim red glow, as it was more than forty years ago when this was Admiral Bull Halsey's flagship at Leyte Gulf, thirty-five years ago when she steamed with the fast carriers off the east coast of Korea, nearly twenty years ago when her thunderous salvos of gunfire saved the lives of U.S. Marines ashore in Vietnam, and much more recently when she was protecting Marines in Lebanon. Now, more than four decades after doomsayers called Pearl Harbor the end of the line for battleships, she steams on yet again with the same red glow from the bridge, the same imposing superstructure, and the same guns which have for so long been a source of awe. This ship, designed in 1938, has accommodated to the passage of time and, in a sense, triumphed over it through the installation of today's technology.

During the nocturnal walk about the forecastle comes the realization that there is much more to the ship than steel, guns, and missiles. Hundreds of Navy men breathe life and purpose into her inanimate elements. It is they who give her a soul and they who inherit the legacy from thousands of *New Jersey* men who have gone before. Many of them have probably had feelings similar to those expressed by one of Herman Wouk's characters in *The Caine Mutiny* when he came aboard with the idea of seeing Admiral Halsey. "Can't you feel the difference between the *New Jersey* and the *Caine*?" he asks. "This is the Navy here, the real Navy." I had that feeling myself upon reporting to the crew of the *New Jersey* in 1969 after service in a much smaller ship, the LST *Washoe County*, off

**Right:** During the late 1960s, *New Jersey* returned to the firing line during the Vietnam War.

**Opposite page:** Lowering a 16-inch projectile through a main deck scuttle.

the coast of Vietnam. Being part of the *New Jersey*'s crew was more than a source of pride; it was a genuine thrill.

Among my most pleasant moments I count a day in June of 1969 when we arrived at Alameda, California. The deep blue sky of Northern California was a dramatic backdrop as hundreds of *New Jersey* men in dark blue uniforms lined up on that towering superstructure and listened as a band ashore played a serenade of welcome. A similar feeling came in the spring of 1983, during a brief visit to the ship. The sun was sparkling off the water as the *New Jersey* completed her refueling one morning from a fleet oiler. As I gazed down from that same superstructure, the hoses from the oiler were unhooked, and the *New Jersey*'s general announcing system played the familiar strains of "Victory at Sea".

The men who have served in the *New Jersey* at various times in the more than forty-three years since her first commissioning have tucked away many of their own special memories of time spent on board, and it is just such memories that form this book. Crewmen have been most generous in sharing their recollections through the medium of oral history and through personal letters. This, then, is a collective insiders' view of what it has been like to live and work in a great battleship in war and peace. To be sure, these men are only a fraction of the total, but in many ways their experiences are representative; one man may speak for dozens or hundreds. All the commanding officers still living have been kind enough to grant interviews. The book places special emphasis on these officers, because they, in their time, have borne the final responsibility for the operation of the ship and the welfare of her crew. And it is they, through the force of their styles of leadership, who have stamped a personality on the ship for a given period.

Even so, running such a vast enterprise is far from a one-man operation. A warship exists as an instrument of national will, and it takes hundreds of men to enable her to execute that will and to spend the thousands of hours of training and preparation needed to be ready to do so. These are real people, with all their strengths and foibles. In walking about the ship, in daytime or at night, the echoes of the past mingle with the sights and sounds of the present. And there is a certain knowledge that the men who have dwelled here have been, since 1943, the very essence of the USS *New Jersey*.

# Acknowledgements

This book would not have been possible without the cooperation of a great many people, particularly past and present crew members of the *New Jersey* who have shared their memories and personal photographs. In some instances, pictures have been pulled out of scrapbooks so they could appear in this volume. Those who have contributed their recollections, either through interviews or letters, are listed in the bibliography. Thanks to all.

The following have provided pictures from their personal collections: Commander Buford D. Abernathy, Captain Edward S. Addison, Captain Clyde B. Anderson, Rear Admiral John C. Atkeson, Arthur D. Baker III, Captain John R. Bierley, Sherman Brattin, Captain William M. Braybrook, C. J. Brooks, Jr., Mrs. Elizabeth Brunelli, Sergeant Ed Coffer, Mr. and Mrs. J. E. Coleman, Benjamin J. Conroy, Jr., John A. Cummings, Mrs. Richard Donovan, Roger Faw, L. Harlan Goodpasture, Captain Oscar E. Gray, Charles R. Hamilton, Noble C. Harris, John S. Hastings, Commander John J. Hayes, Eugene F. Hayward, Captain Erling Hustvedt, Commander Louis A. Ivey, Boatswain's Mate Second Class Charles Jacobus, Chief Musician Leonard J. Jung, Commander Dudley J. Kierulff, Captain Neville T. Kirk, Mrs. Harolyn Lawton, Rear Admiral J. Wilson Leverton, Jr., Rafael Maza, Rear Admiral Francis D. McCorkle, Mrs. Percival E. McDowell, Captain Harry W. McElwain, Ben Mehling, Mrs. George L. Menocal, Lieutenant Michael R. Nixon, Rear Admiral Edward J. O'Donnell, Commander Joseph M. Parsons, Captain Robert C Peniston, Norman Polmar, Rear Admiral Richard R. Pratt, Mrs. Frank Reagan, Christopher Reed, Commander Harry O. Reynolds, Vice Admiral Robert H. Rice, David O. Rupp, Robert Scheina, Howard Serig, Colonel Lemuel C. Shepherd III, Chief Photographer's Mate Ted Shireman, Captain Archie H. Soucek, Richard Springe, Ted Stone, Robert J. Storm, George R. Teller, Allen Trecartin, and Walter Urban. Rear Admiral Atkeson was specially generous, making available a complete file of *The Jerseyman* newspapers from his time in command, reference copies of the three *New Jersey* cruisebooks from the 1950s, as well as his collection of photographs. Ben Conroy, one of the few officers who made both of the battleship's deployments to Korea, provided a great supply of memorabilia, including a harbor chart of Wonsan, North Korea. Boatswain's Mate Charles Jacobus, an extremely enthusiastic former crew member, provided a tour of his home in Moonachie, New Jersey, including a room in which he has built a replica of his narrow *New Jersey* bunk so he can slide in whenever he feels in a battleship mood.

The following individuals made photographs available from their institutions or provided useful information in seeking the pictures: Alice Creighton and Pam Sherbert of the U.S. Naval Academy Library; Mrs. Jane Price of the U.S. Naval Academy Archives; Charles Haberlein, Agnes Hoover, John Reilly, and Michael Walker of the Naval Historical Center in Washington, D.C.; James Trimble and Paul White of the National Archives; Charlotte Valentine of The Mariners' Museum, Newport News, Virginia; Fred Rasmussen of the Baltimore *Sun*; Tom Freeman of Wide World Photos; David A. Deville of the Naval Reserve Association; Greg Gill and Karl Niederer of the New Jersey State Archives in Trenton; Kathleen Anshant of the *Beacon* newspaper at the Philadelphia Naval Shipyard; Philip Judt of *Salute* at the Puget Sound Naval Shipyard; John Venable of the Charles Edison Fund, who lent the 1950 recommissioning scrapbook of the ship's sponsor, Mrs. Charles Edison; Lieutenant Commander Eric Willenbrock and Lieutenant Commander William Clyde, two hard-working public affairs officers of the *New Jersey*; Patty Maddocks and Mary Sprawls of the U.S. Naval Institute; Dr. Evelyn Cherpak of the U.S. Naval War College; Barbara Shattuck of the National Geographic Society; Richard Hosier and Michael Tuffli of *All Hands* magazine; Bruce Bailey of the Newark *Star Ledger*; and Robert S. Kaplan, who supplied National Archives negative numbers. Joanne Foster of Blakeslee-Lane, Inc., has been most helpful in keeping track of the many photos to be printed and copied. Special thanks to a friend of long standing, Patty Maddocks of the U.S. Naval Institute, for her diligence in tracking down pictures on this and many other occasions.

Alan B. Chesley of Annapolis, Maryland, has brought to this book his great skill and painstaking craftsmanship in producing the superb drawings which depict the *New Jersey* at various stages during her career. Through his work we are able to trace the evolution of a long-lived warship.

In addition to Admiral Atkeson, several individuals lent their copies of *The Jerseyman* for reference use: Willard Bartusch, William Dugan, John Hastings, Leonard Jung, Mrs. P. E. McDowell, Joseph McGowan, and Rafael Maza.

George Hill provided the use of a *New Jersey* cruisebook for reference. Greg Gill did yeoman service in patiently making several hundred copies of pages from issues of *The Jerseyman* in the collection of the New Jersey State Archives.

Dr. Dean Allard, Ms. Martha Crawley, Robert Cressman, Ed Marolda, Wes Pryce, and Michael Walker of the Naval Historical Center provided invaluable assistance by making available documentary records on the *New Jersey's* history. Ms. Olga Mager of the office of the Chief of Naval Operations provided access to *New Jersey* deck logs from the post-World War II era. Frank Uhlig of the U.S. Naval War College drew upon his considerable expertise to supply helpful comments after reading draft versions of the various chapters in the manuscript. Howard Serig, a writer and photographer has been helpful in a variety of ways.

A number of individuals have facilitated the oral interviews with former crew members by putting me in touch with them. Included are Russell Brown of the *New Jersey* Reunion Group (1414 South Western Avenue, Champaign, Illinois 61821) and Chief Signalman David Graham of the American Battleship Association (Post Office Box 11247, San Diego, California 92111). Mr. Ed Hill of the USS *Franks* reunion group helped track down men who were serving in that destroyer when she collided with the *New Jersey* in April 1945. A source of kind and frequent help has been Leon Morrison, vice president of the Battleship New Jersey Historical Museum Society and editor of its informative monthly newsletter. Leon's assistance has undoubtedly made this a better book than it would have been without his participation. For those who are interested in joining this worthwhile organization, the address is Post Office Box BB-62, Middletown, New Jersey 07748.

Captain (now Rear Admiral) William Fogarty and Lieutenant Commander (now Commander) Eric Willenbrock were quite helpful during my two-week visit to the modernized *New Jersey* in the spring of 1983. The stay on board was useful in gaining an appreciation in the changes in the ship since my own service in 1969. More recently, Lieutenant Commander William Clyde and Chief Journalist Lon Cabot have greatly facilitated the work of bringing the story of the ship up to date. Also helpful in that regard is Commander Rich Gano, weapons officer of the USS *Iowa* in the summer of 1985 when I visited. He facilitated my interviews with a number of men in his department who had previously served in the *New Jersey*. Commander T. A. Goodall of Long Beach has also supplied helpful inputs on the recent history of the *New Jersey*.

Thomas Epley of the Naval Institute Press and Lionel Levethal of Arms & Armour Press, Ltd., deserve a great deal of thanks for the vision and support needed to transform this book from concept to reality. Mr. David Gibbons of Arms & Armour has contributed his considerable expertise in the editorial and graphics areas to give the volume its impressive look.

Finally, I am grateful to family members who exercised a great deal of forbearance when they might have preferred for me to be doing other things besides writing a book: my wife Karen and my sons Joseph, Robert, and James.

...NG OF BB-62
...OWN WAYS.
...RD PHILA. DEC.7-1942

# CHAPTER I
# FROM DRAWING BOARD TO WARSHIP
## September 1940–January 1944

High above the Philadelphia Navy Yard and the Delaware River, the December sky was laced with the tracks of American fighter planes, bombers, and blimps. Their presence was part of the celebration of the birth and christening of the future battleship *New Jersey*. Far below, at the head of shipways number two, Mrs. Carolyn Edison, the wife of New Jersey's governor, was celebrating the first anniversary of Pearl Harbor day by opening a bottle of champagne. She did so at 2:16 p.m. by smashing the bottle energetically across the olive drab nose of the still-unfinished battleship. The giant hull, which towered five storeys above the building ways, began to slide and then moved ever more quickly away from Mrs. Edison. Her brown mink coat by now covered with champagne, the governor's wife expressed her jubilation by blowing kisses with both hands as the steel behemoth picked up speed and then hit the water with a splash and resulting wave that drenched the shoes of many who were standing too near the river's edge.

Applause from the crowd of 20,000 mingled with the hooting of the *New Jersey*'s whistle and the pouring forth from her stack of oily black smoke – smoke that was still taken as a sign of industrial progress in a nation not yet accustomed to condemning air pollution. After it hit the water following a sixty-second journey down the ways, the 887-foot-long hull described a graceful arc which ended in an unexpected encounter with the state for which it had been named only moments before. The *New Jersey*, in nascent exuberance, reached across to touch the New Jersey shore of the Delaware River. The encounter was but a brief one. Within minutes, a gaggle of puffing tugboats took the hull in tow and brought it back to the shipyard for completion and readiness for certain combat with an enemy far across the seas. Speeches followed from Governor Charles Edison and Under Secretary of the Navy James V. Forrestal. Singer Kate Smith added the proper closing tone to the occasion by booming out her rousing specialty: "God Bless America".

One year before, almost to the hour, Japanese fighters and bombers had traced deadly patterns above Pearl Harbor – sowing their crop of damage and destruction. Now, on 7 December 1942, a different sort of crop was coming in – one that would prove a bitter harvest for the Imperial Japanese Navy.

The design process for the ship christened by Mrs. Edison is covered in an appendix. On 1 July 1939, with the basic design complete, the contract for the construction of the battleship was awarded to the Philadelphia Navy Yard. The New York Navy Yard would build the first ship of the class, the *Iowa*. The New York yard was thus the lead yard, and its central drafting office would be responsible for the designing of the many changes which inevitably take place between contract design and completion of a ship. Philadelphia, as the follow yard, would incorporate in the *New Jersey* the changes designed for the class.

Even as the hundreds of shipboard compartments were taking shape on drafting tables, the name for the planned BB-62 was a subject of interest. Already in 1937, when it was apparent that a large battleship construction program was in the offing, citizens in New Jersey had begun petitioning the Navy to have one of the new warships named for their state. In addition to many private citizens, those making the request included a variety of politicians and members of veterans' organizations. Especially prominent among the latter, as the campaign picked up in 1938, were veterans of the Spanish-American War, which was then just forty years in the past.

The campaign on behalf of the state bore fruit shortly after the construction contract for BB-62 was awarded to Philadelphia. On 7 July 1939, Secretary of the Navy Claude A. Swanson died after several years of failing health. For a number of months, Assistant Secretary of the Navy Charles Edison had been acting in Swanson's stead. Now he was officially made Acting Secretary, and in that capacity he approved the name "New Jersey" on 11 July. Son of the famous inventor Thomas A. Edison, the Acting Secretary of the Navy didn't have his father's creative genius, but he was a capable businessman and a solid administrator. As Assistant Secretary he had been particularly concerned with improving the speed and efficiency of the Navy's shipbuilding. Since he was a lifelong resident of the state of New Jersey, it was not surprising that the name should be bestowed on one of the new battleships. In another move at the same time, he approved the use of the name "Edison" for a new destroyer, DD-439, to honor his father's contributions to Navy research during World War I.

In the months that followed, the Philadelphia Navy Yard took steps to be ready to build the *New Jersey* and her projected sister *Wisconsin* side by side. The existing shipways were insufficient in both length and supporting capacity for the 45,000 tonners. The shipways were able to accommodate construction of the 35,000-ton *Washington*; her

keel had been laid at Philadelphia in June 1938, and the hull was launched in June 1940. Shipways numbers two and three were lengthened in 1940 to 1,135 feet each – an increase of 325½ feet for the site of the *New Jersey*'s construction. Additional pilings were driven into the Philadelphia mud, and two new sets of ground ways were built to support the massive hull. For the *Washington*, one parallel pair of 9-foot-wide ground ways had been sufficient. Now two more ground ways were needed, a 5-foot-wide one next to each of the first pair.

In that year of 1940, the world was in considerable turmoil. The German war machine was on the march in Europe, and President Franklin D. Roosevelt was so concerned by Japanese designs on East Asia that he began to have the U.S. Battle Force stationed at Pearl Harbor in the hope that it would serve as a deterrent. In the political arenas, FDR was considering an unprecedented third run for the presidency. To disarm his political opponents, the President cited the peril facing the nation and added Republicans to his cabinet as Secretary of War and Secretary of the Navy. Charles Edison's status had changed from Acting Secretary to Secretary of the Navy in January 1940, and in June he left the new job when Roosevelt asked him to step aside in favor of Frank Knox. To sweeten the departure for Edison, Roosevelt offered his support for Edison to run for Governor of New Jersey, to which office

he was elected in the November general election which gave the President his third term.

The physical manifestation of the battleship *New Jersey* began on 16 September 1940, when her keel was laid on the newly enlarged ways. The honor of welding the first two keel plates together fell to former Secretary and future Governor Edison. In the months to come, that keel grew to considerable length, frames were attached, and the collection of steel began to take on a shape that would in time be recognized as that of a ship. In charge of supervising the large work force building the hull were Lieutenant Commander Francis X. "Savvy" Forest and 6-foot 6-inch Lieutenant Commander Allan L. "High Pockets" Dunning. Both were naval constructors with considerable experience in the technical aspects of ship repair and construction.

The building of a warship of the *New Jersey*'s dimensions is a vast enterprise – assembling all sorts of components produced in various parts of the country. Of necessity, they must come together and be put in place in a fairly rigid sequence. Writing in the shipyard's newspaper *Beacon*, Lieutenant Commander Forest paid tribute to the thousands of individuals whose joint efforts went into the *New Jersey*:

"Many of the most necessary parts of the construction [and] the launching of this ship depend entirely upon the

**Above:** Ship superintendents and shop supervisors involved in the construction of the *New Jersey* pose shortly before launching. The tall naval officer standing in the center of the second row is Lieutenant Commander Allan Dunning, assistant hull superintendent; the shorter officer next to him is Lieutenant Harry Reynolds. Reynolds, an assistant machinery superintendent assigned to the shipyard, requested assignment to the *New Jersey* and served in the crew throughout her time in combat. (Courtesy of Commander Harry O. Reynolds, USN[Ret.])

**Right:** Former Secretary of the Navy Charles Edison begins construction of the *New Jersey* on 16 September by welding together the first two keel plates. His father, Thomas A. Edison, was the inventor of the electric light-bulb, phonograph, and many other items. (Courtesy of the Charles Edison Fund)

steady hand of the machinist who scrapes the bearing, of the shipfitter who places the steel, of the shipwright who shores and supports the structure and carefully sets the staging that men's lives may be safe while working. All of the skilled trades, the blacksmiths, the toolmakers and electricians, and others by their own touch, place in the ship that which no specification or plan can provide. Not the least of this coordinated group are the riggers, who place every piece of material in its place, safely handling single weights of hundreds of tons, always with the forethought to ensure that the painstaking labor of the other crafts will not be wasted by a single misstep at the last instant. Nor should we forget that the laborers, sweepers and fire watchers play an equally important part in the building of the ship; for without them the chaos of scrap and dirt, and the many other tasks would be a hopeless burden."

All told, the size of the work force involved in the *New Jersey*'s construction amounted to perhaps 6,000–8,000 men and women, including those in various shops. Considering the turnover which took place during the many months while the ship was under construction, Dunning estimates that the number of individuals who had a hand in the process at one time or another was probably in excess of 10,000. One of those thousands was Sam Kuncevich, a young shipfitter's helper. He recalls the

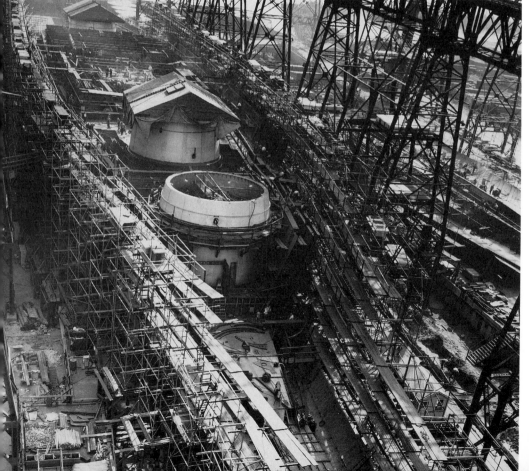

1940–42 period when he was in the yard as a time when there was a "spirit to get things done, to get ships built". After a time, work on the *New Jersey* proceeded around the clock in three shifts. For the day shift, the lunchtime period was a special event. Celebrities were frequently on hand to exhort the yard workers to ever greater efforts and to urge people to buy bonds to finance the nation's war effort. Kuncevich remembers a fight song which included the lyrics, "We're gonna have to slap the dirty little Japs, and Uncle Sam's the guy who can do it."

Throughout the building period, there was a great sense of rivalry with the New York Navy Yard, which had begun the *Iowa* nearly three months before the *New Jersey*'s keel was laid and which would put the *Iowa* into commission three months and one day before the *New Jersey*. In part, there was competition over scarce war materials, which had to be allocated not only to other shipbuilding projects but also to aircraft, tanks, jeeps, and many other things. The allocations were officially set down in the Controlled Materials Plan, although the red-tape CMP came in time to be known more popularly as "Christ, More Paper."

Lieutenant Commander Dunning was in constant contact with steel and armor manufacturers. Certain sketch plates of special treatment steel became particularly critical in the progress of building the *New Jersey* as her scheduled launching date neared. During a visit to Philadelphia, Spider Steigerwalt, a division superintendent for U.S. Steel, asked Dunning if there were any plates he could expedite. Despite the CMP, he was willing to help a friend. Dunning listed his needs, and within a week several railroad cars loaded with steel arrived for the *New Jersey* – plates that were already cut and shaped for specific locations in a battleship. The original address to the New York Navy Yard had been crossed out, and the steel was readdressed to Dunning instead.

The schedule was especially tight with regard to armor plate. Unlike older generations of battleships, the *Iowa* class had internal side belt armor, so the heavy armor was installed while the ship was still on the ways rather than after launching. For the *New Jersey* the supplier of the belt armor was the Midvale Steel Company of North Philadelphia. The armor was routinely shipped from there to the navy yard by railroad cars. For one critical section of lower side belt armor, however, a special shipment was made with a low-bed trailer truck accompanied by police escort to clear the way through city traffic. The plate was still so hot from its final treatment that workmen standing on the plate put an asbestos pad on it to keep their shoes from burning. The lower side belt armor plates weighed about thirty tons apiece and were machined to key to each other in assemblies of three plates. Together with butt straps and adjoining frames, these assemblies weighed about 100 tons for erection on the ship by bridge cranes over the building ways.

The ship's propulsion machinery also had to be installed while the hull was still on the building ways so that decks above the turbines and boilers could be built, and work on construction of the superstructure could proceed. Lieutenant Harry O. Reynolds, who later became a member of the *New Jersey*'s wartime crew, was in the shipyard's machinery department. He remembers that the boiler components were supplied by the firm of Babcock & Wilcox and then erected in the shipyard and lowered into the hull by overhead cranes. Sometime after the keel was laid, construction had progressed far enough to permit building of the boiler foundations, and then the boilers themselves went in during the latter part of 1941. The main engines – one for each of the *New Jersey*'s four propellers – also went into the ship in a prearranged sequence. Reynolds says, "Number four was the last one to go in, and I was on pins and needles as to whether we were going to get it in in time. We had to leave part of the main deck open just forward of number three turret." The engine got in just on schedule.

Plans for the *Iowa* (and thus the *New Jersey*) changed frequently as the building progressed, so Dunning sent a man weekly to the central drafting office in New York to get the latest revisions. Sometimes, he would gamble and go ahead with a preliminary design change before the final version was approved. As a result, three different foremasts were built for the *New Jersey* before the last one was adopted and installed. Other changes included the replacement of the original 1.1-inch guns of the antiaircraft

U.S.S. NEW JERSEY (BB
LOOKING FWD FROM AMID
NAVY YARD, PHILA. JULY 8-
1020-42-B.

**Right:** The bow of the *New Jersey* towers above the bunting-decorated speakers' platform the day of her launching, 7 December 1942. The anchors and anchor chains are suspended from the hawsepipes. (Courtesy of Philadelphia Naval Shipyard)

**Opposite page, top:** The impressive scope of the *New Jersey*'s hull is particularly apparent in this view taken on the day of her launching. The conning tower as yet has no bridge structure around it. The 5-inch guns are in place but covered with canvas rather than their steel mounts. Circular sheds cover the turret barbettes. The light grey paint above the waterline is a holdover from the Navy's prewar color scheme. Before the *New Jersey*'s commissioning, dark blue-grey would become her above-water hue. (National Archives: 19-LCM-BB62/C-4)

**Opposite page, bottom:** A stern view of the *New Jersey*'s underwater hull on 7 December 1942, shortly before launching, shows the protruding shafts to which her propellers soon will be attached. The rudder posts extend down from the hull, inboard of the screws. After poppets help distribute the hull's weight on the ways, as the forepoppets do at the bow. (National Archives: 19-N-94730)

battery with 40-mm. and 20-mm. guns. The war in Europe was demonstrating the vital contribution of antiaircraft guns to a ship's defense, so they were situated all over the *New Jersey*'s topside spaces, along with the necessary magazines and directors. Another big change was the moving of the combat information center from the superstructure to down inside the armored box of the hull. The CIC grew in size to the dimensions of a space on the fourth deck originally planned as a magazine.

The biggest event in the building of the *New Jersey* was her launching. To facilitate the first trip into the water, the ways were built on a slight incline – or "declivity" as naval engineers call it – of $9/16$ of an inch in height for each foot of horizontal length. At the time of launching, the hull of the *New Jersey*, including men on board and attached dunnage, weighed 36,447 tons. This made her the largest U.S. ship launched from inclined ways up to that time. The *Iowa* had weighed 36,346 tons at the time of launching in August 1942; the British liner *Queen Mary*, built in the 1930s, was launched at 36,700 tons.

To get the giant hull of the *New Jersey* waterborne, its immense weight had to be transferred from the fixed supports – keel blocks, cribbing, and shoring timbers – to the sliding ways which would go with the hull into the water. The wooden sliding ways, 17,000 square feet in area, were matched with the ground ways, and the two sets were separated by nearly 100,000 pounds of grease to facilitate sliding when the time came – hence the term "greasing the ways". On top of the sliding ways were wedge riders to carry blocking, each piece of which was specially cut and fitted to the contour of the ship's bottom. At the bow and stern, where the hull was narrower than amidships, boxy poppets were constructed to distribute the ship's weight more evenly on the ways. Once the weight of the ship was on the sliding ways, the hull was held in place by triggers pivoted in the ground ways and held in the cocked position until released by hydraulically controlled pistons.

After Mrs. Edison broke the ceremonial bottle of champagne and pronounced the words which christened the hull *New Jersey*, Rear Admiral Allan J. Chantry, industrial manager of the shipyard, flashed a signal light to alert the trigger pit crew. Frank Bonsack, who had been an employee of the shipyard since before the turn of the century, pulled a lever which opened a hydraulic valve. That knocked out the triggers, and the ship took her minute-long trip to the Delaware River. Even in that short space of time, she got up to a speed of 28.3 feet per second – nearly 20 miles per hour – which was entirely a combination of gravity and momentum, for the hull had nothing except Mrs. Edison's champagne bottle to give it a push. Huge hydraulic jacks were available if the ship had stuck, but they weren't needed.

To add a special flair to the launching, Lieutenant Reynolds had the ship's whistle installed ahead of time

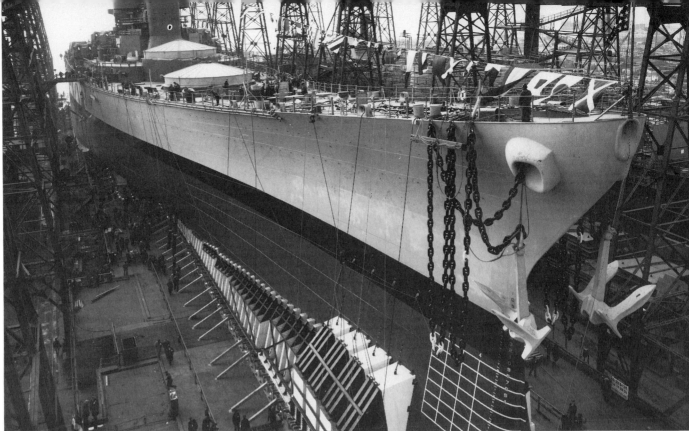

LAUNCHING
VIEW OF
NAVY YARD
1720-

and hooked it up to a steam boiler which had been borrowed from a shipyard crane and hoisted to a position inside one of the *New Jersey*'s smokestacks. In addition, explains Dunning, "Oily rags were thrown into the firebox of the boiler so that black smoke was pouring out of the stack as the deep sound of the whistle echoed against the structural shop next to the building ways." An officer who came to Philadelphia from the New York Navy Yard to observe the launching of the *New Jersey* described the smoke-and-whistle show with scorn – and perhaps a trace of envy – as "typical Philadelphia showmanship".

As the hull went down the ways, one person watching was ten-year-old Joseph Forest, son of the yard's hull superintendent. He held his breath, 'wondering if the ship would break free and whether or not she would float once in the water". She did float, of course, but then a new problem arose. As a means of checking the hull's considerable momentum down the ways, a series of clumps of anchor chain was placed on the riverbank on the vessel's starboard side. To these clumps were attached arresting cables to slew the hull round in an arc to bring it nearly parallel to the course of the river. Shortly before the launching day, the shipyard decided to change the number of slewing cables from three to two to reduce the possibility of having the cables foul each other. It was to prove an embarrassing miscalculation. Because of the extra motion which resulted, the buoyant wooden cradle under the ship was slightly damaged when it struck either a mudbank or submerged pilings on the New Jersey shore, even though the hull itself was untouched.

After the launching the hull was moved by tugboats to a water-filled dry dock so the roller paths on which the turrets would turn could be machined. It was better to perform this operation with the ship afloat rather than still on the ways, because now she was in the position she would be in when the turrets were operated. After the approximately two weeks it took for the turret job to be accomplished, the water in the dock was pumped down so wires could be attached to the floor of the dock and run between the bottom of the hull and the launching cradle. The dock could then be refilled, and the hull was supposed to float free from the cradle secured to the dock floor. The ship started back out of the dock in normal fashion, but when the stern was about 70 feet across the sill of the dock, it would go no farther. The ship was stuck. It could not back out or be pulled into the dock. Dunning remembers the problem vividly, "Thus it stayed for a period of several cold days and nights in January while the ice formed around it. At low tide the ship would list to port and come back upright with the incoming tide."

**The mystery was solved when shipyard divers went down under the ship and found the problem to be one of the wedge riders knocked out of position during the unexpected grounding on the state of New Jersey.** One end of the piece of timber had dug into teeth-like brackets pro-

jecting from the side of one of the large vertical skegs to which a propeller would later be attached. The other end of the timber was jammed into the floor of the dry dock. The wedge rider, which should have come free from the ship, had got into a diagonal position so that it served as a giant latch, preventing movement in either direction. Once the cause was discovered, the solution was to wait for the next high tide to put the ship as nearly as possible in the position she was in when the stoppage occurred. Then with all the power available from dock capstans, dock cranes, and yard locomotives, the *New Jersey* was pulled back into the dock. The troublesome wedge rider was then freed. On reflooding of the dock, the ship floated clear of the cradle, and the undocking proceeded normally.

The *New Jersey* was then moved to the shipyard's pier four for outfitting – the installation of the 16-inch turrets, fire control tower, bridge structure, and all sorts of topside equipment. Much still remained to be done inside the ship as well. Alas, the battleship continued to be plagued by a comedy of errors. In constructing the massive armored conning tower from which the ship would be steered and directed, it was necessary to perform repeated welding operations before she was launched. The cold winter weather of Philadelphia cracked the welded joints, so they had to be burned out and done again. To protect the new joints, a wood-and-tarpaper house was built over the conning tower while the ship was at the fitting-out pier, and the house was heated. During the rewelding, the house caught fire, and flames were leaping up through the framework of the large hammerhead crane alongside.

Lieutenant Commander Dunning was alarmed by the whole turn of events:

"Of course, I rushed down to the dock, and immediately the Marine guards were set up under the captain of the yard and just cordoned off everything so people couldn't go on and off the ship. And here were the firemen throwing water, and I was concerned, because, although we wanted to put the fire out, I didn't want to have this preheated conning tower again quenched with water and crack all the welds all over again. And also I was concerned that the water – fighting a fire aboard a ship afloat there's always that danger that you'll flood the ship to the extent that it will turn over."

The fire, though spectacular, was not dangerous *per se*. The real danger would come if the wooden staging inside the hull caught fire. Dunning was able to get past the Marine guards and send people below to turn off electrical power so no short circuits would set off a below-decks blaze. Fortunately, the fire was put out with no significant damage to the ship, and the outfitting continued.

Next on the schedule was the precarious operation when the gun turrets were to be installed on the barbettes in January. The barbettes themselves had been installed by overhead cranes when the hull was still on the building

ways, and wooden sheds were built over the openings to protect them from the weather. The frameworks, or weldments, for the turrets were constructed in the navy yard's turret shop, where Lieutenant Jim Terry was the officer in charge. His instructions were to build as much of the framework as he could ashore, because construction was easier there than in the cramped spaces aboard ship. The limiting factor was the huge hammerhead crane on the fitting-out pier. The crane's rated capacity was 350 tons, but it had been proof tested to 435 tons prior to the launching of the *New Jersey*, so Terry was authorized to make the turret weldments up to 400 tons. The weldment included the machined upper roller path that would fit into the rollers placed in the lower roller path atop the turret's foundation. The weldment also carried the foundations to accept the gun barrels with their breech mechanisms, the framework to support the turret armor, and all sorts of miscellaneous foundations and stowages.

When the weldment for turret one was ready, a barge went into one end of the turret shop, and the weldment was put on for transfer to the ship. It had been impossible to weigh the finished product, but Lieutenant Terry had been adding the cumulative weights of the various components, and he concluded the turret was about 400 tons at that point. Thus, it was more than a little unsettling

Opposite page, top left: The framework for the *New Jersey*'s turret two is being lifted from a barge alongside the ship in preparation for lowering into the barbette. The structure shown here weighed more than 400 tons, thus overloading the crane's rated capacity of 350. Because turret two is elevated to fire over turret one, it has an extra projectile deck and thus a larger capacity than the other two turrets. (Courtesy of Philadelphia Naval Shipyard)

Opposite page, top right: Having been lifted from the barge, the turret two framework is put in place overtop the barbette. Originally, the Bureau of Ordnance designed a larger turret than this for the *Iowa* class but had to scale back its design to fit the barbette diameter specified in Bureau of Construction and Repair plans for the hull. (Courtesy of Philadelphia Naval Shipyard)

Opposite page, bottom: This picture was taken looking down into the upper shell flat of the *New Jersey*'s turret one just before installation of the turret framework on 13 January 1943. (Courtesy of Philadelphia Naval Shipyard)

Right: The framework for turret one is lowered into position atop the barbette on 13 January 1943. The rows of holes in the framework are to be used for bolting on heavy slabs of armor plate. (Courtesy of Philadelphia Naval Shipyard)

Far right: In this view, looking forward, the lifelines at the bow of the ship can be seen in the background as turret one is put into place on 13 January 1943. In the foreground is the after part of the turret – the booth to be manned by the turret officer and turret captain. The vertical openings in the near bulkhead go into the individual gun rooms for the three 16-inch guns. (Courtesy of Philadelphia Naval Shipyard)

BB-62 - 16" TURRET #2
BEING LOWERED INTO POSITION.
NAVY YARD, PHILA. JAN. 13-1943.
60-43-H.

62 - 16" TURRET #1
ING ARRANGEMENT.
Y YARD, PHILA. PA. JAN. 13-1943
60-43-K.

when he measured the draft at the four corners of the loaded barge and calculated that the crane would be picking up 416 tons – not much safety margin. Once the barge was alongside the ship, the crane lifted the turret weldment, positioned it above the barbette opening, and gradually lowered it into place. Lieutenant Terry, mindful that he would be blamed if a mishap occurred when the turret weight exceeded the 400 tons specified, decided to "hold my tongue and STAY UNDER THE LOAD AT ALL TIMES WHEN IT WAS IN THE AIR!" If the crane failed and the load dropped, there wouldn't be anything left of Jim Terry to answer questions at the inevitable investigation which would follow.

As it happened, the whole thing went smoothly and was followed by turrets two and three. The tops of the barbettes for turrets one and three extended a few feet above the main deck, while that for turret two rose from the 01 level. Turret two is the ship's high turret, extending one level higher to enable it to shoot over turret one. Because of the extra level, turret two has a larger projectile capacity – 475, compared with 405 for turret one and 385 for turret three.

After the turret weldments were in place, the lower structure for each – the electricity deck and projectile handling platforms – was jacked up from inside the barbette and hung from the main weldment so that the portions which would go along with the turret during rotation were moving freely. Armor for the sides and back was put in place and machined to fit together. Up above, the crane lowered the 16-inch guns into place in the framework. Each gun, with its associated breech mechanism, weighed 167 tons. A 16-inch/50 caliber gun means that the length of the barrel, excluding the part in the breechblock, is measured in the number of inches determined by multiplying barrel diameter, 16, times caliber, 50. The result is 800 inches, with the breech mechanism adding 16 more inches for a total of 68 feet.

After the guns were in place, each turret's front plate, weighing more than 100 tons, was threaded on around the guns and attached to the framework. Then came the top armor plates, and the massive turret was entirely enclosed. The weight of the entire rotating turret structure on its path of eighty-four tapered rollers is some 1,850 tons – more than the standard displacement of a number of destroyers which fought during World War II.

The final items in the completion of the turrets included installation of the powder and projectile hoists, training and elevating mechanisms, hydraulic lines, rammers, and so forth. In essence, a gun turret is a huge piece of machinery which has to be put together a piece at a time and connected. The success of the project can be measured by the fact that those turrets are still performing well more than forty years after they were installed.

As the yard work proceeded apace in early 1943, prospective members of the New Jersey's crew were arriving for duty and making their wishes known on details of completion. The ship still belonged to the custody of the Philadelphia Navy Yard and the Bureau of Ships, but the desires of the men who would steam and fight the New Jersey needed to be taken into account, for she would soon be theirs.

The man who was chosen to be the first commanding officer of the new battleship was forty-seven-year-old Captain Carl F. Holden. He had been serving in Washington as communication officer on Admiral Ernest J. King's U.S. Fleet staff and later as Director of Naval Communications. A 1917 graduate of the Naval Academy, Holden had earned a master's degree in electrical engineering from Harvard University and had a solid background of sea duty behind him. Holden was a serious, capable, and ambitious officer. As he later explained to Ensign King G. Brandt, a reserve officer who had come to the ship from duty in Washington, "When I heard the New Jersey was going to be coming down the line, I put my foot out for it." In all likelihood, Holden had Admiral King's support in getting the assignment. There were many more qualified captains in the Navy than there were battleships going into commission.

While yard employees were in the process of completing the ship, future crew members were working also to get her ready to go. Warrant Gunner Robert L. Moore obtained empty powder tanks and dummy 16-inch projectiles in order to check stowage conditions in the projectile flats and the magazines. He wanted to check ammunition battens and also to make sure the ammunition handling wouldn't be obstructed by pipes. Lieutenant Harry Reynolds was down in the engineering spaces, lighting off the boilers and conducting tests of the steam lines. The New Jersey was equipped with high-pressure boilers rated at 600 pounds of steam per square inch, capable, with the geared turbines of the four main engines, of producing 212,000 shaft horsepower and the designed speed of 33 knots.

As more and more of the enlisted crew members arrived, they took up residence in a receiving barracks on the naval base in Philadelphia. They went to the ship daily to become acquainted with their duty stations and to handle such requirements as standing by with fire extinguishers to quell any fires that might break out during welding by shipyard workers.

Sometimes the future crew members got involved in the completion of the ship. Gunner's Mate Second Class Ellis Mamroth reported to the precommissioning detail after several months of on-the-job training in a two-gun 12-inch turret in the USS Arkansas. Commissioned in 1912, she was

the oldest U.S. battleship to perform active service during World War II. Going from the oldest to the newest was a distinct pleasure for Mamroth, especially when he observed that the *New Jersey*'s turret arrangement was much safer than that in the *Arkansas*. In the older ship, he could stand in the turret booth and see the breeches of both guns at the same time. In the *New Jersey*, each turret was divided into three separate gun rooms so that an explosion or problem in one gun wouldn't necessarily disrupt the entire turret. Mamroth recalls working in turret three with manufacturers' technical representatives, such as those from General Electric who helped install receiver-regulators for gun elevation and train.

Morale in the *New Jersey* was high, in part because of the sense of purpose and excitement which accompanied the process of getting the ship ready for war. "By far, my happiest time in the Navy was aboard the *New Jersey*," says Mamroth. "It was essentially what you would call a happy ship." He remembers that Captain Holden seemed to have a lot of regard for everybody in the crew. If there was any sort of gripe about such things as food or living conditions, Holden would set about immediately to correct it. In the early days, prior to commissioning, when the crew consisted mostly of officers and senior petty officers, Holden had a couple of standup meetings with the future Jerseymen in order to encourage them in their efforts.

For Ensign Bill Coyne, an officer assigned to fire control for the ship's antiaircraft gun battery, much of the precommissioning period was spent in "helping to draw up organization plans, battle bills, cataloguing equipment, looking for spare parts, and a myriad of other administrative chores associated with getting the ship ready for active duty". He checked over the four Mark 37 directors which would control the 5-inch guns and familiarized himself with the two plotting rooms for those guns – secondary forward and secondary aft. Each contained a Mark 1 anti-aircraft computer and stable elements through which a gyroscope maintained a true reference plane so that the guns would remain on target even when the ship was rolling and pitching around them. At first, Coyne remembers, he was terrified by the fire control switchboard, a complex maze of several hundred switches which linked up the gun mounts, directors, and computers in various combinations. In time the whole thing turned out to be quite simple and understandable.

Every morning and afternoon, Coyne walked from the shipyard office that had been set up for the ship's precommissioning detail, because he wanted to check on progress being made. "And the progress was astounding," he remembers. "With yard workmen on the job 24 hours a day, 7 days a week, things were happening in a hurry. Equipment would be put aboard one day, and completely wired up and checked out within two days." In that period,

Below: On 14 January 1943, just after installation of turrets one and two, the *New Jersey* sits alongside her outfitting pier at the Philadelphia Navy Yard. In the background are cranes used to install various pieces of top-side equipment. (Courtesy of Philadelphia Naval Shipyard)

Below right: The loop of cable dangling from the overhead indicates that the *New Jersey*'s combat information center was still not finished when this photo was taken. At left is the watch officer's position, including a regular telephone and an intercom. In the center of the photo are the radar scopes. (Courtesy of the Philadelphia Naval Shipyard)

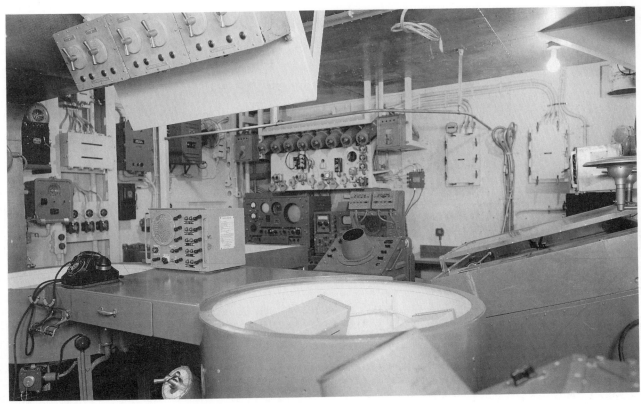

"things were falling into place rapidly as the commissioning drew closer. The battle bill was completed; the ship's organization book was being mimeographed; watch, quarter and station bills were being fleshed out with actual names as more and more of the crew arrived on station; training classes were being held on a daily basis; and equally important, we were getting acquainted with our shipmates, many of whom would become close friends before the war was over."

In the three-month period before the *New Jersey* went into commission, the enlisted men slated for her crew went through a large-scale program of psychological testing, interviewing, and evaluation established by Commander Percival E. "Pete" McDowell, the prospective executive officer. McDowell had had no formal education in psychology, but he had read a good deal about the subject. He saw the *New Jersey* as a giant laboratory in which he could analyze the requirements of the many jobs on board ship and evaluate hundreds of men in order to assign them to the duties for which their skills best fitted them. For instance, those who scored high in verbal skills and speaking ability would serve as talkers on the sound-powered telephone circuits. In a paper written afterwards, McDowell reported that his program "produced almost spectacular results". Other men on board the *New Jersey* viewed the whole thing with a touch of skepticism.

Certainly the testing program achieved better results than if the 90 per cent of the crew with no seagoing experience had been assigned entirely at random, and it also had an interesting side effect engineered by a puckish side of McDowell's nature. Along with the three male interviewers from the Navy's Bureau of Personnel there were two young Navy women who provided clerical help as stenographers. As the day of commissioning approached, Commander McDowell told the two WAVES to go back to Washington and return with white uniforms. Since they had been working with the crew from the beginning, he felt it appropriate that they be in uniform and standing with the men of the *New Jersey* when the ship went into commission.

The day of commissioning fell on Sunday, 23 May 1943, and it turned out to be a warm, beautiful, sunny spring day – an auspicious one for the ship's beginning. The crew was called by reveille at 6:00 a.m. in their barracks, sent for breakfast, and then mustered with seabags and hammocks for the march to the ship. It was still an era when sailors carried hammocks and bedding as part of their luggage from duty station to duty station. Among the men making the march "after we lashed everything in seagoing fashion" was Fireman Second Class Russell Brown. Initially the crew marched in ranks, but things gradually got more ragged and unsteady as the weight of the luggage took effect. "You started out real good," says Brown, "but toward the end you were leaning way over."

Once aboard ship, the men stowed their lockers, made up their bunks, and moved in. The ship was theirs at last. Even though commissioning was largely a symbolic milestone, it nevertheless marked the time when control passed from shipyard to crew. More work was needed before the *New Jersey* could go to sea and fight, but she was essentially complete. As the morning progressed, the men gave the ship a final sweepdown, and the 2,400 officers and enlisted men who comprised the crew began to gather on the fantail in dress whites.

Lieutenant Jim Phelan had the quarterdeck watch as various VIPs arrived for the ceremony. At one point, he dispatched a messenger to tell Captain Holden of an especially important visitor who was scheduled to come aboard. Instead of going to the inside door of the captain's cabin and thus having to state his business to the Marine orderly on duty, the messenger went in through the door from the 01 level weather deck. Hearing the captain was in the shower, he apparently stuck his head around the curtain and told Holden that the officer of the deck had said for him to get down to the quarterdeck right away. About ten minutes later, a highly irritated Holden arrived at the quarterdeck and started to chew out Phelan, saying, "A commanding officer does not take orders from the officer of the deck." Fortunately for Phelan, an official car pulled up just then, and the OOD was spared the rest of the tongue-lashing. It was some weeks before he got up enough nerve to raise the subject with the captain and learn of the unfortunate choice of words the messenger had used when he interrupted Holden's shower.

When it came time for the ceremony, admirals and other dignitaries were everywhere, some of them shepherded by Lieutenant Julius C. C. Edelstein, a reserve officer who had just come from duty at the White House. He looked after civilian VIPs, including Governor and Mrs. Edison, who were on the platform aft of turret three for the ceremony. Present to conduct the formal commissioning was Rear Admiral Milo F. Draemel, Commandant of the Fourth Naval District and the Philadelphia Navy Yard. Admiral Draemel read the commissioning authorization and at 12:38 p.m. directed that the USS *New Jersey* be placed in commission. The American flag, union jack, and commissioning pennant were hoisted, and the first watch was set on the quarterdeck.

Captain Holden then read his orders and assumed command of the *New Jersey*. Throughout his tour in the ship, Holden would be concerned with the welfare of his men and infusing them with a fighting spirit. Lieutenant Edelstein, whose duties included serving as Holden's speechwriter, helped draft the captain's commissioning remarks. Among Holden's words that day were the following:

"This new existence, this new warrior of the deep, yesterday was an 'it', a mere structure of steel, a stout hull

**Right:** Some 2,400 officers and men are formed up on the broad fantail for the *New Jersey*'s commissioning ceremony on the afternoon of Sunday, 23 May 1943. The speakers' platform is at the base of turret three. To the right and below the American flag is the after fire control tower for the main battery, and to the right of that, a Mark 37 director for the 5-inch guns. An official car sits at the foot of the brows at right. Some of the invited guests are on the main deck and others on the pier. (Courtesy of the Charles Edison Fund)

**Right:** Captain Carl F. Holden, the first commanding officer, speaks to the crew during the commissioning ceremony. At right, next to a microphone, is Commander Pete McDowell, the first executive officer. In the background, by turret three, Rear Admiral Milo Draemel, Commandant of the Fourth Naval District, stands with Governor and Mrs. Charles Edison. (Courtesy of Mrs. P. E. McDowell)

powered by mighty engines and studded with cannon. Today this inanimate 'it' becomes 'she', a being endowed with the living character of personality, with a soul and with a purpose. A lovely lady, but a lovely lady who will have her angry moments. . . .

"Notwithstanding the high mechanization of this ultra-modern battleship, we will require as the first and most important quality of a member of this ship's company: that he be a fighting man. A crew of fighting men will make this a fighting ship. . . .

"This is going to be a smart ship. By smart I mean clean, trim, alert, disciplined. That is synonymous with an efficient ship. It is already a powerful ship. It is going to be a fighting ship."

During the period between the commissioning and the second week in July, the crew and the shipyard force worked together to prepare the *New Jersey* to go to sea for the first time. Fuel was taken on from a barge alongside. The men of the engineering plant were gradually getting used to the propulsion plant, and they were also getting used to the chief engineer, Commander Gerald B. Ogle. Ogle knew his business, for he had been assigned to the Bureau of Ships during the design phase for the class, and he had been at the shipyard helping to get the *New Jersey* ready from even before she was launched.

Lieutenant John P. Rossie was head of the *New Jersey*'s A gang, in charge of auxiliary equipment. He recalls that people in the department learned quickly, or Ogle soon got rid of them. A number of the department's officers were mustangs, former enlisted men such as Harry Reynolds whom Ogle had known and worked with prior to reporting. They and the warrant officers served as instructors in drilling new men on equipment. The learning process was complicated by the fact that completion of the ship was still proceeding. As Rossie puts it, ". . . trying to live on a ship when they're working night and day is pretty rough, very noisy". Added to the noise were small fires which broke out from time to time as a consequence of welding operations.

Men in other departments, particularly gunnery, were undergoing intensive training, including being sent to anti-aircraft gunnery schools or to the General Electric plant in Schenectady, New York, to learn more about the turrets' hydraulic controls. Many men traveled to York, Pennsylvania, to be trained on the new 40-mm. quad antiaircraft mounts which were being manufactured by York Safe and Lock Company – one of the many industrial firms which had converted their production lines for the war. Inside the *New Jersey*'s turrets, men were being trained to handle a variety of stations, ranging from handling powder and projectiles far below, to ramming them into the breech ends of the 16-inch guns. A number of classes were held ashore in the shipyard to avoid interfering with the completion of outfitting work on board ship.

**Opposite page:** In this view on the starboard side, looking forward from amidships, the most prominent structure is the *New Jersey*'s forward stack, flanked on each side by a Mark 37 director for the 5-inch guns. In the foreground is a 40-millimeter anti-aircraft mount. On the left, in the background, is the large hammerhead crane on pier four at the Philadelphia Navy Yard. (Courtesy of Philadelphia Naval Shipyard)

**Right:** The long third-deck passageway, running between turrets two and three, is known as "Broadway" because of the amount of traffic it carries from one end of the ship to the other. Entrances to the eight firerooms and four engine rooms are on this passageway. At the top is an I-beam, which can serve as a monorail for moving 16-inch projectiles from one turret to another in an emergency. (Courtesy of Philadelphia Naval Shipyard)

**Far right:** On her commissioning day, 23 May 1943, the *New Jersey* rides high while moored at the Philadelphia Navy Yard's pier four, because she does not yet have her load of fuel and ammunition on board. The bow is still unprotected at the main deck level since the rounded splinter shield for 20-millimeter guns has not yet been constructed. On the *New Jersey*'s jackstaff is a 48-star union jack, flown whenever a U.S. Navy ship is moored or anchored. (National Archives: 80-G-K-885)

For the many hundreds of crew members who were new to the Navy, the training had to cover more than just fighting the ship; it also had to teach them how to live on board ship. They had to adjust to the crowded conditions, lack of privacy, strict discipline and customs, standing in line for meals, and the fact that fresh water was not an unlimited commodity. Commander McDowell, the exec, received reports from the day of commissioning onward about high water consumption and problems in the use of shipboard heads. As McDowell explained, "When we realized that the standards of these boys were the standards of the subway men's room, the railroad and filling stations, the outhouse and third rate hotels, we took action. We devoted two hours of drill and instruction to the use of our equipment and got stopped up drainage under control." In addition, fresh water expenditure was reduced from thirty-five gallons per man each day to less than twenty gallons.

For the senior officers who had come from shore duty and for the vast majority of the crew who were new to the Navy, the vigorous pace of training was the closest thing they'd yet encountered to combat. An exception was Captain Holden, who certainly knew the value of anti-aircraft gunnery, because he was the executive officer of the battleship *Pennsylvania* when she was under attack by the Japanese at Pearl Harbor. Some officers, however, took a jaundiced view of the proceedings. Lieutenant Roman V. "Rosy" Mrozinski was to be one of the *New Jersey*'s turret officers, for he had held a similar position in the heavy cruiser *San Francisco*, a ship heavily damaged by Japanese air and surface attacks off Guadalcanal. Mrozinski

remembers, "Some of the people came from Washington; they had had desk jobs, and they were ready to go out and fight the war right then and there, even in the Philadelphia Navy Yard. And those of us who had been out in the Pacific and had joined the ship thought this was quite a joke; . . . all we wanted to do at Philadelphia was relax and forget about the war."

A group of the junior officers found even the relaxing to be tiring. They got apartments in the area of Philadelphia a bit north of the shipyard. Lieutenant John W. Sullivan, who was Mrozinski's assistant in turret three, explains that there was a real push to get the ship finished, with work going on "Saturdays, Sundays, and everything else. There was a hell of a lot of welding and painting and grinding and so on going on. It was a madhouse, so that's why we had to go ashore if we were going to get any sleep. We all figured . . . that we're going to be gone for a long time, which was a hell of a good assumption. So we tried to live it up instead of sleeping. And, fortunately, youth came to our assistance." Sullivan and his mates needed that youth for the pace they were setting. They sometimes had two dates a night – one in the early evening and another when telephone operators who worked near the officers' apartment finished their stints of switchboard duty.

For Seaman Rafael Maza of New York City, not long out of boot camp and a brief attempt at radio school, initial duty on board the *New Jersey* meant the beginning of a three-month period of mess cooking – peeling potatoes, washing trays, serving food, and swabbing the mess decks. He had no apartment ashore. For sleeping he had to sling his hammock in the mess area when he first reported.

**Far left:** A column of smoke from a steam-powered tugboat punctuates the proceedings as the *New Jersey* is moved away from her berth at the Philadelphia Navy Yard on 8 July 1943, her first time under way on her own power. When her keel was laid less than three years earlier, the schedule called for her to be completed in the spring of 1944. (National Archives: 80-G-82670)

**Left:** The crew gathers informally topside as the ship proceeds downriver on 8 July. Notice the open bridge. There are two sets of viewing slits in the conning tower, one on the 04 level for the pilothouse and another set for the 05 level gun control station. Atop the superstructure is the "bedspring" antenna for the SK air-search radar. Extending from the port side of the ship is the leadsman's platform; men stand there to heave a line with a piece of lead at the end and thus to take soundings on the depth of water. (National Archives: 80-G-82674)

**Below:** The *New Jersey* steams majestically down the Delaware River on the afternoon of 8 July, not long after leaving the navy yard for the first time. The small chain extending from the bullnose leads down to a ring on the forefoot – the bulbous area where the stem meets the keel at the bottom of the bow. From there the chain attaches to a towing bridle for underwater paravanes used to sweep for mine cables in rivers and coastal waters. (Courtesy of Philadelphia Naval Shipyard)

Trying to sleep in a hammock suspended four and a half feet above the deck was a new experience, and it gave him a jolt one night when he fell out of the hammock and onto that hard steel deck. The day began at 4:30 a.m., when he got up to start breakfast preparations, and ended at 7:00 or 7:30 p.m. when things were washed and put away.

Maza's routine – at least in the beginning – was not the fighting for which he had joined the Navy, but he fell in quickly with the Navy's liberty routine. When he got an off day, his interest in baseball took him to Shibe Park to watch the games of the American League Philadelphia Athletics and the National League's Phillies. Both clubs were hapless that year, the Phils finishing seventh and the A's eighth. At other times, the eighteen-year-old Maza went with his new shipmates to Market Street bars to drink beer and listen to the jukebox. Though Maza hadn't been drinking at home before entering the Navy, he and the other younger men followed the example of the older sailors, because, he says, "If you didn't do it, you know, you'd be an outcast."

The men of the *New Jersey* were in their dress white uniforms and at their stations on the afternoon of Thursday, 8 July, when it came time to get the ship under way for the first time. Captain Holden wanted to cut the umbilical cords that had tied the ship to the navy yard ever since the hull had taken shape. Yard pilot John Vitt was at the conn, standing up on the 08 level conning position, because the regular bridge on the 04 level wasn't high enough to permit him to see both bow and stern. Captain Holden stood expectantly nearby, for he was now officially responsible, even if the pilot would be issuing orders to the engines, the helmsman, and the tugs far below. At 1:48 p.m., the last line came free from the shore. The great warship's engines moved slowly astern, and the tugs guided her out into the river and got her headed fair down the channel. After years of planning, building, manning, and training, the *New Jersey* was under way on her own power. As she moved down the Delaware River, the tugs dropped away one at a time.

That night, after hours spent getting the feel of the water, the *New Jersey* anchored for the first time, dropping the starboard anchor in 11 fathoms of water in Delaware Bay. Within minutes, three Navy small craft began conducting a patrol on a circle of 1,500 yards radius around the ship. These craft, which were equipped with sound gear, would make sure that the new battleship wouldn't be caught unaware by a submarine, no matter how unlikely the event in the confined waters of the bay.

In the days that followed, the *New Jersey* was under way during the daytime and anchored at night with patrol boats out. Each morning the yard workmen came out to the ship by boat, and each night they went ashore again. It was a time to test all sorts of equipment throughout the ship to provide further training, to compensate the

**Right:** Under Secretary of the Navy James V. Forrestal, with pipe in hand at center, stands on the 04 level open bridge on 23 July 1943 to observe the first firing of the *New Jersey*'s main battery. The top of turret two can be seen beyond the bridge. Forrestal stands in the narrow catwalk which is all the room officers of the deck have in which to move around. (National Archives: 80-G-82681)

**Below:** The yard tug at left provides an escort as the battleship continues downriver on 8 July. All the way at the stern is the airplane crane used to hoist aboard the OS2U scouting and observation planes. Since the *New Jersey* has no hangar facilities, the planes are stored on the main deck or on the ship's catapults. (James C. Fahey Collection, U.S. Naval Institute)

magnetic compasses, and for the captain and officers of the deck to test the handling characteristics of a vessel that was far bigger than any ship in which they'd ever served. They needed to find out the effect of various speeds, how quickly she would turn, and how big a tactical diameter the turning circle had when the rudder was put over. The ship's planes were catapulted from the fantail to give their pilots practice and to provide training for the crew in launching and recovering them. At times, the ship had to shut down operations and lie quietly at anchor while a thick blanket of fog lay over the bay.

As the month of July passed, the pace quickened on board the *New Jersey*. The crew exercised at general quarters and other emergency drills. Boats brought large numbers of officers and shipyard workers out from the Philadelphia Navy Yard. Others came from the Bureau of Ships and Bureau of Ordnance in Washington. Early on the morning of Thursday, 22 July, a barge brought James V. Forrestal, Under Secretary of the Navy and the man who had made the principal address when the *New Jersey* was launched on 7 December 1942. On that occasion, he reminded his audience that when the keel was laid, the ship's announced completion date was 1 May 1944. That date was still more than nine months in the future, but here was the *New Jersey*, virtually complete and now ready to fire her guns for the first time. The initial shooting was a structural firing to see what effect the 16-inch naval rifles would have on the rest of the ship.

To the ordnance experts from Washington and the navy yard, these tests were routine – another box to be checked off in the overall process of getting the battleship ready for war. For others, the initial firings had a considerably larger

significance. Down in the radio compartment which was his station, Seaman Robert Westcott had a sense of apprehension that was widely shared among the ship's newcomers. "There were all kinds of rumors coming around," he remembers. "The sound from these guns, they say, is going to be so terrible – you know, you're just not going to be able to stand it. And the heat is going to burn the skin off your arms, and all this kind of stuff." In remembering the event years afterward, Westcott likened it to an astronaut being sent into space in a capsule for the first time. Within the experience of most of the *New Jersey*'s crew, there was nothing remotely similar to the firing of these guns to use as a frame of reference.

Throughout the ship, a variety of actions was taking place simultaneously in building up to the big event. Computers and radars were operated so the guns could be trained on a safe bearing. Powder cans far down in the magazines were opened and bags transferred through passing scuttles and then put on hoists that would take them up to the turrets. Projectiles were unstrapped from their positions around the insides of the circular barbettes and then sent upward. In the gun rooms, projectiles were rammed into the gun breeches, to be followed by six bags of powder for each 16-inch shell. Gun captains inserted primers into firing locks in the breech mechanisms. The primers would be fired into the red-colored ends of the rear powder bags, for that section of each bag contained a charge of black powder which would set off the grains of smokeless powder in the six silk bags. Mushroom-shaped plugs sealed off the back ends of the gun breeches so that ensuing chemical reaction would move in only one direction – out the muzzle ends of the barrels.

Ready lights were flashed in turret one to signal to the plotting room on the fourth deck that all was in readiness. Captain Holden gave the order, and at 10:54 that morning the right gun of that turret belched forth a ball of yellow-orange flame and expelled a 16-inch projectile skyward from the starboard side of the ship. One by one, the various guns scattered all over the topside spaces of the *New Jersey* took up the action – the deep, thundering 16-inchers, the sharper, cracking 5-inch, and the staccato sounds of the 40-mm. and 20-mm. antiaircraft machine-guns. Hands and minds worked together to produce a cacophony of noise and a spewing forth of flames.

Down in the secondary battery plotting room, Ensign Coyne was encased by steel armor above and on both sides. For him, the noise and heat of the firing were muffled, but the whole ship seemed to shudder and lurch from the impact of the blasts far above. At the moment of firing, he says, "The ship herself seemed to hold her breath, along with everyone on board." Later, when he returned to his stateroom, he observed the effects of the day's gunnery in another dramatic fashion. Everything that hadn't been properly stowed was jarred loose and strewn about the decks of his room. "In fact," he says, "throughout the ship all hands were learning the hard way that when the main battery fired, everything in the ship had better be adequately secured or one could expect surprising and sometimes distressing consequences."

The firing of the *New Jersey*'s dozens of guns was impressive but not the whole show as far as 22 July was concerned. After the right gun of turret two fired at 12:10 that afternoon, the battleship's speed began gradually to build, reaching 32.4 knots at 4:40 p.m. Ensign Coyne was

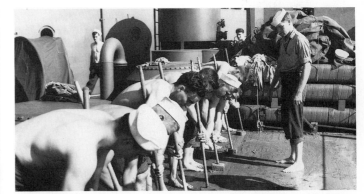

also impressed by this aspect of the *New Jersey*'s performance: "To see and feel that mammoth ship hurtling through the water at more than 30 knots was a unique experience, one that not only inspired pride and confidence in the ship itself, but also tended to impart a feeling of invincibility – a ship that could do this, just couldn't be stopped." Between her guns and her propellers, the mighty *New Jersey* had put on a spectacular show for Under Secretary of the Navy Forrestal.

The remainder of the month of July took the *New Jersey* first to Norfolk for a few days and then into the Chesapeake Bay, where her crew was involved in more general quarters drills and more training. At the end of July and beginning of August, the ship was in Annapolis Roads. For the midshipmen of the Naval Academy who boated out to take a tour of the ship, it was an awe-inspiring experience – particularly so because many of the plebes had never been on board a ship of any sort previously. One such plebe was Midshipman Robert C Peniston, who only a few weeks earlier had been back home in Kansas. Now, having had most of his hair shorn off and many other indignities inflicted by hazing upperclassmen, a trip out into the bay proved a rare treat on a Saturday afternoon. To Peniston, it was "a day I'll never forget, because here's this mammoth ship, just looming in the mist. And then as you get closer and closer, the size just seemed to defy all imagination." He and his classmates visited a turret, a 5-inch gun mount, and the engineering spaces below decks. They were forbidden, however, to go into the officers' wardroom. Instead, they could only peer in with a sense of envy. They were still a long way from being commissioned officers.

After a stay in Annapolis, the *New Jersey* drilled still more in Chesapeake Bay, although several of her training routines were hampered by the shallowness of the water. Probably the two men on board most concerned with keeping the ship from grounding on the muddy bottom were Captain Holden and the *New Jersey*'s navigator, Lieutenant Commander Clayton R. Dudley. Years later, Dudley wrote, "Proceeding in Chesapeake Bay up to Annapolis and back to Norfolk, frequently in waters which were only about six inches deeper than our keel, you can imagine how, as Navigator, I began to grow gray hair and consulted the Tide Tables constantly. . . . I had not served with Captain Holden previously and he had no doubt noticed how I was worried while cruising in Chesapeake Bay – so his confidence in my skill as a navigator was probably not too great. . . . However, by the time we had completed our shakedown cruise, I believe he was well satisfied with my performance." As it turned out, Dudley's tenure as navigator was soon over; he was among the first of the ship's commissioning crew to leave, because he was promoted to the rank of commander right after the shakedown and reassigned.

On 9 August 1943, after a brief stay in Norfolk, the *New Jersey* got under way to begin her shakedown training cruise in the Caribbean. As the battleship moved out into the Atlantic, navigator Dudley could forget about his worries of the Chesapeake and concentrate on enabling the ship to keep to her assigned schedule. He remembers that she did so "Like a passenger train running on a railroad – arriving at predicted navigational positions almost always at the predicted time." While she steamed southward in ever-warming latitudes, the battleship was escorted by the destroyers *Sproston* and *Charrette*, both of which had been commissioned within a few days of the *New Jersey* and were also in the process of shaking down. Their sonars pinged ahead into the waters through which the *New Jersey* would pass. In the captain's cabin, Carl Holden paid close attention to a chart which was marked with colored pins to indicate German submarine sightings of differing degrees of reliability. None of the threats materialized.

On Friday, the 13th of August, the *New Jersey* arrived at the site of her training, the nearly landlocked Gulf of Paria. It is framed on the south and west by the coast of Venezuela and on the north and east by the island of Trinidad. Since the gulf has only two openings – known as the Dragon's Mouth and the Serpent's Mouth – and since both were easily guarded, the gulf presented warships with a safe haven in which to train, free of concern about submarine attack. The first stop in the gulf was Trinidad, where Captain Holden went ashore to pay his respects to the commandant of the naval operating base, and where the crew of the *New Jersey* had some memorable liberties.

Lieutenant (junior grade) Gene Hayward was the number two officer in turret number one. He explains that the crew was cautioned before going ashore on the dangers of drinking local rum and then standing in the hot sun. Recalls Hayward, "Well, that's all they had to say – 'Don't do it' – and, of course, they did it." The potent drink had swift effect on both officers and enlisted men. One junior officer fell from a dock into water that had a covering of oil on top. His white service uniform was instantly transformed to black service. While the officer's cap remained floating on the oil, he and a number of petty officers and non-rated men were hauled back to the *New Jersey* by boat. To Hayward, the liberty parties returning to the ship looked like battle casualties.

The longer some of the men stayed ashore, the worse their condition became. Petty Officer Leonard Jung says that some of the Jerseymen returning to the ship "were as good as dead. They were just passed out." A couple of men tried weakly to climb up Jacob's ladders suspended from the side of the *New Jersey* and faced two perils – possible drowning and being squashed between the boat and the side of the ship. After the futility of these efforts became apparent, says Jung, clearheaded men on deck rigged up the ship's crane on the stern with cargo nets and began scooping men onto the fantail.

Seaman Robert Westcott fell out of a liberty boat on his way ashore. There was further indignity ahead. When the *New Jersey*'s boat brought Westcott and some of his shipmates back so they could return aboard, the garbage grinder at the stern began spewing out its contents onto Westcott's already soaked uniform. Another day ashore in Trinidad brought him a happier outcome. Westcott and a friend decided that bananas were healthier than rum, and after a considerable search they found a place where bananas were growing. They liberated a heavy stalk of the fruit and proceeded to carry it – one end on the shoulder of each man. They managed to transport their prize back out to the ship, eating quite a few of the bananas along the way. Once down in their living compartment, they hung the stalk from the overhead. "And all through the night," recalls Westcott, "you could hear banana peels go plop on the deck. So in the morning, when we got up, all we had was a pile of banana peels, and that stalk was just as clean as anything."

A number of the ship's officers were detached fairly soon after commissioning, because Captain Holden set a high standard of performance for his subordinates. He expected the *New Jersey* to produce topnotch results, and her chances for that would be even better if he got rid of those who didn't measure up. Lieutenant Commander Bill Abhau was then the ship's air defense officer, and he remembers that Holden was "absolutely ruthless in weeding out people that he thought were incompetent. He got rid of two officers that I just couldn't abide, and he got rid of a number that probably – he tended to err on the side of getting rid of them rather than keeping them." Abhau explains that Holden had a friend back in the detail section at the Bureau of Naval Personnel, so the captain would write to Washington and damn an individual with faint praise such as, "I think this officer would do very well in the amphibious force, but he isn't quite battleship caliber." That was the kiss of death on the man's further service in the *New Jersey*.

Based on the recollections of the officers and men who served under his command in the *New Jersey*, Captain Carl F. Holden was a man of many parts – revealing different facets of his personality to individuals at different levels. As commanding officer, he took seriously his role as the ship's chief morale officer. He was concerned about the welfare of enlisted crew members and took a warm, fatherly interest in them – paternal without being patronizing. He spoke to the crew over the general announcing system to inform them – within the strict limits imposed by military security – of what the ship was doing. He took steps to ensure that food and berthing facilities were as comfortable as they could be in an inherently uncomfortable situation on board a ship as crowded as the *New Jersey* was.

To Seaman Bob Westcott, who served with the radio gang and stood communication watches on the bridge,

Captain Holden became an officer with whom he could be unusually familiar, even though Westcott's initial feeling had been that a battleship captain was "almost like God" or at least a disciple. During night watches, however, when little else was happening, the two began chatting. Holden talked about his home in Maine, and Westcott mentioned ham radio operators in that state with whom he had talked. It was the captain's practice to inspect the crew's appearance every other Saturday. During an inspection later in the year, when the *New Jersey* was off the coast of Maine, Holden took hold of a button on Westcott's peacoat, discovered it was loose, and said, "Bob, I think you'd better do something about that button." Two Saturdays later, Holden came by again, checked once more, and said, "I see you took care of your button."

From time to time when the ship was under way, Captain Holden stopped down in the radio compartment for a visit to the men on duty there. Doubtless, he was interested because of his previous service as Director of Naval Communications, and he was interested in the radiomen as well. He put on a set of headphones and listened to the dots and dashes of Morse code as it reported the latest news over a press circuit. On occasion, the radiomen managed to get meat from the ship's butcher shop and cook it in a small skillet on a hotplate they stowed in the compartment. Whenever the metal dogs holding shut the hatch into the compartment were seen to be opening, the radiomen quickly slipped the hotplate and skillet into a tool cabinet because such cooking outside the galley was not authorized. Sometimes the individual who appeared through the hatch was Holden himself, and the smoke and aroma of the frying meat lingered in the air. "Fellows," Holden said to the radiomen once, "I'd swear you've been cooking something in here if I didn't know that you know that it's against regulations." Once the captain left, after his stint of listening to the code, the meat was retrieved from its hiding place, heated up again, and consumed.

With his officers, especially the more senior ones, the captain demonstrated a great deal less tolerance. In fact, it almost seemed there was an inverse relationship between a man's rank and how well he got along with Holden. The officer who bore the brunt of it was Commander McDowell, who had frequent disagreements with the skipper.

Lieutenant John Rossie in the engineering department learned quickly that the captain didn't like to see smoke coming out of the *New Jersey*'s stacks, in part because it fouled the decks and in part because it indicated an improper mixture of fuel and air in the combustion process. "I think [Holden] was a very competent officer," says Rossie, "and we had confidence in the man. . . . You just looked at him, and there's a guy that looked like a commander of a battleship and acted like a commander of a battleship. But he was a little short now and then. If he'd see smoke coming out of the stack, he'd send his messenger around and get ahold of the first engineering officer he could find and bring him up there and give him a chewing-out."

To some of the more senior officers, Holden seemed unpredictable and arbitrary. He was also strict with regard to disciplinary matters. He was the friend of the enlisted men, but not if they got into trouble. The ship's logs for the early months in commission are replete with sentences dispensed at captain's masts and courts-martial. If someone did get into trouble, he was lucky to have it handled at the division or department level rather than reaching the old man.

The *New Jersey*'s skipper prided himself on his navigation; before the war he had been navigator of the battleship *Idaho*. His knowledge of the subject led to an understandable degree of concern in handling the huge *New Jersey*, because there was virtually no precedent or experience in operating such large ships in the U.S. Navy. When the *New Jersey* went to Trinidad during the shakedown period, Captain Holden would not anchor her inside the net provided for protection against submarines; he considered the water too shallow for the ship's draft of more than 35 feet. It was a judgment call, and he concluded there was a greater risk of going aground than of being attacked by submarines, even though the depth of water inside the net had been verified by soundings and was considered sufficient.

From the 13th until the end of August, an intensive period of training molded the crew of the *New Jersey* into a fighting team. The schedule called for the ship to spend most days under way and most nights at anchor – filling the days with incessant drilling. The idea was to do things over and over again in order to improve both speed and reliability – so that the teamwork actions involved in such things as loading and firing the guns would become second nature by the time it became necessary to use those guns against an enemy.

Another purpose of the shakedown was to get the bugs out and correct mistakes. Bob Moore, a warrant gunner in 1943, remembers, "From my point of view our *shakedown* was more of a *breakdown* cruise with 10 per cent regulars and 90 per cent reserve. Knobs were twisted before their duties were explained or one with experience could arrive on the scene." A number of things thus broken had to be fixed when the *New Jersey* got back to a shipyard in the United States. The inevitable equipment failures and malfunctions had a beneficial aspect, says Bill Coyne, "in that they gave the crew valuable experience in trouble shooting and repair which would prove essential in the months to come".

To Lieutenant John Sullivan in turret three, the repeated practice off Trinidad was worthwhile but tiresome. "We worked our ass off," he remembers. A feeling of exhaustion set in after a while, and he would have welcomed a respite,

"but you had the brass driving, and you kept drilling". In this case, the Operational Training Command Atlantic was in charge of the exercises, having acquired a good bit of experience from the steady stream of ships passing through the area for workup on the way to war.

The Gulf of Paria, less than 12° north of the Equator, had the advantage of being a safe haven from submarines, but the crew paid in another way because of having to go through the seemingly endless training sessions in the heat of August. Perhaps the foremost victim of the heat was the *New Jersey*'s rotund chief engineer, Commander Gerald Ogle. Salt was showing up in the condensate produced by one of the condensers, and it was certainly undesirable to feed salty water back into the boilers. So Ogle squeezed through a manhole to get to the saltwater side of the condenser and then to conduct a soap test. By rubbing a bar of soap over a number of tubes, he found in one the leak that was causing the problem. During the time of the test, the August heat so swelled up his body that he was unable to get back out through the manhole by which he had entered. John McCormick, who was Ogle's assistant, describes the remedy, "We had to break out the fire hose and play cold water on him to shrink him. That, with the application of grease on his body, enabled him to get thru the manhole."

On 21 August, the *New Jersey* went alongside the oiler *Mattole*, a ship built shortly after World War I. It marked the first time the battleship refueled under way since going into commission. The officer of the deck for the operation was Lieutenant Oscar Gray, who had come to the ship from the USS *Mississippi*. He remembers that Captain Holden was only too happy to let the experienced Gray take the *New Jersey* alongside the *Mattole* for the maneuver. This new battleship of theirs, which displaced more than 54,000 tons with fuel, ammunition, and stores on board during the shakedown, was the sort of vessel that merited a healthy sense of respect.

Thousands of rounds of ammunition passed through the *New Jersey*'s guns during the shakedown. The anti-aircraft batteries fired at balloons and at target sleeves towed by aircraft. Planes from the light carrier *Monterey*, which was also undergoing shakedown, simulated torpedo attacks against the *New Jersey* to give gunners and fire control technicians a feel for what the experience would be like when the planes were launched by an enemy. The main battery fired both day and night battle practice at target rafts, with the 5-inch guns providing illumination at night by firing star shells. The latter are special projectiles which contain flares, and are equipped with parachutes so that the flares can drift slowly downward and keep targets illuminated for some time.

One of the night practices was conducted in an atmosphere of tragedy. At about 6:00 p.m. on 24 August, the gunnery department was preparing for the upcoming drills by holding alignment checks to make sure that

turrets and plotting rooms were working together. While this was going on, Gunner's Mate Second Class Irving S. Doremus opened a hatch that was in the bottom of the gun pit in turret one and climbed up into the gun pit to get a can of oil near the primer station. The gun captain saw him come up, but he had a mental lapse. When the signal came from the plotting room to match signals, he forgot about Doremus and threw a switch that allowed the guns to go under control of the plotting room. Doremus stepped out from the primer station into the gun pit of the center gun just as the remotely controlled 16-inch barrels were elevated. The huge breech mechanism of turret one's center gun came down and crushed him. He died a few hours later. The crew quickly took up a collection for his pregnant widow.

Late in the afternoon of 31 August, after the training period had concluded, the *New Jersey* left the Gulf of Paria via the Serpent's Mouth. She began the long journey north through the Caribbean and up to Norfolk. While the ship was in Hampton Roads near Norfolk, Rear Admiral Donald B. Beary, Commander Operational Training Command Atlantic, came aboard and gave the *New Jersey* her annual military inspection on 5 and 6 September. Emergency drills were held at anchor on the first day, and the second day was spent in a mock battle problem. The whole inspection was, in effect, an examination which allowed the crew to demonstrate to Admiral Beary and his staff how well it had learned its lessons during the ship's shakedown.

The *New Jersey* concluded her first underway period on Tuesday, 7 September, almost two months to the day since she had first left the pier at Philadelphia. Her return to the shipyard where she was built was marked by a mishap reminiscent of those earlier in the year when she was caught in dry dock and suffered a fire in the shed built over the conning tower. Shortly after noon, the *New Jersey* anchored in the Delaware River to await the high tide that would give her clearance to get alongside a pier.

The ship was under way again in midafternoon, and while she was trying to moor at pier four, one of her paravane chains carried away and was fouled. Then the ship got away from the control of some of the ten tugboats alongside. C. R. Dudley, then the navigator, recalls the circumstances: "The ship was almost as long as the river was wide so when we reached a heading across channel our overhanging bow was above the right bank (on the Navy Yard side) and our stern was in shallow water near the other bank. The bulk of the ship acted like a dam across the river channel." The current shoved the stern aground on the shallow mudbank. The intake of mud fouled the main condenser, stopping the main engines and generators and causing the *New Jersey* to lose electrical power and steering control. Emergency diesel generators went on down in the engineering spaces, but they couldn't get cooling water either, so they soon kicked

Right : The *New Jersey* and the French battleship *Richelieu* lie at anchor off Norfolk in early September 1943. After being damaged by Royal Navy planes at Dakar in West Africa in July 1940, the *Richelieu* was taken over for the Allied cause. She underwent repairs at the New York Navy Yard in early 1943. Soon after this photo was taken, the French battleship steamed across the Atlantic for service with the British Home Fleet.

Below: The *New Jersey* at anchor in early September 1943. This photograph was probably taken within a few minutes of the aerial view of the *New Jersey* and *Richelieu*. Just before heading to Philadelphia for post-shakedown navy yard work, the *New Jersey* still has an open bridge. A piece of canvas has been rigged on the lifelines at the bow to cut down on spray. A metal shield will soon be built. (National Archives: 80-G-204838)

off as well. Lieutenant John Rossie recalls that the engine spaces "were just as black as could be".

If the whole situation was bewildering down below, it had its frightening aspects topside, particularly for one shipyard worker who was in a restroom at the end of pier four. When the stern grounded in the mud, the bow of the *New Jersey* swung around and headed for the restroom. The worker inside saw the bow coming and went tearing out of the place with his trousers still at halfmast. He escaped before the structure was smashed by the bow. Finally the ship was pulled under control and moored to the dock, but the whole episode wasn't quite over. During the yard period which followed the *New Jersey*'s arrival at Philadelphia, a sturdy metal shield was built on the ship's bow to protect the crews of two 20-mm. machine guns being installed there. After the shield was completed, someone in the crew painted on the outside of it the silhouette of an old-fashioned outhouse, much as other ships painted silhouettes of enemy ships sunk or planes shot down. The captain heard about it, and the outhouse symbol was quickly painted over. Division officers then went around asking who had done the painting. Oscar Gray remembers that everyone responded with an astonished "Who, me?" and an imaginary halo above his head.

Because of the brief grounding, it was time to clean out the condensers again. Earlier, while in Norfolk, it had been done, because the scant clearance above the bottom of

**Top right:** This 16 October 1943 photo shows the newly enclosed bridge which was constructed during the *New Jersey*'s post-shakedown yard period at Philadelphia in September and October. She was the only ship of the class to have a rounded 04 level navigation bridge. The *Iowa* went to the Pacific with an open bridge. The two later sisters had their current square-front bridges at the time of commissioning. The windows on the 03 level are part of the flag bridge. Atop the conning tower is the long horizontal antenna for the Mark 3 main battery fire control radar, just installed during the yard period. (National Archives: 80-G-207484)

**Bottom right:** The interior of the newly completed bridge is visible in this October 1943 view as it follows the contour of the previous catwalk around the front of the conning tower at left. At 17.3 inches, the conning tower armor is among the thickest in the ship. The narrow viewing slit through the door at left is typical of those in the conning tower and gives an idea of how limited the visibility was for those in the pilot house. At right are cranks for rolling the bridge windows up and down. (Courtesy of Philadelphia Naval Shipyard)

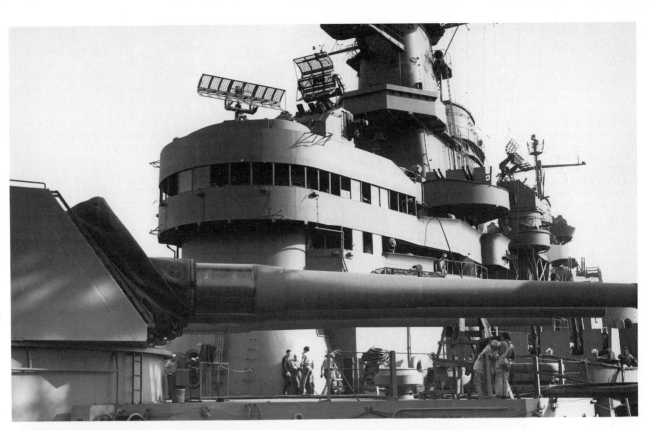

Chesapeake Bay had caused a good deal of mud and debris to be scooped up. When the condensers were opened and dumped into the bilges, says John McCormick, the crew found such things as a four-foot shark, a snake, and hundreds of condoms. This time, at Philadelphia, the "gunk" from the bottom of the river was so hard that it had to be broken up with pickaxes.

Still another foulup occurred on 12 September. A too-sensitive warning system indicated a fire in the powder magazines for turret two. A powder explosion at any time would be a catastrophe, but the effect would be even worse in a shipyard where surrounding facilities might be hit. As a result, Commander Edward S. Addison, the damage control officer, ordered the magazines to be flooded. Later inspection revealed that there had been no fire. Although he realized the necessity for flooding magazines, Lieutenant Gray, the turret officer, was miffed, because his division was forced to "unload every damn stitch of powder in those magazines". Then his men had to clean the magazines, install new insulation, and repaint the interiors.

The problem in the magazines was made even worse by the corrosive effects of the acid-laden water of the Delaware River. John Rossie recalls that hydrogen sulfide fumes from the water turned the wardroom silver black. The water also eroded the copper pipes which ran to the electric condensers and the piping had to be replaced by pipe that was lined with lead solder during a subsequent yard period in Boston.

The *New Jersey* went into dry dock on 20 September as part of the yard period. The time back in Philadelphia was a post-shakedown availability which enabled the shipyard to fix things which had gone wrong during the first underway period. It was also a time for making improvements, such as installing the new 20-mm. guns and gun shield on the bow. Moreover, the ship got a new bridge and a new secondary battle control station, thanks to an early September message from Admiral Ernest J. King, Commander-in-Chief, U.S. Fleet, who had ordered the shipyard period extended for a time in order to make the modifications.

The purpose of the ship's conning tower was to protect the officers inside it who were directing the ship's movements. This was useful for battle, but the narrow viewing slits through the armor were clearly insufficient for normal underway steaming watches. During the shakedown cruise, the *New Jersey*'s officers of the deck stood their watches on an open catwalk around the front of the conning tower, but such an arrangement was scarcely adequate for extended steaming in all kinds of weather, because the bridge personnel were completely unprotected from the elements. Thus, an enclosed bridge was authorized by Admiral King; some *New Jersey* officers recall that Captain Holden made a strong case for a new bridge and got King to agree to it. The resulting bridge

followed the curvature of the catwalk around the front of the conning tower, so it was still cramped, but at least it had a roof and windows.

Another change had been approved by Lieutenant Commander Philip W. Snyder, a naval engineer who was senior assistant on the battleship and cruiser desk in the Bureau of Ships. After the first sea trials, the *New Jersey*'s navigator had submitted an alteration request to improve the ventilation in his sea cabin, which was located in the forward part of the superstructure tower. Commander Snyder disapproved the request because he didn't consider it essential to the ship's operation. On the next trials, Snyder's accommodation turned out to be the navigator's sea cabin – a deliberately diabolical assignment, because the passageway outside the cabin was freshly painted. After an uncomfortable night or two, Snyder returned to Washington and promptly wrote to the shipyard at Philadelphia to authorize improvement of the sea cabin's ventilation "on the basis of proven service experience".

On 3 October, the *New Jersey* got out of dry dock and moored again at pier four. In the ensuing days, she was loaded with 97,920 rounds of 20-mm. ammunition and 107,488 rounds of 40-mm. On the 12th she conducted dock

trials of her engineering plant and then got under way the following day. She went to Chesapeake Bay to test-fire her guns, conduct vibration tests on the engineering plant, and run a battle problem with her crew at general quarters. At Hampton Roads on 17 October, Rear Admiral Beary came aboard to conduct yet another battle problem and military inspection. This was the final exam. On 18 October, Captain Holden was able to send a satisfying message to Admiral Royal E. Ingersoll, Commander-in-Chief, Atlantic Fleet. The message said simply, "Originator reports for duty." The time of training and testing had achieved a satisfactory result; the USS *New Jersey* was at last part of the operating fleet. The crew was able to celebrate with a five-day period of liberty and recreation at Norfolk.

The battleship's first operational assignment was to go to Casco Bay, off the coast of Maine. There was still training to be conducted, but now the *New Jersey* was deemed ready to meet the enemy. When the battleships *South Dakota* and *Alabama* had operated with the British Home Fleet earlier in the year, they and five destroyers constituted Task Force 22 as a "*Tirpitz* watch" – insurance against a possible breakout by German heavy ships.

Admiral King subsequently decided to release the *South Dakota* and *Alabama* for Pacific duty but to keep the *Iowa* and *New Jersey* in the Atlantic for the time being. The latter two ships and a division of destroyers for a time inherited the designation Task Force 22 in the autumn of 1943. While the *New Jersey* had been on her shakedown, the *Iowa* was operating in Casco Bay and off Newfoundland, even farther north. She was not providing the kind of direct support that the *Alabama* and *South Dakota* had, but was an immediately available backstop in case the German heavy ships broke out into the Atlantic and caused the sort of havoc which the *Bismarck* had done during her dramatic but ill-fated voyage in May 1941. In early September 1943, the *Tirpitz* and *Scharnhorst* left Norway briefly to bombard the island of Spitsbergen. After her return to Norway, the *Tirpitz* was damaged later that month in an attack conducted by British X-craft midget submarines. As a result, the German threat had eased even before the *New Jersey* came on the scene. When the *New Jersey* got out of the shipyard at Philadelphia, she was sent north, and this released the *Iowa* to transport President Roosevelt and the Joint Chiefs of Staff to North Africa for a conference of Allied leaders at Cairo, Egypt.

**Below:** An alert photographer on board a minesweeper captured this handsome silhouette profile of the *New Jersey* in Casco Bay off Rockland, Maine, on 26 October 1943. The ship was in the area for a number of weeks in order to be ready to respond if German heavy surface combatants broke out into the North Atlantic. (Courtesy of A. D. Baker III; also Naval Historical Center: NH 45486)

**Right:** The *New Jersey*'s dance band performs at a club ashore in Portland, Maine, in the autumn of 1943 – prior to the ship's departure for the Pacific. These men are already combat veterans, having been members of the cruiser *Northampton*'s band at the time of her sinking off Guadalcanal on 1 December 1942. After survivor leave, they reported to the commissioning crew of the *New Jersey*. (Courtesy of Chief Musician Leonard J. Jung, USN[Ret.])

**Opposite page:** The first issue of the ship's newspaper, then *Clean Sweep Down*, was published in November 1943. The contest to rename the paper brought a $10.00 award to Private First Class Carl W. Ritner of the ship's Marine detachment. His winning entry, *The Jerseyman*, was used on the issue dated 1 January 1944 and those thereafter. (Courtesy of William Dugan)

The *New Jersey* arrived off Maine on 24 October 1943, and Rear Admiral Walter S. Anderson, President of the Navy's Board of Inspection and Survey (InSurv) came aboard to observe standardization trials over a measured mile course off Rockland, Maine. The highest speed achieved during that period was 30 knots. The shallowness of the water – combined with the ship's deep draft – prevented the *New Jersey* from demonstrating her full capabilities. Assistant Engineer Officer McCormick recalls that the water was only 89 fathoms deep, with the result that "we could do only about 29 knots without serious vibrations. I soon found out I could tell the Navigator when we crossed the 100 fathom mark as the vibrations disappeared at that point (this was at high speeds, of course)."

On 2 November, after a brief period in port at Boston, the *New Jersey* entered Casco Bay for the first time. The event was marked by apprehension and caution, particularly because the *Iowa* had been damaged on 16 July when she scraped her bottom against the submerged rock ledge at the entrance to the bay.

One of the junior officers in the secondary battery fire control division during the period of operation off Maine was Lieutenant (junior grade) Les Heselton. His impressions of the time and place are similar to those of many in the crew. He describes Maine in late 1943 as "the coldest spot on earth – cold, damp and windy". When the ship was anchored at night, the practice was to put out picket boats whose mission was to cruise slowly around the ship at a distance of about 50 yards to report the approaches of boats or swimmers – essentially anti-sabotage patrols. The men on watch in the picket boats wore so much protective clothing, says Heselton, that they were too hot at first and then "practically frozen" by the end of a watch. Ensign Bill Coyne also stood boat watches and also remembers the penetrating cold and the frequent showers of spray which turned to ice almost immediately. "In the light of what others were enduring in other theaters," he says, "picket boat duty in Casco Bay was a picnic, but at the time it seemed pretty rough." The most threatening thing Coyne sighted during his boat duty was a floating log or two.

I NO. I.  NOVEMBER 1943  U.S.S. NEW JERSEY

## Now Hear This - - - -

This is by way of an introduction. We hereby present ourself to you.

We are nameless as yet, but will call ourself "Clean Sweep Down" until some clever fellow comes up with a good name and wins a $10 cash prize.

We are your Ship's Paper, which will try to reflect the goings-on in wardroom, gun turrets, engineering spaces, and all the other areas of the New Jersey bounded by port and starboard, fore and aft, above and below.

The ship is our oyster, and we will try to uncover as many pearls as possible. We will be as serious as the occasion demands, and as funny as we possibly can be. We will try to include art, literature, humor, controversy, personalities, and just plain talk within these columns.

Our purpose is to provide a medium for the exchange of information, ideas, and acquaintance among all the several thousand members of this good ship's company. Anything that adds to intrest and convenience of shipmates has a legitimate right to our pages.

This is your paper. It will represent you to your mates on other ships and stations of the Naval establishment. Your pride in your ship should reflect itself in your Ship's Paper All of you are sub-editors and contributing editors, as well as subscribers.

The staff which will carry on the work of putting out this sheet are probably a corny lot, who cant write half as well as the rest of you. So you are invited to take a hand in the publication by contribution, through your division correspondents, of all the material that would possibly be of intrest to any of us or to all of us. Your Ship's Paper is intrested in everything, from gossip to gripes.

But most of all your Ship's Paper is intrested in you, whether working, fighting or playing.

—The Staff

We hope to satisfy.

If it was cold in the boats, so also was it cold on liberty in Portland, Maine, but men went over anyway, even though they had to endure long boat rides. Petty Officer Leonard Jung was struck by the way men huddled over the engines of the motor launches taking them ashore, because any source of heat was welcome. When the men stepped ashore in Portland for the first time, they were herded into a corral and had to wait in it until enough men were on hand for a lecture about proper liberty decorum. Apparently, previous Navy men on liberty there had created a poor image for the service, so the crew of the *New Jersey* was warned to follow strict standards. Both Jung and Fireman Russ Brown remember the precise instructions to have white hats square across their foreheads and all buttons on the heavy blue peacoats buttoned. Some men were sent back to the ship by shore patrol for not having their peacoats buttoned all the way to the top. For both men, the thing to do on liberty was to head for a restaurant and a good steak dinner. Some men holed up in hotel rooms to rest and share a bottle. Seaman Rafael Maza, who had been drinking beer with older shipmates in Philadelphia to prove his manhood, found the test even more challenging in Maine. This time the division's leading boatswain's mate was tossing down double shots. Maza tried but soon got sick, and that was the end of his liberty. As soon as he recovered he was returned to the ship by boat.

For Seaman Bob Westcott, who had a wife at home and couldn't afford a hotel room, an overnight liberty in Portland was a particular trial. After the movies ended at 9.00 in the evening, there was little to do until the next boat back to the ship. One night he crawled into a railroad station luggage rack and wrapped himself in newspaper to try to keep warm. Another night he went to a fishery and chatted with the night watchman, because it at least gave him a warm place to kill time. After such experiences, Westcott would make up his mind, "Boy, I ain't coming ashore next time. I'll stay aboard." But then the next opportunity for liberty came around, and the lure of the beach pulled him over once again, despite his previous resolve.

In November, the members of the *New Jersey*'s crew began to have the benefit of a ship's newspaper, the editor-in-chief of which was Lieutenant Julius Edelstein. For the first few issues, the paper was known as *Clean Sweep Down*, and crewmen were invited to submit nominations for a permanent name. The incentive for the winner was a prize of $10.00, which represented about two weeks' pay for some of the most junior men on board. In early 1944 the title became *The Jerseyman*.

The initial issues of *Clean Sweep Down* offered profiles on the ship's senior officers, with Captain Holden featured in the first one and Commander McDowell in the second. The paper's front page featured a snorting animal labelled "N. J. Bull", which may or may not have been intended as a comment on the contents. Each issue was a compendium

**Above:** The 16-inch guns of the *New Jersey* fire off the starboard beam during operations in Casco Bay in November 1943. Up above the bridge, on the 011 level, yard-arms protrude horizontally from the air defense officer's station. Comparing this photo with the one taken on 8 July shows that the air defense station (also the site for look-outs while under way) has been enlarged with the addition of a small wing on each side. (National Archives: 80-G-207507)

of news tidbits about the various divisions that comprised the ship's company. Featured often were items about engagements, marriages, and births of children. Cartoons, poems, and jokes (frequently feeble) dotted the paper. There were interesting pieces of information – for instance, the crew ate 2,700 pounds of turkey on Thanksgiving that year – and columns of fatherly advice on such topics as getting back from liberty on time, keeping the ship clean, not crowding into mess lines, the safety reasons for not leaning on lifelines, and the necessity to abide by censorship regulations when sending mail home.

Among the early entries in *Clean Sweep Down* were the following:

"I'm glad I am an American
I'm glad that I am free,
I wish I were a little pup,
And Hitler were a tree!"

Father: "Mary, who was that sailor I saw kissing you last night?"
Daughter: "What time was it?"

Doonan: "Why did you ask her for a date?"
Price: "Because she's so different from all other girls I know."
Doonan: "How's that?"
Price: "She'll go out with me!"

Along with the times at anchor, the *New Jersey* was also under way a fair amount during November and the first half of December. She operated with destroyers in Casco Bay and fired both her main battery and antiaircraft guns to keep the crew in practice. The cold weather had an effect on the shooting, along with everything else. Gunner's Mate Ellis Mamroth of turret three was impressed by the layers of ice which built up on the 16-inch gun barrels, including the recoil slides which retract into the turret proper upon firing. When the guns were fired in Casco Bay, good-sized sheets of ice flew through the air after they'd been knocked off the slides by recoil. The ice wasn't able to stick very tightly to the smooth surfaces, particularly because they were lubricated with oil.

According to the ship's World War II cruisebook, some people claimed of the time in Maine that "We were shoveling snow off everything but the deck in the starboard engine room." Certainly snow and ice were problems topside, and some men were injured as a result. A yeoman first class died of bronchial pneumonia.

On Thanksgiving morning, Thursday, 25 November, Ensign King G. Brandt was attending a Protestant church service being held in the mess compartment on the second deck aft. "All of a sudden," he remembers, "there were these terrific vibrations. We couldn't imagine what was going on, but it almost drowned out . . . the minister." It turned out that the New Jersey had been operating her OS2U Kingfisher scoutplanes that morning, and when one of them came back in to hook up to the stern crane, the aviation radioman attempting the hookup, Clinton A. Hanscom, was knocked off the plane by a wave and fell into the sea. His expected survival time in the frigid water was quite short, so Captain Holden immediately kicked up the speed and began turning the ship in order to recover Hanscom. One of the planes got to the chilled radioman, but his waterlogged flight suit made him too heavy to pull aboard the plane. He stayed on the plane's float until a motor whaleboat launched by the New Jersey could pick him up. As it turned out, the heavy leather flying suit which kept the plane from rescuing him had helped ward off the effects of the cold. Even so, he was already turning blue by the time he got back aboard the battleship. He was warmed up in the sick bay by a combination of rubbing and doses of medicinal alcohol. After a day in sick bay he was up and about and soon recovered. What's more, Captain Holden's stock with the crew went even higher because of his demonstrated determination to save one of his men.

When the month of December reached mid-term, the mission of the New Jersey and her accompanying destroyers as a fleet-in-being to counter the German fleet-in-being came to an end, and the ships headed south. From the 16th until the 28th, the battleship was moored at the South Boston Annex of the Boston Navy Yard for last-minute maintenance attention and a period of Christmas leave for crew members. Many of the men had come into the Navy from the eastern part of the United States and thus had a chance to go home during the holiday period. Others, such as Fireman Russ Brown from Illinois, used the time instead to go down to Philadelphia and renew acquaintances with girls whom they had met earlier.

Unexpected Christmas presents came to the men of the battleship from the newly formed State Society of the Battleship New Jersey, spearheaded by a New Jerseyite named Gill Robb Wilson, who was a reporter for the New York Herald Tribune. Each man received a "buddy bag", which was a small ditty bag containing such items as a harmonica, shaving gear, socks, and comb. Each bag contained the name and address of the person who had packed and donated it, so the recipient could write and thank his benefactor. It was a nice touch which helped build a relationship between the ship and the state for which she was named.

Tight security concerning the ship's plans was in force as the old year ended. Crew members were deliberately not told where the New Jersey would be going. Seaman Second Class Roger Faw, fresh out of boot camp, was ordered to catch a ferryboat and train from Norfolk to Boston to join the ship, even though Norfolk was the New Jersey's next destination – something he specifically was not told. Another shipmate, Seaman Second Class Bill Hartley went through the same routine and remembers that his Christmas dinner consisted of sandwiches and coffee on the train northward. Had he known at the time of the ship's schedule, he would have much preferred to spend Christmas with his family in Washington, D.C., and then meet the ship at Norfolk.

For one New Jersey officer, the period in Boston was the end of the line – far sooner than he wanted to leave for other duty. Executive officer Pete McDowell had been on board only seven months from the time of commissioning and very much looked forward to going with the ship to the war zone so he could see the results of his psychological testing and assignment of personnel. But his personality had clashed on numerous occasions with that of Captain Holden, so when the news came through that McDowell had been selected for the rank of captain, he was reassigned right away. On 23 December, McDowell reluctantly turned his job and his spacious shipboard quarters over to Commander Rufus E. Rose, the gunnery officer. Rose celebrated the promotion and the holiday by having his wife and son come aboard for Christmas dinner. He made it a point to visit all the messes and observed that the cooks had done an excellent job. During dinner the general alarm went off, sending the crew scattering. Remembers Rose, "The families could only sit where they were – and feel quite superfluous. Fortunately, the alarm was a false one and we were able to finish the meal – a happy occasion to remember in the days to come."

One New Jersey officer for whom the Boston stop proved especially memorable was Ensign Bill Coyne. Years later, he wrote, "I do remember very vividly having some Boston friends aboard for dinner one evening and walking back to their car with them following the movie in the wardroom. It was a clear moonlit night, and when we were some 200 yards from the ship we turned and looked back. There broadside, silhouetted against the night sky, was that magnificent ship. We stood there, silent, for several minutes, drinking in the beauty, the strength and awesome power of the NEW JERSEY. Many years later I again visited those same friends in Boston. They could still remember the sight of that beautiful ship and the lasting impression it had made on them. It also made a lasting impression on me."

Above: The New Jersey sits at anchor in Casco Bay, near Rockland, Maine, on 28 November 1943. Prominent on her bow are her newly installed 20-millimeter guns and splinter shield. The bridge watch team has reason to be grateful for the recently enclosed bridge because the weather off Maine is seasonally cold in late autumn. (Courtesy Mrs. P. E. McDowell; also National Archives: 80-G-207502)

Shortly after Christmas, the *New Jersey* headed south for Norfolk, where also it was cold. The year 1943 ended with the battleship taking on 324 16-inch high-capacity projectiles while at anchor in Hampton Roads. The first day of January was spent taking on new men and transferring some who had been on board since the commissioning. For nearly all in the crew, their destination was still a mystery, especially because men had been ordered to equip themselves with long underwear and other cold weather gear, and they had even been inspected to make sure they complied.

At 1:37 on the afternoon of Sunday, 2 January, the ship got under way from her anchorage and began standing out of Hampton Roads. The captain, exec, navigator, and pilot were on the bridge, and Lieutenant Rosy Mrozinski was officer of the deck. Lieutenant John Rossie of the engineering department thought the ship was getting under way just so she could move to another anchorage; instead, she took up station in column 2,000 yards astern of her sister ship *Iowa* and began heading south for the Panama Canal. Rossie remembers, "They were trying to fool somebody; they sure fooled me."

Later in the afternoon, when the battleships were clear of Hampton Roads, four destroyers joined the heavy ships and fanned out ahead to provide an antisubmarine screen. Up ahead in the *Iowa*, the officer in tactical command was Rear Admiral Olaf M. Hustvedt, commander of the newly constituted Battleship Division Seven. The admiral had recently returned from duty in Europe, where he had been Commander Task Force 22 when the U.S. Navy was providing support to the British. As the six ships headed steadily to the south, they were on wartime footing – showing no lights at night and zigzagging to foil any submarine attack. Such precautions were still prudent, although no longer so vital as they had been in 1942 and 1943 when German U-boats posed much more of a menace in the Caribbean and along the Atlantic seaboard.

With the warming of the weather, the men of the *New Jersey* began to get a better idea of their destination. In the meantime, they had to put up with the discomfort of storm-tossed seas in the traditionally rough Cape Hatteras region off the Carolina coast. On 4 January, for instance, Seaman Second Class James V. Grimm received a fracture to the upper part of his left arm when heavy seas washed him against the shield of a 20-mm. gun mount on the fantail. The battleships had to slow down, because the destroyers couldn't keep up in the rough weather.

Friday, 7 January was a long day for the *New Jersey* as she made her laborious way through the locks of the Panama Canal. She had been designed so she would just barely fit through those locks, and now her dimensions were put to the test for the first time. She had less than a foot of clearance on each side. After passing into the Pacific for the first time in her career, she stopped overnight for liberty in Balboa, Panama Canal Zone. For the vast majority

of the ship's crew who had been ashore in a foreign country before only in Trinidad, the experience in Panama was quite a revelation. For Philip Fuller, a member of the *New Jersey*'s band, "Getting into the city of [Balboa] and seeing the conditions there at that time, I think, opened a lot of our eyes to the fact that all the world isn't like America."

The men of the *New Jersey* went on liberty at the same time as those of the *Iowa*, and a rivalry sprang up that was to last for quite a while. The two sister ships had gone into active service within a few months of each other, and the men from each battleship felt that theirs was the better one. Seaman Second Class Roger Faw observed that the men of the *New Jersey* and *Iowa* "were constantly at each other's throats". Almost anything could start a fight. One barroom brawl erupted when the men of one ship felt that a Panamanian woman performing in the bar had been mistreated by some of the men from the other ship. Even so, that fight was an exceptional one, according to Faw, because, "I guess that was the only fight I can remember seeing and knowing what started it." In most cases things broke loose merely because the men of the *Iowa* and *New Jersey* were together. For Seaman Rafael Maza, who was in the *New Jersey*'s fourth division along with Faw, his ability to speak Spanish was a boon to his shipmates. He was able to serve as interpreter and keep his friends from getting cheated in their transactions with the local ladies.

The stop in Panama afforded the last opportunity for the *New Jersey* to take on fuel before her long transit to the South Pacific. Even so, she wasn't supposed to fill the fuel oil tanks above the waterline, explains John Rossie, because of fleet practice. The feeling was that oil above the level of the water was more likely to catch fire than that below. The Panama fueling facilities delivered the heavy black oil at well over 1,000 gallons a minute, a considerably faster pumping rate than the *New Jersey*'s fueling gang was used to.

Each fuel tank was equipped with a vent pipe routed to an overboard terminal point. The vent served two purposes, as an escape path for the air in the tank that was displaced during the filling and as a relief pipe to prevent overpressure in the case of overfilling. For some reason, one of the ship's tanks did get too much oil that night and, inexplicably, the vent pipe from the tank led not overboard but to a small storeroom adjacent to the tank. The storeroom was fitted with a duct connected to the exhaust ventilation system of the A division berthing compartment. The oil from the over-full tank quickly filled the storeroom, which was sealed off by a watertight door. The fuel then continued up the ventilation duct to the A division compartment and rained down upon sleeping men. Machinist's Mate First Class William Chambers, in a bottom bunk, awoke with the odd sensation of finding himself awash in fuel oil, because it covered the deck of the compartment to a depth of a foot or more. Wearing only his skivvy shorts and a coating of oil, Chambers scrambled along the deck, falling into the black pool at one point. He managed to get up a ladder and to the quarterdeck with the urgent message that pumping should be stopped, which it was.

Rossie remembers that Chambers's quick thinking may well have averted a much worse problem. In addition to flooding the berthing space, a considerable amount of the fuel was drawn through the vent by an exhaust fan and found its way to one of the boiler uptakes. Uptakes are spaces above the firerooms from which blowers pull air for combustion. When the cleanup crew opened the uptake space sometime later, they found the deck covered with oil to within a few inches of the top of the protective coaming surrounding the air intake openings to the boiler which was steaming for auxiliary purposes. Had the pumping not been stopped when it was, the fuel oil would have topped the coaming and flowed into the combustion air intake and then into the operating boiler, possibly causing an explosion and fire.

Even without that potential problem, things were bad enough. The compartment had to be cleaned and re-painted. The smell of the oil then lingered in it for months afterward. Lockers were flooded with oil, and men's uniforms had to be replaced. Moreover, the flooded store-room contained a large stock of spare parts for electronic equipment, and all of them were ruined by the oil. Lieutenant August B. Cook, an ex-enlisted man who served as the New Jersey's radar material officer, had to scramble around during the night seeking replacement parts, because the ship was due to leave for the war zone the next day.

Late the next morning, Saturday, 8 January 1944, the Iowa got under way from Balboa, and the New Jersey followed shortly past noon. In appearance, the two sister ships traveling together were a marked contrast. The Iowa was painted in a crazy-quilt "dazzle" camouflage pattern of grey, black, and white – a confusing mixture of shapes designed to minimize detection and determination of the direction in which the ship was headed. For a submarine seeking to set up a torpedo firing solution, the target's course is all-important. The Iowa still had the open cat-walk around the conning tower, for her trip to deliver President Roosevelt to North Africa had kept her away from a shipyard at the time the New Jersey was getting an enclosed bridge. The New Jersey was painted all over in a dark bluish-grey. The intent of that particular camouflage scheme was to make the ship blend with the sea, especially when viewed from above or from a distance. The teakwood decks had been painted over so that the light color of the planking would not stand out against the dark sea when viewed from the air.

During the next two weeks, the Iowa, New Jersey, and their destroyers maintained a course that was nearly west-southwest, with a speed generally around 20 knots or slightly higher. The battleships could easily hold that pace with half their boilers on the line. Each day the New Jersey held practice general quarters drills; for Seaman Roger Faw the drills were a useful means of breaking the monotony of the transit. Other than that, there was an endless round of chipping, painting, cleaning, swabbing decks, and stand-ing watches. For the turnbuckles holding the lifelines at the edges of the main deck to their stanchions, Faw and his mates might one day have to chip off the grey paint and polish the turnbuckles to a high luster, then repaint them again soon afterward. Recalls Rafael Maza of the trip, "They kept us pretty busy. You know, they didn't give you time to be bored, really. If you weren't sweeping, you were mopping. If you weren't mopping, you were painting."

A device which was useful both for keeping the men busy and for preparing to handle their coming combat duties was the loading machine on the 02 superstructure deck between the two smokestacks. It was a mockup of part of the machinery inside each 5-inch gun mount and provided training for the guncrews through the use of dummy projectiles and powder cases. The loading crew took the ammunition out of the loading machine hoist, loaded it into the breech of the barrel-less "gun", then hit a lever to ram projectile and shell casing into position. The repeated practice developed speed, coordination, and perspiration. Seaman Second Class Bill Hartley says of loading machine drill in the equatorial regions, "I'll guarantee that would bring the sweat out of you."

One of the normal traditions of the Navy was dispensed with during that January transit because of the urgency of getting the battleship out to the war zone. Customarily, the ceremony associated with crossing the Equator includes much hijinks and merriment. The pollywogs who have never been across the line before – and that was nearly everyone in the New Jersey – are the victims of playful mischief on the part of the shellbacks who have been through it already. Pollywogs often have their heads shaved, backsides pounded, and suffer the indignity of crawling through a chute filled with garbage. There was no such ceremony when the New Jersey crossed into the South Pacific for the first time on 13 January. Instead, the men were all handed wallet-sized cards which Executive Officer Rufus Rose signed on behalf of "Davey Jones" and "Neptune Rex".

With their arrival at Funafuti Atoll in the Ellice Islands on 22 January, the battleships and their escorts entered a lagoon that was filled with ships – the battleships Washington and North Carolina, aircraft carriers, supply ships, tankers, and transports. Seaman Rafael Maza was awed by the sight of all the naval vessels: "When we went there and we anchored, I never, never in my life had seen so many ships together. I never will forget that. That was tremendous."

The preliminaries were over at last. The USS New Jersey had joined the fleet that was fighting Japan.

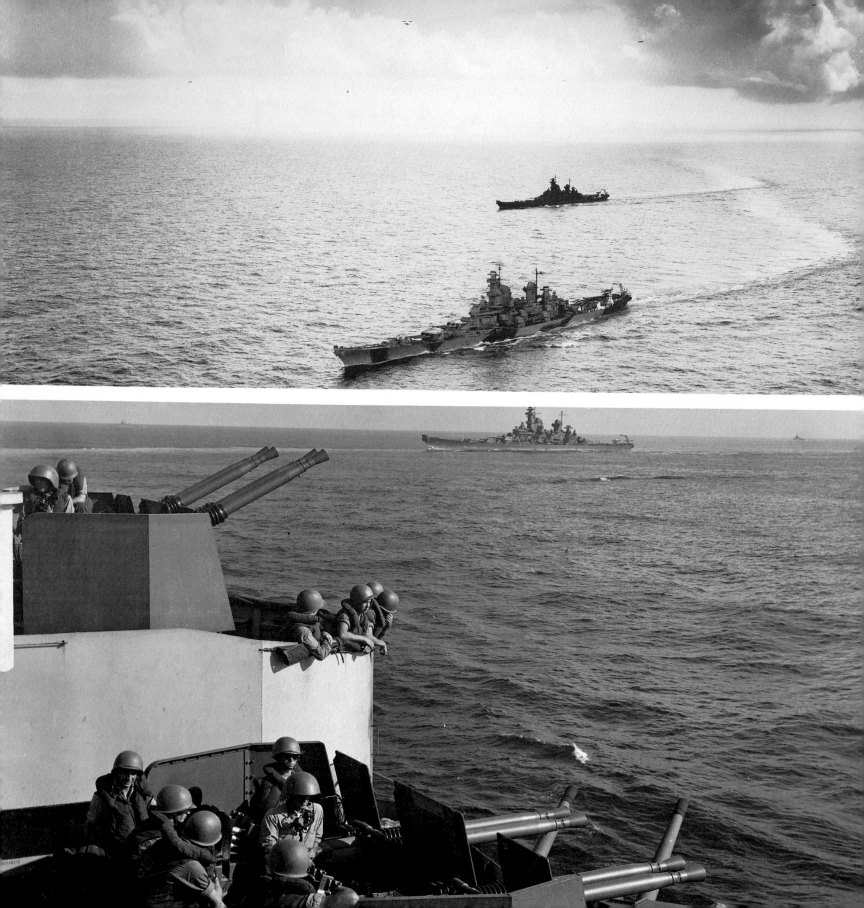

# CHAPTER II
# WORLD WAR II – EVERYTHING
# EXCEPT A BATTLESHIP
## January 1944–August 1945

The *New Jersey*'s main engines scarcely had a chance to cool at Funafuti Atoll before she was off and running again. The crew's sea legs, developed during the three-week voyage from Panama, remained in use, right away, because this was not a liberty stop. The Central Pacific offensive against Japan – built around amphibious landings and carrier air strikes – was moving into high gear.

Soon after arrival at Funafuti, Captain Holden reported to Rear Admiral Frederick Sherman in the carrier *Bunker Hill*. Joining Holden in going to the pre-operation conference for the Marshall Islands were Rear Admiral Olaf Hustvedt, Commander Battleship Division Seven, and Captain John McCrea of the *Iowa*. Commander Roland Dale, the *Bunker Hill*'s air group commander, got the impression that the battleship officers expected their ships to win the war. As Dr. Clark Reynolds reports in *The Fast Carriers*, combat veteran Sherman soon set them straight by saying, "I don't care whether or not you can shoot your 16-inch guns, but you'd better know how to use your anti-aircraft batteries." Aircraft carriers were now the top dogs.

The *New Jersey*'s crew was already preparing for an early departure. Radarman Third Class Joseph McGowan and many of his shipmates stayed up long into that night of 22–23 January to bring supplies aboard. Radar technicians, including Robert Parmelee, were also busy because of problems with the SG surface search antenna. The repairmen finished about daylight and were met by Lieutenant August Cook, the colorful radar material officer described by another member of the *New Jersey*'s wardroom as a "capricious genius".

Cook took the men to his stateroom and telephoned the wardroom for four glasses and four cans of pineapple juice. He then broke out some bottles of alcohol he had smuggled aboard in Philadelphia by telling the officer of the deck they were radar repair parts. He conveniently disregarded the prohibition against alcoholic beverages on board U.S. Navy ships, although the bottles did have a connection – as reward – with radar repair. After the technicians finished their drinks, Cook told them, "All right you bastards, don't say nothing to nobody. Just go up and go to sleep."

Less than twenty-three hours after her arrival, the *New Jersey* was under way once more. She and the *Iowa* soon joined Sherman's Task Group 58.3. Included, besides the flagship *Bunker Hill*, were the light carriers *Monterey* and *Cowpens*, the heavy cruiser *Wichita*, and nine destroyers. Two of the warships dated from 1939, but the other thirteen in the task group had been in commission less than a year. Altogether, there were four such task groups which comprised Task Force 58 under Rear Admiral Marc Mitscher. As the force steamed northward, Captain Holden told the *New Jersey*'s crew members their destination. Kwajalein Atoll was considered the heart of the Marshalls, though not the most heavily defended part.

At about 3:00 a.m. on 29 January, the men of the *New Jersey* were roused from their bunks, given coffee and sandwiches, and sent to general quarters. Joe McGowan described the scene in a letter written shortly afterward: "My battle station was Air Defense aft so I was able to see everything. It seemed funny, everybody was quiet and you said so long to your friends and went at it." In the darkness that morning, some 700 planes took off to attack Kwajalein; they achieved complete surprise and success. No Japanese planes came within sight of the *New Jersey*.

Once control of the air was achieved, battleships – principally old ones – began giving the boomerang-shaped Kwajalein Island a "Spruance haircut", named for Vice Admiral Raymond Spruance who, as Commander Central Pacific Force, was in overall command of the operation. The murderous gunfire mowed down palm trees, buildings, and Japanese.

Task Group 58.3 then steamed west, while an enemy scout plane trailed during the night, until daybreak on Sunday, 30 January. The battleship's crew took it as the precursor of a large attack. Wrote Joe McGowan afterward: ". . . while [we were] just getting ready to sit down to Sunday dinner the Japs started to come in. Everybody ran like everything for their battle stations and me cursing them for interrupting my dinner. Then I began to worry. I had no gas mask or flash clothing to protect me from burns. Everything down by my bunk. I started to hope they wouldn't use gas. In fact I begged them not to. As it was they didn't get as far as us before they had to go home."

From the 30th until 1 February, the day of the amphibious assault on Kwajalein, Sherman's task group operated between Bikini and Eniwetok in the Marshalls. Carrier planes pounded the latter with bombs in order to keep Japanese forces there from threatening the Kwajalein landings. After three days of bombing at Eniwetok, wrote

**Above:** Admiral Raymond A. Spruance, left, Commander Fifth Fleet, with his flagship captain, Carl F. Holden, 8 April 1944 at Majuro Atoll. The two are standing near the turret two barbette. (Naval Historical Center: NH 62516)

**Above right:** A small Japanese trawler pours out smoke after being hit by 5-inch projectiles from the *New Jersey* during the Truk strike of 16 February 1944. (From the *New Jersey*'s after-action report; courtesy Naval Historical Center)

Sherman, "Everything above ground had been obliterated and the island looked like a desert waste."

The Marshalls campaign turned out as close to a textbook operation as possible. The Japanese Combined Fleet chose not to contest it, and the U.S. Navy ended up in possession of a new fleet base in the Marshalls, Majuro Atoll, 250 miles southeast of Kwajalein. It had a large, protected anchorage, much closer to the scene of future operations than was Funafuti. The *New Jersey* arrived at Majuro late on the morning of 4 February and anchored. The gathering of ships was even bigger than that at Funafuti, and now there was a chance for liberty of a sort. Landing craft borrowed from the amphibious forces present came alongside to ferry men ashore for beer, barbecue, baseball, and swimming.

The stay at Majuro also brought the battleship her first embarked flag officer, Vice Admiral Spruance. His previous flagship, the heavy cruiser *Indianapolis*, moored alongside for the transfer on 9 February of the Central Pacific Force (also known as Fifth Fleet) officer staff, enlisted support personnel, and the office files that went with them. Shortly after Spruance's arrival, a message received in the *New Jersey*'s radio central brought the news that President Franklin Roosevelt had just nominated Spruance for promotion to four-star rank.

The man nominated by FDR was a lean, quiet individual, known for his shrewdness and his fondness for swimming and long walks. Ensign King Brandt of the *New Jersey*'s communication staff came to know the taciturn Spruance through his messages. Spruance, remembers Brandt, "could say more in about ten lines than any other naval officer I ever ran into". Brevity was desirable when radio messages had to be laboriously encoded before being sent

out. The admiral was not one for oral small talk either, as Lieutenant Commander Bill Abhau of the ship's gunnery department discovered. He recalls that Spruance frequently paced on the 01 superstructure deck outside flag quarters. Staff officers came out to walk with him and brief him on various matters, and the admiral often indicated his position either by nodding or shaking his head – not saying anything at all. On one occasion in 1945, it fell to Abhau to escort Admiral Spruance to the movie about to be shown on the fantail. Abhau says, "I quickly learned that all he wanted to hear from me was, 'Good evening, admiral'". Of the methodical flag officer, Abhau observes, "When Spruance was in command, everything happened just the way it was laid down in the plan. Somehow, the Japanese always conformed."

There was, however, at least one occasion when events didn't go according to plan and barely escaped causing what would have been embarrassing damage to the *New Jersey*. In the first two years of the war, Truk in the Caroline Islands was considered an impregnable stronghold for the Japanese Combined Fleet. Now it had to be neutralized so the Fifth Fleet could proceed with its plans to capture and occupy Eniwetok. Admiral Mitscher's task force was assigned to attack by air, and Admiral Spruance elected to lead a surface task group against Japanese warships escaping from Truk Lagoon.

Late in the morning of 16 February, a task group consisting of the *New Jersey* and *Iowa*, the heavy cruisers *Minneapolis* and *New Orleans*, and four destroyers assembled under the tactical command of Admiral Spruance and began a counterclockwise circuit about Truk. The events of the day were mostly anticlimactic, because the bulk of the Japanese fleet had fled shortly

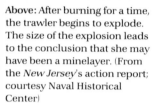

**Above:** After burning for a time, the trawler begins to explode. The size of the explosion leads to the conclusion that she may have been a minelayer. (From the *New Jersey*'s action report; courtesy Naval Historical Center)

**Above right:** Smoke towers 300 feet skyward as the Japanese trawler erupts in a dramatic explosion. (National Archives: 80-G-210972)

before. Even so, 16 February brought plenty of excitement, not least because it marked the first time the *New Jersey* fired her guns in anger.

At midday, a Zero fighter plane dropped a near-miss bomb which came close to the bridge of the *Iowa* on the side where Admiral Hustvedt was eating lunch. The *New Jersey* took the plane under fire, but it got away. The effect down inside the ship was electric. For the men below decks throughout the war, action had to be seen through the words of whomever was on the bridge serving as battle announcer. Lieutenant Harry Reynolds was at his battle station down in main engine control that day, listening to reports over the general announcing system. Suddenly a report came down, "There are Japanese airplanes overhead." The men in main control, who had been relaxed and doing nothing more taxing than watching the turning of the engine revolution counters, bolted out of their seats with a sense of shared peril.

During the course of the afternoon, the *New Jersey* fired at more aircraft; sank the trawler *No. 15 Shonan Maru* at close range; shot at the destroyer *Maikaze*, which was later finished off by the cruisers; barely escaped being torpedoed by the light cruiser *Katori*; and then was involved in a long-range stern chase in which 16-inch projectiles from the *New Jersey* straddled the fleeing destroyer *Nowaki* before she escaped.

The battle against the trawler was pitifully one-sided. She was only a few thousand yards away from the *New Jersey*, so she was dispatched with the ship's 5-inch and 40-mm. guns. Seaman First Class Rafael Maza was in a 5-inch mount on the port side. He recalls, "We were so excited that we kept feeding those damn guns, and the horn was blowing – cease firing, cease firing. And we kept

loading that silly thing – we were so nervous." The reason for the order to cease fire was that the trawler erupted in a spectacular explosion which blew smoke and debris high in the air. Maza contends, with tongue in cheek, that if it hadn't been for the explosion the tiny trawler would have sunk from the weight of the 5-inch projectiles hurled at her by the battleship.

Before the *Katori* was sunk by the cruisers, she unleashed a spread of torpedoes which passed between the *Iowa* and *New Jersey*. None exploded, and at least one broached after passing through the *New Jersey*'s wake. Radar Technician Parmelee was in the combat information center on the fourth deck ". . . when those torpedoes went by us. I was right next to that 16-inch magazine, and I wasn't scared too many times, but that was one damn time I was scared."

Spruance's biographer, Commander Thomas B. Buell, recounted in his book *The Quiet Warrior* that the admiral's chief of staff, Captain Charles J. Moore, was mortified that the torpedoes came close to hitting the flagship *New Jersey*. Normally, a fleet commander would have passed tactical command to a subordinate, such as Rear Admiral Hustvedt in the *Iowa*. Spruance's staff was used to making strategic decisions rather than tactical ones, so Moore wasn't quick enough to realize that torpedoes were being fired at the *New Jersey* and to take appropriate action to get the formation out of the way. As Buell explains, "It had been a near thing, and the torpedoes had missed the battleships through luck alone." In a sense, Truk was the Japanese equivalent of Pearl Harbor, so Spruance's command of the task group may have been his way of flaunting the dramatic growth in American naval power since 7 December 1941. It also gave him a chance to act, in essence, as a battleship division commander in combat.

The day of battle was still not over because of the fleeing *Nowaki*. Only the two forward turrets were used, because the *New Jersey*'s progress would have been impeded by turning to fire turret three. As it was, recalls turret two officer Oscar Gray, the ship weaved back and forth about ten degrees either side of a true trailing course in order to avoid the shock damage to the raised bow which might have resulted from shooting directly over it.

Turret two opened with a salvo of three projectiles, followed shortly by a salvo from turret one. The latter knocked the SG surface search radar out of commission but didn't affect the Mark 8 main battery fire control radar. Lieutenant Commander Abhau of the gunnery department was impressed by the latter, because the signal on the radar scope was so precise that fire controlmen could see the splashes of the 16-inch projectiles falling near the target. Commander Dale of the *Bunker Hill* was in an aircraft over the *Nowaki* to spot the fall of shot. He recalls that "this was a real smart [destroyer] captain. As soon as he saw the belch of the 16-inchers, he changed course about 45 degrees and held it until the shells splashed, which were then well off in deflection, then he resumed his base course." Dale and his wingman were unable to slow the *Nowaki* by strafing her. Overall, the *New Jersey* fired for nine minutes as the destroyer's range opened from 32,200 yards to 35,000, unleashing eighteen of her 16-inch shells; they came close but not close enough.

On the morning of 17 February, the *New Jersey* rejoined Task Group 58.3 to resume her role of conforming to the movements of the carriers. That less-than-glamorous duty continued until she anchored in Kwajalein Atoll on 19 February. Two and a half weeks earlier, the amphibious assault had been mounted there, and now the conquering fleet came in to have a close look at the target it had struck previously from afar.

The five-day stay at Kwajalein was the first time that most of the men of the *New Jersey* encountered the effects of war at close range. The guns of the old battleships had devastated the island, and the rifles of American soldiers had created many, many corpses. The stench from the rotting bodies reached out to the *New Jersey*'s anchorage in the lagoon. When Lieutenant Roman "Rozy" Mrozinski went ashore, he saw an American soldier, sitting among the corpses and flies, happily eating a can of captured Japanese pineapple. The soldier offered some, but Mrozinski hadn't much of an appetite at that point. Lieutenant Gray saw a Japanese pillbox heavily damaged by naval gunfire, so he went inside for a closer look and came face to face with a detached Japanese head suspended from the top of the pillbox by a soldier with an unusual sense of humor. Other soldiers brought along enemy heads when they came out to the *New Jersey* for a shower and hot meal, but Captain Holden soon put a stop to that practice.

Those who did go ashore from the ship were propelled by a sense of curiosity but took with them a sense of caution as well, for snipers were still active. Sometimes, the earth-moving blades of the Seabees' bulldozers served as shields to fend off stray bullets. Seaman Bob Westcott decided to be something of an entrepreneur when he discovered the paucity of pure drinking water ashore. On board ship he filled up canteens with cold water and began peddling it to the soldiers on the beach for a dollar a swallow. He was stopped as soon as the officer of the deck found out.

Inevitably, some of the *New Jersey*'s men sought to carry away war souvenirs from the battered island. One of the men in the FA division took a Japanese antiaircraft fuze to the ship. His division officer, Lieutenant (junior grade) Les Heselton, offered to disarm the fuze by removing the cap. In the process, the last bit of powder exploded, shattering Heselton's left index finger and "shooting down" a model plane that was hanging in the secondary battery plotting room. "Thus," remembers Heselton, "the AA fuze fulfilled its mission in a minor way."

One other event of the stay at Kwajalein was Spruance's formal promotion to full admiral on 21 February. That was the first time he had an opportunity to take the physical exam required for promotion. Once he passed the physical, he was able to wear on his khaki shirt collar the four-star insignia made for him in the *New Jersey*'s machine shop. His blue and white four-star flag was hoisted from high in the ship.

On 25 February, after a brief trip from Kwajalein, the *New Jersey* anchored at Majuro. That day's issue of *The Jerseyman* featured heavy coverage of Admiral Spruance's arrival, and it also carried an article about the only crew member born on board the ship. That was SuzyBelle, a small black-and-white terrier who served as the Marine detachment's mascot. Her mother, LuluBelle, had given birth to her in August 1943 in the first sergeant's stateroom. Soon SuzyBelle acquired a Marine-like nickname, Spike, and made it clear that she preferred the company of Marines rather than sailors. The feeling was reciprocated, although Private First Class Dale O'Bryen wasn't pleased when ordered to clean up Spike's droppings.

The *New Jersey* spent much of the next month anchored at Majuro while awaiting ensuing stages of the Central Pacific campaign. Admiral Spruance was absent for nearly a week, having been summoned to Pearl Harbor to be briefed by Admiral Chester Nimitz, Commander-in-Chief, Pacific Fleet, on Joint Chiefs of Staff decisions concerning future strategy. Spruance's forces were to bypass Truk and capture the Marianas Islands to the north in order to provide the Army Air Forces with bases for long-range bombing of Japan.

While Admiral Spruance was away, the *New Jersey* and *Iowa* went out for a practice session which proved unexpectedly hazardous for their health. It was intended

Above: Spike, mascot of the *New Jersey*'s Marine detachment, sits atop a hatch on the fore-castle. She was born in a ship-board storeroom in 1943. (Courtesy Mrs. Frank Reagan)

as the range closed, giving her gun and ammunition-handling crews practice against a supposedly easy target.

In the *New Jersey*'s lower handling room, down near the bottom of the ship, Seaman First Class Robert Knoll had the job of taking powder bags out of the flameproof passing scuttle and carrying them over to put on the hoist up to the turret. In an adjacent magazine, other men took the bags out of the aluminum containers in which they were stored, catching a whiff of the ether used as a preservative, and put the bags into their side of the scuttle so they could go through to Knoll. The handling room and magazines were separated by a stout bulkhead in order to confine the effects of a possible mishap.

All went well until the two ships got in to 19,000 yards. Then, more than two hours after the battleship bombardment started, pinpricks of light began flashing on the beach. The Japanese had waited until the American ships got within range of their 6-inch guns – transported to Mille after being captured from the British at Singapore – and then opened fire themselves. Splashes were soon straddling the *New Jersey*. The Japanese guns had the right bearing but were off in range. Storekeeper Third Class Willard Bartusch was standing on one of the *New Jersey*'s superstructure decks when a Japanese projectile went over the ship from port to starboard. Says Bartusch, "I felt the heat, but I didn't realize what it was until somebody said that was a shell that hit the water on the other side."

Inside turret two Lieutenant Oscar Gray had his periscope trained forward on the *Iowa* when he saw two flashes as enemy projectiles hit the sister ship, causing minor damage on her port side. Up in the *New Jersey*'s exposed air defense station, Lieutenant Commander Bill Abhau was watching the enemy shore batteries through a pair of binoculars mounted on a metal splinter shield. While his eyes were fixed to the binoculars, he said something to a Marine lieutenant who was stationed topside with him, but there was no answer. Abhau turned around to look; when he found the lieutenant behind the foundation of the main battery director, he asked, "What are you doing back here?"

The lieutenant replied, "You just can't dig a foxhole in these steel decks."

Abhau admits he was not feeling comfortable himself at that point, especially because the two battleships continued to stay within range of the enemy guns, even while the Japanese were peppering away at them: "We didn't turn, we didn't change speed, and . . . the pair of guns that was shooting at us had too good a [fire control] solution. They managed to keep one short and the other one over the whole time. But it would have been a lot more comfortable if we'd turned or done something."

The situation on board the *Iowa* was an unusual one. Even though Admiral Lee was senior to Admiral Hustvedt and in overall command of the operation, he did not have tactical command of the battleship formation. Years later,

strictly as a training session at bypassed Mille Atoll in the southern Marshalls. The two battleships, still new to the war zone, would get their first opportunity to practice shore bombardment against live targets. They would be joined by four destroyers and the carrier *Lexington*, back from the repair of battle damage in the United States and in need of training for her new air group.

Rear Admiral Willis A. "Ching" Lee, Jr., was on board the *Iowa* in overall command of the Mille Striking Group, while Rear Admiral Hustvedt remained in the same ship and had command of the two-battleship bombardment unit. The striking group arrived off Mille on the morning of 18 March. With Spruance away from the *New Jersey*, the *Iowa* was again temporarily senior ship, so she had the honor of opening fire first with her 16-inch guns. The two battleships proceeded methodically to send 1,900-pound high-capacity projectiles toward defense installations on Mille. The *New Jersey*'s three turrets were firing in rotation

in his oral history reminiscences with the U.S. Naval Institute, Hustvedt said, "I should like to record here my appreciation of the fact that Admiral Lee, although he was a very interested observer of the operation . . . never at any time interposed anything which could be interpreted as an interference with the plan which I had issued in my short operation order nor with the movements as they were executed by the forces under my command." Lee may have offered suggestions, because Frank Pinney, then assistant gunnery officer in the *Iowa*, remembers that Lee told the ship's captain that he should clear out to save his ship and ammunition for more worthwhile targets than those on Mille. Being damaged on an easy practice run was surprising and led Lieutenant Harry Reynolds of the *New Jersey*'s engineering department to summarize the operation by saying, "We looked silly at Mille."

On Sunday, 19 March, the day after the Mille bombardment, the *New Jersey* anchored in the lagoon at Majuro Atoll. Admiral Spruance returned from Hawaii, and so the *New Jersey* was once again fleet flagship. Upon the *Iowa*'s return to port, her skipper, Captain McCrea, received a message from the commanding officer of the fast battleship *Alabama*, asking the cause of the hole in the side of the new ship. Captain McCrea puckishly replied, "Rats."

The stay at Majuro was brief, for the mobility and striking power of Task Force 58 were again to be put to use, this time at the Palau Islands in the Western Carolines. The objective was 2,000 miles west of Majuro and more than 1,000 west of Truk. The *New Jersey* was part of Rear Admiral Alfred Montgomery's Task Group 58.2. In some ways, the strike was reminiscent of the mid-February attack on Truk. That had been the base for the Japanese Combined Fleet. After it escaped Truk, it moved to Palau. There, it would be in a position to harass General Douglas MacArthur's planned landings at Hollandia, on the north coast of New Guinea, in April.

In an effort to avoid detection during the long journey westward, Task Force 58 looped south toward the Equator. On the way, however, the American force was seen and reported by Japanese search planes, so the element of surprise was lost. The date of the carrier strike, which was also to include aerial mining to bottle up ships in Palau harbor, was advanced from 1 April to 30 March.

On the night of 29 March, the *New Jersey* encountered her first night air attack of the war. Surprisingly, the first warning of the incoming raid came when her main battery fire control radar detected Japanese planes at a range of 30,000 yards. The SK air search radar picked them up a minute later. Shortly before 9:00 that night, the 5-inch battery was ordered to open fire. The secondary battery fire control radars indicated that one plane was shot down. Although no explosion was visible in the sky, the bursting 5-inch projectiles could be seen on radar in the vicinity of the plane, and then there was no more blip for the plane. Another aircraft turned away and disappeared

when the first was apparently shot down. The *New Jersey*'s 20-mm. and 40-mm. guns were also chattering away during the enemy raid, which included torpedo planes. Since the light antiaircraft guns were not controlled by radar, they were supposed to shoot only when the men firing them could see their targets visually. Analysis after the battle concluded that the gunners had been over-anxious during the ship's first night action. Other bugs in the system showed up as well.

Lieutenant Commander Abhau, all the way topside in the air defense station, found it useful to have Lieutenant (junior grade) Bill Coyne down in the combat information center as an air defense liaison officer who could keep watch on the various plotting boards in CIC which kept track of range and direction of incoming raids. He was then able to pass the information to Abhau by sound-powered phone, and Abhau, in turn, used the information to direct the anti-aircraft batteries.

On 30 March, Admiral Mitscher's aircraft went after their targets and achieved considerable success, both in bottling up ships with their mining and in destroying enemy aircraft and small vessels. Alas, as at Truk, the big ships, including the Combined Fleet flagship *Musashi*, had been tipped off and were able to escape. On 1 April, after two days of strikes on Palau, all three of Admiral Mitscher's task groups attacked Woleai, another of the Japanese-occupied islands in the Carolines, but the opposition and results were small. Then the ships turned their bows toward the east and the long run back to Majuro.

The Palau operation provided the crew of the *New Jersey* with yet more knowledge of the ways of a battleship in a carrier war. Although they had already learned a lot since their joining, more than two months earlier, Radar Technician Bob Parmelee recalls that some of the officers in the FA division carried with them for too long the notion that the most important part of a Mark 37 antiaircraft director was its optical rangefinder. They had been brought up to believe, "If you can't see it, you can't hit it." However, as the attack on 29 March demonstrated – and as many more would during the war – radar-controlled gunfire is effective, and at night it's the only way. Parmelee had been experiencing difficulties keeping the fire control radar operating, because men kept stepping on coaxial cables and breaking connections. But once the value of the gunnery radar became apparent, Parmelee no longer had trouble getting support for it. After a while, the situation reversed. He says, "If the radar wasn't pluperfect, we caught hell. It was a complete turnaround."

As the Pacific campaign progressed, everyone on board was concerned with sleep. Fireman Sherman Brattin, for instance, was assigned to one of the *New Jersey*'s boiler rooms. Though the temperature often reached 90°, it was still reasonably comfortable, because one could stand underneath a blower and get a steady breeze. No such solution was available, however, in the B division berthing space. Brattin's bunk was next to a boiler uptake which carried hot exhaust from the boilers to the stacks topside. It was too hot to be tolerable, so he began sleeping on the deck in the compartment.

For Russ Brown, a machinist's mate in the boiler division, the berthing compartment became inconvenient because of all the general quarters drills to which the ship was subjected. In addition to those at dawn and dusk, which were designed to provide maximum alertness at the times most likely for submarine attack, there were also calls to battle stations when Japanese planes approached. To avoid the treks from the berthing compartment to his battle station in forward diesel, Brown just remained at his battle station at night. He explains, "You just threw a blanket on the steel grate and slept on that."

Shipfitter William Dugan found the R division berthing compartment too crowded for comfort, so he sometimes slept out on deck topside. He recalls with fondness the

Below: Having shed his shirt, a *New Jersey* man takes some sun in front of the two forward turrets. Notice the rifling at the muzzle end of the right gun of turret one. A wartime censor has retouched the Mark 8 radar antenna atop the forward fire control tower. (U.S. Naval Institute Collection)

cool nights in the Pacific, although rain showers sometimes disrupted sleep. As a result, there was frequently a good deal of competition to get protected spots under turrets, whaleboats, or stacks of life rafts. For Leonard Jung, a musician in the ship's band, the narrow separation between individual bunks in the four-tiered racks caused problems. They were so close together in some cases that people had trouble turning over once they were in bed, especially if the man above was heavy. Thus, Jung also found sleeping on deck to be preferable. As a pillow, he used his folded-up hat, previously white but dyed dark blue to make detection difficult at night. After a night on deck, his left hipbone was frequently sore in the morning.

The days and nights on the way back to base passed relatively quickly, for the ship was heading away from the threat rather than toward it. On 18 April, at Majuro, the *Indianapolis* came alongside, and on the following day she received Admiral Spruance and his staff. He was headed for Pearl Harbor to work on planning for the forthcoming Marianas campaign, and the *New Jersey* would soon be off to support the landings at Hollandia, New Guinea.

In the meantime, there was a bit of surgery to be performed on the nine barrels of the 16-inch guns. The firing during the 1943 training and shakedown period – along with that at Truk – had extruded the hard metal liners so that they had pushed out beyond the ends of the barrels. There was a danger that the liners could crack and keep the guns from being fired. Warrant Machinist Leo Hicks sought help for the problem from repair ships at Majuro, but they were too busy to provide much assistance. The solution came from a machinist's mate second class named Ewald who had run a small machine shop in New York in civilian life and had become adept at finding ways to accomplish what his customers wanted. In this case, he took a turbine motor that was used to run brushes in a boiler to clean it. He mounted that on a yoke that hooked onto the ends of the gun barrels and attached a gearing mechanism and a cutter blade made of tool steel. The motor then turned the blade so that it went round and round the barrel, shaving off a continuous sliver, perhaps 1/16 inch thick, of the extruded liner. One by one, the protruding liners were shaved down.

On 13 April, Task Force 58 left Majuro for New Guinea. The *New Jersey* was again in Rear Admiral Montgomery's Task Group 58.2. The naval force arrived off Hollandia for air strikes on 21 April, the day before General MacArthur's amphibious landings. As expected, the *New Jersey* didn't get in sight of land, and the aviators of Task Force 58 met little opposition from the Japanese. Because of the effectiveness of bombing strikes on New Guinea by the Fifth Air Force, Mitscher's task force hadn't been needed to support MacArthur, but it was better to be safe than sorry.

Although the trip to Hollandia was not memorable in terms of enemy action, the crew of the *New Jersey* did form lasting impressions of the heat in the equatorial region. Ensign King Brandt had found the rain squalls in the Marshalls refreshing, but there was no such relief off New Guinea. When the ship was closed up during general quarters, there was often little air moving, especially because blowers had to be turned off to avoid the possibility of fire spreading through ventilation ducts.

Lieutenant Julius Edelstein often didn't bother to take off his flameproof oilcloth mattress cover. When he got into bed, he generally just flopped down on top of the oilcloth. Decks and bulkheads were bare of insulation, so heat radiated into his room. The temperatures of more than 100° produced pools of perspiration which couldn't be absorbed into the bedding because the mattress cover was waterproof as well as fireproof. Fire Controlman George Teller had the opposite problem. He took the mattress cover off to sleep, so when he put it back on, he kept the accumulated sweat in the mattress from evaporating. Teller also recalls that Hollandia was the first place where the men of the New Jersey encountered use of flares by the Japanese. Planes flew over at night and dropped flares to illuminate the American ships. The crews of these ships, including the New Jersey, were then obliged to go to battle stations to be ready for possible attack. Fatigue set in, and Teller recalls that, "You built up a certain numbness after a while."

One consequence of the heat, recalls Rafael Maza, who was a seaman in the fourth division, was that many of the ship's crew members developed heat rash with itching, peeling skin. It was especially uncomfortable around the crotch and between the legs, so sick bay had many customers for a purple ointment which provided some relief and doubtless produced some interesting-looking sailors.

When Task Force 58 was released to leave the area, Admiral Mitscher was not content to return the carriers to Majuro with their magazines still full of bombs and ammunition that weren't needed at New Guinea. He scheduled another strike at Truk on 29 April, because it was still a formidable Japanese air base. During the attack, a low-flying Zeke fighter out from Truk flew through the American formation and came under fire. The New Jersey suffered by virtue of being at the center of the Task Group 58.2 formation during much of the operation. She had fired fewer than a dozen rounds of 40-mm. when the plane passed astern of her, because that was the only time she had a clear bearing. One New Jersey crew member recalls that she was sometimes referred to as "the ship with the wooden guns" because she was so often restricted in her ability to shoot.

On the afternoon of 30 April, after the air strikes had eliminated Truk as a major Japanese base, the New Jersey was released from Task Group 58.2 to join up with the rest of the battleships. For the first time in the Central Pacific campaign, the recently promoted Vice Admiral Lee had a chance to operate the battle line together. The New Jersey

and Iowa joined the North Carolina, Massachusetts, Indiana, Alabama, and South Dakota. Ponape, the largest of the Carolines at 19 miles in diameter, was considered a suitable target because it offered potential as an alternate Japanese air base after Truk was hit.

Altogether, the New Jersey fired ninety rounds of 16-inch ammunition and 154 of 5-inch. Air spotters reported that she had caused considerable damage to Japanese barracks buildings. It was the New Jersey's best shore bombardment to date, but there was one member of the 5-inch gun crew who wasn't able to participate in the gunnery. Seaman Roger Faw of the fourth division felt abdominal pains when he reported to his general quarters station, so he went to the sick bay for treatment. The first doctor who examined him told Faw he was probably just constipated, but the ship's senior medical officer recognized the symptoms of an inflamed appendix and proceeded to operate during the course of the shore bombardment. Faw had only a local anesthetic during the appendectomy, so he was alert enough to realize that the doctor interrupted work whenever a 16-inch salvo was coming up.

During the New Jersey's operations with the fast carrier task force, her movements were controlled by a rotation of officers of the deck on the bridge. Captain Holden relied on three lieutenants, all Naval Academy graduates: Rozy Mrozinski and Gene Hayward of the class of 1939 and Oscar Gray from 1940. Day after day, they trudged to the cramped bridge around the conning tower, alert for signals from the task group flagship, keeping abreast of carrier movements, watching the radar scope, listening to messages on the voice radio, guiding the ship while destroyers were alongside to refuel, and generally keeping track of the tactical picture in their heads. Each of these officers could count on spending eight of every twenty-four hours on the bridge, and all three had turret divisions to run as well.

Later in the year, Lieutenant John Sullivan, Gray's classmate, moved into the rotation when Mrozinski left. Sullivan remembers Mrozinski as a stolid, stonefaced man in whom lurked a mischievous sense of humor. He also considered Mrozinski the ship's best officer of the deck, someone who knew tactics thoroughly and was calm under fire. Says Sullivan, "An atomic blast 1,000 yards away wouldn't faze him." Neither, apparently, did Captain Holden. On one occasion, when the captain was sitting in his chair on the bridge and appeared unnerved by the tactical situation, Mrozinski walked over, patted the captain on the head, and said, "Just relax. Everything's under control." Normally, such familiarity would not be tolerated by a senior officer, but Holden's future prospects depended on these OODs keeping him out of trouble – and both he and Mrozinski realized that.

Oscar Gray recalls that all the bridge windows had to be rolled down when the guns were to be fired so they

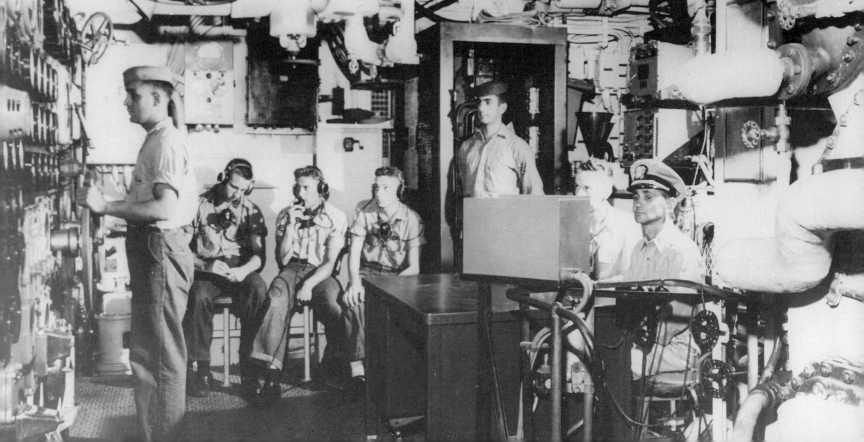

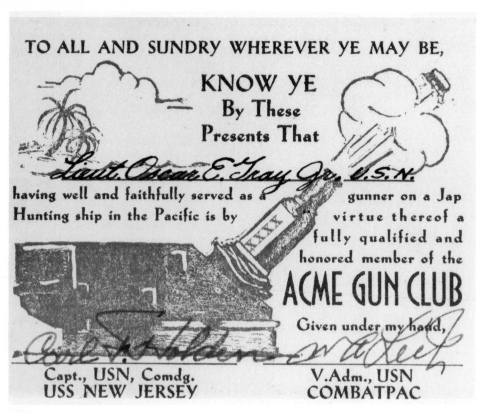

TO ALL AND SUNDRY WHEREVER YE MAY BE,

KNOW YE
By These
Presents That

*Lieut. Oscar E. Gray Jr., U.S.N.*

having well and faithfully served as a
Hunting ship in the Pacific is by

gunner on a Jap
virtue thereof a
fully qualified and
honored member of the

ACME GUN CLUB

Given under my hand,

Capt., USN, Comdg.
USS NEW JERSEY

V.Adm., USN
COMBATPAC

**Above:** One of the ship's OODs carried this wallet card countersigned by the skipper and Vice Admiral Willis Lee. The gun club was named for the Acme beer consumed at Pacific anchorages, and that is why this turret's gun is a beer bottle and the projectile is a bottle cap. (Courtesy Captain Oscar E. Gray)

wouldn't be shattered by the blast. "When we got an AA attack," he says, "the 40-mm. gun that sat on turret two [just forward of the bridge] . . . was very staccato, and it would practically tear the teeth right out of your head – the concussion." Gray's recollection is in line with that of many other *New Jersey* men – that the smaller guns were harder on the ears than the 16-inch.

Among the many considerations of an OOD in formation with a variety of other ship types is matching his ship's movements to those of the rest, especially the aircraft carriers. That means close coordination with the throttlemen in main control and other engine rooms, for it is they who must feed in the proper amount of steam to the turbines to ensure that the ship accelerates and decelerates properly. Lieutenant Commander John McCormick, the assistant engineer officer, rigged up three different sets of acceleration curves – a slow one to match the relatively slow pace at which aircraft carriers moved up to speed, a faster one to match the 27-knot, 35,000-ton battleships, and a third for times when the *New Jersey* was steaming with quick-starting destroyers. Says McCormick, "In this last condition we just opened the throttle and took off at great speed."

The *New Jersey*'s OODs and machinist's mates were able to rest for about a month when the ship arrived at Majuro once more on 4 May. On the 14th, the *New Jersey* got a new occupant in her flag quarters in the person of Vice

Admiral Willis Lee, Commander Battleships Pacific. He had been with the *New Jersey* at the bombardments of Mille and Ponape, and now he was embarked. In reality, he was using the ship only as a hotel for himself and his ten-officer staff during the period between operations. His favorite flagship was the USS *Washington*, but she had been damaged in a collision with the *Indiana* on 1 February 1944, so Lee had switched to the *North Carolina*. Now, that ship was headed to Pearl Harbor for rudder repairs, and Lee moved again, to make his home in the *New Jersey* for the next three weeks. Vice Admiral Mitscher was also in Majuro on board the carrier *Lexington*, so the period offered them a chance to work on the planning necessary for the Marianas. On 30 May the *Washington* – along with many other ships – stood in to Majuro and later that day embarked Lee and his staff.

Two members of the *New Jersey*'s supply department found an interesting pastime during the period the ship was at anchor. Seaman Third Class Wesley Krstich and Seaman Second Class James Russo wrote a letter to the New Jersey state chamber of commerce to propose a pinup contest in which photos of girls who lived in the state would be forwarded to the ship for posting on bulletin boards. An excerpt from their letter was published in the 17 May edition of the *Newark Evening News*. Altogether, more than seventy photos arrived. Among them was a beguiling shot of five-month-old Harolyn Cheryl Meyer. Her father was Lieutenant Harold Meyer, an Army Air Forces pilot from Clifton, New Jersey; he had recently been shot down over Europe and taken prisoner. The photo of baby Harolyn was the overwhelming winner in the crew's voting later in the year. The *New Jersey*'s generous men then pitched in to donate to the baby girl a silver napkin ring and war bonds that would mature to a value of $3,200. Years later, the tale had an even happier ending. Harolyn used the money to pay for her education at New Jersey's Caldwell College, married shortly after her graduation in 1965, and became a schoolteacher and mother.

One advantage of the relaxed pace in port was that it gave the *New Jersey*'s crew a chance to attend regular worship services, uninterrupted by demands of underway watches and frequent trips to battle stations. The ship had a Protestant chaplain, Catholic chaplain, and an unofficial Jewish lay leader. Father James J. Gaffney sometimes found an unconventional approach to be the most effective means of serving the needs of the crew. Musician First Class Leonard Jung was at one of Gaffney's services to provide musical accompaniment, but the singing by the congregation was lackluster. Thereupon, Gaffney said, "For Christ's sake, why don't you guys sing those goddamn hymns?" Having thus gotten his men's attention, he continued, "Now I shocked you, didn't I? I'll tell you why. You know, my stateroom is right near the bottom of this one ladder where a lot of you fellows gather to shoot

**Right:** This was the front cover of the shipboard newspaper on the first anniversary of commissioning. (Courtesy William Dugan)

**Far right:** This is the front page of a special supplement to *The Jerseyman* of 31 May 1944, providing biographical details on the temporarily embarked flag officer, Willis A. Lee, Jr. (Courtesy William Dugan)

**Bottom right:** This picture of the baby Harolyn Cheryl Meyer earned her election as Miss *New Jersey* in the summer of 1944. (Courtesy Mrs. Harolyn Lawton)

*The Jerseyman* — Anniversary Issue

VOL. 2 NO. 9 — U.S.S. NEW JERSEY — May 31, 1944

Happy Anniversary

**SISTER CONGRATULATES SISTER**
- TWO WISHES MADE -

On May 23, the U.S.S. IOWA sent a message to her sister ship the JERSEY, congratulating the younger of the two sisters on her first birthday. The IOWA dispatch and the reply from the JERSEY to the senior member of the "family" follows:

From IOWA to NEW JERSEY

"ON OCCASION OF NEW JERSEY'S FIRST BIRTHDAY ALL HANDS IN IOWA SEND BEST WISHES IN THE HOPE THAT DURING THE COMING YEAR THE TWO SISTER SHIPS MAY DEAL THE ENEMY SOME RIGHT SMART BLOWS."

From NEW JERSEY to IOWA

"YOUR SISTERSHIP THANKS YOU SINCERELY FOR YOUR MESSAGE AND JOINS MOST HEARTILY IN YOUR WISHES FOR JOINT QUOTE RIGHT SMART BLOWS UNQUOTE AGAINST THE ENEMY DURING THE COMING YEAR."

In addition to greetings received from sistership IOWA, the NEW JERSEY was honored by a call from the Division Commander, who made special point of wishing us "happy hunting" on this, our first birthday.

- RESTRICTED SUPPLEMENT -

*The Jerseyman*

- NOT TO BE MAILED HOME -

VICE ADMIRAL W. A. LEE

He raises his Flag in the New Jersey

One day recently the NEW JERSEY became for the second time in a month a flagship, with the arrival on board of Vice Admiral W.A. Lee, Commander Battleships, U.S. Pacific Fleet.

Again it was the JERSEY's good luck to have a "fighting admiral" aboard, one of the most famous "flags" in the fleet.. famous, that is, among fighting men. Admiral Lee bears a good-natured tolerance toward the press, but prefers to keep out of its way.

Born in the "Daniel Boone country" of Kentucky, Admiral Lee learned to handle a rifle almost before he could carry one. By the time he entered the Naval Academy in 1904, he was as good a shot as there could be found in the north central hills of Kentucky (he still keeps his home in the little town of Owenton where he was born). At the Academy the young plebe could shoot more accurately than his teachers. He became a member of the Academy rifle team, and for many years after graduation was the star shot of the Navy rifle team. He went to the Olympics in 1920 as a member of the American rifle squad and helped to hang up some kind of a record when his team won five firsts, a second, and a third.

In 1910 on Asiatic station (where he came by his nickname of "Chink"), young Lee participated in the famous inter-club Shanghai rifle shoot; in 1924 he was back in Asia and took part in the inter-club Hongkong shoot.

"I hope to be doing some shooting in that same general neighborhood in 1944", Admiral Lee remarked with a slow grin. It is more than possible.

Admiral Lee got two stars in 1941, he added a third in 1944. In September, 1942 he arrived at Tonga Tabu from Navy Department Duty as Assistant Chief of Staff to Cominch. He took over the U.S.S. WASHINGTON and U.S.S. SOUTH DAKOTA as COMBATDIV 6. In November of that year there took place the Battle of Savo Island, the only heavy ship surface engagement

*(Continued on Pg. 2)*

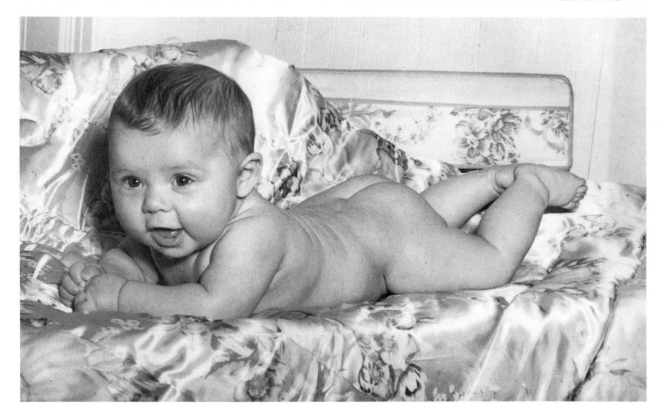

the breeze. The language I hear all the time is so sickening. How did it sound coming from me?" Fire Controlman J. P. Loughan, who was also at the service, believed Gaffney made his point most effectively.

The stay in port came to an end on 6 June when the *New Jersey* departed and soon linked up with Admiral Montgomery's Task Group 58.2 on the way to the Marianas. Thirty-two minutes into the new day of 12 June, the persistent bong-bong-bong sound of the *New Jersey's* general alarm swept through the ship. Men jumped from their racks, from on deck, or whatever other place they had found to pass the night. Watertight doors and hatches were shut and dogged down. Helmets, life jackets, and sound-powered telephones were donned. Finally, at 1:45 a.m. the radar screens throughout the ship were clear of bogeys, and the crew was allowed to go back to bed. The respite was a short one, for at 3:33 enemy planes dropped flares to illuminate the task group, and at 3:35 the ship was again called to general quarters.

The *New Jersey* and the carriers, cruisers, and destroyers with her were zigzagging through the June night at 20 knots, mindful of the possibility of attack from below as well as above. At 4:00 a.m. came still more flares. Surrounded as she was by friendly ships, the *New Jersey's* antiaircraft battery was in a "guns tight" condition. Then, out of the night, an undetected Japanese Betty torpedo bomber roared in directly at the starboard beam of the

*New Jersey* at an altitude of 300 to 500 feet. It dropped a torpedo and then, at a range of 800 yards from the ship, turned sharply to the right to parallel the ship's course.

At 4:04, Gunner's Mate Third Class V. D. Griffin, manning a 20-mm. gun on the starboard side, saw the plane and began firing, soon to be joined by three other guns. Within seconds, Lieutenant John Sullivan, who was conning on the bridge, saw the Betty's left engine nacelle catch fire: "A small glow of orange spread and spread, and the thing crashed in front of us." As the torpedo passed 2,500 yards astern of the *New Jersey*, Sullivan ordered a slight change of course to port to avoid passing too close to the burning aircraft. When ammunition expenditure was counted afterward, all four guns had fired only eighty-one rounds. A grateful Captain Holden promptly advanced Gunner's Mate Griffin from third class to second.

The following day, 13 June, the *New Jersey* and the six other fast battleships under Admiral Lee were withdrawn from the carrier task groups to make a pre-invasion bombardment of Saipan and Tinian islands, because D-day at Saipan was scheduled for 15 June. The islands had been significantly fortified with coast defense and antiaircraft guns in anticipation of an American invasion, so it was desirable to knock out as many as possible. Alas, explains historian Samuel Eliot Morison in his history of the Navy in World War II, the bombardment by the fast battleships that day was a failure. Because they had been

**Below:** The *New Jersey's* dark grey paint job and fire-belching 16-inch guns were the basis for her wartime nickname, "Black Dragon." This, one of the few World War II pictures showing the ship firing her 16-inch guns in anger, was taken during the bombardment of Tinian in mid-June 1944. (National Archives: 80-G-253608)

spending almost all of their time with the fast carriers, they hadn't had an opportunity to practice the slow, methodical approach to sighting in on a land target and then applying corrections until it was destroyed. What's more, the battleships' scout plane pilots didn't have sufficient experience to be able to distinguish targets, and the valuable battleships were forced to fire from too far off the beach in order to make sure they wouldn't run into mines. Heavy 16-inch projectiles were flying all over the place, but they were destroying only such things as farmhouses and sugar mills. Morison endorsed the words of one sailor who wryly observed that the 13 June firing was "a Navy-sponsored farm project that simultaneously plows the fields, prunes the trees, harvests the crops, and adds iron to the soil." The following day, the much more skilled old battleships showed how the job should be done.

For the Marianas campaign, the Fifth Fleet mustered a vast armada of 644 ships. Many of them were amphibious warfare ships and landing craft, and on 15 June they disgorged their cargo of Marines on the beaches at Saipan. Thus, the gauntlet was so defiantly thrown down that the Japanese fleet could no longer avoid a fight. The Marianas were too close to the home islands to be lost without a serious challenge to the American invaders. From the Philippines to the west came the First Mobile Fleet, commanded by Vice Admiral Jisaburo Ozawa.

Before the fleets tangled, the men of the *New Jersey* observed mass death in progress. Dr. William Robie, one of the officers in the *New Jersey*'s medical department, looked at Saipan through one of the spotting scopes for the 16-inch turrets and saw Japanese civilians walking off cliffs and plunging to their deaths. Remembers Robie, "You could just see them walk to the end and go off in the ocean so they wouldn't be captured."

Task Force 58 had two principal objectives during the Battle of the Philippine Sea, as the engagement off the Marianas came to be known. The one considered more important by Admiral Spruance was to protect the amphibious transports of Vice Admiral Richmond Kelly Turner's landing force at Saipan. The second, if possible, was to seek out and destroy the Japanese fleet. On 18 June, the *New Jersey* joined with six other battleships, seven heavy cruisers, and fourteen destroyers to form Task Group 58.7 under Vice Admiral Ching Lee. This was to be the battle line which would stand between the carrier task groups and the heavy ships of the Japanese if a surface battle loomed. One carrier group was assigned to provide air cover for the battle line.

The surface battle never took place. Lee declined Mitscher's suggestion of a gun battle on the night of 18 June. Lee was cautious because his ships had been integrated into the carrier groups for so long that they hadn't had much chance to drill together in tactical maneuvers. He may also have expected that he would get a better chance under more favorable conditions later.

Spruance, filled with concern that the Japanese might try an end-around to get at Turner's transports, quickly endorsed Lee's decision, and Task Force 58 went eastward on the night of 18–19 June instead of toward the enemy.

The battle which ensued on 19 June is one of the classics in naval annals, known as the "Marianas Turkey Shoot" because of the more than 350 Japanese planes which were shot from the sky that day. As a result of the overwhelming success on the part of fighter pilots in their F6F Hellcats, only a relative handful of enemy planes reached the battleships. When they came, Rafael Maza, a member of the gun crew for one of the 5-inch mounts, opened a hatch to see what was going on. He says, "When you stuck your head out there, the sky was black with explosions. You thought something was coming your way." After that, he decided it was safer and wiser not to open the hatch.

Dr. Robie's battle station was in the wardroom, where the mess tables were prepared to be used for surgery if necessary. Later in the war, when Robie was promoted to lieutenant, he was moved to the after battle dressing station, down inside the ship's armor belt. He explains, "I was much more comfortable up in the wardroom, where I could see what was going on than after I got promoted and got down protected by the armor. You know, up there topside that helmet [seemed] 40 inches thick and didn't weigh anything. And it was big enough you just crawled up in it, and when the bullets were flying, you were just invincible. Psychologically, you weren't aware that you just had a tin helmet on your head. You just felt protected, and I guess we never really thought about it." Logically, he believes people were safer down below, but they felt trapped and left out of the action.

At various times during the battle, the *New Jersey*'s 5-inch, 40-mm. and 20-mm. guns were firing at a Zeke fighter, a Jill fighter, and a Tony fighter – nicknames assigned by the Americans so that lookouts and gun crews wouldn't have to struggle with trying to pronounce the actual Japanese names. The *New Jersey* was credited with a "sure assist" for her 20- and 40-mm. fire in downing a Tony also being attacked by two American planes. The ship also damaged one Zeke and one Tony. Seaman Art Scott, whose job was to elevate and depress the barrel of a 20-mm. gun on the port side, felt vulnerable in his exposed position in the superstructure. But there was also a sense of satisfaction afforded by the vantage point. He says, "I guess seeing enemy planes shot down made me feel I was personally doing my share."

Down in the engineering spaces, Russ Brown was trying to follow the progress of events topside through what he could hear. The reports from the ship's battle announcer helped diminish the sense of isolation, and he had another source of information on the approach of enemy planes: "Normally, if you could hear the 5-inchers fire, you knew they were quite a ways away. And when the 40s came on,

you could tell that they were getting closer. And when the 20s started firing, you knew they were right on top of you."

For Ensign Val Winkelman there was no question of being able to look up and see what was going on; the problem was trying to hit anything. When the ship was operating at high speed in a formation, the propellers – which were practically underneath his quad 40-mm. mount on the fantail – set up such a vibration that it was hard for Winkelman to keep his gun sight on the target. Unlike the radar-controlled 5-inch guns, the 40-mm. mounts depended on the officer operating the director being able to see the enemy planes. The gun sight was supposed to compute the necessary angle by which to lead the enemy plane, but Winkelman remembers that the job called for a good deal of human proficiency as well. Later in the war, Fire Controlman First Class J. P. Loughan was able to rig up a system in which the 40-mm. mounts in the center of the *New Jersey* were hooked into the radar-controlled Mark 37 directors which aimed the 5-inch guns. The parallax angle was too great, however, to permit linking in the 40-mm. on bow and stern.

When the aerial slaughter of 19 June was over, Task Force 58 was released from protecting the transports and thus free the next day to attack the Japanese fleet. The strikes of carrier planes were launched at long range late in the afternoon. The night of 20 June 1944 has become justly famous as the time when Task Force 58 ships, including the *New Jersey*, turned on searchlights to serve as beacons for the returning planes. In the darkness, with gasoline tanks in their planes nearly empty, the American fliers scrambled desperately to get back aboard.

Down in the engineering spaces, Lieutenant John Rossie was listening on the phones to a fireman who was topside for the purpose of reporting the color of the ship's smoke. The aim was to ensure that the smoke reflected the proper mix of fuel and air in the boilers, but he was also able to serve as an auxiliary battle announcer for the benefit of the engineering department. The man topside, watching an aircraft carrier steaming nearby, reported, "They're pushing planes off the front and landing them on the back." Lieutenant John Sullivan watched as planes came in, "They'd make an approach on the *New Jersey*, thinking we were a carrier, and then pull up at the last minute. . . . It was a bloody mess that night." As fuel tanks ran dry, pilots who couldn't find a deck on which to land ditched in the sea instead. Out came life rafts and whistles. Seaman Roger Faw, peering into the night from a spot topside on the battleship, frequently heard the shrill sound of pilots' whistles as the downed fliers entreated destroyers to come alongside and pick them up. Rescue operations went on into the following day, with both destroyers and seaplanes picking up Task Force 58 airmen.

On the morning of 21 June, the *New Jersey*, as part of Admiral Lee's battle line, was detached to proceed westward in pursuit of Admiral Ozawa's fleet but didn't even come close. On 24 June, the *New Jersey* again joined a carrier group, Task Group 58.3 under Rear Admiral John "Black Jack" Reeves. On the 25th the *New Jersey* got in the air-sea rescue business, an unexpected role for the battleship. That afternoon, Lieutenant W. A. Butt, one of the pilots in the *New Jersey*'s aviation division, landed his OS2U Kingfisher scout plane off the island of Guam, which was still held by the Japanese. He picked up three fliers from a USS *Lexington* plane. While the rescue was in progress, Japanese shore batteries opened up on the Kingfisher, splashing shells nearby but not hitting it. With three extra men on board, the plane was too heavy to take off, so Butt taxied over to the destroyer *Caperton* to drop off his passengers, then flew back to the battleship.

While the rescue of the *Lexington* men presented an unusual hazard, just operating the catapult planes from the *New Jersey* was frequently hazardous enough. The normal procedure called for the Kingfisher to sit at the rear of the catapult and rev up its engines. Ideally, when the plane was to go off to starboard, for example, the launching officer would wait until the ship had rolled all the way to starboard, then give a signal to the launching petty officer to yank the lanyard that fired the powder charge underneath the movable sled on which the plane sat. There was a one-second delay between the giving of the signal and the firing of the powder. With a great whoosh, the plane jumped forward. By that time, the ship was on an up-roll, giving the plane a small boost as its 450-horsepower engine clawed the air to gain altitude. The pilot held his hand on the throttle and elbow into his stomach so that he wouldn't inadvertently pull back on the stick when the force of the catapult shot came.

Throughout the remainder of June and all through July, the battleship continued to operate with Task Force 58 in the vicinity of the Marianas, supporting the carriers while they conducted air strikes. Marines landed on Guam on 21 July and on Tinian three days later. From 25 July until the 27th the *New Jersey* was with the carriers during strikes against Palau, because U.S. forces were about to seize the western Carolines, in part to take control of Ulithi Atoll as a fleet anchorage and staging area for the forthcoming campaign against the Philippine Islands.

During July, the *New Jersey* was under way continuously, except for a few brief stops in Saipan harbor, a sheltered anchorage for providing fuel and stores to destroyers. The *New Jersey* was able to replenish her own supply of fuel when necessary from fleet oilers, but her supply of food grew ever lower, for by late July she had been away from Majuro for nearly two months. Chili beans and rice became daily staples in the diets of *New Jersey* men who, until then, had for the most part experienced considerable satisfaction from the mess deck and wardroom. Fireman Sherman Brattin, who had grown up on a farm during the Depression of the 1930s, found that both the quantity and variety of food in the battleship were "better than what I had at home". Fresh meats were eaten for a while after the *New Jersey* had been in a port to stock up, but then her men had to fall back on canned meats such as Spam and Vienna sausages. Shipfitter William Dugan remembers: "There were times when we had Spam for breakfast, Spam for dinner, Spam for supper. You had it fried, baked, in soup – every way you could think of, we had Spam." On one occasion, when the *New Jersey* later pulled into one of the islands to get mail, Dugan received a letter from his wife. He turned to a shipmate nearby and asked, "Hey, Hack, what do you think my wife is sending me? A box of Spam."

For Fireman Russ Brown, who had eaten only his mother's cooking before joining the Navy, shipboard food took some getting used to. But after a while, he says, even the powdered eggs and powdered milk "got to where they didn't taste too bad. In fact, some of the fellows would go in a dark corner of the mess hall to eat, and you couldn't see what it was." Nearly all who served in the ship during the war agree that the highlight of the food was that from the bakery – freshly made bread, rolls, and pastries. Musician First Class Leonard Jung kept a jar of peanut butter in his locker. Every so often, he explains, the bakery "gave us a hot loaf of bread; it would be so hot you'd have to juggle it. And then I put peanut butter on that, and, oh man, that tasted real good." But then came that summer of 1944, when the flour grew old. One day when Jung was having his customary slice of bread, he found what seemed to be caraway seeds in it. Actually, they were dead weevils, but, Jung says, "After a while, you didn't even bother to pick them out. They're not the most appetizing thing, but [they] didn't hurt anybody."

Another thing the men of the *New Jersey* missed, of course, during the long periods at seas was feminine companionship. Commander Edward Addison, the ship's first lieutenant, had a whimsical touch in putting the situation to verse. One poem was addressed to his wife Nellie, back home in Norfolk, Virginia:

"I don't like the atolls at all, my Dear,
I don't like the atolls at all.
And I'll broadcast my grief to each white coral reef,
And I'll salt up the sea as I bawl.
Oh, I want to go home to my Honey!
The home site is sounding its call,
But it isn't the fighting that induces my writing
That I don't like the atolls at all –
It's just that I miss you, my Darling,
Separation is wormwood and gall –
And since this is my reason, you can't call it treason
That I don't like the atolls at all, my Dear,
That I don't like the atolls at all!"

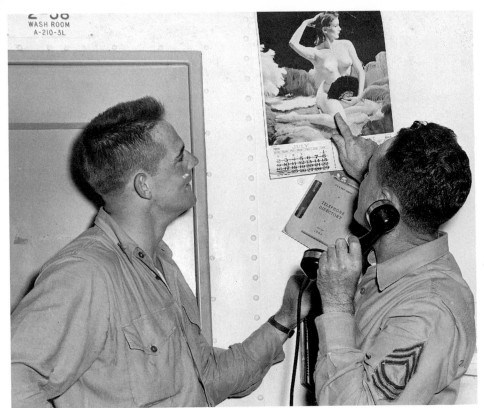

**Above:** The month is August 1944 as two *New Jersey* Marines check calendar art near a wash room on the second deck. (Courtesy Mrs. Frank Reagan)

coming aboard as Commander Third Fleet. He explained in his postwar autobiography that members of his staff had been shipboard observers during the Marianas campaign and came up with a list of improvements to be incorporated into the *New Jersey* when she was designated to receive the Third Fleet flag. Halsey wrote, "On the basis of their recommendations, the *New Jersey*'s flag plot was extensively altered, and when we put to sea, it was the best in the fleet." All electrical cables were replaced and much new communication equipment put in. Halsey even arranged for the installation of a ladder so that he could go directly from the flag mess on the 02 level to the flag plot one deck above.

For many of the battleship's men, who had been without real liberty for about seven months by the time of arrival on 9 August, Hawaii itself wasn't as important as being ashore in a civilized area. They were mainly interested in wine, women, and song – with precious little emphasis on the singing. By 1944, Hawaii was swamped with American servicemen, so many of them that there were long lines waiting to get into the brothels. Men coming in from the sea went from bar to bar, drinking in good cheer, with headaches to follow.

Shipfitter Second Class Bill Dugan ran into a chief petty officer with whom he had served in the battleship *Arkansas* earlier in the war. His former shipmate was obliging enough to lend Dugan a chief's uniform to give him some added social standing. They went to Aiea, overlooking Pearl Harbor, and found a recreation area which was terraced in such a way as to parallel the Navy's hierarchical structure. At the bottom of the terraced slope, enlisted men had to stand in line for beer, with a two-bottle limit. Chiefs – including honorary chief Dugan – got to sit at tables and got three or four bottles at a time. Up above were the officers who presumably had even more privileges.

Rafael Maza, a seaman in 1944, has souvenirs of Honolulu to this day, for he got tattooed there. Marine Private First Class Dale O'Bryen found the Hawaiian culture attractive during his forays ashore: "I listened to Hawaiian music every chance I got. Of course, I had my picture taken with the Hawaiian girls and their grass skirts." Fireman Sherman Brattin went ashore with a religious group that had formed on board the *New Jersey*. The men went to parks and other recreation areas, including swimming at Waikiki and the beachfront Royal Hawaiian Hotel. The latter had been set aside as a haven for submariners between war patrols, but Brattin recalls that, "We'd kinda walk around the fence every once in a while and get in on the beach side there, just to say we'd been in there, really." Others went to the local armed forces' YMCA, and still others, such as Fire Controlmen J. P. Loughan and George Teller, to steakhouses because they offered more substantial main courses than Spam. Especially popular was a place called P. Y. Chung's.

Speaking of the feminine gender, one should recall that the Navy habitually refers to a ship as "she" and that Captain Holden described the *New Jersey* as a "lovely lady" in his commissioning speech. In fact, he used that nickname for her throughout his time in command. Addison had some fun with that one also:

"I am a wolf in sheep's clothing,
And my past is decidedly shady.
Even here in the Pacific,
My love life's terrific;
I'm riding the lovely lady."

The long period since taking on stores finally came to an end when the *New Jersey* spent about four hours on 4 August at one of Addison's unlikable atolls, Eniwetok in the Marshalls. As was frequently the case when stores were brought aboard, large numbers of *New Jersey* men were summoned to form working parties. A fair amount of the food never got to the intended storerooms, because it was shanghaied on the way. Fruit, whether canned or fresh, often seemed to get diverted. The forbidden fruit invariably tasted better than the mess deck fare.

The stay at Eniwetok was short, because this time the *New Jersey* didn't have to take on provisions for a long operation. The ship had been ordered to steam to Pearl Harbor for alterations to her flag plot so that she could accommodate Admiral William F. Halsey, Jr., who was

On 22 August, as the rest and recreation period was approaching its end, the *New Jersey* took on a hefty load of ammunition. In the period just before getting under way, she also took on a hefty load of Third Fleet staff personnel. Early in the year, Admiral Spruance had brought with him about thirty officers as the Fifth Fleet staff; Halsey had double that number for the Third Fleet. And these were not two dissimilar fleets that had to be administered; they were essentially the same ships but designated differently now that Halsey was in charge. Lieutenant (junior grade) Bill Coyne of the *New Jersey* observed that, "Admiral Halsey's staff was not only larger but also noisier and more flamboyant." One member who attracted his attention was a Naval Reserve commander, Harold Stassen, who served as Halsey's flag secretary. He had previously been a "boy wonder" governor of Minnesota and later mounted several unsuccessful attempts to be President. The chief of staff was Rear Admiral Robert B. "Mick" Carney, who later served as Chief of Naval Operations from 1953 to 1955. One of the *New Jersey*'s newly reported junior officers, Ensign Roland "Bud" Bowler, explained years afterward that the statement, "That's what Admiral Carney says", had a way of ending debates.

Bowler, fresh from the Naval Academy, had to put behind him what he'd picked up at Annapolis and learn now about his seagoing job. He began studying the practice of visual communications with Chief Signalman E. L. Wilkes serving as his mentor. In Bowler's view, "The chief was clearly in charge of me. There was no doubt in his mind, and that was okay with me. I was a brand, spanking new ensign, and he just took me under his wing and kept me there for a year. He was happy when he thought I had learned enough to be essentially on my own, and to me, that was normal."

Bowler was one of many new crew members who came aboard in Hawaii, because that was the first convenient place in months to turn over a significant number of personnel. The Hawaii interlude was a time of departure for many of the plankowners who had been with the ship since her commissioning fifteen months earlier.

Dr. Robie found a disadvantage in the arrival of such new men. He discovered that, for the most part, the young men who comprised the ship's crew were typically quite healthy, for they had gone through a number of physical screening processes to get into the Navy and on board the ship. However, they did bring with them a flurry of coughs and colds and, in so doing, infected the men who had been on board and not exposed to these germs.

During the cruise west and south from Hawaii, the days fell into a pattern for the new crew members, especially as they were indoctrinated into the ways of the ship. The process was speeded by a repetition of the sort of drills that had been the order of the day during shakedown the year before – firing, firing, and more firing of the guns. One of these practices involved repelling simulated night

Opposite page, top: Commander Gil Slonim, left, a Japanese language specialist on the Third Fleet staff, goes over captured enemy charts with Rear Admiral Robert B. Carney, Halsey's chief of staff. (National Archives: 80-G-471152)

Opposite page, bottom: Oahu lies in the background as the New Jersey clears Pearl Harbor on 31 August 1944 after a period of modifications to accommodate Admiral William Halsey as Commander Third Fleet. (James C. Fahey Collection, U.S. Naval Institute)

Right: OS2U floatplanes sit on both catapults as the New Jersey steams away from Pearl Harbor on 31 August 1944 to return to the war zone. (James C. Fahey Collection, U.S. Naval Institute)

destroyer torpedo attacks from ships of the New Jersey's screen. The battleship fired 5-inch star shells for illumination of the attacking destroyers.

Lieutenant Commander Bill Abhau, the assistant gunnery officer, remembers, "When the star shell spread broke, I could see every one of the destroyers with the naked eye, didn't need glasses." He checked the radar and the star shells – which were 5-inch projectiles with flares in them – were the right distance above and behind the destroyers. The senior officer in the destroyers, however, claimed that the flares had come too close to the ships. Captain Holden was furious and sent for Abhau and Lieutenant Commander Baxter Russell, the gunnery officer. The two of them listened to a tongue-lashing until Russell could take it no longer. He defended his gunners, saying that people were so used to star shells being too far from their targets that when they came down in the right place, they looked too close. Holden decided it was time for Russell to move on to other duty, and Abhau became the department head. Abhau had mixed feelings about the episode – happy to be promoted but sorry that Russell had to depart for supporting his men when he was convinced they were right. Abhau explains, "I had learned by that time not to try to reason with Holden when he was angry." Interestingly, Abhau recalls that Commander Gerald Ogle, elevated from chief engineer to executive officer a few months earlier, apparently concluded that his promotion chances were not too strong. He was more willing than his two predecessors to stand up to Captain Holden. As a result, he was an effective executive officer for the New Jersey and ended up being promoted to captain after all.

There was one other untoward incident during the transit. On 28 August, the day after the star shell episode, one of the ship's Kingfishers crashed while the pilot was trying to land about 2,000 yards off the starboard quarter. The pilot and his rear seat man were rescued by the USS Hickox, a ship of the screen, and then the OS2U was sunk by destroyer gunfire.

On 4 September, the journey out from Hawaii ended when the New Jersey and her escorts anchored at Seeadler Harbor, Manus Island, in the Admiralties. The following day, the New Jersey was under way again, first with Task Group 38.5, then joining 38.2. The task groups were part of Task Force 38, the Third Fleet counterpart of Task Force 58 with which the New Jersey had been during the first half of the year while in the Fifth Fleet.

On the 12th, the battleship received a contingent of Japanese prisoners from the destroyer Marshall. With hundreds of curious sailors and Marines standing around watching, the Japanese were stripped of their clothes, bathed on deck, deloused, given haircuts by one of the ship's barbers, and then dressed in dungarees of the type worn by the crew. On one such occasion, when a prisoner was being marched along the main deck, Admiral Halsey was standing on one of the superstructure decks. Seaman

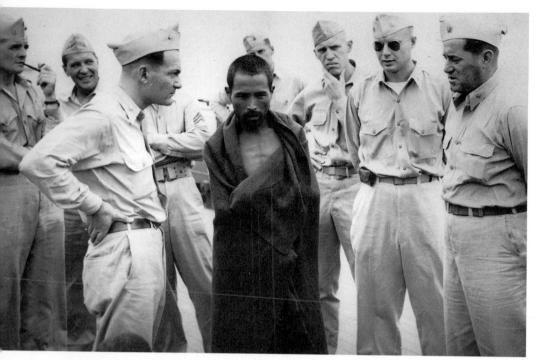

Above: A Japanese prisoner, brought aboard the *New Jersey* in the autumn of 1944 for interrogation, is surrounded by U.S. Navymen and Marines on the battleship's fantail. (National Archives: 80-G-283330)

Rafael Maza was nearby and heard Halsey say to one of the Marine guards, "Make that son of a bitch look up to me." The guard did, and the prisoner did.

Once the Japanese got through their experience topside, they were taken down and put in cells of the ship's brig, below and aft of the mess deck. Private Don Kelly was one member of the ship's Marine detachment who served guard duty. He recalls Commander Gil Slonim, the Japanese language officer on Halsey's staff, coming down to interrogate the prisoners and reassuring them about their fate. The Japanese were initially fearful, for they thought they had been transferred to the *New Jersey* to be executed. Each day, when no shootings took place, the prisoners smiled more and more. Even though the brig, down near the hot, steamy ship's laundry, was cramped and uncomfortable, the Japanese – according to Kelly – "were just smiling all the time, . . . just as happy as could be to be in that brig".

From 12 until 14 September, the *New Jersey* was in Rear Admiral Gerald Bogan's Task Group 38.2 as it conducted air strikes on the Visayan group in the southern Philippines, for the reconquest of the Japanese-occupied Philippine Islands was a prime item on the Third Fleet agenda for the upcoming autumn season. From the Philippines, the *New Jersey* moved to join a surface group in the Palaus on 17 September in order to be on call to provide counter battery fire during the U.S. invasion of Pelelieu and Angaur, but her guns were not needed. The month of September wound down, and the battleship steamed to newly occupied Ulithi Atoll in the Carolines.

Just as the capture of Kwajalein in the Marshalls had enabled Majuro to be taken over as a fleet base, so the conquest of the Palau group permitted the Third Fleet to move into the vast lagoon at Ulithi. It would serve as the principal base during the coming offensive to recapture the Philippines. After arriving on 1 October and giving the crew liberty at Mog Mog Island of the atoll, the *New Jersey* and other Task Force 38 ships had to sortie on 3 October because of the approach of heavy weather. They returned on 4 October. The postwar cruisebook commented that the typhoon ". . . hit like a bolt out of the blue. It was a question of which was rougher – the typhoon, or Mog Mog liberty?"

Landing craft provided trips from the ship to Mog Mog, a place remembered by J. P. Loughan for the customary routine of "two beers and a fight". Those who didn't drink could opt for sodas or else sell their beers to those who were not easily satisfied with only two. Since Loughan was interested in neither beer nor fighting, he often stayed on board ship. The island was also a place for swimming, softball, baseball, and other sports in which the inter-ship games could serve as an outlet for the rivalries that sprang up between various vessels. For Sherman Brattin, a denizen of one of the *New Jersey*'s boiler rooms, the island was a pleasant contrast to the shipboard world of steam and steel. On the beach at Mog Mog, he could get out and stretch his legs by running around its perimeter, or he could search for odd-looking seashells and rocks to take home to Missouri. Leonard Jung of the ship's band has still another recollection of the island – as a place for high-stakes gambling. He recalls "hundred dollar bills floating around; they didn't have anywhere else to spend it".

Although Ulithi was one place for gambling among the crew, it was far from being the only venue, for the "sport" was widespread on board the *New Jersey* as well. It was taken for granted on paydays, no matter how much against the rules it was. Blackjack was popular, and so was crap shooting. Both officers and enlisted men participated enthusiastically. The officers had both low- and high-stakes versions; the crew had many games at a variety of levels. Rafael Maza recounts his observations in the fourth division living compartment: "They would gamble after lights-out under the red lights that they had in the compartment, set up a blanket and roll dice there all night."

The red lights which illuminated the interior of the *New Jersey* went on when the bugler played taps over the general announcing system and stayed on until another bugler sounded reveille the next morning. (Sometimes, remembers Robert Moore, a warrant gunner during the war, the bugler would play a jazzed-up, swinging version of reveille, provided a complaisant officer of the deck was on watch.) The red lights were sufficient at night for those who had to be awake, but not bright enough to prevent sleep. Throughout the night, men such as Shipfitter Bill

Dugan regularly patrolled inside the ship to watch for leaks of water or fuel and otherwise to make sure that things were secure. One night, the red lights showing the way, Dugan approached the machine shop on the second deck. There he was suddenly brought up short when he saw a body strung up to the overhead and swinging to and fro in harmony with the rolling of the ship. He approached ever so cautiously, thinking perhaps one of his shipmates had decided to kill himself. He got up close and shined his flashlight on the body – only to find that it was the dummy the ship's officers threw over the side from time to time so they could practice making man-overboard recoveries. Such dummies are habitually known in the Navy as "Oscar", and on this night "Oscar" had been the pawn in a practical joke.

In October, American forces were to redeem General Douglas MacArthur's famous pledge to return to liberate the Philippines. To make the way easier, Task Force 38 ranged far to the west to launch air strikes on Okinawa and Formosa. The fleet went closer to the Japanese homeland than any American ships since Jimmy Doolittle's famous flight from the carrier *Hornet* to Tokyo in April 1942. As at the Marianas, the air battle off Formosa was one-sided. Japanese carrier planes went ashore to help fend off the attacking Americans, and this time the Japanese lost approximately 550 planes. But they did not go down easily, sending a number of raids against Task Group 38.2 and leading Bob Moore to remember, "There were so many GQ's when Boggy Bogan was in charge we were about worn out." The most striking memory for J. P. Loughan is a night when the American ships were dramatically silhouetted by air-dropped flares. Fortunately, the Betty

torpedo planes mistimed their approach and were shot down before the flares could do them any good.

The Battle of Leyte Gulf toward the end of October was a source of great controversy, because – as was the case at the Marianas in June – the U.S. Navy did not score the knockout blow it had been seeking against the Japanese fleet. Unlike the Marianas, this time the Japanese felt compelled to come close and fight it out. They mounted a three-pronged effort aimed at attacking the American amphibious forces at the Leyte beachhead. Vice Admiral Shoji Nishimura's southern force was devastated by Rear Admiral Jesse Oldendorf's old battleships in the Battle of Surigao Strait. Vice Admiral Takeo Kurita's center force, including the giant battleships *Musashi* and *Yamato*, was to approach through the Sibuyan Sea and San Bernardino Strait to attack the transports. And wily Vice Admiral Jisaburo Ozawa, Spruance's adversary at the Marianas, came in with a northern force consisting of aircraft carriers and the converted battleship-aircraft carriers *Ise* and *Hyuga*. Since the carriers' air groups had been pulverized in the Formosa operation, Ozawa's role was to act as a decoy so that Kurita's center force could get through to Leyte Gulf. Admiral Halsey, eager to knock out the Japanese carriers, fell for the ploy and charged northward with Task Force 38.

Part of Halsey's plan was that Vice Admiral Lee, the battle line commander, would form Task Force 34 – to be composed of fast battleships and supporting vessels in the event of a surface engagement. On 24 October, many of Kurita's ships were hit in the Sibuyan Sea and a number sunk, including the giant battleship *Musashi*. Afterward, his force appeared to head west, away from the transports

Below: The fleet flagship *New Jersey* is prominent in the foreground as the Third Fleet lies anchored in Ulithi Atoll in late 1944. (James C. Fahey Collection, U.S. Naval Institute)

at Leyte, so Halsey decided not to activate Task Force 34 after all. A contact report from an American scout plane during the night indicated that the center force had again turned east and was headed for San Bernardino Strait. Both Lee and carrier commander Marc Mitscher considered it prudent to form some of the battleships into Task Force 34 so that they could stay behind and guard the strait. They sent messages to the Third Fleet staff on board the *New Jersey* to call attention to the new contact report, but the Third Fleet Commander was unmoved. Halsey decided to take all the fast battleships with him, thus keeping intact the antiaircraft capability of Task Force 38 for the impending duel with Ozawa's nothern force.

Kurita's center force then made its way through the unprotected strait. The only thing standing between it and the American transports was a group of destroyers, destroyer escorts, and jeep aircraft carriers. They performed heroically in standing off the Japanese heavy ships. Vice Admiral Thomas Kinkaid, Commander of the Seventh Fleet, had expected Lee's Task Force 34 to be at San Bernardino Strait and sent a series of increasingly frantic messages asking for help. Halsey continued north until a radio dispatch came in from Admiral Nimitz, asking him where Task Force 34 was. It was meant as a nudge and certainly achieved its purpose. Lieutenant John Sullivan was the officer of the deck on the *New Jersey*'s navigation bridge when Nimitz's message arrived. He says that Halsey was so mad that he threw his cap down and stamped on it.

Late on the morning of the 25th, the *New Jersey* turned south. She was in Task Group 34.5 under the tactical command of Rear Admiral Oscar Badger in the *Iowa*, for Badger had relieved Olaf Hustvedt as Commander Battleship Division Seven. The force initially had to slow to refuel the escorting destroyers. As the evening progressed, the task group built speed to 28 knots. The *New Jersey* and *Iowa* were the only battleships in the Third Fleet that could go that fast.

During the night, a surface contact was detected on the ship's radar. Lieutenant (junior grade) Bill Coyne was adjacent to the main battery plotting room forward, where "The atmosphere was tense as all hands watched the target being tracked on the [Mark] 8 rangekeeper. But not a shot was fired; nor did either we or the target alter course and speed. Obviously the decision had been made that our presence in Leyte Gulf was more important." As it turned out, Kurita's force had become concerned and turned around, going back into San Bernardino Strait without ever attacking the U.S. transports. One of the stragglers from Kurita's force, the destroyer *Nowaki*, was sunk by surface gunfire on the morning of 26 October. (This was the destroyer which escaped the *New Jersey*'s salvos at Truk in February.) Task Group 34.5 was hampered by an engineering casualty in the *Iowa* which slowed her speed to 24 knots. By the time the *New Jersey*, *Iowa*, and their escorts reached their objective, it was too late. The transports were safe, but the Japanese fleet had escaped again.

Samuel Eliot Morison contended that the missed opportunity may well have been providential for the Americans, because a force of only two U.S. battleships would have been outgunned by Kurita's four. During the greatest naval

Below: Fire controlmen in front of the control panel in main battery plot. The controls can set up many different combinations of directors, guns, and range keepers. (National Archives: 80-G-469932)

battle in history, the *New Jersey* was the fleet flagship, but she didn't fire a single shot. For her crew the reaction was a mixture of disappointment and relief. Marine Private Donald Kelly says, "We had a great deal of confidence in our gun crews, particularly our main batteries. And we thought, sure, if we had the opportunity, that we would have done a heck of a fine job. So I would say a sense of extreme disappointment that we didn't close with the enemy." Rafael Maza, on the other hand, remembers that the married men in the crew were making out their wills and had trouble sleeping during the night of the approach to San Bernardino Strait. They were just as glad that the planned encounter didn't take place.

With the benefit of a great deal of hindsight, we can observe after the battle that the U.S. Navy missed two golden opportunities to eliminate the bulk of the Japanese battle line – because of Admiral Lee's caution at the Marianas in June and because of Halsey's impulsiveness in chasing after the decoy carriers and unwittingly leaving San Bernardino Strait to be defended by small boys. In the process, the *New Jersey* was deprived of fulfilling the role for which she was designed and built – to fire her 16-inch guns against the heavy ships of the enemy. Retired Rear Admiral Wiliam Abhau, the *New Jersey*'s gunnery officer during the Battle of Leyte Gulf, has done a splendid job of putting the ship's World War II experience into perspective: "We were part of the antiaircraft protection. We did a good deal of shore bombardment. We also served as . . . an underway refueling ship and as a hospital ship. In fact, we did everything except be a battleship."

In late October and early November, the *New Jersey* was back to her antiaircraft duties in Task Group 38.2 during air strikes on Luzon, the main island in the Philippines. As so often during the war, the *New Jersey* refueled destroyers in between periods when the task group met up with oilers at a fueling rendezvous. There were also other reasons for destroyers coming alongside, and on the afternoon of 4 November, the USS *Colahan* made an approach on the *New Jersey*'s port quarter for a transfer of personnel and movies. During the course of the maneuver, the *Colahan* apparently lost steering control, so that her starboard anchor raked the *New Jersey*'s port quarter, tearing loose two chocks, ripping out numerous lifeline stanchions, and sheering off rivets at the deck edge.

The transfer of movies between the *New Jersey* and other ships was a frequent occurrence during the war, for they served as one of the main forms of recreation with the ship at sea. Also popular were books from the *New Jersey*'s library. A writer whose work Seaman Bob Westcott particularly admired was Zane Grey, who wrote novels of the American West. Westcott enjoyed going topside to the main deck at a time he was off duty and sitting down to read in the shade of the aircraft crane on the fantail. He found Grey's descriptions of the western landscape so realistic that, "You could almost smell the pine needles" or "reach out and pull a leaf off the tree".

Radio programs, beamed into speakers in the living compartments, were also sources of entertainment. Music was frequently featured, as were news broadcasts put on by some of the ship's officers who read reports received on the radio circuits. Or there might be propaganda broadcasts from Japanese stations, which had the strongest signals until armed forces radio stations were set up late in the war. Tokyo Rose was unintentionally amusing because of her skewed versions of the truth. She often mentioned the *New Jersey* by name, either reporting that the ship had just been sunk or was about to be. Also subjects of derision by the crew were Japanese melodramas intended to influence American servicemen. One scenario featured a Marine who surrendered, went to Japan, and married a Japanese girl with whom he lived happily ever after.

Gunner's Mate Ellis Mamroth remembers playing bridge and Monopoly with FM division members on top of the stable element or Mark 1A computer in the main battery plot. In the turret with his fellow gunner's mates he played hearts, pinochle, cribbage, and acey-deucey. Mamroth's turret three also had a phonograph and record library which included many popular tunes as well as the type then known as hillbilly music and now as country and western. He says that many divisions had individuals who had personal musical instruments and so could keep their fellows entertained.

Another attraction was the "gedunk", which sold soda pop and various forms of ice cream. For Storekeeper Third Class Willard Bartusch, keeping the soda fountain sup-

**Below left:** Admiral William F. Halsey, Jr., Commander Third Fleet, sits in his chair on the flag bridge as the *New Jersey* steams toward the Philippines in December 1944. (National Archives: 80-G-471106)

**Below:** The bow of the pitching *New Jersey* rises out of the water in November 1944 as she steams in company with the carrier *Hancock*. (Bureau of Aeronautics photo 291047; courtesy of Arthur D. Baker III)

Above: Admiral William Halsey eats holiday dinner with the crew in the flagship's mess deck on Thanksgiving 1944. (National Archives: 80-G-291498)

his stateroom desk when the Third Fleet staff departed, a going-away present.

On at least one occasion at Ulithi, a number of nurses from a hospital ship were brought to the *New Jersey* in the admiral's barge and were escorted to the flag quarters for socializing with the Third Fleet staff. Some of the crew members resented the nurses, the whiskey, and other things which seemed to come the way of the staff but not the ship's company. On the other hand, many of the *New Jersey*'s men were very much taken with the admiral, because he was friendly and interested in them.

Sometimes Halsey showed up in Gunner's Mate Mamroth's turret. "He just seemed to pop in, sit down, shoot the breeze, have a cup of coffee with the fellows," says Mamroth. "We would have gone anywhere he said, without any question. I mean, just from the standpoint of confidence in what he could do." Sometimes Halsey went to the berthing compartments to say hello to the men. Once this happened when the band had been playing and was changing out of uniform afterward. "Well, what do you do?" asks Musician Philip Fuller. "Do you salute an admiral when you're in your shorts? But all he did was he stood around and talked to us." When he encountered men out on deck, sunbathing perhaps or just relaxing, Halsey was not one who expected them to jump to attention. He also endeared himself to the crew by going through the messline from time to time to see that they were well fed.

For a number of the *New Jersey*'s officers, the presence of a staff – especially one as large as Halsey's – was not so popular as with the enlisted crew members. For one thing, the staff took up a good many staterooms that would normally have been filled by ship's company officers. The latter had to crowd even closer together. At its height during the war, the combination of ship's company and staff personnel was probably around 3,000 men – possibly more. Dr. Robie remembers that Admiral Spruance's people were more willing to take what was available in the way of staterooms than Halsey's were.

After a brief stop at Ulithi in mid-November, the *New Jersey* was again under way with Task Group 38.2 late in the month for more air strikes against the island of Luzon. By this time, the kamikazes, Japanese suicide planes, were beginning to wreak havoc on the Third Fleet. Previously, Japanese planes had been frequently intercepted and either shot down or driven away by the combat air patrol of fighter planes before they could get within gun range of the big ships. Now, with the normal instincts of self-preservation having been overcome, the pilots of the suicide bombers bored their way through. Much of the time, they aimed for the carriers, both because the carriers' planes were doing damage to the Japanese ashore and because the carriers and their unarmored flight decks were a good deal more vulnerable than the thick-skinned battleships.

plied was a chore, because whenever the gedunk was open there was a line all the way up the port passageway. Sometimes the place ran out of ice cream before everyone could be served. Philip Fuller of the ship's band enjoyed getting chilled pineapple juice from the gedunk and drinking it topside. Of his shipboard relaxation, Fuller recalls, "Some of the most pleasant hours of my life were spent on the *New Jersey*. You'd sit on the fantail at night and look up at the Southern Cross, and it was beautiful. The waves would get that white [cap] as they would crest, the phosphorescence. And you'd watch the flying fish alongside."

While some of the *New Jersey*'s crew members were satisfied with the products available at the gedunk, others wanted stronger stuff. A number of them liberated alcohol used in ship's equipment and then cut off both ends of a loaf of bread and poured the stuff through to strain out impurities. In order to preserve the supply of alcohol, the ship's doctors began mixing it with croton oil, a severe laxative which apparently could not be strained out by bread. Other men tried making their own. The wooden tubs in which shipments of Coca-Cola syrup came to the gedunk were highly prized because the empty ones could be used for brewing concoctions such as raisin jack.

For a number of Third Fleet staff officers, and for Admiral Halsey himself, supplies of real liquor arrived in mail bags or pieces of luggage. There were some embarrassing moments, such as the time one of the bags banged against the deck, broke open, and spilled part of its contents. "Scotch whiskey was running all over the deck," says John Rossie, who was an officer in the ship's engineering department. Admiral Halsey's brand was Black & White, which featured drawings of black-and-white scottie dogs on the label. Lieutenant Harry Reynolds of the engineering department found a bottle of Scotch on

On 25 November the *New Jersey* was the guide in the center of Task Group 38.2 when a Zeke fighter dived on the *Hancock* and was disintegrated by a combination of gunfire from the carrier and the *New Jersey*. A section of burning fuselage landed on the *Hancock*'s flight deck. Soon afterward, two more Zekes dived on the *Intrepid*, Admiral Bogan's flagship. The *New Jersey* splashed one, which exploded and crashed into the water. The battleship's gunners also hit the second, but it succeeded in crashing onto the *Intrepid*'s flight deck and started large fires. Within minutes, the *New Jersey* also fired on planes going after the *Iowa* and the carrier *Cabot*; a kamikaze crashed into the latter. The *Essex* was also hit during the day. Harry Reynolds, who had been down in main engine control, says, "I went up on the topside after general quarters secured, and there were four carriers burning."

When planes were getting in as close as they did during the kamikaze strikes of 25 November, the dozens of 20-mm. guns on board the *New Jersey* were in frequent use. They were short-range weapons whose aiming and shooting depended strictly on the abilities of the men looking through the crosshair-and-concentric-rings arrangements of the gun sights. Many of those manning the 20-mm. guns were members of the *New Jersey*'s Marine detachment. Private Dale O'Bryen's job was as loader on a gun near turret two. He remembers that the noise was "terrific" when a lot of guns were firing at once, but then adds, "I remember that it would get so exciting that you would forget about the noise and everything else. You would just be interested in the plane you were shooting at. If a plane blew up in front of you, then everybody kind of cheered like a ball game, and you had to make sure you didn't spend too much time doing that."

The Marines and sailors in the *New Jersey*'s crew had a friendly rivalry, which included trying to outdo one another and also passing jibes back and forth. There was a fair amount of good-natured kidding, remembers Don Kelly, who was a Marine private. He got used to being referred to as a "seagoing bellhop", while the Marines referred to the sailors as "deck apes" and "swabbies". The rivalry extended to their prowess in gunnery, but the Marines won easily when it came to military appearance. Even Kelly admits, "Of course, with so much time on our hands, we would just literally spend half our life either shining our shoes or shining our pistol holsters or the brass." They also spent time keeping their rifles cleaned and working out with weights and a punching bag in order to keep in the fighting trim of their Marine counterparts ashore. Time was available for these pursuits because the Marines did not have to do nearly so much of the ship's work as the naval crew did.

Both Marines and sailors got another shot at Mog Mog liberty in Ulithi before the Third Fleet sortied again on 11 December. With landings on the island of Luzon scheduled for early in the new year, the Task Force 38 fighter planes sought to knock out the kamikazes at their fields before they could get airborne, rather than when they were over the American fleet. During the Third Fleet run-in toward Formosa in September, bad weather had been an ally, shielding the fleet's approach until it was time for the strikes to begin. In mid-December, by contrast, weather was a ferocious enemy of the American ships approaching Luzon.

The problem was already apparent during the noon hour on Sunday, 17 December when Admiral Halsey was seated at the lunch table in the flag mess. Through an open door, he could look out and see the difficulties the destroyer *Spence* was having in trying to take on fuel alongside the *New Jersey*. The *Spence* was rolling wildly in the heavy waves and having trouble maintaining steering control. Both fueling hoses to the destroyer parted, and the effort had to be abandoned.

Below: Antiaircraft gun crews watch from the *New Jersey* as an explosion rocks the carrier *Intrepid* following a kamikaze attack off northern Luzon on 25 November 1944. (Steichen Collection, U.S. Naval Academy Library)

Admiral Halsey has been much criticized for persisting in his efforts over the following two days to refuel the fleet and continue the planned schedule of air strikes rather than making escape from the storm his first priority. The *New Jersey* was in a typhoon which grew even worse on the 18th, with mountainous seas and winds and spray blasting past at more than 100 knots. Normally, the battleship was able to plow through the seas that treated destroyers as corks, but this time, even the *New Jersey* was rolling noticeably. In his postwar memoirs, Admiral Halsey wrote that the storm peaked at midday on 18 December, adding, "No one who has not been through a typhoon can conceive of its fury. The 70-foot seas smash you from all sides. The rain and scud are blinding; they drive at you flat-out, until you can't tell the ocean from the air. At broad noon I couldn't see the bow of my ship, 350 feet from the bridge."

Down inside the mighty *New Jersey*, the 3,000 men were learning firsthand what a typhoon can do to a battleship. Lieutenant Harry Reynolds, eating dinner in the wardroom, was summoned by the engineering officer of the watch to number three engine room. There, Reynolds heard "the damnedest popping and snapping around the high-pressure turbine. . . . I went down underneath, in the lower level, and it was the sliding feet of the high-pressure turbine." Normally rock-solid, the turbine was moving back and forth, perhaps an eighth or 3/16 of an inch, in time with the rolling of the ship. Reynolds rounded up a grease gun, gave the zerk fittings on the track a few shots of grease, and the loud noises stopped.

Dan Scanlon, tending a boiler in one of the firerooms, had to take someone else's word for it that the waves outside the ship looked like mountains. He and Russ Brown, who was also in B division, went for close to a week during the mid-December period without seeing daylight. Crewmen were emphatically warned not to go topside, so they stayed below and kept the *New Jersey* running. Brown explains what it was like down in the depths of the giant battleship during the height of the storm: "When the screws were down in the water, it wasn't too bad, but when the ship tossed and the screws came up out of the water, the whole ship would shudder." Topside, the incredible force of the unbridled Pacific bent back solid metal shields on 20-mm. guns. In the rolls of 20°–25°, metal billets being stored for the machine shop flew around like missiles in the smokestack uptakes, and bottles of shaving lotion in lockers crumbled to piles of broken glass.

Though sleeping was tough for men not used to the stormy conditions, eating was even more difficult. The mess cooks didn't even try to set up the spindly-legged mess tables. Instead, they just served sandwiches and coffee. People had to hang on just to be able to fill their cups. Warrant Officer Bob Moore went to the 02 deck topside to have a look. There the water stung like a spray of BB pellets when it hit his face.

Gradually, the storm abated, and when it did new troubles were apparent. Some of the 20-mm. projectiles had been wrenched loose from their stowage places and were washing back and forth in the waterways alongside the edges of the wood planking on the main deck. Lieutenant Commander Wally Howe of the construction and repair department courageously went out and disposed of the live ammunition, gingerly picking up the projectiles and tossing them over the side.

Elsewhere, some destroyers had rolled so badly that their masts were nearly parallel to the water before they righted themselves. A few kept on going when they reached that point. One was the *Fletcher*-class destroyer *Spence*. Her inability to fuel from the *New Jersey* on the 17th was apparently compounded by a decision on the part of her commanding officer not to take on saltwater ballast. When the roll was called by voice radio after the storm, the *Spence* was no longer around to answer, and neither were the older destroyers *Hull* and *Monaghan*.

On Christmas Eve, after a period of normal steaming in the wake of the storm, the *New Jersey* pulled into Ulithi Atoll and anchored. That morning, the ship's Marines, including Private Dale O'Bryen, were gathered on the stern, aft of turret three, to pose for a group picture. Then, all of a sudden, the Marines started to break ranks. The photographer, who had his back to the sea, hollered at the Marines to get back together, but they didn't, because they saw something that the photographer didn't – 5-inch projectiles landing around the ship. Ships in one of the carrier task groups were practicing antiaircraft gunnery against drone targets as they approached Ulithi. J. P. Loughan became concerned when he looked out and saw that the drones were closer to the *New Jersey* than to the firing ships. If 5-inch projectiles go up and don't explode, they must come down somewhere, and one went right through the main deck on the *New Jersey*'s fantail, not far from where the Marines had been standing. The projectile also went through the second deck and finally rattled around inside a head on the third deck before coming to rest in a wash basin. Seaman Second Class Robert Clower received a number of wounds in the leg from the wayward shell, and two other men sustained superficial injuries. Lieutenant George Van Vleck, the *New Jersey*'s bomb disposal officer, tossed the projectile over the side after it was cooled by a fire hose.

Later in the day, Chester Nimitz, recently promoted to the rank of five-star fleet admiral, flew in to Ulithi for a conference with Admiral Halsey. When Nimitz came aboard the *New Jersey*, a five-star flag was flown aloft, the first such occasion in a Pacific Fleet warship. With him, Nimitz brought a decorated Christmas tree for the *New Jersey*'s wardroom. Nimitz's biographer, Professor E. B. Potter, noted that the admiral was disappointed because the battleship's officers preferred an artificial tree the crew had made from nuts, bolts, and scrap metal. Ensign Allen

FR.57

Trecartin, one of the *New Jersey*'s scout plane pilots, had duty as in-port officer of the deck at Ulithi. He recalls that the total number of stars from all the flag officers on board the ship during Nimitz's visit was forty-five. One of them was Rear Admiral Gerald Bogan, who recounted in his oral history that Halsey showed color movies, taken from on board the *New Jersey* during the kamikaze ordeal of 25 November. One showed Bogan's flagship *Intrepid* when she heeled to port and burning gasoline poured over the side. "It was a solid sheet of red," remembered Bogan.

With the *New Jersey* in port over the holiday period, it was time for many sacks of mail to be brought aboard and eagerly seized upon by the crew – probably a bigger morale-builder than anything. When the mail arrived, remembers Fireman Russ Brown, a letter might remark that one he had sent home earlier had been heavily cut up by one of the ship's censors. And the cutting was literal; portions which indicated where the ship was or what she might be doing were cut from the paper with a razor blade. The result sometimes looked like a doily. The alternative was self-censorship, in order to encourage the ship's officers to withhold the blade. As a result, say Brown, "You'd start out, 'I'm feeling fine', and there just wasn't much else to write about."

Even before the onset of the New Year of 1945, the *New Jersey* was under way once more with Task Group 38.2. The Third Fleet carrier force was again on the prowl, conducting air strikes against Formosa and Luzon, then proceeding through the Bashi Channel between Formosa and Luzon and into the South China Sea. Admiral Halsey's foremost goal at that point was to sink the two Japanese half-battleships *Ise* and *Hyuga* which had escaped Third Fleet guns at Leyte Gulf because of the turn south on 25 October. The pair got away again this time. However, carrier planes from Task Force 38 struck along the

Indochina coast – later Vietnam – and at Formosa, Hong Kong, and the Chinese mainland.

On 26 January, the day after the *New Jersey* returned to Ulithi, she got a new commanding officer, Captain E. Tyler "Slim" Wooldridge. The weather during the change of command ceremony was such that Admiral Halsey was wearing non-regulation khaki shorts and short-sleeved shirt when he presented Holden with a Bronze Star medal for his command tenure. A day later, Halsey and his Third Fleet staff were gone as well, because it was time to shift to the Fifth Fleet organization once again. Since Admiral Spruance preferred to have his flag in the cruiser *Indianapolis*, that left the *New Jersey* available for Rear Admiral Oscar Badger, Commander Battleship Division Seven. He and his staff embarked on 29 January, because his previous flagship, the *Iowa*, was leaving for overhaul.

Within a few days, the *New Jersey* had antiaircraft practice, and Admiral Badger meant to show that he was boss. Planes were to tow target sleeves, two at a time, for the *New Jersey* to shoot at, so Badger called the gun boss, Commander Abhau, to the flag bridge. "Young man," said the admiral, "I don't want to see one sleeve go across the ship today, and I don't care how much ammunition you use." On the first eleven passes, the ship's guns shot down both sleeves. On the twelfth, they hit only one of two, but by that time Badger had evidently become bored with the string of successes, so he didn't see the failure.

Lieutenant John Sullivan had a similar experience with Badger on another occasion, when the *New Jersey* was bringing aboard 16-inch powder from a merchant ship alongside. Sullivan discovered that some of the powder bags were so rotten that the pellets of powder were falling out. Admiral Badger came along and decided to exert his authority. In what Sullivan remembers as Badger's "usual God-almighty way", the admiral told Sullivan that the powder was satisfactory and should be sent to the magazines. Naturally, if something untoward had happened, the responsibility would have been on Sullivan and the ship's crew, so as soon as the admiral had departed the scene, the defective bags were once again brought back up and returned to the merchantman.

From 10 February to 5 March, the *New Jersey* was in Rear Admiral Frederick Sherman's Task Group 58.3 during its wide-ranging attacks against the Japanese. In this period, planes from the carriers of Task Force 58 struck at the Japanese home islands for the first time. Then they went on north to hit Iwo Jima in the Bonin Islands, and Admiral Badger embarked temporarily in the *Indiana* to command a shore bombardment group. Iwo was to provide a land base for American bombers to use against Japan, particularly for strikes in connection with the eventual landings planned for the enemy's home islands. The *New Jersey* was with Sherman's task group northwest of Iwo Jima when the Marines hit the beach on 19 February.

On the way back from the Bonins, the carriers again hit Tokyo, and then the task group headed toward Okinawa so that the carrier planes could conduct photo reconnaissance. During the early morning hours of 26 February, a period of low visibility, a Japanese picket boat passed inside the formation of American ships. Because the *New Jersey* was unable to identify by radar which vessel was the enemy's, she withheld her fire. Some of the other "friendly" ships were not so cautious, with the result that 40-mm. tracer shells whizzed close by over the bow of the *New Jersey*.

After returning to Ulithi on 5 March, the *New Jersey* had a respite of only a little more than a week before she had to be on the go again. It was a time to take on provisions and relax, including watching movies topside on the fantail. On the evening of 12 March, the ship's crew gathered as usual in front of the screen and put down the galvanized buckets that were sometimes used for washing clothes but for movies were turned upside down to serve as chairs. When the word was passed over the general announcing system that an air raid warning was in effect, it didn't faze the men of the *New Jersey*. Explains Russ Brown, who was among the crowd, "We had our seats for the movie; we weren't about to move." A plane came up from astern and flew along the starboard side. A number of men thought it was a U.S. pilot showing off. Commander John McCormick, the ship's engineer officer, saw the bluish flame of the plane's exhaust as it passed. It was a kamikaze which crashed into the stern of the carrier *Randolph*, anchored ahead of the *New Jersey*, killing twenty-five of her men and injuring another 106. When the plane exploded upon hitting the carrier, the fantail of the *New Jersey* was cleared in no time, leaving behind only a sea of overturned buckets.

During that period in Ulithi, the *New Jersey* got a new executive officer. Commander Bob Rice was a former submarine skipper who had been picked for the job by Captain Wooldridge, breaking the pattern in which the two previous execs had been *New Jersey* department heads who moved up. When Rice got to the *New Jersey*, he directed that his Marine orderly walk ahead of him – rather than the normal practice of following behind – so he could help the newcomer find his way around inside the huge, much-compartmented *New Jersey*. If the size of the ship was a bit much at first, so were the nightly telephone calls Rice began getting. When he answered, he was confronted with foul language, presumably from new men who didn't want to be in the war. The callers were also pouring abuse over the phone lines to other authority figures, Captain Wooldridge and Chaplain Leonard Goode, so all three soon had their telephones disconnected.

A few days after departure from Ulithi on 14 March, the *New Jersey*'s Task Group 58.3 proceeded to Kyushu, Japan, for air strikes on 18 and 19 March. On the 18th, the battleship's Kingfishers were launched to attempt a rescue of a *Bunker Hill* pilot who had been shot down near Kyushu.

One of the OS2Us, flown by Lieutenant W. A. Ethridge, went in and snatched the pilot from heavy seas.

The following day, 19 March, the *New Jersey* was able to refute the charge of having "wooden guns". The ship's air defense officer was Lieutenant Commander Archie "Zeke" Soucek, who recorded the ship's performance in a personal log. His station was on the 011 level air defense platform, all the way at the top of the ship, where he wore a set of sound-powered phones which connected him with the secondary battery plotting rooms and the four Mark 37 directors for the 5-inch guns. Beside Soucek were officers to relay his commands to the machine-gun batteries, one officer for the 40-mm. and one for the 20s. It was their job to make sure that guns were assigned to all appropriate targets and that one set of guns stopped and another started as a plane flew from one side of the ship to the other.

The morning of 19 March held favorable conditions for the attackers, because they could dive out of low clouds; gun crews had only a short time to react. At 7:15 a plane did get through and dropped two bombs on the carrier *Franklin*, which was steaming near the *New Jersey*. At 7:41 a Judy dive-bomber plummeted out of the clouds and flew

forward along the port side of the *New Jersey* in an attempt to crash on the *Essex*. The battleship's machine-guns knocked off the plane's tail, and it crashed "very close" to her starboard bow. At 8:13 another Judy came out of the low ceiling and went straight for the *Bunker Hill*; the *New Jersey*'s 40-mm. brought the plane down in flames. At 1:21 p.m., a Zeke fighter headed for the *Bunker Hill*. This one was hit by the *New Jersey*'s 5-inch battery, which, in Soucek's words, "turned him into a ball of flame and scattered bits of wreckage all over the ocean". At 2:18 another Zeke passed the *New Jersey*'s stern, headed toward a carrier. The *New Jersey* claimed credit when the plane was knocked down off her starboard beam by 5-inch shell bursts. At 2:31 the battleship fired on another Judy, which was splashed by U.S. fighters. Either by herself or with the assistance of gunfire from other ships, the *New Jersey* shot down more than a half dozen enemy planes that day. When Soucek was able to climb down from his lofty perch at day's end and crawl into bed, he had been on the air defense station forty-one continuous hours.

Many other men in the ship were finding sleep hard to come by. One was Fire Controlman George Teller. Fortunately, he had an assignment that helped. He was given a

**Below:** The dark grey bulk of the *New Jersey* stands out against the sky as she refuels the *Allen M. Sumner*-class destroyer *Borie* on 16 March 1945. Notice the many spectators on board the battleship. (National Archives: 80-G-315391)

pair of dark goggles and directed to go topside and wear them while lying on a cot and looking up. His purpose was to detect any Japanese planes that were trying to dive on the task group from out of the sun. Teller thinks he probably spent more of his lookout time sleeping than watching for planes.

In many stations, men were able to have a modified type of general quarters during periods when the ship was not under attack but had to remain ready. Crew members had by then long since learned to sleep on steel decks, metal gratings in the engineering spaces, and even in their seats inside the gun mounts. Battle messing became a useful alternative when men weren't able to get normal meals from the galley. Sometimes the crew subsisted on coffee and sandwiches. At other times, they opened up boxes of K rations of the type used by troops fighting ashore. Included in the rations were such things as crackers, candy, bouillon, cheese, and small cans of meat.

On 22 March, the *New Jersey* joined Rear Admiral Arthur Radford's Task Group 58.4 for operations in the vicinity of Okinawa. On the morning of the 24th, she shifted to a bombardment group under Admiral Badger. Also included were five destroyers and the battleships *Missouri* and

*Wisconsin.* In the morning, the ships shelled the island of Kutaka Shima and in the afternoon bombarded the southeast coast of Okinawa.

Soon it was back to work in the carrier task groups, first Rear Admiral J. J. "Jocko" Clark's 58.1 and then back to Radford's 58.4. Easter Sunday, 1 April 1945, was the day Okinawa was invaded. The *New Jersey* continued to operate about 50–60 miles off the coast with her task group. She got a profound jolt on the night of 2 April. At 9:08, just after the last dusk combat air patrol was recovered, Task Group 58.4 was turning out of the wind and heading south for a fueling rendezvous. The *Fletcher*-class destroyer *Franks* had been serving as plane guard astern of the USS *Yorktown*, Radford's flagship. When released from that duty, she was to return to her normal screen station on the outer circle of the task group.

The *New Jersey* was plowing through the dark, cloudy night at 23 knots when her officer of the deck, Lieutenant Gene Hayward, spotted the lights of the *Franks* close ahead, crossing the battleship's bow from starboard to port. At 9:14, Hayward saw that the destroyer was on a collision bearing and shouted "Right full rudder emergency" to the man on the *New Jersey*'s wheel and ordered the engines to back at full power. Had he not done so, the mammoth dreadnought might have cut the *Franks* in half. The destroyer frantically sounded her whistle, and at 9:15, the two ships sideswiped each other, port to port. The *New Jersey*'s huge anchor, high above the water, ripped through the bridge of the *Franks*, sending the captain and officer of the deck crashing down onto the main deck and injuring both badly. The *New Jersey* continued her turn to starboard while the destroyer sent showers of sparks into the air, rolling back and forth and banging into the solid side of the battleship with each roll to port. Hayward then shifted the rudder to left full to swing the *New Jersey*'s stern clear of the passing *Franks*.

In the destroyer, Quartermaster First Class Mike Bak thought his ship had been hit by either a torpedo or mine. Wearing only his undershorts, he made ready to abandon ship. Fortunately, the hull of the *Franks* was intact. She stayed afloat, and Bak stayed on board. Robert Huff had just climbed into his bunk on board the *Franks* when he heard the emergency alarm and felt heavy vibrations. He jumped out of bed and ran topside. There, he says, "... all I could see was the enormous hulk of the NEW JERSEY looming above me." Quartermaster W. B. Middleton was on watch on the destroyer's bridge. He recalls his ship being dead in the water after the collision with her recognition lights left on for a while so she wouldn't be run down by other ships in the task group. In the *New Jersey* Russ Brown saw one of his shipmates writing a letter with a pen that he dipped into an open bottle of ink. When the crunch of collision came, the fellow was so unnerved that he spilled his ink and started running. Lieutenant John Sullivan went to the bridge from the wardroom and there

Below: Seen here in a photo taken from the deck of the *New Jersey* in December 1944 is the *Fletcher*-class destroyer *Franks*. On the stormy night of 2 April 1945, the *Franks* and *New Jersey* collided. (National Archives: 80-G-470279)

found OOD Hayward beside himself because he hadn't been able to avoid the collision. It would comfort Hayward afterward to realize that he had prevented the incident from being much worse.

Because the *Franks* was only 1,500–2,000 yards away from the *New Jersey* when on her plane guard station, the whole affair had taken place in just a few minutes. Hayward's commands on that stormy night, when the visibility was marginal, were based mostly on the automatic reaction that grows out of training and experience. He recalls that Captain Wooldridge treated him splendidly thereafter, grateful for what Hayward had done, because it reflected on Wooldridge as well.

On board the battered destroyer, the commanding officer, Commander David R. Stephan, was so badly injured that he died two days later as a result of fractured ribs having punctured his left lung. His officer of the deck, Lieutenant (junior grade) Bob Numbers, was injured but survived. Ensign Mark Lillis, the junior officer of the deck, recalls that Stephan ordered the destroyer's engines to back when she got within about 1,000 yards of the *New Jersey*. Hayward, recounting the event from a perspective nearly forty years afterward, believed that the smaller ship might have made it safely across the *New Jersey*'s bow if she had kept going. The truth, of course, can never be known. The decision to cross the *New Jersey*'s bow was a dangerous one, and perhaps the decision to reverse the engines the fatal one.

The *New Jersey* sustained negligible damage from the encounter. Less than half an hour after the accident, she regained her station as the formation guide. Two days later, just to keep in practice, her gunners fired on target drones. They shot down both, and one of them almost fell on the ship. On 7 April, the planes of Task Force 58 went after the Japanese battleship *Yamato* and her consort of cruisers and destroyers steaming west of Kyushu. This was a ship version of the kamikaze effort and proved not nearly so effective as the airborne type. Though Admiral Spruance would have preferred to sink the Japanese giant with his battle line, Admiral Mitscher's planes could do the job more quickly, and so they were sent in for the kill.

The next day, the *New Jersey* shifted once again to Task Group 58.3, but her activities in support of the Okinawa campaign were nearly finished. On the 11th, she did open fire with 5-inch and machine-guns on a Zeke and hit it. The plane crashed in flames about 3,000 yards away. On the 14th, Captain Wooldridge announced to the crew that the battleship was going back to the United States for overhaul, and the men were understandably enthusiastic. On 16 April, the *New Jersey* arrived at Ulithi, where Admiral Badger gave a farewell talk to the crew. Two days later, he transferred his flag to the *Iowa*.

The *New Jersey* made the journey to Pearl Harbor in company with the heavy cruiser *Minneapolis*. The stay in Hawaii was a brief one, less than twenty-four hours, and then the battleship resumed her journey eastward. The man in the captain's sea cabin during the voyage to Bremerton, Washington, was making the trip reluctantly. Captain Wooldridge would have much preferred that the *New Jersey* remain in combat, because he was on board her to get the big ship command experience he needed for promotion to rear admiral.

Edmund Tyler Wooldridge was a supreme gentleman and a brilliant officer. He was known for his expertise in the field of personnel and was a highly capable administrator. Indeed, he went on to four-star rank. On the other hand, he lacked a number of the qualities possessed by Carl Holden, whose highest active duty rank was rear admiral. While both were ambitious officers intent on doing a fine job on board the *New Jersey*, Holden had a special relationship with the crew that Captain Wooldridge was never able to achieve. The commissioning skipper had a feeling and sensitivity for the men's wishes and needs that his successor did not. Holden also had a sense of dash and an ability to handle the ship in action that Wooldridge did not achieve. Wooldridge probably also suffered in the crew's eyes if only because he was not Carl Holden, the man they had come to love because he cared about them and in whom they had developed a great sense of confidence.

When it came to the matter of enforcing regulations, Holden had started off as strict when he took command, because that was the way he had been brought up in the Navy. Gradually, though, as the ship got into steady combat, things had eased up, because combat itself is demanding enough. When Wooldridge came on the scene, he resumed the strict enforcement of regulations. The trouble was that the crew wasn't starting at the same point as Captain Wooldridge was, and so they saw the tightening as an unfortunate contrast.

Captain Wooldridge was an abstraction to the enlisted men at large, for they didn't get to know him personally. Few had the opportunity, of course. One who did was Marine Private First Class Dale O'Bryen, who served as Captain Wooldridge's orderly, summoning people to see him, handing him his binoculars and coffee and so forth. O'Bryen observed that Wooldridge had a physical condition in which his hands shook so noticeably that he could take only a half cup of coffee at a time. As O'Bryen, Commander Rice, and others close to the captain realized, the condition didn't affect the captain's ability to think or act, but word of it still got around among the crew and reinforced their impression of him.

On 6 May, the *New Jersey* arrived at Puget Sound Navy Yard, Bremerton, Washington, after stopping for two days at anchor to offload her ammunition. The shipyard period was to be long enough to allow the crew to go home on leave in two installments. For the half not on leave at a given time, there was enjoyment to be had in Seattle, where there were USO-sponsored dances and other attrac-

tions. Seaman Bob Westcott and others even found a way to enjoy the ferryboat ride over and back. They bought bags of popcorn and then tossed pieces of it in the air; seagulls were so eager for it, he remembers, that they never missed a piece of the corn. "And I can remember Seattle itself," he says. "It seemed like you were always walking uphill." He didn't notice the downhill part, only the climbing.

One member of the first leave contingent was Fire Controlman First Class J. P. Loughan. He recalls riding the train for four and a half days to get home to Boston to be married. The Pullman car going to Chicago was occupied entirely by *New Jersey* crew members on leave. Loughan

Right: Steaming at 18 knots during trials in Puget Sound on 30 June 1945, the *New Jersey* sports her new Measure 22 camouflage paint – navy blue up to the main deck and haze grey above. (Courtesy Arthur D. Baker III)

remembers, "We were able to persuade the porter to leave the bunks made up, and we just slept when we felt like it. So it wasn't all that bad. It's just that we were anxious to get home." He was married within a few days of getting home and then had a nine-day honeymoon in New York City. The toughest part was leaving to head back to the ship, especially since he had no idea when he would see his bride again.

Roger Faw, then a seaman first class, was in a delegation of *New Jersey* men which went to Seattle by ferryboat and was kept all in a group until they had bought their train tickets. He recalls that those in charge "were afraid that we would probably get on the beach, get drunk, lose all of our money, and wouldn't have fare home. And they were absolutely right." As it was, Faw lost his wallet, identification card, and leave papers. The shore patrol in Chicago fixed him up with temporary papers and sent him on his way east to home in Washington, D.C. There he received a telegram from a Bremerton barmaid who had found his wallet and later mailed it to him. Once he was back on the West Coast, he gave her a carton of Lucky Strike cigarettes every time he went on liberty until the ship departed.

For married officers such as Lieutenant Commander Archie Soucek and Lieutenant Bill Coyne, the leave period was a time to get acquainted with their families, eat their wives' cooking, and spend some time with their children. For Soucek that included Archie, Jr., who had measles. Coyne and his wife went to Vancouver, Canada, for two weeks of vacation and then settled into a government-owned cabin in Port Orchard, Washington, for the duration of the overhaul. "The cabins were sparsely furnished," he explains, "with a wood stove for cooking and heating, but after 18 months at sea it was a welcome change. The overhaul was completed in record time . . . and all too soon we were heading back to the war zone."

As to the ship herself, there was a fair amount to be accomplished in a relatively short time in order to get the *New Jersey* ready to go back out to finish the job against the Japanese. Probably of foremost concern was overhauling the engineering plant, because it had logged many thousands of miles of demanding, high-speed steaming. To make spotting the ship more difficult for kamikazes, a new device was installed to generate smoke screens. The *New Jersey* also received a new, roomier, square-front bridge in place of her rounded one. The new one was of the same type that was built into the *Missouri* and *Wisconsin* during original construction and added to the *Iowa* as part of her early 1945 navy yard period.

Inevitably, the work was wrapped up, and it was time to go again. Many of the *New Jersey*'s men treated their last night in port as if there would be no tomorrow – at least

**Right:** Anchored off Blake Island in Puget Sound, the *New Jersey* loads ammunition from barges on 2 July 1945. During the yard period just completed, a new tripod mainmast has been stepped from the after stack. (James C. Fahey Collection, U.S. Naval Institute)

**Below left:** Newly installed radar antennas are evident in this 30 June 1945 trials shot. An SP height-finder is on the new mainmast and SK-2 air search on the foremast. (Courtesy Arthur D. Baker III)

**Opposite page:** A Japanese projectile splashes off the port bow during the *New Jersey*'s 8 August 1945 bombardment of Wake Island, her last combat action of the war. (Courtesy Vice Admiral Robert H. Rice)

not one for on-the-beach "steaming". The town of Bremerton was not big enough to contain that boisterous, rowdy last night, which included much drinking and destruction of property. Typical was an incident in which someone took a stuffed moosehead down from a tavern wall and followed it out through a front window.

Fireman Russ Brown says, "It started out real peaceful until some of them got a few too many drinks, and they had the fire department out, washing guys down the street. They deserved it, because they had just taken over the town. I don't care where you looked, there was a sailor operating whatever was going on." Roger Faw agrees: "I can vouch for what happened that night, and that was about the wildest night I guess I ever saw." And Faw unquestionably saw some wild ones during his time in the Navy.

The ship got under way for sea trials on 30 June. She anchored to take on ammunition, and only the officers and chiefs got liberty. Dan Scanlon remembers the restriction partly as punishment for the mayhem before leaving and partly as a means of preventing more such problems. Captain Wooldridge had a busy time of it while the ship was at anchor on 2 July, handing out a fistful of punishments at mast and informing the crew that he'd received too many reports on their foul language in Bremerton. Roger Faw, who hadn't returned to the ship on time because he was with a girl, stood before the captain at mast and was awarded a punishment of restriction to the ship. "Now do you think it was worth it?" asked the captain.

"Yes, sir," replied the undaunted Faw, so the captain increased the severity of the punishment and repeated the question. Faw still thought the girl had been worth it, so then Wooldridge asked if Faw thought she was worth a court-martial. No, she wasn't, and so Faw ended up with his restriction to the ship, which was really no punishment at all with the New Jersey about to head back to the war and not much liberty in sight anyway.

On leaving the Pacific Northwest area, the New Jersey proceeded south to San Pedro, California, in company with the light cruiser Biloxi and destroyer Norris to undergo a period of refresher training that would bring the crew back up to speed. Again, the men were kept on board, because the captain didn't want anyone jumping ship at a time when he was determined to get her back to excel in combat. During part of the period after leaving Bremerton, Commander Rice assumed temporary command, because Captain Wooldridge was suffering a painful case of bursitis, so bad that he couldn't get up and get dressed. He received shots from the ship's medical department and was soon able to take over again.

Before leaving the United States, about a dozen men were dropped off and left behind when Commander Rice discovered that there was a group of homosexuals on board the ship. He explains, "The Navy had a very stern policy with respect to that sort of thing, and I think quite properly so. It detracts from other interests, such as duties." On 19 July, with the crew training completed, the New Jersey stood out of San Pedro harbor and headed west for Pearl Harbor, an intermediate stop on the way back to the war. The stop was a brief one.

On 8 August, still farther west, the New Jersey stopped near Wake Island long enough for a practice bombardment. The island had been seized by the Japanese soon after the beginning of the war in December 1941, but by 1945 it was so far beyond the drawn-in Japanese defensive perimeter that it was more liability than asset. Still, it provided a live target for the 16-inch and 5-inch guns of the battleship and got her men into the spirit of combat again after the West Coast layoff. As at Mille in March 1944, the Japanese were spirited enough to send some shells zinging out at the New Jersey. The four salvos fell between 200 and 2,500 yards short, and Captain Wooldridge quickly conned the ship out of harm's way. One of the ship's spotting planes – SC-1 Seahawks now in place of the old Kingfishers – had its main pontoon and wing float damaged by enemy fire, but the other planes were unhit. Warrant Officer Bob Moore says of the practice bombardment: "We had the Japs up and running at 17,000 yards when we broke off the engagement. Our five-inch battery was deadly."

At 4:30 p.m., after shooting much of the day except for a lunch break of sandwiches and coffee, the New Jersey gathered up her escorts – the light cruiser Biloxi and four destroyers – and began steaming southwest.

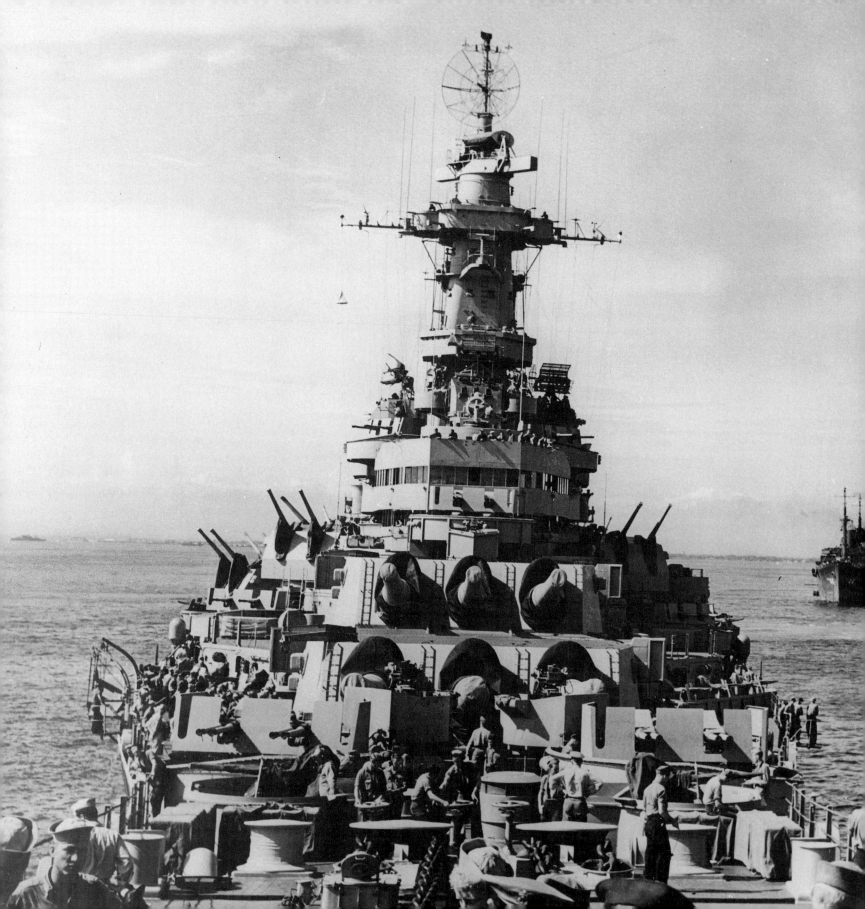

# CHAPTER III
# POSTWAR DOLDRUMS
## August 1945–June 1948

As the *New Jersey*'s heavy anchor chain rattled out through the hawsepipe at Eniwetok Atoll on the evening of 9 August, plans called for the Third and Fifth fleets to support the invasion of Japan's home islands. On 20 August, Admiral Halsey was scheduled to arrive at Eniwetok in the *Missouri* and transfer his Third Fleet staff to the *New Jersey* for the final campaign of World War II.

After supper that night, members of the crew went out on deck to relax, have a smoke, and survey the vast lagoon of Eniwetok. As the men talked, the air was buzzing for the first time with rumors that the war was nearly over. On 6 August, an American atomic bomb had been dropped on Hiroshima. The Soviet Union had come into the war against Japan, and that very day, 9 August, an atomic bomb was dropped on Nagasaki. The home islands had been reeling for weeks under relentless air and naval pressure. The noose had reached the choking point, and Japanese leaders were scrambling to find a formula for peace.

Despite the high-level negotiations, the commonplace was still necessary. On 10 August, the cargo ship *Durham Victory* came alongside the *New Jersey* to supply 16-inch ammunition. The war was not yet over, so it was prudent to be ready for whatever lay ahead. Manhandling the heavy ammunition was hot, hard work, especially in August at torrid Eniwetok, only 11½° north of the Equator. For the first time in months, crew members were allowed to swim off the side of the battleship.

At 5:00 a.m. on the 11th, Captain Wooldridge was awakened and presented with what he described as ". . . two startling pieces of information. One was to the effect that Japan had made proposals to surrender provided the emperor was left in power and, second were the urgent sailing orders for the *New Jersey* to proceed to Guam." The captain sent his orderly to summon the ship's navigator, Commander Myers Keithly, so he could prepare to get the ship under way. Later that morning, the *New Jersey* and five escorting destroyers began their journey, which ended two days later in Apra Harbor. Guam had become the forward headquarters of Fleet Admiral Chester W. Nimitz, Commander in Chief Pacific Fleet and Pacific Ocean Areas. He was conferring with Admiral Raymond A. Spruance, Commander Fifth Fleet, and his staff concerning the coming landings in Japan. As the *New Jersey* bided her time, diversions were provided for the war-weary crew. A

boxing ring was set up on the fantail for intramural matches, and on one occasion the fantail was a concert hall as the Pacific Fleet band played from an impromptu stage on top of turret three. Meanwhile, the rumor mill continued to grind. The ship's cruisebook *War Log* said of the Guam stay: "The scuttlebutt now took on some rare and fantastic forms – everyone from Chiang Kai-Shek [President of China] to Hedy Lamarr [movie star] was coming aboard, and we were expecting to be the surrender ship at Tokyo."

The Japanese cabinet accepted surrender terms on 14 August. Reaction on board the *New Jersey* was subdued. The crew was still far from home and apprehensive about what lay ahead in Japan. In a letter he wrote to his wife on 15 August, Captain Wooldridge explained: "We still don't trust the Japs and realize that all opportunities for treachery will probably be used; this means that we will remain on a complete war footing until we have actually disarmed the Nips."

On 16 August, with the fighting ended, Admiral Spruance and his staff embarked in the *New Jersey*. Admiral Halsey would remain in the *Missouri* and be responsible for receiving the surrender of the Tokyo area and northern Japan. Spruance would take over western Honshu and the islands of Kyushu and Shikoku.

Captain Wooldridge was disappointed, explaining in a letter home that if the surrender negotiations had taken place two weeks later, Halsey would have been on board the *New Jersey* by then. She would thus have been his flagship at the time of the surrender in Tokyo Bay. Many in the crew believed that their ship deserved to be the site of the formal Japanese capitulation, but then came word that President Harry S Truman had chosen the *Missouri* instead. She was named for his home state, and his daughter had christened the ship. The *New Jersey*'s men harbored a feeling of disappointment for some time.

The next stop after Guam was Manila, where the *New Jersey* arrived on 21 August. The ravages of war were much in evidence. The city itself was 85 per cent destroyed, and the harbor was littered with wrecked Japanese ships. Some were completely underwater, while the masts and stacks of others protruded above the surface as a menace to navigation. In heavy rain, Wooldridge, navigator Keithly, and a harbor pilot gingerly threaded their way through the maze to bring the *New Jersey* to her anchorage.

The captain and navigator, both of whom spent much of their time on the bridge when the ship was under way, had formed a bond. Both were submariners. Wooldridge had specifically requested a former skipper, concluding that someone who had commanded his own vessel would have an appreciation of the kind of information a captain expects from his navigator. During the westward journey, the two of them played nightly games of cribbage in the navigator's charthouse or in the captain's sea cabin just aft of the bridge. (When Captain Wooldridge left the ship a few months later, he took with him a case of cigarettes as Commander Keithly's payment of his cribbage debts.)

While in Manila, Admiral Spruance held planning meetings with General Walter Krueger, whose Sixth Army had been designated to occupy the Japanese islands of Kyushu and Shikoku, as well as the western part of the main island of Honshu. Also involved in the meetings was General of the Army Douglas MacArthur, who was to be Supreme Allied Commander for the surrender. MacArthur planned to wait two weeks before beginning the occupation so that the Japanese Emperor would have time to prepare his people.

The Philippine economy was in ruins. Surprisingly, children had fistfuls of American money, but there was little to buy from local sources. "Hey, Joe, you want to sell your watch?" was a common question. *New Jersey* radioman Bob Westcott remembers, "They'd buy your watch; your shoes right off your feet; your shirt – they'd buy anything. . . . Not only the kids, but naturally all the women were in business." The women were selling, not buying. Westcott went into an enterprising, though dubious business of his own. He began making and selling one-tube, one-earphone radio sets with parts from the *New Jersey*'s storerooms. One of his shipboard superiors soon ordered him to stop.

As the officers and men of the battleship walked the streets of Manila, which was feeling the effects of the hot summer sun, their nostrils were invaded by the sweetish smell of rotting human flesh. They saw people digging amid the rubble of the city and watched the passage of horse-drawn carts, for the only motor vehicles were those of the American military forces.

One young officer from the *New Jersey* was struck by the great sadness he encountered. Bud Bowler, then an ensign, explained later that the local inhabitants "were still battered and bedraggled and sad – and obviously undernourished. I didn't see any happiness at all among the Philippine people. That was kind of startling. You would have expected a great deal of exuberance to carry them over any remaining hard times, but they were just beat to a pulp, from my observation. . . . They were clearly showing the impact of the long occupation [and] mistreatment at the hands of the Japanese."

Some crewmen saw Manila liberty primarily in terms of what it offered that shipboard life did not – a chance to get drunk. The men of the battleship were warned before going ashore of the dangers of wood alcohol. The Japanese had been burning it in their trucks when gasoline grew scarce, and they left supplies of it behind. Enterprising Filipinos colored the fuel to look like liquor and poured it into whiskey bottles, which they sold to the American sailors. Despite the warnings, Lieutenant John Rossie of the engineering department observed that a few men from the ship suffered ill effects from drinking the wood alcohol. One, for instance, was so disoriented that he walked over the side of the ship and had to be fished out of the water.

After staying at Manila from 21 to 28 August, the *New Jersey* steamed to Buckner Bay, Okinawa. There she remained for two weeks while Admiral Spruance's occupation fleet assembled. Halsey's Third Fleet was already in action against the Japanese when the surrender came and thus available to move into Tokyo Bay. Sufficient ships were now available for both the Third and Fifth fleets to exist simultaneously, but it still took time for Spruance's to come together.

On 2 September, while the surrender ceremonies were taking place on board the *Missouri*, Admiral Spruance was hundreds of miles away, because Admiral Nimitz had not

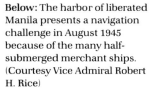

**Below:** The harbor of liberated Manila presents a navigation challenge in August 1945 because of the many half-submerged merchant ships. (Courtesy Vice Admiral Robert H. Rice)

directed him to be present. One logical explanation is that the Americans were still concerned about the possibility of last-minute Japanese treachery and so didn't want to have all the top U.S. naval commanders in one spot. Probably the most noteworthy thing which happened for the *New Jersey* on 2 September was that Lieutenant (junior grade) Tom Mullaney, the disbursing officer, brought aboard $2.4 million worth of Japanese currency for the crew to spend on liberty in Japan.

The stay at Okinawa afforded the opportunity for high-ranking visitors to confer with Admiral Spruance. One was a khaki-clad Army officer, General Vinegar Joe Stilwell, who had earned fame fighting the Japanese in the China-Burma-India theater. He had taken command of the U.S. Tenth Army on Okinawa and would be in charge of accepting the surrender of all Japanese forces in the Ryukyus Islands. Much more nattily dressed than Stilwell was Admiral Sir Bruce Fraser, Commander-in-Chief, British Pacific Fleet. He strode aboard through two rows of sideboys, wearing a snappy set of tropical white shorts, white shirt, long white socks, and white shoes.

Yet another guest soon after the war's end was Rear Admiral Carl F. Holden, the previous commanding officer. Because of his popularity with the crew he received a rousing welcome upon his return. When he stepped onto the quarterdeck, he remarked to Captain Wooldridge, "What a beautiful deck. How did you get it like that?" He was used to seeing it covered with camouflage. Getting the paint off after the war's end had been a real chore. The men of the deck force had to scrape "holystones" back and forth over the wood until the layers of paint were removed – a back-straining job.

When the battleship left Buckner Bay on 13 September, she was able to steam toward Japan at a leisurely 16 knots, and she was able to operate with her running lights burning brightly – after some 200,000 miles of Pacific steaming at darkened ship. As the *New Jersey* approached Japan, she was greeted by a touching and symbolic event. Her destination was the port of Wakayama at the eastern entrance to the heavily mined Inland Sea of Japan. Pulling out after loading hundreds of just-released Allied prisoners of war was the USS *Sanctuary*. As the hospital ship passed on the *New Jersey*'s starboard side, the ex-prisoners let forth a cheer for the battleship, and the men of the *New Jersey* applauded the newly liberated POWs.

The Fifth Fleet flagship arrived at Wakayama on 15 September and left the following day. She reached Tokyo Bay on 17 September, just over two weeks after the surrender signing, and moored to a buoy at the former Japanese naval base in Yokosuka. At that point, Admiral Spruance took command of all U.S. naval forces in Japan. In addition to keeping control of the islands already assigned to the Fifth Fleet, he took over eastern Honshu from Admiral Halsey and Hokkaido from Vice Admiral Frank Jack Fletcher. Among Spruance's responsibilities as naval occupation commander were the disposal of Japanese chemical warfare weapons; sweeping of American mines (a task capably handled by the Japanese); and repatriation of soldiers of two nations. The latter involved sending home Americans who had been in Japanese hands and bringing back Japanese from outlying areas of the Pacific.

As soon as the fighting ended, the American public began exerting considerable pressure to "bring the boys home". This pressure had demonstrable effects in faraway Japan. Demobilization was to be based on a point system. Those who had enlisted for the duration of the war were to be released in a priority sequence based on the number of dependents they had and the number of points they had accumulated by virtue of length of service in the war zone. This meant that many thousands of American GIs and sailors had to be transported to the United States, and it also meant that ships of the occupation fleet would be losing crew members. Under the system the most experienced – and thus most valuable – crew members would leave soonest.

The Fifth Fleet's staff operations officer, Captain Edward M. Thompson, noticed that Admiral Spruance seemed not to be adjusting to the fact that he was no longer a combat commander. Even though it might have made more sense, for example, to set up the fleet communicators ashore in Japan, Spruance insisted on keeping them on board the *New Jersey* so that the fleet wouldn't be robbed of its mobility. Moreover, Thompson was directed to send only operational radio messages, not administrative ones. Asking people in a particular port how many soldiers they had for travel home to the States was considered administrative and thus not permitted. Thompson was, as a result, somewhat stymied in knowing where to send "Magic Carpet" ships to pick up loads of men. The *New Jersey* herself would not be going home right away to be part of the victory parade and Navy Day celebrations in the United States in late October. Because of her overhaul at Bremerton, she had been to the States most recently of the available battleships and so was tapped as flagship for the occupation forces.

To the *New Jersey*'s crew the occupation role offered an opportunity to see firsthand the land of their recently conquered enemies. Sports and recreation programs were set up, and the customary liberty pastimes were rediscovered – drinking and sex. Sometimes men had to stand in line for as much as an hour to buy a bottle of Japanese beer, and there was also a good deal of competition in taking pleasure with Japanese women. The unhappy consequences were fighting, rape, and venereal diseases. To counter these ills, Admiral Spruance and his fleet medical officer, Captain Morton D. Willcutts, authorized houses of prostitution under U.S. Navy control. Navy medical personnel were in charge of sanitation and protection against VD.

Lieutenant Leonard Goode, the *New Jersey*'s Catholic chaplain, argued that such a program condoned sin, and he had other objections as well. He recalls that he and his Protestant counterpart, Lieutenant R. J. Hawkins, met with the Fifth Fleet staff officers, "and we pleaded with them not to do this since we had information from missionaries in Japan about the rampant disease in these houses. We were told to leave the decision to the medical department and to go 'say your prayers'."

Commander Bob Rice, soon to be relieved as the *New Jersey*'s executive officer, later described the reaction: "One morning, my chaplain . . . came to me and said could we make the wardroom available for a meeting of fleet chaplains. I said, 'Certainly, we could do that.' It seemed natural to me they should come to a big ship with plenty of space. But later on, I learned the purpose of this meeting was to decide what should be done about Admiral Spruance's and the fleet surgeon's plan to create a bordello in the interests of the health of the crew." The protest was picked up by newspapers and congressmen in the United States, and Spruance was forced to cancel the program.

The feared Japanese treachery did not come to pass, but *New Jersey* men were still wary about the reception they would encounter. Hank Kubicki, one of the buglers, remembers that the Japanese "were more standoffish than anything. I think they were afraid of us as much as we were apprehensive of them." For the most part, the people were docile but understandably reluctant to warm up to their conquerors, although there were exceptions. In part, relationships grew out of the generosity of the Americans who were willing to share food and other items. There was also interchange as a result of the widespread American desire to take home souvenirs, particularly Japanese swords. Barter seemed to work in some cases, with Americans trading such items as shoes and cigarettes which were readily available for purchase on board ship. Seaman Harry Fagan of the *New Jersey* tried to get the sword of a Japanese policeman, who was reluctant to give it up. Fagan finally desisted when someone explained to him that a policeman's sword constituted his badge of authority.

Barter wasn't the only means of obtaining local goods; there was also the large supply of Japanese currency obtained in Okinawa. Because he was sending home a good deal of his pay to support his wife and two young children, Radioman Bob Westcott had only $15.00 on the books. He decided to draw out all of it and was surprised by the large handful of Japanese paper money he received. As he went from shop to shop, he didn't know the price of anything, "so when I'd buy something, I'd just hold my hand out, and they'd take what they wanted. And I had a lot of money when I came back." Among his purchases was a kimono, which he proudly presented to Mrs. Westcott when he got discharged and went home to New Jersey. He was somewhat deflated when she looked inside the garment he'd bought in Japan and found a California label.

Bugler Hank Kubicki and several shipmates visited a local bathhouse, where they saw that Japanese of both sexes were in the tub. The Americans doffed their uniforms and got into the water, although they did keep on their skivvy shorts as a matter of modesty. Afterward, Kubicki got a massage as a young Japanese woman walked on his back with her bare feet. "That was one of the most relaxing moments of my life," he remembers. "Her heels and toes going up and down your spine – it was just absolutely gorgeous." Even though the woman administering the massage with her "educated toes and educated heels" spoke little English, she readily communicated that the Americans were allowed to do no touching of their own. When a sailor reached for her, she could certainly say "No!" After the experience, the *New Jersey* men put their uniforms back on and returned to the ship, but had to carry their still-wet shorts.

As one means of keeping some control over the Americans who were going ashore for liberty two nights out of three, a midnight curfew was imposed. There were restricted areas in the port city of Yokosuka, so a more popular spot was Yokohama, which was reached by trips in LCUs – large, open landing craft. Even with the midnight limit, some men could get thoroughly drunk by that time. Commander Zeke Soucek was serving as command duty officer one night in Japan when a landing craft brought men back to the ship. Many of the men were "tanked up", according to Soucek, and some were vomiting and urinating in the open well deck of the landing craft. The skipper of the LCU said something which evidently raised his passengers' ire, and spanner wrenches of the type used to tighten fire hoses were soon flying around. Even after the men were brought back aboard the *New Jersey*, some started throwing wrenches down into the boat, one just missing the landing craft's skipper. Finally, the ship's master-at-arms force was able to restore order.

The officers of the fleet were accorded liberty privileges not given to enlisted men. Groups of them were able to go off for a few days' leave in Japanese resort hotels in an undamaged part of the country. Soucek went with a group which included Commander Bernard F. Roeder, Jr., who relieved Bob Rice as exec. Their jeep took them over rocky, bumpy roads and included a picturesque view of the Japanese countryside. As Soucek remembers, "We'd go through these little Japanese towns, where . . . the water coming down from the mountain would run through the city in what we call gutters. . . . The housewife would come out with a pan and gather up some water and go back in the house with it. Or she'd come out there and squat with her pan and vegetables, using the ditch like a sink. Or she'd come out holding her baby . . . by the knees, and that was the johnny where the baby went. It was an all-purpose ditch."

**Right:** Photographed at Yokosuka in October 1945 are the ship's pilots, standing on the fantail in front of one of their SC-1 floatplanes. Left to right: L. Harlan Goodpasture, Allen L. Trecartin, Glenn Harris, Jr., and G. E. Percival. (Courtesy L. Harlan Goodpasture)

**Below:** Pilot Allen Trecartin flies one of the *New Jersey*'s new SC-1 Seahawks above the clouds and a Japanese volcano in the autumn of 1945. The ship got the SC-1s in place of OS2Us when she returned to the United States in the spring of 1945. (Photo by L. Harlan Goodpasture; courtesy Allen Trecartin)

Certainly there were more esthetic experiences. During her time in Yokosuka, the fleet flagship was frequently in view of beautiful Mount Fuji, the snow-capped volcano which is much revered in Japan. Charles Mathias, an officer from the occupation fleet, recalls, "I must say that the morning watch [4:00 to 8:00 a.m.] was one of the most beautiful experiences I ever had, to watch the sun coming up on Fujiyama and see it change color from just being a grey shadow on the horizon, and then to have the sun touch the top of the mountain and turn it first to a sort of gold and then to pink and finally, pure white."

Although life on board the *New Jersey* generally fell into a routine of maintenance work, watch-standing, and liberty, two of the ship's officers found the autumn of 1945 to be anything but routine. Lieutenant Commander John Sullivan and reserve Lieutenant John Yeager were detached for three months' duty ashore in Japan. When General MacArthur's occupation troops had moved into the country, some inadvertently detonated Japanese naval weapons, such as mines and torpedoes. Thus, naval ordnance officers were called for, and Sullivan and Yeager got the job. Assigned to help them were a couple of Japanese – a former Imperial Navy captain who had been educated in the United States and was fluent in English, and a kamikaze pilot who didn't get into action before war's end. Yeager managed to commandeer an Army jeep as their transportation, and the group traveled widely. At one point, the Americans were challenged by two U.S. Army sentries for allowing the Japanese to ride in the jeep with them, in contravention of standing orders. By then, the *New Jersey*'s officers had become good friends with the Japanese, but as a ruse they glibly told the Army sentries that these were prisoners to be tried as war criminals – and on their way they went.

On Thursday, 8 November, the *New Jersey* got a new occupant in her flag quarters. Raymond Spruance was relieved as Commander Fifth Fleet by Admiral John H. Towers, who had become the Navy's second aviator more than forty years earlier. Spruance was piped over the side and rode away in a barge en route to relieve Admiral Nimitz as Commander in Chief Pacific Fleet. When he left the *New Jersey*, Admiral Spruance was concluding the last seagoing assignment in a career that stretched back nearly to the turn of the century.

The departure of Admiral Spruance led to the ship getting a new captain. Captain Wooldridge had been selected for rear admiral. He couldn't hold that rank as the ship's commanding officer, but he was eligible for the promotion as soon as a vacancy occurred. The fleet operations officer, Captain Thompson, went to Spruance with the suggestion that Wooldridge could take the place of a cruiser division commander whose flagship was also in Yokosuka. Thompson volunteered to command the *New Jersey*. Spruance and Thompson were not on the best of terms, and so the admiral turned down the proposal. As

Opposite page, top: Snow-capped Mount Fuji is in the background as the *New Jersey* lies at anchor in Yokosuka harbor in the autumn of 1945. She serves as flagship for Admiral Raymond Spruance as the occupation of defeated Japan gets under way. (Courtesy Vice Admiral Robert H. Rice)

Opposite page, center: The crew, already beginning to decline in numbers, gathers on the fantail on 8 November 1945 at Yokosuka for the Fifth Fleet change of command. (Thomas Buell Collection, U.S. Naval War College)

Opposite page, bottom: The outgoing and incoming Fifth Fleet commanders greet visitors on 8 November. Second from left is Admiral Raymond Spruance, concluding the final seagoing command of his long career; second from right is Admiral John H. Towers. (National Archives: 80-G-355329)

Right: In this aerial view of Yokosuka in late 1945, the *New Jersey* is in the right foreground. Just beyond her is the *Nagato*, last surviving Japanese battleship, and to the left are U.S. cruisers. (Photo by L. Harlan Goodpasture)

soon as Spruance was relieved, however, Thompson presented his plan to Admiral Towers. Towers agreed and sent off a message to the Bureau of Naval Personnel, which also approved. On 17 November, only nine days after Spruance's departure, Wooldridge left also.

The new commanding officer presented a contrast to the old in his manner of operating the ship. Wooldridge, a former submariner, was perhaps awed by the great size and bulk of the *New Jersey*, for he was timid in conning her. Thompson, on the other hand, was inclined to be bold. He had the added advantage of having been conning officer of the fast battleship *Massachusetts* while serving as executive officer when she was first commissioned. In 1942, during the Allied invasion of North Africa, he had kept the *Massachusetts* away from enemy gunfire and torpedoes as she dueled with the French at Casablanca.

Near the end of the month, on 28 November, the *New Jersey* was to get under way for the first time since arriving in Yokosuka. Thompson concluded that one means of winning the crew's confidence was to put on a bold display of shiphandling. The ship was moored to a buoy near the berth of the Japanese battleship *Nagato*. Rear Admiral Wooldridge, as senior officer for the maneuvers that would follow, offered tugboats to help the *New Jersey* move away from the *Nagato*. In order to demonstrate his self-confidence – and possibly to show up his cautious

predecessor – Thompson declined the tugboats and twisted the *New Jersey* clear with her own engines.

Several officers who served under Captain Thompson in the *New Jersey* have offered their assessments of him. One calls him "a wonderful skipper . . . a very, very fine officer, and he let you do your job". This same individual added, in speaking about Thompson, "He was a little on the heavyset side. He didn't present quite as clean a military appearance as some of the other officers, but as far as being an all-around good officer, it was a pleasure to work under the gentleman." Gunnery officer Soucek remembers that Captain Thompson "was well-loved on board; we all liked him, and we had good camaraderie with him, enjoyed him very much. But when he got angry, by golly, he'd get angry, and his face would get red, and boy, he didn't mince any words. He'd tell you what was what, but he was still very well liked."

Commander Myers Keithly, the navigator who had been brought aboard by Captain Wooldridge, remembers Thompson as "a very bold man", likable, outspoken, and abrupt. He was not aloof, as Wooldridge had been in dealing with subordinates. On one occasion several months later, Keithly recalls that Captain Thompson "scared the hell out of me" by running along parallel to the breakwater at Long Beach Harbor, then having Keithly turn at just the right instant to go through the narrow opening

into the harbor. Although Keithly was nervous about it at the time, he doesn't believe the captain was risking all that much, because Thompson was such a good shiphandler that he could have rescued the situation if anything untoward had happened.

During her first three days at sea under Thompson, the *New Jersey* spent a lot of time training – exercising at general quarters, maneuvering in company with Rear Admiral Wooldridge's new flagship *Pasadena*, and firing her antiaircraft guns. The crew was already turning over, because experienced men were leaving quickly now that the war was over. Performance suffered, including a foulup between ships. At one point, recalls Zeke Soucek, the *New Jersey* got so close to the stern of the *Pasadena* that "I could have thrown a potato and hit that ship."

During the entire time Captain Thompson was in command of the *New Jersey*, there wasn't a single opportunity to fire the main battery, but he did enjoy the rare occasions, such as this, to fire the antiaircraft guns. By this time the battleship was already so undermanned that Soucek had to pool his men in order to assemble gun crews. One of the newly arrived gun crew members was Seaman Harry Fagan, who remembers that some of the shots nearly hit the aircraft flying past instead of the target sleeve it was towing. The pilot reported afterward that he didn't want to work with the *New Jersey* until her gunnery improved.

There were several reasons for the letdown in crew performance during that period. First, there was no longer a war on, with its built-in self-preservation instinct which improves men's shooting. Second, there was considerable loss of experience. Finally, the two-month layoff while in port might have dulled the edge of even a wartime crew.

Discipline had to be tightened up during this period, because the beginning of peacetime had brought some slackness. Strict standards were still largely in place, but crew members no longer felt the previous incentives to observe them. A number of men were just biding their time until they could be discharged and return to civilian life. Even when punishment was necessary, however, Captain Thompson dispensed it reluctantly. He explained years later that "a perfect day for me was to have the chief master-at-arms come up and say, 'No men at mast today.' . . . I hated to hold mast, [but when he did hold it] I always went on the assumption 'hit 'em hard and hit 'em quick'. Three days' solitary confinement on bread and water, administered on the spot, is a damn sight more effective than thirty days' loss of pay submitted two weeks later."

The need to exercise the *New Jersey* as a warship was not the only reason to get under way after the long stay in port. The water of Yokosuka Harbor was polluted by the effluents of the all-purpose ditches Commander Soucek had seen in his travels. The crew of the cruiser *Pasadena* had been so wracked by dysentery that she was nearly disabled prior to Admiral Wooldridge's arrival. The condition hadn't been so bad on board the *New Jersey*, because the ship's doctors had dispensed tablets to make the water safe for drinking. Even so, some men in the *New Jersey* did have problems, and it was worth a trip to sea to flush out storage tanks and fill them with new fresh water made by the ship's evaporators.

Throughout the autumn of 1945, crew members left in droves to return to the United States for reassignment or discharge. The manning problem was rampant in most other ships as well. Rear Admiral Charles Wellborn, Jr., was then on board as chief of staff to Admiral Towers; he recalls the period as a time when the battleship served principally as a hotel and communications facility for the fleet commander. He says that Admiral Towers referred to their function then as "counting LSTs". The LSTs, a type of large amphibious landing craft, were being immobilized wherever they were when their crews dwindled to the point of rendering them incapable of getting under way. At least the *New Jersey* could still operate.

Most of December 1945 and January 1946 were spent at a buoy in Yokosuka, interrupted for a brief period each month by operating at sea with the *Pasadena* and accompanying destroyers. Some new men reported to beef up the crew slightly and to compensate for the many who had been detached. One such was reserve Ensign Dan Duffy, whose case illustrates the disorganized state of naval personnel in the year after the war. He had previously served in the heavy cruiser *Louisville* and then was in San Francisco following VJ Day. A personnel officer on duty there seemed to think Duffy was having too much fun, so he was sent out by ship to join the crew of the *New Jersey* for a trip to – of all places – San Francisco.

On 18 January, Admiral Towers's two-month stay in the *New Jersey* ended as he relinquished command of the Fifth Fleet to Vice Admiral Frederick C. Sherman.

Sherman's stay was brief; on 28 January, he shifted to the USS *Iowa*, swapping flagships with Rear Admiral John W. Roper, Commander Battleship Division One. Hundreds of passengers reported to the *New Jersey* for transportation to the United States. Among them was the man with whom Admiral Spruance had conferred in Manila, General Krueger. The old warrior and his staff were going home, and that would justify cranking on a few more knots than permitted under normal postwar economies.

The great day came at last on Tuesday, 29 January 1946. At 1:00 p.m., the crew was mustered at quarters, and the master-at-arms force searched the ship for stowaways. At 1:58, the anchor chain was slipped from the mooring buoy, and the battleship was under way for San Francisco. During the trip, recalls Dan Duffy, war correspondents showed films taken in one of the Japanese cities hit by an atomic bomb. General Krueger explored the giant dreadnought and learned something about her operations. On one occasion, he was chatting with the navigator, Commander Keithly, who sought to explain to him the sextant used in measuring the angle between the horizon and various stars for celestial navigation. The general cut short the conversation by saying, "I was surveying the west coast of Luzon with a sextant before you were born."

Keithly did have a new plaything to help with the navigation – a spherical metal calculator devised by the Japanese to solve the celestial triangle and provide the

components for fixing the ship's position. It was among the booty liberated from caves in the vicinity of Yokosuka. A more serious concern was in operating the *New Jersey* during the return transit after she had lost so many experienced people, including nearly all the qualified helmsmen. Keithly and a chief quartermaster shared the steering duties until they could break in replacements.

New officers of the deck were needed also. Captain Wooldridge had sought to hang on to his turret officers as OODs and junior officers of the deck. But they were being swept out in the demobilization, and so a new group of men came under instruction. One of them, Lieutenant (junior grade) Bob Moore, found it a new experience after serving in a fire control division throughout the battleship's wartime service. His training was enhanced a month later with the arrival of a new senior watch officer. White-haired Lieutenant Bob Pearson had spent the war piloting newly constructed LSTs down the Mississippi River and had much useful shiphandling experience to pass on to his new shipmates.

When the *New Jersey* reached San Francisco on 10 February, she steamed beneath the Golden Gate Bridge, timing her arrival for the high tide. Some families of crew members were on hand to welcome the long lines of sailors standing on the main deck. Among those sailors was Fireman Russ Brown, who remembers that the ship was welcomed by a boat with a band on board; included in

**Below:** Home at last from the war, the *New Jersey* steams under the Golden Gate Bridge at San Francisco on 10 February 1946. (AP/Wide World)

the tunes played for the crew was "Jersey Bounce". As a whole, though, this was a much more subdued celebration than that which greeted the bulk of the fleet upon its return the previous autumn. By February, the freshness of victory had worn off, and so the *New Jersey*'s arrival was anticlimactic. As with the surrender gathering in Tokyo Bay, fate and poor timing had conspired to place the ship elsewhere when the crowds gathered.

Despite the letdown, the men were still thrilled to be back, particularly the passengers who had been overseas for a long time. Hundreds of them were disgorged at San Francisco, along with still more crew members to be discharged from the service. Less than six hours after anchoring in San Francisco Bay, the ship was under way once again, to Long Beach in southern California. This, for a time, would be the *New Jersey*'s base. Men could get used to Stateside liberty again, including such simple pleasures as eating fresh food. Zeke Soucek remembers the enjoyment he had by gorging himself on salads and fresh milk upon reaching California.

During the next few months, the doldrums which had beset the *New Jersey* in Yokosuka became even worse in Long Beach. Still more men left for discharge, and the ship lay anchored for weeks at a time. Boredom became a shipmate of the crew, for the *New Jersey* had no real purpose. A rare break in the schedule came when one of the crew members who knew a talent agent in Hollywood arranged for a variety show to be presented on board by entertainers Marilyn Maxwell and Jack Carson.

In early 1946, the Navy was trying to decide what to do with the *New Jersey* and hundreds of other warships as well. Many of those were being laid up, because the Navy no longer had the money or manpower to operate them. Moreover, with no significant potential naval enemy in sight, the need for the vast wartime fleet no longer existed.

On 26 March, after having been anchored in port for a month and a half, the ship got under way long enough to move in and moor to a pier at the naval shipyard in Long Beach. A beneficial side effect of the long time in port was that it allowed the crew members to get away on leave for extended periods. One was Seaman Harry Fagan, who rode by train to his home in Brooklyn. After an enjoyable stay of several weeks, he bought a bottle of whiskey, which he planned to use as part of a birthday celebration once he returned to the *New Jersey*. He and several shipmates were on the westbound train. In the evenings, the other men repeatedly implored Fagan to share a shot of the liquor with them to help them get to sleep in the day-coach seats in which they were riding. He turned them down, he remembers, jealously saving his treasure for a party.

On the night Fagan and his mates got back to Long Beach, they stepped up to the quarterdeck and saluted the officer of the deck to ask permission to return aboard. The OOD, one of the officers from the ship's Marine detachment, informed the men that he was going to inspect their luggage. Fagan quickly decided to return ashore and throw his bottle away, because it was better to do that than to be punished for trying to smuggle liquor aboard ship. The

Marine had been kind to Fagan by giving him the chance to get rid of the bottle rather than searching him on the spot. On the other hand, Fagan had to face the rebukes of his buddies from whom he had kept that bottle night after night on the train.

During those months in Long Beach, the personnel turnover continued. When the ship did get new men, they were frequently inexperienced seamen second class, straight from boot camp. They were given some training about the ship, but there were precious few knowledgeable petty officers left to do any training. For the officers as well, life was a desultory affair. To escape the boredom of the ship's routine Ensign Duffy applied for training in Navy schools. He had already been to fire-fighting school, but he went again, if only because it gave him a chance to visit relatives nearby. He passed up a course in recognition of Japanese planes, which surely had outlived its usefulness, and applied instead for one in ice cream-making. Alas, that one was cancelled.

In late April, the pace of activity picked up, although only temporarily. Late that month and through early May, the *New Jersey* got under way frequently in the area off Long Beach to train with the *Iowa*. Rear Admiral John Roper, as Commander Battleship Division One, was embarked in the *New Jersey* for the local operations. There were steering exercises, man overboard drills, launching of planes from the fantail catapults, fire drills, seamanship drills, gunnery drills, underway replenishment practice, antiaircraft practice, navigation and shiphandling drills,

and a surprise military inspection to test readiness. For Captain Thompson, it was an all-too-rare chance to operate the ship, but it still had limited value, because the *New Jersey* was so pitifully undermanned.

One thing that did happen in 1946 was that the *New Jersey* was called to account for the supplies she had used in the war. When Commander Hank Kretz reported in mid-April to take over as the supply officer, he found that, "Nothing seemed to balance; suppliers were demanding payments for items that they claimed were forwarded to the ship but for which no records or receipts could be found; some items were found to have been lost when the supply or other ship carrying them over was sunk; others were still floating around somewhere in the Pacific." In addition, the wardroom mess bill was a month in arrears. Eventually, he got things straightened out, in part by assessing the officers one extra mess bill, in part by submitting dummy vouchers, and in part by getting Washington's blessing to write off some accounts.

Another task that fell to Kretz was preparing for an assignment which turned out to be a mirage. He was to get the *New Jersey* ready for duty as host ship for VIPs at the atomic bomb tests scheduled for July at Bikini Atoll in the Marshall Islands. The ship had understandably been stripped down for wartime, in large part to remove fire hazards. Now her roomy flag quarters could get new carpeting and furnishings. Provisions for the trip were put into storerooms. But once the ship had been made nearly ready to go to Bikini, her participation in the tests was

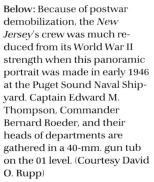

Below: Because of postwar demobilization, the *New Jersey*'s crew was much reduced from its World War II strength when this panoramic portrait was made in early 1946 at the Puget Sound Naval Shipyard. Captain Edward M. Thompson, Commander Bernard Roeder, and their heads of departments are gathered in a 40-mm. gun tub on the 01 level. (Courtesy David O. Rupp)

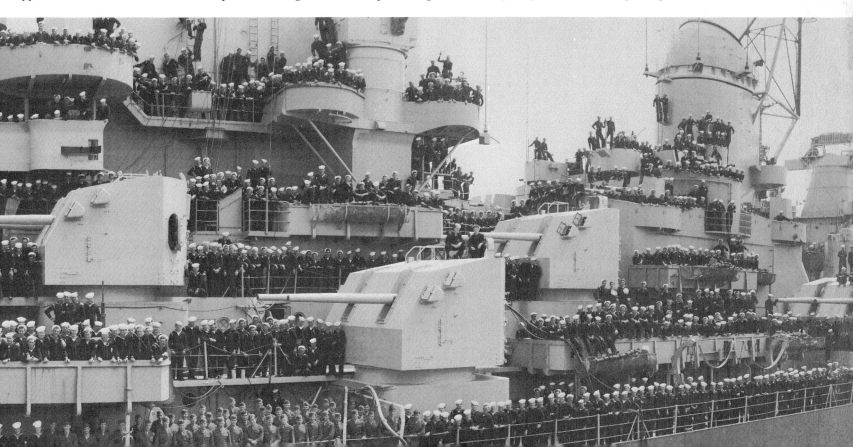

cancelled. She would go into deeper hibernation instead. The New Jersey and Iowa got under way together from Long Beach on 29 May to proceed to Puget Sound Naval Shipyard. There they would sit beside a pier, because they no longer had enough men to operate.

En route, the two ships anchored on 1 June at the naval ammunition depot at Bangor, Washington, and unloaded the tons of powder and projectiles which had been on board since war's end. During the process, which lasted two days, the New Jersey's magazines and projectile flats were unburdened of more than 1,000 16-inch projectiles and more than 11,000 of 5-inch. There were more than 100,000 rounds of 40-mm. antiaircraft ammunition and more than 85,000 of 20-mm. It was a big job, and in competition with the Iowa's crew, the men of the New Jersey got done slightly sooner. Zeke Soucek, the gunnery officer, has an especially vivid memory of the offloading: "I remember one time when we had the tongs on a 16-inch shell and lifted it off the ship, and the davit was swung over so that the shell was hanging above the barge, which was already loaded with a lot of ammunition. And something happened; that shell started to slip out of the tongs. I was standing there watching, and there wasn't a thing I could do except pray. And I didn't even have the sense to duck or anything. Well, it hung on, and boy, we lowered in a hurry to get that thing down so it wouldn't have a distance to fall. We got it down safely."

Once the ammunition was offloaded, the two battleships reached the shipyard on 4 June. As if she hadn't already lost enough, the New Jersey then gave up still more of her men, these to be assigned to cruisers. Lieutenant (junior grade) Roy Lee Vaught had reported as electrical division officer in February. At the time, his division numbered about 140, because the ship still had to generate her own power when she was anchored. Upon arrival at Bremerton, the battleship hooked up to power cables from the shore, and so the division soon melted from 140 to about thirty, and even that left the E division better off than some. The wartime crew of nearly 3,000 men had been reduced to around 400. The battleship was manned with a crew little bigger than a destroyer's.

The rest of 1946 was a time of drabness. She lay moored the entire time, much of it alongside the Iowa until that ship returned to more active service in late October and departed Bremerton. Rear Admiral Roper was relieved of his duties as Commander Battleship Division One on 23 June and left two days later. Commander Battleships Cruisers Pacific Fleet, with headquarters in Long Beach, also took on the duties of division commander.

The months passed, and on 5 August, the dormant New Jersey got a new commanding officer. Captain Thompson had maneuvered to get command the previous fall, but the New Jersey turned out to be a hollow prize. This officer who took such delight in bold shiphandling ended up with few opportunities. There had been little to do during

the long transit from Japan or the long in-port periods at Long Beach and Bremerton. Only the couple of dozen days of training maneuvers had given him a chance to practice his craft, and even then the battleship wasn't able to fire her big guns. Captain Thompson's command tour was a short one, only eight and a half months, and the satisfactions were few. As he put it, "If it had been active and operating, it would have been something else, but just to be tied up to a damn dock at Bremerton was no fun."

The new skipper was a handsome submariner, Captain Leon J. Huffman. Nicknamed "Savvy", he finished high in his class of 1922 at the Naval Academy, standing 27th of the 539 graduates that year. Hyman G. Rickover, who later became famous for developing nuclear submarines, stood 106th in the class. There are few recollections of Huffman from his time in the New Jersey, because the period of hibernation offered little chance for the crew to see him in action. He is generally remembered as being an able and eager athlete – bowling, golfing, and playing softball, among other things. A junior officer who served in the New Jersey during that period describes Huffman as "Sort of reserved, austere, very nice-looking, always in good physical shape, always in perfect uniform."

Sports provided one outlet for the crew, which had little of real consequence in the way of military duties to pass the time. There were too few men to operate the New Jersey, so they did their best to keep the ship reasonably clean and rust-free, but even those efforts were only partially successful because of the shortage of manpower. Electronic gear and fire control equipment were kept going, but help was required there. Lieutenant Commander Noble C. Harris, combat information officer, sometimes had to depend on manufacturers' representatives to take care of electronic gear, because he didn't have sufficient qualified technicians as part of the crew.

In midsummer, a new batch of ensigns reported from the Naval Academy, and they were assigned make-work duties. One of the new ensigns was Elmer Kiehl, who recalls that the ship had three brows, or gangways, while she was at Bremerton. At most other times, she had two brows, one for officers and the other for enlisted men. The third one was installed for the carrying of ship's garbage to the pier, and that was the one assigned for watchstanding by the ensigns.

Kiehl remembers that one of the few occasions for contact with the commanding officer came during inspections of the ship. Kiehl says that the crew felt a sense of excitement – a mixture perhaps of anticipation and apprehension – when Captain Huffman was due to come around. There was still a considerable gulf between officers and enlisted men, and the captain was a remote figure at the top of the officer pinnacle. Kiehl says, "I can remember being on one of the ammunition-handling platforms, in the lower part of the barbette, when he came sweeping through, and everybody was excited that he was

coming. Everybody was anticipating, and, of course, he swept around, and he found a couple of things wrong and a couple of things good and sort of patted everybody on the head, and went sweeping out again. Did it very well, as I remember."

To escape from the shipboard routine, Ensign Kiehl patronized illegal after-hours gambling establishments in Bremerton. Perhaps it was the appeal of forbidden fruit that added to his enjoyment. "If you were an ensign and young and eager," he reminisces, "you could go out and wait until 3:00 or 4:00 [in the morning] and come back to the ship, get up in the morning, and make quarters. And then spend the rest of the day dodging authority, which was trying to give you something to do that wasn't necessary."

During the forlorn months in Bremerton, some watches still had to be stood, and meals cooked and clothes washed, and the ship kept reasonably clean. But the clear sense of purpose which had invigorated the *New Jersey* during the war was no longer in evidence. As a result, there was an inevitable concern about morale. Commander Kretz, the supply officer, sought to keep some of the men in his department interested by instituting a storekeepers' training course which would be beneficial in preparing them for advancement. Training on radar in the combat information center was one of the few useful pursuits available for eighteen-year-old Seaman Second Class Harold Gill, fresh out of school. After reporting to the ship, he says, "I spent the next 3 or 4 months . . . learning about plotting and running the gear since there were very few of us [and] not much to do."

Recreation was another means of keeping men interested, and that didn't always mean hanging out in bars or engaging in the shipboard crap games which sprang up on paydays. (One enlisted man remembers winning $600 with the dice and blowing it all in a "super weekend" in Vancouver, British Columbia.) A duck-hunting club was established on the nearby Hood Canal for the benefit of the *New Jersey*'s men. The crew built several rafts which were towed out into the canal and used as duck blinds. To supplement the rafts, Hank Kretz requested two used boats and outboard motors from the shipyard's supply department. He got a negative reply, so he sent a message to the Bureau of Ships in Washington, explaining in detail why he wanted the boats and motors. Within forty-five minutes, Kretz remembered, he received an information copy of a message from the Bureau of Ships to the Puget Sound Naval Shipyard. The yard was directed to provide the ship with two brand-new boats, instead of the old ones he asked for, and four outboard engines instead of the two he requested. The recreation project turned out to be a huge success.

By autumn of 1946, the Navy had decided to put the *New Jersey* in mothballs. In October, Lieutenant Commander Bill Dobie reported to take over over as main battery officer

and principal assistant to Commander Soucek, the gunnery officer. Dobie explains that the assistant did not have "exciting prospects since the ship was already commencing its *first* inactivation. The Gunnery Department personnel level had been drawn down to about 100 souls, from a normal complement of about *900*. We barely had enough bodies to handle all of the 'mothballing' procedures required. The work was hard, not too exciting – more like being a mechanical embalmer." Because the ship was preparing for the reserve fleet, Dobie stepped up to become the gunnery officer, a department head, when Soucek was transferred to other duty. At that point, Lieutenant Commander Dobie was only six years out of the Naval Academy. By way of contrast, Commander Rufus Rose, class of 1924 at the Naval Academy, had been a commissioned officer for nearly nineteen years when he became the *New Jersey*'s first gunnery officer in May 1943.

A brief bit of excitement came on the afternoon of 24 October, when the attack cargo ship *Sylvania* was passing astern in order to moor alongside to starboard. A combination of wind and current caught hold of the *Sylvania* and sent her crashing into the battleship. The collision did superficial damage to a number of items of topside equipment in the *New Jersey*, breaking a number of lights and bending a 40-mm. gun barrel in the gun tub all the way aft on the starboard side.

The remainder of the year dribbled out in the frequently rainy Pacific Northwest, and the process of inactivation moved beyond the preparatory stage of conducting inventories and making up work lists. Soon after the beginning of 1947, on 11 January, the *New Jersey* was drydocked and subsequently underwent an InSurv (inspection and survey) visit to determine in detail her material condition. Such an inspection can be part of the mothballing process as a means of establishing specifically what would be required to restore her to active condition when the time came. In this instance, the call to active service was much sooner than expected. Before the inactivation could get well under way, the Navy found a mission for the *New Jersey*, and it turned out to be the highlight of her postwar service. She would be part of the Navy's first overseas midshipman training cruise since before the war.

The inactivation was halted, and the process was reversed. In three months, the crew doubled in size, to approximately 800. These men didn't even constitute a normal peacetime allowance, but they would permit the ship to steam and shoot, and there would be hundreds of additional men in her bunks once the midshipmen arrived. All told, the midshipman squadron was to embark more than 2,000 students from the Naval Academy and various NROTC units around the country. Gunnery officer Dobie remembers that the buildup was helpful in numbers, but even so, many of the men were woefully short of experience in battleship gunnery and procedures. He recalls the time as an exciting challenge for a thirty-year-old gun boss who didn't have nearly the wealth of talent to draw upon that his predecessors enjoyed. Finally, about two weeks before the *New Jersey* was due to leave the shipyard, a turret captain arrived. He was a lifesaver for a crew with virtually no experience in firing 16-inch turrets.

The work of putting the ship back together continued in all departments, and on 12 March she emerged from dry dock. On St. Patrick's Day, she took on a full load of fuel oil which made her ride about a foot lower in the water, and in early April she loaded enough ammunition to increase her draft a good deal more. She also took on provisions for the forthcoming voyage. Supply officer Hank Kretz remembered of the job, "I think every cigarette company in the United States sent two or three representatives in order to be sure that their brand of cigarettes was going to be exposed in the best possible way to the midshipmen." All the while things were being loaded aboard, the ship had been gradually reawakening, undergoing the various tests and trials which would certify her once again ready for sea.

An incident which occurred on the morning of 2 April 1947 remains vivid for those who were present. The ship was moored alongside a pier at the naval magazine at Bangor, Washington. Shortly after 5:30 a.m., the loading of ammunition began. After about six hours came a mishap which gunnery officer Dobie describes especially well:

"The approved procedure for on-loading and handling all 16" projectiles was to first receive the projectile on deck using the depot slings which had a special cross bar for 'quick release' once the projectile had been lifted from the dockside flat car and lowered in place to the deck on board; then the depot slings were opened (using the 'special quick release cross bar') and transferred to the shipboard slings which had no cross bar. This obviously took time, but the transfer was for *very* good reasons which should become apparent as my tale unfolds.

"One of my ensigns . . . on his own initiative and wanting to speed up the procedure, ordered the Turret II loading crew to leave the 'depot sling' on one of the [2,700-pound] dye loaded armor-piercing projectiles for lowering through a trunk to the shell flat level of Turret II using the shipboard hoist. Well – as the projectile was being lowered the 'cross bar' of the depot sling hit the coaming of the trunk hatch at the 2nd deck level, and the projectile was released to fall about five deck levels. The projectile base struck the top of a fresh water-filled double bottom, punching a crescent-shaped hole, with spectacular results – all in blue color. [Projectiles carried dye in them for use when shooting against other ships. The idea was that when a number of battleships were shooting simultaneously, they would use different colors of dye and thus would know which ship's shots were falling closest to the enemy.] The projectile dye cap broke, dye mixed with a column of water, and there was a blue stain for several deck levels up. I was aft when this misfortune occurred.

When this was reported to me I went forward with my Gunner [a warrant officer] . . . to 'investigate'!

"When we arrived at Turret II's projectile striking down hatch we were met by one very shaken Ensign, and a bunch of frightened youngsters – all probably expecting the projectile to detonate (or something!). At the very least, they knew that they had done something very wrong.

"The Gunner and I climbed down the trunk, had a set of *shipboard* slings lowered, attached them to the projectile and had the round hoisted. At the same time the projectile was being hoisted to the main deck we ordered that it be set to one side of the main deck and then be transferred dockside for examination and handling by the depot. The Gunner and I then started the long climb up about six decks. Lo and behold, when we arrived topside we were surprised to see the lifelines of the ship being secured – and our projectile nowheres in sight! It seems that our same Ensign, still well-meaning, still concerned that we had a 'time bomb' on our hands – and definitely not understanding my orders – had deep-sixed the round, believing this was the safest thing to do under the circumstances."

Ensign Robert C. Peniston was in charge of loading on turret two, and his memory differs somewhat from Dobie's. As Peniston recalls it, the loading was proceeding satisfactorily when the ship's fire control officer came along and said things were moving too slowly. Despite Peniston's protests, the officer ordered the quick-release yard sling used, and it wasn't long before the accident occurred. As he looked down into the ammunition-loading hatch, he saw a big splash of dye from the base of the projectile. In Peniston's recollection, it was the turret two division officer, and not he himself, who then put the projectile on a dolly, rolled it over to the edge of the deck, and heaved it overboard, producing a big plume of water. Lieutenant Commander Dobie was understandably disturbed by the turn of events, but Peniston remembers Captain Huffman as being surprisingly placid about the whole thing, "rather than raise hell like you would expect".

The story has a sequel. In the years that followed, both Peniston and the *New Jersey* went their separate ways. Twenty-two years later, they were reunited. In August 1969, Captain Robert Peniston was ordered to command the ship in which he had served as an ensign. As part of the process of refamiliarizing himself with her, he climbed down to take a look at the spot where the projectile had landed in 1947. The dye was long since gone, but he could still see a 16-inch half-moon shape embossed into the steel of the deck.

Once the ammunition loading was completed, the *New Jersey* got under way from Bangor on 5 April for a journey down the West Coast. Her appearance was now somewhat different from when she had entered the shipyard. In place of her previous two-tone camouflage pattern she was now haze grey except for the black smokestack caps. On her bow were painted small black hull numbers, whereas they were white throughout the rest of her career. Along with the changed appearance, there was a new sound. The battleship filled the air with the chatter of 20-mm., 40-mm. and 5-inch gunnery. The antiaircraft guns which had been silent for nearly a year were getting their chance once again.

A two-day stop at Long Beach on 8–9 April was marked by a departure inspection conducted by Commander Cruiser Division 13 and two of his ship captains. Once they had satisfied themselves, the *New Jersey* was on her way south to the Panama Canal. Her all-day trip through the canal on 20 April marked her return to the Atlantic for the first time since 1944.

Test-firing of the antiaircraft guns was a nearly daily feature of the trip, because the new men needed lots of practice. Finally, the turret crews got their opportunity. When the 16-inch guns opened up on 21 April, they were doing so for the first time since the end of the war. The big guns got more of a workout as the ship practiced shore bombardment in the Caribbean, part of an overall refresher training program conducted with the *New Jersey* operating in and out of Guantanamo Bay, Cuba. Day after day was occupied with steaming and shooting. The training effort culminated on 8 May in a mock battle problem. The following day, the ship headed north. When the *New Jersey* arrived at Bayonne on 13 May, it marked her first visit to the state for which she had been named.

The fourth anniversary of the ship's commissioning was celebrated with a flourish on 23 May. New Jersey Governor Alfred E. Driscoll attended the ceremonies, as did former Governor Walter E. Edge. Rear Admiral Carl F. Holden, who had put the ship in commission as skipper four years earlier, flew up from Norfolk to attend. As he spoke to the assembled guests, he held in his arms 3½-year-old Harolyn Meyer, the ship's pinup girl during the war.

The most substantial event of the day was the ship's change of command. Relieving Captain Huffman was Captain George L. Menocal, who had been head of the foreign languages department at the Naval Academy following a variety of destroyer duty during World War II. He would do much in the succeeding months to put his imprint on the ship and the crew, though his methods were certainly not welcomed by all. A short, swarthy man, he was a Naval Academy classmate of Huffman, but he finished well below him in the 1922 class standings.

The day after the change of command, the *New Jersey* headed south for Hampton Roads. She spent several days at Norfolk and took aboard a number of Naval Reservists to help fill out the crew. She needed these men for her coming cruise to northern European waters. Reserve centers were canvassed, and a number of men volunteered for a temporary return to active duty. One who did so was Ensign Charles McC. Mathias, Jr., a Naval Reservist who was drilling at Baltimore while attending law school. He is now a U.S. Senator for the state of Maryland.

The *New Jersey* anchored on 3 June in Annapolis Roads. The stopover there afforded the crew opportunities for liberty in Annapolis, Baltimore, and Washington. It was also the occasion for accepting a challenge from the *Wisconsin*'s baseball team. Thanks to the lusty hitting of Ensign Carl Alberts, who had a three-run homer, the *New Jersey* team won, 6–3.

A rainy mist was in the air on 7 June as a procession of motor launches plied back and forth between the Naval Academy seawall and the squadron of ships anchored offshore. Up the accommodation ladders came 518 Naval Academy midshipmen of the classes of 1948 and 1950. The former had but one more year before graduation; the latter had completed only one year. The men of 1948 would dress and be treated much like junior officers. The new sophomores, known as "youngsters" in Naval Academy jargon, would live in similar fashion to the junior enlisted men. They would sleep in enlisted living quarters, eat in the general mess, and carry out the same types of duties. The only distinction was that the white hats of the midshipmen carried dark blue stripes around the rims to distinguish them from crew members.

Noise and confusion temporarily took hold of the battleship's forecastle as boat after boat brought its human cargo. Pyramids of gear collected on deck – seabags, suitcases, and other luggage. Soon enough, the third-class midshipmen were taking their gear below and finding bunks. Two of the prospective members of the class of 1950, Midshipmen William J. Aston and Alexander G. B. Grosvenor, wrote of their time in the *New Jersey* for a later issue of *National Geographic* magazine. Of their arrival in the berthing compartment, they wrote: "Our pipe bunks – and they were comfortable too – were stacked in tiers of four, lining the bulkhead (walls or ship's side) and grouped compactly in columns, fore and aft, two tiers wide, but with enough room to scoot out quickly. We were each assigned a locker, so tiny it left us skeptical. How could we cram all the gear in our two bulging bags into that small space? Nevertheless, after much refolding and rolling, our 'white works', 'skivvies', etc., were squeezed in."

For the midshipmen, many of whom had probably never been to sea before, the cramped nature of shipboard living spaces was an education in itself. It was nothing like the three-man rooms they had known in Bancroft Hall at the Academy. In fact, part of the purpose of this indoctrination cruise was to give the midshipmen – both those of the Naval Academy and the approximately 200 men from the Naval ROTC units of various universities – an idea of what life was like for the enlisted men who would eventually be working for them once the midshipmen became officers.

In about an hour and a half, the midshipmen were aboard; shortly before 10:00 a.m., the *New Jersey*'s anchor chain was heaved in through the hawsepipe, and the ship was under way in company with the *Wisconsin* to rendezvous with the rest of the ships in Task Force 81, the training squadron. The *New Jersey* dutifully followed 1,500

Below: The heavy ships of Task Force 81 lie at anchor in Annapolis Roads on 6 June 1947. Front to back are the *New Jersey, Wisconsin, Kearsarge, and Randolph.* (National Archives: 80-G-438757)

Below right: Midshipmen relax in a berthing compartment. The bunks have thin mattresses atop pipe frames. The shiny metal lockers seen at left were the type used in enlisted berthing on board the *New Jersey* until 1969. (Photo by Alexander G. B. Grosvenor © 1948 National Geographic Society)

**Above:** A 16-inch gun of the *New Jersey*'s turret three frames the picture as the battleship steams in company with the carrier *Kearsarge*. Next to the lifelines are 20-mm. mounts. (Ted Stone photo; courtesy The Mariners' Museum)

**Above right:** Captain George Menocal, the *New Jersey*'s skipper, helps himself during a meal in the chief petty officers' mess in 1947. Beyond Menocal is the executive officer, Commander Bill Leverton. (Courtesy Rear Admiral J. Wilson Leverton)

yards astern of the other battleship, because the *Wisconsin* was carrying Rear Admiral Heber H. McLean, Commander Battleship Division One. BatDiv One had for all practical purposes gone out of business in 1946 when the *New Jersey* was tied up pierside at Bremerton. Now that the ships were steaming, the division was reactivated.

The two battleships joined the remainder of the ships off Cape Henry, Virginia, and set course for Rosyth, Scotland. With them were two fleet carriers, the *Kearsarge* and *Randolph*; the destroyers *O'Hare, Cone, Stribling*, and *Meredith*; and the dock landing ship *Fort Mandan*. The latter, an amphibious warfare vessel, was included so that her covey of landing craft would be available to provide liberty boats in European ports.

The Atlantic crossing was made at a leisurely pace in order to give the midshipmen and reservists plenty of time for underway training, and it is also likely that the new crew members were getting an indoctrination as well. Overall, the crew of the *New Jersey* had too many chiefs and not enough Indians. Commander Bill Leverton was the executive officer, and he particularly remembers the ship being overpopulated with chief petty officers, to the point of having to expand the chiefs' quarters to accommodate them. The chiefs were there in disproportionate numbers, because these were career Navy men, not war-enlistment people. Since quite a number of them had been

in the service since before the war, they now enjoyed a good deal of seniority. And even for those who had left to join the reserve, a cruise such as this was a strong lure. The upshot of the skewed manning was that a number of chiefs wound up doing relatively menial jobs, such as standing burner watches on the boilers, because there were not enough junior people to do them.

The officers' wardroom was a curious amalgam as well. The division officers were largely "mustangs" – former enlisted men. There were few Naval Academy graduates in the crew; of the Academy men who were there, the preponderance were ensigns not long out of Annapolis. These two groups were from far different social and educational backgrounds, but the mustangs had the advantage of being senior to the Academy ensigns and were not hesitant about reminding the new men that they had been out fighting the war while these ensigns were still hitting the books at Annapolis. Moreover, the mustangs were sorely needed in the talent-depleted ship for their technical expertise in such specialized areas as gunnery and engineering.

Leverton recalls that the ex-enlisted men weren't the well-rounded type of officers that could be assigned to the Pentagon, for example, but they were top-notch in their specialties. Even so, throwing the two groups together in the wardroom probably made both a bit uncomfortable.

Above: Heavy seas wash over the fantail as the *New Jersey* steams across the Atlantic toward Scotland on 15 June 1947. (Courtesy Commander Dudley J. Kierulff)

Above right: Midshipmen eating in the *New Jersey*'s mess deck in 1947. The mess tables, a type used until the 1950s, were triced up to the overhead between meals, leaving a large, open area. (Photo by Alexander G. B. Grosvenor © 1948 National Geographic Society)

Senator Mathias remembers that Commander Leverton was "distressed, because the mustangs had imported a number of the customs from the chiefs' mess to the wardroom. One of the most obvious of which was a big bowl of toothpicks on the wardroom table." Part of the overall wardroom atmosphere which was assuredly different for the ex-chiefs was the method of summoning officers to dinner. Each evening, one man with a fife and one with a drum paraded up and down the passageways in officers' country, playing a tune to announce the meal.

Down in the crew's mess, conditions were less elegant than in the wardroom. In 1947, Ted Kosmela was a seaman striking for quartermaster. After he had served in a small, rocket-armed landing ship during World War II, the *New Jersey* was the epitome of what Navy life should be. The mess deck was roomy, even if the benches and tables, with their spindly, foldup legs, had to be set up for each meal and folded away in between times. Since the tables weren't fast to the deck, as they would be later in the ship's career, things got a bit hectic on the occasions when the big ship was in heavy seas. As Kosmela recalls, "When she rolled, she laid over there, and she stayed on that side for a while. And all the damn tables – and, of course, all the chow in that mess hall – just went to that side. And then, when you came up and got righted and everybody got squared away, it flopped on the other side."

Even though Kosmela served in the *New Jersey* for only a few months, the experience was a vivid one, and even now he can recite a good many details. The bulkheads were painted green and the decks grey, although the most heavily travelled portions of the passageway decks were left as bare steel to save wear and tear. During the war, decks and bulkheads were routinely left unpainted to prevent paint from adding to fire hazards.

Senior petty officers lived in the same compartments as the rest of the men in their division. They served a valuable function as leaders; says Kosmela, "You learned by watching those old salts with the hashmarks on their arms. If they didn't like something, they were quick to let you know about it. If somebody was dirty, or the sacks weren't made up right, or the compartment was dirty, they were after you." Besides being disciplinarians, petty officers were advisers, teachers, and perhaps father substitutes for young sailors who had left home not long before. To Kosmela there was a warm, fraternal atmosphere that he treasures even now: "There was absolutely no privacy, but you didn't mind it."

Being a quartermaster was a delight for Kosmela, because the duty of winding the ship's clocks gave him a legitimate reason to roam the ship to an extent permitted to few enlisted men of that time. At night, when he was quartermaster of the watch, he enjoyed going down to the

bakeshop to get some fresh bread or rolls, telling a white lie that the food was for officers. At other times, he enjoyed standing out on deck at night, listening to the sounds as the ship made her way through the dark sea, watching the play of moonlight on the huge grey smokestacks aft of the bridge. Some days, to escape the usual routine, he would invent an excuse to walk up to the bow. There he would peer down through the hawsepipes, high above the water, and enjoy a time of quiet solitude. "All the noise was behind," he explains, "and then you'd turn around and you'd look at that big, beautiful ship."

There was no chance for quiet solitude on the morning of Sunday, 8 June, when the *New Jersey* broke from her training routine long enough to take a drink from the fleet oiler *Chemung* during the voyage to Scotland. The midshipmen who were topside that June morning saw the *Chemung* up ahead, linked by heavy black fuel hoses to the *Wisconsin*, which was on the oiler's port side. The midshipmen writing for *National Geographic* described the event, "Slowly our skipper conned the *New Jersey* into position on the opposite side. Inch by inch we crept up, until we were only 100 feet from the oiler's bridge. Because of the armored conning tower, steersmen on duty could see only dead ahead, so they never knew how close the steel monsters were. Eyes glued to compasses and ears tuned to captains' voices, they kept the ships on steady course hour after hour. A veteran officer told us that even in wartime simultaneous refueling of two battleships was as rare as 'sun off Cape Horn'."

The midshipmen had an enforced training regimen which acquainted them with operations throughout the ship. They stood watches on the steering wheel (although certainly not while alongside the oiler), life buoy watch on the rail, lookout watches high up in the air defense station, and engineering watches. They learned seamanship and navigation, engineering, ordnance, and gunnery; included in the latter were taking apart and cleaning a 40-mm. anti-aircraft gun. Noble Harris, combat information center officer, set up a duplicate CIC in the flag plot and arranged for midshipmen to send their own radar reports to the bridge by sound-powered telephone. In this capacity they served as a backup for the ship's radar gang. In addition to all these different kinds of hands-on training, further instruction came in the form of training films which were shown to the future oficers.

One event which gave the midshipmen a feel for the way enlisted men lived was the field day set aside for cleaning the ship thoroughly. The day began at 5:30 when the boatswain's mate of the watch passed the word over the ship's announcing system, "Reveille! Reveille! Heave out and trice up." On came the normal lights in each berthing compartment, and off went the red lights which provided the only illumination during the night, because they wouldn't interfere with the ability of the eyes to adapt quickly to darkness.

After reveille had hauled sailors and midshipmen from their sleep, the men got dressed and went up on deck. With scrub brushes they went carefully over the wooden decks, their feet bare because a man with a hose was close behind. Sometimes, holystoning was called for, so large GI cans were filled with a caustic solution of bleach, salt-water soap, water, and boiler compound. (Kosmela remembers the solution as being "so powerful it almost smoked".) In addition, sand was sprinkled on the wooden

**Right:** Midshipmen hold drill on a loading machine in the *New Jersey*'s superstructure, thus preparing them for operation of 5-inch gun mounts. (Photo by Alexander G. B. Grosvenor © 1948 National Geographic Society)

**Right:** The *New Jersey* approaches the cantilevered Firth of Forth Bridge shortly before her arrival at Rosyth, Scotland, on 23 June. (Courtesy Captain Neville T. Kirk)

decks to add still more abrasiveness when the holystones, which were made by drilling holes in boiler bricks, were scraped monotonously across the wood. Inside the ship, other men were sweeping and swabbing, cleaning the tops of lockers, and reaching into tight corners to clean out accumulated grime. Others were polishing up mirrors, sinks, urinals, and shower stalls. When all were finished, the decks were clean enough to sleep on, and the men of the *New Jersey* were famished. As Kosmela puts it, "When you had breakfast, it felt like the noon meal – you had been at it so long."

After the battleship had been at sea for two weeks, the midshipmen had received sufficient training and practice to man the guns. While firing at drones and target sleeves, the antiaircraft guns were operated entirely by midshipmen, with officers in the mounts only as safety observers. Gunnery officer Bill Dobie remembers that it was useful to have Naval Academy staff members on board from the departments of seamanship and gunnery to provide advice to the none-too-experienced ship's crew.

In charge of the training detail from the Academy's faculty was Commander John D. Bulkeley, who had won a Medal of Honor early in World War II for his exploits in PT boats in Philippine waters. His boat successfully evacuated General Douglas MacArthur from beleaguered Corregidor in 1942 and took him to safety in Australia. Some of the *New Jersey*'s officers and enlisted men got the impression that Commander Bulkeley mentioned his wartime heroics a bit too often. He was overbearing in pointing out infractions and usually managed to work into the conversation something along the lines of, "I was there in the big war; where were you?"

On the bright Sunday morning of 22 June, Task Force 81 steamed past the sheer cliffs of Scotland's Cape Wrath and then to Dunnet Head and the sometimes-turbulent waters of Pentland Firth, which separates Scotland from the Orkney Islands. Scotland was green and lovely, with the fields coming right down to the water's edge.

The scene was on the dismal, rainy side the following day when the task force entered the Firth of Forth and passed ships of the British Home Fleet at Rosyth, Scotland. The ships of both nations rendered honors to one another as they passed. Ensign Mathias was out on deck to take in the scene: "The bands played the national anthems, and there were gun salutes; it was one of the most thrilling moments in any sailor's life – this whole experience of these two great fleets passing."

Although a battleship as large and powerful as the *New Jersey* is a joy to handle in the open sea, with room to roam and stretch her sea legs, things get a good bit more difficult when she reaches constricted waters. Whenever the ship got into a situation that required close-in maneuvering, Captain Menocal frequently dispatched his Marine orderly to a stateroom far down in the ship so he could summon Lieutenant Commander Dick Peek to the bridge. Peek was a Naval Reserve officer from Buffalo, New York. During the war he had gained a good deal of ship-handling experience as commanding officer of a destroyer escort, so the captain called on him to conn the *New Jersey* through tight spots in the midshipman cruise.

As the ship made her approach to Rosyth, there were already indications of the hospitality to come. The U.S. task force steamed through a group of fishing boats, and as the ships and their thousands of sailors passed, an officer on board the *New Jersey* overheard a reaction. A Scottish voice from one of the boats remarked, "It'll be a hot time in Edinburgh tonight." When the *New Jersey* passed under the great cantilever railroad bridge across the firth at Rosyth, her mast barely cleared the lower span. From that span, as recounted in the *National Geographic* article, "five hooky-playing Scottish children leaned out and waved a large American flag".

During the trip across the Atlantic, the *New Jersey* had had to bring up the rear as far as the battleships were concerned because of the rear admiral on board the *Wisconsin*. The situation was dramatically reversed when the task force reached Scotland. Soon after the anchor chain had been made fast to the mooring buoy at Rosyth, Admiral Richard L. Conolly's four-star flag was hoisted on board the *New Jersey*. He was Commander U.S. Naval Forces Eastern Atlantic and Mediterranean, normally headquartered in London. For the duration of the ship's visit to Northern Europe, he became a seagoing flag officer and took considerable pride in showing off the *New Jersey*.

The arrival of the training squadron was the signal for an outpouring of good will on the part of the Scots. Commander Charles K. Duncan, executive officer of the *Wisconsin*, was on that ship's forecastle to help supervise mooring. He recalled years afterward that "Immediately after we were shackled up [to a buoy], someone handed me a program of events about two inches thick. They contained the most meticulous detail of such items as to what cars would meet our people, how many were to go, and where they were to go. I found when I opened it that three events had already passed." He added, "It nearly killed me, not the hospitality, but trying to get the midshipmen where they were to go, because the people opened their homes. We had invitations that could not be filled. Particularly after about the third day I had to order people on lists to go to parties because the people of Scotland were so hospitable."

The same sort of quota system was set up on board the *New Jersey*, involving both the ship's company and the midshipmen. As the cruise went on, it became a rather demanding ritual. Lieutenant (junior grade) Bob Moore tried to hold back and hope the invitations would be filled up before his name was called, because he needed a chance to recover from all the kindness that had been showered upon him and his shipmates.

**Left:** Two of the *New Jersey*'s midshipmen on a date with Scottish girls during the visit to Rosyth. (Photo by Alexander G. B. Grosvenor © 1948 National Geographic Society)

**Below:** The *New Jersey* moored to a buoy at Rosyth, Scotland, on 27 June 1947. In the foreground is an American flag on a boat carrying members of the battleship's liberty party ashore. (Courtesy Captain Neville T. Kirk)

Ensign Mathias was invited to a party at the home of Rear Admiral Frederick Dalrymple-Hamilton, the senior officer at His Majesty's Dockyard in Rosyth. (As a captain, Dalrymple-Hamilton commanded HMS *Rodney* during her famous encounter with the German battleship *Bismarck* in 1941.) The party was, Mathias remembers, almost like a Gilbert and Sullivan event, highlighted by Scots in kilts doing a sword dance, pipers, and "lots of gin, lots of gin". The admiral's wife had an extraordinary social faculty, even though blind. Mathias explains, "Although hundreds of people went through the receiving line, she could then call you by name later in the evening just from recognizing voices."

The Scots were so generous in their hospitality for the visiting American Navymen that they gave until it hurt. On one occasion, a group of U.S. officers went into a pub for a drink and absently asked if there was something to eat as well, although they had surely been well fed on board ship. After some conferring, the Scots broke out a can of potted meat and made sandwiches for their guests. In so doing, they were sharing from their own scarcity, for they had not yet recovered from the food rationing of the wartime years.

On another outing, a group of officers from the *New Jersey* accompanied Admiral Conolly on a visit to the castle of a Scottish lord. It was a dreary, cool day as most of the guests toured the castle grounds. The battleship's two Marine officers stayed behind in the castle with the sixty-ish sister of the lord, and the three of them knocked back the better part of a crock of fine Scottish whiskey. The sister and her drinking companions were unsteady by the time the chilled, wet tourists got back to the castle from viewing the dogs and horses. For consuming too much of a rare Scottish export product, the Marines spent some time confined to their quarters after returning to the ship.

Since taking over as skipper of the *New Jersey*, Captain Menocal had been terribly demanding about keeping the ship clean and squared away. Junior officers feared his wrath if he found something amiss while they were on watch. He was also a stickler for the observance of proper honors and ceremonies, and there were plenty of them with a four-star admiral and his staff embarked. Ensign Elmer Kiehl stood officer of the deck watches on the quarterdeck when the ship was in port. He says, "It was like going into battle, practically, to go out there and have the deck during that period, for fear that you would make some gross error and have the whole world come crashing down on you."

An important individual on the quarterdeck was the ship's bugler. There was a set of rules for these honors and ceremonies, but it seemed that every admiral and every consular official had his own special variations. Kiehl well valued the bugler's contribution:

"The rules were not so specific that anybody knew exactly what to do. The officer of the deck didn't know; the

receiving captain didn't know. They knew the general outline of the ceremony, ruffles and flourishes and a certain number of sideboys and everything, but there were little details. . . . The bugler – that was his profession; he'd been up there all his life, watching people come and go, and he wasn't a dumbbell. He had figured out what to do in situations . . . when the arriving personage violated the rules. He knew how to handle it and make it look like it was all pro forma. . . . If you, as an ensign, understood that he knew better than you what to do, and you somehow or other transmitted that information on to him, he would protect you to some degree. If he thought you were a super jerk and conceited, he would not protect you."

The visit to Rosyth lasted six days, and then the *New Jersey* and *Wisconsin* were off to Oslo, Norway, marking the first time big ships had been there since the war. Other ships from the training squadron went to ports in Denmark and Sweden. Sightseeing, dances, and parties were the order of the day, as well as shopping expeditions on the part of the prosperous Americans. To a degree, this prosperity sparked resentment and coolness on the part of the Norwegian men. They were interested in seeing the American ships and the technology they incorporated, but they did not like the well-heeled visitors barging in and dating their girl friends. The midshipmen writing in *National Geographic* told of one Norwegian mother "who insisted that a midshipman date her son's fiancee while the poor lad remained home!" It's no wonder some of Norway's young men were physically attacking midshipmen ashore.

Because of the far northern latitude and the time of year, it was daylight or at least dusk almost around the clock. That was the occasion for all-night partying by some of the Americans, and it led to an embarrassing incident. Norway's King Haakon VII, who was raised in a naval tradition, was quite taken with these wondrous modern warships that were visiting his land, so Admiral Conolly invited him to the flagship.

The rail-thin King, wearing the uniform of a Norwegian admiral, boarded the *New Jersey* by accommodation ladder and proceeded on a guided tour, evincing a good deal of interest in the things he saw in the way of weapons and mechanical equipment. Then, because he had been accustomed to the quarters in smaller, older ships, he asked to see an officer's stateroom. Eager to please, Admiral Conolly led the King to a room and flung open the door. The occupant had been one of those out much of the night, and now he was recovering with a peaceful snooze rather than taking part in the reception for King Haakon. One who was on board the *New Jersey* at the time remembers of the slumbering officer that "If it had not been for the fact that he had the Congressional Medal of Honor strapped firmly around his neck, I think he would have been picked up bodily by the admiral and stuffed through the porthole."

Opposite page, top: Top-hatted Charles Ulrich Bay, U.S. Ambassador to Norway, prepares to descend the *New Jersey's* accommodation ladder at right after a visit to the ship at Oslo in July 1947. (U.S. Naval Institute Collection)

Opposite page, bottom: Left to right in this photo taken on board the *New Jersey* on 2 July at Oslo are Rear Admiral Heber H. McLean, Commander Battleship Division One; Captain George L. Menocal, commanding officer; Admiral Richard L. Conolly, Commander U.S. Naval Forces Eastern Atlantic and Mediterranean; King Haakon VII of Norway. (Courtesy Commander Dudley J. Kierulff)

Below: Rows of F8F Bearcat fighters line the deck of the carrier *Randolph*, foreground, as she and the *New Jersey* arrive at Portsmouth, England, on 9 July 1947. (UPI/Bettmann Newsphotos)

Seaman Kosmela, the quartermaster striker, also recalls Conolly's time on board, because the admiral was pleased with the appearance of the flagship's bridge during an inspection tour. The painting and polishing to make it what Captain Menocal referred to as "my jewel box" had been successful, although there was a price to be paid for the sparkling look. A number of *New Jersey* officers remember that Menocal was ready to chastise for the slightest infraction of procedure or appearance of sloppiness. The captain could be charming and courtly with visitors, then suddenly turn and inflict his temper on a ship's officer for a stray cigarette butt or some grease leaking from a lubrication fitting. The captain took a more kindly approach toward the enlisted men and was more popular with them than with the officers.

To get between ship and shore, the *New Jersey's* sailors rode liberty boats. The going and coming presented marked contrasts. When leaving, liberty parties were carefully inspected to make sure that their uniforms were impeccable – hair cut, faces clean-shaven, and shoes brightly polished. Each man stepped up to the oficer of the deck, saluted, presented his liberty card, asked permission to go ashore, and then filed down into the waiting boat. During the ride to the boat landing, petty officers enforced a strict regimen. Each man had to sit in his place, being careful to keep his hands and arms off the boat's gunwales. Hours later, when it was time for the return trip, many of the men were drunk, white hats pushed to the back of their heads, shoes scuffed, and demeanor much less

military than before. Kosmela says of the men of the master-at-arms force, "They were just happy to get everybody back on board." Sometimes even that was difficult. One time, in the early hours of the morning, a boat was returning to the *New Jersey* with a load of drunken midshipmen and sailors. The coxswain misjudged the running of the tide, and when he tried to go around the bow of the ship, he got set down on the anchor chain. The boat rode up the chain and ended up in an almost vertical position, says Kosmela, before gravity took effect and returned it to the water.

The departure from Oslo was a memorable one, highlighted by the performance of Crown Prince Olav, who is now Norway's King. As the *New Jersey* and *Wisconsin* steamed out to sea, headed for Portsmouth, England, Prince Olav went out in a 50-foot motor launch to bid them farewell. The mouth of Olsofjord was choppy that day, causing the boat to lurch about considerably. Midshipmen Aston and Grosvenor described the scene: "Through the passing of our ships, the Prince adhered to the adage of the sea, 'One hand for the ship and one for yourself.' Never before had we seen a boat do four-dimensional gymnastics. Yet at all times the Prince had his right hand raised smartly in salute as *Wisconsin* fired the 21 guns reserved for chiefs of state and for royalty."

In England, following a transit marked by rough seas, the men of the *New Jersey* got the red carpet treatment once again, particularly because of the reservoir of good will Americans had built up during the war. At Portsmouth midshipmen visited Lord Nelson's famous flagship *Victory* from the Battle of Trafalgar. Their host on board the memorial vessel was Admiral Lord Fraser, who had last encountered the *New Jersey* at Buckner Bay, Okinawa, in September 1945. Twenty midshipmen were lucky enough to be invited to a garden party thrown by King George VI at Buckingham Palace. Princess Elizabeth had recently become engaged to Prince Philip, and the two of them filtered through the crowd.

One of the future officers described the event:

"Our midshipmen's group had long since dissolved, each seeking to get the closest view of the royal party. While elbowing my way into the path of the slowly advancing group, I noticed our captain had caught the eye of an ushering Air Force officer. This unexpected opportunity of meeting the Princess and her fiance was not to be lost because of the intervening crowd. By a bit of fancy dodging and ducking and numerous apologies, I was soon standing nervously with two other shipmates, waiting to be introduced to Elizabeth and Philip. After the presentation their naturalness and friendly nature quickly put us at ease. Soon we were chatting gaily and even joking as if with an old acquaintance. Philip seemed extremely interested in the Academy, and we swapped a few tales of Dartmouth and Annapolis. . . . Our talk, which lasted for 10 to 12

minutes, was finally interrupted by the fidgeting ushers, who realized that we had more than tripled the usual allotment of time. With words of congratulation and good luck, we moved off into the crowd."

There were also some touching encounters with British commoners. While the *New Jersey* was tied up at the royal dockyard jetty in Portsmouth, a number of local people were invited to come aboard to eat a meal in the wardroom. A mother and a little boy about five years old were sitting with Commander Dudley Kierulff, the supply officer. Kierulff was startled when the boy pointed to butter and bread on the table near him and asked, "Mum, what is this?"

"Why, that's butter."

"We don't have that at home," he said. "And look – white bread. Ours is dark."

As Kierulff observed, "It sort of wrings your heart. We had excellent bakers aboard and when we left Portsmouth, we left many loaves of 'white' bread ashore at the officers' mess for delivery to the needy."

Lieutenant Commander Neville Kirk, a Naval Academy professor who made the cruise in the *New Jersey*, had a similar experience. When he went by train to visit relatives in Leeds, he took along a substantial box lunch prepared on board ship so he wouldn't have to deprive the British. At noontime during his ride, he broke out his meal and noticed a little girl looking on with wonder at his hefty ham sandwiches and thick slice of dessert cake. He shared with the people in his compartment and remembers that they were "pathetically thankful" for the food. During his trip, he visited an uncle who put him up for the night and then served him a breakfast of synthetic oatmeal. To Kirk, it tasted like sawdust, so he flushed it down a toilet when his uncle wasn't looking.

Along with food, English woolens were rationed and could not be purchased by the British without coupons. The American Navymen were granted exemptions, but their purchases had to be delivered to the ship under bond and locked in a storeroom until the *New Jersey* was on her way home – thus to avoid black market operations by crew members. The supply officers of the American task force were directed in their cruise instructions not to purchase any produce while in England, because to do so would deprive the local citizens. U.S. Navy refrigerated stores ships provided the *New Jersey* and other task force ships with fresh food in order to keep them from living off the local economies.

On 18 July, after thousands of British citizens had visited the *New Jersey*, Admiral Conolly's flag was hauled down, and Task Force 81 departed. This time the midshipmen and crews of the training vessels were headed south for Guantanamo Bay, Cuba. Within a week, they were soaking up tropical sun and watching hundreds of flying fish skimming along the Gulf Stream. There were daily gunnery

drills, and the usual watches to stand, but nightfall brought moments of relaxation as the mids had a chance to watch movies on a screen set up in the open air on the fantail. Midshipmen also used the site to stage an evening of entertainment featuring musical numbers, standup comedians, and a series of skits which gently made fun of some of the ship's officers and the officers who had come aboard to help with the training program.

The *New Jersey* reached Guantanamo Bay on 1 August, but Midshipman First Class Dick Springe decided to forgo liberty the following day, a hot Saturday, because he didn't want to go through the hassle necessary to take a shower. He had discovered early in the cruise that the crew members berthed near the midshipmen in living compartments on the main deck had an advantage in using showers. The men of the ship's company could go to and from the head clad in towels, because there was a direct route from their berthing compartment. Midshipmen were advised not to use that compartment as a passageway, so they had to go out onto the weather deck to get to the head and thus had to be in the uniform of the day.

On 2 August, after deciding to remain on board, Springe received from home a letter which described a picnic and all sorts of good food. He checked the ship's supper menu and decided he'd rather go ashore after all than endure the three-colored lunchmeat ("red, grey, and green," he says) to be served that night. After taking a shower and getting into his liberty uniform, he had to wait in one line after another. As the disgruntled Springe recalls, "There was 'the line' for the liberty launch, another for the shuttle bus, a dusty ride to the Marine PX, and a long wait in that chow line – watching the steak dinners go by – only to find that when I could order, all that was left were large cans of warm tomato juice!"

Following that stop in Cuba, the ship set sail for Culebra, a small island near Puerto Rico. The island was raked by

the 16-inch and 5-inch guns. It was the first time during the cruise that the big guns had fired, and they blasted old Army tanks ashore with devastating accuracy. Despite the inexperience of his crew, gunnery officer Bill Dobie and his senior petty officers had trained their people well. Alas, such capability was to be short-lived, because the ship's days of active service would soon be over.

As the cruise wound down and the ships of the task force headed home for the United States, night gunnery and submarine warfare were the main themes of the training. Midshipmen were dispersed to destroyers and submarines. The submarines made simulated torpedo-firing runs on the battleships.

At night target sleds towed by tugs were used to sharpen the battleships' gunnery against enemy vessels, in contrast to the land targets they had fired at on Culebra. The *National Geographic* description said,

"These night-firing exhibitions were spectacular and, in fact, enjoyable once we got used to the roar of the 16's and the ear-splitting cracks of the secondary battery. Barrages began with the 5's firing star shells to light up the targets. Then, its turrets trained, the main battery let go with 2,700-pound calling cards. These weighty shells are sped by brilliant orange flames flashing 30 feet beyond the muzzles. Instantly, light vanishes, and the ship is left in darkness. As your ears recover, you hear the shell cleaving the distant atmosphere. The sound resembles the swoosh of a jet plane. Long after firing has ceased, you remember the shell's weird moan."

The days and nights at sea came rapidly to an end. The midshipmen, many of them with their first substantial oceangoing experience behind them, had gained a new maturity during their two-month trip. They had acquired a jaunty saltiness and a remembrance of battleship life that would stay with them from then on. On the night of 25 August, the first classman with the lowest class standing (known as the "anchor man") followed tradition by going to the *New Jersey*'s forecastle to knock open the pelican hook with a hammer and send the anchor to the bottom of Chesapeake Bay off Annapolis. With the coming of the following dawn, motor launches came out to take the midshipmen ashore, and the *New Jersey* was soon on her way again.

She arrived on 28 August at New York City, where several thousand visitors came aboard. Then the ship proceeded to an anchorage in Gravesend Bay and began offloading her ammunition, much of it left from the laborious loading at Bangor, Washington, earlier in the year. Once the ammunition was removed, the *New Jersey* went on 3 September to moor at the Naval Supply Depot in Bayonne, New Jersey, just across the harbor from New York City.

The new lease on life offered by the cruise to Europe had merely delayed the inevitable. Now the inactivation could

**Above:** During air-bedding day, midshipmen and crew members drape mattresses and blankets on lifelines and a 40-mm. gun tub on the *New Jersey*'s fantail. (Photo by Alexander G. B. Grosvenor © 1948 National Geographic Society)

**Above right:** The *New Jersey*'s broad fantail gets the nickname "splinter beach" as midshipmen and crew members flake out on the teakwood deck for sunbathing. (Photo by Alexander G. B. Grosvenor © 1948 National Geographic Society)

**Right:** Tugboats move the *New Jersey* up the ice-covered East River in February 1948. The SK-2 radar antenna has been removed from the foremast to enable the ship to pass beneath the Brooklyn Bridge on her way to the New York Naval Shipyard for inactivation. (Thomas Kinkaid Collection, Naval Historial Center)

be put off no longer. It was a result of the very heavy cutting of the national defense budget. Navy man-power was drastically reduced, and that meant there would not be enough bodies to keep the *New Jersey* going even in a reduced status. The *Wisconsin* was also to be decommissioned, and the *Iowa* would follow a year later.

On 3 September 1947, the very day she arrived at Bayonne, the process of taking apart the *New Jersey* began when the large SK-2 radar antenna was removed from her foremast to facilitate her trip two days later to the New York Naval Shipyard at Brooklyn. The radar antenna would not have safely cleared the Brooklyn Bridge.

On 12 September, Rear Admiral McLean, the division commander, shifted his flag from the *Wisconsin* to the *New Jersey* and remained until 27 October. One afternoon, Admiral McLean's official car pulled up at the ship's forward brow as Machinist's Mate Third Class William Tiernan was leaving the *New Jersey* to go on liberty. When the petty officer saw McLean emerge from the car, he snapped to attention and saluted, whereupon the admiral instructed his driver to take Tiernan to the navy yard gate because a heavy rain was imminent. Remembers Tiernan, "The downpour started, and we approached the Gate with the Admiral's flags still flying. A Marine guard opened the car door and smartly saluted, and out stepped a Third Class Petty Officer. I was rather amused, but the Marine remained impassive."

In the days and weeks at Brooklyn, the process of mothballing the battleship continued, accomplished mainly by the crew, with some technical assistance from shipyard personnel. It was done at a fairly leisurely pace, because the decommissioning date was not to be until the end of the following June. In the interim, dehumidification equipment was installed in the interior of the ship to prevent rust. Plastic cocoons were lowered over the 40-mm. anti-aircraft guns to protect them from the elements. Exposed equipment was covered over with a framework of tape in crosshatch squares, and then a plastic preservative substance was sprayed over the tape to form a watertight shield. Storerooms were inventoried to make sure spare parts were on hand for possible reactivation. Cosmoline preservative was put into piping to keep moisture from building up. In the wake of World War II, the scientific mothballing of ships had been perfected, and the process was used hundreds of times as the vast wartime fleet shrank to one more suited to the era of *Pax Americana*. When it was time for the *New Jersey* to join the other mothballed war veterans, the process had been well set down in available publications.

For the crew, inactivation led to a workaday existence, much like many another job, and certainly without the excitement and differing experiences of the summer cruise. To provide some incentive for the leading chief petty officers, Commander Leverton set up a procedure whereby specific divisions were assigned certain spaces to inactivate in a given amount of time. If they got done before then, the men of the division were given open gangway for liberty ashore.

As the old year of 1947 left the calendar, the first watch of 1948 was observed with the traditional poetic entry in the ship's deck log. Ensign Robert A. Weir had the quarterdeck duty in the lonely hours after midnight and wrote a log entry which concluded as follows:

"We welcome our last new year,
Aboard this 'Mightiest of the Sea',
For the thing we used to fear,
Has finally come to be.

"At last the proud NEW JERSEY,
With her head still on high,
Steams into the 'moth ball' sea,
To find her place to die.

"But her deeds will live forever,
With those who love her dwell,
And the hearts of her men never
Shall willingly say 'Farewell'."

In the following weeks there was a brief interruption to the period in the shipyard when the ship steamed out again to Gravesend Bay to pump off her supply of aviation gasoline and to offload the rest of her ammunition. While the *New Jersey* was making her approach to the assigned spot for dropping the hook, Captain Menocal ordered the anchor party on the forecastle to "let go". Commander Jim Dyer, the ship's first lieutenant, called up by sound-powered telephone to the bridge and said the order was premature, because the ship was still going too fast. Twice more, he was ordered to drop the anchor, and on the third such order, he finally did, ordering the forecastle cleared as he did so. Because the ship still had so much way on, the anchor chain came up out of its storage locker at a much faster rate than it should have and was undulating about three feet in the air as a result. Fortunately, nothing untoward happened.

Captain Menocal's days in command of the *New Jersey* were rapidly coming to an end. By this time, he had perhaps concluded that he was not going to be selected for rear admiral, and there was certainly no more future for him on board the *New Jersey*. Surely the inactivation process in the shipyard, where the vessel returned after getting rid of her ammunition, would be a dreary thing. He put in his papers for retirement and then began holding a round of farewell lunches and dinners in his quarters on board ship. He entertained a number of guests with meals featuring spectacular flaming desserts, fueled by his private supply of brandy. He landed a job with the overseas division of General Motors Corporation and was on his way to a second career. On Valentine's day, Captain Menocal was relieved as the *New Jersey*'s commanding officer by Commander Leverton. The ship's chief petty officers gave the captain an engraved watch as a going-away present. Noble Harris, by then the ship's operations officer, observed that Menocal was "pretty emotional about [his departure], and he was pretty shook up. It was a big day for him."

Following Menocal's departure, the short, slender, good-natured Leverton continued to perform pretty much the same duties he had as exec. A ship captain's job is to operate the ship, and that role was eliminated by the *New Jersey*'s moribund status. About all that was left was internal administration of the battleship, which is what an executive officer does normally. The biggest change was that Leverton no longer had to serve as a buffer between Menocal and the ship's other officers. He no longer had to find a way to remain loyal to the captain on one hand and protect the junior officers on the other. To this day, Leverton remains loyal to Menocal, saying of him, "He was a nice, lively type, and he was a good ship's captain. . . . He used to get the whole crew out and tell them about smartness and shipkeeping. . . . If you've got a ragged pennant flying, everybody in the Navy can see it and know you've got a ragged ship. . . . If you take care of the little things, you take care of the big ones at the same time."

As more and more of the battleship – by now riding high in the water with her ammunition removed – was closed up, the crew moved off and into a barracks vessel known as an APL. The APL was alongside the *New Jersey* until late March when the ship was moved into dry dock for further inactivation, including the sealing up of the underwater openings in the hull. More and more, this once-active dreadnought was becoming an inert hulk. She came out of dry dock in late April, and once more took up position alongside a pier in the shipyard. One brief interruption to the routine came on 6 May when she was presented with a plaque by the State Society of the Battleship New Jersey to commemorate her exploits during World War II. On 29 June, all her shoreside connections, including electricity and fresh water, were cut loose. The APL was taken away, and a group of tall-stacked, steam-powered tugboats came alongside to shepherd the lifeless *New Jersey* across the harbor to the state for which she was named. Again, she tied up at Bayonne, now to be her mothball fleet berth.

The fiscal year ended on Wednesday, 30 June 1948, and so also did the first period of commissioned service for BB-62. Two four-star admirals were on board for the farewell, Admiral H. Kent Hewitt, who had commanded the naval task force for the North Africa invasion in 1942, and

**Below:** Shepherded by a gaggle of tall-stacked, steam-powered tugboats, the *New Jersey* is towed on 29 June 1948 from Brooklyn to her reserve fleet site across the harbor at Bayonne, New Jersey. (Ted Stone photo; courtesy Howard Serig)

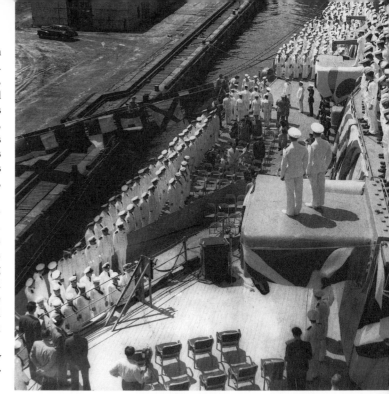

Thomas C. Kinkaid, with whom Commander Leverton served in the Aleutians during the middle part of the war. Just over five years after the ship went into commission, only thirteen plankowners from the original crew were still part of ship's company. They had a place in the first row as various speakers said their piece to honor what might, under some circumstances, have been the *New Jersey*'s final passing from the Navy. (After the national ensign was lowered, it was cut into thirteen pieces, recalls Boatswain's Mate Rafael Maza. Each of the thirteen plankowners, including Maza, received a piece.)

In his remarks that day, before reading the decommissioning orders and directing that the flag be hauled down, Commander Leverton said, "I must confess that this occasion is, in many ways, a depressing one. To me it is depressing because I am being instrumental in retiring this wonderful ship from active service. We are indeed fortunate that our country does not need to retain in active service this mighty and proud ship. She has no potential foes worthy of her steel. Lesser ships are able to maintain the inviolability of our shores and sea frontiers."

He need not have been depressed. All too soon, the *New Jersey* would again have "potential foes worthy of her steel".

# CHAPTER IV
# KOREA, MIDSHIPMEN, AND KOREA AGAIN
## September 1950–July 1953

With each passing day that she sat idly at Bayonne, New Jersey, the battleship bearing the state's name took on more of the dismal appearance of her surroundings. She was moored alongside the Bayonne Naval Annex, a concrete peninsula jutting into New York harbor. In the midst of an industrial area, the *New Jersey*'s paint faded, and she took on a patina of grime. Fortunately, the effects of time, weather, and pollution were easily reversed.

During the ship's time in the mothball fleet, the world at large kept turning, and war broke out once more. The Communist North Koreans launched an invasion of South Korea in late June 1950. An ambitious Secretary of Defense, Louis Johnson, had gone on a cost-cutting spree to eliminate fat from the nation's budget. In his hacking, though, Johnson went well beyond fat. Thus, by the time war came, the U.S. Navy was down to one active battleship and had only a few aircraft carriers in each ocean.

In the wake of the North Korean attack, the U.S. Navy scrambled to reinforce the Western Pacific. The sole battleship, the USS *Missouri*, was hurriedly pulled from midshipman training and steamed to Korea, where she began shore bombardment in mid-September. Within a few days, the Department of Defense announced that it was going to bring out a battleship from the reserve fleet.

On 26 September 1950, workmen went aboard the *New Jersey* at Bayonne. They used cranes to remove the plastic igloos which protected 40-mm. gun mounts. Crowbars produced screeching sounds as they pried away a framework of wood from around lifeboats. Seals were removed from around hatch edges and from the recoil mechanisms of 16-inch guns. Covers were taken from radar antennas and winches. Down below, divers examined the underwater hull to look for covered-up openings. In the engineering spaces, men began checking lines and joints. During the days and weeks that followed, more progress was made, including turning off, disconnecting, and removing dehumidification machines.

By October, a new crew was being assembled. The Naval Reserve was called upon, in large measure. In many cases, the recall to active duty was an unwelcome surprise for World War II veterans who had settled into comfortable civilian jobs and begun raising families. Even for those who were single, it was to be quite a change from the routine.

Seaman Joe Brooks had been a Navy storekeeper in the closing days of the war. By 1950, he was working for the telephone company in Washington D.C., and drilled in the Naval Reserve. He thought, "They'll never get me," but one night he came home and discovered a registered letter telling him to get his affairs in order and report for processing at the naval station in nearby Anacostia. After taking a physical exam and waiting about ten days, he saw his name show up on the *New Jersey* list, then headed for Bayonne.

In Bloomfield, New Jersey, Gunner's Mate First Class Bob Storm got his letter and was on board the battleship about a week later. His physical exam was little more than telling a doctor at the New York Naval Shipyard that he felt fine. For Storm, who had just gotten a good job and moved into a new home two weeks earlier, the transition was an abrupt one. His Navy pay would be a good deal less than the civilian salary that was to be the basis for his monthly mortgage payments. By law, the mortgage couldn't be foreclosed in such circumstances, but he would have to make up the difference once released from active duty. That obligation, said Storm, turned out to be "a bitch on wheels for a while".

Officers were soon coming in as well. Lieutenant (junior grade) Ben Conroy was a regular officer who had been on active duty since his graduation from the Naval Academy in 1947. He quickly grew tired of hearing complaints from the *New Jersey*'s reactivated reserve officers who talked about how much more pay they were making in civilian life. Conroy had been drawing low Navy pay all along, so he felt little sympathy.

David Rupp and Eugene Duncan of York, Pennsylvania, reported to Bayonne after brief stops at Anacostia. Geographic proximity played a large part in the early callups to return the ship to the fleet. Many of those reporting were from New York, New Jersey, Pennsylvania, Massachusetts, and Ohio. When Duncan stepped aboard soon after the opening-up process began, the *New Jersey* still had the appearance of a dead ship, what with life jackets and other paraphernalia lying about. George Hill, a seaman, was recalled to duty from his home in Maryland. He soon set to work, as did other future crew members, joining forces with the yard workmen who were taking seals off guns, chipping, painting, and cleaning up.

Hill and other men were given bunks in the escort carrier *Mission Bay*, moored forward of the *New Jersey* at Bayonne, until the living compartments in the battleship

Far left: The *New Jersey* lies quietly in her reserve fleet berth at Bayonne, New Jersey, on 1 June 1949. (USN photo 442943; courtesy Robert Scheina)

Left: Reactivation for Korean War service begins 26 September 1950 at the naval annex in Bayonne, New Jersey. One of the first steps, shown here, is the removal of the plastic covering from the 40-mm. quad mount atop turret two. (UPI/Bettmann Newsphotos)

Below left: Crew members remove protective seals from the muzzles of turret one guns in October 1950. (National Archives: 80-G-423415)

Top right: Crew members made a substantial contribution to the reactivation of the *New Jersey* for Korea. Here they wirebrush the hull and apply primer paint in early November 1950. Moored ahead are two escort carriers. (U.S. Naval Institute Collection)

Right: On 3 November 1950, more than two weeks before recommissioning, the galley is already reactivated and serving meals. (National Archives: 80-G-421955)

were ready to be occupied. Rupp remembers that paint flaked off bulkheads and tumbled to the deck when the previously sealed and dehumidified compartments were opened to the atmosphere. New paint was applied, and the reactivation teams went from space to space to make them livable. In the weeks that followed, the galley was reactivated and meals were again served in the ship.

In addition to the housekeeping details, there was much work to be done to the thousands of pieces of equipment throughout the giant ship. During the mothballing, equipment was cleaned and often given a coat of the gummy preservative known as cosmoline to seal out moisture. After the cosmoline was removed, the equipment had to be tested and perhaps repaired to make sure it was in operating condition.

Gunner's Mate Storm had particular difficulty removing cosmoline from hydraulic lines in turret one. He and other men got rid of it a little at a time by pumping hydraulic fluid into the lines, running equipment, and pumping the fluid out. The insides of the gun barrels had also been given a preservative coating. Here the solution was to wait and shoot out the cosmoline when the guns were fired for the first time.

Turret one underwent alteration in appearance during the reactivation with the lopping off of the two protruding "ears" which housed the ends of the optical rangefinder. The rangefinder was not high enough off the water to be effective. If visual rangefinding were needed, turret two's system was still intact. Moreover, fire control radar was likely to be more effective, so the visual system was strictly a backup.

Commander Charles Coley was ordered in from the Naval ROTC unit at Cornell University to become the New Jersey's executive officer. He was the senior man in the prospective crew for several weeks before the eventual commanding officer, Captain David Tyree, reported. Coley apportioned incoming men among the various department heads. The initial basis for planning, training, setting up watchbills, and so forth was the ship's organization manual in use at the time of decommissioning. As time passed, the manual was updated a bit at a time.

In choosing a captain for the first battleship reactivated for Korea, the Bureau of Naval Personnel took into account Tyree's postgraduate education in ordnance, battleship duty in the old West Virginia, and service as gunnery officer of the heavy cruiser Salt Lake City at the outset of World War II. Soon after he reported, Tyree found a welcome source of information in Carl Holden. By 1950 the first skipper was a rear admiral and commander of the nearby New York Naval Base. He was delighted to show Tyree his scrapbooks and tell him about preparing the "Lovely Lady" for the earlier war. Holden, however, declined an invitation to attend the recommissioning ceremony at Bayonne on 21 November, perhaps because he didn't want to upstage the new captain and perhaps

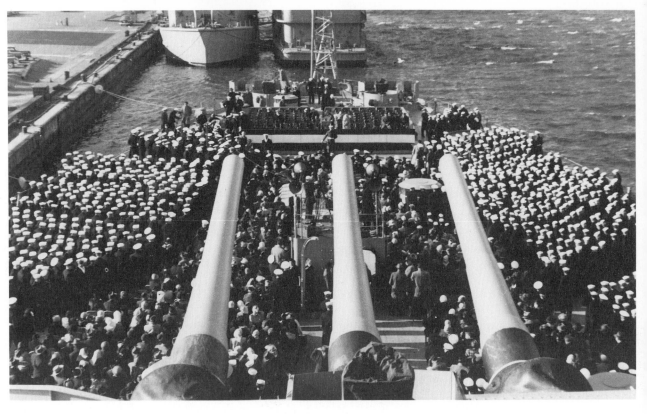

because he didn't trust his emotions in an event which would closely parallel the one he had gone through in 1943.

One benefit Holden got by staying away was that of avoiding the windy, bitterly cold weather. Robert Plumb wrote for *The New York Times*, "A gale was blowing across Upper Bay, whipping a white meringue on the moss-green water." The *New Jersey*'s enlisted men stood and shivered on the main deck aft, wearing their white hats and Navy blue peacoats, many with their collars turned up. The members of the Marine detachment wore heavy coats also and had chin straps tucked securely under their chins to keep hats from blowing away.

The principal speaker at the ceremony was Fleet Admiral William F. Halsey. His five-star personal flag blew stiffly at the main truck during his speech, which was delivered with chattering teeth and cut short because of the cold. Vice Admiral Oscar Badger, who also had had his flag in the *New Jersey* during World War II, was another of the speakers, as was Governor Alfred Driscoll of New Jersey. Mrs. Charles Edison, clad in a fur coat – as she had been during both the launching and first commissioning – was also among the assembled dignitaries. Both she and her husband made a warm impression on a cold day.

For the assembled guests and crew, it was a welcome relief when the formal ceremonies ended and the party began. Receptions were held in the mess deck, wardroom,

captain's cabin, and admiral's mess. Cakes were decorated with icing forming silhouettes of the ship. Punch was ladled out of the ornate punchbowl which was part of the *New Jersey*'s silver service, though many of the people present preferred hot coffee as an antidote to the weather. If anyone doubted that there is a romantic element about great ships, that notion was dispelled by a woman naval officer who didn't eat her piece of commissioning cake. Instead, she wrapped it in a napkin and told those nearby that she planned to take it home and put it under her pillow.

The day after the *New Jersey* went back into commission, she returned to Brooklyn, which was where she had undergone part of the inactivation process in 1948. Her engineering plant was not yet ready for propulsion, so she was towed as a dead ship on 22 November to the New York Naval Shipyard by a collection of 16 tugboats. Within a few hours, she was put into dry dock.

A number of problems, such as inoperative equipment, can be expected during the course of a ship's reactivation, but in the *New Jersey*'s case there was also a large unexpected problem from the weather. With many of the crew off the ship for Thanksgiving holiday, the captain and executive officer were eating dinner with the crew when a violent storm blew up. The combination of wind and rain was such that Commander Coley had a genuine fear that the rising water of the harbor might leap over the caisson

Right: On 22 November, the day after recommissioning, the *New Jersey* is towed to the New York Naval Shipyard at Brooklyn for the rest of her reactivation. (UPI/Bettmann Newsphotos)

at the end of the dry dock and threaten the ship's balance on the keel blocks. Sandbags and other barriers were put into place, but fortunately the rain stopped and the wind died down.

In the waning days of the year, as the ship moved closer to being ready for action, her crew did also. Dozens of men were sent to damage control school at Philadelphia and antiair gunnery school at Dam Neck, Virginia. The *New Jersey* became more and more shipshape as compartments and equipment were declared ready for active service and checked off. Storerooms were topped off, and other needed equipment and spare parts were provided by the cooperative Bureau of Supplies and Accounts. A limited amount of new equipment was installed for radio communication, but essentially the idea was to restore the battleship to her 1948 condition. Because only a little more than two years had passed, she did not need extensive modernization. Indeed, little things rather than big ones were often what caused problems. While the dehumidification gear was quite effective at restricting rust and other corrosion, it had an unfortunate side effect in that it dried out rubber gaskets, wood, and electrical insulation. Gaskets could be replaced, but the insulation problem manifested itself in a series of electrical fires which broke out with some frequency during the period at Brooklyn and even for a while after the *New Jersey* went to sea.

On 16 January 1951, the *New Jersey* made the short trip back to Bayonne, and she did so under her own power this time. Soon she was off to Norfolk, which was her new home port. A year earlier, the *Missouri* had run aground in the Hampton Roads area, and it took two embarrassing weeks before she was refloated. Shortly before Captain Tyree was to take the *New Jersey* into Norfolk, one of his seniors in the chain of command warned, "Whatever you do, don't run that damn ship aground. The Navy's gotten a black eye already, and you don't want it to happen again." Tyree was cautious in handling the *New Jersey* throughout his command tenure and especially so that first trip.

After two weeks in Norfolk, during which the *New Jersey* took on supplies and ammunition, she headed south for Guantanamo Bay, Cuba, to begin a shakedown period for the crew. The days were long and the work hard as the fleet training group based in Cuba put the ship's men through a great many drills and practice sessions. The antiaircraft guns were tested, including 5-inch, 40-mm., and 20-mm. There were only a few remaining of the latter.

On 23 February, for the first time since recommissioning, the *New Jersey* fired her 16-inch guns. When Seaman Joe Brooks, high up in the Spot I forward fire control station, got his initial chance to aim a 16-inch barrel, he was understandably nervous: "I didn't know whether to fire on the uproll of the ship or the downroll of the ship or when. I think my first one wound up in the water. . . . But they didn't get upset; they knew it was all new to us." He was supposed to fire at the peak of the uproll, when the ship was steady for just an instant before beginning to roll the other way.

Back on the fantail Boatswain's Mate First Class Leo Meyer was in charge of a 40-mm. mount. His crew had a full supply of eagerness, if not accuracy, in the early going. When a ram-jet drone or a plane towing a target sleeve approached from the stern, the mounts on the fantail got to open fire considerably earlier than the ones farther forward in the ship. As a result, Meyer was almost always reporting more rounds expended than other mounts. Just getting shells in the air wasn't enough, of course, but Commander Coley observed that the ship was making progress.

The main battery fired against a towed sled and conducted shore bombardment against the island of Culebra, not far from Puerto Rico. There were also engineering casualty drills, a mock battle problem, and a simulated response to a type of weapon then still relatively new. On 1 March, the signal "Prepare for defense against atomic attack" was passed to the crew. The procedure called for men to take cover if a blast occurred and to shield themselves as much as possible for ninety seconds. Once the immediate danger was past, teams from the damage control division would go out with Geiger counters and mark off areas considered contaminated. Men with fire hoses were then to wash the contamination off the ship, and those crewmen who were found to be contaminated would go for ten-minute scrubdowns. The *New Jersey*'s three decontamination stations, including a large head all the way aft in the superstructure, were just off the main deck in order to keep the radioactivity from spreading to the interior of the ship, which was tightly sealed off during general quarters. In a more conventional damage control reaction assignment, the crew simulated response to a 16-inch projectile hit amidships.

After the shakedown ended, the *New Jersey* conducted a 32-knot full power run on the way north to Norfolk. Lieutenant (junior grade) Ben Conroy stood on the fantail and watched with wonder as the propellers threw up a rooster tail of spray which went well above the level of the main deck.

The battleship arrived at the Norfolk Naval Operating Base on 19 March, and the crew welcomed a period of liberty after their full days of training. Seaman Charles Jacobus discovered Norfolk's disadvantage as a liberty spot: "Two many sailors and not enough women." As a result, Navy enlisted men congregated in a series of bars which lined both sides of a four- or five-block section of Norfolk's East Main Street near the waterfront. Jacobus found that one challenge was to try to have a beer in each place. He says, "You'd be going back and forth across the street; you just wouldn't make it to the end, because you couldn't stand up at the time." Certain bars were frequented by sailors from particular ships, to the point that men from other ships were not welcomed. Sometimes interlopers were invited politely to leave; in other cases, they were removed bodily.

The time originally planned for the post-shakedown shipyard availability at Norfolk was extended as a result of a casualty in turret one during the shakedown. The powder hoist for the turret's center gun "completely disintegrated" in the words of Gunner's Mate Bob Storm and fell all the way to the bottom of the barbette. At the shipyard in Portsmouth, Virginia, one section of the turret's roof had to be removed so that a new hoist could be installed.

On 6 April, the *New Jersey* came afloat in her dry dock and remained there several more days during dock trials before going out for a speed run. After a stay at the naval operating base, the ship got under way for Panama to relieve her sister ship *Missouri*, due in from Korea. As in 1945, the men of the *New Jersey* again had the feeling that the *Missouri* would get the lion's share of the publicity, no

matter how well their ship performed. George Hill, then of the *New Jersey*'s supply department, recalls that he and his shipmates referred to the younger ship as "Truman's Mule".

Seaman David Rupp went all the way to the top of the *New Jersey* for sightseeing on the way through the Panama Canal on 20 April. He had to shield himself as the temperature got up to 92°. Down on the main deck, members of the gunnery divisions didn't have the luxury of getting out of the sun. Boatswain's Mate Leo Meyer was supervising the placing of fenders made of manila line down between the ship's sides and the nearby walls of the locks. As the *New Jersey* went into each lock, fenders went over the side one by one, and each man stayed with his fender. As the ship moved farther forward, a continuing string of men put in still more fenders, with some of the later ones being pulled out and carried forward when they were no longer needed at the stern.

**Below:** On 16 March 1951, the *New Jersey* makes a full-power run while en route from Guantanamo Bay, Cuba, to Norfolk. The catapults have been removed from the fantail, and a helicopter sits among the ship's boats. (U.S. Naval Institute Collection)

Going through Gatun Lake in the center of the canal offered the *New Jersey* a rare opportunity for a fresh-water washdown without the need to use water from the evaporators. Fire hoses were broken out, and deck sailors began the process of spraying the topside and each other. Lieutenant (junior grade) Conroy was one of several bystanders who got blasted. He turned a corner and was drenched when he ran into a steady stream of water. He retired to his stateroom long enough to change into a dry uniform, then found a safe spot from which to observe the fun and frolic. The festivities came to a halt when Commander Coley appeared on the scene and directed people to keep their attention on the task at hand.

Some of the sailors in the crew seized upon the opportunity to inflict some mischief on their Marine brethren. Joe Brooks observed someone saying, "Let's go get the Marines and bring them topside." That was all some men needed to inspire them to go below and drag out a number

of the Corps' finest. "They were like sacrificial lambs," says Brooks. "The deck divisions proceeded to wet them down something fierce. So from that point, there was no love between the . . . deck divisions and the Marine detachment."

On another occasion, later in the deployment, the Marines sought to get even and decided they could outpull the deckhands in a tug of war. Out to the fantail came the detachment, one man carrying the guidon, and strains of "From the Halls of Montezuma . . ." on their lips. As inspired and strong as the Marines were, the contest was really no contest at all. They would have done far better challenging the sailors to a marksmanship contest or arm-wrestling or just about anything else. Handling lines was everyday business for the deck hands, and they proceeded to haul the Marines about the deck.

The *New Jersey* stayed overnight at Balboa on the Pacific side of the Canal Zone, and then the *Missouri* arrived the

next morning for turnover briefings. Officers from the *New Jersey* went over to learn from their opposite numbers as much as they could about operations in the Far East. Captain Tyree learned, for example, in talking with Captain George Wright, that the harbor pilot in Sasebo, Japan, was extremely capable and could be relied on to take the ship in and out through a tricky channel beset by currents.

On the last day of April, the *New Jersey* arrived at Pearl Harbor. Some of the crew headed for the local dives, while those with more expensive tastes, such as Seaman Joe Brooks of the FM division, spent their time drinking in the Surf Bar at the Royal Hawaiian Hotel. Between his liberty expenses and his penchant for shooting craps, Brooks found it necessary to write home to his parents for money from time to time. His mother couldn't understand why he needed so much; his father understood, grumbled about what he accurately suspected to be true, then sent the funds anyway.

The time available for drinking was brief, for the *New Jersey* was soon on her way to a fleet operating area near the Hawaiian island of Kahoolawe so the officers and men could get one additional session of training. Both the main battery and antiaircraft battery got workouts. One of the ship's motor whaleboats put a shore fire control party ashore on the island to spot gunfire, and the ship's helicopter was sent aloft to provide aerial spotting as well. On 4 May, the ship took departure for Japan.

Captain Tyree was widely perceived among the officers and crew as both a gentleman and a gentle man. He reinforced that perception as the *New Jersey* steamed independently on her journey westward. Charles Jacobus was boatswain's mate of the watch one night when the sea was unusually smooth. The bridge was illuminated with dim red lights, and Jacobus was taking it easy when he heard the familiar cry of "Captain on the bridge" and sprang to attention. Once Tyree had been briefed on steaming conditions, he sent down to the galley for a fresh pot of coffee and a supply of cups. Then he and the boatswain's mate went from man to man in that night's watch section, Jacobus carrying the coffee and Captain Tyree, the cups. As each man received a cup of coffee, he got a tangible sign that the captain knew of his contribution to the ship and cared enough to show appreciation.

On 12 May, the *New Jersey* reached port in the Far East, passing through submarine nets in Tokyo Bay and mooring to a buoy in the harbor of Yokosuka, Japan. The conning officer on the bridge lost sight of the buoy long before the ship got close because of the vessel's long, sloping bow. So Commander Coley, who had previously commanded a destroyer himself, went to the bow and maneuvered the ship from there, passing orders to the bridge by phone while keeping an eye on the buoy below. Once the ship was in position, a wire was sent out, and then an anchor chain followed so it could be hooked onto the eighty-pound shackle on top of the cylindrical buoy.

On the day after arrival in Yokosuka, the *New Jersey* embarked the Seventh Fleet Commander, Vice Admiral Harold M. "Beauty" Martin, and his staff. On the 15th the *New Jersey* got under way in company with the carrier *Philippine Sea*, light cruiser *Manchester*, and three destroyers, heading for a rendezvous with Task Force 77 off the east coast of Korea in order to provide antiaircraft protection if needed. The task force, which was built around *Essex*-class carriers, was the principal striking arm of the Seventh Fleet and was roughly comparable to one of the several task groups which constituted Task Force 38/58 during World War II.

On the evening of 19 May, the *New Jersey* and two escorting destroyers were detached from Task Force 77 and sent to bombard shore installations in North Korea. It was a pattern of operations that would be followed throughout the remainder of the war – alternating periods of shore bombardment on the bombline and task force operations with the aircraft carriers. The first firing mission for the 16-inch guns came on the morning of 20 May, when the *New Jersey* commenced bombardment at 5:00 o'clock at Kansong, a city not far north of the famous 38th parallel which divided North and South Korea. After firing for an hour and a half, the ship moved north and hit Kosong. The goal in both places was to interdict the movement of enemy supplies from north to south.

After the second mission, the *New Jersey* moved still farther north to an enemy stronghold known as Wonsan. It was a center of transportation for the North Koreans. In the evening of 20 May, the ship moved into Wonsan harbor and anchored. At 11:10 that night, she began firing her 16-inch battery and continued well past midnight. Shortly

after 3:00 a.m., there was a flurry of excitement when a fire started in one of the 40-mm. mounts after burning particles from one of the 16-inch guns ignited oil which had splashed from an open can in the mount onto life jackets and canvas ammunition covers. One 40-mm. shell exploded in the fire, and several others were thrown over the side. Within minutes, a repair party had extinguished the fire.

In many cases, even after daylight came, the men of the *New Jersey* had to depend on spotters because targets such as railroad yards and road intersections were on the other side of mountains. Occasionally, a red light appeared in the sky some 20 miles distant, beyond a mountain, to reward the *New Jersey*'s gunners for their efforts. The noise of the explosion didn't reach the ship until a number of seconds after the appearance of the red flash.

At about 9:30 a.m. on 21 May – six months to the day since recommissioning – some of the men topside noticed splashes in the water on the port side of the ship. The splashes were walking progressively closer to the *New Jersey*, at 9:32, one of the enemy's guns – probably 4- or 5-inch – found the range. Inside turret one, Gunner's Mate First Class Bob Storm was looking through his periscope when it suddenly went blank. One of the enemy projectiles hit the port side of the top of the turret and broke into pieces. One of the pieces shattered the periscope, others inflicted superficial damage, and still others landed in the water on the port side. Encased in the turret's heavy armor, Storm didn't hear or feel a thing.

Up on the bridge, Quartermaster Third Class Roff Grimes was standing anchor watch. He quickly called down to main control to tell the engineers to be ready to stand by

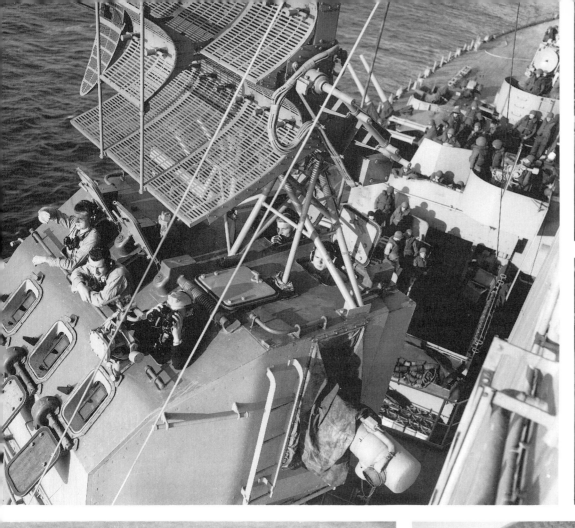

for engine orders. The shrill, urgent voice of an undoubtedly upset boatswain's mate of the watch rang out through the ship on the announcing system: "All hands, man your battle stations! The Reds are firing back at us!" Within seconds, the great battleship was a surging mass of men, heading from whatever spot they'd been in when they got the word to wherever their battle stations were. Among the many were Seaman Robert Osterwind and Seaman J. H. Dezekon. Both were on the port side when an enemy shell exploded near them, sending fragments toward the ship. Pieces of shrapnel ripped through Osterwind's life jacket and pierced the left side of his chest. Another piece went into Dezekon's left arm. Boatswain's Mate Leo Meyer was nearby and directed a man from his division, who was on station on a 40-mm. mount, to send word for medical help. Osterwind was already dead by the time he reached the wardroom casualty treatment station. He was the only man ever killed in action on board the New Jersey.

Seven minutes after she was hit, the New Jersey was firing back at the enemy gun battery. It was in the mouth of a cave on a rocky peninsula named Kalmagak which jutted into the harbor. Seaman Joe Brooks was in one of the plotting rooms on the fourth deck when general quarters was sounded. His battle station was in Spot I, up on the 010 level. Normally, he climbed ladders up the side of the ship to get there but concluded that wouldn't be prudent in this case. Instead, he pushed his bulky body as quickly as it could go up through the inside of the ship, including the normally off-limits officers' country. Once inside the pointer's chair for aiming the 16-inch guns, he explains, "I was winded. I was hot, and my face was radiating heat." His gun sight soon fogged up, so he turned on a fan to clear it. As the sight was clearing, the main battery officer, mustang Lieutenant Commander Robert Beadle, told Brooks and the man in the trainer's position next to him where the target was on Kalamagak. Brooks was able to see gun flashes still coming out of the mouth of the cave. The trainer got the guns lined up in bearing, and Brooks cranked handwheels which set the proper elevation. Firing one projectile at a time, the New Jersey was first too short, then off to the right. Then, says Brooks, "The third one went right in the cave, and that has got to be the biggest all-time thrill I have ever had in my life."

Both 16-inch and 5-inch guns were involved in the bombardment. While it was in progress, turret three was trained as close to the superstructure as it could get in order to bear on the North Korean positions. Boatswain's Mate Meyer recalls that two New Jersey enlisted men were wounded by gun blasts from the turret when they were climbing a ladder they shouldn't have been. The battleship also damaged herself in the process. The enormous concussion from the 16-inch guns, fired too close to the superstructure, badly buckled a watertight door, a splinter shield for a 40-mm. mount, and a basket in which life-

saving floater nets were stored. In addition, steam line connections were torn loose.

The New Jersey's counter battery fire silenced the enemy, scoring a direct hit on the gun emplacement and direct hits on two other caves. After about six or seven minutes, the battleship ceased fire and finally got under way from anchor shortly after 10:00 a.m. to leave the harbor. It was the last time the New Jersey fired in Wonsan while at anchor.

Throughout the ship, there was an air of disbelief. Seaman George Hill could see a difference in men's faces after the incident, adding that "Everybody got a deep concern then that we were in war." Joe Brooks, despite the triumph he felt over scoring a hit on the enemy's gun emplacement, was a troubled young man that night of 21 May. He and many other men had the shakes. As he put it, "Here we are over there for two days, and we've lost one man already. What the heck do we have to look forward to?" He couldn't fall asleep as he lay in his bunk, so he decided to go to the ship's post office on the second deck for a chat with the chief postal clerk, who was a fellow reservist Brooks knew from home. When Brooks got there, he told the chief, "I'm having one heck of a time. I can't go to sleep."

"I think I've got just the thing," replied the postal clerk, who got a bottle of soda and mixed up a drink for Brooks with a miniature bottle of liquor from a supply he had smuggled aboard.

"I drank that," remembers Brooks, "and went back to my compartment and slept like a top."

Not everyone tried to sleep in compartments; some had their bunks in the 16-inch turrets. There were a number of void spaces where bunks were fitted, and being in the turrets gave men a head start in getting equipment turned on and warmed up when general quarters was sounded. During the early part of the deployment, the equipment didn't need to be warmed up. The weather off Korea was so chilly that pointer motors, trainer motors, and so forth were kept running to provide some warmth for the turret inhabitants, because the regular heaters were not working. Gunner's Mate Bob Storm estimated that probably a dozen men slept in turret one; his bunk was in the right gun room. The turret also contained a small hiding place for a coffeepot and hot plate.

Throughout the rest of May, the ship fired against Yangyang in North Korea. Her big guns dropped a bridge span, destroyed three large ammunition dumps, and annihilated a large number of enemy troops. On 24 May, one of the New Jersey's spotting helicopters was lost during an attempt to rescue a pilot from the carrier Boxer. Lieutenant (junior grade) George Tuffanelli was flying the helo when it ran out of fuel. There was general concern that Tuffanelli and his crewman, Aviation Machinist's Mate J. B. Williams, were lost, but the two of them made their way across mountains to a friendly airstrip. From there

they were flown to a rendezvous with the destroyer *Arnold J. Isbell*, which returned them to the *New Jersey* on 27 May.

Near the end of the month, the *New Jersey* headed for Sasebo, Japan, to take on ammunition. It would be a frequent port of call for the ship during her two tours of Korea. Handling the heavy 16-inch projectiles and accompanying powder was difficult at best, so it was considered safer for the battleship to take on ammunition in port rather than under way. Quartermaster Roff Grimes steered the ship in and out of port, and he – like Captain Tyree – developed a great admiration for the harbor pilot, whom he remembers as having been a high-ranking officer and battleship skipper in the Imperial Japanese Navy during World War II. The pilot, who gave his commands to Grimes in English, handled the ship beautifully. The harbor entrance was surrounded by high, craggy rock formations and had a twisting course to follow through a channel swept free of mines. The pilot knew the points of reference on land and used them to indicate which courses to steer and when to turn. Captain Tyree was grateful to be able to trust the pilot who had the conn. Years later, Tyree recalled of the Japanese officer, "He knew just when to put that rudder over and just how close he could come to that bank and so on. It was the most marvelous piece of ship-handling I ever saw. . . . I can't remember how many times we went in and out, but every time we did, he was the one that had the conn. I would no more have been able to do that than fly a kite, because he knew that channel, every inch of it."

On board during the next venture to Korea were Admiral Arthur Radford, Commander in Chief Pacific Fleet, and Vice Admiral C. Turner Joy, Commander U.S. Naval Forces Far East. They were treated to a bombardment of Wonsan. In time, a number of the ship's officers and men adopted a cynical view of the routine when high-ranking visitors embarked. Lieutenant (junior grade) Ben Conroy was assigned to the ship's combat information center. He recalls, "We could almost lay odds that once we picked up this particular VIP or group of them we'd be back up to Wonsan again. Not that there were not always targets which could be profitably exploited, but I think a lot of the reason for our multiple visits there was simply the fact that we were on display and affording the VIPs an opportunity to view, from relative safety, bombardment of enemy strongholds."

After Wonsan and sending the visitors off by helo, it was back to steaming with Task Force 77. On 7 June, the *New Jersey* took on provisions at sea from the stores ship *Graffias*. The battleship's wartime complement of some 2,400 – augmented by the officers and enlisted men of the Seventh Fleet staff – had a large collective appetite. Among the many items which came over by highline that day were 990 pounds of spaghetti, 2,016 pounds of sauerkraut, and twenty-nine gallons of worcestershire sauce.

The *New Jersey* also refueled that day, taking on a supply of oil from the USS *Ashtabula*. That meant that it was time for oil king Frank Oliver, a boilerman first class, to take over. His headquarters was the oil shack down on the third deck, close to amidships. From there he used a set of phones to direct the disposition of incoming fuel. He told the oiler when to start pumping and when to stop, and he also kept in touch with men throughout the ship to tell them how much fuel should go into which storage tanks, and the men responded by opening and closing various valves in sequence. Oliver also had to keep track of amounts when the *New Jersey* was on the delivering end – sending out oil to escorting destroyers to keep their tanks topped off.

During normal underway steaming operations, Boilerman Oliver had a crew of men who went around the ship each night at midnight to take soundings of the fuel tanks. The practice was to empty each storage tank only down to the waterline so there would still be liquid to absorb the impact if that area of the ship were hit by a torpedo. It was necessary to alternate the emptying of port and starboard tanks so that balance was maintained and the ship didn't develop a list. From storage tanks, fuel was pumped to service tanks, of which there were two on each side of each fireroom. When the battleship as a whole got down to about 65–70 per cent of her capacity of two and a half million gallons, it was time to schedule another replenishment and start the whole cycle over again.

On the morning of 12 June, the *New Jersey* was steaming about 60 miles off the Korean coast in company with the carrier *Princeton* and other ships of Task Force 77. Gunner's Mate Bob Storm had just come up from eating breakfast and was relaxing under the rear overhang of turret one. The destroyer *Walke* was off the starboard beam. Then, recalled Storm, "All of a sudden, the whole goddamn destroyer comes up out of the water." The *Walke* had run into a floating mine which did serious damage on her port quarter and killed 26 members of her crew. Some of the bodies were trapped below decks and could not be recovered until the *Walke* was drydocked.

Nine of the dead were transferred from the *Walke* to another ship, and that evening their bodies were brought aboard the *New Jersey*, because the battleship had a refrigerated morgue. The battleship's end of the highline transfer was supervised by Commander Coley, the executive officer, and Lieutenant Boyd Hughes, the first lieutenant. Coley recalls: "I remember distinctly cautioning all concerned to take extra care to see that none of the bodies were lost over the side. We completed the transfer successfully; however, one of the bodies almost slipped out of the stretcher, and I always had a horror of losing a body over the side and trying to explain to the powers that be how it happened." The dead were to be delivered to Yokosuka, Japan, the next port, and from there shipped back to the United States for burial. Seaman George Hill, below decks

in the *New Jersey*, was reminded anew of the realities of war when he saw the nine coffins built in the battleship's carpenter shop.

During June, the *New Jersey* operated for a while under the tactical command of Commander Task Element 77.15. That was Rear Admiral Arleigh Burke, Commander Cruiser Division Five, embarked in the heavy cruiser *Los Angeles*. Burke, who became Chief of Naval Operations four years later, had a reputation from his World War II destroyer days as an officer with a great deal of zest and dash. When he was transferred to the *New Jersey* by highline for a conference with Vice Admiral Martin, Commander Coley saw him come over and later described the event: "I remember his grinning and kicking his feet during the transfer, as if he was really enjoying the transfer, and I believe he did." Nearly all other dignitaries arrived by helicopter when the *New Jersey* was at sea.

There was also a highline incident involving a *New Jersey* enlisted man, but he wasn't so happy as Admiral Burke. The battleship's police force was composed of petty officers who were given badges and designated masters-at-arms. One in particular performed his duties with a considerable degree of zeal and managed to make himself thoroughly unpopular in the process. When he was due to be transferred from the battleship by highline, Boatswain's Mate First Class Leo Meyer was in charge of the detail. He recalls being approached by some of the ship's enlisted men who said, "You're going to dunk him, aren't you, boats?" ("Boats" is an informal form of address for a boatswain's mate.)

"I don't know," Meyer told them and proceeded to set up the highline rig, which was attached to a strongpoint near the bridge.

Captain Tyree had evidently got wind of the possibility, because he called down and said, "Now, I don't want you to dunk him, Meyer."

The petty officer acknowledged the captain's order, but the men taking a strain on the line slacked off anyway – Meyer contends he was powerless to stop them – and the master-at-arms had a brief period underwater, chair and all. So Captain Tyree called down again, "Meyer, what did I just tell you?"

"Sorry, sir, the ships surged in," answered Meyer. No further action was taken in the case.

The port of Yokosuka offered a number of pleasures for the *New Jersey*'s crew when they arrived on 15 June after nearly a month of Korean operations. George Hill enjoyed the boat ride from ship to shore, because it gave him a chance to glance back at the graceful, majestic-looking *New Jersey* and to feel a thrill of pride in being part of her crew. On arrival at the naval base, he often went for a boxing workout in the gym, had dinner, and went to the base library afterward to read books about the *Bible*. "After that Wonsan harbor," he explains, "I thought I'd get a little closer to God, and I did a lot of *Bible*-reading." Boatswain's

Mate Meyer found solace of a different sort. He and a number of shipmates preferred to ride trains to Yokohama, which they considered cleaner than Yokosuka. They liked Japanese beer and Japanese nightclubs, particularly because the latter had a touch of elegance. In those days before air-conditioning became commonplace, large blocks of ice with flowers frozen into them were put in the middle of the nightclub floor. Fans blew on the ice to distribute its cooling power. For Seaman Charles Jacobus, Japan was alluring because of its "accommodating women" who offered "Stateside beds" rather than the customary oriental tatami mats.

Being in port also meant standing quarterdeck watches. Seaman Joe Brooks particularly enjoyed standing duty with big, handsome, spit-and-polish First Lieutenant Claude Kirk of the ship's Marine detachment. Kirk, who later served as governor of Florida from 1967 to 1971, had a good-natured side which probably helped his political career. Brooks, for example, told Kirk that where Brooks came from, Arlington, Virginia, Marine lieutenants were used as messenger boys in the Pentagon. Kirk didn't take offense and was willing to joke with the enlisted men on watch with him.

When the *New Jersey* was in port, she had two brows or gangways. The forward one was used by the ship's officers and visiting VIPs who came aboard. The after brow, where the officer of the deck stood his watches, was used by the enlisted men for coming and going and was also the place from which the ship's routine was dictated by announcements and bugle calls. Seaman Jacobus considered the Marine bugler exceptionally proficient – "just a pleasure to listen to, very good". For the young Jacobus, the end of the day was a moment of quiet satisfaction as he lay in his bunk, thought about the pleasures of being part of a great ship, and heard the notes of the preparatory tattoo and, five minutes later, taps itself.

After the stop in Yokosuka, the *New Jersey* was off to Sasebo and then again to Wonsan. During the course of July, the *New Jersey* continued to alternate between shore bombardment and periods with the carrier task force. A bombardment on 6 July near Kansong was in support of United Nations troops, effecting a limited push against the enemy. As she did customarily during her Korean War operations, the *New Jersey* flew the United Nations flag in addition to the U.S. national ensign. Captain Tyree considered close support of friendly troops to be the most difficult and satisfying of the ship's achievements during the 1951 deployment. It required greater precision than other types of bombardment because of the danger of injuring friendly forces, but it also offered the opportunity to save the lives of friends who were close to the enemy.

Marine Lieutenant Kirk was often up above in a helo to act as spotter during the fire support missions. Other times it was an Army or Marine spotter in an aircraft, and still other times the firing was spotted and corrections sent

Far left: Members of the *New Jersey*'s band sit under the barrels of turret three to play after noon chow. (Courtesy PHC T. E. Shireman)

Left: A 5-inch gun of the *New Jersey*'s secondary battery fires at Kosong, Korea, in the summer of 1951. (National Archives: 80-G-432930)

Below: Turrets one and three are trained toward the rugged mountains of North Korea as the *New Jersey* patrols her shore bombardment station off the coast in the summer of 1951. (Courtesy PHC T. E. Shireman)

by a shore fire control party on the ground. Even before the first round was fired near friendly troops, Captain Tyree insisted that the navigator, combat information center, and plotting room should all have the same solutions on the bearing and range of the target from the ship. "If any one of them showed a discrepancy," said Tyree, "we would stop and find out why. And, as a result, as far as I know, we never hurt any of our own people." After the opening ranging shot, the spotters then pulled the fall of shot in closer and closer to the front lines between friend and foe, the place where the exploding 16-inch projectiles could do the most good.

This sense of caution was typical of Tyree throughout his tour in command. Boatswain's Mate Jacobus recalls that Tyree often had a troubled look on his face while on the bridge. Ensign Bob Watts, who stood junior officer of the deck watches during the deployment, observed that the captain was "pleasant but nervous". He chain-smoked cigarettes, and Watts was fascinated to see that the ash on the captain's cigarette often got as long as an inch and a half before the skipper would knock it off into one of the butt kits positioned throughout the bridge. To the junior officer, the skipper didn't appear comfortable enough with the *New Jersey* to enjoy his time in command.

Few of the *New Jersey*'s men had such an opportunity to observe Captain Tyree at close range. One who did was executive officer Coley, who offers another facet of the skipper's personality: "Captain Tyree was a soft-spoken individual, not demanding, with a genuine concern for the crew and officers in the order given. He was not an out-going individual, but after knowing him, you soon discovered his sincere concern and capabilities. He used the public address system to keep the crew informed. In short, he had their welfare at heart and made every effort to see that their needs were met. As a shiphandler, he was about average."

In many Navy ships, there is a traditional – even stereo-typed – description of the roles of the captain and executive officer. The captain is the warm, fatherly type who is concerned about the welfare and morale of the crew. The exec is the stern disciplinarian who looks after the internal running of the ship, ensuring that duties are performed, standards are met, and punishment meted as necessary. In the *New Jersey*, says Coley, this pattern prevailed during the first Korean cruise.

On 16 July, while the battleship was operating at high speed with the carriers, a shortage of feedwater developed in the tanks serving boilers seven and eight. In a com-pounding chain of events, one problem led to another. Because of the low water problem, the boilers were shut off, which stopped the supply of steam to main lubricating pumps in number four engine room. That, in turn, led to the loss of lubricating oil pressure to number three main engine, and the loss of main steam also prevented the immediate stopping of number three propeller shaft.

Because the shaft kept turning for two or three minutes without lubricating oil, bearings were wiped in both high- and low-pressure turbines, and other damage was done as well. The shaft was locked as soon as possible, and the *New Jersey* dropped out of formation to work on the problem.

With her speed restricted and the repair apparently beyond the capability of the ship's force, the *New Jersey* was soon ordered to the shipyard at Yokosuka. An examination of the problem revealed that her engineering personnel had not taken corrective action quickly enough when trouble developed and had failed to recognize conditions that indicated potential casualties. It could well be that the problem was a consequence of the ship's relative newness back in commission. Training on how to deal with propulsion plant casualties had somehow not been completely sufficient for those on watch that morning.

Fortunately, the solution was at hand in Yokosuka, where the shipyard work force was almost completely Japanese. The *New Jersey* didn't need to go into dry dock; she was repaired while moored to a buoy in Yokosuka harbor. The irony of the situation struck Captain Tyree when he went down to observe the work in progress by the Japanese: "It hadn't been so awfully long before that we were all trying to kill each other." He recalled that a lot of the work accomplished by "swarms of people" was done

by hand. "They knew what they were doing, and they did an outstanding job. We weren't there very long."

Once the problem was fixed, the *New Jersey* was again off to Korea. In late August, she fired at enemy troop concentrations and North Korean transportation facilities. Places hit included Kansong, Sapyong-ni, and Changhang. Major General Edward M. Almond of the Army Tenth Corps praised the *New Jersey* for the devastating effect on enemy morale, causing great damage to enemy equipment and inflicting a large number of casualties. The thanks and congratulations received by the ship were typical of many such messages which expressed gratitude for her accurate and effective shooting. To Commander Coley, they were the best sort of reward for the work the ship was doing. Many of the letters from ashore indicated that the *New Jersey* was able to accomplish destruction that aircraft had not been able to.

When the *New Jersey* was out of range of enemy guns, the firing was often carried out at Condition III by whichever of the three sections had the watch. These watches with only part of the guns manned sometimes went on both day and night, and the latter caused problems for those trying to sleep. Lieutenant (junior grade) Ben Conroy had a stateroom in the superstructure, with only a bulkhead separating him from a 5-inch gun right outside. It took some time before he was able to sleep through the repeated sharp cracking of the 5-inch guns.

**Right:** The library aft of the mess deck provides magazines, books, and a comfortable place to relax while off duty. In this September 1951 photo, the man second from right is Seaman David Rupp, ship's librarian and chaplains' assistant. (Courtesy New Jersey State Archives)

Sometimes, as in World War II, the *New Jersey* employed a system of command duty officers on the bridge in order to give the captain a break. One night Commander Coley had the duty on the bridge when one of the turrets fired, and he heard two explosions quite close together. The first had the normal thundering boom, followed immediately by what he remembers as "a sort of mushy sound". The second was caused by a premature explosion of the projectile itself, the ship having been given a supply of old projectiles. The next morning, a number of pieces of shrapnel on deck further demonstrated that the projectile had indeed destroyed itself almost immediately after leaving the gun. During the course of the tour off Korea, there were a number of such prematures.

During the first Korean cruise, the *New Jersey* had two chaplains. The Protestant was Commander Chester Hults, and the Catholic was Lieutenant Peter Brewerton. In his capacity as the chaplains' yeoman, 30-year-old Seaman David Rupp sometimes prepared the answers to incoming letters and sought only the signatures of his bosses. In many cases, this was easy, because the same types of letters showed up over and over, frequently having to do with problems back in the States – a missing allotment check or a pregnant woman trying to locate her baby's father. When a member of the family of a *New Jersey* man died, Rupp set the paperwork in motion to arrange for emergency leave. Sometimes, members of the crew used Rupp as a sounding board on what to say to the chaplains. For instance, a Catholic sailor who had just had his first sexual experience with a girl, wanted Rupp's advice on whether to confess to the priest.

On Sundays Rupp set up for chapel services, and every morning he arranged the library to serve as chapel for early mass. It was convenient, because the library had a bunk in it for Rupp. On Friday nights, Rupp turned the library into a mini-synagogue, complete with gefilte fish and matzos, so the supply officer, Commander Herman Strock, could conduct Jewish services. Rupp even accommodated a group of crew members he terms "holy rollers", who had their own church. That group's organ music and accompanying vocal efforts got so loud that their particular brand of religion had to be terminated in the *New Jersey*.

As the ship's librarian, Seaman Rupp kept the library stocked with the latest issues of periodicals, as well as books that were supplied by the Navy Department. As often as possible, the ship received a supply of *Stars & Stripes*, a daily newspaper published in the Far East by the Defense Department. Members of the crew were particularly interested in sports. The paper enabled them to keep track of that year's baseball pennant race, which was eventually won by Bobby Thomson of the New York Giants with a last-inning home run at the Polo Grounds. George Hill remembers that the recalled Naval Reservists in the crew were especially eager to get news of progress in peace negotiations with the Communists. The reservists wanted the war to end so they could go back home. Hill estimates that two-thirds of the men recalled from civilian life were unhappy with their lot and would just as soon have been elsewhere.

Among other diversions during the deployment was the perennial favorite – gambling. In his role as disciplinarian, Commander Coley was concerned about the pernicious effects gambling could have in the crew. He couldn't prevent the wagering but did try to limit its ill effects. One tactic was to deputize different masters-at-arms just before paydays so that gamblers wouldn't always know whom to be on guard against. Coley recalls that a prime concern was the welfare of the gamblers' families. On one occasion a report came to him that about $600 had been stolen from a petty officer, who said it was a bonus he had received for reenlisting. He had been planning to send it home to his family, but a shipmate had taken it from him. Coley then checked the ship's post office and discovered that a money order had recently been sold for just about the amount of the missing money. The buyer was hauled up and asserted he had won the money from the newly reenlisted man in a dice game. The loser had invented his story, because he didn't want his family to know what had really happened to the money.

Fire Controlman Joe Brooks remembers that it was standard practice to play records on the fantail during those evenings when movies were shown. One night, while Vice Admiral Martin was embarked, a tune that was played while the crew gathered before the show included the playful lyrics "The admiral's daughter is down by the water; she's out to get your dinghy." Admiral Martin was due to watch the show that night, and an officer from his staff apparently considered the song to be in poor taste. He picked the record off the machine and hurled it over the side. Brooks remembers that word of the officer's action got back to Admiral Martin, and the officer was disciplined for unauthorized destruction of the crew's property.

Sometimes the crew's off-duty time was spent in pursuits which contained a useful measure of training. Boatswain's Mate Charles Jacobus gathered men together after ship's work ended and taught them various aspects of marlinspike seamanship, such as knots and splices. Several became skilled enough to be able to tie eye-splices and back-splices blindfolded. He taught them how to make pieces of line into quoits, which were then tossed at sawed-off pieces of swab handle in a game similar to horseshoes. Another game was to place two buckets at some distance from each other and try to toss stiff-bristled wooden scrub brushes into them – a cross between horse-shoes and basketball.

As summer turned to autumn, the *New Jersey* continued her superb shooting. On 5 October, while the ship was operating in the Hungnam-Hamhung area off North Korea, Lieutenant George Tuffanelli, a *New Jersey* helicopter pilot, rescued Lieutenant H. C. Engle, Jr., a flier

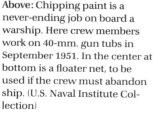

Above: Chipping paint is a never-ending job on board a warship. Here crew members work on 40-mm. gun tubs in September 1951. In the center at bottom is a floater net, to be used if the crew must abandon ship. (U.S. Naval Institute Collection)

from the carrier *Bonhomme Richard*. Engle had been shot down in a river ten miles south of Wonsan. Thanks to cover provided by spotting planes from Task Force 77, Tuffanelli and his crew were able to brave heavy small arms fire by the enemy and pick by the grateful Engle. The injured pilot was brought back aboard the *New Jersey* for medical treatment.

The demands of plotting targets, firing the guns, and looking out for hostile fire from ashore in such places as Hungnam and Wonsan were such that simply steaming with the carriers seemed easy by comparison. In one of his letters home, Lieutenant (junior grade) Ben Conroy wrote, "When we're in Task Force 77, it's like a vacation." He had earlier got another sort of relief from the normal underway duties when he and Radarman First Class Arthur Fowler went ashore to spend several days with the Army. Their mission was to coordinate gunfire spotting missions between ship and shore and to encode radio messages going to and from the ship. They were in an area in North Korea known as the "Iron Triangle" of Pyonggang-Kumha-Chorwon, south of Wonsan. For Conroy, the time ashore provided a revealing glimpse of how the other half lived. Coming from the ship, where alcohol was prohibited, Conroy was surprised to find that the Army officers always seemed to have a good supply of liquor and beer. One Army officer advised Conroy to open a can of beer and leave it by the cot in his tent overnight. When Conroy woke the next morning with a bit of a headache, the warm beer seemed to do the trick in getting rid of it.

The young naval officer developed an admiration for aerial spotters when he flew over enemy areas in one of the Army's helicopters. There was great visibility, but virtually no protection against gunfire from the ground. One of his most vivid memories of the time spent living with the Army was that of being close enough to the enemy lines to hear Chinese bugles in the distance. When the time came to return to the *New Jersey*, the ship wasn't able to pick up the men when expected, so they rode a torpedo plane out to the USS *Boxer* and from there a helo hop to *New Jersey*.

Toward the end of the deployment, there was some turnover in the *New Jersey*'s crew, including the release of some of the reservists who had been recalled from civilian life. In World War II, men were generally in for the duration, but this time conditions for release were not so stringent, in part because the demands for manpower were far lower. Seaman George Hill was able to be released on a hardship basis, because his wife was having trouble getting settled in at home without him. Gunner's Mate Bob Storm went home because his enlistment expired.

At the same time, new crew members were arriving. One of them was a big bear of a man – 6 feet 6 inches tall and probably in the neighborhood of 250 pounds. He wasn't assigned any specific duties at first, so he wandered throughout the ship to see what was where. One morning he pulled on a navy blue knitted watch cap and a khaki uniform without insignia, then proceeded down to the engineering spaces as part of his continuing education program. After emerging from the long, long third-deck

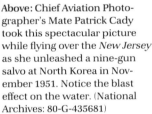

Above: Chief Aviation Photographer's Mate Patrick Cady took this spectacular picture while flying over the *New Jersey* as she unleashed a nine-gun salvo at North Korea in November 1951. Notice the blast effect on the water. (National Archives: 80-G-435681)

Above right: The nine-gun salvo is also impressive when photographed from the bow by Ted Shireman. (Courtesy PHC T. E. Shireman)

passageway known as "Broadway", which opens onto the engine rooms and firerooms, the new man found a ladder and climbed up to the mess deck. He got himself a compartmented aluminium tray and pushed it along the serving line where it was filled with breakfast.

When the big fellow sat down at a mess table and began eating, some curious crew members started passing the time of day with him. "Chief, how long you been aboard?" one asked.

"I just got here a couple of days ago," said the fellow in khaki.

"Are you going to stay long?"

"I don't know. You know the Navy. I don't know whether they'll let me stay very long or not."

Fairly soon after that, someone came along and recognized that the big man in khakis was Captain Francis D. McCorkle, who had just reported aboard on 1 November to familiarize himself with the ship before taking over command from Captain Tyree. He welcomed a period without duties or responsibilities to explore the ship at his leisure to find out what made it run, what the men were like, and a host of information that would be useful to him as commanding officer. The Tennessee-born McCorkle had enough down-home informality to his personality that he enjoyed the opportunity to pretend he was a chief petty officer rather than immediately demanding all the honors and perquisites that went with his rank.

In early November, with McCorkle along for the ride, the *New Jersey* went to bombard such places as Iwon,

Tanchon-Songjin, Chongjin, and Kansong. Targets included bridges, tunnels, buildings, railroad yards, rail junctions, bunkers, caves, gun emplacements, and enemy troops. Lieutenant (junior grade) Conroy felt "pretty damn cold" because the ship was operating up near the Siberian border. There were splashes and airbursts near the ship but no hits.

The five-day interdiction mission ended on 6 November and then the *New Jersey* headed to Task Force 77 for a short interval and then on to Sasebo, Japan. There she picked up British Rear Admiral Alan K. Scott-Moncrieff, who would be embarked in the ship as a spare flag officer while Admiral Martin took the flagship around for an inspection trip into the Yellow Sea off the west coast of Korea. On 13 November, the *New Jersey* used the spotting services of planes from the Australian light carrier *Sydney* while firing on enemy targets in the Chang-San-Got peninsula. That particular bombardment put the battleship's total of 16-inch rounds fired during the Korean deployment past the 3,000 mark. During World War II, she had fired fewer than 1,000 of her big projectiles in anger.

The next stop was Yokosuka. On 17 November, Captain McCorkle relieved Captain Tyree as commanding officer, and Vice Admiral Martin used the ceremony as an occasion to pass out a fistful of medals and other awards to the men who had made a success of the *New Jersey*'s deployment to the Far East.

Four days later came the event which the men of the *New Jersey* had been waiting for. The *Wisconsin*, fresh from recommissioning and a midshipman cruise to Europe, arrived to take over as Seventh Fleet flagship. The navigator who brought her into Yokosuka was Lieutenant Commander Elmo R. Zumwalt, future Chief of Naval Operations. On 22 November, a signalman hauled down Admiral Martin's three-star flag from the *New Jersey*'s yardarm, and its twin went fluttering up on the *Wisconsin*. Captain McCorkle quipped that the *New Jersey* rose about 15 inches out of the water when the fleet staff transferred to the other battleship. There would no longer be a need for officers to fight for seats in the wardroom or enlisted men at movies. Ben Conroy used two terms to describe the departing guests: "staffbastards" and "flagbastards", all run together, just as inhabitants of the Old South used to refer to "Damnyankees".

On 24 November, the ship got under way, and Captain McCorkle poured on the speed going through the submarine nets guarding the entrance to Yokosuka harbor. He had to squeeze the 108-foot beam through a 200-foot gap in the net and decided that the best way was to rush right through so there would be less chance for the current to swing him into the net. The *New Jersey* formed a column with the heavy cruisers *Toledo* and *Helena* and headed for Hawaii. She was able to get an overnight liberty for the crew there on 1–2 December, then took on a load of VIP passengers for the next leg of the voyage, to Long Beach, California. Included in the group was Colonel Wilburt S. "Bigfoot" Brown, described by Executive Officer Coley as "One of the most colorful characters in the long history of the Marine Corps." McCorkle decided that Brown, as the senior officer on board, rated Admiral Halsey's old cabin, and the other guests, including the president of the University of Hawaii and other educators, had suitable accommodation elsewhere.

Captain McCorkle and the visitors seemed to gravitate to Colonel Brown's quarters, because he was an entertaining storyteller. One of the educators surveyed the opulent surroundings in the flag quarters and made a speech directed at Brown and McCorkle: "Oh, you fellows have got it good in the Navy. I got in the wrong business. Just look over there at that mahogany table. Look at this deep rug. All air-conditioned. Now, when you get ashore, you've got PXs, you've got movies, you've got a commissary. This is a wonderful life."

Bigfoot took it all in for a while, then responded, "Doctor, it certainly gives me encouragement to think that a man of your intellectual caliber could so appreciate the fine life we live in the military. Now I haven't seen my wife in two years; she's back in Mississippi. And yes, there is a movie; there is a commissary; there is a PX in New Orleans, but all that is 500 miles away from her. I've tried to explain to her all the things you're saying. I just wish you could talk to her; maybe you could persuade her."

The *New Jersey* stopped briefly at Long Beach on 8 December to give part of the crew liberty. One group of

VIPs was dropped off and another taken aboard. The second group included several New Jersey businessmen, as well as the mayor of Trenton and the president of Lenox China Company. Then it was on to the Panama Canal for the trip through on 14 December. The ship arrived back in Norfolk on 20 December in order to be home in time for Christmas. For some reason, the use of Norfolk as home port continued for all the battleships during the Korean War, even though the ships could have saved about three weeks' travel time on each deployment had they been based at Long Beach, the traditional battleship home port, rather than on the East Coast.

The Christmas season was a time of great change in the *New Jersey*'s crew. Many of the recalled reservists were going home, and other crew members were transferring to different duty stations. Captain McCorkle had the feeling he was being robbed of a good deal of his talent, especially since the ship was being drawn down to overall numbers which were more in keeping with her peacetime allowance than her wartime complement. On 4 January, Rear Admiral H. Raymond Thurber and his Battleship Division Two staff moved aboard. The division had been activated to provide an administrative home for the battleships now that enough had been brought out of mothballs to keep the *Missouri* company.

On 11 February, the *New Jersey* entered the naval shipyard at Portsmouth, Virginia. The period in the yard offered the opportunity to scrape marine growth off the ship's bottom, further update her communications and electronic equipment, and perform some of the other maintenance and repair work which was deferred during the hurry-up reactivation at Bayonne and Brooklyn. There were several topside changes. The two remaining 20-mm. guns were removed from the forecastle. The large rounded splinter shield which had been painted with an outhouse in 1943 was removed from the bow also, replaced by a much smaller shield just above the bullnose. At the very top of the ship, the circular, dish-like antenna for the SK-2 air-search radar was removed and replaced by a smaller, rectangular one for the SPS-6.

As the *New Jersey* went through the overhaul, she had a new executive officer. Commander Paul Joachim brought to his capacious shipboard cabin a tankful of fish and the palette of a skilled oil painter. One of the enlisted men was also a quite talented artist. Quartermaster First Class P. H. Stevens had executed a drawing of Seaman Robert Osterwind which he gave the dead boy's parents in a solemn ceremony on board ship shortly after the *New Jersey* returned to Norfolk in December 1951.

In early 1952, the ship's library near the mess deck got a number of new books. Included was Herman Wouk's best-selling novel about the World War II Navy, *The Caine Mutiny*, which contained a passage set on board the *New Jersey*. There were some removals from the library shelves as well, because this was the time when Senator Joseph

**Right:** Boatswain's Mate Third Class Aaron Richardson uses the boatswain's call to alert the crew while passing the word over the general announcing system in December 1951. (Courtesy BM2 Charles Jacobus)

**Far right:** Storekeeper Third Class Edward Coletti adds up the prices of ship's store purchases made by Sal Cusumano in early 1952. (National Archives: 80-G-437222)

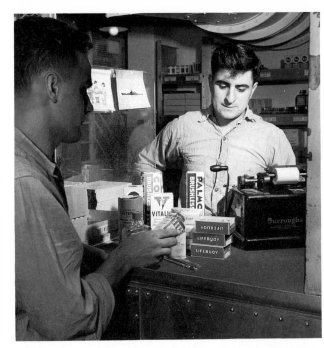

**Right:** Captain Francis McCorkle, seen from the rear at left, and Rear Admiral Ray Thurber, right, inspect the *New Jersey*'s Marine detachment on 2 February 1952. (Courtesy Mrs. Richard Donovan)

McCarthy of Wisconsin conducted congressional inquisitions in an attempt to expose Communists, real and imagined. In that Red-hating atmosphere, the Navy Department apparently decided it should be above reproach, So David Rupp, the ship's librarian, was visited one day by a lady from the Navy's library service in Washington. She spent two mornings going through the *New Jersey*'s collection, throwing into boxes books that were by Communist authors or deemed to be subversive for some other reason. Rupp went along as part of a working party that included a Marine and two sailors as they carried the boxes of books to the Portsmouth city dump. The only proscribed book that sticks in Rupp's mind was a dictionary of slang and unconventional English. Subversiveness was in the mind of the beholder.

The stay in port gave the ship's crew a chance for some activities not possible at sea, and one of those was basketball. The ship's team won four straight games to win the tournament played among vessels of her type command, the Atlantic Fleet Cruiser Force. To get to the finals, the *New Jersey*'s men beat teams from the *Salem, Baltimore*, and *Albany*. Ten of the battleship's players were picked for the type command all-star team. Among the *New Jersey*'s top scorers were Jim Mabry and Owen Cunningham.

There were other forms of recreation, including the inevitable movies. Two officers of the deck delighted in adding a personal touch when standing watch in port. The standard practice during the watches in the early evening was to announce the name of the night's film and the cast of characters. Lieutenant (junior grade) Ben Conroy always managed to have the boatswain's mate of the watch slip the name of Spanish pianist Jose Iturbi into the list. Lieutenant (junior grade) Ben Dowd went a step further, putting a name quite similar to his own into the cast. As Boatswain's Mate Charles Jacobus remembers, the word was passed as follows: "The name of the movie to be shown tonight will be 'Japanese War Bride', with Don Taylor, Shirley Yamaguchi, and also starring Benjamin P. O'Dowd." Another event of quarterdeck watches was the mustering of restricted men and prisoners at large. The mustering place was supposed to be the quarterdeck, but just for the heck of it, Conroy sometimes called for the musters to be held elsewhere. Once he announced that the muster would be on top of turret three, which was in

sight of his post at the after brow. Dozens of curious crew members came topside to see if the men really were being mustered on the turret. Sure enough, they were.

The battleship left dry dock on 16 April and then, except for sea trials and the loading of ammunition, spent much of the remainder of April and May alongside a pier at the naval operating base in Norfolk while preparing to operate once again. By early May, the crew was down to 1,920 officers and men, nearly 85 per cent of whom were from east of the Mississippi River. The crew comprised 1,754 Navy enlisted, 103 Navy officers, 61 Marine enlisted, and two Marine officers.

When the *New Jersey* headed south for refresher training, McCorkle's dachshund Heiny was living in the captain's sea cabin. The dog wasn't able to find a place to relieve himself, so he stopped eating and drinking. When the ship anchored at Cuba on 5 June, the captain made sure that his dog was in the first boat ashore. A few days later, Heiny wandered by a boatswain's locker and discovered that the boatswain's mate in charge of the space used a sawed-off tree stump as a stool. Heiny immediately began using it for something else.

Even though the squatty dog found it difficult up and down the ship's many ladders, he did like to follow the captain about, and the dog in turn was followed by the skipper's Marine orderly who sometimes had to reach down and lift Heiny over hatch coamings that were too high for him. The dachshund didn't endear himself to the new navigator, Lieutenant Commander Ray Wilhite, by nipping at him a time or two when he went to report something to Captain McCorkle. The dog had a repertoire of tricks. For instance, when Captain McCorkle asked Heiny, "Would you rather be a soldier or be dead?" the dachshund immediately rolled over and played dead, receiving a dog biscuit as a reward. Then, when the skipper asked, "Would you rather be an alert sailor?" the dog stood at attention and received another biscuit from the grinning captain.

The refresher training was a time for new officers of the deck and many other men throughout the huge ship to get concentrated training in their duties and to experience battle problems and casualty drills. Lieutenant Donald Poe of the battleship division staff observed what was going on and appreciated the fact that Admiral Thurber and Captain McCorkle let the junior officers sit in on discussions of professional topics. McCorkle would have preferred to spend the time with his own officers and men and have the staff anywhere other than on board the New Jersey. This was especially the case in regard to Admiral Thurber's preferred anchorage near the officers' club. Once, when leaving that spot, the captain had to give perhaps as many as 100 orders for changes to the engines in order to get the giant New Jersey twisted around and on her way out of the bay. The next time McCorkle got into that anchorage, he told Admiral Thurber he was going to back the ship out, and he did, because it was much easier.

The big captain with the big ship relished the opportunity to maneuver her, and he was extremely good at it, which was not surprising in that he had reported aboard after a tour of duty as chairman of the Naval Academy's department of seamanship and navigation. Through long years of experience, he had developed a trait known as a seaman's eye. He was able to estimate the distances to objects and to other ships, and he grasped well the combinations of rudder and engines that would produce desired results in getting where he wanted to be.

The same enthusiasm with which he handled the steel monster came through in his approach to the crew. During the short time in which Commander Coley served as McCorkle's exec, he observed that the skipper had a number of qualities one associates with a politician. The captain had a gregarious nature and was eager to "press the flesh" with his shipboard constituents. Just as he had done when he first reported aboard, McCorkle liked to wander all over the ship and see things for himself. He learned the names of men, where they were from, and what they did in the overall scheme of things. So informed,

he would later get on the general announcing system and tell all who were listening that he had learned that Joe Newell was doing a great job as ship's tailor; Quartermaster Roff Grimes was a splendid helmsman; Chief Yeoman J. A. Williams was a hotshot on paperwork; and sailmaker Charles Metzell was to be commended for the fine muzzle bags on the New Jersey's 113 guns. Though the approach was similar to that of an old-time ward boss, it was also highly effective.

Fireman Allan Frank got to meet Captain McCorkle more directly than he would have liked. One night he came up out of a fireroom in order to go to the head. He put his hands through a hatch to pull himself up to the mess deck, and he ran right into the skipper. McCorkle, despite the fact that he was wearing only a T-shirt and khaki trousers rather than the full trappings of his rank, was still the captain; Frank was petrified. Words would not come, not even "Good evening, captain". McCorkle quickly realized what the problem was and humored Frank in order to allow him to compose himself. He went through the usual routine of asking Frank his name, what division he was in, where he lived, and so forth. After a bit more light talk, he said good night and continued making his way through the passageways of the ship he loved so dearly.

While the ship was in Guantanamo for training, there were opportunities to go ashore nights and weekends. Some men got their entertainment fishing for sharks from the fantail; the galley provided leftovers to use as bait. During a break from Cuba, liberty at Haiti's capital city of Port-au-Prince offered a chance to buy a variety of items ranging from live chickens to gold earrings. Briefings prior to the weekend visit warned crew members against attending native voodoo rituals. During the course of the stay at Haiti, the fatherly Admiral Thurber took Lieutenant Poe and another member of his staff out for dinner and then staked them for gambling at a local casino. It is little wonder that Poe recalls his battleship staff duty with much pleasure.

While in Guantanamo, Captain McCorkle donned his white service uniform, complete with white gloves and high, choke collar. Then the entire crew lined up at division parade and he went up and down the ranks, noting the military appearance of the men. He remarked that shoes here might need more work, and a haircut there had gotten a bit too shaggy. McCorkle was, however, especially impressed when he came to 6-foot 5-inch Fireman Dick Molinaro, one of the few crew members he didn't have to look down to. The skipper was so struck by the appearance and military bearing of the A division sailor that he called him "the best looking man on the ship". Extra liberty back in the States would be the reward for the fireman's efforts in preparing for the inspection.

The Caribbean liberty ports were not so inviting as those the New Jersey was to hit during a coming midshipman training cruise, so it was a relief for many in the crew to put this phase of training behind them. The ship headed for home after a round of gunnery drills which involved firing the main battery at towed targets and at the island of Culebra. The *New Jersey* got into port at Norfolk on 3 July, just in time to full-dress the ship with signal flags from stem to stern in honor of Independence Day.

In preparation for the trip to Europe, McCorkle was pleased to learn that the ship would again be the beneficiary of the generosity of the State Society of the Battleship New Jersey, which was reactivated when the ship was. The group sent the captain a high-fidelity record player for his cabin, flown in by a New Jersey National Guard aircraft so he could have the machine for entertaining overseas. Asked if there was anything else he'd like, the skipper said he had admired a state seal when he visited the *Missouri*, so an attractive plaque showed up from Walter Margetts, treasurer of the state of New Jersey.

McCorkle also sent to Tiffany's in New York to see about spending some money donated by the state. He wanted to augment the elaborately decorated silver service which had first been presented to the original USS *New Jersey* shortly after the turn of the century. Captain Tyree received the service when the ship went back in commission for Korea, and it was displayed in the captain's cabin, which had the advantage of a Marine guard on duty at all times. The silver was worth guarding well; when new, it had cost $10,000. By the early 1950s, it was appraised at $50,000 but considered almost priceless, because Tiffany's didn't know if it had the craftsmen to reproduce the set if something happened to it. The ship had received another $10,000 from the state during World War II and finally got around to spending it during the Korean War. This time the same amount of money brought a few additional place settings in the form of plates and goblets.

The cruise began on 19 July after the ship had taken on 731 midshipmen from the naval ROTC units of twelve different colleges and universities. The *New Jersey* steamed in company with the light cruiser *Roanoke*, oiler *Severn*, and seven destroyers, in her first trip across the Atlantic since the midshipman cruise of 1947. One thing which was necessary during the transit was getting the gun battery aligned. Commander Bill Braybrook, recently reported aboard as gunnery officer, was bothered by the large fire control corrections which had to be applied during the shooting in the Caribbean. He worked with fire control officer Stu Sadler and Warrant Gunner Kermit Mintz. They discovered that the alteration of the former 20-mm. gun position on the bow had upset the bench-mark used as a reference point for aligning the ship's gun battery. The time at sea, says Braybrook, was "comfortably warm and delightfully calm, with good clear weather and sharp horizons. Under ideal conditions, we undertook to carefully realign the main and secondary batteries." By making careful measurements and adjustments, the gunnery department was able to get all the ship's guns

aligned, so that it would have been theoretically possible to fire the main battery using either the 5-inch or 40-millimeter directors.

During the training cruise, Boatswain's Mate Third Class Charles Jacobus enjoyed the idea of having the third class midshipmen working for him as if they were nonrated enlisted men. Jacobus told the half-dozen or so midshipmen assigned to him that they would have two minutes after reveille to get topside for their morning cleaning stations. The first morning, both the midshipmen and ship's company deckhands were slow in meeting his requirement. So he put it to them, "Tomorrow morning, I want you up here before me." The next morning, the midshipmen hurriedly pulled on their dungarees. They raced topside, and there was Jacobus, who had slept up there overnight just to play a trick on them. He didn't have any trouble after that in getting them to their stations promptly.

On 30 July, the *New Jersey* and her consort of destroyers approached the English Channel as they neared the end of their transatlantic journey. Down in the combat information center, Midshipman First Class Lee Douglas from Harvard was standing a training watch. All was going routinely, and there were few contacts to track by radar. Then one of the radarmen announced that he was tracking a "skunk" (as surface contacts were designated) headed toward the *New Jersey* at a speed of about 40 knots. One of the watch officers announced that it had to be a "bogey" (air contact), because no skunk could go that fast. After some double-checking, the watch officer finally became convinced that it was a surface ship and relayed the word to the officer of the deck on the bridge. More incredulity surfaced there, until finally the realization came that this must be the new passenger liner *United States*, which had set a transatlantic speed record during her maiden voyage earlier in the month. The radar also showed another large contact tracking along near the *United States*.

The next concern for the battleship was getting past the two oncoming ships, because there was not a great deal of room for maneuver, and the *New Jersey*'s escorting destroyers were fanned out in front of her in a bent-line screen. Ensign Bob Watts, the officer of the deck, became increasingly concerned during that evening watch, because a turn in either direction would bring the *New Jersey* and her screen into the path of the oncoming liners. The Battleship Division Two staff had tactical command. Watts kept calling flag plot on his squawkbox to alert the staff, but he got no results. He finally called Captain McCorkle, who came charging out of his sea cabin. Once McCorkle was aware of the problem, he sent out an impromptu signal by voice radio to the destroyers: "All small boys take cover on Onrush." "Onrush" was the *New Jersey*'s voice call sign and thus a quick means of identifying her to the destroyers.

Like chickens following the directions of a mother hen, two of the destroyers scooted out into a line ahead of the battleship and two fell in astern. Thus, the *United States* and the other ship would have to pass only a single column of ships rather than go through the pickets of a fence. Out of the night roared the mammoth *United States*, nearly 1,000 feet long and lit from stem to stern so that she appeared as a seagoing city. She passed close aboard on one side of the *New Jersey*, and the second liner went past on the other side. The sea giants passed quickly in the darkness, and then the liners disappeared astern.

Years later, McCorkle reminisced about the event and said he took comfort during the unexpected meeting because he knew that the liners would be handled correctly by their officers when speeding past at distances measured in hundreds of yards. Said McCorkle, "You knew damn well those ships were run by professionals that were good." The liner captains could have said the same of him.

The *New Jersey* arrived off Cherbourg on the last day of July and was guided to her berth alongside a dock. Four days later, RMS *Queen Mary* arrived and moored astern of the *New Jersey*. The French were trying to increase the flow of commerce through Cherbourg, and having two such large ships in at the same time was a dramatic way of showing off the port's capability.

Almost as soon as the *New Jersey* arrived, Lieutenant Poe and other staff members were off on tours which had been set up through American Express by members of Admiral Thurber's Battleship Division Two staff. The Paris tour, for example, had a package price of $36.50 for midshipmen and officers and $30.00 for enlisted men. A special train took the men to Paris, and then they could both go sightseeing on their own and take tours in buses with English-speaking guides. For $6.50 they could take buses from Cherbourg to see the island of Mont-Saint-Michel. Naturally, the tour brochure provided by American Express advised the Navy men that they should be sure to protect their funds with travelers' checks.

Captain and Mrs. McCorkle and the dog Heiny stayed in Cherbourg so they could entertain important visitors. One day a group of wives of local dignitaries came aboard, and they were dressed to the nines. The captain met them at the quarterdeck and thought to himself, "My God, are they shipshape!" He was especially struck by seeing one whose hat looked to be about two feet in diameter. Groups of schoolchildren and various other Frenchmen came aboard to tour the ship.

While some *New Jersey* men took tours, others found their amusement in Cherbourg. After liberty call, Boatswain's Mate Jacobus and some of his buddies set out to walk up one of the streets of the port city. Meanwhile, on board the *New Jersey*, members of the duty gun gang for turret one were swabbing out the 16-inch gun barrels. The turret was trained so that it pointed straight down the street on which the sailors were walking. Jacobus learned that some members of the liberty party had put out the word in town that once in a while some of the guns got fired accidentally, no doubt leading to some feelings of discomfort on the part of French shopkeepers. Jacobus and his mates were more convivial toward their hosts. When they saw a crowd of Frenchmen repairing a stretch of pavement, the sailors invited them into a tavern for a beer, and another, and another. "The road work never got done until the next day," says Jacobus.

From Cherbourg, the *New Jersey* went on to Lisbon, Portugal, staying from 11 until 15 August. There were the usual honors and ceremonies involving the admiral and captain. Lieutenant Poe of Admiral Thurber's staff was particularly impressed by the work done by Commander Eugene Fluckey to prepare for the visit. Fluckey was a World War II Medal of Honor winner as a submarine skipper. By 1952, he was U.S. naval attaché in Portugal, and he pitched in with enthusiasm and thoroughness in setting up parties and other events for the benefit of the midshipmen and the ship's crew. There were more tours through American Express, and the people from the battleship also had a chance to go to Lisbon's Campo Pequeno Arena for a special bull fight, set up in honor of Admiral Thurber. He was the guest of honor in a box seat and was rendered frequent obeisance by the Portuguese. Lieu-

**Below:** The British passenger liner *Queen Mary* arrives at Cherbourg, France, on 4 August 1952 and prepares to moor astern of the *New Jersey*. (Courtesy Mrs. Richard Donovan)

tenant Poe considered the Portuguese bullfights considerably more civilized than those he had heard about elsewhere, because there were heavy leather covers on the horns, and the matadors didn't kill the bulls. Says Poe: "All the pageantry is there and the spectacle and so forth, but the bloodshed is eliminated."

After five days in Portugal, it was on to Guantanamo again. There were the inevitable post-liberty disciplinary cases to be dealt with. On some occasions at captain's mast, the skipper sent men to Ship's Serviceman First Class Mike Danese for chastening in the *New Jersey*'s laundry. Danese was a giant of a man, about as tall as McCorkle and a good deal broader amidships. With a cigar in his mouth and tattoos on his forearms, he was not the sort whom a young enlisted man could take lightly. Laundry temperatures as high as 120° were such that men often had to work in their skivvies. Add to that the chore of washing some 40,000 pounds of laundry each week in the summertime. Danese's twenty assistant laundrymen were probably so grateful to go on liberty when they got a chance that they didn't want to do anything amiss that would cause them to have extra duty in the battleship's sweatbox.

On the way home from Lisbon, the *New Jersey* ran into heavy seas. The weather got so bad, remembers Allan Frank, that, "There were lines going into the head to throw up. The stench of the head, plus the humidity and the heat below decks, was unbearable." There were lifelines through the mess decks to help men keep their balance, and there was water on the decks, sucked in through ventilators even when hatches were closed. One of the midshipmen told Frank he was going to get out of the Navy as soon as he could get back to his university's NROTC unit to resign.

Once the seas had calmed somewhat, Midshipman Roger Taylor gloried in the weather. He took pleasure in going up on the slender "long snout" of a bow as the ship plunged into head seas. There, looking out at the turbulent water and then back at the main part of the ship, he had a feeling almost as if he were on the long bowsprit of an old sailing vessel. Although there was a certain sense of vulnerability, he recalls, "you felt that the vessel following you was a huge juggernaut that the sea couldn't hurt".

While in Guantanamo for the second time in a few months, the *New Jersey* carried out more training maneuvers. For instance, Admiral Thurber directed

**Right:** Ship's servicemen strikers John Nelencamp, left, and Charles Manley contend with mountains of clothes in the *New Jersey*'s laundry in January 1952. (National Archives: 80-G-437215)

McCorkle to make a tug of the *New Jersey* and conduct a drill at towing a destroyer-type vessel. The skipper wasn't keen about the maneuver, which was unusual for a battleship, but the *New Jersey* carried it off without difficulty.

Before her return to Norfolk, the *New Jersey* took aboard Captain Warner Edsall. He was destined to command the *Missouri*, but she was undergoing overhaul at the Norfolk Naval Shipyard, and he wanted to spend some time getting the feel of a ship of the class before he took over his own. In the process of spending time on the 04 level bridge, Captain Edsall discovered that it was different from that on the *Missouri*, and he preferred the *New Jersey*'s setup. McCorkle explained to the visitor that the 04 level had been altered during the overhaul earlier in the year, and he summoned Lieutenant Commander Wilhite to provide a thorough tour. The navigator showed Edsall around, and then the visitor said, "There's one place on this level that you haven't shown me, and that's your sea cabin. Do you mind if I see that?"

"Not at all," answered Wilhite, who forgot for the moment that he had given Quartermaster P. H. Stevens permission to use the cabin as a drying room for some of his oil paintings. So Wilhite unlocked the door, reached in to flip on the light, and then stood aside so that Captain Edsall could go in. Wilhite himself stood outside to wait. When Edsall came back out, he had a glazed look in his eyes. So, as Wilhite puts it, "I looked in real quick to see what the hell had surprised him so much, and every wall was a nude on black velvet. He probably thought I was a sex maniac of some kind. But they were all in there drying. [Stevens] had gone into a nudes-on-black velvet phase."

After arriving in Norfolk on 4 September, the day Captain Edsall took command of the *Missouri*, the *New Jersey* had a brief stand-down period to give the married men some time with their families. She spent the latter part of September and much of October at sea in training exercises, largely in the lower Chesapeake Bay and in the Virginia Capes operating area of the Atlantic. From 21 September to 4 October, the *New Jersey* played the role of training ship for a group of Naval Reservists, eighteen officers and ninety-one enlisted men, from five different naval districts. The men ranged from chief petty officers, with World War II experience, to some young men who had never been on active duty.

Much of the training conducted by the *New Jersey* that autumn involved running through various competitive exercises and drills prescribed by the Navy for determining relative rankings among ships in the category of battle readiness. The *New Jersey* was competing with the other ships in the Atlantic Fleet Cruiser Force for the sought-after Battle Efficiency E, which is awarded annually to the ship considered to have the highest proficiency overall in preparation for battle.

Some of the mid-October training was for the benefit of Captain Charles L. Melson, who reported aboard to relieve

Captain McCorkle as commanding officer. McCorkle let his successor take the conn to become familiar with the ship. And when she was going in and out of port, several other officers, including operations officer James Darroch and navigator Ray Wilhite, handled the ship so Melson would be reassured that he had capable subordinates to help him. Even so, the new captain faced a psychological hurdle once he relieved McCorkle on 20 October and had the responsibility on his own shoulders.

On 8 November, Rear Admiral Clark Green relieved Admiral Thurber on board the *New Jersey*, and that same day the ship got under way the first time under Captain Melson's command. Years later, in recording his oral history with the U.S. Naval Institute, Melson said:

"The first time we got under way, everything went along nicely. We started down the channel. The only trouble was the channel didn't seem to be wide enough. It looked to me like we were wider than the channel. These were all first impressions. We went to sea and operated for about a week, came back in, and again that channel didn't look big enough, particularly when something else was coming down the channel, coming out when you were headed in. . . . Actually, I guess all these impressions were exaggerated, because it was my first time that it was my sole responsibility. I'd seen the same thing happen under McCorkle, but it didn't impress me the way it did when I was the one that had to give the orders."

Elsewhere in his oral history, Melson said that he never

did develop a great deal of confidence during his tenure as skipper. He had a tough act to follow in the area of ship-handling, and he got the job done, though not with the same flourish.

In November, while operating in rough weather off the Virginia Capes, Captain Melson was impressed by the *New Jersey*'s ability to plow through the water "as steady as she could be". He was particularly struck by the action of the narrow bow, because it sometimes quivered back and forth as a result of wave action and the flexing of expansion joints. Melson later said, "I used to stand there and watch this bow shake like that and wonder if it was going to stay on. But it did through a lot of rough weather with no problem."

On one of the dreary weather occasions, the *New Jersey* was in company with the USS *Coral Sea*, which had Rear Admiral Charles "Cat" Brown embarked as carrier division commander. Fog set in while the carrier's air group was in the air, so then the task group began steaming around at high speed in search of a patch of clear weather through which the planes could descend to be brought back aboard. The task group went into relatively shallow water so that the combination of shallowness and speed sucked the *New Jersey*'s stern downward. At one point, observed Melson, "the geyser at the stern was higher than my bridge". The planes were recovered, and the incident ended.

Much of December was spent at anchor in Hampton Roads after the operations ended, and then the *New Jersey*

arrived at the naval operating base at Norfolk for the holiday season. An impressive array of Christmas lights was strung on the battleship, including having each of the big guns outlined with lights. A Christmas tree was placed on top of turret two and a lighted cross in the superstructure. Santa Claus came aboard and was greeted at the quarterdeck by the in-port officer of the deck, Lieutenant (junior grade) Ben Conroy. When the ship's next cruise-book came out the following year, the red-suited visitor was listed as Jose Santa Claus because of Conroy's practice of inserting the name Jose Iturbi into movie cast lists.

In this case, Santa Claus was portrayed by one of the ship's warrant officers, Chief Machinist Pervy F. Parrish. He was the hit of a party staged in the after mess deck on Christmas Eve for the benefit of some seventy children of *New Jersey* crew members. The event got under way with cartoon movies for the children, and then Parrish arrived to have the kids sit on his lap. First the youngsters received stockings filled with candy and nuts, then came the big presents, which were paid for by the ship's welfare and recreation fund. For the boys there were games, trucks, tractors, and fire engines. The girls got dolls, dollhouses, and other toys and games. Then came ice cream and brownies to round out the celebration.

As the evening moved on, Lieutenant Robert Bonner, newly reported as the Protestant chaplain, served a candlelight communion service in the mess deck. Less than an hour later, the same mess deck – decorated with candles, ferns, and poinsettias – became the site of Father

**Below left:** The *New Jersey*'s bow plunges into heavy seas while in the Virginia Capes operating area in late November 1952. The ship experienced winds up to 53 knots and 10-foot swells as the result of an extra-tropical cyclone. (Courtesy Captain Clyde B. Anderson)

**Below:** The ship is decorated with lights while at Norfolk's pier seven during the Christmas season in 1952. Notice the lighted cross above the *New Jersey*'s bridge. (Courtesy Captain William M. Braybrook)

Peter Brewerton's midnight mass. On the holiday itself came the *New Jersey*'s Christmas dinner, at which the 1,100 persons present, including crew members, families, and guests, ate eighty turkeys and 800 pounds of ham. Jose Santa Claus was a most welcome visitor to the battleship in December 1952.

As the New Year of 1953 got under way, Captain Melson settled in as skipper. He was widely viewed by those who served under him in the *New Jersey* as a very friendly man. He was smoother and less flamboyant than McCorkle. Both men impressed their subordinates as fatherly types to be liked and trusted, but the men still couldn't get too close to the new captain. To Fireman Jacob Brown of the interior communication shop, Melson was "somebody you felt like you could turn to for counsel rather than a game of cards". On one occasion, Brown had to repair the telephone in Melson's sea cabin. It was right next to the skipper's bunk so that officers of the deck could reach him easily. Brown thought the most convenient way to fix the phone was to lie in the bunk, and he soon got so comfortable that he fell asleep. The next thing he was aware of was Captain Melson shaking him by the shoulder and asking, "Are you done with the repair, son?" Brown was finished and soon on his way out, but the captain wasn't reproachful. In fact, Brown thought the skipper seemed amused by the whole thing.

Commander Joachim took a sterner tone with a sailor when he concluded that the quality of the ship's bugling wasn't up to snuff. Navigator Ray Wilhite had tried the quartermaster at several tasks, and the young man wasn't successful at any of them, so bugling was still another attempt to find a niche for him. Joachim told the quartermaster that playing the bugle wasn't his calling either, whereupon the quartermaster retorted, "Commander, what do you expect for $95.00 a month – Harry James?"

In mid-January, during a training period off Cuba, the *New Jersey* was put through an operational readiness inspection by Admiral Green, Commander Battleship Division Two. Previously, Admiral Thurber had been unsuccessful in attempts to have the division commander and his staff serve in the combat area. Instead, the job remained that of working on the East Coast to prepare the battleships for what they would encounter overseas. Green's operational readiness inspection (ORI) was, in effect, grading the crew on how well it had learned the lessons imparted during several trips to Guantanamo Bay over the preceding months.

Commander Bill Braybrook, the gunnery officer, was especially eager to show off the results of the thorough job of realigning the gun batteries the previous summer. Braybrook remembers that the ship had saved eighteen target projectiles for the 16-inch guns and built the ORI salvo plan around those eighteen projectiles. The ship fired six salvos of three guns apiece, using one gun from each turret per salvo. Shooting at a towed target sled, the

*New Jersey* scored eighteen hits, and the 5-inch guns performed beautifully as well.

It was useful to have such tests before sending the ship back to the combat zone because of the high turnover of personnel since the last time she had been to Korea. For men such as Seaman Apprentice Roland Blanchette, new to the ship in November 1952, the repeated training periods were essential as a means of working into the crew and providing practice at his battle station. In fact, he rotated among several stations in a 5-inch mount, including serving as hot shellman and pointer. The hot shellman stood behind the breeches of the mount's two barrels, and he wore a pair of long asbestos gloves. In most cases, the hot brass shell casings were ejected automatically from the mount when the guns fired. However, when the barrels were at high elevations for shooting at aircraft or sleeves, the hot shellman had to reach in, pull out the hot shell case, and toss it out through a scuttle at the rear of the mount. Later, Blanchette got to be the pointer who sat on the left side of the mount and wore a pair of earphones so that he could get directions on the elevation of the barrels for a particular target. He used his handwheels for changing the elevation only when the mount was in local control. When it was in automatic control by a director, the guns matched up by remote control with targets picked up by fire control radar.

The *New Jersey* reached the Norfolk Naval Shipyard on 26 January and remained there for about a month. On 24 February, Admiral Green transferred his flag to the *Iowa*, and the next day the *New Jersey* moved to an anchorage in Hampton Roads to load ammunition. The time in the Norfolk area before heading overseas provided a study in contrasts as far as liberty activity was concerned. Seaman Apprentice Blanchette had saved a couple of hundred dollars to buy a 1950 model Ford. As a result of having wheels and being able to stay with a Norfolk family when he was off duty, there were some of the advantages of home. Seaman Apprentice Don Hood, fresh out of a training period at Bainbridge, Maryland, resembled many of his shipmates in frequenting the establishments on East Main Street, explaining, "The sailors were lonely and away from home, so they'd go to a bar and get drunk." Ensign Rodion Cantacuzene, the assistant navigator, concluded that many of the people who ran downtown businesses that catered to Navymen were parasites. Sailors hocked watches and other items to get money, and it was soon gone. Merchants sold a variety of wares, especially jewelry, that put sailors into debt. If a man missed an installment payment, the merchant repossessed the item and started the process again with someone else.

When he was on board ship instead of ashore, Seaman Apprentice Hood was attached to the *New Jersey*'s "dog" division, "dog" being the word for the letter D in the phonetic alphabet then in use. Essentially, the men in that division were the ship's sidecleaners, responsible for cleaning and painting the hull from main deck to water-line. Usually they worked from a scaffold hung over the side of the ship, sometimes from floats alongside, and occasionally from boatswain's chairs. Because of the way the ship's side curves inward at the bow, the scaffold work got a bit tricky. First the men went over the side, then pulled themselves in and used pieces of line to tie the scaffold to padeyes welded to the side of the ship. Thus held in place, they did their painting. Paint rollers were not yet in common use at that point, so Hood and his fellow side-cleaners had to apply the haze grey paint with thousands of strokes of 4-inch-wide paintbrushes. During that period in early 1953, the sidecleaners painted the ship's hull number 62 on both bow and stern with much larger numerals than used previously. The Navy as a whole was changing to large white numerals shaded in black, so the *New Jersey* followed suit.

The period in Norfolk was broken up by an enjoyable ship's party. Half the crew went on 20 February and the other half the following night. Beforehand a crew's com-

Below: Sidecleaners are supported by a stage suspended over the side as they brush a new coat of haze grey paint onto the hull. (Courtesy BM2 Charles Jacobus)

mittee investigated no fewer than fourteen possible locations before settling upon the spacious Norfolk Municipal Auditorium. The most important considerations were capacity, ability to serve beer and liquor, and willingness to accommodate the entire crew – both black and white. Entertainment was provided by bandleader and saxophonist Tex Beneke's group. The party was quite successful, and even Commander Joachim got into the swing of the thing, taking over the string bass for a while and playing with Beneke's group.

Not nearly so pleasant as the party was the last hurdle to be cleared before deployment, an administrative inspection conducted on 3 March. Admiral Green led the inspection party, which was composed largely of officers and men from the *Iowa* rather than members of Green's staff. The *Iowa*'s department heads inspected their counterparts in the *New Jersey* to make sure their paperwork and administrative practices were up to snuff. Admiral Green's party toured the living spaces, galley, bake shop, wardroom, and various ship's service facilities. Green took a flashlight and white cloth on his tour, checking to see that messing facilities were clean and sanitary. In the wardroom, for instance, he had a white-jacketed steward roll back the green baize tablecloth and pull out leaves from an officers' mess table to make sure all was in order. The *New Jersey* passed her inspection easily, and the admiral gave her an upcheck to proceed to Korea.

Once wives, sweethearts, and other interested parties had been kissed good-bye, the *New Jersey* got under way from Norfolk at 10:19 a.m. on Thursday, 5 March. She spent nearly all that month under way without escort, going through the Panama Canal on 9 March, stopping from the 17th until the 19th at Long Beach, California, and then heading for Pearl Harbor. The visit in Hawaii was only two days, because the *New Jersey* had business to attend to in the Far East. The stop was long enough for Fireman Jacob Brown of the IC gang to make his first attempt at riding a surfboard; it was a disaster. In addition to picking up a ferocious sunburn after spending weeks down inside the ship, Brown found that the tide was for a while carrying his surfboard out to sea faster than he could paddle back in. He was exhausted by the time he got back to the beach.

The Hawaii stop gave Captain Melson a pleasant opportunity to attend a reception given by Admiral Arthur Radford, Commander in Chief Pacific. Melson also spent time with staff officers in Radford's operations section so that he could be briefed on what was happening in Korea. On 26 March, the *New Jersey* departed from Pearl Harbor with Captain Melson at the conn. After the ship passed the sea buoy, which marked the end of the channel out of the harbor, Commander Joachim came to the bridge to show Melson a radio message which had arrived just before the ship got under way. It reported that Captain Warner Edsall, a Naval Academy classmate of Melson's back in 1927, had just dropped dead on the bridge of the *Missouri*

while conning her out of Sasebo, Japan. He suffered a heart attack and died instantly. The executive officer held up the message, because he didn't want Melson to have to think about his friend's untimely death while in the midst of maneuvering his own ship.

On 5 April, the *New Jersey* arrived in Yokosuka and was met by a U.S. Navy warrant officer who would serve as pilot to conn the battleship into the harbor and bring her along-side the *Missouri*. Quartermaster Second Class Roff Grimes, the sea detail helmsman, was at the wheel as the *New Jersey* followed the pilot's directions while putting her starboard side along the port side of the Seventh Fleet flagship. As he got in close, the pilot cut the *New Jersey*'s speed, and pusher boats gradually eased her over next to the *Missouri*. Then lines went over, and the *Missouri* used her winches to reel in the dreadnought to port. "It's easy to tie up alongside somebody who's tied to a dock," explains Grimes, "but when you've got somebody anchored and your movement moves them, it's a little bit more difficult."

On 6 April, the Seventh Fleet Commander, Vice Admiral Joseph J. "Jocko" Clark, shifted his flag to the *New Jersey* to continue the fleet's direction in the effort against Korea. Clark was aggressive, eager, and ready to take matters into his own hands if he wasn't satisfied with the way things were going. In his oral history, Melson said, "I'd heard many stories about Jocko Clark. Some of them made me wonder what kind of life I'd live as flag captain, but I say here and now I never dealt with a more pleasant indi-vidual. The whole time he was on board the *New Jersey*, he never once corrected me or told me how to do anything.

He said, 'Do this or do that,' and that was it. I saw a lot of him, and I found him a very interesting individual and a very competent officer."

Within a few days, the new fleet flagship was off to Sasebo and soon after that joined up with Task Force 77. For the small percentage of *New Jersey* men who had been on board in 1951, there was considerable similarity in the pattern of operations – steaming with the carriers and bombarding the shore.

At 5:15 on the morning of 13 April, the *New Jersey* went to general quarters, and at 6:24 her main battery started pumping out shells at targets in the Chongjin area. She steamed on courses parallel to the coast, usually staying 11 to 13 miles offshore in order to avoid mined areas. One floating mine was spotted close to the battleship's port side, so the destroyer *Laws* was summoned to sink it with rifle fire. Aircraft from Task Force 77 provided spotting services for the *New Jersey*, and other planes from the carriers alternated their air strikes with the battleship's bombardment in a coordinated attack. Among the targets for the first main battery mission were a telephone head-quarters building, a suspected enemy telephone exchange, a weather station, and a warehouse. That day, the *New Jersey* fired 104 rounds of 16-inch high capacity ammuni-tion, all with full powder charges.

As the deployment proceeded and the ship got more comfortable with steaming closer to the shore, many of the missions were fired with reduced powder charges because they produced less wear on the gun barrel liners. On occasion, that would prove to be a problem. Lieutenant Stu Sadler, the fire control officer, was surprised once when the aerial spotter didn't see the fall of shot at all. Sadler then discovered that the man operating the Mark 8 range-keeper in the plotting room had set the equipment for reduced charges and thus had the barrels at near maximum elevation for a target about 12–14 miles inland, which was about as far as the reduced charges could propel a projectile. Unfortunately, the turret loaded full service charges, sending the 16-inch projeciles much farther inland than the spotter was prepared for.

Other problems could happen near those 16-inch powder bags, as Seaman Apprentice Don Hood learned in one of the magazines. Safety rules dictated that men had to take off their shoes and rings and belts and anything else that might cause a spark. Hood vividly remembers the day when ". . . we were all sitting around there, and it was hot. Nobody's talking. This one sailor pulled out a cigarette lighter, and he was playing with it, clicking the top back and forth, back and forth. Nobody really sensed what he was doing at first, and then, when it hit everybody, we liked to kill him. If he'd struck that cigarette lighter, we'd all been gone." Perhaps the fellow's judgment was numbed by the effects of the ether used as a preservative inside the large aluminium powder storage cans. Even so, he never should have had the lighter in a magazine at all.

**Below:** Newly arrived in the war zone, the *New Jersey* transfers outgoing mail to the destroyer *Trathen* on 17 April 1953. One member of the destroyer's crew at the time was Chief Machinist's Mate Jackson K. Parker, who is still on active duty after more than 44 years of naval service. (National Archives: 80-G-484374)

**Right:** *New Jersey* signalmen communicate with another ship by flashing light on 18 April 1953. At right, an officer uses "big eyes" binoculars. (Photo by R. C. Timm, National Archives: 80-G-K-16323)

**Far right:** Empty brass powder cases litter the deck after firing by the ship's 5-inch mounts in the spring of 1953. (National Archives: 80-G-K-16303)

**Opposite page, bottom left:** This remarkable photo displays both the advantages and disadvantages of the *New Jersey*'s living compartments. There is a good deal of camaraderie but also an obvious lack of privacy. (National Archives: 80-G-K-16306)

**Opposite page, bottom right:** Three crew members stand watch in an engine room, operating the throttle and relaying orders by sound-powered phones to the other engine rooms. Left to right: Fireman John M. Hernandez, Machinist's Mate Fireman James Cronin, and Machinist's Mate Fireman Robert E. Plank. (Photo by R. C. Timm, National Archives: 80-G-K-16325)

Despite the occasional foulup, the *New Jersey* was again doing some spectacular shooting, as she had in 1951. On 15 April, the target was in the Kojo area. Two days later, it was in the area between Hungnam and Songjin. On 20 April, it was back to potent Wonsan, which still had an inexorable attraction for U.S. warships. True to form, there was a VIP on board in the person of John Floberg, Assistant Secretary of the Navy for Air.

Ensign Rodion Cantacuzene, the assistant navigator, was on the secondary conning station with the executive officer and two bearing takers – a team prepared to take over if the bridge personnel were disabled. The young officer, who hadn't even bothered to strap on his helmet or tie up his life jacket, noticed that Quartermaster First Class Sam Delvecchio, one of the bearing takers, had a dogging wrench in his pocket. "What's that for?" asked the ensign.

"Just in case somebody gets excited," Delvecchio told him. Cantacuzene was still calm at that point, gazing over at the enemy coast of Korea through his binoculars. The next thing he knew, a shell whizzed overhead, making a sound like that of a truck. Cantacuzene heard a lot of movement down below on the bridge. Soon Lieutenant Commander Wilhite, who was navigating on the 04 level, noticed that no one was standing up except himself and Quartermaster Grimes, the helmsman. Captain Melson was in the pilothouse, cautiously giving steering orders and standing up from time to time to look through the narrow viewing slits. Shells were soon falling on both sides of the *New Jersey*, and when Cantacuzene had a chance to take stock at one point, he discovered that he had strapped on his protective gear without being conscious he had done so. Seaman Roland Blanchette was a hot shellman in a 5-inch mount on the starboard side. His mount captain, Gunner's Mate Third Class D. E. Klotz, had a hooded opening at the top of the mount so he could see outside. He invited Blanchette up for a look. The seaman saw splashes in the water and asked, "What the hell is that?" When Klotz told him they were enemy projectiles walking their way toward the *New Jersey* Blanchette ducked back down into the mount and concluded that being shot at wasn't so comfortable as being on the delivering end.

The enemy fire came to an end after about twenty-five rounds, the closest of which landed about 10 yards off the port side. A souvenir-hunting Marine hopped down from a 5-inch gun mount during the action and ended up with burned finger from touching a hot shell fragment. He applied for a Purple Heart but instead got a reprimand for leaving his post. Secretary Floberg, who had observed the action from the 05 level above the bridge, appeared to Captain Melson to have got a kick out of the whole experience.

During April, the *New Jersey* went briefly to the South Korean port of Pusan and the crew manned the rail when President and Mrs. Syngman Rhee came aboard for a visit. It was one of several times the flagship paid that honor to the President of the Republic of Korea. May was spent much as April had been, with more and more shore bombardment. By 1953, the likelihood of air attacks on the carriers was deemed much less than it had been in 1951, so the *New Jersey* spent most of her time firing at Korea's east coast. This was especially the case after the Communists launched a vigorous offensive in mid-May in an attempt to strengthen their bargaining position during armistice negotiations. In late May, the *New Jersey* went around into the Yellow Sea off Korea's west coast. On 25 May, she bombarded targets near Chinnampo, within range of Communist MiGs based in Manchuria, but she was not attacked. Her firing concentrated on enemy gun emplacements in caves on Amgok Peninsula. The *New Jersey* operated in concert with the U.S. destroyer *Chauncey* and two British ships, the heavy cruiser *Newcastle* and the aircraft carrier *Ocean*. Aerial spotters reported the results of the *New Jersey*'s bombardment as "good to excellent" and a news service reported the bombardment being temporarily interrupted by etiquette. According to the Associated Press, the *New Jersey* was firing away when the two British ships passed near her. She suspended bombardment long enough to render the customary whistles and salutes, "and then, etiquette taken care of, let fly again at the Reds".

Along with the gunnery missions, the *New Jersey* continued to be, as she had been in 1951, a gigantic admiral's barge for the Seventh Fleet Commander. There was a small airfield ashore designated K-18, and it was frequently the *New Jersey*'s lot to crank on the steam and get into a position from which Clark could take a helicopter ashore in order to confer with Army and Air Force commanders. Ensign Cantacuzene thought it would be preferable to have a destroyer deliver the admiral and to leave the *New Jersey*'s bombardment uninterrupted. As he bent over a chart one day on the way to K-18, the assistant navigator said to Chief Quartermaster W. M. Brown, "I wonder who the goddamn fool was that thought this up."

Cantacuzene then heard a good deal of scurrying and breath being sucked in, and he heard a voice saying, "I was." He turned slightly, peered under his arm, and all he could see was a blue uniform with one broad gold stripe and two narrow stripes on top. It was Admiral Clark, who continued, "Young man, why am I goddamn fool?" Cantacuzene proceeded to put forth his theories about the lower fuel consumption rate of a destroyer and the battleship's usefulness in responding to call fire missions on the bombline. Clark then explained the reason for taking the *New Jersey* and added, "Son, do your course and keep your nose clean. And if you get promoted to vice admiral, you can do it your way. But in the meantime, we're going to do it my way." (The admiral's way meant less time away from the action for him.)

**Above:** The crew mans the rail to honor a visit on 14 April 1953 at Pusan, South Korea, by President and Mrs. Syngman Rhee of the Republic of Korea. (Photo by R. C. Timm, National Archives: 80-G-K-16319)

**Top right:** During his 14 April visit to the Seventh Fleet flagship, President Rhee is flanked by the *New Jersey*'s skipper, Captain Charles Melson, left, and the fleet commander, Vice Admiral Jocko Clark. (Courtesy John S. Hastings)

**Center right:** In this May 1953 photo, radiomen listen to Morse Code on headphones and turn it into messages with the typewriters in front of them. (National Archives: 80-G-K-16289)

**Bottom right:** *New Jersey* chief petty officers engage in favorite Navy pastimes, drinking coffee and playing acey-deucy. (National Archives: 80-G-K-16287)

Cantacuzene answered with a meek "Yes, sir," and Clark walked out of the charthouse. Just as he was leaving, Captain Melson was coming in, so Clark said, "Charlie, I haven't been called a goddamn fool in fifteen years." The assistant navigator noticed a very shocked look on his captain's face at that moment.

In the midst of the high-level maneuverings, the enlisted men of the *New Jersey* were following off-duty routines which often had to do with food. Fireman Allan Frank was once in a working party when his fireroom crew was called upon to help break out provisions from a storeroom. As was so often the case, some of it never made its way to the galley. The boilermen and machinist's mates had discovered that the void spaces above the boilers were crosshatched with a checkerboard pattern of metal slats. These were ideal for storing canned goods and other nonperishable items. If things got hungry on a watch, the men broke out their information sheet to see that such and such an item was so many spaces over and so many back.

Seaman Roland Blanchette had grown uncomfortable in the confined spaces of a 5-inch mount, so he requested transfer to the S-1 division, where he served first as a butcher and then as a baker. The bakers were popular throughout the ship and could trade their wares for head-of-the-line privileges at the ship's store, free ice cream concoctions at the gedunk, and other things. And they freely gave away their pastries and bread. At one point, however, the chief commissaryman decided that too much of a sweet tooth wasn't a good thing for the men of the *New Jersey*, and so he decided to eliminate their between-meals snacking. The cutoff produced a good deal of unhappiness in the crew, and so it was up to the E division to rectify matters. The electrician's mates suddenly concluded that it was just the right time of year for the annual inspection of the bakeshop fans, so they were all removed. Naturally, a bakeshop without fans can get uncomfortably warm. Within a day or two, the chief commissaryman surrendered, and the flow of pastries resumed.

In the middle of May, more than 250 *New Jersey* crew members went ashore for a three-day rest and recreation period at Japanese hotels in the Yokosuka area. The highlights were top-quality food, the chance to sleep in real beds instead of crowded berthing compartments, freedom from the demanding shipboard routine, and a variety of forms of recreation. The hotels, which were run by U.S. armed forces special services, offered such things as boating, sailing, fishing, golf, horseback riding, and sightseeing. In addition, each hotel had nightly dances for the men. Some men were granted even longer R&R periods. Fireman Jacob Brown, for instance was gone long enough to get away from the Yokosuka area, traveling to Beppu,

where he saw a large statue of Buddha. At that point, only eight years after the end of World War II, Brown observed that Americans were well received in the land they had conquered.

The tenth anniversary of the ship's commissioning was observed on 23 May 1953, when Captain Melson pulled out his sword and cut a birthday cake. Ten days later, on 2 June, there was a celebration of a different sort when the *New Jersey* was at Sasebo, along with a British carrier, HMS *Ocean*. It was the coronation day in London for Queen Elizabeth II, and her subjects around the world wanted to honor her. A few of the *New Jersey's* men ashore on liberty that day took exception to the laudatory remarks, and the inevitable row ensued. A number of the *New Jersey's* officers were invited to festivities on board the *Ocean*.

Cantacuzene observed afterward, "I have never had such a serious bout of drinking in my life. I prided myself on being a Seventh Fleet sailor, but I'd never seen anything like that in my life. We ended up playing leapfrog, and that was pretty rugged, because you were leaping over people and heading toward a steel bulkhead to see who got there first. I didn't win. I didn't even try to win, because I wasn't about to bang my head. But the Brits did, with gay abandon. We all came back feeling miserable, but I felt we had a great deal to do with Her Majesty being coronated properly."

In mid-June, back in Korean operations, the *New Jersey*, heavy cruiser *St. Paul*, and the aircraft carriers worked together to support U.N. efforts to recapture the Anchor Hill area which had been taken by the enemy a month earlier. This followed a period of several days earlier in the month when the *New Jersey* had been frustrated in her efforts to provide shore bombardment because of poor visibility. Admiral Clark later recounted in his autobiography, *Carrier Admiral*, that he considered unobserved battleship gunfire to be essentially wasted, and so shooting was curtailed when it wasn't possible for spotters to get the shells on target.

Early on the morning of 16 June, Lieutenant Henry J. Airey, flying an F4U-5 Corsair night fighter from the USS *Philippine Sea*, was returning to his ship after a close-air-support mission ashore. His engine died, and his radio was already deceased as well, so he decided to land near friendly ships offshore to eliminate the need for a pre-arranged rendezvous. His Corsair's hydraulic system was in bad shape, and he couldn't get his flaps down, so he made a high-speed ditching near the *New Jersey*. Lieutenant (junior grade) W. H. Williamson was aloft almost instantly in the battleship's helicopter "Jersey Bounce". Along with his crewman, Airman J. L. Spahr, Williamson hoisted Lieutenant Airey into the hovering helicopter at 7:07 a.m. and carried him back to the waiting deck of the *New Jersey*.

As she had in 1951, the *New Jersey* again made Sasebo her most frequent logistic support base. One such replenishment took place on 21 June, when the ship made a dawn arrival. As she approached the Japanese port, Ensign Cantacuzene saw what he had come to expect – fishing boats from horizon to horizon. Initially the ship slowed down so she wouldn't swamp any of them, but then she maintained course and speed, because it was easier for the boats to get out of her way than vice versa. It even seemed to be a game as the boats zipped in close under the bow of the giant grey battleship, being lost from sight for a time to those on the bridge. Then they popped up again on the other side, hoping they had transferred any evil spirits that might have infested the boats onto the arriving behemoth.

Cantacuzene's boss, navigator Ray Wilhite, enjoyed the Sasebo stops as a rare interlude from the demanding periods off the bombline when he got little sleep because of the need to spend so much time on the navigation plot

when close to shore. Thus, most of his time at Sasebo was spent asleep. On 21 June, the *New Jersey* took on 650 tons of ammunition, 130 tons of fresh provisions, 83,000 gallons of fresh water, and thirty-three bags of mail. The ship's post office was at the same time sending out an estimated 100,000 letters and thirty-five bags of parcel post. Shortly before sunset, the *New Jersey* hoisted anchor and again stood out to sea, headed back to Korea.

When the members of the crew weren't busy writing all those letters, many of them took advantage of the hobby shop on the 02 level or worked on projects they'd picked up while in port in the Far East. Fireman W. T. Pritchard, for instance, built a gasoline-powered model airplane, while Electronics Technician W. R. Dunham preferred auto racers. Commander Ed Standish of the Seventh Fleet staff enjoyed building HO gauge model trains, and Radarman Third Class J. C. Dicken built an *Iowa*-class battleship of wood. Gunner's Mate J. A. Larson was one of many who worked on leather goods. Various types of leather, lacing, and tools were provided in the hobby shop. Commander Brick Ganyard, the engineer officer, liked to paint, but he wasn't in a class with Commander Joachim. The chief engineer went for paint-by-number pictures such as a depiction of Christ's last supper.

Another diversion during the war was the system of remote broadcast outlets in messing and berthing compartments throughout the ship. In those days before closed-circuit television, radio station WRNJ had three different channels that Jerseymen could choose from during the hours of station operation. Seaman Apprentice Danny White hosted a "hillbilly hour" which featured both records and his singing; Chief Boilerman D. E. Stuber had a sports show; and Seaman Apprentice Nait McIntire and Seaman Gene Muir played disc jockey and responded to crew requests. The armed forces radio network supplied tapes of popular music, hit radio programs of the time, and sports events. In some cases news and sports programs were beamed live into the ship's berthing compartments.

After a time, remembers navigator Ray Wilhite, Admiral Clark changed the method of operation for the ship around Wonsan, observing that the destroyers that went into the harbor didn't get fired at from ashore if the *New Jersey* was around to cover them. The enemy might shoot at the *New Jersey* if she was firing, but there was no fire from ashore if the battleship was present but not shooting. So the ship went to Wonsan more and more to keep the enemy quiet. Then Wilhite persuaded Captain Melson to have the *New Jersey* sit outside the harbor, because she could still strike back at the enemy, but her own vulnerability was reduced. As the navigator said to the captain, "If you're going to go in a room with a stick that's twice as long as the other guy's, you don't close to the length of his to make it a fair fight."

June and July were months during which the *New Jersey* fired more and more rounds at a variety of enemy

targets ashore, supporting friendly troops against the enemy, bombarding enemy facilities, and continuing to try to interdict the flow of supplies and transportation to those waging war against the United Nations forces. A comparison of the pace of the *New Jersey*'s two Korean deployments can be seen in the number of 16-inch projectiles fired. From May to November of 1951, the total got just slightly above 3,000 rounds in six months. In 1953, from mid-April to late July, only about three and a half months, the *New Jersey* put out just over 4,000 16-inch rounds. The shooting was especially hectic in late July, recalls fire control officer Stu Sadler; it was a deliberate attempt to put pressure on the negotiations at Panmunjom. Round after round was fired at certain targets until they were reduced to piles of molecules or became gaping holes in the ground.

The Seventh Fleet flagship made things lively right up to the end. Late on the night of 25 July, she sent an armed spotting crew ashore in a motor whaleboat. The boat pro-

ceeded to a point just offshore so that the men could be in position to detect an approaching train if one came. The idea was to hit the train while it was moving to see if the battleship could knock it off the track. No trains came along, so the boat returned to the ship at 1:22 a.m. and the battleship sent a few 16-inch calling cards ashore to blast a tunnel entrance and adjoining railroad track.

An hour after reveille that same morning, the *New Jersey* arrived off Wonsan and at 8:34 began blasting away at gun emplacements and bunkers. She ceased firing at 12:30 p.m. after putting out 191 rounds of 16-inch. That was the Korea swansong, for at Panmunjom the negotiators finally worked out their differences sufficiently to sign an armistice at 10:01 a.m. on 27 July with Admiral Clark present to witness the ceremony. The war was finally over after 37 months of fighting. The guns of the *New Jersey* had helped to hasten the process of transforming the Korean War from a news story to an entry in the history books still to be written.

# CHAPTER V
# THE IN-BETWEEN YEARS – PEACETIME AND LIBERTY PORTS
## July 1953 – August 1957

With the last stroke of a pen on the armistice documents at Panmunjom, the role of the *New Jersey* changed dramatically. The giant warship was no longer fighting a war – nor would she for another fifteen years. During the years in between wars, the large black and white hull number 62 on each side of her bow would be seen in many an overseas liberty port as the *New Jersey* carried out for her crew that favorite promise of Navy recruiters: "Join the Navy and see the world".

The ship's routine became different almost immediately, particularly for those who had been standing long, long hours of watch throughout the ship. A case in point was Lieutenant (junior grade) Bob Watts, an officer of the deck in regular rotation and also during general quarters and special sea detail. He recalls that he felt fatigued almost from the time the ship got to Korea and then "stayed bone-tired until the armistice". Photographer's Mate Third Class John Hastings was taken aback, as *New Jersey* men had been eight years earlier, by the experience of going topside at night. After months of operating darkened during wartime, the *New Jersey* and other vessels were all lit up. "It was a beautiful sight," says Hastings, "but one that took a while to get used to."

On 27 July 1953, the day of the armistice, the *New Jersey* was back with the carriers of Task Force 77. On the 28th,

she arrived at Sasebo, Japan, and her crew spent two days loading ammunition; the old habits were hard to break. The crew mustered aft on 1 August, when Vice Admiral Jocko Clark passed out decorations to 27 officers and enlisted men of the *New Jersey* and to 21 Seventh Fleet staff members. Captain Melson received a Legion of Merit.

From 20 to 27 August, the crew enjoyed a port visit in the picturesque British crown colony of Hong Kong. Because of her deep draft, the *New Jersey* anchored in outlying Junk Bay rather than in the inner harbor that is most often seen on postcards. As a result, the Seventh Fleet flagship became an object of scorn in local newspapers. Hong Kong residents wrote letters to the papers, indicating that their civic pride was wounded. They argued that the *New Jersey* ought to be ashamed for not coming in where she could be better seen.

If the ship wouldn't come to the people, they would go to the ship. Residents of Hong Kong were invited to visit on the afternoon of 26 August if they could provide their own transportation. Commander Bill Braybrook was command duty officer and had the dubious distinction of presiding over mass confusion. In the early afternoon, he recalls:

"The water was black with boats, hundreds of them! All in a race to be first alongside. You've never seen a 'horde' until you've seen a bunch of Chinamen! The boats came crashing toward us. When the first few got alongside, the others merely jammed into them and the people started walking toward the accommodation ladder from boat to boat. Soon there were literally hundreds of them jammed together. . . . In a short time there was a steady stream of Chinamen – including women and children – streaking up the ladder. . . . It took 20 minutes to get 4,000 Chinese on board and three hours to get them off."

While hundreds of sampans were milling around next to the armored sides of the grey giant, a large junk came charging into their midst under full sail – scattering the sampans like matchsticks. One boat overturned near the ship's accommodation ladder. Private First Class Stephen Peliotes and Seaman Ronald Donne dived into the water and rescued the boat's occupants, including a small baby. They began administering artificial respiration to the infant until the arrival of Lieutenant (junior grade) William D. Hoskin, one of the ship's doctors. All the people who had been in the water made a full recovery.

Below: At Sasebo, Japan, on 1 August 1953 the crew musters for presentation of awards by Vice Admiral Jocko Clark, Commander Seventh Fleet. At left is the ship's HO3S helicopter, nicknamed "Jersey Bounce." (Courtesy *All Hands* magazine)

Meanwhile, chaos had taken firm hold topside. Fortunately, some English-speaking visitors were located to serve as interpreters in an effort to keep the situation at least somewhat under control. Lieutenant Stu Sadler, the fire control officer, was unlucky enough to have the duty that day, and his biggest problem was still ahead. This was the matter of getting the visitors off the ship. The Chinese were determined to leave in the same boats in which they came. It had been a free-for-all as people stampeded aboard in the first place, but they weren't about to stampede off. Sadler had the complicated task of rounding up the right set of people at the top of the accommodation ladder and the right boat at the bottom. The problem finally eased as both the number of people on the ship and the number of waiting boats grew smaller and smaller. The duty section was vastly relieved when the whole thing was over.

Much more pleasant were the experiences of the crew members who went ashore to take tours of such exotic sites as Tiger Balm Gardens and to avail themselves of the vast array of merchandise for sale. Some merchants even came aboard and set up shop on the fantail. To Seaman William Hunt, a radioman striker, it looked like a "farmers' market" with all sorts of trinkets and wearing apparel on sale. Yeoman Third Class Jack Cruppenink bought a powder blue cashmere sport jacket and grey gabardine

trousers at a tailor shop ashore. First he and his buddies got measured, then drank beer furnished by the tailor so they could pass the time while waiting for their outfits to be done.

Some men, of course, headed off for the drinking and wenching that they could have found anywhere, but others took time to appreciate their surroundings. Fireman Jacob Brown was struck by the diversity of cultures. Hong Kong was one of the fabled outposts of the vast British Empire, which in those years still held considerable sway. In contrast were the Chinese of many different social strata. Fireman Allan Frank of B division observed the gulf between squalor and luxury. Years later, he reflected, "I guess when you're a young kid, the splendor and the glory are what stand out. As [I] got older, [I] realized that while I was having a good time . . . there were people probably starving over there that I never even thought about. I guess it's part of getting wise as you get older."

Next after Hong Kong was a trip to the island then popularly known as Formosa, now as Taiwan. An important part of the mission of the U.S. Seventh Fleet was to provide support for the island, so the *New Jersey* steamed there to spend some time off the coast on 28 August. Captain Melson was part of the welcoming committee for what he recalled in his oral history as "the midshipmen of the Nationalist Chinese Naval Academy and what must have been all the officers of their navy. I'd never seen so many. They came out in destroyers alongside and boarded. We made a short trip up and down the coast during the day and fired some guns for their benefit, and then sent them home."

After stops at Sasebo and Yokosuka, Japan, the fleet flagship went for a liberty call at Beppu on the island of Kyushu. On 15 September, the *New Jersey* arrived at Pusan, a port at the southeast corner of South Korea, for a ceremony which put the capstone on her contribution to the waging of the Korean War. On the following day, the crew of the Seventh Fleet flagship manned the rail – the third time they had done so during the 1953 deployment – in tribute to a visit from President and Mrs. Syngman Rhee of the Republic of Korea. Other dignitaries were on hand as well. The occasion was the presentation by Rhee of the Korean Presidential Unit Citation to the U.S. Seventh Fleet for the period from July 1950 to July 1953. Vice Admiral Clark, as fleet commander, accepted the award on behalf of the ships, aircraft, and men who comprised the fleet during that period.

A twenty-one-gun salute to South Korea was obligatory. Commander Bill Braybrook, the gunnery officer, had to keep his fingers crossed over the performance of the saluting guns, which dated from the Spanish-American War. There was a pair of guns on each side of the ship, mounted on the 01 level, just aft of the admiral's promenade deck. Navy tradition prescribes a five-second interval between shots of a gun salute. Because the guns were so

old and unreliable, the procedure called for three men on each gun – one to load, one to pull the firing lanyard, and one standing by with a rawhide maul to slug the breech wedge if necessary to make sure the shell seated properly and didn't misfire. To see that there would be no interruption, Chief Warrant Gunner Jesse Marcum stood near the saluting battery with a stopwatch. At the proper time, he pointed to the gun that was to fire, and the gun captain jerked the lanyard. If it didn't fire, Marcum pointed to the other gun and hoped it would shoot. In the meantime, the gunner's mate on the first gun was slugging the breech with the maul to see if he could get the shell seated sufficiently for the firing pin to be released by the next jerk of the lanyard. Once, Braybrook remembers, "During a 21-gun national salute, we fired 22 guns! I was standing on the 01 deck forward. I was counting. After the 22nd round went off, I looked casually toward the flag bridge [and] the navigation bridge to see who was sending for the gun boss. But nobody said a word. Only the gunner and I were counting."

The lack of reaction was probably symptomatic of something that Lieutenant Commander Ray Wilhite, the *New Jersey*'s navigator, noticed while serving as majordomo of honors and ceremonies. The ship had been doing so well for so long that excellence was taken for granted. She had had a great deal of practice in her role as fleet flagship, and Wilhite and the Marine detachment skipper, Captain Joe Odenthal, had the ability to adjust as necessary to just about anything as they coordinated sideboys, band music, announcements on the public address system, boatswain's pipes, and so forth. On the occasion of one visit by President Rhee there had been a plan for a complex sequence of people arriving by boat and helicopter, but the schedule got upset at the beginning. Admiral Clark's chief of staff reacted somewhat uneasily, so Wilhite reassured him by saying, "If we screw it up, we'll screw it up so magnificently that they'll think that's the way it's supposed to be done." That visit – like the one at which President Rhee presented the citation – went off with no problem.

The *New Jersey*'s gunnery in late July may have had a hand in the armistice, and when peace came it was time for competitive exercises once again. On 22 September, while operating out of Sasebo, Japan, the ship fired a gunnery exercise, both to shoot for score in the battle efficiency competition and to put on a show for a visiting combat camera team that was making a Navy film on the battleships of the *Iowa* class. The gunnery exercise was based on both speed and accuracy, and the ship's shooting was magnificent. Only turret one fired that day, because its repeated on-the-mark salvos demolished and sank the target sled before the other turrets got to shoot. The turret achieved that result while firing in local control with the aiming done by pointers and trainers rather than by the plotting room and its more sophisticated equipment. There were still more firing exercises on 1 October.

Above: Radarman Seaman E. E. Lockley operates a radar repeater in the combat information center, September 1953. (National Archives: 80-G-629466)

than 3,000 men on board for the homeward journey in 1953, and they had a chilly ride during that late October trip. In addition, it was rough because of heavy seas through which the ship passed. Relief came on the fourth day, off Wake Island.

Before the storm abated, Yeoman Third Class Jack Cruppenink had to go high in the ship to avoid being hit by flying water. When he looked out upon the angry seas, the escorting destroyers were going up and down so much that he thought of them as submarines – now you see them, now you don't. One member of his division didn't get out of his bunk for several days because the *New Jersey*'s rolling made him so nauseous. Cruppenink and other helpful shipmates brought food to their living compartment to keep the unhappy man going.

Fortunately, most *New Jersey* men didn't have such tender stomachs. They found the cruise a pleasant one, especially after the seas flattened, because they had been released from their wartime responsibilities. Lieutenant (junior grade) Bob Watts was no longer standing bridge watches day after day. With a new skipper about to take over and ready to set up his own rotation of officers of the deck, Watts was taken off the watch bill completely. That was both good and bad; the routine was so restful that it was boring. Fireman Jacob Brown didn't have such difficulties. He recalls that the trip homeward "was a very jubilant time for us. It was the least military of all the time that I was aboard. There were not as many drills as usual, and the atmosphere was more relaxed."

The 3,400-mile journey from Yokosuka ended when the *New Jersey* arrived at Pearl Harbor on Friday, 23 October. Fireman Charles Huntington of the A division was particularly struck by the moment when the majestic *New Jersey* steamed past the submerged hulk of the *Arizona*, which had been on the harbor bottom since the Japanese attack in December 1941. The *New Jersey*'s crew was called to attention by the bugler as their ship passed her long-gone predecessor.

The next day, 24 October, was Captain Melson's last in command of the *New Jersey*. The new skipper, Captain John C. Atkeson, embodied the qualities most valued in a destroyerman, especially during the Battle of the Komandorski Islands in the Aleutians in World War II. Then a lieutenant commander, Atkeson was in command of the destroyer *Bailey* and took her in to launch torpedoes against Japanese cruisers, even though they were hitting his ship with heavy projectiles. His courage earned Atkeson the Navy Cross.

The *New Jersey* was under way again on the morning of 26 October. She soon completed the main battery firing exercises that had been suspended off Sasebo the month before when turret one destroyed the target raft. This time, turret two ripped a target structure to shreds, but there was another available, and turret three was able to get its qualification shooting accomplished as well. Captain

With the winding down of the Far Eastern deployment, the weekly issues of *The Jerseyman* published maps of the Pacific which showed the progress of sister ship *Wisconsin* as she made her way westward to relieve the *New Jersey* at Yokosuka as fleet flagship. The newspaper's issue of 9 October carried a front-page cartoon which showed a grinning *New Jersey* alongside a scowling *Wisconsin*. The former was about to head home, while the latter's period in the Orient was just about to start.

The long-awaited day came on 13 October when the *Wisconsin* loomed out of the mist at Yokosuka and gingerly came alongside. Seaman Roland Blanchette and others in the *New Jersey* sought out crew members of the newly arrived battleship so they could swap their Japanese money for American greenbacks to be spent in Hawaii or back home. Others weren't so eager to go home. Fireman Jacob Brown was one of several who sought to swap duty with *Wisconsin* men. Brown wanted to stay in the Far East because he had found his rest and recreation periods in Japan so enjoyable. As it happened, he didn't get his request submitted soon enough. Once he got back to the United States, he decided he was just as glad he hadn't received what he asked for.

On 16 October, the *New Jersey* was freed from both the *Wisconsin* and from her mooring buoy, and began the eastward journey to Pearl Harbor. The ship was jammed with passengers. Just as she had been when returning to the West Coast from Japan in early 1946, she was again bringing home the boys after the conclusion of a war across the far Pacific. Including the crew, she had more

Atkeson also practiced during the trip. He hadn't served in battleships since he was a junior officer and so had the carpenter shop construct a large wooden raft to use as a reference point for maneuvering the ship in the open ocean in order to get an idea of her handling characteristics. After several hours of figuring out rudder and engine combinations and becoming comfortable with the *New Jersey*, Captain Atkeson let the secondary battery pepper away at the raft until it was demolished.

As Captain Atkeson was settling into his new duties, the ship had a relatively new executive officer as well. He was Commander Fred Chenault, whom one officer recalls as "a brilliant guy, really a sharp individual. . . . He knew everything that was going on on board ship. He ruled much like Captain Atkeson in that he would tell you what to do and expect you to do it and left you pretty much alone unless things got fouled up." The exec used psychology effectively. Lieutenant Commander Ray Wilhite, the navigator, observed that Chenault was a very intelligent officer who "hid behind the pose of a dumb country boy. . . . He would get the department heads in and make them think of what he wanted done in the first place. And since they thought of it themselves, they thought it was a great idea. When I accused him of it one time, he said, 'Don't tell them.'"

A junior officer also impressed by Commander Chenault was Ensign Rodion Cantacuzene, who was himself moving into a new job in the *New Jersey* with the arrival of peace. During the operations off Korea, Cantacuzene had served as assistant navigator under Wilhite. Now he was moving in to take over the third division and turret three because Bob Watts was due to leave shortly. One thing that Watts taught him was the value of crane room coffee in exercising leadership. The space below the fantail contained the machinery for operating the crane which was originally installed to recover floatplanes during World War II. The boatswain's mates of the third division gathered there each morning to drink coffee and plan their day. Says Watts, "You knew you were accepted by them when they invited you down to have coffee with them."

Cantacuzene carried on the tradition in third division. When the bugler blew reveille, the new division officer was up in short order to enjoy the fresh morning breeze. But more than that, he was topside to drink a cup of coffee with his leading boatswain's mate and to show his men that if they had to get up early, he would get up early as well. He showed his concern in other ways. When the Marine detachment held marching practice on the fantail and made black marks on the deck by grinding in the rubber heels of their boots, Cantacuzene got the Marines to help out with holystoning for a while so they could see how hard it was to clean the marks off. After that, the Marines were much more careful in their stepping.

Besides running the fantail, Cantacuzene had to learn his duties in connection with turret three. There he relied on Gunner's Mate First Class Bob Moore. The turret officially rated a chief petty officer, but the new division officer was in no sense disappointed, explaining that Moore was the "finest gunner's mate I've ever known, and I've known some neat ones". Cantacuzene did have to do some things himself. About once a quarter he got into the breech end of each gun of his turret and lay on a canvas sled with a piece of line attached. He was then pulled slowly through the length of each barrel so he could use a flashlight to inspect the lands and grooves of the rifling to check for cracks, erosion, and the buildup of copper from the base rings of the projectiles. In addition to pulling Cantacuzene's whole body on the canvas sled, the men of the turret crew sometimes pulled just his leg by joking that they were going to take a coffee break and leave him stranded for a while halfway through a barrel.

With each reveille and daily swabbing of the teak decks, the *New Jersey* moved closer to Long Beach. She arrived on 30 October and stayed only a day. To make up for the months overseas, the crew was broken into various leave parties, the first of which left from California. Yeoman Jack Cruppenink had lined up a flight while still on board ship and was soon on his way to visit his parents in Illinois. Fireman Charles Huntington and several others got on a Trailways bus and stayed together until they got to their individual dropoff points – Kentucky, Illinois, Missouri, and so forth.

The next stop after Long Beach was Panama. The trip through the canal on 9 November took longer than expected. The *New Jersey* ran aground going into one of the locks, because it was the dry season, and the people running the canal had tried to conserve water when filling locks. During the approach to the locks at Miraflores, the bow got in all right, and then Lieutenant Stu Sadler, the officer of the deck, looked out to the side and noticed that the lifelines on the main deck were not moving in relation to the lifelines on the edge of the lock. The ship was stuck about one-third of the way into the lock. Lieutenant Commander Wilhite, the navigator, knew what the problem was because he'd once had a school roommate whose father worked for the Panama Canal Company. Wilhite recalled that the bottom "corners" of the locks were rounded. The pilot had allowed in enough water to go under the ship's keel, but he hadn't taken into account the bilge keels which caught on the rounded corners. There was nothing to do but wait until more water was able to run in from Gatun Lake and raise the level a foot or two so that the ship could float free.

In nearly any other situation, the grounding of a capital ship of the Navy would make her skipper's day an extremely unhappy one. In the Panama Canal it is the pilot, rather than the ship's captain, who is responsible. Captain Atkeson sent for some coffee and leaned back in his chair on the bridge to smoke a cigar, for he had fancied cigars since his destroyer days.

The next stop after Panama was to be Norfolk, but Captain Atkeson decided he'd like to stop first in Cuba, on 11 November. He recalls, "I requested permission to go into Guantanamo so I could clean the sides from rubbing against the side of the canal. I didn't say anything about my brother being down there." The skipper's elder brother, a rear admiral, was commander of the naval base at Guantanamo.

When he approached the anchorage at the Cuban base, the new skipper relied too much on his small-ship experience. He wanted to make a snappy approach – barreling in, backing down quickly, and dropping the anchor. What he didn't take into account was the momentum built up by a ship of more than 50,000 tons displacement. Irrepressible Quartermaster Second Class Roff Grimes was on the helm as the New Jersey came in at too high a speed. He recalls hollering out to Atkeson, "You better back the damn thing down."

By the time the backing bell did take effect, it came within a whisker of being too late. Lieutenant Stu Sadler was on the bridge, and as he looked over the side, he noticed that the ship was still moving forward at a good clip after the anchor was dropped. Part of smart seamanship consisted of having the boat booms and accommodation ladders swung out over the side simultaneously with the dropping of the anchor. With the ship still moving ahead, remembers Sadler, "We nearly tore the accommodation ladder off, and at the same time the anchor [chain] kept peeling out of the hawsepipe at a considerable rate."

The anchor chain acquired a momentum of its own and was jumping high off the deck as it sped out. The ship's boatswain ordered the forecastle evacuated, and himself climbed over the lifelines, ready to jump some 30 feet down into the bay if he saw red-painted links of chain coming up through the hawsepipe. That would mean the chain was near its end. The end might have ripped loose from its mooring in the chain locker below and possibly killed anyone still up on deck when it whipped overboard at high speed. The reversing of the ship's giant propellers finally arrested her forward motion. When she came at last to a stop, yellow anchor chain was up on deck; the red links were not far behind. On the bridge, recalls Grimes, a chastened Atkeson apologized to those around him, then went off to visit his brother.

The New Jersey was under way for Norfolk later the same day after getting the canal scrapes painted over. Down in number two fireroom, Fireman Allan Frank, a Naval Reservist, was standing watches, as he had been for the nearly two years since he joined the crew. In that time, he had seen both Europe and the Orient, but the price had been hour upon hour in hot, steamy firerooms – performing some of the least desirable duties on board the ship. The temperature was generally above 100° and was especially difficult to take when operating in the tropics. At the end of a four-hour watch, Frank's shoes sometimes

had a squishy feel because of the sweat that had rolled down his legs and collected in his shoes. He couldn't even roll up his shirt sleeves because of the hazard of touching a hot metal surface.

An important part of Frank's watch routine was to make sure that everything sounded right, for he had stood so many watches that his ears told him when something was amiss. If a watch was slow, he might sit and shoot the breeze with others, and that was likely to be the only breeze stirring in the hot fireroom. Every hour on the hour, he walked around to read gauges and record his findings.

Main control informed the fireroom and other engineering spaces by sound-powered telephone when there was to be a speed change so the men on watch could react. When the ship increased speed, it was necessary to feed more air into the boilers for the burning of the increased flow of fuel oil. That meant a louder whine from the blowers on the boilers. Men had to shout to make themselves heard over the whine of the blowers, the rush of hissing steam, and the lop-lop-lop sound of the propeller shafts as they turned over. When a watch ended, Frank often took pleasure in stepping up to the weather deck to relax. When one got topside, he says, "All you hear is the water slapping the side of the ship, especially at night. So it's an eerie silence."

On 14 November, the New Jersey brought Frank and his shipmates back to their home port. As usual, Quartermaster Grimes was at the helm on the way in, using his skill to keep the ship out of the mud on the long approach up Thimble Shoals Channel to Norfolk. There was so little water under the keel that he had to steer something of a sinuous course, putting the rudder five degrees to the right, then shifting to five degrees left as soon as the rudder took effect, and so forth. The deep-water part of the channel was narrow, and the mud had a suction effect which would have pulled the hull against the bank if Grimes hadn't used the constant-helming technique to push her away.

At long last, the New Jersey cleared the channel and moored to pier seven, across from the Missouri, which had last been seen half a world away in Yokosuka the previous spring. Brows were put in place, loved ones greeted warmly, and the sweet celebration of homecoming began. Rear Admiral Clark Green, Commander Battleship Division Two, came from his flagship, the Missouri, to welcome Captain Atkeson to Norfolk. The new skipper had already been welcomed to the ship by his crew. The New Jersey's communication officer was Lieutenant Commander Jim Pringle. He says, "By the time we reached Norfolk on our return from Korea, all hands conceded that Captain Akeson was the finest officer that they had ever served under.... I have never served in an organization with such outstanding morale."

Part of Captain Atkeson's popularity lay in the swashbuckling spirit he brought from his destroyer days; this

Right: The USS *Missouri* awaits across the pier as tugboats ease the *New Jersey* in at Norfolk's pier seven on 14 November 1953. At far right is the heavy cruiser *Newport News*. (Courtesy *All Hands* magazine)

Below: The view from the *New Jersey*'s signal bridge as she comes home on 14 November. The *Missouri* is at left. (Norfolk *Virginian Pilot* photo; courtesy Rear Admiral John Atkeson)

**Above:** On 30 January 1954, Rear Admiral George R. Cooper, left, relieved Rear Admiral Clark L. Green, right as Commander Battleship Division Two on board the *New Jersey*. (Courtesy Rear Admiral John Atkeson)

serviceman can be punished for not returning on time – wrote a letter explaining that it was to blame for his tardiness. As soon as Huntington came up before Atkeson at captain's mast, he presented the airline's letter. Atkeson responded with a smile on his face and said, "Oh, a Christmas card."

"No, sir, I wish it was," said the young fireman. As soon as the skipper read it, he dismissed the case. Huntington thanked the captain profusely and went on his way.

Christmas on board the *New Jersey* at Norfolk in 1953 was much the same as it had been a year earlier. This time Santa Claus was portrayed by Chief Boilerman John Jones. When the 1954 New Year's issue of *The Jerseyman* was published, Chief Santa Claus Jones told an inquiring photographer: "I am going to resolve to visit church more frequently this year than I did last. I always make the resolution not to drink and for the past six years I have kept it fairly well."

During much of January, the *New Jersey* was in the Caribbean for a training period. Embarked was Rear Admiral Green, who had shifted his flag from the *Missouri* two days after the *New Jersey*'s arrival in mid-November. One event of the January cruise was a practice firing of the main battery, held at Culebra Island for the benefit of Green and his boss, Admiral Lynde D. McCormick, who was Commander in Chief Atlantic Fleet. McCormick was an old battleship hand, having commanded the USS *South Dakota* during World War II. On 30 January 1954, shortly after the *New Jersey*'s return to Norfolk, the ship served as the site of the division change of command when Green was relieved by Rear Admiral George R. Cooper.

Even before that, the ship's bowling team, under the officer in charge, Lieutenant (junior grade) L. R. Brandsma, had flown from Guantanamo to Norfolk to take part in the annual Battleship Cruiser Force bowling tournament. The *New Jersey* squad won the tournament by beating teams from the *Iowa, Missouri, Mississippi,* and *Baltimore.* Top individual honors for high scores went to two *New Jersey* men, Boatswain's Mate Third Class Donald Dunn and Commissaryman First Class James Caldwell. Later in the year, the *New Jersey* team finished third in the 1954 Atlantic Fleet bowling tournament.

On the nights of 8 and 9 February, the crew had its annual ship's party at the Norfolk municipal auditorium. Many of the battleship's men enjoyed Chick Ciccone's dance band and the various floor show acts. Included among the latter was Mallie Theimer, billed at the time as "the world's champion fire baton twirler". In addition to putting away a large buffet spread, the men of the *New Jersey* did a good deal of drinking as well. One officer who attended was Commander Edward "Tex" Winslow, who had relieved Commander Braybrook as gunnery officer. Some thirty years after the event, Winslow called it "Truly a party to end all parties. There are probably some old stiffs still lying around."

was the kind of officer that men wanted to take them into battle if they had to go. Then, too, he had a sort of rumpled look and an outwardly gruff manner, which gave him the air of a salty sea dog. In truth, the gruffness was mostly a facade, for he was softhearted underneath. His department heads liked him because he left them alone to do their jobs. If something important needed correcting, he raised hell about it. But he was not the sort who hounded people about details. His job was leadership; he left the managerial side of things to subordinates.

One enlisted man who got to see the Atkeson touch at close range was Fireman Charles Huntington, who had a girl friend in Illinois. He decided that the leave he'd taken from Long Beach wasn't enough, so he requested and got leave for the holiday period. On the way back to the ship after Christmas, a malfunctioning plane caused him to miss a flight connection. The airline – knowing that a

**Above:** Ensign Louis Ivey, the first black officer in the crew of the *New Jersey*. (Courtesy Commander Louis Ivey)

the items that came out of the seabag was a jumper with the rating badge of a commissaryman first class and four hashmarks down the left sleeve to indicate his years of service. He had been in the Navy since 1938. Mueller's young-looking face had evidently earned him that sort of ribbing before, so he strung Blanchette along for a while before springing the trap.

One cold night in February, Ensign Louis Ivey reported to the *New Jersey* for duty after being commissioned through the Naval ROTC unit at Penn State University. Ivey was the first black officer to serve in the *New Jersey*, and he soon got evidence that President Harry Truman's executive order of July 1948 requiring "equality of treatment and opportunity" in the armed services was not always observed. When Ivey woke after his first night in one of the officer staterooms, he discovered that the man who had been in the room left during the night. Then the roommate reasserted his claim, and Ivey had to move twice before settling into a junior officer bunkroom he remembers as the "ensign locker".

Ivey, who later left active duty and became a successful surgeon, moved cautiously in establishing relationships with his shipmates. He was assigned initially to the boiler division and later became division officer for the *New Jersey*'s radiomen. He decided to be cautious, concentrating on doing his professional duties well. He gained respect as a naval officer and then established social relationships only as they grew naturally with some of the friendlier junior officers.

Norfolk was still highly segregated in the mid-1950s. Since Ivey wasn't accepted at the places white officers frequented, he had two alternatives. One was to spend time with the small circle of black naval officers in the area, and the other was to stick largely to the naval base in Norfolk. The latter was federal property and thus integrated by law. Later, when the ship went overseas, conditions were easier, especially in Mediterranean ports, so Ivey was able to go ashore with his shipmates. Even so, he had to pick his friends carefully, because a number of officers let him know, in a variety of ways, that they didn't welcome his presence. One of the ship's doctors told Ivey that his upset stomach was probably the result of having "a tough time adjusting to white man's food". Ivey recalls that he was able to fire back rejoinders to some digs of that sort, keeping things within bounds so that differences didn't have to be resolved by more senior officers. He earned the respect of those seniors by doing his professional duties superbly and keeping his cool.

Ivey was especially welcomed by the black enlisted men, because they viewed his arrival as a tangible manifestation of progress. They sometimes came to him to talk about problems in their workplaces, because they felt more comfortable with him than with their own division officers. Ivey's most frequent contact was with the black stewards in the wardroom. They made things as easy for him as they

The size of the crew had been reduced when the *New Jersey* got back from the Pacific, as it had after the first deployment to Korea in 1951. With the war over, the battleship's manning came back down to its peacetime allowance, and there was a good deal of turnover also with old faces leaving and new ones coming. One of the latter reported in February and started unpacking his seabag in the S-1 division berthing compartment where Seaman Roland Blanchette and some of the other commissarymen were playing cards. The new fellow, who didn't have his jumper on, had a fresh crewcut and looked about nineteen years old, just out of boot camp. Blanchette decided to haze him a little to put him in his place, so he started asking a few questions. The new man answered by saying that he was Gordon Mueller and had gone to boot camp at Great Lakes. Mueller kept on answering questions as he put his uniforms and other gear into his new locker. One of

could, knowing that his relationships were not always easy with his fellow officers.

In February and March, the *New Jersey* was in and out of Norfolk training her new crew and dozens of visiting Naval Reservists in the Virginia Capes operating areas off the coast. Among the reservists on board for training was Radarman First Class Leonard Sanders, who lived in New Orleans and worked in civilian life as a cartographic drafts- man for the Army Corps of Engineers. Back in May 1943, Sanders was a member of the *New Jersey*'s commissioning crew and served in the ship for the remainder of the war.

As the crewmen manned their stations throughout the ship during the training periods, they were linked by various interior communications circuits, principally sound-powered telephones. These phones were designed to operate independently of external power sources, so that a failure of the ship's electrical system wouldn't affect them. Generations of Navy men have worn sound-powered telephones, each set composed of two black earphones and a mouthpiece. Inside the rubber covering of the mouthpiece is a diaphragm. When the speaker pushes a button on the mouthpiece, the diaphragm vibrates and establishes an electrical current sufficiently strong to transmit the sound to other stations on the circuit. IC Electrician Third Class Wayne Amend discovered that the ship's setup permitted various stations to be isolated by plugging in and switching individual circuits around. This came in handy when someone was talking on the phones

when he shouldn't have been. The IC men were able to isolate the offender and nail him for not observing proper phone procedures.

While at sea, the ship's supply of fresh water – both for boiler feed water and for human use – was produced by evaporators maintained and operated by the A division. Their function, as the name suggests, was to evaporate seawater, draw off the resulting steam, and recondense it to make fresh water. The salt was collected in tubes in the evaporators and disposed of.

During the course of his A-gang duty, Fireman Charles Huntington discovered that he and others who stood watch in the *New Jersey*'s forward diesel engine compartment were beneficiaries of their World War II counterparts. Some inventive soul had devised a makeshift, steam-operated coffee maker. There was a container to hold fresh water, and steam was diverted from a regular line to make a circular path through a coil around the water container. When a man felt ready for a cup of coffee, he put in some fresh water and tossed in coffee grounds. A strainer was then used when pouring the resulting brew into a coffee cup.

In late March, the *New Jersey* arrived in Norfolk and began a great deal of preparation to serve as the site of the Atlantic Fleet change of command ceremony on Monday, 12 April. Lieutenant Commander Richard Brega, who had taken over from Ray Wilhite as navigator, went through a lot of "planning, sweat, and worry" to get the ship ready for

all the hoopla. The Atlantic Fleet staff, with headquarters at Norfolk, provided a good deal of guidance on protocol and so forth. On the day itself, the battleship's crew mustered on the fantail. Hundreds of guests were on hand as Admiral McCormick turned over the fleet to Admiral Jerauld Wright. The Chief of Naval Operations, Admiral Robert B. Carney, lent his presence. He inspected the Marine Corps honor guard and sat on the speakers' platform during the ceremony itself. As a rear admiral in 1944–45, Carney lived in the *New Jersey*'s flag country while serving as Admiral Halsey's chief of staff.

A week later, it was back to routine business as the *New Jersey* got under way in company with her sister ship *Iowa* and two destroyers for the 1954 Atlantic Fleet Group Landing Exercise. The ships provided simulated naval gunfire support for an amphibious landing exercise off Onslow Beach, North Carolina. Then, in mid-May, the *New Jersey* was off to New York City as the featured naval attraction for Armed Forces Day. Captain Atkeson took the ship past the Statue of Liberty and up the Hudson River. She moored at pier 88 on Manhattan's west side. Governor Robert Meyner of New Jersey came aboard for a visit, and so did thousands of the good people of New Jersey and New York. For many in the crew of the battleship, it was the first opportunity for liberty in the nation's largest city. Few were left from the commissioning crew which had helped activate the *New Jersey* at Bayonne and Brooklyn more than three years before.

On Saturday, 15 May, the *New Jersey* sent a contingent of officers and men to march in an Armed Forces Day parade down Fifth Avenue. The turret three officer, Lieutenant (junior grade) Rodion Cantacuzene, had a difficult time getting crew members motivated for the parade. It was, he remembers, a real test of leadership. He solved the problem by telling potential paraders that they would get liberty half an hour earlier than their shipmates and adding, "Look, there are going to be thousands of girls there. This isn't Norfolk."

Marching aside, any *New Jersey* man who didn't have fun that weekend wasn't trying very hard. Seaman Ray Nelson of the seventh division found enjoyment in the music of such New York clubs as Birdland and Basin Street. Storekeeper Second Class Jim Sullivan toured Times Square, watched a couple of movies, and attended a rehearsal for Ed Sullivan's "Toast of the Town", then the most popular variety show on television. Electronics Technician Third Class William Wright went to the Empire State Building, played shutterbug, and visited the oldest chess club in the country; his only gripe was that the taxi fares were too high. Seaman Jim Donovan of Q division was in Times Square after dark and found it "like a huge carnival with all those lights".

Sunday, 16 May, was a beautiful warm spring day. Tens of thousands of people – both tourists and local residents – were out to enjoy the plesures of the season. Some 7,000 of them found that pleasure in touring the battleship. Other thousands, including *New Jersey* crewmen, were at city baseball parks. Half the National League teams were on display that day within subway hailing of the *New Jersey*. The New York Giants, featuring Willie Mays, split a doubleheader with the visiting Milwaukee Braves at the Polo Grounds. Over at Ebbets Field in Brooklyn, the Dodgers won one and lost one against the Cincinnati Redlegs. Yeoman Third Class Jack Cruppenink was delighted by the seats he had for ball games that weekend and liked the price best of all. The generous ballclubs admitted servicemen in uniform free of charge.

On Sunday evening, men from the battleship were picked as contestants on Bert Parks's "Break the Bank" quiz program. Ensign A. J. Coldwell, junior officer in the third division, was teamed with an Army sergeant, and the two answered enough questions correctly to collect $200 in prize money.

The men of the *New Jersey* were understandably reluctant to leave on Monday morning when tugboats backed their ship away from the pier for her trip to Newport, Rhode Island. In Newport, Fireman Charles Huntington of A division had an enjoyable visit with his brother, who was in the crew of the destroyer *Black*. His brother twitted him by casting an eye at the anchored battleship and saying smugly, "I think we can sink it." Then the two of them went off to see the latest in monster movies, "Creature from the Black Lagoon".

Meanwhile, Captain Atkeson was making his ship available for a baker's dozen of flag officers who were on board for an Atlantic Fleet type commanders' conference. Some thirty years later, Atkeson asked plaintively, "Can you imagine having thirteen admirals aboard at the same time?" There were other guests as well. Clarence Williams and his ten-year-old grandson got a tour of the ship and a meal in the recently established first class petty officers' mess. In 1913 and 1914, Williams was in the crew of the coal-burning battleship *New Jersey*, which was commissioned in 1906, decommissioned in 1920, and sunk in 1923

by Army bombing tests conducted by Brigadier General Billy Mitchell.

After Newport, Norfolk, and Annapolis, the *New Jersey* prepared to get under way on Monday, 7 June, to begin the summer midshipman cruise in company with the battleship *Missouri*, heavy cruisers *Macon* and *Des Moines*, escort carrier *Siboney*, the fleet oilers *Nantahala* and *Allagash* and a covey of destroyers. With the Korean War over and the Seventh Fleet flag having moved from the *Wisconsin* to a heavy cruiser, there was a rarity that June day with all four ships of the *Iowa* class in one place. As Commander Battleship Division Two, Rear Admiral George Cooper realized that this was probably the last opportunity to get all four ships operating with one another. Because of wartime commitments, it had never happened before, and it wasn't likely to take place again because the impending decommissioning of the *Missouri* had already been announced.

Admiral Cooper took his request for such an event to the *New Jersey*'s former skipper, Captain Melson, who by now was chief of staff to Rear Admiral Ruthven Libby, Commander Battleship Cruiser Force Atlantic Fleet and also designated as task group commander for the upcoming midshipman cruise. Atkeson recalls that Libby was disgruntled by the suggestion but eventually consented. Thus for several hours on that sunny Monday, the four giant dreadnoughts gathered for formation steaming, photo taking, and maneuvering drills. Midshipman Joe Ballou, just through with his first year at the Naval Academy, found it an extremely impressive introduction to life at sea. He recalls that the *New Jersey*'s general announcing system made the crew aware of the historic nature of the occasion. When the exercise was over, the *Iowa* and

*Wisconsin* steamed back to port, and the *Missouri* and *New Jersey* joined up with the midshipman task group.

With the oiler *Allagash* in company for the slow cruise to Europe, it was convenient for the *New Jersey* to go alongside for a drink. At his customary station at the wheel was Quartermaster Second Class Roff Grimes. He admired Atkeson's approach style, coming alongside the oiler quickly and smartly. He also liked the captain's willingness to change course during a replenishment if sea conditions called for it. This could be difficult, because both the oiler and the battleship had to maneuver in tandem while linked by wires and hoses, but it was sometimes necessary in rough seas because of a handling problem.

Grimes also pats himself on the back for his ability to steer the ship within fine tolerances during a replenishment, a judgment confirmed by the officers who served with the quartermaster. Grimes preferred a course which put the sea on the starboard bow during replenishment, for the oiler was invariably to starboard. As he stood in the pilothouse, Grimes looked out through the narrow viewing slits in the front, but also frequently out the open side hatch of the armored conning tower to keep an eye on the movement of water between the battleship and oiler and also the markings shown on the distance line rigged between the ships. While the captain was out on the starboard wing of the bridge sending in orders to the pilothouse, Grimes was relying on what he calls an innate gift – a sixth sense, perhaps – which enabled him to anticipate the order the skipper would give him. It took time for the captain's order to be repeated by the phone talker on the wing of the bridge. By the time the order got to Grimes, he was usually already carrying it out. His mind had been working in tandem with the captain's, so the conditions which dictated a steering command on the part of Atkeson had already dictated the same thing to Grimes, and he reacted accordingly.

Grimes particularly admired Atkeson's shiphandling skill when it came to the *New Jersey*'s 19 June arrival at the port of Vigo, Spain, on the Atlantic coast, just north of the border with Portugal. The United States and Spain had recently concluded an agreement for use of Spanish bases by U.S. military forces, and the *New Jersey*'s visit was part of the process of implementing the agreement. It was, however, the first time in more than twenty-five years that a U.S. battleship had visited the port, and certainly no previous battleship there had been so large. The Spanish simply weren't prepared. As Grimes remembers, "When we were going into Vigo, they sent out a little one-lunger tug, and it couldn't even have moved one of the hawsers." Photographer's Mate John Hastings was among the hundreds of crew members out on the main deck. He says, "Those of us who were standing at division quarters all started looking up at the 08 level [where the captain and pilot were], wondering how much longer this show was going to go on. We were all smiling. Some guys were

Below: The only time all four sisters steam together, 7 June 1954. Front to rear: *Iowa, Wisconsin, Missouri, New Jersey.* (National Archives: 80-G-638279; courtesy Norman Polmar)

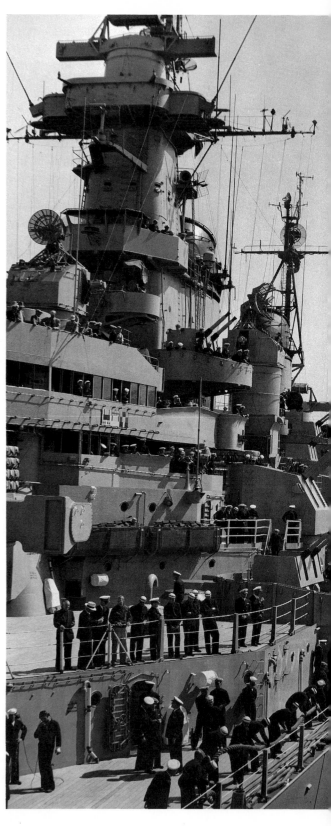

Opposite page, top: At Vigo, Spain, on 19 June 1954, the Spanish tugboat cannot move the New Jersey, so small boats carry the battleship's mooring lines to the dock. (Photo by L. Zamora; courtesy Rear Admiral John Atkeson)

Opposite page, bottom: The New Jersey uses her main deck winches and capstans to pull herself alongside the dock. (Photo by L. Zamora; courtesy Rear Admiral John Atkeson)

Left: The battleship is secured to the dock at Vigo. Notice the two different types of radar antennas atop Mark 37 fire control directors; circular Mark 25 above the bridge and the parabolic Mark 12/22 combination on the port side. (Photo by L. Zamora; courtesy Rear Admiral John Atkeson)

starting to giggle. I think the bosuns [and] deck division guys were near tears trying to keep a straight face [and] be polite." With the little tug pushing mightily but getting nowhere, says Atkeson, he took the conn for the *New Jersey* and "worried it alongside the dock". He got the ship reasonably close by using the rudders and engines. She was still too far away for the normal practice of throwing over light heaving lines first and letting people ashore use them to pull in the mooring hawsers. In this case, boats carried the ends of the mooring lines to the dock. They were attached to bollards, and the shipboard ends were put on winches and capstans. Then the ship essentially pulled herself alongside the dock. The entire feat won for captain Atkeson the admiration of the *New Jersey*'s crew. (Several days later, when it was time for the battleship to get under way, the winch trick obviously couldn't be used in reverse. Instead, a towing hawser was delivered to a nearby U.S. destroyer, which pulled the *New Jersey* away from the dock until her own engines could take over.)

The bright side of the unusual landing was soon apparent to the crew. The deep water right up to the dock had enabled the *New Jersey* to moor in the middle of town. There was no need to anchor out and endure the long boat rides that were customary in nearly every overseas liberty port the battleship visited. Midshipman Joe Forest was struck by the warmth of the welcome extended by the town of Vigo, saying, "We were berthed alongside the quay and were met by bands and dancing groups and many senoritas, all of whom were well chaperoned." There was a party for the ship, tours, and basketball games. On 22 June, ten Catholic crew members received the sacrament of confirmation from Cardinal Fernando Quiroga y Palacios.

One drawback encountered by those on liberty in Vigo was that very few of the local residents spoke English. When they left the ship, men frequently walked for quite a time during the course of their explorations, taking pictures as they went and communicating by gestures. After several hours of walking one day, Fireman Charles Huntington and some of his buddies decided it was time to return to the ship, and they preferred to ride a taxi rather than retrace their steps. They weren't able to explain their intended destination to the cab driver in words, so one of the sailors got out a piece of paper and sketched the outline of the *New Jersey*. The driver understood that readily enough and drove the sailors back to their floating home.

After the five-day visit to Vigo, the *New Jersey* spent 3 to 10 July in Cherbourg, France. Crew members took tours to London, Paris, and elsewhere. Ensign Lou Ivey and fellow junior officers Ron Esper and Bob Nishman had a rollicking good time on the four-day tour of Paris which cost only $42.25 for train transportation and for lodging. They bought *Lady Chatterley's Lover* and other books which were still forbidden in the United States. Once in Paris they went from night spot to night spot. Ivey recalls,

"It was just amazing the things that we saw that were not customary back home [such as topless dancers], . . . and for that very reason, we couldn't close our eyes. We stayed up all night almost, drank champagne. We had a tremendous time."

Midshipman Joe Ballou and some friends took a guided tour of Parisian nightclubs, stopping for a drink at each of several. To their surprise, they found an obscure, unpretentious place to be more enjoyable than those with famous names. Yeoman Second Class Conrad Johnson said of his experience in the French capital: "It was something wonderful, and all men who were given the opportunity should have taken it. The night life in Paris is fabulous. There were many things to see and it was a holiday for photobugs." Johnson was one of several who provided his recollections for the next week's edition of *The Jerseyman*. The ship's paper of the time was informative, and it well served the interests of the crew. The editor in chief was Journalist Third Class John Dickey. His staff included two seamen, James Hankers and George Ethier, to handle news and sports, and two photographer's mates, third class John Hastings and striker Alex Lambert.

Each week the staff assembled an issue averaging six pages. About half was devoted to the ship and her crew, and the other half comprised news and features supplied by the Armed Forces Press Service. The latter included news on defense developments, a great deal of sports news, cartoons, crossword puzzles, and the inevitable two cheesecake photos each week. Popular individuals such as Doris Day, Marilyn Monroe, and Zsa Zsa Gabor were pictured, of course, and so were a good many starlets who haven't been heard from since except by family and friends. An exception was a Texas beauty named Kathryn Grandstaff, who was pictured in a June 1954 issue of *The Jerseyman*. When she appeared in the paper later in the year, her name had been changed to Kathryn Grant, and still later it was changed to Mrs. Bing Crosby.

While some men were off touring glamorous capital cities, others found enjoyment in Cherbourg and its environs. One such was Fireman Charles Huntington. He went on liberty with two other A division firemen, Rex Reynolds and Bob Asbury. During the course of their travels, they bumped into some French sailors and had fun swapping hats with them and taking pictures of one another. As noontime approached one day, the Americans went to a Cherbourg bakery and bought a long loaf of French bread. Then they went to another store where they got the bread cut into three pieces and filled with meat. Next was a cheese store where the three of them communicated through their gestures that they wanted to sample small pieces of various cheeses. When they hit upon one they especially liked, they bought a good-sized wedge of it. Finally, they bought a bottle of wine. With all their goodies, they went to a place where they could sit with their backs against a building which was still scarred by bullet holes from World War II. They looked out over a beautiful inlet from the sea and ate one of the most memorable meals of their lives.

The stay in France came to an end on 10 July when the *New Jersey* got under way for Guantanamo Bay. It was back to the work and training routine which had been so pleasantly interrupted by the stops in Spain and France, but even at sea, there were things to do to enjoy the off hours. Roland Blanchette recalls the nightly movies, pingpong, games of chess, and adds, "There was a piano in the library, and someone was always playing honky-tonk or something on the piano.... Some of the guys would get together, and there would be an accordion and a guitar and a banjo, and they'd just have a jam session." Lieutenant (junior grade) Rodion Cantacuzene had never heard country music before joining the *New Jersey* and found that he enjoyed the sessions on the mess deck even more than the playing by the ship's official band. Gunner's Mate First Class Bob Moore, whom Cantacuzene respected highly for his professional capabilities, was also an accomplished guitarist. Moore and other members of the Mess Deck Boys were part of a combination smoker and happy hour on the evening of 24 July. The evening on the fantail included boxing, wrestling, a boatswain's pipe contest judged by Chief Boatswain Ed Oberbroeckling, and a one-hour variety show.

When the *New Jersey* reached the Caribbean, she did her only firing of the 16-inch guns during the course of the cruise. High on the 011 level, where he was watching the firing, Midshipman Joe Forest was knocked backward by the enormous concussion. Being assigned to the *New Jersey* that summer was a particular pleasure for Forest, because he was the son of the officer, Lieutenant Commander Francis Forest, who was hull superintendent during the *New Jersey*'s construction at Philadelphia in the early 1940s. He explains, "It was a great thrill for me to sail in that wonderful ship, especially after having watched her construction and knowing that my father had been instrumental in her design."

The crew found that Guantanamo in the summertime was unpleasantly hot. Men slept topside a good deal, and a favored few got to benefit from the rare cases of spot air-conditioning in the ship. One who did was Interior Communication Electrician Wayne Amend, who had a bunk in the compartment which housed the ship's gyro-compasses. There was a danger that they would overheat and tumble, thus making them incapable of supplying the ship's true heading to the dozen or so gyro repeaters at various places in the ship. Petty Officer Amend and a few other men got bunks in the gyro compartment. The draw-back was that they were the ones who had to answer complaints about telephone troubles during the night, but it was more than worth it to stay cool.

Included in the training at Cuba was a landing exercise involving the ship's Marine detachment, which was com-manded by Captain Harry Randall. The Marines from the *New Jersey* and the other ships in the task group were sent ashore in landing craft after climbing down the sides of their ships on nets. Once ashore, remembers Sal Triola, the Marines were marched a number of miles into the Cuban jungle, ending up in the wee hours of the morning. Squad leaders such as Corporal Triola were given a map and compass and told to lead their men to a tower on the beach around daybreak. Despite the play-acting elements of it, the operation was realistic enough for Marines who'd been on board ship for months and hadn't been able to practice their land-warfare specialties. Reaching the tower, says Triola, was "a glorious occasion". The whole thing was something less than that for Photographer's Mate Third Class John Hastings who went along to take pictures of the operation. It was a far cry from running the ship's darkroom.

On the last day of July, after the Marines had rejoined, the *New Jersey* got under way for home. After offloading her ammunition from 9 to 12 August, she arrived at the Norfolk Naval Shipyard in Portsmouth on Friday the 13th to begin her first large-scale overhaul since being recom-missioned. This one, which would include a dry dock period from 23 September to 2 November, was more extensive than the shorter overhaul in the same shipyard in early 1952. For one thing, she got a beefed-up after mast with an SPS-8 height-finding radar antenna on it for increased capability in aircraft detection. In the area of radio communications, teletypes were installed to copy fleet broadcasts, so as not to have to depend on the old CW (continuous wave) Morse code transmissions which had been the norm for so many years. Jim Pringle, who was then the ship's communication officer, recalls it as the "beginning of the end for the old time radioman". He explains that the ultimate test of a good radioman in the CW days was being able to copy a fleet broadcast while drinking coffee and having a cigarette. The radioman was positioned at a typewriter and had a set of earphones on his head. Through training and experience, his hands and brain were able to convert the dots and dashes in the earphones to words on paper. To take his hands from the typewriter to smoke or drink coffee meant the radioman had to keep the train of thought imposed by the code and then catch up again after the hands returned to typing.

Besides the changes in the *New Jersey*'s electronics setup, there was a renewal in the most basic equpment of all – the big guns. The ship got a new set of liners for her 16-inch gun barrels. The gunnery officer, Commander Tex Winslow, learned from shipyard workers that there was excessive wear at the breech ends of the rifled barrels. In some cases the insides tended to be elliptical rather than round. Heavy firing had extruded portions of the liners beyond the ends of the barrels, and the extra metal had to be shaved off. The fact that metal was coming from the muzzle ends meant that there was less back down the rest of the barrels. As Winslow puts it, "Only the skillful use of the very flexible fire control system compensates allowed good shooting." There is a limit to such flexibility, so in late September all nine gun barrels were lifted out by crane and taken ashore. The old liners were extracted and new ones were installed. It was the first regunning of the *New Jersey*'s main battery since her commissioning in 1943.

One task which fell to the gunnery department during the overhaul was preparing for a potentially expanded capability for the 16-inch battery. Projectiles were developed to accommodate atomic warheads. Such weapons were tied up in the great inter-service rivalry with the Air Force. Being able to fire atomic projectiles from battleships would give the Navy one more arrow in its quiver. The ones under development were built in prototype form and tested ashore. Lieutenant Commander Ray Peet relieved Commander Winslow as gun boss during the overhaul. Peet, who eventually retired as a vice admiral, recalls that members of the *New Jersey*'s crew were given special weapons clearances and sent to schools to learn about the new projectiles. The former gun boss adds, "To my knowledge, we never had one on board, but we had the dummies, and we were all prepared to receive the nuclear projectiles." In the end, they lost out. Fissionable material was still scarce at the time, and gun-type weapons required relatively more of it than did air-dropped bombs. Furthermore, battleships were already on the endangered species list.

Shortly before the beginning of the overhaul, the *New Jersey* got a new executive officer, Commander Dick Pratt. To him the five months in the shipyard "seemed like an eternity and it was hard to see such a beautiful ship torn to pieces, as is always the custom in a yard". Hoses were running everywhere to provide essential services, and filth and grime and clutter seemed unavoidable concomitants in the process of improving the *New Jersey*'s material condition for further service. Despite the noise and discomfort that went with the overhaul, Rear Admiral George Cooper, the division commander, chose to make the *New Jersey* his flagship throughout the autumn, except for brief periods.

The new exec quickly formed impressions of Captain Atkeson. Pratt was amused, for instance, by the skipper's practice of driving a "disreputable old jalopy" and parking it in the commanding officer's reserved spot next to the brow. Atkeson struck Pratt as an old-shoe type, so a run-down car was perfectly in keeping with the image. The exec also observed the same outwardly gruff manner that others detected in the captain, explaining, "Though he looked as if he was going to tear someone apart, he never did – his bark was worse than his bite. He loved the ship and the crew performed well under his leadership."

The long in-port period afforded the opportunity to take part in activities that weren't so convenient during normal operations. Many of the ship's crew members were sent away to Navy schools. Seaman Dick McDowell went to fire fighting and damage control schools in the Norfolk area. Crewmen joined sports teams which sprang up in baseball, softball, bowling, boxing, and basketball. Chick Ciccone played for another ship's party in early October.

On 14 December, the *New Jersey* left the shipyard and went out for full power trials the next day to test the overhaul work done on her engineering plant. Propeller shafts had been rebuilt, and blades themselves were repaired where they were nicked and scarred. Normally, screws in that condition were replaced, but in this instance, they were built up with welding and then ground down to their proper shape. Four of the ship's boilers were rebricked, and many other smaller jobs were accomplished as well, including cleaning and repairing some sixty oil tanks and repairing fuel lines. The full power test was a success as the newly overhauled battleship built up to 31 knots during her trials on 15 December.

With the holiday season at the end of 1954, crew members were granted leave. To lessen the likelihood of traffic accidents, the ship chartered buses for leave parties going to New York and Washington. The price charged for each crew member was nominal, and the buses were convenient as well. During the holidays, there were two leave parties, each comprising about 35 per cent of the crew. As soon as the second leave party got back, on 3 January 1955, the *New Jersey* left the shipyard at Portsmouth and went out to Hampton Roads to anchor and reload her ammunition.

Shortly past noon on Monday, 10 January, the battleship got under way from anchorage and began steaming to

Below: The basketball squad was one of several teams which represented the ship in Atlantic Fleet Battleship-Cruiser Force athletic competition. (Courtesy Rear Admiral John Atkeson)

Above: The *New Jersey* as seen from the beach at Guantanamo Bay, Cuba, during post-overhaul shakedown training in early 1955. (Courtesy Charles Hamilton)

Above right: A launcher, lashed down on the main deck, sends a drone skyward to be used as a target during antiaircraft practice in 1955. (Courtesy Charles Hamilton)

warmer weather at Guantanamo Bay, Cuba. That first night at sea was a rough one. By the time lights went out throughout the ship at the playing of taps, the *New Jersey* was off Cape Hatteras in the Carolinas, traditionally a rough stretch of water. In the early hours of the 11th, the barometer dropped steadily. The wind kicked up to 40 knots and gusted to 55. Down in the K division berthing compartment, Photographer's Mate Striker Chuck Hamilton was suffering mightily. He had just reported aboard after three years of shore duty, and this was his first night at sea. He couldn't have had a much worse beginning. "I thought I was going to die," remembers Hamilton, who then adds, "I knew I was going to die." Trying to stay in his bunk was so bad that he took his mattress and found a storage room, where he put the mattress on the deck and moaned for two hellish days until the weather improved.

The shakedown training which the ship was to undergo in the Cuba area was in many respects similar to the shakedown in the same area in early 1951 following reactivation. This time, however, there was a nucleus of holdovers so the crew wasn't starting from scratch. The executive officer, gunnery officer, and chief engineer were new, while the skipper, operations officer, and navigator were holdovers. The normal practice during the 1950s was to give a battleship captain a tour of just about one year in command. That had been the case with Captain Tyree, Captain McCorkle, and Captain Melson. All took command in the autumn and were relieved in the autumn. In Atkeson's case, the tour of duty lasted about a year and a half so he could provide his experience in leading the rest of the crew through the shakedown.

When the *New Jersey* reached Guantanamo Bay on 13 June, Seaman John Evans of Q division was dispatched from the bridge to the forecastle to raise the union jack as soon as the anchor hit the water. The union jack is essentially an American flag without the red and white stripes. During that period it featured a blue field with forty-eight

white stars. By tradition, it flies from a jackstaff on the bow of a Navy ship while she is anchored or moored, and the national flag flies from the stern. During normal underway operations, the American flag flies from the mast and the union jack is not used. In this case, Evans was new to the job because he had reported aboard during the overhaul. Shakedown training can take many forms, including a lesson on what's involved in raising a small flag. As soon as the anchor was released, chain began rumbling out through the hawsepipe, getting louder and faster until the brake was eventually applied. Evans remembers, "The first time we come in there to drop the anchor, I'm up on the forecastle. The whole thing's shaking like a son of a gun, and the dust is flying. . . . I was petrified." Evans had another interesting job during the shakedown in connection with his duties on the bridge. He rolled down the many plexiglass windows which went around the bridge on the 04 level to prevent them from being shattered by the concussion from firing the 16-inch guns.

Lieutenant Commander Peet, the new gun boss, was pleased with the ship's shooting performance during the shakedown, giving much of the credit to Lieutenant Commander Joe McGinnis, the assistant gunnery officer, who provided the continuity in that department. McGinnis, recalls Peet, was a former enlisted man who "was outstanding in training gun crews. I think in large measure the credit for our performance down there in Guantanamo is due to Joe McGinnis."

The fleet training group in Guantanamo imposed all sorts of casualty control drills and battle problems to improve the crew's ability to react in the event of emergencies. Lieutenant Commander Jim Pringle devised a means of outwitting the training team. The *New Jersey* had received some walkie-talkies, and by chance Pringle discovered that they could be used to communicate between the bridge and after steering as long as the antennas were fairly close to the sound-powered telephone system. Thus,

**Above:** Captain John Atkeson, left, leads a party of visitors during a stop in the Dominican Republic on 14 February 1955. In the fancy uniform is General-issimo Rafael Trujillo. The structure just to the right of Atkeson is a movie booth with three circular ports for the projectors when showing films on the fantail. (Courtesy Rear Admiral Richard Pratt)

**Above right:** Captain John Atkeson shakes the hand of a department head as he prepares to leave the ship following his rainy-day change of command on 18 March 1955. (Courtesy Rear Admiral John Atkeson)

when the fleet training group people imposed simulated casualties at the same time to both the steering system and the sound-powered phones, the walkie-talkies were whipped out and steering orders sent by that means. As Pringle explains, "It worked beautifully but got a 'low horrible' from [the fleet training group] because it wasn't according to the book." One of the men involved in presenting the critique after the 1 February battle problem was the fleet training group's chief staff officer, Captain Dana B. Cushing. Cushing had been the *New Jersey*'s navigator when she first went into combat in early 1944.

On Saturday, 12 February, the *New Jersey* ended her training period for the week with main battery shore bombardment qualification at the island of Culebra. Then came a visit to the port of Ciudad Trujillo in the Dominican Republic. The idea was to give the crew some liberty and to demonstrate support for a U.S. ally in the Caribbean. The crew went on liberty on Sunday, and the next day there was an official visit from President Hector B. Trujillo and from his brother, the head of state, Generalissimo Rafael Leonidas Trujillo. The president arrived in civilian clothes, while the general was wearing a uniform heavily encrusted with gold. Bolts snapped open on rifles as the Marine detachment was inspected, and then the Trujillos were given a guided tour of the ship. Their bodyguards, wearing civilian clothes, had bulges here and there where they carried their concealed sidearms. Photographer's Mate Charles Hamilton joked to a shipmate that the bodyguards were along to protect all the gold on the general's cap and uniform.

Pleased with the visit, General Trujillo invited the *New Jersey*'s officers to a banquet ashore. The officers scrambled to get into their dress whites and catch buses to the large gymnasium where the fete was to be held. No drinking was permitted before Trujillo arrived. Finally the skipper and dictator showed up, and the more junior officers got to quench their thirsts after waiting an hour and a half. Then came the meal. Commander Joe Parsons, the operations officer, was struck by the fact that the general had an official food taster with him to check things before he would partake himself. When it got down to the eating, says Jim Pringle, "I don't recall what was served but I do recall hearing the amazed gasps of our officer hosts when the Generalissimo clapped the Captain on the back and roared with laughter and the Captain returned the clap on the back with equal gusto. It was a fine party but the next morning was quite painful and there was no loud talking in the wardroom."

A new member of the *New Jersey*'s wardroom who had a special degree of rapport with Captain Atkeson was Ensign Ted Walker, whose father was a contemporary and friend of the skipper. One of Ensign Walker's chores was to take the captain's pay to him, either on the bridge or in his cabin, on payday. On one occasion Atkeson asked Walker how things were going, and the young supply officer began ranting about his problems. The captain replied, "Now, Ted, I want you to understand. You only have two or three really good fights in your lifetime. Save it for something that's important. The Navy's been going to hell for almost 200 years, but it's not there yet. And you probably are not going to make it go any faster or slower."

In late February, the *New Jersey* returned to Norfolk. On 1 March, the ship got a new flag officer, Rear Admiral William B. Ammon, who had just relieved Admiral Cooper as Commander Battleship Division Two on 28 February. The stay was a short one, lasting only until 18 March, when Ammon shifted his flag to the *Wisconsin*. The same date, 18 March, marked the end of Captain Atkeson's command tenure. It rained steadily, so the change of command ceremony had to be held in the ship's wardroom. The rain did stop by the time Captain Atkeson was ready to depart. Instead of the enlisted men who normally serve as side-boys on such occasions, this time the double row of men at the end of the brow was composed of the battleship's department heads and assistant department heads. Captain Atkeson went down the row shaking hands with the officers who had served under him. When the time came at last for Atkeson to go, remembers Jim Pringle, "There wasn't a dry eye in the whole line-up when he was piped over the side."

Captain Edward J. O'Donnell, the new skipper, reported from a tour of duty as assistant superintendent of the Naval Gun Factory in Washington, D.C., where the *New Jersey*'s guns had been manufactured more than ten years before. Though the turnover period with Atkeson was brief, O'Donnell knew that the previous skipper had left things in great shape for him. The *New Jersey* was in fine material condition as a result of the recent yard overhaul, and the crew was in a good state of training because they'd just come through the shakedown at Guantanamo. With those concerns taken care of, remembers O'Donnell, all he had to do was run the ship, and he had a talented group of enlisted men and officers to accomplish that. One of them was the exec, Dick Pratt, who had already been selected for the rank of captain. The selection had been made when Atkeson was still skipper, and he reacted in his usual bluff way, saying, "I'll be damned if there is going to be more than one captain on this ship!" Captain O'Donnell, on the other hand, did not mind, so Pratt soon had a fourth stripe sewn on each sleeve of his blue uniforms.

The change of command was on a Friday, and the new skipper was due to get his feet wet in a hurry. Early the next Monday morning, 21 March, the *New Jersey* got under way from the naval operating base and steamed to a rendezvous with her sister ship *Wisconsin*. The two heavy ships comprised a task unit which simulated a surface raiding force, somewhat reminiscent of the role played by the German ships *Prinz Eugen* and *Bismarck* in the early part of World War II. The two U.S. battleships, recalls O'Donnell, hugged the Atlantic Coast while heading south, because their mission was to intercept an "enemy" force coming out from the Caribbean. When they got down to North Carolina, the two separated and steamed in parallel 20 miles apart. The battleships successfully surprised and intercepted the opposing force, built around a U.S. aircraft carrier.

Captain O'Donnell got a surprise of his own after the *New Jersey* returned to Hampton Roads on 28 March. Since the ship was anchored out, crew members had a boat ride of some forty minutes in to the fleet landing. Captain O'Donnell took his gig when making the trip, and as soon as he arrived he stepped out and went off to conduct some business. There to meet the boat were the wives of two *New Jersey* officers who were in the duty section, Lieutenant Commander Jim Pringle and Ensign Ted Walker. The women were going to ride out to join their husbands for dinner, and so when they saw a *New Jersey* boat arrive and a tall gentleman in civilian clothes step out, they didn't give it much thought. They jumped aboard the boat and ordered the coxswain to take them to the ship. Since Captain O'Donnell was still so new, the wives didn't recognize him, and the gig's coxswain was apparently too awed by their tone of voice to tell them that he was supposed to wait at the landing for the captain and take him back to the ship. When the gig pulled up alongside the *New Jersey*, Lieutenant Commander Pringle, as command duty officer, was there to meet it and was aghast to see that the captain wasn't in the boat and his own wife was. He had time to contemplate the possible penalties for hijacking a captain's gig. Back ashore, Captain O'Donnell had to cool his heels until the gig could get back for him. He understood the situation when it was explained, and the two officers involved got off with no more than a case of temporary anxiety.

In early April the ship went to Mayport, Florida, for a port visit and open house at Easter weekend. When the *New Jersey* arrived on 8 April, a Florida congressman was due for a visit, so Captain Pratt, the exec, was keeping an eye on the pier as the brow was being put in place so that he could spot the arrival of the distinguished visitor. Instead, he saw an attractive, scantily clad woman who was either a stripper or prostitute and was doing a bit of advertising for the benefit of the battleship's crew. Pratt rushed down the brow to tell her to get out of sight before the congressman and other guests began arriving. The sight of the exec rushing frantically to reach the woman created an interesting scene for the men all over the ship who were watching.

A local organization in Mayport set things up so that the unmarried *New Jersey* officers would have a pool of girls to date during the weekend's social affairs. All the girls were white, but the person who organized the gathering approached Ensign Lou Ivey and said, "We knew you would be coming. If you'd like a date, we have made arrangements to call someone, and she will come and meet you. But we didn't want to be so presumptuous as to have one standing here for you." As it turned out, remembers Ivey, the girl standing by in the wings was "very, very attractive, very elegant, very super". That, however, was the only time in his *New Jersey* experience that such a special effort was made to look out for him. Everywhere else the ship went, he was on his own.

On Monday, 11 April, the *New Jersey* got under way. Two days later, Rear Admiral Clarence Ekstrom, Commander Carrier Division Six, and his staff were ferried by helicopter from the carrier *Ticonderoga* to the *New Jersey*. He remained for two days of operations, including a spectacular firepower demonstration for the benefit of VIPs on board the carrier. Ekstrom wanted the *New Jersey* to put a salvo of projectiles just aft of the carrier. Captain O'Donnell told him, "I'm game if you're game." Then the problem was turned over to Commander Peet, and it was something that he enjoyed working on with the skipper, because both were ordnance specialists. Peet knew that if the 16-inch barrels were pointed at the carrier at the time of firing, there was no danger of hitting her, because the ships were on parallel courses. The speed of the carrier and the time of flight would cause the projectiles to drift astern. The carrier was nearly over the horizon when the *New Jersey* fired, and the nine projectiles landed in a tight pattern in her wake. It was a "very impressive" demonstration, remembers O'Donnell.

The latter part of April and much of May were spent in conducting individual ship exercises in the Virginia Capes operating area. For part of the time, the *New Jersey* performed tactical maneuvers in company with the *Wisconsin*. She did spend some time in her home port. With a midshipman cruise coming up, a number of the ship's crew members from the New York area wanted to head for home while they had the chance. Just as the ship had been accommodating over the Christmas and New Year's holiday leave period, so also did the *New Jersey*'s chaplains charter liberty buses on other occasions while in Norfolk. William Hunt, who was a seaman in the communications division, recalls that men going on the chartered buses were given early liberty on Fridays as an incentive to keep them from driving and facing the possibility of being involved in wrecks or coming back late for some other reason.

One man who frequently took advantage of the bus rides was another New Yorker, Seaman Ben Mehling. He recalls that the bus picked up *New Jersey* men at pier seven and then drove to a ferryboat for the one-hour trip to Cape May at the southern end of New Jersey. Once the bus began rolling again, Mehling and his shipmates went to sleep. The aroma of pig farms around Secaucus, New Jersey, invariably woke him up, and then he looked forward to seeing the lights of New York City as the bus approached.

Weekends were spent seeing his family and friends in New York, and then he and the other men from the ship gathered at the port authority bus terminal in midtown Manhattan on Sunday evening for the ride that would get them back to the ship in time for quarters on Monday morning. The men brought beer, sausages, olives, and other things to eat and drink. They all shared what they had brought. Once the meal was out of the way and the bus had moved south a number of miles on the New Jersey Turnpike, says Mehling, "The lights would go out, the jumpers would come off, and everybody would go to sleep. They'd be sleeping on the floor and they'd also be sleeping, believe it or not, on the baggage racks."

In contrast with the streetwise New Yorkers who served in the *New Jersey*, there were also crew members from the interior of the United States. One was Wayne Amend, who had joined the *New Jersey* back in May 1952, when he was eighteen years old. As did many others while on board the ship, Amend changed from a boy to a man. He reported aboard right out of boot camp and A school and was soon advanced to the rate of fireman. It had not been too much

earlier when he came out of the little town of Fond du Lac, Wisconsin, so he was inclined to keep his ears open and mouth closed when older members of the crew – those in their twenties and thirties – spun tales of the various ports they had visited and their romantic conquests in those ports. Amend also had to put up with the normal hazing and fool's errands that boots are sent on, such as being dispatched to get some "magnetic flux" or a "bucket of steam".

As time passed, Amend gained experience and confidence. In 1953 he was advanced to interior communication electrician third class. As a petty officer he began to enjoy the pleasure of overnight liberties in Japan rather than the back-by-midnight "Cinderella liberties" which were the lot of the nonrated men in the crew. In 1954, Amend went still another rung up the ladder, to petty officer second class. Now he found that he was one of those individuals to whom newcomers were looking for guidance, and, yes, for those sea stories that are an inextricable part of the baggage that a sailorman carries around with him. As he neared the end of his three-year cruise in 1955, Amend made it a point to act kindly toward the younger fellows coming in, because he recalled what he had gone through not all that long ago. He gave the new men a hand in being introduced to shipboard life and allowed them to discover, as he had, the special qualities that go with being a battleship man.

On 31 May, the *New Jersey* arrived at Annapolis to take on midshipmen for another training cruise to Europe. Now that the Korean War was over, the battleships began to settle into a regular routine of training the future officers. Because the *Iowa*-class ships no longer had either their wartime crews or their wartime missions, they were well suited to train some 700 midshipmen apiece each year. There was also room for a group of VIP guests of the Secretary of the Navy.

The midshipmen, of course, spent their summer taking orders, while the SecNav guests generally had to do nothing but enjoy themselves. One educator in the visiting group went overboard on the tourist routine, often going around with three or four cameras hanging by straps from his neck. Near the end of the cruise the midshipmen got their revenge in a happy hour, a time at which they are allowed to poke gentle fun at their shipmates. The best of the skits involved a talented, funny midshipman named Orv Wright who dressed up as Captain O'Donnell, including wearing oversized captain's shoulder boards. Wright's roommate impersonated the professor with all the cameras. Wright, pretending to be the skipper, then made remarks about the various guests. When he got to the shutterbug, Wright brought down the house by asking, "Where the hell does SecNav get these guys?"

On the evening of 18 June, shortly before the *New Jersey* reached her first liberty port of the cruise, the crew settled in for a boxing and wrestling smoker, with the smokes donated by the welfare and recreation fund. Ensign Ted Walker got final proof of just how pungent Captain Atkeson's cigars had been. The former skipper smoked a brand that caused Walker to say, "If they tasted half as bad as they smelled, they were just terrible." Once Atkeson left, the market for his brand evaporated. The ones he didn't take with him were marked down in the ship's store to a nickel apiece and then a penny, but no one bought them. The last straw came when the supply department took boxes of Atkeson's brand out to the fantail and tried to give the cigars away before smokers. Still no takers.

The first stop on the liberty schedule was Valencia, Spain, which the *New Jersey* visited from 20 to 27 June. Before being turned loose on the Spanish populace, the men had been given a generous number of lectures on the importance of protecting themselves against venereal disease. Some houses of prostitution were okay, but others were declared off-limits, and it was up to the shore patrol to enforce the prohibition. Photographer's Mate Third Class Chuck Hamilton did not welcome shore patrol duty. It was relatively easy to go up and down streets and warn men against going into certain places, but he also had to go inside at times and interrupt sailors and midshipmen in their encounters with the women. As Hamilton puts it, "You've got to get these guys out of the rooms, and that's not the easiest thing to do."

The city of Valencia was quite generous in its provision of hospitality for the visiting American warships. Among the various festivities ashore were the mayor's cocktail party at city hall for officers and midshipmen; a tea dance in the port captain's building; a concert in the patio of the captain general; a dance for officers and midshipmen at a local yacht club; and a snipe regatta between Spanish and midshipmen crews; the concert, which was held on the evening of 24 June, drew more than 600 American Navymen – officers, enlisted, and midshipmen. The featured work was composer Anton Dvorak's "New World Symphony". It was an appropriate tribute for a group of new world sailors receiving hospitality in the old.

Because the Spanish organize their days and nights in different fashion from Americans, the *New Jersey* had to adjust her daily shipboard routine to accommodate local customs. What with dinner often not beginning until late in the evening – by American standards, that is – Captain Pratt put taps an hour later than usual and let the men of the battleship wait until 7:00 in the morning before hearing the first strains of reveille.

Some of the *New Jersey*'s junior officers had a bit of a problem not with Spanish customs but with the difference between U.S. and British practice in regard to drinking on board ship. Lieutenant (junior grade) Dick Abrams, the assistant first lieutenant, had the quarterdeck watch one

evening while the ship was anchored at Valencia. Outfitted in dress whites and carrying the long spyglass which is the OOD's symbol of authority, he could see that nearby Royal Navy destroyers were lit up, and their officers appeared to be lit up as well. Abrams says, with a feeling of remembered envy, "All the babes from the shore would come out there, and they'd entertain them, and they'd have a party on board. . . . And we would patrol around the teak deck and mutter curses under our breath at hearing all these limeys parked next door to us in these little destroyers having a ball."

One Naval Reserve officer who made the cruise was Commander Neville Kirk, a Naval Academy history professor who had been along on the *New Jersey*'s 1947 midshipman cruise to Europe. Back then, the officers wore their uniforms when they went ashore on liberty. This time it was civilian clothes, and Kirk had the misfortune to tear the trouser leg of his summer suit when he came too close to the jagged edge of an automobile's mudguard. As a result, he had to endure the rest of the visit in Valencia's 95° heat while wearing the heavy woolen suit he had brought for the upcoming stop in England.

The *New Jersey* arrived at Weymouth, England, on the morning of 4 July, and at noon that day the ship fired a 21-gun salute to honor Independence Day. The British were good sports; HMS *Maidstone*, a nearby submarine tender,

answered with a twenty-one-gun salute. The people of Weymouth were extremely hospitable to the visiting Americans. Dances were held on two evenings for U.S. enlisted men, and the local people frequently invited the Americans into their homes after meeting them during chance encounters in town.

As part of the experience of sharing friendship and cultures, British and American teams competed against each other in a variety of sports, including water polo, tennis, golf, and sailing. The British weren't up to baseball, so the *New Jersey*'s team played an exhibition game against a team from the destroyer *Basilone*.

Midshipmen and crew members had the opportunity to take American Express tours to London and Paris. Commander Kirk observed that the lusty morning appetites of the midshipmen seemed best satisfied by the big breakfasts available in British hotels. There they filled up on such things as finnan haddie, sausages, bacon and eggs, fried tomatoes, and kippered herring. All that was a far cry from the continental breakfast of rolls and juice that they might have had elsewhere and an even farther cry from the disturbing food shortages Kirk had observed when he and the *New Jersey* visited Britain in 1947.

After the visit ended on 11 July, the *New Jersey* and other ships were once again under way, this time for Guantanamo – the traditional wrapup port for the mid-

**Below:** The ship is dressed with signal flags in honor of a holiday. This shot shows results of the late 1954 overhaul, including the addition of support legs to the after mast so it can accommodate the SPS-8A height-finding radar. (Courtesy Captain Clyde Anderson)

shipman cruises before heading back to the States. Having already suffered the indignity of the torn trousers and an unventilated stateroom, Commander Kirk experienced still further unpleasantness one day when he tried to give a lecture to a group of midshipmen on the fantail. Things were going along fairly well until the ship picked up speed, which had two unfortunate side effects. The relative wind increased dramatically, and so did the vibrations of the propellers. Kirk, who was known for his captivating classroom manner back in Annapolis, was more like a contortionist during this lecture. He tried simultaneously to keep the microphone and lectern from bouncing all over the place, to prevent his notes from being blown over the side by the wind, and to shout to be heard above the noise of the wind and vibration.

After the ship reached the Caribbean, she went through the usual gunnery drills, exercising the main and secondary batteries against towed targets. The *New Jersey* had a new supply officer by that time. Commander Ralph Meilandt reported aboard at Weymouth on 4 July and relieved Commander Clyde Maddock the next day. By the time the ship got south to the gunnery area, Meilandt was able to fire the 16-inch guns. That was, he says, "the result of a bit of forgivable bribery" given to Lieutenant Joe Ellis, the main battery officer.

In late July, the results of the 1955 rear admiral selection board were announced. Captain Charles Melson, the *New Jersey*'s commanding officer in 1952–53, was on the list, but his successor, Captain Atkeson, was not. Atkeson was one of the few *New Jersey* skippers not selected for flag rank, and the news came as both a shock and disappointment to the crew. Ray Peet, the gunnery officer, remembers that a feeling of sympathy for the former skipper "just permeated the whole ship".

It could well be that Atkeson was the victim of poor timing. When the Naval Academy's class of 1927 – of which both he and Melson were members – came into the zone for possible promotion, there was a new Secretary of the Navy, Charles Thomas. He had already selected Arleigh Burke, a junior rear-admiral, as Chief of Naval Operations, and he charged the selection board to go for younger officers than had been the norm. Atkeson might have made it under the rules in effect the year before. Captain Atkeson had an aversion to duty in Washington, D.C., and the workaholic pace expected there. That may also have weighed against him, but the men of the *New Jersey* had found him a success at the essence of the naval profession: commanding a man-of-war at sea.

Atkeson's successor, Captain O'Donnell, had the task at the end of the 1955 midshipman cruise of summarizing his observations in a report to the cruise commander. O'Donnell declared that the training regimen imposed on the midshipmen was too onerous. In particular, he said that the cruise journals – consisting of questions to be answered concerning every shipboard department – were unrealistically difficult. O'Donnell wrote, "The first classmen [seniors] were required to complete two assignments per day at sea. To accomplish this, after a full day of watches, drills, and instruction periods utilized all the free time of the conscientious individual."

A number of members of the Naval Academy football team, including all-America end Ron Beagle, were among the midshipmen in the *New Jersey* that summer. Because of the need to get back to Annapolis to begin fall practice, the football players were transferred from the battleship to a destroyer by highline and thence ashore. When the first of the football players made the trip in a chair suspended from the highline, the pages from his cruise journal fluttered in the air and were borne away by sea breezes. Presumably he couldn't be graded on his notebook and would have to be given special consideration because of the accident which had befallen him. By curious coincidence, as man after man made the trip to the destroyer, notebook after notebook came open, and the sea swallowed hundreds of pages.

On 3 August, the *New Jersey* and other ships of Task Group 40.1 arrived at Annapolis to offload their Naval Academy midshipmen. She next proceeded to Hampton Roads, then got under way on the ninth and joined the *Iowa*, *Des Moines* and *Macon*. The four heavies steamed together for several days, sometimes in diamond formation, while evading hurricane Connie. When she got back to port, the *New Jersey* stayed only a short time, getting under way again from 16 to 19 August to steam with the

*Iowa* while avoiding the effects of hurricane Diane. Between them, the two East Coast storms killed more than 400 people that summer.

As soon as the *New Jersey* returned to Hampton Roads, Captain Richard Pratt was detached, having been relieved as exec at sea on 18 August by Commander Charles Conway "Connie" Hartigan, Jr. Lieutenant Pierre Vining, who was then the *New Jersey*'s main propulsion assistant, observed that the arrival of Hartigan to join Captain O'Donnell meant that the ship had "a tall, smiling Irishman for skipper and a short, smiling Irishman as exec".

Without exception, O'Donnell is remembered by those who served with him for his pleasant disposition. Dick Brega, who was the navigator, recalled the skipper as having a commanding manner and air of dignity, yet not pompous or overbearing; he had time to be friendly with those who worked for him. In fact, he made it a point to seek out crew members. Dick Pratt, the exec, says, "I think, without any question, that O'Donnell was a superb administrator." He also says the captain had a tremendous sense of humor and the kind of contagious laugh that made people feel comfortable in his presence.

In the area of shiphandling, Captain O'Donnell was inclined to be more cautious than Atkeson. O'Donnell's specialty was gunnery, which is why he spent a good deal more time with the gunnery officer than his predecessor had. And O'Donnell shone in human relations as well. Seaman Ben Mehling was up on the bridge chipping paint one day when he was summoned to the captain's cabin by O'Donnell's Marine orderly. O'Donnell told him to sit down and offered him a cup of coffee, which was even more unexpected than the invitation had been. O'Donnell then told young Mehling that he had received a gift from the seaman's mother and wanted to tell the sailor of his gratitude. He also asked if the youngster wrote home often. Mehling sheepishly admitted that he didn't, so the captain suggested it would be a good idea and also gave him a card that he had written to thank Mrs. Mehling for the gift. It was to be an enclosure for the letter he was encouraging the young *New Jersey* man to write.

When he did write home, Mehling probably didn't go into too much detail about what he did on liberty in Norfolk. As was the case with so many others, he frequently made his way to the bars on East Main and Granby. A favorite with him and his shipmates was the Savoy on East Main. The proprietor knew the crews of various ships had their favorite hangouts, so he put a big picture of the *New Jersey* on one wall of the Savoy. It worked; as Mehling puts it, "If you were going to meet a *Jersey* sailor, anybody from the 'Big Jay', you went to the Savoy." Dick McDowell, a seaman in the *New Jersey*'s fifth division, was another of the many who went there. The customers were drawn in part by the owner's willingness to make no-interest loans to *New Jersey* men to tide them over between paydays. It was a change from the loan-sharking practices of some of the Norfolk predators who lent money at high interest rates. The idea of the loans without interest was to build up good will and, of course, to keep men coming back time and again.

For some men in the crew, such as Fireman Charles Hungtington of the A division, a beer or two was usually sufficient, so he avoided the scene downtown and looked instead for other off-duty pastimes. Sometimes he spent entire weekends at the Norfolk USO, playing pingpong, checkers, pool, cards, reading, or watching television. In the mid-1950s, TV was not yet the universal phenomenon it would later become, so a comfortable place to sit, relax, and watch a set for a while had novelty value as well as being entertaining. Huntington also enjoyed going to Norfolk's Ocean View amusement park on the waterfront.

On 23 August, Rear Admiral Edward N. "Butch" Parker shifted his flag from the heavy cruiser *Des Moines* to the *New Jersey*. Parker had previously commanded the heavy cruiser *Newport News* and was involved in a succession of destroyer billets before that. He was skipper of the four-stacker *Parrott* as the U.S. Asiatic Fleet was undergoing its death throes in early 1942 and then commanded the USS *Cushing* when she was sunk by Japanese battleship fire in the Battle of Guadalcanal on the night of 13–14 November 1942.

The *New Jersey* was about to begin a tour with the Sixth Fleet in the Mediterranean, the first of her career. She would be taking a cruiser's place in the deployment rotation, so it was appropriate that Parker, who was Commander Cruiser Division Six, should be embarked. The cruise began on Wednesday, 7 September, as the *New Jersey* got under way from Norfolk and began making her way across the Atlantic. On the 17th the battleship pulled in at Gibraltar and anchored for a stay which lasted until the 20th.

Members of the crew had a chance for liberty at this gateway to the Mediterranean. Many of them, including Seamen John Evans and Dick McDowell, visited the famous "rock" for which Gibraltar is best known. They were given tours by the British military men on duty there, climbing up through caves to the top and enjoying the magnificent view. There were a few distractions, however, in the form of numerous apes which had shore duty on the rock and didn't take all that kindly to visitors. Evans tried to touch a small one, and its mother came right after him. "I thought she was going to chew me right up," he says. As soon as he walked away, she relaxed.

From 22 until 28 September, the *New Jersey* visited Valencia, Spain, her second trip there in a short space of time. Valencia was the place where Photographer's Mate Chuck Hamilton had the duty of chasing men out of the brothels while on shore patrol. This time he had difficulties of another sort, but at least they were connected with his rating. One of the battleship's chaplains asked him to provide photo coverage of a religious service which members of the crew would be attending in Valencia. Hamilton himself had to remain on board ship because of other duties, so he sent Seaman Apprentice Jimmy Barnes, who had been in the engineering department until a short time before. Hamilton had been shorthanded, so he recruited Barnes for the photo lab, even though Barnes's only "qualifications" were a desire to help and the fact that both he and Hamilton were from Baltimore. During the religious service, Barnes apparently got rattled, because when he got back to the ship, he had what Hamilton recalls as "the clearest, blankest film you ever saw in your life. That's the first time I ever got chewed out by a chaplain. I didn't know chaplains talked like that, but he sure did."

After leaving Valencia, the *New Jersey* joined up with the Sixth Fleet for a period of operations. Since there was no war in progress at the time, the ship's role was to remain ready if needed and to demonstrate that readiness to Mediterranean nations. Certainly, there were the usual aircraft carriers on station with the Sixth Fleet, but a battleship added still more muscle. As O'Donnell explains, "It seems to me that there has not been a sufficient appreciation of what's involved in the gun as part of your essential firepower. When you can use it . . . it's the cheapest and most effective, the most satisfying to the customer, way of going."

In terms of economy of resources to get the job done, that was also a concern of the engineering department and was reflected in the department's annual standing in the type command fuel effiency ratings. The results had recently been posted for the type command engineering competition for fiscal year 1955, which had ended on 30 June. In fiscal year 1954, the *New Jersey* finished in sixteenth place of the sixteen ships in BatCruLant. Now, with Commander Fred Bitting having taken over as chief engineer and determined to run the ship more economically, she had pulled herself all the way up to fourth. Bitting's philosophy included the use, for instance, of only as many generators as were needed for the ship's power requirements, rather than always having some extras operating just for good measure. Especially important was the sparing use of fresh water, because that was more of a variable than fuel for propulsion. Each gallon of fresh water which had to be made by the evaporators required that much more use of fuel oil. One of Commander Bitting's tactics was to plug up most of the holes in shower nozzles in the officers' heads. Earlier in the year, before Admiral Parker was embarked, two other members of the wardroom conspired to borrow a shower head from flag quarters, then passed it back and forth for use until water restrictions eased up. Bitting's methods weren't always popular, but they did produce a significant boost in the ship's competitive standing. When the fiscal year 1956 engineering results were published a year later, the *New*

*Jersey* had moved up a notch to third place in the type command standings.

While the officers were dealing with minor irritants such as shower nozzles, they had a quite pleasant existence in the ship's wardroom mess. Lieutenant (junior grade) Dick Abrams enjoyed the atmosphere with the silver service, white tablecloths, folded cloth napkins, and meals served by stewards. There was a degree of formality about the whole thing. Since Captain O'Donnell had his own mess, Commander Hartigan, as exec, was president of the wardroom mess and sat at the head of the senior table. The places for the rest of the officers were determined by their seniority. The ensigns had their own tables. One of those ensigns was Ted Walker, who now says facetiously, "You really didn't want to be promoted to jaygee or lieutenant, because then you had to go up and be polite."

Walker and others remember that the officers ate well in that wardroom, paying about $45.00 a month for their food, which was a good-sized chunk out of an ensign's pay in those days. The general mess was free for the enlisted crew members. The Navy did not make as much effort then as it does now to cater to individual tastes, says Walker, but people were given plenty to eat. An example of a crew's mess "meal of the week" in late September included mulligan soup, Waldorf salad, sweet pickles, grilled rib steaks, french fried potatoes, buttered lima beans, cream-style corn, orangeade, crackers, parkerhouse rolls, milk, coffee, and dessert.

One officer who was getting the feel of the *New Jersey* during that cruise in the Mediterranean was Commander Clyde Anderson, who reported aboard in August as operations officer. The son of a chief petty officer who joined the Navy in the nineteenth century, Anderson had been used to seeing battleships since he was a boy in the 1920s. Now he made a close acquaintance with the *New Jersey* and initially expressed a sense of "surprise that any ship so massive, so solid, with such a sense of permanence, could still be so beautiful". He discovered her comfortable handling characteristics as well as her appearance and had the experience a number of times of taking her alongside replenishment ships in the Mediterranean. He kept careful track of both range and bearing to the other ship during an approach so that he would know when to ease back on the battleship's power. If he waited too long, the *New Jersey* would shoot on past. If he did it too soon, the battleship would be pushed away by the propeller wash of the other ship against her bow before she got into place.

Because the Sixth Fleet was a highly mobile one, not tied to fixed bases, the *New Jersey* depended a great deal on taking on fuel, stores, and ammunition from other ships while under way. As was the case from the beginning of the ship's active service, supplies of food which came over in replenishments were considered fair game by the crew. Seaman Wayne Begandy of EX division once joined a couple of buddies in filching a case of pears. Begandy was spotted, however, and the long arm of a chief master-at-arms nailed him. Then came the interrogation, and Begandy stoically refused to divulge the names of his accomplices, so it was he alone who served the sentence. For a week, he had to carry that case of pears around with him whever he went – to muster in the morning, to meals in the mess deck, to the movies, and to his work in the print shop.

The *New Jersey*'s time in the Mediterranean was a pleasant period in which fleet operations alternated with enjoyable port visits. One of the latter came between 5 and 13 October at Cannes on the French Riviera. Some crew members did the beach routine, while others went by bus to the town of Valburg in the French Alps. Seaman Dick McDowell learned to ski there on a beginners' slope opposite the hotel where he and other *New Jersey* men stayed. Others went ice skating, and there were also toboggan rides available. Seaman John Evans had a good time taking pictures until he lost his light meter in the snow.

Between port visits, the *New Jersey* and other Sixth Fleet ships gradually worked their way eastward across the Mediterranean. A number of them anchored briefly in Suda Bay, Crete, on 19 and 20 October, and the *New Jersey*'s sailors had a swim call. Sure, there had been plenty of chances to go swimming on the beach at Nice when the ship was in France, but this was a sort of bonus – liberty while on board ship. Marines armed with rifles went out in a boat to keep watch over crew members as they swam. Seaman Evans found out why the Marines were there soon after he dived into the water from a 5-inch gun mount. He remembers, "I dove, and I just kept on going down and down and down, and I saw a shark. I turned around and I came back up. There's no way that Marine could have helped me out." It was the first and last time Evans dived from such a height. As soon as he could, he scrambled up the cargo net draped over the side of the ship and sat out the rest of the recreational swimming.

The Marines in the crew, of course, had many other duties besides protecting against shark attacks. Corporal John Walsh, for example, drew guard duty in the brig on a regular basis. Men were confined there for two principal offenses, unauthorized absence from the ship and fighting. The latter usually took place after too many drinks ashore. Sometimes those in the brig were on bread and water, in which case they were only exercised, not made to work. The prisoners on regular rations were put on work details so their days wouldn't be completely wasted.

Sergeant Sal Triola served as sergeant of the guard when it came his turn, and every fifth day he had a day's duty as the ship's bugler. His duty period ran from reveille to taps, and he used a microphone to send his musical messages throughout the *New Jersey* and thus to regulate the ship's routine. On the days between his stints, the bugling was done by the Navy members of the crew. Triola really

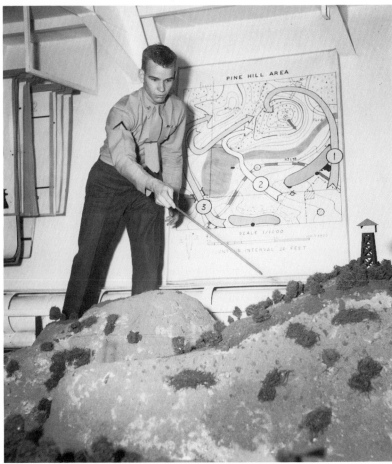

considered bugling secondary to his other duties and was most proud of his role in helping to train others. For instance, when Captain Lemuel C. Shepherd III, the commanding officer for the detachment, wanted to set up a classroom deep within the ship, Triola helped. Some members of the ship's crew had been apprehensive prior to Shepherd's arrival, because his father was then the Commandant of the Marine Corps. There was a natural concern that Captain Shepherd might try to wear his dad's stars, but that didn't prove to be the case. As Triola puts it, "He was just a human being, and he was concerned about his people. . . . He was a magnificent man." Shepherd was friendly and approachable and treated his men as any other Marine captain would. Thus Triola was more than happy to pitch in on making a classroom out of a storeroom. Triola built a plaster of Paris landscape which matched up with a terrain map, and so Shepherd and others were able to teach classes in map reading and the ways in which Marines ashore use various types of terrain for tactical purposes.

From 22 until 27 October, the *New Jersey* was anchored in Phaleron Bay, the port for Athens, Greece, and yet another visit. Captain Shepherd's Marines always had a prime role to play in the ceremonial aspects of port visits. Because of the diplomatic mission of the ship and her men, the Marines assigned to shipboard detachments were carefully chosen. They weren't fresh out of boot camp but had some seasoning so that the ones that went to the *New Jersey* and other ships were, in Shepherd's words, "for the most part, very good Marines". In essence, he says, ship detachments were "gold-plated", taking out potential troublemakers so they couldn't cause embarrass-ments overseas. Admiral Parker thinks there must have been an additional qualification for some – that they be more than 6 feet tall. The routine for visiting a port was that Admiral Parker would go ashore and call on senior dignitaries in the area, and then the dignitaries would be invited to come aboard. The ship visit was frequently timed so the guests could have lunch in the flag mess. There was also the routine of coming aboard and passing between two rows of saluting sideboys and then inspecting the Marine guard. The Marines were almost invariably taller than the visitors and so helped create a psychological impression about the strength and power of the United States. It was an impression that was reinforced in no small measure by the imposing strength and majesty of the *New Jersey* herself. As Parker explains, "This was a period of time when we were trying to do things to put iron in the back of some of those people under pressures from the Soviets. So the bigger we could make the United States appear, the more likely they would feel that we could help them."

Tall Marines could be helpful in other ways as well. Perhaps the most magnificent physical specimen in the detachment was Sergeant Don Henderson, who was 6 feet 2 inches or so, had broad shoulders and a slim waist. It was he who had the duty of serving as payroll guard when Ensign Ted Walker was handing out money to the crew on paydays. That was still a time when men stood in line and stepped forward with pay chits made out for the amount of money they were due to receive. Each chit was signed and marked with the fingerprint of the man's right index finger as protection against someone claiming another man's pay. There were numerous pay lines with a supply

officer at each, but it took several hours to pay the entire crew, especially since there had to be lines for watch-standers and stragglers. When a man stepped up with his pay chit, Walker counted out the amount of cash indicated, and then a petty officer recounted it as a double check before the money was handed to the recipient. Then, in the case of the Marines, recalls Walker, the amount of money immediately started diminishing. A number of senior Marine noncoms were standing by to take a dollar for Marine Corps relief, a dollar for Red Cross, a dollar for the Marine Corps ball, and so forth. With tongue in cheek, Walker says that, "The kid didn't have any money left when it was over."

Sergeant Henderson, a black man, was highly thought of by his *New Jersey* shipmates. Private First Class Walsh and Sergeant Triola were embarrassed that they couldn't go on liberty with Henderson in Norfolk because of segregation laws still in effect. Walsh had grown up in New England and says, "It was hard for me, as an individual, to understand that." In the home port, the white Marines left the ship with Henderson, and then they had to go their separate ways. Overseas, it was different. Sal Triola says that Henderson is "the most superb guy I've ever met in my life. . . . I walked on liberty with that man through all of Europe."

In the diplomatic realm, the *New Jersey* was even-handed in her visits to two nations whose people had long harbored feelings of animosity toward each other. On 27 October, the battleship weighed anchor in Greece and steamed to Istanbul, Turkey, where she arrived the following day and rendered a twenty-one-gun salute. As part of the international relations game, the Turks invited the *New Jersey* to supply a delegation to march in their Republic Day parade. After approval came from Washington, Captain Shepherd led the Marine detachment, color guard, and band. The whole affair was mounted on a tremendous scale, and Captain Shepherd felt as if he were "standing right in Red Square, because there were just thousands of banner-carrying youth groups that preceded us. . . . I can remember seeing the Turkish reviewing officer standing there holding a hand salute for the first hour. I don't know whether he did it for the whole eight hours or not, but I saw it for the first hour."

One effort at international relations was marred, though not seriously, by an amusing miscue. The mayor of Istanbul, an especially short man, came to the ship and inspected the Marine detachment, each member of which had a rifle with a chrome-plated bayonet attached. When one Marine brought his rifle smartly to the port-arms position, the silvery bayonet knocked off the mayor's top hat and startled him until he realized what had happened.

Wayne Begandy, who was an eighteen-year-old seaman in late 1955, looked back on his liberty experience with a degree of regret years later: "Just out of high school, and you don't take advantage of what you can see and what

you can learn in the different ports, and I regret that part of it – that I wasn't smart enough to realize what I was seeing and where I was." Seaman Ben Mehling also had a sense of disappointment; he found both Greece and Turkey picturesque and wished afterward he had taken a camera. At the time one of his concerns was the Turkish coffee, which he considered terrible: "They put three tons of sugar in the smallest cup I've ever seen." Ensign Ted Walker was drinking stronger stuff, having gone ashore with Lieutenant Joe Ellis and Lieutenant Commander Hank Short. They went to the posh bar atop the Marmara Roof of the Istanbul Hilton, and each of them had three or four drinks. When the bill came, the drinks cost about $3.50 apiece, so Walker was awfully glad he didn't lose when the officers rolled dice to see who would pay the bill. "Had I lost," he explains, "it would have been my liberty money for the rest of the time in the Mediterranean."

An individual who redeemed himself in Turkey was Seaman Apprentice Jimmy Barnes, the hapless photographer who came back with blank film in Spain. In Istanbul the assignment was to go to the local USO and photograph an exhibition of belly dancing put on for visiting American sailors. Once again, Chuck Hamilton, the leading photographer's mate, briefed Barnes on using the Speed Graphic camera. Barnes was evidently inspired, because, says Hamilton, "He did the best job of shooting belly dancers I've ever seen. I mean, the detail was perfect." Barnes's photos later showed up in both *The Jerseyman* and the cruisebook for the *New Jersey*'s 1955 operations. That cruisebook was marked by an imaginative touch. The staff invited the leading cartoonists of the day to submit

**Left:** This petition, signed by hundreds of *New Jersey* crew members, offers support to the Naval Academy football team for its 1955 game against West Point. (Courtesy Charles Hamilton)

**Right:** Captain and Mrs. E. J. O'Donnell in the crew's mess during Thanksgiving dinner at Trieste, Italy, in 1955. (Courtesy Captain John Bierley)

drawings which tied in the *New Jersey* with such characters as Dick Tracy, L'il Abner, and Dagwood Bumstead. One cartoon showed a grizzled chief petty officer saying to his men, "There's been a security leak – every time we hit a liberty port there's my wife."

On 3 November, the battleship got under way from the Dardanelles and refueled the next day from the oiler *Mississinewa*. On the fifth, the *New Jersey* began operations with a carrier task group built around the USS *Lake Champlain*. On 7 November, the 5-inch and 16-inch guns conducted a firing exercise at Porto Scuto on the island of Sardinia. It was one of the few times during the deployment that the big guns got an opportunity to fire. Captain Shepherd went to the island as part of the shore fire control party observing the gunfire. Since he hadn't had much training or experience at spotting, he mostly observed the work of the Navy men in the party. One of those naval officers was Lieutenant (junior grade) Joe Metcalf, a member of Admiral Parker's staff. Twenty-eight years later, in the autumn of 1983, Metcalf was a vice admiral in command of the U.S. Second Fleet. He led the expedition which secured the island of Grenada in the Caribbean.

On 9 November, there was another swim call, and two days later the *New Jersey* visited Leghorn in Italy. The next stop, from 22 until 28 November, was Trieste, Italy, a port at the northeast end of the Adriatic Sea and long a bone of contention between Italy and Yugoslavia. The visit to Trieste offered the crew opportunities to visit Munich and Venice, and it also offered the Navy an opportunity to collect intelligence. The port had recently been released from the protection of the United Nations Security Council, and the *New Jersey* was the first U.S. warship in some while to visit. Photographer's Mate Hamilton was sent up in the ship's helicopter to take aerial pictures of the shoreline. He also took radar scope pictures of the port, as he had done also at Istanbul. The pictures left the ship as soon as they were taken so that they could be put in a data bank for use by intelligence officers in Washington. Lieutenant (junior grade) Charles Mumford was one of the officers assigned to the *New Jersey*'s combat information center. He likens the radar scope photos to the medical practice of taking electro-cardiograms. Each picture provides a basis for comparison with shots taken at other times and thus shows changes which occur.

The Thanksgiving holiday fell on 24 November, while the ship was at Trieste. Along with the roast turkey and baked ham were shrimp cocktail, oyster dressing, pumpkin pie, mince pie, fruits, vegetables, and other treats. Joining the crew for dinner in the mess deck were Captain and Mrs. O'Donnell. The skipper's wife had come to the Mediterranean to follow the ship during part of the cruise. Seaman Dick McDowell of the fifth division was pleased that the O'Donnells ate with the men and that the captain took time to ask crew members how things were going. If there were problems – then or at other times – the skipper worked through the exec and division officers to get things taken care of.

Trieste brought unhappy news for Admiral Parker, the embarked Commander Cruiser Division Six. He had been having trouble for some time with pain in his left foot and had taken medication for a suspected case of gout. The

**Above:** Three members of the *New Jersey*'s crew have a snack while on liberty in Cannes, France, in October 1955. At left is Photographer's Mate Third Class Charles Hamilton. (Courtesy Charles Hamilton)

U.S. consul in Trieste happened to know an Italian doctor who had worked with the U.S. Army there, and the doctor indicated that the admiral's trouble was probably cancer. Parker sent off a message to the Bureau of Naval Personnel in Washington to report the tentative diagnosis, and then the ship got under way on 28 November. En route to Cannes, France, a message reached the ship on the 29th, detaching her from Task Group 60.3. She was diverted to Naples, Italy, where Parker reluctantly left his flagship on the last day of November and flew to Washington. At nearby Bethesda, Maryland, the diagnosis was confirmed, and his foot was amputated. Eventually fitted with an artificial leg, Parker remained on active duty into the early 1960s and was promoted to vice admiral.

After the interruption, the *New Jersey* continued westward and made port visits at Cannes, France, and Barcelona, Spain. The latter, which lasted from 17 December until 3 January 1956, is remembered with special fondness by many of the crew. Wayne Begandy, then a seaman, says, "The people were fantastic. I fell in love, as every eighteen-year-old does. It was just great. I went on liberty every night." One prosperous Spanish gentleman took Begandy and several of his shipmates to dinner on one of the few occasions when the young sailor wasn't with his newfound love.

Commander Clyde Anderson, the operations officer, met a good many Spanish people and found that the population of Barcelona included a fair number of British men who were in businesses there and married to Spanish women. On one occasion, one of these couples had come out to have dinner on board, and so they reciprocated by inviting Anderson and Jim Pringle, the communication officer, to their home for dinner. "Fine, what time should we come?" asked Anderson.

The prospective host answered, "Oh, come early so we can have a drink before dinner. Come around 10:00 or 10:30."

On Christmas Eve there were religious services on board, but many of the crew went ashore. Captain O'Donnell and Commander Hartigan led a contingent of 300 men who marched from the fleet landing to Our Lady of Bethlehem Church for midnight mass. One who went was Seaman John Evans, who had some misgivings about the experience, because many of the townspeople were left without seats when the men of the battleship marched in and sat down. Even though a large number of the Spanish had to stand, they were nevertheless friendly toward the visitors.

Barcelona is also remembered for two ship's parties which took place on successive nights. The advance man for the port was Lieutenant Commander Hank Short, a stocky mustang officer who was officially the ship's damage control assistant and unofficially her liaison man with local police forces. He found out ahead of time which places the men should stay away from. The city had a fairly well defined red-light district, and there were also some clip joints. Captain O'Donnell proposed to Short that the ship put a few extra shore patrolmen on duty to protect the crew from being defrauded, but Short replied, "Captain, there's no way you're going to keep a damn fool from wasting his money." For the parties themselves, the ship paid top dollar to hire the lavish Rialto nightclub. Department store windows carried notices inviting Spanish girls to show up for dinner and dancing, and they could also bring their mothers as chaperons. O'Donnell recalls that the Barcelona police were stationed at the door, and any time they recognized a professional hooker, she was invited to leave.

The first day of January was marked by more than the beginning of the new year, for the ship also got a new flag officer to replace the departed Admiral Parker. The new commander of Cruiser Division Six was Rear Admiral John H. "Savvy" Sides. A highly intelligent officer, he had spent the previous three and a half years in Washington as director of the Navy's fledgling guided missile program.

The first stop of 1956 was at Palma, Mallorca, in the Balearic Islands, some 135 miles southeast of Barcelona. It was the spot for the wetting-down party of three officers in the *New Jersey*'s medical-dental department. Actually, the three had been promoted to their new ranks back in November, but Palma offered the first real chance for a party without interfering with the holiday season. Included were new Captain John Bierley, the senior medical officer; Captain Harold Siemer, the senior dentist;

and Lieutenant Jack Gehring of the medical service corps. Cut-rate liquor supplied from Sixth Fleet stores came in handy, because two of the officers involved had objections to possible alternative means of celebration. Dr. Bierley explains, "Siemer objected to candy as a gift because he did not wish to contribute to tooth decay; I, as a physician, had always inveighed against tobacco in all its forms; Gehring objected to nothing."

On the morning of 16 January, after she had stopped for a few days for another visit to Gibraltar, the *New Jersey* got under way for Norfolk, steaming in company with the heavy cruiser *Des Moines*, which had just been relieved as Sixth Fleet flagship. Captain O'Donnell was highly gratified to receive a message from Commander Sixth Fleet: "Your outstanding conduct record and excellent performance of duty have reflected credit upon you and Sixth Fleet. Goodbye and good luck. Vice Admiral [Ralph] Ofstie." The message was especially welcome because of the emphasis placed since the beginning of the cruise on the importance of good conduct ashore. The men of the *New Jersey* were in a very real sense ambassadors for their country.

During the week-long voyage back to the States, the *New Jersey* and *Des Moines* conducted a number of drills, including gunnery exercises. After the arrival in Norfolk on 25 January, Admiral Sides remained embarked in the battleship for three more weeks. He shifted his flag to the

command ship *Northampton* on 15 February, the day after the *New Jersey* moved to the Norfolk Naval Shipyard for a brief period of upkeep following her overseas deployment. The routine of yard work was broken on 22 February when the *New Jersey* followed Navy tradition by dressing ship with flags in honor of George Washington's birthday. On 28 February, she began heading south for Guantanamo and the annual "Springboard" exercise to provide a training period to prepare the crew for the ship's coming operational readiness inspection.

On Saturday, 3 March, the crew donned dress uniforms for a captain's inspection and honor ceremony. Sweltering Guantanamo was not the crew's favorite spot for an inspection. Private First Class John Walsh of the Marine detachment felt relieved when he was able to get back down inside the ship and out of the sun. He recalls, "The polish was melted right off [our shoes] because of how extremely hot it was." At the honor ceremony crew members were given such things as Good Conduct Medals, mess cook of the month awards, and certificates for completing a high school equivalency course.

Seaman Ben Mehling spent much of each working day on the bridge as part of the quartermaster gang, then took his mattress up to sleep on the bridge at night. The sky above Cuba was beautiful, clear blue. At night the heat had dissipated, and a slight breeze blew past as Mehling counted stars before falling asleep. After such pleasant evenings, the routine was for the ship to weigh anchor in the morning and go out for the day's training operations, which sometimes included the firing of the guns.

On 13 March, Rear Admiral Henry Crommelin, Commander Battleship Division Two, came aboard from the *Wisconsin* to give the *New Jersey* her annual readiness inspection and battle problem. The *New Jersey*'s crew then got a breather from their training in the form of a weekend visit to St. Thomas in the Virgin Islands from 17 until 19 March. Then it was back to Guantanamo Bay and still more training before returning to Norfolk at the end of the month.

Following just over a week at anchor in Hampton Roads, the *New Jersey* went out for training exercises on 9 April in company with the carriers *Coral Sea, Forrestal*, and escorting destroyers. The *Forrestal*, which had just been commissioned the previous October, was the first of the Navy's "super carriers", and she was involved in a training period that was especially intensive because of her status as first of a class. She was, indeed, the biggest ship the Navy had ever had up to that time. The skipper of the *Forrestal* was Captain Roy Johnson, a Naval Academy classmate of Captain O'Donnell in 1929. Johnson wanted to demonstrate that the *Forrestal* could operate in heavy weather and was concerned about the ability of destroyers to serve in the plane guard role in case of a crash. So he asked O'Donnell to use the *New Jersey* as a plane guard, which O'Donnell did.

Below: Two F7U Cutlass fighters sit on the recently commissioned carrier *Forrestal* during heavy weather exercises with the *New Jersey* in April 1956. (National Archives: 80-G-760836)

The months of April and May were spent largely in the Norfolk area and operating off the Virginia Capes. On 12 May, Commander Battleship Division Two and members of his staff came aboard to conduct a surprise administrative inspection. Late in the month, the *New Jersey* offloaded much of her fuel so she could lighten her draft and get through the York Spit Channel on her way up the Chesapeake Bay to Annapolis. There she got a new commanding officer. Captain Charles B. Brooks became the twelfth skipper of the *New Jersey* when he took command on 31 May, not far from his old office, for he had been secretary of the Naval Academy's Board since 1953. Brooks had previous fast battleship experience as executive officer of both the *Indiana* and the *Iowa*. Much earlier in his career, he was officer of the deck in the old *New York* when she was commanded by Captain Husband E. Kimmel.

The cruise began on 5 June; the other heavy ships accompanying the *New Jersey* and a flock of destroyers were the battleship *Iowa* and the heavy cruisers *Des Moines* and *Macon*. The first stop was Oslo, Norway. The *New Jersey* arrived there on 20 June, just before mid-summer's night, which was practically no night at all because the sun set briefly at about midnight and then came up an hour or so later. Commander Clyde Anderson joined an Air Force colonel whom he had met at the Armed Forces Staff College and who was now on duty in Norway. They spent the night cruising a fjord in a large boat, stopping at every little point of land. They were invited ashore for a drink at each place, and then they'd go off to find another host and hostess. After a while, many boats converged for a grand picnic, warmed by bonfires on the edge of the fjord. Finally the tired celebrants straggled back to their homes – and in Anderson's case, his ship – at about 7:00 in the morning. Midshipman Third Class Rich Milligan from the Naval Academy spent the long night in a cabin up in the Norwegian hills. The people he was visiting held a party and passed the time by playing old American phonograph records, including those of Frank Sinatra.

Seaman Dick McDowell was much taken by the beautiful scenery in Norway, the opportunities for sightseeing, and the friendliness of the people. He and other shipmates such as Ben Mehling were taken with the girls. They all looked the same – blonde, blue-eyed, and with milky skin. Brunettes and redheads were rare. Mehling was pleasantly surprised by the friendliness and hospitality of the Norwegians, for as he puts it, "It was unusual for people to treat you that way, because sailors are not the most welcome persons in the world." He gave the natives tours of the ship when he had the duty and visited in their homes when ashore.

In 1955, the *New Jersey* had spent 4 July in England, and then did so a year later. This time she was at Portsmouth instead of Weymouth. Ben Mehling found a pub called the Red Lion, which he tried to drink dry. He took some umbrage in midafternoon when he was invited to go out

and sit on the sidewalk so the proprietor could clean up the place and have his customary tea. After a time, Mehling and his mates were allowed back in again to slake whatever thirst had built in the meantime. Still, it took some getting used to. "We were a little mad," he says, "because who the heck in America has tea in the afternoon?"

Portsmouth marked the completion of the *New Jersey* tour of duty for Commander Hartigan, the executive officer. His place was taken by Commander Harry McElwain, who came to the job reluctantly, because he had been told by his detailer in the Bureau of Naval Personnel that the *New Jersey* was scheduled for decommissioning. The *Missouri* had been decommissioned in 1955, and all too soon it would be the turn of the *New Jersey*. Another who felt unhappy at the projected turn of events was the new skipper, Captain Brooks. He remarked to some of his officers that even if 16-inch guns became obsolete, the *New Jersey*'s hull, power plant, and armor protection made her highly suitable for adaptation to any new weapons the Navy might develop, especially guided missiles. Clyde Anderson recalls that Brooks was even then thinking of the huge Jupiter missiles the Army was using. As it turned out, the large ballistic missiles were scaled down and found their way into the fleet via the Polaris program.

Captain Brooks bore a physical resemblance to Captain O'Donnell, for he also was tall and even more slender. He also had a pleasant smile and friendly manner but was not so outgoing and gregarious as O'Donnell. He had more of the reserve and aloofness traditionally associated with the commanding officers of large ships. McElwain recalls that his relationship with Brooks was excellent. The captain told him, "Okay, Harry, you run the ship internally, and I'll take care of the external part." And that's just the way it worked. As a seaman, Brooks was competent but not flashy. Lieutenant Pierre Vining was the *New Jersey*'s main propulsion assistant. He remembers Brooks as a man who had "universal respect from people on board". Ben Mehling, one of the quartermasters, saw Brooks frequently on the bridge and considered him "a little sterner than Captain O'Donnell". To Mehling, Captain Brooks's presence was more overtly felt than O'Donnell's had been. Brooks was more likely to get involved in correcting small details than O'Donnell, who put his confidence in trusted subordinates for that function. As Mehling says of Brooks, "He wouldn't yell at people, but he'd make sure it was right." Commander Fred Bitting, the engineer officer, was especially struck by Captain Brooks's sense of loyalty to his officers and crew, backing them in their dealings with outsiders.

The biggest project in the ship's print shop during that summer of 1956 was the forty-eight-page paper-covered cruisebook for the midshipmen. Along with pictures of liberty ports and shipboard training, there were group

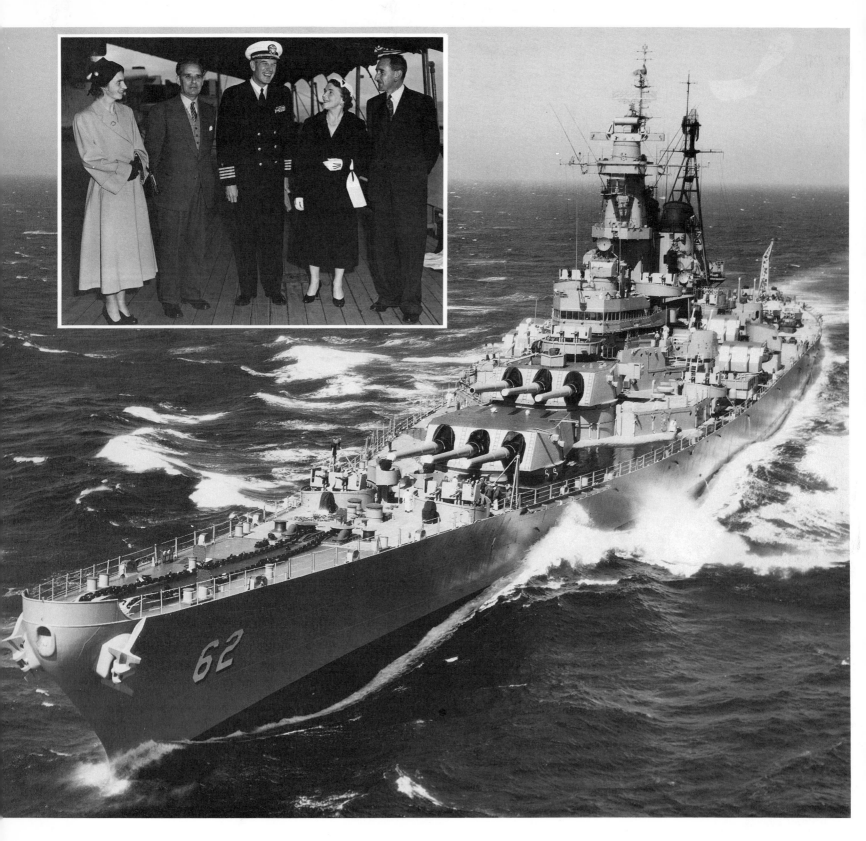

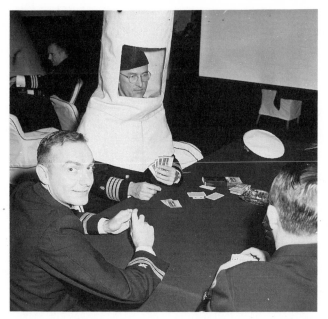

photos of the midshipmen. The NROTC types were largely from eastern universities, and there was the Naval Academy contingent as well. Among the latter was nineteen-year-old Rich Milligan from Matawan, New Jersey. He had just completed his plebe year at Annapolis. Nearly thirty years later, he became commanding officer of the *New Jersey*.

Back in 1956, Milligan was sleeping in the same four-tiered pipe frame bunks as other crew members and sharing the primitive, trough-type heads which didn't have individual stalls. That was the basis for one of the most interesting shipboard practical jokes. The troughs were on an incline so the sluicing salt water could serve to flush them. When one or more young sailors were ensconced on the seats above the trough, some mischievous character would put a wad of toilet paper in the trough and set fire to it, then watch with glee as it produced hot seats down the line. Another stunt, recalls Ben Mehling, took place in berthing compartments. A sleeping man often draped an arm out of the bunk, and his not-so-kind shipmates would fill the hand with shaving cream, then tickle his face with a feather. When he scratched or smacked the itch, he got a face full of shaving cream.

After winding things up in England, the *New Jersey* got under way on 10 July for the obligatory trip to Guantanamo Bay to complete the training routine for the midshipmen, and then to Annapolis, where she arrived 31 July to drop off the midshipmen. Then it was on down to Norfolk to spend much of August. On 23 August, the *New Jersey* again became a flagship with the embarkation of Commander Second Fleet, Vice Admiral Charles Wellborn, and his staff. This was a repeat visit for Wellborn. Back in the autumn of 1945, when the *New Jersey* was flagship for the occupation of Japan, Wellborn – then a rear admiral – had been in the ship as chief of staff to Admiral John Towers, Commander Fifth Fleet. In this case, Admiral Wellborn would be wearing his "NATO hat", Commander Striking Fleet Atlantic, for a coming exercise off the coast of Europe.

Fortunately for the crew, there were to be additional liberty ports as part of this last, brief deployment prior to the beginning of her pre-inactivation overhaul. She left the Norfolk naval operating base on Sunday, 26 August. Once the battleship was out into the Atlantic, she was involved in the communications exercise "Gulf Stream" from 4 until 8 September as she proceeded toward Lisbon, Portugal. The stop there lasted from the 12th until the 15th, and then she headed north for Scotland. She was at Greenock from 18 to 25 September. Seaman Ben Mehling and others went to a hall where a large dance contest was held. The various contestants had numbers on their backs so the best couples could be picked out by the judges. Even though prizes were being given, Mehling and his buddies were restless and departed, because they wanted something with more kick than the Coca-Cola which was the main drink in the dance hall.

Back on board ship, life became a lot more pleasant for Dr. John Bierley with the arrival of a new first lieutenant, Lieutenant Commander Frank Kalasinsky. Previously, Bierley, who had an aversion to cigarette smoke, had been forced to leave when the concentration got above a certain level in the wardroom. Kalasinsky invented a canvas hood which could be attached to an air duct in the overhead of the wardroom. It flared at the lower end to permit air to escape and had an isinglass "window" through which the doctor could look while playing cards or watching a wardroom movie.

On 25 September, the *New Jersey* departed Greenock for Oslo, Norway, and from the 26th through the 28th the Striking Fleet staff on board the ship conducted Exercise "Whipback", a simulated air operation off the coast of Norway. It was laying the groundwork for a full-scale NATO exercise the following year. On shore at that same time, the Allied Command Europe was conducting Exercise "Whipsaw". The *New Jersey* was acting as flagship of a simulated task force of NATO ships, including carriers, cruisers, and destroyers. The role of the "constructive" – imaginary, that is – task force was to support NATO operations in the area of Norway, The Netherlands, and Belgium. Part of the test was to observe the weather and sea conditions that such a task force would encounter when operating a NATO mission so far north. There was also a hint of something else the NATO ships would encounter. Says Admiral Wellborn, "I recall that at one time during this trip we tracked by radar a 'snooper' plane, undoubtedly Russian, that followed us for some time but was never actually sighted." The *New Jersey*, remembers Harry McElwain, the exec, had an electronic intelligence

team on board for the exercise. The team set up shop high in the tower structure above the bridge, listening for radio transmissions and observing when it was likely that the ship was picked up on radar.

While it was obviously useful for the defense of the free world to conduct such exercises and maintain naval readiness, Lithographer Third Class Wayne Begandy had some misgivings about the whole thing. The print shop where he worked printed a confidential annex to the Striking Fleet operation order. Says Begandy, "Every time we were printing, there was an officer in the print shop with us. Every piece of paper had to be accounted for. We had to get a security clearance and the whole thing. We were in the middle of the Arctic, and there was nobody around us. . . . Because we had the flag aboard, when we had to empty trash over the side, we had to go topside in our undress blues. I couldn't believe it, because there wasn't even a polar bear around."

From 29 September until 4 October, the *New Jersey* was at Oslo, the second such visit in a brief period, for she had just been there in June during the midshipman cruise. Commander McElwain, the executive officer, observed that the crew was delighted with the prospect of seeing the place again. A number of them took up with the same girl friends they'd been seeing during the previous visit. Not all were so lucky. John Evans, then a seaman, recalls, "I looked, but I didn't find her." Admiral Wellborn received an official call from Crown Prince Olav, the same individual who had so valiantly saluted the *New Jersey* and

*Wisconsin* from his wildly tossing boat during the ships' visit to Oslo in 1947.

In Oslo, as elsewhere, the ship's senior petty officers had a powerful motivational tool to make sure that work got done, uniforms were squared away, and that men carried out the orders they were given; that tool was the liberty card. Each sailor had to have one to go ashore, and so it was a simple matter to withhold the card until things were right. This was part of an informal disciplinary system at the division level. Only relatively serious offenses got to the executive officer and captain's mast. For day-to-day things – including the proper performance of duty – the petty officers had considerable power, either in assigning extra duty or holding back privileges. One of those in charge of seeing that things were done correctly in the E division was Electrician's Mate First Class Arthur Smith. He says, "I was a firm believer that if somebody told you to do something, you did it, and then maybe you questioned later on. . . . But you didn't question [beforehand], because it would be in the back of your mind that if you did, somebody would put a foot up your rear end."

Vice Admiral Wellborn and his staff left the *New Jersey* on 3 October, and on the following day she began the long journey home to Norfolk, arriving on the 15th. In the following weeks she was in and around Norfolk, then spent the latter half of November and the first part of December at the Norfolk Naval Shipyard in Portsmouth. On 13 December, the *New Jersey* got under way for Bayonne, New Jersey, and arrived the following day. There to greet her were two mothballed veterans of the Pacific campaign in World War II, the carriers *Franklin* and *Enterprise*. On 20 December, tugboats pulled the battleship away from the pier at Bayonne for a planned trip to the New York Naval Shipyard in Brooklyn. The tugs got her too far away from deep water, and she grounded. Her main condensers filled with silt, and the main generators soon kicked off – not the best news for Commander Fred Bitting, the chief engineer. He recalls that the emergency diesel generators then came on automatically, but their intakes soon filled with mud also, and they went off the line. The ship had no propulsive power and no electricity until she could be brought back alongside the dock and hooked to shore power. Bitting recalls that it was a dirty job to open and clean the condensers, and then she was able to go to an anchorage at Gravesend Bay before proceeding on 21 December to the shipyard in Brooklyn.

Soon after the beginning of the new year of 1957, on 7 January, the *New Jersey* again went out to Gravesend Bay, this time to offload her ammunition. She got rid of more than 500 16-inch projectiles, more than 9,000 5-inch projectiles, a commensurate amount of powder, and more than 75,000 rounds of 40-mm. ammunition. On 11 January, she returned to Brooklyn, and on the 17th her Marine detachment was disbanded – yet another sign of the growing momentum toward decommissioning. This great warship would gradually lose those elements which had made her an active part of the fleet since that cold, windy day in November 1950 when she was recommissioned for service in the Korean War. The life-draining process would be a two-step affair. The first, which began on 15 January, was a $1 million preinactivation overhaul which concentrated primarily on the engineering plant: boiler work, reduction gears, and fuel oil piping and heating coils. After that would come the inactivation itself over at Bayonne. The period at the naval shipyard in Brooklyn ended on 19 April, when the *New Jersey* cast off from her pier and steamed over to the naval annex at Bayonne, where she was put into dry dock. Some of the inactivation process had already started at Brooklyn, and now the mothballing became the main focus of activity.

Because of the electrical equipment and cabling which had to be inactivated throughout the ship, one man who had a large job during the mothballing process was Electrician's Mate Smith. In preserving a motor, for instance, Smith's men completely stripped it down, cleaned it, replaced bearings as necessary, and reassembled it. He was also in charge of batteries and the other electrical aspects of boats, including running lights, wiring, and starters. Other gangs of electrician's mates worked on switchboards, generators, pumps, lighting, ventilation, and the hundreds of other facets of the huge vessel's electrical system.

Elsewhere in the ship, the inactivation process was largely similar to that of nine years earlier, including

sealing up the ends of the guns, putting waterproof covers over exposed items, and sealing up holes in the hull while in dry dock. The cosmoline which had caused so much difficulty during the Korean War activation was eschewed in favor of thin film rust proofing. The latter was a liquid which could be sprayed on in various thicknesses to seal out moisture. It remained tacky to the touch and could be removed by the use of petroleum-based solvents. Captain Brooks, who was saddened by having to be involved in the mothballing process at all, was especially unhappy about the requirement to go through the preservation checkoff list on the 40-mm. gun mounts. On 13 May he sent a long letter to Captain John Miner, commanding officer of the *Wisconsin*. That battleship was scheduled to go through the mothballing process after the *New Jersey*, and so Brooks wrote to prepare Miner for what he would be up against. In discussing the gunnery aspects, Captain Brooks wrote, "We made a strong effort to get rid of our 40-mm. mounts since I feel that they would be one of the first items to come off in case these ships are recommissioned. We were unsuccessful however, and had to accomplish the normal inactivation procedures for the 40-mm. batteries." Brooks's prophecy was fulfilled ten years later. When the *New Jersey* was reactivated for Vietnam, the 40-mm. mounts were removed.

There were more mundane concerns, some of which involved the matter of what the crew did when not required to be assisting in the inactivation process. Younger members of the crew frequently went to New York City for liberty. Seaman John Evans got good, free seats whenever he went to a big league baseball game. He saw the Dodgers play in Brooklyn during their last summer there before moving to Los Angeles. Lieutenant (junior grade) Charles Mumford, a bachelor officer, made it a point to try to see at least one Broadway show and one off-Broadway show each week. Some were free; others meant he had to be around the cancellation windows at show time. The hardest ticket to get was for "My Fair Lady", starring Rex Harrison and Julie Andrews.

For more senior members of the crew, especially those with families still in the ship's home port of Norfolk, the weekends were made for commuting back and forth. Lieutenant Commander Pierre Vining noticed that Captain John Bierley, the non-smoking physician, picked his car pool partners carefully so he wouldn't be gasping for air all the way to Norfolk and back. A couple of warrant officers bought a used car for weekend journeys to Norfolk. Electrician's Mate Arthur Smith observed: "That looked like a typical hoodlum's car, because it was an old Cadillac, and it had side curtains on the windows. They had the concealed places where I guess the mobsters used to keep their guns or something like that."

Commander Ralph Meilandt, the supply officer, had two principal responsibilities during the inactivation – making sure that all the allowance list items were on board the ship and all the "strip ship" items were removed. Equipment and spare parts which would be needed for reactivation were to be on board, but consumables and other items which might be used by other ships had to be removed. In going through the allowance list requirements with Commander Bitting while back in Brooklyn, Meilandt had discovered that the main shaft bearings called for on the allowance list couldn't be found on board the ship. Accordingly, a requisition was put in for the huge bearings to be fabricated. Later, the engineering department discovered the necessary bearings were on board after all. They had been welded to a bulkhead down in "Broadway", the long third deck passageway, and subsequently painted over and hidden by other gear. The search had been inspired by the arrival of a new set of bearings which came to Bayonne on railroad flat cars. Meilandt remembers, "The extra set of bearings were returned to Philadelphia. We weren't entirely surprised to see them again when someone in Philadelphia decided to send them back to us again – the flat cars reappeared alongside the ship a couple of day before our decommissioning. . . . Once more, I sent them off to Philly."

As the time of decommissioning drew nigh, Commander McElwain, the exec, found it necessary to make some disposition of the several thousand dollars remaining in the ship's welfare and recreation fund. He wanted to give it to charity, but instead the crew voted for what McElwain describes as "a hell of a big decommissioning party". For one night the *New Jersey* took over a ballroom at the Waldorf Astoria Hotel and really did things up right. There was even a Miss USS *New Jersey* in the person of actress Julie Newmar, who was appearing in a New York produc-

tion of "L'il Abner". She visited the ship and also attended the party ashore. Speaking of her ship visit, Ben Mehling says, "I remember one time she was going down a ladder. She was going below deck, and I don't think any woman had so many helpers in her life. . . . She was friendly, very friendly." At the party itself Mehling discovered there was a good supply of girls, and there was also a paddy wagon outside – just in case. He remembers, "It was a happy occasion, yet it was a sad occasion, because every guy was going somewhere else, and you never know when you're going to meet them again."

When it came time for the decommissioning ceremony on 21 August, there were only a few hundred crew members left to observe and participate in the *New Jersey*'s passing from the roster of Navy ships. The mothballing was complete, and the only thing remaining was to hold the funeral service on the fantail. Captain Brooks read the decommissioning order and turned the now-silent battleship over to Captain Charles Hopper, commander of the New York group of the Atlantic Reserve Fleet. Among the guests that day was Mrs. Pierre Vining, wife of the officer who had been the *New Jersey*'s main propulsion assistant. She found the whole occasion so sad that she vowed never again to attend a ship's decommissioning. Lieutenant Commander Vining himself was philosophical. He and his shipmates had lost their home and indeed the institution which had bound them together for months or even years. Though they would no longer have a physical association with the *New Jersey*, they had the memories of shared experiences that would always remain with them. As Vining says today, "I don't think I've ever been in a ship that had such a great spirit."

**Below left:** The quarterdeck plaque honoring the ship's battle history is no more than a prop in this 1957 publicity photo. The *New Jersey*'s executive officer, Commander Harry McElwain, is shown with an aspiring starlet, for whom the publicity was not sufficient to make her a star. (Courtesy Captain Harry McElwain)

**Below right:** Actress Julie Newmar, Miss USS *New Jersey* of 1957, poses on a 16-inch gun barrel that has already been sealed off as part of the inactivation prior to decommissioning. (Courtesy Captain Harry McElwain)

# CHAPTER VI
# POLITICS AND THE VIETNAM WAR
## August 1967 – December 1969

Even though the *New Jersey* was designed and built well after the age of sailing ships, she was still very much subject to the political winds which blew strongly during the 1960s. Her truncated Vietnam career was dictated probably as much as or more by political considerations than military ones. Even before she went to Vietnam, much had happened on the national and world political scenes in the ten years between mothballing and demothballing. Cuba fell under a Communist regime, the Berlin Wall was built, the Cuban Missile Crisis raised the chilling specter of nuclear war, and the United States became increasingly involved in a war in Southeast Asia.

Initially, the battleship remained discarded and forgotten as the chill political winds stirred the world scene. In the summer of 1962, as part of a consolidation of the Atlantic reserve fleet, she was towed from her berth at Bayonne, New Jersey, to the Philadelphia Naval Shipyard. The growing U.S. involvement in Vietnam after the summer of 1964 compelled the examination of possible reactivation of one or more *Iowa*-class battleships to support U.S. Forces ashore in Vietnam. Unlike the *New Jersey*'s reactivation for Korea, the decision process this time was

especially long because Admiral David L. McDonald, the Chief of Naval Operations, was steadfast in his opposition to bringing battleships out of mothballs.

Richard Russell of Georgia was a powerful member of the Senate, serving on both the Armed Services and Appropriations committees. After 1964, 1965, and 1966 passed with no decision to bring back a battleship, he said in early 1967, "I will insist on it this year." With his power of the purse, Russell had a great deal to say about paying for the Vietnam War. He got his way. In late May, the Department of Defense announced that it had approved the opening up and inspection of the *New Jersey*. The Navy had already selected her, because she was in better material condition than her three sisters. The so-called inspection actually constituted the opening phase of reactivation – that which would take place during Admiral McDonald's brief remaining tenure as CNO. On 1 August, the same day he retired, the Department of Defense announced officially that it was going to reactivate the *New Jersey* for Vietnam war duty.

The initial steps included moving the ship in mid-June from her mothball fleet berth between the *Iowa* and

**Right:** This view of the Philadelphia Naval Shipyard from 6,000 feet on 20 July 1966 shows dozens of mothballed ships, including the three *Iowa*-class battleships at the right center. (Photo by Joseph Garfinkel; U.S. Naval Institute Collection)

Opposite page, top left: This 21 September 1967 picture, taken shortly after drydocking, shows the effects on propellers and skegs of ten years in the mothball fleet. (U.S. Naval Institute Collection)

Opposite page, center left: Seen in November 1967 while in dry dock is the tunnel formed by the skegs leading forward from the inboard propellers. In the center are the two rudders. (USN photo K-43090 by PH3 J. T. Bullington; U.S. Naval Institute Collection)

Opposite page, bottom left: The New Jersey in dry dock at night during reactivation. (USN photo K-42810 by PH3 J. T. Bullington; U.S. Naval Institute Collection)

Opposite page, top right: The fantail helicopter pad is largely in place as reactivation transforms the New Jersey. Note the 40-mm. gun mount still in place atop turret three. (Courtesy Philadelphia Naval Shipyard)

Opposite page, bottom right: Clutter is the order of the day in this 16 February 1968 picture, taken during reactivation. In the foreground is turret two with a 40-mm. gun tub on top. (Courtesy Philadelphia Naval Shipyard)

Right: Tugboats move the New Jersey away from her reserve fleet berth at Philadelphia on 11 June 1967. (Courtesy Philadelphia Naval Shipyard)

Wisconsin to a pier in the shipyard proper; sandblasting the exterior of the ship; removing dehumidification units; taking the fuel out of the ship's tanks; and removing allowance items and spare parts so that they could be inventoried. Once the reactivation began officially on 1 August, the Philadelphia Naval Shipyard immediately instituted a three-shift, six-day-a-week working schedule and stepped that up to seven days a week before the month was over.

Part of the process involved ripping out and removing things that were outdated. The 40-mm. guns were taken off, electronic gear pulled out for replacement, messing and berthing spaces stripped, and so forth. The resulting clutter was evident when the prospective commanding officer, Captain Richard Alexander, reported to Philadelphia. Alexander observed of the New Jersey, "That thing was the biggest shambles inside when I arrived six weeks after it had been first opened that I ever saw any ship in, in a shipyard, other than new construction." Alexander was disappointed by what he considered an over-long schedule for the battleship's reactivation. She was not to get to Vietnam until some fourteen months after the official start of the yard period. He would have preferred that the shipyard cut corners and not carry out as extensive a modernization package as the one provided. He believed that the need for the New Jersey's bombardment capability off Vietnam was so urgent that she should have been hurried out as quickly as possible.

Captain Alexander had extensive experience in destroyers and had compiled a superb record since being graduated from the Naval Academy in 1944. He reported from the Bureau of Naval Personnel and before that had a topnotch tour of duty as skipper of the guided missile destroyer Semmes. Bill Thompson, who was serving as

public affairs officer in the office of the Secretary of the Navy in 1967, observed of the *New Jersey*'s prospective skipper, "Everybody said he had 'flag officer' written all over him." Also on the secretary's staff at that time was Captain Andy Kerr, a Naval Academy classmate of Alexander. Kerr remembers of Alexander: "He had a reputation of being right in controversial issues, of taking positions that were not in accordance with the common wisdom of the time and having prevailed and been proven right in the end. This reputation resulted in Dick being considered one of the real comers in the Navy of our rank. . . . His selection for flag rank was a foregone conclusion. He was truly a fair-haired boy if there ever was one, and he clearly deserved that position."

In the course of his discussions with officials in Washington and during a trip to ships off the coast of Vietnam to observe bombardment operations, Captain Alexander learned how the battleship was to be employed. She was to support ground troops in South Vietnam, and she was to participate in the Sea Dragon bombardment effort off North Vietnam, shelling enemy coastal supply routes as a means of interdicting the flow of war materials from north to south. These were essentially the same missions the *New Jersey* had performed off Korea fourteen years earlier. In her interdiction role, she would be able to take some of the load off American pilots who were being shot down in considerable numbers while attacking targets such as the bridge at Thanh Hoa in North Vietnam. Alexander found that the comment most often made to him in the autumn of 1967 about the ship's potential contribution was, "If you can get the Thanh Hoa bridge, you'll bring back the big gun." In reflecting on the matter, Captain Alexander came up with roles for the battleship that would be potentially even more valuable – effecting a lodgement to neutralize the enemy transportation center at Vinh and enforcing a blockade against the port of Haiphong. The latter would have shut off the arrival of war materials at the source rather than having to attack the flow of supplies after they reached Vietnam. For political reasons, Haiphong was not cut off until 1972, and then it was achieved through the sowing of naval mines.

On board ship at Philadelphia, department heads and other members of the crew were gathering. Captain Robert Peniston was then involved in making officer assignments at the Bureau of Naval Personnel. He helped assemble a formidable array of talent for key positions throughout the ship. Lieutenant Dick Harris, who had served as a gunfire spotter in Vietnam, was an exception in that he got assigned to the *New Jersey* on his own initiative rather than being handpicked. Once at the ship, Harris quickly became aware that Captain Alexander made it a practice to question members of the nucleus crew with whom he wasn't already acquainted. The captain frequently knew the answers already, so this gave him a means of finding out whether prospective *New Jersey* men knew the ship

and their jobs – and whether they would give him a straight answer if they didn't know something. Fire Controlman First Class Rick Crawford was nearby on one occasion when Captain Alexander was questioning a young enlisted man about the number of exits off "Broadway", the long third-deck passageway which provided access to the engine rooms and firerooms. Crawford considered the new man overmatched by the captain, especially since Crawford – himself a senior petty officer – thought the ship so big and complex that "I was worried about leaving bread crumbs to find my way back."

Even while Alexander was trying to get the ship and her crew ready for duty overseas, his mind was also on another matter – the so-called "Arnheiter Affair". In late 1965 and early 1966, Lieutenant Commander Marcus Aurelius Arnheiter had served for ninety-nine days as commanding officer of the radar picket destroyer escort *Vance*. His overzealous style of leadership and his questionable practices while the *Vance* was off the coast of Vietnam led to his being summarily relieved of command after such a short time. Alexander, who had known Arnheiter for a number of years and had been involved in getting him command of the *Vance*, took up the deposed skipper's cause. He argued that Arnheiter was removed from his ship without due process and had been undermined by a disloyal group of junior officers. Explains Alexander, "I decided to intervene only when [Commander Cruiser-Destroyer Force, Pacific Fleet, Rear Admiral Walter H.] Baumberger, after a thorough review of the case, recommended that Arnheiter *be restored to command*." Captain Alexander had a private meeting with Secretary of the Navy Paul Ignatius in Washington on 7 November 1967; soon afterward the captain released to the press copies of a twenty-seven-page statement he had written on Arnheiter's behalf and presented to Ignatius.

Admiral Thomas H. Moorer, who had relieved Admiral McDonald as Chief of Naval Operations, did not like being bypassed in the Arnheiter case. He considered Alexander's statement "somewhat intemperate" and did not respect Alexander's judgment in releasing his statement rather than pursuing the matter through internal Navy channels. In late December, Captain Alexander was asked to request a transfer from the *New Jersey* to shore duty, and he complied. His once-promising career ended less than two years later when he retired from active duty, never having been selected for the admiral's stars which earlier seemed so likely. Once again, he had taken a courageous but controversial stand, but this time he was undone by it.

Captain Alexander's replacement was Captain J. Edward Snyder, Jr. Both he and Alexander were in the Naval Academy's class of 1945, which was graduated a year early because of the push to get officers out to the fleet during World War II. The new man had earned a master's degree in nuclear physics and had a solid background of big-ship experience, having served in the battleship *Pennsylvania* and the heavy cruisers *Toledo* and *Macon*. In mid-December, he was about to begin driving across country from Washington to California to take command of the heavy cruiser *St. Paul*. Instead, he was to report to Philadelphia the following month to take Alexander's place.

There was an understandable concern about what effect the change would have on the crew. As it turned out, it was slight. Snyder says, "I was concerned to see whether or not the ship had formed any loyalty. I was quickly relieved to realize that there were less than 200 in Philadelphia, therefore less than 200 people who even had the opportunity to know Captain Alexander intimately, and that the work load . . . was so strenuous in those days that people didn't have time for sessions and discussions."

An officer who reported aboard with a good deal less fanfare than Snyder was Ensign Chris Reed, who came in wintry February when the *New Jersey* had completed the dry dock portion of the reactivation but was still uninhabited and chilly inside. Reed was struck by the maze-like interior of the ship, which was divided into hundreds of compartments. He recalls, "The cramped interior dimensions of the ship were always a surprise to visitors." His long, narrow stateroom – when he later moved in – seemed to Reed little more than a passageway with lockers on one side and bunks and desks on the other.

One individual who was able to make things less cramped than previously was Chief Ship's Serviceman Lew Moore. In two previous wars, the ship's store had been a small affair at which customers lined up at a window and bought items such as shaving cream, toothpaste, and cigarettes from the man on duty behind the counter. Chief Moore was involved with the shipyard in constructing a new, much larger walk-in retail store which would allow crew members to come in and browse as they would in a Navy exchange ashore.

When Chief Moore began laying in stock to sell in the new ship's store and gedunk, he was under the impression that Marines would again be part of the ship's company, as they had been during World War II and Korea. However, Secretary of Defense Robert McNamara had decreed there would be no Marines, because he put great value on cost-effectiveness 'and wanted the *New Jersey*'s return to service to be as austere as possible. Captain Snyder was disappointed by the ruling. He was thinking not so much in terms of their ceremonial function as of their potential value in manning a couple of 5-inch mounts. Familiar with the sort of competition that springs up between Navy and Marine gun crews, he reasoned that the attempts to outdo one another would improve overall performance. Chief Moore's concerns were of a different sort. He had bought lots of canned sardines and a type of candy known as Jujubes, because they had been popular with Marines in his past experience. Once the ship got into commission, he found himself with a lot more sardines than the *New Jersey*'s sailors seemed willing to buy. He hit upon a gimmick long known to manufacturers of breakfast cereal – offering a premium to help move the product. In this instance, he offered condoms with the sardines. Along with the expected increase in sales came a protest from the ship's Catholic chaplain, Lieutenant Commander John Byrnes.

Among the enlisted crew members who reported to the ship at Philadelphia was Seaman Tom Feigley, who had just completed two months of boot camp and six months of gunner's mate school. At the outset, he says, "We were doing, really, the menial labor – painting and scraping. There wasn't too much work for us; the shipyard was doing everything. As we went along, we got doing more and more." Feigley was assigned to turret three, the one that Gunner's Mate First Class Bob Moore had served so well as turret captain during the Korean War. By early 1968, Moore had retired from active duty as a chief petty officer and was part of the shipyard crew which was reactivating the turrets for Vietnam. Feigley and others were there not so much to help reactivate turret three as to learn the workings of the equipment. Supervising the training was the new turret captain, Senior Chief Gunner's Mate George Petrovitz, whom Feigley considers "probably one of the smartest mechanics I ever met, inside or outside the Navy".

Even as the nucleus crew was at work in Philadelphia, another group of *New Jersey* men, known as the balance crew – for they would provide the balance of the ship's manpower – were undergoing training at Navy schools in San Diego. Fire Controlman First Class Rick Crawford, who had initially reported to Philadelphia, was among those in a fifteen-week main battery school at San Diego. He recalls that the director they used in their training was from a light cruiser, the range keeper and fire control radar from a battleship, and the power drives from a heavy cruiser. The

Left: In the foreground is Captain Richard G. Alexander, prospective commanding officer of the *New Jersey* until reassigned following his spirited defense of Lieutenant Commander Marcus Arnheiter, shown behind him. (UPI/Bettmann Newsphotos)

instructors were from a previous generation of big-ship fire controlmen who provided both classroom instruction and hands-on drill with the gear.

Walt Migrala and several other ensigns fresh from Officer Candidate School got to San Diego late one week and were informally attired when they went to the fleet training center to get the lay of the land and to find out where they would be going when they officially reported the following Monday. Their attempt at getting a jump on the situation backfired. When they said they were part of the *New Jersey*'s pre-commissioning unit, the petty officer on duty at the training center didn't understand that they were on only a preliminary scouting trip. Instead he escorted them in to see Commander James Elfelt, slated to be the battleship's executive officer. Elfelt took a look at the casually clad group and announced, "I don't know where you guys came from, but out here we report for duty in the full uniform of the day. You guys are starting out in a hole." They dug their way out of it by serving as shore patrol officers for the ship's party held in San Diego.

Migrala remembers that the training offered in San Diego took into account the many different jobs to be done on board the battleship and the varying skill and experience levels of the prospective crew members. Among other things, men received lookout training, fire fighting, damage control, and practice working with underway replenishment rigs. As at Philadelphia, the training had a secondary effect in getting future shipmates working together and forming associations. They were already on their way to becoming *New Jersey* men before they boarded chartered aircraft in March for the long cross-country flight to Philadelphia.

The *New Jersey*'s messing and berthing spaces had been readied just in time for the influx of men from California. One of those reporting with the balance crew was Fire Controlman Second Class Tom Mumpower. When he got to the ship, he was delighted to see that she was air-conditioned and that the FM division berthing compartment had tables useable for letters or playing cards.

In time, each living compartment would have a television set also, part of a closed-circuit system donated by the State Society of the Battleship New Jersey; the society had also been reactivated. The TV system could be hooked up to an outside antenna for picking up commercial programming when close to land. At sea the closed-circuit setup could be used for showing movies or videotapes. Lieutenant Dick Harris was one of a number of officers who brought in their own TV sets for use in their staterooms. They got wired into the system and thus had, in effect, cable television long before it became popular nationwide. The TV setup had an additional function; Captain Snyder had some of the crew members go about the ship carrying cameras and pretending to be network reporters. If yard workmen were slacking off, a camera pointed in their direction generally got them moving more quickly.

The ship was, of course, the focus of a great deal of public interest during her reactivation period. Ensign Scott Cheyne reported to the ship as the new public affairs officer and had to cope with the avalanche of interest and attention being showered upon the *New Jersey*. Fortunately, he was able to draw on the skills of Lieutenant Commander Brayton Harris, the public affairs officer assigned to the staff of the Fourth Naval District at Philadelphia. Gradually, as Cheyne learned more and became more comfortable in his new job, he was able to take on the load himself. That load included answering letters from both children and adults all over the country. Among them were letters from former crew members who provided advice on various pieces of equipment they remembered and how they should be reactivated.

There was also a media blitz, because newspapers, magazines, radio, and television all wanted a piece of this great human interest story. Cheyne and Harris were swamped with requests from reporters who wanted to be on board when the *New Jersey* went out for her first engineering trials in the Atlantic. Because of safety considerations and the need for climbing steep ladders, Lieutenant Commander Harris established a ground rule that the trials could be covered by male newsmen only. Reporters called in to make reservations, and the resulting list included only men's names. Thus, there was considerable surprise when a woman wearing a miniskirt and black textured stockings showed up on the morning of 26 March and announced, "I'm Toni Franzolini of the *Courier-Times* in Levittown [Pennsylvania]." Sure enough, a reservation had been made; the person approving the request had mistakenly assumed it was Tony rather than Toni. She was allowed to go aboard rather than create ill will. The ship then proceeded on down the river, and Captain Snyder slowed at Wilmington, Delaware, to allow the newspeople to transfer to the Navy tug *Menasha* for the trip ashore. One of the other reporters, Baxter Omohundro of the Ridder newspaper chain, remembered afterward that the woman from Levittown was "the center of considerable attention as she descended the Jacob's ladder in her miniskirt. Some of the more ungentlemanly newsmen applauded and made photographs during her departure."

One man from the news media became a stowaway – sort of. In addition to the male-only ground rule, there was one that stipulated that the reporters had to leave at Wilmington and not stay for the three-day cruise. Photographer Neil Leifer from *Sports Illustrated* stayed with unofficial permission because he was working on a photo book for the *New Jersey*'s crew. When he didn't show up with the group coming back from Wilmington, Lieutenant Commander Harris in Philadelphia sent a message to the ship for Leifer to be removed, but by then the weather was too rough. Despite the temporary embarrassment, Leifer served the ship well. His one book eventually became two: *Dreadnought Returns* and *Dreadnought Farewell*.

Together, they comprise a spectacular pictorial documentation of the *New Jersey* between 1967 and 1969.

The trials themselves went satisfactorily, especially on 27 March when the *New Jersey* conducted a full-power run which included building up to maximum speed – reported as 35.2 knots in the ship's official history for the year. Ensign Chris Reed formed indelible memories from the trials that day:

"The ship had settled into her taut high-speed transit jiggle, with which we grew so familiar in later months. Because of her great length she pitched very little. At speeds beyond twenty-five knots or so, her slight roll became segmented into one- or two-degree increments so that she made several distinct steps in a full roll cycle. During the test something minor had gone awry with boiler seven or eight and as we raced through the nearly calm seas we left an impenetrable trail of roiling black smoke. Seven-eighths of the plant was generating the classic light brown haze, but from one of the uptakes in the after stack there boiled up the sooty rebellion of the lone dissenter. The smoke trail was all the more spectacular because there was no wind to disperse it. It continued back to the horizon in an unbroken plume, while directly below it, sparkling rose and gold in the setting sun, the ship's wake arrowed to the same vanishing point on the horizon."

Below: Thousands of spectators have already gathered on the pier on recommissioning day, 6 April 1968. (Courtesy Philadelphia Naval Shipyard)

As the ship raced along, her movement created a relative wind that made walking difficult for those topside. The forced-draft blowers on the air intakes of the giant stacks howled vehemently. Prongs of the radio antenna which sprouted horizontally from the mainmast began vibrating like tuning forks and broke themselves off. The ship's speed built up an inertia which manifested itself dramatically during the most strenuous test of all – going from all ahead flank to all back emergency. Underwater, the giant propellers came to a stop, reversed direction, and gradually began to bite into the sea. A smoke float was thrown over the side when the engines were reversed. The ship hurtled forward for another two miles before she finally came to a stop and began to go astern.

When the *New Jersey* got back to pier four at the Philadelphia Naval Shipyard on 28 March, a broom had been raised on one of the signal halyards to signify a "clean sweep" on her engineering trials. There would be real sweeping as well, because the world's only operational battleship had little more than a week to clean up for the commissioning ceremony on Saturday, 6 April. In the meantime, two events served to put a damper on the ship's coming-out party. On 1 April, a war-weary President Lyndon Johnson put all but the southern panhandle of North Vietnam off limits for bombing and shelling by U.S. forces. He hoped thereby to bring the North Vietnamese to the bargaining table to make peace. There would be no chance to hit the Thanh Hoa bridge after all.

The second happening was the assassination of civil rights leader Martin Luther King in Memphis, Tennessee, on 4 April. Almost instantly there was a backlash of racial violence in a number of large U.S. cities. On 5 April, Philadelphia Mayor James Tate declared a state of limited emergency, akin to martial law. He prohibited public gatherings of more than eleven people and closed bars throughout the city.

The Saturday of the ceremony was a beautiful, warm, sunny early spring day. The disturbances were relatively minor and had more to do with the battleship than with Dr. King. Anti-war demonstrators gathered to stage a protest against a ship which was obviously headed for Vietnam. One group planted a 10-foot-tall "peace tree" about 100 yards from the naval base; forty-nine protesters were arrested, handcuffed, and hauled away in police vans for violating the ban against public gatherings. On the Delaware River side, the Coast Guard was, for the most part, successful in holding back the fifteen or so boats that were attempting to break through to the gleaming grey battleship. The boats sported such signs as "Retire the USS New Jersey – Rebuild Philadelphia" and "Battleship No – Hospital Ship Yes".

Standing on the deck of the battleship, Ensign Chris Reed heard one of the protesters using a bullhorn to read a prepared statement. At the end of it, he exhorted *New Jersey* men to refuse to serve in what he and his comrades

considered an unjust war. Part of the plan had been to throw a garland of flowers up and snare the bow with it, a giant game of ring toss. The protesters failed because they had not counted on the great height of the bow above the water; the flowers fell far short. Fireman Bill Sosnowski was also in ranks, and he and other members of the crew got mostly amusement from the futile efforts of the demonstrators. Men of the battleship laughed when fireboats on the river periodically shot water at the protesters.

Even more important were the feelings that the ship herself evoked among crew members – feelings of pride and of being special because such a large crowd had turned out for the show. Hundreds of VIPs were gathered on the fantail, and thousands more sat in chairs on the pier. Captain Snyder soon demonstrated that he was concerned about the crew. When it came his turn to speak, he picked up the podium which had been facing the VIPs and turned it 90° so that he could address the crew members' families on the pier. "Now," he said, "I'm talking to you families out there. And these other people – as far as I'm concerned, they're not even here." It was a grandstand move, and Snyder would make many more of them during his command tenure. Though he wasn't a psychology major, he might as well have been, for he knew how to inspire a crew and make the men feel good about themselves. Lieutenant Carl Morse was assigned to the shipyard and had had a large role in getting the battleship ready for this day. One of his strongest memories is that of Captain Snyder's head-turning and podium-turning speech: "It made quite an impression on the crew and on the families. It was the coolest move he could've ever done."

All too soon, however, the festivities were over, and it was time to get back to work again. More trials were on the docket, this time a check by the Board of Inspection and Survey. On the morning of 15 April, the *New Jersey* eased away from the pier for the 86-mile, eight-hour sea detail trip down the Delaware River to the Atlantic. The officer of the deck for the sea detail was Lieutenant Carl Albrecht, a superb shiphandler whose primary job was as main battery officer. He had been assigned to the *New Jersey* because of his experience with the 8-inch bag guns of the cruiser *Macon*. His service in that ship and the cruiser *Long Beach* had given him both an expert seaman's eye and familiarity with handling large ships. He was so capable that Captain Snyder habitually relied on him for handling the ship in restricted waters. Albrecht remembers that the Philadelphia sea details were made easier than they might have been by the fact that the Delaware River pilots' association undoubtedly sent one of its best men to work with so important a ship.

On the morning of 17 April, off the Virginia Capes, the *New Jersey* began test-firing her guns. Turret one was trained around to a bearing of 110° relative to the bow. As a result, the guns pointed somewhat abaft the starboard beam and would impart the maximum stress to the super-

structure. The test was to see how well the ship could withstand the concussion produced by her own guns. It took some forty seconds before the first projectile splashed down in the Atlantic and created a green-colored fountain of spray. A dye-loaded projectile was used to help spot the impact point. Ensign Walt Migrala was manning a secondary battery director in the after part of the superstructure. He had listened with interest as turrets one and two were fired, but when turret three was trained around and pointing forward of the beam, he had the feeling he could almost reach out and touch the barrels. His director wasn't needed for the big guns, so he closed all the hatches and hunkered down inside. Later, off Vietnam, the firing would become routine, but there was still a sense of caution when the experience was so new.

Down in the projectile deck for turret three was Seaman Larry Pousson. "The first gun we fired," he says, "one or two lights would go out. The second gun, a couple more lights would go out; the third gun, a couple more lights. Then when we loaded up and fired a broadside, a whole bunch of lights went out. It definitely cleaned the dirt out of the overhead." The tests did what they were supposed to do; they demonstrated the weaknesses in the ship's ability to withstand the shock of firing. Some of the new electronic gear was knocked out, fluorescent light fixtures crashed to the deck, ductwork fell, and new plumbing developed minor leaks.

Altogether, eighteen rounds were fired that day, all with the barrels trained to their limits. For the most part, the ship survived, but Ensign Jack Hayes observed that some yard workmen's tools didn't. The workers, who had come along to continue their tasks on board ship, put their toolboxes inside a circular shield that had once protected a 40-mm. gun mount. The muzzles of the guns from one turret were almost directly over the toolboxes when the flame and concussion erupted. The muzzle blast crushed the toolboxes around the tools, just like shrink-wrapping a piece of plastic around an item before displaying it for sale in a retail store. The outlines of wrenches and pliers were embossed into the covers of what was left of the metal toolboxes. Some life rafts were blown out of their holders, and an accommodation ladder stored forward of turret three was wrecked by the concussion. On 18 April, the *New Jersey* returned to Philadelphia, again wearing a "clean sweep" broom.

The long stay at Philadelphia came to an end on Thursday, 16 May, when the *New Jersey* got under way and began the long odyssey that would take her to Southeast Asia. As she headed out with her crew paraded on deck in white uniforms, the battleship glided past her still-mothballed sisters *Iowa* and *Wisconsin*. She was saluted by bright red fireboats sending triumphant streams of water into the sky. Her progress down the Delaware River to the sea was filmed by a camera crew for the soon-to-be-released Navy film entitled "The American Dreadnought".

On Monday morning, 20 May, the *New Jersey* reached Hampton Roads near Norfolk. Her crew spent three reveille-to-taps days taking on some 2,500 tons of projectiles and powder. She went to sea on 23 May, the twenty-fifth anniversary of her first commissioning, to fire dozens of rounds of 16-inch and 5-inch. The shooting a month earlier had been to test the ship structurally. This time the weapons department wanted to calibrate the guns and fire control equipment. A target was towed by the fleet tug *Shikora*, and the high-speed transport *Beverley W. Reid* was used as a reference for indirect fire.

During the weekend of 25–26 May, the battleship was moored at her former home port of Norfolk, the first time she had been there since late 1956 when she left for her pre-inactivation overhaul at Brooklyn. Her nostalgic appeal acted as a magnet during two days of general visiting. It was the first time the ship was opened to the masses after recommissioning, and the masses came – nearly 32,000 people during the two days. Navy bands were on the pier, welcome-aboard phamphlets printed for distribution to the guests, and Radioman Second Class George Stavros of the crew broadcast a description on loudspeakers every half hour to tell visitors of his favorite ship's capabilities. Some of the guests recognized one another and held private reunions. One man who had served in the *New Jersey* during World War II met a Korean War crewman and observed, "Oh, you're a newcomer".

On the morning of Wednesday, 29 May, the *New Jersey* pulled away from Norfolk's pier seven and headed for Panama. Her departure was scarcely noticed because of the flurry of activity connected with a search for the missing nuclear submarine *Scorpion*. Her remains were later found on the bottom of the sea in the Eastern Atlantic. During the southward trip, recalls Radarman Bob Fulks, the *New Jersey*'s crew members in radio central and the combat information center were listening carefully in the hope of hearing a distress signal from the submarine. It took five days for the battleship to steam down to Panama. She anchored at Cristobal on the morning of 3 June, and the day-long transit took place the following day.

The squeeze was a tight one, as usual. The *New Jersey*'s beam was just over 108 feet at its widest. Seaman Larry Pousson found out just how little clearance there was in the 110-foot locks when he stood with the toes of his shoes flush with the side of the ship and looked straight down. He says, "You couldn't really tell where the side of the ship ended and the lock itself started." He observed deck seamen using fire hoses to quell the smoke produced when the sides of the ship scraped against the lock walls.

Along the sides of the canal Ensign Chris Reed saw enthusiastic Americans demonstrating their support and encouragement for the giant dreadnought. One woman held over her head a homemade sign which said, "Give 'em hell, New Jersey." Reed was not really encouraged, because he and other junior officers thought considerable hazards faced the *New Jersey* in the war zone. In 1967, Egyptian patrol boats had sunk the Israeli destroyer *Elath* with surface-to-surface "Styx" missiles, and the news media had been full of speculation about what might happen to the battleship. The Communists could gain a powerful proaganda advantage by using a small missile boat to damage the huge ship and send her back to base for repairs. She was a sufficiently tempting target for there to be a basis for concern on the part of crew members. Probably more were concerned than cared to admit it.

Once the ship got through the canal, she was in the Pacific for the first time since late 1953. Captain Snyder was interviewed during the northward journey by two southern California newspapermen, Bob Zimmerman of San Diego and Buck Lanier of the ship's new home port, Long Beach. The captain revealed to the newsmen that the Department of Defense had recently granted his request that more enlisted men be added to the crew, raising the enlisted total from 1,400 to 1,556. The number of officers remained at seventy. Austerity has its virtues, but the original manning had been too lean for the ship's intended mission. In his repertoire of motivational tools, Snyder was to dwell on that small crew size – telling the men of the *New Jersey* that they must be twice as good as their World War II predecessors because they could operate the ship with half as many. What he didn't tell them was that the

job was smaller this time. The manpower-hungry 40-mm. and 20-mm. guns were gone, there was no embarked flag officer to support, and the ship no longer had enough engineering personnel to steam at high speeds for extended periods as she had done during World War II.

On 11 June, the *New Jersey* arrived in Long Beach and was escorted by an enthusiastic group of small craft. She moored at the naval shipyard's huge Pier Echo, near the retired Cunard liner *Queen Mary*, which was on her way to being converted to a hotel and tourist attraction. The first weekend in port was a time for more general visiting of the sort allowed in Norfolk. Once the visiting was over, the *New Jersey* steamed to San Diego on 17 June to begin six weeks of intensive training – the equivalent of a shake-down – to prepare the crew for the coming deployment to Vietnam. Gunner's Mate Seaman Larry Pousson considered the crew of turret three well drilled already. Senior Chief George Petrovitz had been training the ammunition handlers slowly and carefully. First they walked through all the movements, emphasizing safety at each step. Only after they had mastered the procedures did they begin to try to pick up speed. At first it took about two minutes to load a 16-inch round and the associated powder. Gradually the time was reduced to about thirty seconds. The projectile decks were kept oiled to facilitate the movement of heavy shells, and two-man teams were able to move one of the large projectiles by sliding it along the deck with the aid of a piece of line powered by a mini-capstan; the process was known as parbuckling.

Both Pousson and Fire Controlman First Class Rick Crawford felt that the people from the local fleet training group were at a disadvantage. "We wound up having to

teach them," Crawford says. For one practice shore bombardment at San Clemente Island, off the coast of southern California, the targets were old automobiles which had been painted yellow to make them stand out. Firing from 20,000 yards, the *New Jersey* showered the cars with shrapnel. The weapons officer, Commander Pete Roane, commented dryly, "I think we've put the yellow cab company out of business."

The battleship returned to port on 2 August to spend a month getting a final tuneup at the Long Beach Naval Shipyard. The time in home port provided a rare opportunity for the married men to be with their families, and the single men had a good time as well. Seaman Larry Pousson went to an area of Long Beach known as the Pike. It had an amusement park and the sort of bars and restaurants that catered to the tastes of Navy men – "dives, really," says Pousson in retrospect. For some of the ship's chief petty officers, recreation was to be found as near as the chiefs' club on the naval base adjacent to the shipyard. On Friday and Saturday nights, the chiefs danced with women they met there. As friendships ripened during the course of an evening, a chief might ask, "Would you like to go aboard the *New Jersey* for breakfast?"

"Sure, why not?" would come the answer, and the time between taps and breakfast was spent comfortably in a spare bunk in chiefs' quarters. "See you next week," a woman might say afterward.

"Okay, sweetheart," came the reply from a chief who knew that he would soon run out of next weeks.

After adding still more ammunition to the supply picked up in Norfolk, the *New Jersey* spent 30 August on a leisurely family day cruise off the California coast. One of the attractions of the day was watching the ship's newly installed closed-circuit television system playing a videotape of one of the summer's practice shore bombardments. Wives, children, and girl friends got to see where their men worked, and all were treated to a barbecue on the ship's broad fantail.

All too soon, the halcyon days of August were over. Vietnam was beckoning. The beginning of a deployment is a time of mixed emotions for the men of a warship's crew. Those with families must say goodbye to dear ones for periods which usually last from six to nine months. And the bachelors no longer have the opportunity to go ashore nearly every night to whoop it up on liberty. On the other hand, the professional Navy man knows that he is truly performing his job – doing that which years of education and training have prepared him for – when he makes a combat deployment. The officers and enlisted men were about to experience the culmination of the months of hard work which had led to this cruise. For the *New Jersey* herself, a third war was just over the horizon.

A huge crowd of families, friends, and well-wishers was on Pier Echo at Long Beach for the departure on the morning of Thursday, 5 September 1968. After a four-day trip, the *New Jersey* arrived at Pearl Harbor on 9 September. On her bow for entry to the harbor, the battleship carried a colorful lei. The stopover in Hawaii was brief, but there was time for more general visiting, and another 10,000 people trooped aboard. There were also two nights of liberty. Ensign Walt Migrala and another *New Jersey* officer left the ship and were walking along a pier on the way to a good time when they spotted a ship much smaller than their own. She was 306 feet long and only 37 feet in the beam – DER-387. She was the USS *Vance*, previously commanded by Marcus Arnheiter. Her presence in Pearl Harbor caused Migrala to reflect on what a large role the small ship had played in the selection of the commanding officer who would shortly take the *New Jersey* to war.

On 11 September, the *New Jersey* left Pearl Harbor accompanied by the guided missile destroyer *Towers*, which was to provide antiaircraft and antimissile protection when the battleship got to Vietnam. The destroyer would serve as an insurance policy since the *New Jersey* herself was not equipped with antiair missiles. On 17 September, the battleships changed course to swing south of Guam in order to avoid typhoons Carmen and Della. Later that day, she was overflown by two Soviet Tu-95 "Bear D" reconnaissance planes. They went over the battleship and destroyer three times, dropping down to as low as 1,000 feet for good photographic coverage. Captain Snyder hoped that the planes' intelligence-gathering would pick up the fact that he had had two of the now-

empty 40-mm. gun tubs painted blue inside. One of his stunts was to have small "swimming pools" topside on the battleship. Many crew members were out on deck during the overflight. Radarman Bob Fulks recalls that sailors were sending quite a few "universal hand signals" skyward. One of the fads of the time for antiwar activists was to raise the old V-for-victory sign but to call it instead a peace sign. In this instance, the battleship's men were giving the Soviets only half of the peace sign.

The *New Jersey* passed through San Bernardino Strait in the Philippines on 21 September. The Catholic chaplain, Lieutenant Commander John Byrnes, honored the occasion by describing the Battle of Leyte Gulf for the benefit of the crew. Lieutenant Commander Carl Albrecht observed that attendance at mass picked up considerably as the ship got ever closer to gunline duty. The morning of 22 September brought her to Subic Bay in the Philippines. There the finishing touches were put on her preparations for Vietnam.

Departure from Subic Bay was on the 25th, and the next day the battleship had a final antiaircraft practice. On 27 September, the *New Jersey* rehearsed with a DASH – drone antisubmarine helicopter. Certainly she wasn't going into the antisubmarine business, but the ship had been equipped to control the small, unmanned craft with the idea that a DASH version with a television camera (known as "Snoopy DASH") could be used for spotting gunfire. The battleship herself would not carry the helos but would borrow them from destroyers, as she did in this instance from the USS *Fechteler*. (As it turned out, manned spotter planes served the purpose in Vietnam, and the DASH was seldom used.) Also on the 27th, the *New Jersey* fired one last shore bombardment practice. The targets were barren coastal mountains in the Tabones range in the Philippines.

During the two-day transit to Vietnam, Machinist's Mate First Class Dan Norton died of natural causes; his body was stored in the morgue until it could be delivered ashore in Vietnam. On 28 September, Gunner's Mate Seaman Harold Shaw was hit with a case of appendicitis. Lieutenant Commander John Denby, the battleship's surgeon, performed an emergency appendectomy on that day with the ship's other physician, Lieutenant Commander James Quinn, acting as anesthetist. And there was a bit of surgery on the top of turret one. Fire Controlman Rick Crawford recalls that the main battery plotting room was conducting transmission checks and inadvertently trained turret two when its barrels were so low that they lopped off periscopes from the top of turret one.

The *New Jersey* arrived off Danang, South Vietnam, on the morning of 29 September, and nearly three dozen news media people came aboard. The world's only active battleship was to be in the world spotlight. The media scrutiny manifested itself in reporting on something even before the ship went into action. Under the rules in force at

**Top right:** A projectile sits in a loading tray before being rammed into the breech of a 16-inch gun in March 1969. (Photo by PH2 Kenneth Barrett; U.S. Naval Institute Collection)

**Bottom right:** In one of the main battery plotting rooms, Fire Controlman Dennis Stark has his right hand on the trigger that will fire a 16-inch gun. His left hand controls the salvo alarm. (Courtesy Howard Serig)

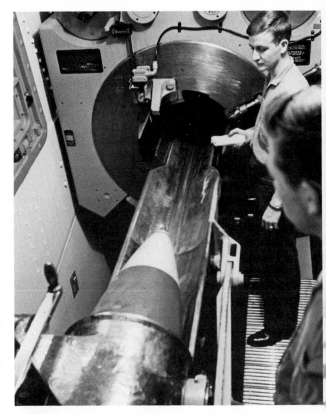

the time, the men of the *New Jersey* would be eligible for an extra $65 apiece combat pay for September since they would be going into action on the last day of the month. Captain Snyder told the crew over closed-circuit television of their good fortune, and the information later showed up in some news stories with the suggestion that the schedule had been so arranged as to give the crew extra money.

Finally, it was Monday, 30 September. The morning dawned grey and choppy. Shortly after 7:00 a.m., the crew was called to general quarters. The initial target was an enemy supply dump a few miles north of the Benhai River which separated North and South Vietnam. The klaxon-horn salvo alarm sounded its warning buzzer three times. At 7:32, simultaneous with the third buzz of the alarm, the right gun of turret two blasted out a 1,900-pound projectile amid a wreath of bright orange flame. Fifty-four seconds later, the shell landed, and a Marine Corps TA-4 Skyhawk spotter plane reported that the initial shot landed only a few hundred yards from the intended target – fine shooting. Adjustments were made, and the target was soon eliminated. Later in the morning, the Marine jet came under fire from antiaircraft batteries on the ground. They were soon silenced by the *New Jersey*'s guns. The appreciative spotter aircraft then flew to within close range of the ship, dipped its wings in salute, and radioed, "Welcome to the war".

One of the reporters on board to report the first day's firing was retired Marine Colonel Robert Heinl, a writer who had campaigned long and hard for more gunfire support capability in the fleet. Being on hand for the first shot was a joyous experience. During World War II, the new fast battleships had operated in support of the carriers, and it had been the old battleships which were best at shore bombardment. Now that the *New Jersey* was an old battleship herself, Heinl wrote afterward, she was shooting as well as the old battleships of 1945. He considered that such fine technical performance "could only have come from . . . the highest quality of command of the ship". Lieutenant Commander Albrecht knew Snyder as a demanding skipper, but one whose demands were reasonable. The skipper was not a gunnery expert, but he certainly knew enough about what could be expected of the guns in terms of accuracy – and he meant to get it. Beneath Snyder's sometimes frivolous exterior was an officer with a technical mind and high professional standards.

For the men of the *New Jersey*, who had been training and drilling for months, the first day on the gunline was – to some at least – anticlimactic. Fire Controlman Crawford remembers it as "just like a day at the office". And, after all the apprehension about possible retaliation, Lieutenant Commander Albrecht felt "a little bit of a letdown" that there had been no reaction at all on the part of the enemy. The enemy did bare its fangs during the ship's second day

Above: A pallet of 16-inch powder cans makes the highline journey from the ammunition ship *Haleakala* to the *New Jersey* during operations in the Tonkin Gulf. (Courtesy Naval Historical Center)

on the gunline. On 1 October, the *New Jersey* fired at targets 7 to 12 miles north of the demilitarized zone which ran between North and South Vietnam. In the process, the North Vietnam antiaircraft artillery hit a TA-4 jet which was on its way to spot for the battleship. The pilot radioed that he was losing fuel and would have to ditch his plane at sea. Chief Radarman MacDonald Shand, down in the ship's combat information center, acted as air controller, giving the damaged plane the course to fly to safety. The Marine plane flew out to the *New Jersey*'s position, where both the pilot and his rear seat observer ejected. They were picked up within a few minutes by the USS *Towers*, the *New Jersey*'s "shotgun" escort.

The *New Jersey* did more shooting north of the DMZ in the days which followed, and on 2 October she had her first underway replenishment off the gunline, taking on ninety-six 16-inch projectiles, 644 5-inch projectiles, and associated powder. She was alongside the ammunition ship *Haleakala* for some four hours. Just as Captain Snyder had demonstrated his confidence in Lieutenant Commander Albrecht by using him as sea detail officer of the deck, he also gave him the conn for underway replenishments. Though Snyder didn't direct the ship's movements personally, remembers Albrecht, the captain was very much in charge. He set the tone for each shiphandling situation by indicating how he wanted it executed. In the case of an underway replenishment, the skipper wanted it

done smartly, with the snap and precision that were hallmarks in the destroyer force. Captain Snyder, of course, would have borne the ultimate responsibility had anything gone wrong.

Within a relatively short time after beginning gunline operations, the crew settled into a pattern of firing and rearming. The ship went to general quarters when she was on a firing mission, and those who had to be topside were outfitted with helmets and flak jackets for protection. It was a tiring routine, especially for those who had underway watch stations. Radarman Third Class Bob Fulks, for instance, had a variety of watch duties in the combat information center. He might be manning – at any given time – a plotting board, dead reckoning tracer, or radiotelephone. If the firing missions and accompanying general quarters came when he would normally be on watch, fine. If the battle stations were manned when he would have been off watch and sleeping or otherwise relaxing, he had to go back to CIC anyway. With some exaggeration, he recalls, "It seemed like we were either at general quarters or on watch twenty hours out of twenty-four."

The ship often fired both day and night missions while off North Vietnam. At night, the ship shot at prearranged targets, putting out what was known as H & I fire – harassment and interdiction. This was a time when no spotting planes were available, so there could be no corrections to ensure that the projectiles were falling on target. Critics

**Right:** Steaming in the Gulf of Tonkin on 6 October 1968. (Courtesy Chris Reed)

have argued that H & I was largely a waste of ammunition; other individuals believe it had value in forcing enemy soldiers to back off and keep their heads down.

During the daytime, jet aircraft were used for spotting, because their speed made them less vulnerable to antiaircraft fire and surface-to-air missiles than were propeller-driven types. Ensign Walt Migrala, the junior officer in turret three, observed that the 16-inch rounds frequently had a time of flight as long as seventy-five or eighty seconds, depending on the ship's range from the target. He explains, "We'd count down so the jet pilot could hear us counting down. Right before the fall of shot, he'd dive down in the plane to see where the rounds landed." By staying high except when it was time to spot the fall of shot, the jets were reducing their exposure to enemy fire.

On the evening of 7 October, a Navy S-2 surveillance aircraft reported a concentration of enemy smallcraft moving along the coast of North Vietnam near the Song Giang River. In the parlance of the day, these were water-borne logistics craft. The abbreviation, WBLCs, was pronounced "wiblicks" as a kind of oral shorthand. Such craft were considered lucrative targets (abbreviated "LucTars") for the Sea Dragon gunfire forces of which the *New Jersey* was a part. The interdiction strategy sought to choke off enemy war materials on both land and water. Thus the *New Jersey* and her escort, the *Towers*, took the enemy craft under fire with 5-inch guns and destroyed eleven of them before the remainder were able to beach themselves on the coast. The enemy junks showed up as phosphorescent pips on the surface search scopes in CIC and the fire control radars of the Mark 37 secondary battery directors. Ensign Chris Reed watched radar pips wink and go out, one by one, as the enemy vessels were destroyed. Lieutenant Dick Harris was in one of the 5-inch directors that night; he recalls it as one of the few times off Vietnam when the ship fired a mission by radar control from the directors themselves. Normally, the 5-inch guns were used for shore bombardment, and the mission was run from either a secondary battery plotting room or from the combat information center. That night also marked one of the very few times in the ship's career when she fired at enemy surface vessels.

The *New Jersey* continued to move her operations farther and farther north up the coast of Vietnam. On 12 October, she fired at targets 75 miles above the DMZ, using A-7 Corsair II attack planes from the carrier *America* to spot rounds sent against heavily fortified caves at Vinh. She shot at the caves on the following two days as well, although heavy monsoon rains kept spotters from seeing the targets much of the time. During one of these missions, the heavy rain set off the nose fuze of a 16-inch high-capacity projectile, leading some in the crew to believe that the *New Jersey* had been fired upon from the shore. During the afternoon of 14 October, the *America*'s A-7s were again on the job, and this time the battleship fired for

**Above:** Off-duty recreation in one of the berthing compartments in October 1968 includes playing cards and watching the closed-circuit television set in the background. (Courtesy New Jersey State Archives)

**Opposite page, top:** Chief Boilermaker Rex Walton posts mock battle damage on a status board in damage control central during a drill in November 1968. At left is Lieutenant Commander John Hubitsky. (Courtesy Howard Serig)

**Opposite page, bottom:** Lieutenant (junior grade) Walter Migrala stands watch as officer of the deck on the 04 level bridge. To his left is a radar repeater with a rubber hood attached so daylight won't obscure the view of phosphorescent pips on the scope below. (Courtesy Naval Historical Center)

thirty minutes at coastal artillery positions on the island of Hon Matt. The spotter in the Navy plane reported one secondary explosion and the destruction of one artillery position. Then he exclaimed, "You've blown away a large slice of the island; it's down in the ocean." The exploit was widely trumpeted in the world's news media, leading to reports that the *New Jersey* had sunk an island.

In the middle of the month, the world's only active battleship moved south and fired her 16-inch and 5-inch guns in support of friendly ground forces in contact with the enemy. She supported U.S. Army troops in the II Corps area of South Vietnam, providing preparatory fire for a battle from 23 until 27 October. After the *New Jersey* had softened up the area, only seven Americans were lost in the operation, compared with 301 enemy killed.

On 26 October, while the battleship was bombarding targets in and around the demilitarized zone, Machinery Repairman Third Class Bill Sosnowski was on watch in the after diesel compartment. He was all the way in the stern of the ship, at about the level of the waterline, assigned to start up the emergency diesels if the situation warranted. Unless there was an emergency, however, there wasn't really much for him to do, so he was passing the time by listening to a stereo through a set of headphones. As a makeshift alarm he put a cylindrical dogging wrench on one of the metal dogs holding the compartment's hatch shut. When he heard the wrench crash to the deck, that meant the dogs were being opened, and he was about to have company. Thus warned, Sosnowski scrambled to throw the stereo headphones into a hiding-place. Soon the hatch opened, and in came Captain Snyder, executive officer Jim Elfelt, and others. Sosnowski stood and saluted, then was told to carry on with what he was doing. The officers went to the starboard side of the compartment, which ran from one side of the ship to the other that far aft,

and asked him, "Did you hear anything?" Naturally, he hadn't heard anything except stereo music, a piece of information he omitted in giving his negative report. The *New Jersey* had just been fired upon for the first time during the Vietnam deployment, and the skipper wanted to know if there was any evidence she had been hit.

Those topside had observed perhaps a dozen splashes in the water; the closest one was about 500 yards short. Lieutenant (junior grade) Dick Rockwell, the officer of the deck, had immediately kicked on some speed and turned the ship to seaward so the enemy would have the smallest target aspect at which to aim. Turret three kicked out some retaliatory fire. By the time an aerial spotter was able to get over the enemy position, the mobile artillery piece – which was probably about a 4-inch gun – had disappeared. Radio Hanoi was soon claiming to have achieved a direct hit on the *New Jersey*. The expectations were thus fulfilled that the North Vietnamese would try to score propaganda points by hitting the battleship. In this instance, both the claims and the fears that had gone beforehand were exaggerated. Captain Snyder was his usual flippant self in reporting the incident to Saigon by radio, saying that it "appeared from the bridge that six to twelve golf balls were driven off Cap Lay in our direction. Next time I will try to get more excited." Snyder recalls that Commander Elfelt was a valuable "balance wheel", restraining some of the wilder messages the captain proposed sending at various times. Even with the exec's calming influence, a number of colorful messages emanated from the *New Jersey* during Snyder's tenure.

On 27 October, Navy Day, 50 men from the Third Marine Division came aboard to visit. Some got their first hot showers in thirty days and marveled at the comforts of seagoing life. They were accorded laundry service, haircuts, ship's store buying privileges, Navy chow, and a special cake made in their honor. Staff Sergeant Robert Gauthier spoke to the crew over closed-circuit television, saying, "You are doing more to improve the morale of the men on the beach than anything else in the war. Every time we go on patrol, someone says, 'The big one is out there. Nobody better mess with us or she'll get them.' You are saving lives out here . . . American lives. And we thank you." The *New Jersey* was a friendly haven for soldiers and Marines throughout the deployment, and many of them brought messages of gratitude similar to Sergeant Gauthier's.

On the night of 30 October, about six rounds of enemy artillery were fired at the *New Jersey*, again from Cap Lay. This time the closest round fell some 3,000 yards short. On the morning of 1 November, the battleship moved south to a position off Danang for replenishment. Lieutenant Commander Carl Albrecht, who had the conn, noticed that the ammunition ship *Haleakala*'s black boot topping rose steadily higher out of the water as she relieved herself of 417 tons of projectiles and powder. The whole period

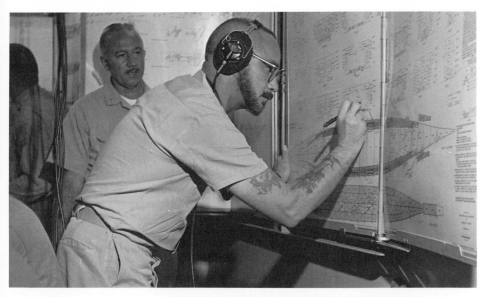

alongside, including the return of empty powder tanks, took more than seven hours.

During the course of that long replenishment, the *New Jersey* intercepted messages from the Joint Chiefs of Staff indicating that all of North Vietnam was now off limits to U.S. bombing and shelling. Again, the battleship's operations were to be dictated by political considerations. Within a few days, Vice President Hubert Humphrey was to face Richard Nixon in the presidential election. Humphrey had been hampered by his support of the Vietnam War, and now President Johnson was making a conciliatory gesture which might aid in the bargaining for peace. Whatever the motivation, the bombing halt put the *New Jersey* out of business in the principal role for which she had been reactivated – bombardment of North Vietnam. Although the move obviously didn't single out the battleship, her crew had a tendency to view it in terms of themselves and their ship. They thought about all the work they had done to get the ship to this point and the fact that they were just getting far enough north to demonstrate the ship's real capabilities.

As is often the case with initial reactions, there were many overreactions. The war wasn't being fought for the benefit of the USS *New Jersey*; she was an instrument to be used in executing national policy. However flawed U.S. policy toward Vietnam may seem in retrospect, it is unlikely that the use of the *New Jersey* in North Vietnam's southern panhandle during that period would have made a substantial difference to the war's outcome. Had she been used to enforce a blockade, or had there been U.S. ground operations in North Vietnam for her to support, she could have had considerably more impact than she did in trying to interdict supplies once they got into the country. Even at the time, though, things were not so bad as they seemed at first. There was still a useful role for the *New Jersey* under the strategy being pursued. By firing in support of allied ground troops in South Vietnam, she could do more in terms of the direct saving of American lives than by firing at the supply trail. In the months that followed, *New Jersey* men discovered that there was considerable satisfaction in saving those lives.

For much of the deployment, Walt Migrala and other officers who stood bridge watches directed helmsmen to steer northerly courses. The engines were slowed to bare steerageway, just enough to counter the prevailing north-to-south current and keep the ship essentially stationary. Down in the main battery plotting room, Fire Controlman Second Class Tom Mumpower was frequently assigned to keep the Mark 13 main battery fire control radar locked on a reference point ashore. When there was a call-for-fire mission, the target was plotted by the Mark 48 fire control computer which solved the trigonometry problem involving the ship, reference point, and target. The Mark 48 computer then fed an offset bearing and range to the Mark 8 rangekeeper. The latter, in turn, transmitted orders to the

Opposite page, top: The fantail helo pad serves as a resting spot for two UH-1 Hueys in between flights in December 1968. Hundreds of visitors came aboard off Vietnam via helicopters. (Courtesy Howard Serig)

Opposite page, center: With the forelock of black hair dangling in front of his face as usual, Captain Ed Snyder gives Republic of Korea Army officers a tour of the *New Jersey*'s mess deck in November 1968. (Courtesy Howard Serig)

Opposite page, bottom: The heavy cruiser *Canberra* comes alongside the *New Jersey* at Subic Bay, Philippines, in November 1968. (Courtesy Howard Serig)

guns to put them at the correct bearing and elevation. The higher the barrels were elevated, the farther they would fire.

To verify the accuracy of the fire-control solutions, they were double-checked by the watch team in the combat information center and triple-checked by the team in the command control center, which was the former flag plot on the 03 level. When all the solutions were in agreement, triple C gave the okay, and a fire controlman in the plotting room sounded the salvo alarm and squeezed the brass trigger which sent a projectile on its long flight ashore. When the ship was moving, the Mark 48 computer provided constant updates. When the *New Jersey* was firing at multiple targets or shifting targets, the fire controlmen reacted as needed. They also reacted when given inputs from the spotters, who were either in the air or on the ground. Radarmen such as Bob Fulks manned the radio-telephone links to the spotters, and it was the radarmen's job to repeat carefully what they heard to ensure that the fire controlmen were getting the right spotting information. The fire controlmen then fed the corrections into the computer to bring subsequent rounds on target.

For targets that were relatively close to the ship and didn't require heavy firepower to knock them out, the 5-inch secondary battery was available, ten guns on each side of the *New Jersey*. Just as the 16-inch guns were fired almost always to port because of the ship's northerly heading, so also did the port side 5-inch guns get much more of a workout. Lieutenant Dick Harris, in charge of the starboard side 5-inch battery, often sent his men over to spell gun crews on the other side and thus to help even the workload.

Another consequence of shifting operations south of the demilitarized zone was that the shipboard routine became a lot easier than it had been. No longer did the whole crew have to go to general quarters when the ship fired. One turret at a time had the duty under Condition III. If it was turret one or two, the topside portions of the forward part of the ship were off-limits, but the crew was permitted to go aft for sunbathing or other relaxation. When turret three was firing, the forward part of the ship was available.

In this setup, a portion of the ship was always kept on alert, but the remainder of the crew could do its normal work and then rest when not required to be on duty. Fire Controlman Mumpower remembers, "I used to enjoy the trips topside, onto the fantail. There was a lot of camaraderie after a day on the gunline. . . . We'd go topside – the engineers or weapons types or whatever and bat the breeze back and forth. It was good time. You needed a chance to relax, and you had that opportunity back there." Gunner's Mate Striker Tom Feigley sometimes found it hard to realize that he was in a war at all, because there was little of the excitement or danger that one normally associated with combat. On the other hand, he says, "It's probably the hardest physical work I ever did in my life." In

addition to the long hours on watch, both shooting and the handling of powder and projectiles during replenishments meant that the gunner's mates and other men of the turrets did a great deal of strenuous manual labor.

Captain Snyder was aware of the need to keep the crew interested and supplied with diversions. When there were visitors on board – and there were hundreds during the course of the deployment – he asked them to tell the crew what a great job the *New Jersey* was doing. The guests ranged from admirals and generals to junior enlisted men. Captain Snyder gave the crew a sense of mission and self-esteem, and he also did something else – he played on the theme that battleship men had more important things to do than be bound by petty rules. In the past, as a flagship for numerous admirals, the *New Jersey* had been a spit-and-polish show ship. Snyder emphasized that she was now a working ship, so he allowed men to go topside without hats; enlisted men could wear T-shirts rather than dungaree shirts. It was a subtle means of thumbing the nose at authority. In addition to such superficial things, Snyder displayed a genuine concern for his men. Unlike many skippers who spend their underway time glued to the bridge and sea cabin, Snyder was wont to roam the ship. He picked officers of the deck in whom he had great confidence and left them alone to do their jobs. They could reach him by telephone if they needed him, or in emergencies call him on the public address system, but for the most part he left them alone. That meant that he could go around and poke his nose into all sorts of things. He frequently picked up an aluminium mess tray, filled up on the mess line, and sat down at a table to eat and talk with crew members. Says Radarman Bob Fulks, "He made a special effort to come down and be with the crew, to let them know that he was concerned about the welfare of the crew. He was . . . easy to talk to, a heck of a captain."

Sometimes Captain Snyder did his roaming in a bathrobe. Personnelman Third Class Hank Strub saw the captain in the personnel office late at night at times when Snyder would rather chat than sleep. Or the skipper might be down in the bakeshop at 2:00 in the morning, sampling a freshly baked loaf of bread. And he habitually showed up at the weekly birthday parties in the mess deck. Each week a cake was baked and decorated for all the men who had a birthday that week, and they were given head-of-the-line privileges in the mess line. Snyder remembers that he got awfully sick of birthday cake after a while, but more important was the message he was sending to his men – that he cared about the *New Jersey*, and he cared about them.

The crew had a couple of ways of keeping up with the outside world during their deployment to Vietnam. One was through news programs which came in on the Armed Forces Radio and Television Service or news reports read on camera by crew members in the television studio. The other was through publication of the *Daily Bugle*, the

ship's newspaper which was named by Ensign Scott Cheyne after a fictitious paper he'd seen in Scrooge McDuck cartoons. Pete Holste, who was a journalist third class, recalls that members of the newspaper's staff made trips to radio central several times a day to pick up the latest news copy which had come in by radio teletype. Chief Journalist Jim McDonough handled the sports news, always an item of interest, and Holste and Journalist Third Class Bob Schweitzer worked on straight news. The whole thing got typed up as news came in, was printed in the print shop on the third deck, and then was collated and stapled for distribution to the crew. It was scheduled to come out as officers and enlisted men were gathering for movies in the evening.

On 8 November, the *New Jersey* was detached from the gunline and traveled at high speed to Subic Bay in the Philippines to give crew members their first liberty ashore in a month and a half. She stayed there from 10 until 20 November. As for liberty, the tastes of the crew members varied widely. Personnelman Andy Lavella says that he and other chief petty officers spent so much time playing slot machines in the chiefs' club that "you could have scraped the silver off our fingers". Radarman Third Class Bob Fulks thought the U.S. naval base in Subic Bay was fine, but the adjoining city of Olongapo left much to be desired. As a result, he tended to stick around the base enlisted men's club, recreation hall, movie theater, and gymnasium. Warrant officer Ed Flamboe discovered the unsafe nature of Olongapo one day when he was carrying some money in his shirt pocket. He felt sharp jabs in his ribs, and when he reacted to those, a confederate of the jabbers took advantage of Flamboe's distracted attention to grab the money from his shirt.

On the other hand, many of the junior members of the crew took special delight in the pleasures of Olongapo. Ensign Chris Reed observed that, "It was a young sailor's dream come true. . . . Terrific music, plus there was booze, and there were girls. And the girls, by and large, were attractive – better than average . . . and a lot of the sailors just fell in love with the whole thing. . . . It was like a [school] dance, except that you could get drunk, and you could take a girl home." One *New Jersey* petty officer considered Olongapo "heaven". He says, "It was a place where you could go, and you could get drunk. You could get yourself a girl, and she'd [even] feed you . . . all for under $10.00."

At least one man had too good a time. Ensign Frank Swayze was the *New Jersey*'s discipline officer and was confronted with the case of a third class commissaryman. The shore patrol apprehended the petty officer when he was running down a street, roaring drunk and wearing only shoes and a T-shirt. Recalls Swayze, "The story he told was sufficiently bizarre that I believed it – up to a point." The man said that he had been riding in a jeepney (a local taxicab built on a jeep body) in Olongapo. He

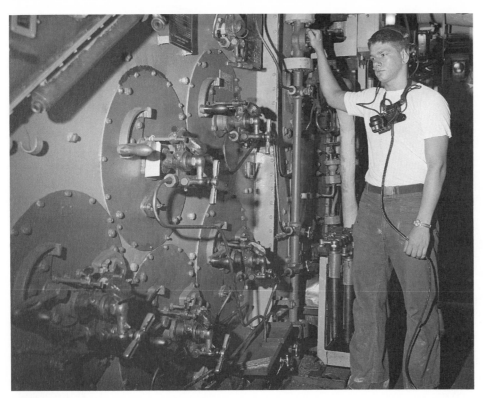

Above: Fireman Apprentice Gary LaPuma stands boiler front watch in one of the battleship's firerooms. (Courtesy Howard Serig)

claimed that he was kidnapped, taken to a house, stripped of his clothes, and tied to a bed. When one of the captors started abusing him, the cook said, he burst his bonds, fought off the kidnappers, and ran from the house. That's when the shore patrol got him. To make things worse, he attacked an innocent Filipino while he was in custody and waiting to be returned to the ship. As the strange narrative unfolded, Swayze tried to stifle his sense of amusement and finally failed. He laughed out loud, which probably added to the sense of misery the cook was experiencing.

Though he was inclined to make things as easy as he could for the sake of crew morale, Captain Snyder generally showed that he meant business when it came to captain's mast. Swayze recalls that the skipper often had several dozen cases to deal with when the ship went back to sea after a period in port. Snyder himself recalls that one tool he found especially useful was what is known in the Navy as a "suspended bust". To "bust" an enlisted man is to reduce him in rate, as from petty officer third class to seaman, for instance. The penalty meted out at mast often depends on the nature of the testimonial the individual's chief and his division officer are willing to make on his behalf. If a man was habitually in trouble, he might well get a stiff sentence. If, on the other hand, he was someone of normally sterling performance who had a one-time misstep, the tendency was to sentence him to a reduction in rate but to suspend the sentence for six months. If he performed well and kept his nose clean for that period, the

sentence was not carried out, and he retained his pay-grade. In effect, he was put on probation, and the slate was wiped clean unless he got into further trouble in the meantime.

When the *New Jersey* got back to the gunline in Vietnam, she resumed firing mission after mission on behalf of her constituents ashore. Most of the time, the men of the battleship could not see their targets, because they were over the horizon. The only real idea of what was happening at the end of a projectile's long, high trajectory came in the voice radio messages received from spotters. Ensign Chris Reed got the impression that spotters occasionally called in rounds when they didn't really have a legitimate target; they just wanted to see what a big bang looked like. Ensign Scott Cheyne, the public affairs officer, got the chance to see a big bang on one rare direct-fire mission when the target for the 16-inch guns was in sight of the ship. He describes the experience:

"This mission was such short range – we were shooting against a hillside, some suspected Viet Cong position or something – that you could follow the trajectory of the bullets their entire flight, and you could actually see them impact. . . . The bullets would hit into the hillside, and you could see the shock waves, concentric circles ripple out in the trees. It was the most eerie sight I've ever seen, really strange. The sound, of course, travels slower than light. . . . Several seconds would elapse, and then you could hear the concussion, . . . the shells exploding."

The ship's firing for 25 November was her biggest one-day score of the year 1968. She fired eight different main battery missions and was credited with destroying 117 structures and thirty-two bunkers. In addition, she set off eight secondary explosions in enemy storage areas near Quang Ngai, South Vietnam. Her projectiles killed an estimated forty enemy troops, and spotters gave her credit for damaging ninety-three structures, tearing up 110 meters of trenchline, and destroying a number of tunnel complexes. Cost-conscious Secretary of Defense Robert McNamara had imposed a limit of sixty-five rounds per day on the ship's main battery. Snyder recalls that he observed the limit in spirit but not always to the letter.

On 2 December, forty-five men from the Third Marine Division came aboard to spend a two-day rest and relaxation period on board the battleship. Accompanying them was the division's assistant commander, Brigadier General Robert B. Carney, Jr., son of Admiral William Halsey's World War II chief of staff. On 8 December, the *New Jersey* fired seven missions in support of Operation "Meade River". When she kocked out an enemy bunker south of Danang, the spotter reported that the resulting crater looked big enough for the foundation for an eight-story building.

Soon, it was time for another trip to Subic Bay, where the *New Jersey* arrived on 10 December and took on ammuni-

Right: Marine Corps visitors to the *New Jersey* on 2 December 1968 include Brigadier General Robert B. Carney, Jr., son of Admiral William Halsey's World War II chief of staff. (Courtesy Howard Serig)

Far right: A reluctant crew member is offered a stalk of celery after having crawled through a garbage-filled chute as part of his initiation. (Courtesy Howard Serig)

Below: A mock beauty contest is part of the initiation silliness when the *New Jersey* crosses the equator on 15 December 1968. (Courtesy Howard Serig)

tion, food, and general stores. On Friday the 13th she headed for the Equator in company with the destroyer *Towers*. Those who had not already made the crossing would have to undergo an initiation in order to be transformed from pollywogs to shellbacks. Among the events connected with the crossing was a "beauty" contest in which an officer or enlisted man from each division dressed up in women's clothing. The aim was to look either as attractive as possible or as gross as possible. Virtually all entrants were at one extreme or the other.

On 15 December, the day of the crossing, Fire Controlman Second Class Tom Mumpower had to pretend he was the pet dog of Chief Al Gambetta. Mumpower sat at Gambetta's feet during breakfast and ate dry cereal from a paper plate. Says Mumpower, "There was a chunk of shredded wheat and maybe a Cheerio or two, and the only moisture that was allowed to touch that was what was already in my face." Out on deck, Senior Chief Boiler Technician Walt Hosta served as "royal baby" for the initiation, which meant that his ample abdomen was smeared with grease, and pollywogs had to kiss it. Shellbacks lined up from bow to stern with pieces of fire hose to use as shillelaghs to whack the new men as they crawled by on hands and knees. For the most part, the pollywogs who got to go later in the process felt luckiest, because the hose-swinging arms of the shellbacks were weaker and more tired by then. Following the ordeal of running the gauntlet of bottom-slappers, pollywogs got stalks of celery shoved in their mouths, and then they had to crawl through a chute filled with garbage. At long last, the messy new shellbacks got to wash off.

Fortunately, the line-crossing ceremony was a prelude to a port visit in Singapore from 16 through 20 December. Ensign Chris Reed was struck by the variety of cultures to be seen. There were ultramodern apartment buildings, twenty and thirty stories high, and they had bamboo poles sticking out of many windows to serve as impromptu clothes dryers. Ensign Ron Kaderli, a merchant ship enthusiast, found Singapore to be a living museum, because there were in the area some old vessels which looked as if they had been around from the time of World War I or possibly earlier. Gunner's Mate Third Class Tom Feigley was one of many who shopped for souvenirs and found that the items for sale didn't have established prices. The system of haggling had been institutionalized and was thus the accepted way of doing business.

After a good dinner one evening in Singapore, Ensign Frank Swayze and several of the other junior officers went out in search of entertainment. "We were looking for a place that ·might have a dancing girl or something like that," he says. They tried to cross the language barrier sufficiently to tell their cab driver they were looking for girls. A flicker of realization finally seemed to come to him, and the driver headed off on a road into the jungle. The officers arrived at last at a tin-roofed hut. They found inside a single 8-millimeter movie projector and a stack of stag films, six in black and white and two in color – not quite what they had in mind.

On 22 December, after winding up the Singapore trip, the *New Jersey* returned to her station off Vietnam's demilitarized zone. After two days of shooting, it was Christmas, and the men of the battleship celebrated by watching a show presented by Bob Hope and a troupe of entertainers which included nineteen gorgeous girls. The group, which included Les Brown's band, Ann-Margret, and former football player Roosevelt Grier, arrived by helicopter and presented a ninety-minute show from the top of turret one. Fire Controlman First Class Rick Crawford served as escort for Hope because the younger sailors were all vying to be with the pretty girls. Crawford found Hope to be "as funny off the stage as he was on the stage". Among other things, Hope made a crack during the show about the *New Jersey*'s size, saying, "This is Wake Island with a rudder." He also indicated that his idea of a good time would be to go on a double date with *Playboy* publisher Hugh Hefner and take the rejects. And after Ann-Margaret told Hope she wanted him both to sing and dance, he said to her, "Okay, but if I require mouth-to-mouth resuscitation, remember . . . no fellows!"

Having women on board was obviously unusual for a man-of-war, but the crew members proved adaptable. Chief Lew Moore's laundry took care of cleaning clothes for the visitors. He recalls that the girls "sent their skivvies

Top left: Comedian Bob Hope atop turret one to deliver his Christmas show to the *New Jersey*'s crew in 1968. (Courtesy Howard Serig)

Bottom left: The bow is jammed with the audience for Bob Hope's Christmas program. The platform in the center contains lights, camera, and cue cards. (Courtesy Howard Serig)

Above: K. W. Bowman and Stuart Goldman decorate a Christmas tree in the crew's lounge in December 1968. (Courtesy Howard Serig)

and all down to the laundry, and we washed them and sent them right back – no problem." Even more surprising was a request made on behalf of one of the girls in the troupe. She had run out of birth control pills, and the "den mother" accompanying the girls asked if there were any available on board the *New Jersey*. There were, and the request was fulfilled.

Christmas came and went rapidly, and then the ship resumed her firing missions during what little was left of 1968. The New Year's holiday was a time for muted celebration on board ship. This was one night when the rule against consumption of alcoholic beverages on board a Navy ship was at least bent. The chief petty officers managed to get a small supply of wine to add a bit of kick to the grapefruit juice punch they concocted in chiefs' quarters. As midnight approached, Chief Personnelman Andy Lavella went up to the helo deck and looked shoreward from where the *New Jersey* was quietly lying to. "You could see the Marines," he recalls. "They were probably shooting the rounds off just for the joy of it, because the whole sky was lighting up over there. Whether 'Charlie' [the Viet Cong] was firing back at them or what, they were just making noise there. I thought, 'Gee, it's too bad we don't fire over there. We really could make some.'" For once, the *New Jersey* remained silent.

During that middle part of the deployment, Warrant Officer Ed Flamboe – newly promoted to that status and

new on board as well – was getting on-the-job training on what a warrant officer is supposed to do. As an enlisted electronics technician, he had long found both pleasure and satisfaction in trouble-shooting a piece of equipment, finding the problem, and repairing it. He loved to get his hands into the gear, and so he indulged himself after reporting to the *New Jersey*. Then one day, Electronics Technician First Class Ron Sousa came to Flamboe's stateroom and diplomatically gave him the best advice he ever got on how to be a warrant officer. Flamboe remembers Sousa telling him, "I realize you like to get your hands in, but you kind of destroy the confidence of the technicians when you do. Stand back and let them at it." It was a great leadership and management lesson – that people have to be allowed to try things themselves and learn through their mistakes rather than having the boss do the job for them.

A different sort of problem in officer-enlisted relations involved Bill Partain, the ship's warrant carpenter. From time to time, Ensign Chris Reed of the FA division would go to the carpenter shop, approach one of Partain's men, and ask him to do a certain job in the weapons department office if he had time. The jobs got done, but after a while Partain came to Reed to complain that he was jumping the chain of command. Reed explained that he'd just been trying to save time for Partain by not getting him involved. The warrant officer finally had to yell at the ensign to get him to understand, "When you ask an enlisted man something, no matter how you phrase it, it's an order. And you can't order my men around." Reed got the message – that he should make his requests through Partain, because it was Partain who was responsible for the work of the carpenters and the priorities of the projects they were doing.

Warrant officer country was on the port side of the second deck, beneath the barrels of turret two's guns when they were fired overhead. The turret's firing sometimes made sleeping difficult, and it caused Ed Flamboe a different sort of problem at one point during the deployment. The repeated jarring imparted by the big guns damaged the bevel gears which turned the antenna for the SPS-6 air search radar. Some of his electronics technicians went up the foremast and retrieved the two gears which were supposed to mesh at a 45° angle with their stems perpendicular to each other. Ordering replacement gears through the supply system would take some time, and the radar would be useless in the meantime. Thus Flamboe sought to have replacements made in the *New Jersey*'s machine shop. One machinist's mate third class responded to the challenge with particular dedication. First he worked up computations, then stayed up all night making replacements from scratch. Unfortunately, the shank on one gear was too long, so the machinist's mate put it in a vise to cut it down. When he did, the gear popped out, slid across the steel deck, and was smashed.

Since there was no use crying over spilled milk, he immediately spent four more hours making another one. Then Flamboe and a couple of his technicians went up the foremast and installed the new gears, ducking behind the foremast for protection whenever turret two's guns were going to fire.

During the first thirteen days of 1969, the *New Jersey* supported troops in South Vietnam. From 11 to 13 January, she provided direct support for Operation "Bold Mariner", an amphibious landing on Batangan Peninsula by two Marine Corps battalion landing teams. On the 13th, the ship was released to proceed to Subic Bay. On 14 January, men in turret three had to move some 16-inch projectiles to different positions on the shell deck. The gunner's mate who was supposed to be supervising was elsewhere, and the consequences were nearly fatal. During the course of fastening in one of the projectiles, Seaman Andy Tobias didn't hear the alarm which warned that the movable deck was being rotated. Gunner's Mate Third Class Tom Feigley was one of those on the projectile deck. He recalls that the man at the controls was not in position to see Tobias from his station. As the deck moved, Tobias's body got caught between a projectile hoist and a clump of projectiles. Slowly he was crushed into an ever more narrow space. When the movement was finally stopped, Tobias had suffered traumatic injuries, including compound fractures of both upper and lower legs, a crushed pelvis, and severe damage to many blood vessels. Feigley and others immediately began parbuckling projectiles away from Tobias.

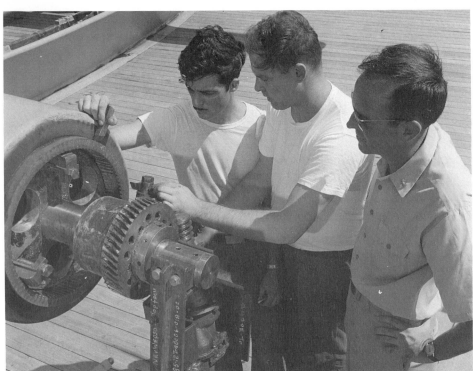

Below: In this November 1968 gag photo, Lieutenant Commander John Denby, the ship's surgeon, observes the "circumcision" of a 16-inch barrel. Machinery repairmen Charles Grosser and Earnie Roberts use an orbital lathe to shave off the portion of the liner which has been extruded beyond the end of the barrel proper. (Courtesy Howard Serig)

They were afraid that pulling away the last one might do still more damage, so a husky seaman named Johnson – no doubt fueled by a supply of adrenaline – knocked it out of the way. Tobias was put on a stretcher and transported up through the long third-deck passageway that runs between the forward and after turrets. Sick bay and the operating room were in the forward part of the ship, so it was essential that he be moved.

Tobias, in shock and weak from the loss of five pints of blood, nearly died during the course of the surgical repair performed by Lieutenant Commander John Denby. The ship had what Denby describes as a "walking blood bank" in the form of the hundreds of men on board; volunteers responded quickly and donated blood which matched Tobias's type. Denby's skillful work saved both the young man's life and his legs. It was a masterful, perhaps even miraculous job. After a night in sick bay, Tobias left the ship as soon as she reached Subic Bay the next day. He and Denby were flown by helicopter to the hospital at Clark Air Force Base in the Philippines.

As the *New Jersey*'s surgeon, Denby was a holdover from the time when the smaller ships of the fleet looked to battleships for types of underway medical treatment they themselves could not provide. Destroyermen who needed appendectomies in World War II were highlined to battleships. The surgeon, of course, was also supposed to be ready to deal with injuries sustained in combat. By now, the role was pretty much an anachronism because of the availability of helicopters and the unlikelihood of battle damage. Providence was kind to Seaman Andy Tobias in putting a skilled surgeon on board the *New Jersey* on 14 January 1969.

The battleship's stay in the Philippines lasted until 20 January. She steamed to Yokosuka, Japan, where she arrived on the 25th for more upkeep and liberty. The ship's arrival prompted a demonstration on the part of Japanese socialists, but the *New Jersey* was probably more of a pretext than anything else, for such demonstrations were a regular occurrence. They were arranged primarily for internal Japanese politics rather than against the United States.

Dress blues and peacoats were definitely called for on liberty – much in contrast to the liberty uniforms in the Philippines. Personnelman Third Class Hank Strub rode one of Japan's efficient electric trains to Kamakura to see the great Daibutsu, a giant statue of Buddha. During the course of wandering around the town, he became chilled, so he put his thumb up and hitched a ride. He thought it was awfully nice of the Japanese man who picked him up. When they got to the train station, the driver stuck out his hand and asked for a fare. He wasn't a taxi driver, but had taken advantage of the opportunity when he saw it. Strub was grateful, even if it did cost him.

Fire Controlmen Tom Mumpower and Rick Crawford rented a real taxi and had the driver take them on a sightseeing tour. One of the places they visited in Yokosuka was *Mikasa*, the battleship which served as Admiral Heihachiro Togo's flagship at the Battle of Tsushima Strait in 1905, during the Russo-Japanese War. Now encased in concrete, it is a memorial and museum. While the Americans were visiting the Japanese battleship, hundreds of Japanese were visiting the American battleship. Warrant Officer Ed Flamboe was standing watch as officer of the deck one day when a Japanese dignitary came to call. Captain Snyder rushed out of his cabin and began walking across the broad 01 promenade deck to greet the visitor. Characteristically, he was hatless, so his steward came chasing after him to give the captain his scrambled-egg cap for the welcome at the quarterdeck.

During his watchstanding at Yokosuka, Flamboe developed the same high regard for Japanese craftsmanship as had Captain Tyree during the Korean War. Some of the planks in the *New Jersey*'s teakwood deck were damaged and needed replacement. One workman from the local ship repair facility was especially adept at such work, remembers Flamboe. After looking at the spot in the deck which needed to be filled, the workman surveyed it visually from several angles but didn't take a single measurement. Then he walked over to his wood supply, sawed off a board, and dropped it into place with just the right amount of space around the edges for caulking to be put in.

The ship got under way again on 5 February, and within a few hours of leaving port she ran into gale force winds with gusts up to 65 knots. Lieutenant Commander Carl Albrecht, the main battery officer, talked to his principal subordinates and directed them to make sure their turrets were secured for heavy seas. As soon as sea detail was over, Albrecht grabbed an early lunch and then headed for his stateroom to take a noontime nap. He put a large electric fan next to his bunk. While he was sleeping, the ship took a heavy roll, and the fan toppled onto Albrecht's bunk. It nearly amputated his little toe. Filled with embarrassment, especially after cautioning his turret officers about the weather, Albrecht wrapped his foot in a towel, donned a bathrobe, and then hobbled through the wardroom where the senior officers were having lunch. It wasn't his first choice of a route, but it was the most direct way to sick bay. A hospital corpsman sewed up his toe, and he returned to his room to spend the rest of the day in bed.

Topside, the heavy seas damaged exterior fittings. The ship arrived off Danang on the morning of 10 February and immediately began gunfire support of Korean troops fighting there. On 14 February, she fired a mission into the demilitarized zone when a U.S. observation aircraft came under fire from the ground. The next day, the men on board the ship received information that the Communists were setting up a rocket site for night firing from the southern half of the DMZ, about 11 miles northeast of the U.S. Marines' post at Con Thien. Opening up about dusk

with her main battery, the ship fired until well after dark. A ground observer reported twenty-five secondary explosions and seven fireballs which rose 500 feet.

On the afternoon of the 15th, Chief Lew Moore was manning a 5-inch mount, because he had been a gunner's mate before converting to ship's serviceman. His ears and mind had become so accustomed to the routine of the ship that a break in the pattern was disturbing. He heard the first two buzzes of the salvo alarm but then didn't hear the customary roar of a 16-inch projectile being sent on its way. There was a misfire in the center gun of turret two. After repeated attempts to fire the gun were unsuccessful, there was a two and a half hour cooling-off period to see if the round would be fired by a residual spark in the breech. When it wasn't, the crew went to general quarters, and two men went into the center gun room: Lieutenant Roger Glaes, the turret officer, and Chief Gunner's Mate Harold Sykes, the turret captain. Outside in the turret booth, peering through a circular window into the gun room, was Lieutenant Commander Albrecht. The main battery officer recalls that he was describing "in excruciating detail exactly what was going on" for the benefit of Captain Snyder and Lieutenant Commander Roy Short, who had replaced Commander Pete Roane as weapons officer. Glaes and Sykes risked their lives as they went in to clear the unfired round. First they took out the firing lock and pumped in water with a hand pump. Then, cautiously, they opened the mushroom-shaped plug which sealed the breech of the gun. Fortunately, nothing happened. When

Right: Grains of powder are visible through the ripped covering of a 16-inch reduced powder charge which did not explode during a firing attempt in February 1969. The quilted area at left is the red-colored ignition pad, covering the black powder into which the primer is fired. (Courtesy Howard Serig)

the two men looked in, they saw the problem. The powder bags were reduced charges and thus smaller in diameter than the full service charges. The last bag had tilted to a cockeyed position when the gun was raised to firing position after loading. When the primer was fired at the askew bag, it missed the red ignition pad and black powder at the rear end of the bag. Instead it burned a hole into the silk portion of the bag. Sykes and Glaes, much relieved, pulled the bag out of the breech, and the emergency was over. The ever-curious Captain Snyder came to the turret and insisted on seeing the bag before

Lieutenant Glaes energetically heaved it into the South China Sea. New powder was put into the gun, the breech closed, and the projectile was cleared from the barrel. Snyder says he prohibited the use of reduced powder charges after that incident.

The *New Jersey*'s most noteworthy exploit of the Vietnam War occurred in the early morning hours of Saturday, 22 February. At 1:06, while she was firing an unobserved mission, the ship's combat information center received an urgent radio call for help. A Marine outpost about 1,000 meters south of the demilitarized zone was being attacked by a large number of enemy troops. The *New Jersey* promptly began firing salvoes of 5-inch pro-

Opposite page, top: One of the 40-mm. gun tubs at the stern serves as a repository for empty 5-inch powder cans after the charges have been used in firing. (Courtesy Commander John Hayes)

Opposite page, bottom: A salvo of 5-inch projectiles is in the air at left after the firing of the secondary battery on the starboard side. (Courtesy USS New Jersey)

jectiles, first with two mounts and then with four. The 16-inch guns joined in as the action intensified. The *New Jersey*'s guns were augmented by those of the Coast Guard cutter *Owasco* nearby.

The calls for fire from both ships came from one spotter, Marine Lance Corporal Roger Clouse. Radarman Third Class Bob Fulks marveled as he listened to the crackling of the radiotelephone net in the ship's combat information center. Speaking of the spotter, Fulks says, "He was very calm, very cool, as I recall, very skilled in what he was doing, even though he was facing immense odds. . . . He did a heck of a job, and he was on it all night." Warrant Officer Ed Flamboe was also fascinated by what he heard over the radio that night, because the spotter's transmissions were punctuated by the staccato bursts of machine-guns firing close by. The initial rounds from the two ships offshore were directed at positions practically on top of the Marines' outpost. As the ships fired on and on through the night, their gunfire moved the enemy forces back and away from the Marines. Fire Controlman Rick Crawford stayed in the *New Jersey*'s plotting room that night, even though he was no longer on watch, because he was captivated by the unfolding drama. He looked at grid coordinates where the spotter was calling for fire and noticed that, after a while, the spots formed a circle. The Marines were surrounded by the enemy.

Down below, Lieutenant Dick Harris was busy, even though his 5-inch guns on the starboard side were not involved. Following usual practice, the ship was heading northward at slow speed, and so the port side guns were engaged. Harris sent his men in relays to relieve tiring gun crews on the port side, because the business of loading 5-inch projectiles and powder cases into the breeches as fast as they could be loaded was physically demanding. Harris also had his men transfer 5-inch ammunition from starboard to port in order to replenish supplies steadily being exhausted. That meant carrying the powder and projectiles across "Broadway" and thence to the handling rooms on the other side.

By 5:00 a.m., the firing by the two ships had forced the enemy troops to diminish the intensity of their attack. They began withdrawing. Finally, at 6:33, the attack had been completely repulsed, and the firing ceased. When the crew went out on deck that morning, they found the area of the port side mounts knee-deep in empty powder casings. After the cases had been ejected from the mounts, there hadn't been time to stop and clear them out of the way. The demand for fire was so heavy that the shooting went uninterrupted, and the brass casings piled higher and higher. The battleship fired 1,710 5-inch rounds that night. The paint was scorched off the gun barrels because they had grown so hot from the repeated firing. Gunner's Mate Second Class Mike Lucas, one of the mount captains, observed, "We kept up a barrage of four-, six-, and eight-gun salvoes until dawn. The guns became so hot that the

grease on the recoil slides was bubbling, and an hour after we finished firing the barrels were still hot to the touch." On shore, grateful Major Ron Smaldone, who was in command of the outpost that was nearly overrun, expressed his evaluation in one sentence: "If it hadn't been for the *New Jersey*, they would have zapped our ass."

The intense firing that night had started from Condition III and was quickly upgraded to Condition I for the people of the 5-inch mounts. It demonstrated the flexibility of the partial battle manning which allowed most of the crew to relax when not required for duty. Gunner's Mate Larry Pousson remembers that men in Condition III watches could lie on deck and sleep in turrets if they weren't being called upon to fire at a given time. When completely off duty, the gunner's mates enjoyed watching closed-circuit TV, chatting, and playing poker. Ensign Chris Reed was one of many who purchased stereo equipment when the ship was in Japan, because listening to music was a popular pastime. Personnelman Third Class Hank Strub built a model of the *New Jersey* during off-duty hours in the personnel office. He got a Revell brand plastic kit from a Navy exchange. Since the model had the ship outfitted as she was during World War II, Strub had to do some improvising to show her as she appeared in 1969. Whenever he had a question about how something had been changed topside, all he had to do was step outside and take a look.

There were also poker games in the chief petty officers' quarters. Andy Lavella, the chief personnelman, remembers that Captain Snyder used to visit fairly frequently and josh with the chiefs. One greeting was "How's the game going tonight?" Chief Ship's Serviceman Lew Moore says that Snyder used to kid the chiefs during the daytime as well, once remarking, "What's going on? The lights are on in here." It was the responsibility of the chief petty officers to make sure the work was done, not to do it themselves unless it was beyond the capability of the enlisted men working for them. Thus, recalls Moore, chiefs' quarters was often dark during the day, a sort of sleepy hollow.

Despite their propensity for entertainment, the *New Jersey*'s chiefs had a vital role in the running of the ship. Chief Moore recalls that Captain Snyder's frequent visits were a way of reinforcing his support and confidence in the chiefs. He depended on them in matters large and small, and they, in turn called on knowledge gained during long years of service to see that their divisions performed well in their particular specialties. In the ship's laundry, for instance, it was Moore who was summoned to the captain's cabin when Snyder's shirt collar and cuffs weren't done properly the first time. Moore remembers that Snyder "relied on his chief petty officers, and he told them so. If you were a chief and you screwed up, he was the first one to greet you. But he backed his chiefs up all the way, and I've got to give him credit for that. Like he said, 'You guys have got the experience.'" In Moore's case, that experience went back to 1943. Another chief, Boatswain's Mate C. W. Holmes, had served in the old *Mississippi* and there were others from World War II.

Between 14 February and 9 March, the *New Jersey* spent twenty-four consecutive days in support of the Third Marine Division. Most of that time she was keeping station in the relatively small area just south of the demilitarized zone. As the deployment wound down, the heavy cruiser *Newport News* came alongside the battleship on 13 March to receive turnover material for her scheduled relief of the *New Jersey* on the gunline. General Creighton Abrams of the Army was Commander U.S. Military Assistance Command Vietnam, and he had previously told Captain Snyder of his efforts to get the battleship extended in her Vietnam deployment because of the valuable contribution she was making to the war effort. His request was not approved, and the ship was scheduled to go back to Long Beach, then return to Southeast Asia in the fall when she could do the most good – during the season of monsoon rains.

Rear Admiral Thomas Rudden, Commander Task Group 70.8, came over by highline from the *Newport News*. Machinery Repairman Third Class Bill Sosnowski of the *New Jersey* had gone from the machine shop to the fantail

to dump some metal shavings into the world's largest garbage disposal – the Pacific Ocean. He observed that the men of the cruiser were paraded at quarters in dress uniforms, while the battleship's crew was in customary less-than-formal attire. Snyder had already made the point, though, that the *New Jersey* was a working ship. Rudden agreed and hailed the crew by saying, "Your performance out here has been nothing short of magnificent. You have fully justified every effort that was made to get you on the line as quickly as possible."

The battleship made a five-day stop at Subic Bay in mid-March before returning to the coast of Vietnam for one final line period before heading home. She was back on station from 21 March to 1 April. The last spotter-observed mission was fired on the evening of 31 March at a bunker complex three and a half miles northeast of Con Thien. The aerial observer reported seven bunkers destroyed. After midnight, the ship fired unobserved missions which qualified the crew for combat pay for the month of April. As she wound up her Vietnam efforts, the battleship had amassed 120 days on the gunline. In that time she fired nearly twelve million pounds of ordnance – 5,866 16-inch rounds, and 14,891 of 5-inch.

**Below:** The *New Jersey* rendezvouses with the heavy cruiser *Newport News* off Vietnam on 13 March 1969. (Photo by PH2 H. Spencer; U.S. Naval Institute Collection)

The next stop after Vietnam was Subic Bay, where the ship stayed for 2 and 3 April, and then to Yokosuka from 6 until 9 April. The crew had hoped to wind up the Far East cruise with an even more exotic port visit, which was the basis for one of Captain Snyder's more whimsical tricks. While in a crew's berthing compartment toward the end of the Vietnam stint, the skipper picked up a telephone, acted as if he were calling the bridge, and pretended to tell the navigator to break out charts for Australia. Rumors raced through the length of the huge ship, and before long it was accepted as gospel that the *New Jersey* would visit Australia and New Zealand before going back to the States. The single men were delighted. The married men reported in letters home that the cruise was going to be extended. Some of the men's wives began lodging protests with Navy officials and members of Congress. Since the ship did not go to Australasia – which she had not been scheduled to visit in the first place – the wives smugly congratulated themselves and one another for what they viewed as a successful protest campaign.

Unlike the *New Jersey*'s visit to Japan in January, the one in April was low key. Then the battleship set her course for Long Beach, leaving Yokosuka on 9 April as part of Task Group 77.7, which included the aircraft carrier *Coral Sea* and three destroyers. The men who had gone to the coast of Vietnam and earned plaudits for their service were now mentally tasting the pleasures to come once they reached Long Beach. A state highway patrolman from California was flown aboard to give traffic safety lectures to men who hadn't been behind the wheel of a car for many months.

On the morning of 15 April, the *New Jersey* was only four days and 1,800 miles away. Lieutenant Dick Harris was looking forward to the homecoming with his family. He recalls, "We were all listening to the San Diego or Long Beach radios. . . . We were that close. I remember them passing the word, 'Stand by to list to starboard'." The ship heeled over as she made a long turn to port. Petty Officer Bill Sosnowski and Lieutenant (junior grade) Walt Migrala were two of many crew members up on deck as the battleship was headed east toward the rising sun. Soon, however, the sun was behind them, and they were pulling away from the *Coral Sea*. A voice radio message had come in, ordering the battleship to turn west. Surprise and disappointment filled the vast dreadnought. Captain Snyder briefed the officers, and then the word began to filter

Below: In March 1969, the *New Jersey* fires a nine-gun salvo toward targets in South Vietnam. (USN photo 1137972 by PH2 Kenneth Barrett; U.S. Naval Institute Collection)

down. Fire Controlman First Class Rick Crawford got an inkling when the FM division officer, Lieutenant (junior grade) Larry Whitman came down to main battery plot and asked if the ship had any shore bombardment charts of Korea; she hadn't.

As the word eventually came out, a U.S. Navy EC-121 electronic intelligence plane had been shot down by North Korean aircraft, killing all thirty-one crew members. This was something of a repeat performance of the North Koreans' seizure of the U.S. intelligence ship *Pueblo* just over a year earlier. Back in Washington, recalls Admiral Thomas Moorer, then the Chief of Naval Operations, the Joint Chiefs of Staff were urging retaliation to prevent still further attacks. The Nixon Administration, newly in office, was hesitant to start a round of hostilities with North Korea when it was already bogged down in a war against North Vietnam. While no immediate retaliation was authorized, it was within the power of the Joint Chiefs to order naval ships to the scene so they could be ready, just in case. The *New Jersey* was one of the ships so ordered.

Reaction throughout the ship was mixed. As had been the case when the bombing halt was ordered at the beginning of November, some men were disbelieving, but international politics had again forced a change in the ship's mission and schedule. At the same time, says Carl Albrecht, there was a sense of excitement. Maybe the ship would be getting into the kind of action she had been denied in North Vietnam. As a result, he says, many people were thinking, "Boy, let's get over there."

The unexpected diversion from original plans spawned a host of difficulties back in the United States. By midweek, officers at the Long Beach naval base knew that the ship would not be coming in on Saturday morning, the scheduled arrival time, but they were forbidden by Washington to say anything for security reasons. Thus, many relatives of crew members did not learn of the schedule change until too late and showed up in Long Beach. Mrs. Sally Elfelt, wife of the ship's executive officer, took charge. Nearly 200 families in the area provided temporary lodging for relatives of *New Jersey* men, but even that wasn't sufficient, and so the base movie theater became a dormitory. The whole thing was a huge fiasco, especially for those who had traveled long distances to meet a ship that didn't arrive.

Far to the west, the *New Jersey* arrived at Yokosuka on 22 April. In the thirteen days since she had last been in that port, she had steamed 7,042 miles at an average speed of 22.4 knots. Her crew wasn't permitted liberty; instead, they spent seven hours in port taking on provisions. Then the ship headed out to get lost in an operating area which was centered about 175 miles southeast of Yokosuka. On 24 April, she rearmed from the ammunition ship *Paricutin*, taking on 837 tons of ammunition during ten hours alongside. It was the biggest replenishment of the deployment. The ship's orders were to stay out of sight. Even while a force of four aircraft carriers, three cruisers, and twenty-two destroyers was parading ostentatiously in the Sea of Japan near Korea, the *New Jersey* was kept hidden in the background. Obediently, she steamed around in her holding area at eight knots to conserve fuel. Shortly after noon on 26 April, the ship received a most welcome message, directing her to head for the United States. At 12:35 in the afternoon, her conning officer, Lieutenant (junior grade) Randy Ghilarducci, ordered "Right full rudder, all engines ahead full, indicate turns for 22 knots, steer course 090." The trip back to the Far East had proved an empty gesture. Fortunately, the *New Jersey* hadn't joined the other ships off Korea itself, or her long trip would have been even longer.

After the few days she had spent in aimless meandering, the battleship once again caught the bone in her teeth. She was making homeward-bound turns as steam surged through her turbines. Eagerness mounted once more. As the ship reached Long Beach on the morning of 5 May, Captain Snyder was interviewed by radiotelephone for the benefit of the news media. If the level of hostilities continued as it was in Vietnam, Snyder told the listening newsmen, "Only an idiot would not send the *New Jersey* back." A crowd of more than 1,000 people gathered on Pier Echo to welcome the battleship. Her first mooring line hit the pier at 9:43, and as soon as the brows were over to the pier, there were conspicuously happy reunions between crew members and those who had waited behind for so long. For some wives, the wait had been too long. Looking shoreward from the deck of the *New Jersey*, Personnelman Hank Strub saw a group of men dressed much more formally than the casually clad Southern California crowd. The men in coats and ties carried briefcases, and in the briefcases were divorce papers to be served on returning crewmen. Welcome home from the war!

During the next month, the ship settled in for a refit period, and crew members were given early liberty on days when they weren't in the duty section. Into this atmosphere, the author reported to the *New Jersey* at the Long Beach Naval Shipyard on 20 May to join the crew and to begin a period of training and indoctrination for the planned deployment to Vietnam in the autumn.

The *New Jersey* had done a splendid job during her first deployment to Southeast Asia, despite the change in role soon after she arrived on the scene. Credit for a ship's performance comes principally to her commanding officer, so there were expectations that Captain Snyder would be on the selection list for flag rank. Lieutenant Commander Carl Albrecht was the *New Jersey*'s command duty officer one evening when Captain Snyder called down from a dinner party he was hosting in the captain's cabin and told Albrecht that he had been receiving congratulations on being chosen for rear admiral. He wanted Albrecht to track down the official selection list as quickly as he could. There was a Captain Ed Snyder on the selection list, but it was Edwin K. Snyder, skipper of the *Newport News*, not J. Edward Snyder of the *New Jersey*. The *New Jersey* Snyder was selected for rear admiral two years later.

On 2 June, Rear Admiral Lloyd Vasey, Commander Cruiser-Destroyer Flotilla Seven, moved aboard with his staff so that he could command that summer's Pacific midshipman training squadron. For Vasey, who had served in the USS *Mississippi* upon graduation from the Naval Academy in 1939, there was a touch of nostalgia to be on board another battleship three decades later and to find so many similarities. The only major difference, he says, is that men no longer slept in hammocks. The training period began on 9 June when the *New Jersey* got under way for a two-week period in the southern California area. On board were 104 midshipmen from the Naval Academy and NROTC units. It was a far cry from the 700 midshipmen the *New Jersey* routinely took aboard each year during her cruises in the 1950s. By the late 1960s, midshipmen were dispersed much more widely throughout the fleet.

After the offshore training, which included shore bombardment requalification at San Clemente Island and observation of missile-firing exercises, the crew got one last liberty weekend in the Long Beach/Los Angeles area. On Monday morning, 23 June, the battleship got under way as flagship of Task Group 10.1. In her wake as she began her journey northward were the fourteen destroyers which comprised the remainder of the training squadron. The *New Jersey*'s austere reactivation package had specified that she was not being equipped to serve as a flagship, and so her communications gear was limited accordingly. Her flag quarters were not supposed to be reactivated, but Captain Snyder got around that by fixing them up as the "Fleet Admiral Halsey Memorial Suite". Now they were indeed serving as flag quarters for Admiral Vasey and his staff, and the battleship's radio spaces were swamped while trying to handle the communications for fifteen ships, not just one. Two officers who got very little sleep during the early part of the midshipman cruise were Lieutenant Tom Thornton, the ship's communication officer, and Ed Flamboe, warrant electronics technician.

The arrival at San Francisco on 24 June was an impressive one, with so many ships stretched out astern of the *New Jersey* in column. The battleship passed under the Golden Gate Bridge and moored at the naval air station at Alameda. By mid-1969, the nation's mood had swung

**Right:** Among the hundreds of newsmen who besieged the battleship during the Vietnam War are these at a press conference at Alameda, California, on 24 June 1969. Captain Ed Snyder puffs on his pipe as Rear Admiral Lloyd Vasey responds to a question. (USN photo by Ken Smith; courtesy of Rear Admiral Lloyd Vasey)

Right: Lined up are some of the more than 10,000 people who visited the *New Jersey* at Alameda, California, on 25 June 1969. (Photo by Paul Stillwell)

Below: The *New Jersey* steams under the Golden Gate Bridge upon her arrival at San Francisco on 24 June 1969. (Courtesy Rear Admiral Lloyd Vasey)

considerably in the direction of opposition to the Vietnam War. Lyndon Johnson's presidency was shortened as the war became increasingly unpopular. On the night of the ship's arrival, Admiral Vasey's official car was surrounded by unfriendly people who used him as a symbol upon which to vent their frustration over the course of the war. The next day, however, the appeal of the *New Jersey* herself was demonstrated when 12,730 people came to see the ship during general visiting. Vasey recalls, "Throngs of visitors stood quietly and almost in reverence to visit Admiral 'Bull' Halsey's Flagship."

A few days later, the battleship was under way once again, steaming farther up the Pacific Coast and arriving on 30 June at Tacoma, Washington, to help that city celebrate its 100th anniversary. More visitors came aboard, although this time their numbers were curtailed. Because the ship was anchored instead of moored to a pier, visitors had to stand in line to catch boat rides to the ship. I particularly recall one evening when I stood beach guard watch during the general visiting. I had a radio link with the *New Jersey* and was expected to maintain a semblance of order over the shore end of the boating expeditions. One young woman in a miniskirt rode out to the ship early in the evening, accompanied by a *New Jersey* crew member whom she had evidently met while he was on liberty. At taps I called out to the ship by radio and was assured that all the tourists had gone ashore. But an hour or so later, a boat heading in toward the landing contained Miss Miniskirt, and this time she was with a sailor other than the one who had taken her to the battleship. She looked considerably rumpled at this point, and I overheard a few snickers from *New Jersey* men about her experiences in the "lower handling room" – a term I now realized could apply to more spaces than just those adjacent to the powder magazines.

As the clock edged toward midnight, I had to preside over the loading of the drunk and tired into boats returning to the ship. There was one pot-bellied first class petty officer who seemed to be resisting suggestions to get him into the liberty boat. From a position overlooking the boat, I told a couple of shore patrolmen to get the obviously intoxicated man aboard and keep him as quiet as possible. He reluctantly acquiesced, but once in the boat, he pointed a finger up at me and admonished, "Hey, you in the Navy suit, if you're lucky you might grow up to be a battleship sailor some day." Things were not all that different from the *New Jersey*'s first midshipman cruise back in 1947, when young Ted Kosmela observed that boat behavior was much more strictly enforced when crew members were going ashore than when they were returning to the ship.

On the morning of 5 July, the *New Jersey* prepared to go to sea once more. As some of the crewmen were coming aboard at the end of their liberty, they brought with them a girl wearing a Navy uniform. Her hair was tucked under a sailor's white hat. She managed to make it and was put into hiding. The girl's cohorts from the crew began taking her food, and she was having sex with them in return for her expected passage to Hawaii. Alas, the secret was too good to keep, and the men with her took to bragging. Machinery Repairman Third Class Bill Sosnowski heard the rumors that were spreading through the mess deck, and the rumors reached topside as well. Since she wasn't discovered until the ship was at sea, she had to be removed by a Coast Guard helicopter.

At about noon on Saturday, 12 July, the great grey dreadnought and her brood of destroyers swept past Diamond Head and through the narrow channel into Pearl Harbor. During the ten days the ship was in Hawaii, many crew members took tours, and many more went to Waikiki Beach. After the sunning session each day, Lieutenant (junior grade) Scott Cheyne and other officers from the *New Jersey* gathered at the Army officers' club at Fort DeRussy to have dinner and a few cold beers before heading back to the ship. Near the end of the time in Hawaii, on Sunday, 21 July, astronaut Neil Armstrong made history by becoming the first man to walk on the moon. Warrant Officer Ed Flamboe went to the officers' club swimming pool that day to sunbathe and listen to moonwalk reports on the loudspeaker. He fell asleep next to the pool, and when he woke up, he had "a sunburn like you wouldn't believe. . . . I had blisters on the top of my feet."

From Pearl Harbor, the training squadron ships got under way once again and steamed to San Diego, arriving on 28 July. The battleship moored at the North Island Naval Air Station in Coronado. Two days later, the *New Jersey* left for Long Beach, and on the morning of 30 July the main battery used the decommissioned fleet minesweeper *Raven* as a target. It took twenty-six rounds of 16-inch fire to spell nevermore for the *Raven*.

On the last day of July, the *New Jersey* arrived once again at her home port, disembarked her midshipmen and admiral, and got ready for one final month of preparations before the scheduled fall deployment to Vietnam. Three weeks later, Captain Robert Peniston reported aboard to begin turnover conferences with Captain Snyder. This was a homecoming for the new commanding officer, because the *New Jersey* was the first ship Peniston had gone aboard as a Naval Academy midshipman in 1943. She was also the first ship in which he served as a commissioned officer, reporting for duty as an ensign in 1946.

On the morning of 21 August, the day after he arrived from duty in the Bureau of Naval Personnel, Captain Peniston was in the office of Commander Jim Elfelt, the executive officer. A telephone call from Washington reported that the Secretary of Defense was just about to announce that dozens of Navy ships were to be decommissioned. The name at the top of the list was the USS *New Jersey*. This was the ultimate political assault on the *New*

*Jersey.* Even while American soldiers and Marines were fighting and dying in South Vietnam, the *New Jersey* would be withdrawn from service. She wouldn't be making that second trip to Vietnam after all. Peniston was stunned, because his dream assignment had fallen apart after one day. The rest of the crew got its shock later in the morning when Captain Snyder passed the word over the general announcing system that the ship was to join the mothball fleet instead of the Seventh Fleet.

Lieutenant Dick Harris observed that it was "a pretty low day for everybody, a very low day. I don't think anybody thought it should happen." Personnelman Third Class Hank Strub considered it a great mistake, but recognized that those in the ship had no control over their own destiny. He said, upon reflection, "I guess the *New Jersey* was a pawn and got involved in that particular chess game, and we lost." One crew member who didn't take the whole thing lying down was Radioman Second Class George

Stavros, who began an intensive campaign of writing letters to congressmen in an effort to get the decision reversed. It was too late.

During the remaining two weeks that the ship had in Long Beach, the crew members were able to bring their families aboard for a one-day cruise reminiscent of the one held a year earlier just before the deployment. On 27 August, Captain Peniston took command, and Captain Snyder made his valedictory speech. During the course of his prepared address, he said, "War is hell, and it is also expensive, and the American people have tired of the expense of defending freedom. And so this year when the winter monsoon comes to Vietnam . . . the American boys who looked to the 'Big J' for their very lives must look elsewhere." As the public mood had soured on the U.S. involvement in Vietnam, so also had Congress soured on continuing to pay for the war. The Department of Defense considered the battleship a target in its efforts to cut costs.

**Below:** The *New Jersey* approaches Puget Sound Naval Shipyard on 8 September 1969 at the end of the last voyage of her Vietnam War period of service. On the fantail are crew members' automobiles which have been ferried up from Long Beach, California. (Courtesy *Bremerton Sun*)

**Right:** Captain Robert Peniston wears a pained expression following arrival at Bremerton on 8 September. At left, equipped with long glass and grey gloves, is the in-port officer of the deck, Lieutenant (junior grade) Chris Reed. (Courtesy Captain Robert Peniston)

As officer of the deck at Long Beach that evening, a few hours after Captain Snyder's departure, my curiosity got to me. I walked from the quarterdeck to one of the old gun tubs that Snyder had used as a swimming pool. It was already painted haze grey inside instead of light blue. Captain Peniston was setting a different tone immediately – one of dignity and formality. Even though he was to be in command only long enough for the *New Jersey* to be inactivated and decommissioned, he was going to be a traditional battleship captain.

The *New Jersey* had been scheduled to depart for Vietnam on Friday, 5 September, one year to the day after she started her war cruise in 1968. Instead, on 2 September 1969, she moved out to an anchorage off Seal Beach, California, to spend three days offloading the tons of ammunition she carried. Soon, she would be off for the Puget Sound Naval Shipyard at Bremerton, Washington. On the morning of Saturday, 6 September, there was a subdued pierside ceremony in Long Beach. Captain Peniston sat on the speakers' platform ashore, dabbing a handkerchief to his eyes, for the hurt touched him deeply. Then he returned to the ship and climbed to the 08 level bridge for what seemed then the last time a battleship would get under way on her own power. At 9:00 a.m., to the strains of the Navy hymn, "Eternal Father, Strong to Save", the *New Jersey* edged slowly away from the pier. Peniston emphasized smartness and tradition. Years afterward he recalled that the ship's warrant boatswain, ruggedly built Joseph Heeney, came to him to express appreciation for the manner in which the *New Jersey* got under way. Peniston explained that "two bells were sounded, the bugle was sounded for being underway, followed by the long blast for clearing the berth almost simultaneously".

As the *New Jersey* made her way to the harbor break-water and headed for sea, the day was hazy. Coming from

**Right:** Ensign Robert Peniston and his bride Fran pose in front of the *New Jersey*'s turret one in January 1947. (Courtesy Captain Robert Peniston)

**Far right:** The same couple in front of the same turret during the ship's family day cruise off Southern California, 25 August 1969. (Courtesy Captain Robert Peniston)

the other direction was a squadron of minesweepers returning to Long Beach after a deployment to the Western Pacific. On the bridge of the USS *Esteem* was Lieutenant (junior grade) John Lewis. Because of the haze, the four small ships were using radar navigation to find their way into the Long Beach harbor channel. Suddenly Lewis saw the silhouette of a huge ship emerging from the gloom, and he knew she must be the *New Jersey*. He climbed as high in the *Esteem*'s superstructure as he could get. Then, he says, "As we rendered honors she glided past like some great alp moving silently out to sea."

As the steel-grey sea lapped at the battleship's sides during the journey northward, Captain Peniston stuck to the bridge. That's where he considered a battleship's captain should be when she was under way. On Monday, 8 September, the *New Jersey* made her way through the tree-lined waters of Puget Sound. She arrived at Bremerton in the late afternoon and moored. On the other side of the pier were three long since decommissioned cruisers, the *Pittsburgh*, *Quincy*, and *Pasadena*. Their faded grey paint was mottled by the droppings of hundreds of passing seagulls. To every appearance, the cruisers had died but had never been given a decent burial. Lieutenant (junior grade) Chris Reed looked over at the sickly old ships and felt, with a considerable sense of sadness, that he was seeing the future of the *New Jersey*.

Once the ship's officers had had a chance to sort things out with shipyard officials at Bremerton, recalls Jim Elfelt, the executive officer, it became more obvious than ever how precipitous the inactivation order had been. He felt that the ship had been hustled out of sight as quickly as possible in order to minimize the chance that supporters could organize and overturn the decision. Back in the 1950s, the *New Jersey*'s crew had known months ahead of time when she was going to be mothballed. In this instance, however, there had been only two weeks between the order and its execution.

Captain Peniston was in an awkward position. His personal feelings were completely against the decommissioning order. As a naval officer, however, he was compelled to follow orders and keep a lid on the whole thing. The Navy was deliberately downplaying all publicity in an attempt to avoid discussions about what some would obviously see as the folly of reactivating a ship for one deployment and then putting her back into mothballs again. He recalls the position he took: "This was a proud ship, and there was nothing I was going to do that would bring any dishonor on it. I did find that I had to measure my words very carefully because the subject was *very* sensitive."

For the crew at large there was much to be accomplished. Complicating the task were the steady rains of the Pacific Northwest which drummed upon the ship day after day. For a while, food was served on board, and then the crew moved off and occupied barracks ships which

afforded them a far lower standard of living than they had known in the *New Jersey*. Personnelman Hank Strub and others moved into a house trailer just to get away. They had a huge job, because everybody in the ship had to be transferred. That meant paperwork to be typed from early in the morning until late at night. After coping with service records and transfer orders for hours at a time, a stop at Bill's Tavern was obligatory before heading for the trailer.

Warrant Officer Ed Flamboe's electronics technicians had inactivation duties which ranged from the top of the ship to the bottom. Topside, they had to clean and preserve antennas for storage ashore. When they were unable to get crane services as soon as they wanted, they lowered the antennas with block and tackle instead. For cleaning out the heavy black fuel oil which had filled up voids deep inside the ship, they organized a bucket brigade because no hose-and-pump arrangement would

do the job. Flamboe's men worked out a schedule which assigned quotas for how much oil was to be dumped each week. It served as a useful motivator, because they always managed to meet the quota by Thursday and earn themselves long weekends ashore.

Senior Chief Storekeeper Al Scarselletta was one of a number of *New Jersey* men who made a trip to the mothballed *Missouri*, berthed at Bremerton, so they could get an idea what the *New Jersey* would be like at the conclusion of the process. Back on board their own ship, one of the storekeepers' chores was to check air vents. Scarselletta's men found one of the vents that hadn't been cleaned for an especially long time. The evidence was a sailor's hat dyed dark blue. It had evidently been there since World War II, when white hats were turned into blue hats to reduce their visibility topside at night.

Chief Ship's Serviceman Lew Moore found a definite morale problem during the inactivation, and there was no real cure for it. The crew had lost the collective sense of purpose which had sustained them since the days in Philadelphia. As Moore remembers, "Nobody wanted to do anything. . . . To tell a guy to do something – where it would normally take him fifteen minutes to do a job, it took him an hour and fifteen minutes. Everybody was biting each other's head off."

There were some chances to get away on liberty. Personnelman Andy Lavella and some of the other chiefs enjoyed spending weekends with a fellow they met in the chiefs' club at Bremerton. He was retired Chief Machinist's Mate Orville Greenwood, who had served in the old *Pennsylvania*. His home on Bainbridge Island was a haven for visits by the *New Jersey* men, and they reciprocated by inviting him to visit their ship. When Greenwood got down into the *New Jersey*'s engineering spaces, he was, remembers Lavella, "like a kid in a candy store". Gunner's Mate Tom Feigley and others in the third division spent off-duty hours at the home of Gunner's Mate Wesley McGee in Everson, Washington, up near the Canadian border.

Finally, on 17 December, it was time to close out the log and end the third chapter in the *New Jersey*'s life story. The day was cool, rainy, and overcast – much in contrast with the beautiful spring weather in Philadelphia just twenty months earlier. Rare are the times when men serve in a ship from commissioning to decommissioning, but that was the case for a number of the *New Jersey*'s officers and men in the late 1960s. Two who did were Radarman Bob Fulks and Machinery Repairman Bill Sosnowski. As they stood in ranks that day in Bremerton, their peacoats gave them some protection against the cold, but no protection whatever against the chilling sense of sadness and loss they felt.

Andy Lavella, the chief petty officer who had served on board longest, lowered the national ensign at the fantail. Senior Chief Al Scarselletta, as the *New Jersey*'s senior enlisted man, lowered the commissioning pennant and

presented it to Captain Peniston. The captain was especially sad, because this grim day in Bremerton was in such contrast to what he had expected the ship to be doing in December of 1969. As he remembers, "I think all the crew were betting that I would break down, but I didn't." Many in the crowd that day did resort to tears, because this was commonly believed to be the end of the battleship era. In his brief command tenure, Peniston's legacy was to preserve the *New Jersey*'s sense of honor and to oversee the inactivation so that she would be well preserved in a material sense as well. As he neared the end of his formal remarks, he said, "The hour cometh and now is to say farewell. But, before doing so, my last order to you – battleship *New Jersey* – is rest well, yet sleep lightly, and hear the call, if again sounded, to provide 'firepower for freedom'. She will hear the call, and thanks to her magnificent crew, she is ready."

Left: The 16-inch projectiles on deck await transfer to the barge alongside during offloading of ammunition at Seal Beach, California, in early September. (Photo by PH2 John Cary; U.S. Naval Institute Collection)

Right: A saddened Captain Peniston leaves the ship following decommissioning at Bremerton, Washington, on 17 December 1969. (Photo by Tom Brownell, *Seattle Post-Intelligencer*; courtesy Captain Robert Peniston)

# CHAPTER VII
# FROM MOTHBALLS TO LEBANON
## July 1981 – June 1984

Top left: In mothballs at Bremerton, Washington, the *New Jersey* is second from left. Other ships include the *Missouri* at far left, two guided missile-cruisers, and three *Essex*-class aircraft carriers. (Photo by David R. Frazier)

Bottom left: Two Navy tugs at the stern act as propellers and rudders for the *New Jersey* as the commercial tugboat *Shelley Foss* tows her on 27 July 1981. (Photo by PHC Terry C. Mitchell; courtesy Norman Polmar)

With each passing year of the 1970s, the World War II-built ships in the mothball fleet at Bremerton, Washington, became older and older – or else they ceased to age further. The end of the line came for a number of them which were sent to be scrapped. Two battleships remained, however, their dehumidification machines humming steadily. In June 1979, the *New Jersey* was moved from amid the other decommissioned vessels to a spot on public display: right across a pier from her sister *Missouri*.

As the decade drew to a close, the *New Jersey*'s grey paint had faded, but it was apparent that she had not faded from the consciousness of those concerned with U.S. interests in an unfriendly world. The autumn of 1979 was not a happy one. Iranian militants seized the U.S. embassy in Tehran, and the Soviets invaded nearby Afghanistan. It was a time when the United States was perceived in some parts of the world as weak and unable to exert its accustomed influence. The atmosphere was made to order for a man named Charles E. Myers, Jr., a former Pentagon official who had become a part-time defense consultant and part-time unofficial lobbyist. Myers made the case for battleship reactivation in the November 1979 issue of the magazine *U.S. Naval Institute Proceedings*. To describe the intended role of the *New Jersey* and her sisters, he used the term "interdiction/assault ships", because it was less fraught with controversy and emotion than the word "battleship". Myers was tireless; he put together a detailed paper and talked, whenever he could, to congressmen, congressional staffers, uniformed military officers, and civilian officials in the Department of Defense. The Chief of Naval Operations, Admiral Thomas B. Hayward, actively supported the idea.

The administration of President Jimmy Carter exerted considerable pressure in 1980 to defeat the reactivation measure in Congress and finally succeeded. The victory was only a temporary one, though, coming as it did at a time when Carter himself was solidly trounced by Ronald Reagan in that year's presidential election. The new President brought with him a Secretary of the Navy, John Lehman, who had a vision of a much-enlarged U.S. fleet. Recommissioned *Iowa*-class battleships would serve two purposes. They would symbolize the nation's intent to rearm itself in the wake of the setbacks of the late seventies, and the ships would have a substantive role as well with their 16-inch guns and new missile batteries. What's more, they would be relative bargains. The cost of bringing the *New Jersey* back from mothballs and modernizing her would be roughly comparable to that of a new guided missile frigate, a ship with only a fraction of the battleship's combat capability.

When battleship proponents got support rather than active opposition from the civilian officials in the Defense Department, congressional approval was relatively easy. Without such support the margin of defeat in 1980 had been close. Part of the reason for the success in 1981 was that Secretary Lehman made the battleship program almost a personal crusade, pledging that the modernization would be accomplished on time and within budget.

President Reagan's signature was still fresh on the defense legislation that summer when things began stirring in Bremerton. Plans were made to tow the *New Jersey* from there to the Long Beach Naval Shipyard, which would perform the reactivation. The date chosen to begin the tow was 27 July, in the middle of the highest tide period of the season. At 5:30 that morning, after the last mooring lines had been cast off, the commercial tug *Shelley Foss* pushed the *New Jersey* away from the pier. Two fleet tugs were placed at the stern so their screws and rudders could substitute for the battleship's. The USS *Moctobi* was made up on the *New Jersey*'s starboard quarter, and the USS *Takelma* was in a similar position to port. Both tugs were listed outboard three degrees to tilt their superstructures away from the battleship and minimize the likelihood of damage. The *Shelley Foss* then sent up a tow wire through the port hawsepipe, which had been cleared by putting one of the *New Jersey*'s huge anchors in a newly created notch in the spray shield on her forecastle. The push-pull tow progressed, although the *Moctobi* had to be replaced by the USS *Quapaw* because of engine difficulties.

Once the group of vessels was clear of restricted waters, the *Shelley Foss* was released, and the *Quapaw* and *Takelma* took up positions ahead of the battleship and began pulling. Late in the morning of 28 July, the *New Jersey* passed through the Strait of Juan de Fuca for the first time since September 1969, and she was southward-bound in the Pacific. Aided by the Humboldt Current, the cluster of vessels proceeded southward at speeds averaging just over seven knots. Outside the Long Beach breakwater, six harbor tugs met the *New Jersey* on 6 August and took over the job. They guided her in alongside the giant Pier Echo, which had been her home during the Vietnam War.

Chief Personnelman Andy Lavella had lowered the American flag when the *New Jersey* was decommissioned in December 1969. By the summer of 1981, he had retired from active duty and was working in northern Virginia. Such was his enthusiasm for his former ship that he traveled across the country to welcome the *New Jersey*. She was soon to begin the reawakening process that would transform a nearly forty-year-old inert hull into one of the most modern warships in the fleet.

The program laid down for her return to service was indeed an ambitious one. Within a year and a half, she was to be reactivated and undergo major surgery which would include the removal of four of her ten 5-inch gun mounts and the installation of launchers for thirty-two Tomahawk missiles and sixteen Harpoon missiles. This would not be an "austere" reactivation of the type which had cost $23 million back in 1967–68. This time the price tag would be $326 million. A rundown of the major items in the modernization program is included in Appendix 4.

Chosen to command the *New Jersey* was Captain William M. Fogarty. He had previously served as chief engineer of the antisubmarine carrier *Wasp* and then put the destroyer-escort *Jesse L. Brown* into commission as first skipper in 1973. The shipyard experience thus acquired would prove invaluable in coping with the tightly scheduled milestones that lay ahead for the *New Jersey*. In addition, Fogarty had demonstrated that he was an articulate spokesman for the Navy. The latter ability would be especially needed because of the unusual nature of the job for this prospective commanding officer. Not only would he have to fulfill Secretary Lehman's promises that the *New Jersey* would come in on time and on budget, Fogarty would have to try to convince thousands of people that reactivation of the other three *Iowa*-class ships would also be worthwhile. Fogarty performed this public role superbly in the months ahead, making dozens of appearances and being interviewed by members of the media.

The decision to bring back the battleship struck a resounding chord in many Americans. Thousands visited the *New Jersey* in Long Beach soon after her arrival, and other thousands volunteered to serve in the crew. Many Naval Reservists wanted to be recalled to active duty. Men

**Below:** On her way south for reactivation, the *New Jersey* is shown being towed by the fleet tugs *Takelma* and *Quapaw* on 2 August 1981. (Photo by PH1 Corinne Kelly; courtesy Arthur D. Baker III)

**Right:** The *New Jersey* in dry dock at Long Beach, 19 November 1981. The anchor is temporarily mounted on the bow because of the use of the hawsepipes for tow wires during the trip from Bremerton. (Courtesy Long Beach Naval Shipyard)

Left: Amidst a web of dry dock scaffolding, a shipyard worker washes off one of the *New Jersey*'s four propellers. (USN photo by Cheryl May Campbell; courtesy Norman Polmar)

Right: The *New Jersey* in dry dock on 5 February 1982. The hole in the forefoot, at the bottom center of the photo, was used years before with paravane chains. (Photo by PHAN J. Steinessen; courtesy Norman Polmar)

were willing to come out of retirement, and many who were still in the Navy yearned for a taste of battleship life. When it came to selecting the crew, Captain Fogarty was pleased with the names submitted by the Naval Military Personnel Command (formerly the Bureau of Naval Personnnel) to fill key officer and enlisted billets on board the *New Jersey*.

Some of the crew members were selected from among the thousands of volunteers, but for the most part they came through standard channels, in part because crew members were needed sooner than the volunteers could be screened and in part because a substantial portion of the *New Jersey*'s crew at any time is made up of nonrated men fresh from boot camp or Navy schools. Some reservists and retired personnel were recalled for service in the battleship because their experience with 16-inch guns and fire control equipment was sorely needed. A high percentage of the volunteers had to be disappointed. Boatswain's Mate Second Class Charles Jacobus of Moonachie, New Jersey, for instance, made the first cruise to Korea on board the *New Jersey* in 1951. He was still a drilling reservist thirty years later and volunteered to go back once again, but it was not to be.

Some of Captain Fogarty's discussions on personnel had to do with the size of the Marine detachment, which was settled at two officers and forty-two enlisted men, sufficient to man one 5-inch gun mount and to have some left over for other duties. The Navy men in the ship's crew were to discover that the Marine Corps had sent some of its finest. The battleship was a prestige assignment, and the reputation of the Corps would be judged by the actions of these few good men. As it turned out, there was a harmonious relationship between sailors and Marines. The latter were accepted as exactly what they were – members of the crew – and not treated as outsiders. Even so, there was a Marine Corps pride that could not be quelled. Once the ship went into commission, the eagle, globe, and anchor insignia was painted on the outside of the Marines' 5-inch gun mount all the way aft on the starboard side.

The *New Jersey*'s crew as a whole was to comprise about fifty fewer men than it had for Vietnam, when there were seventy officers and 1,556 enlisted men. This time, in addition to the forty-four Marines, there were to be seventy officers and 1,460 enlisted men. Some of the first crew members began showing up in the late summer and early autumn of 1981, not long after the ship herself arrived. They were struck by the immaculate condition in which she had been left by the decommissioning crew. One man in both groups was Senior Chief Gunner's Mate Don Davis, who served in the *New Jersey* in 1956 and again in 1968–69. After having retired in 1975, he was recalled to duty because his turret experience was a rare commodity. After Davis arrived in September and had had a chance to look around, he told a reporter for *All Hands* magazine, "Nothing has changed. The first thing I did when I went aboard this time was go back to the chiefs' quarters. My name was still on the old locker. . . . On the bulkhead in the second gun turret, there's a brass plate with the names of the last turret crew to serve aboard. My name's on top as turret captain."

Lieutenant Commander Chris Johnson came in October 1981 as the prospective navigator. There was not much navigating to be done in a ship which would shortly go into dry dock, so he spent his time initially going through the vessel to become familiar with her many, many compartments. He saw how solidly she was built, and he poked through the files which had been left behind by his predecessors. All that he learned reinforced the sense he felt that this vessel represented a tangible link with the Navy's past. He explains, "It's always very special to bring a ship back to life. I've been on a commissioning crew of a new ship, and it's not the same. The ship doesn't seem to have a spirit yet, and yet you walk aboard *New Jersey*, and if you have any sense of history, you feel Bull Halsey here. And you feel the sense of that message: 'Where is Task Force 34?'"

Another of the early arrivals was Storekeeper Second Class Richard Wolpin. His first task was to commute some 20 miles north each day to a government warehouse near the town of Florence. He and the storekeepers working with him matched up the shipboard allowance lists with stocks of parts coming in from the Naval Supply Center in Oakland, California. Some of the parts were needed for the reactivation itself, while others would equip the battleship's many storerooms. The quantities of various items allocated were based on usage rates compiled during the ship's active service in the late 1960s. In other cases, the allowance lists were educated guesses, based on the experiences of other ships, because some equipment and weapons, such as the Phalanx close-in weapon system, weren't around in 1969. The storekeepers also had to see that supplies of consumables were laid in, both for the shipyard period and beyond. Two items sure to be called for often were toilet paper and paint.

Gunner's Mate First Class Carl Farmer encountered a number of supply problems, which was certainly not unexpected in putting such an old ship back together. It wasn't always easy to convert a part number to the federal stock number needed to order it. And even when ordered, some items were no longer available because there hadn't been any demand for them in a long time. Thus it might be necessary for the shipyard to manufacture items such as gaskets that were needed in a turret, and then a contract could be let to get new gaskets flowing into the supply system. In addition, it was a time-consuming process to go through all the systems in a turret and untie the knots which had developed with age. Hydraulic lines were a perpetual problem. Because of the special attention paid to finishing the reactivation on time, the schedule was a demanding one for the shipyard workers and the future crew members working with them. Farmer remembers that after mustering at quarters in the morning, the Navy men sometimes had to work until 8:00 or 9:00 at night before being able to knock off.

Fortunately, many of them didn't have far to go when the day's work came to an end. Moored near the ship were the living quarters. There were three berthing barges – two YRBMs and one APL – and one messing barge. Captain Fogarty and his prospective executive officer, Commander Richard McKenna, moved early to make the routine on board the barges parallel as closely as possible that which the crew would experience once they moved aboard the battleship. There were watches to be stood, quarters for muster, compartment cleaners, and even a closed-circuit television system that was later transferred to the *New Jersey* herself.

For the most part, the men who would form the crew of the *New Jersey* were involved more with training for their jobs than with the modernization and reactivation work. Schools were set up at the naval weapons station at Seal Beach, California, for the men who would be in gunnery and fire control. Experienced crew members such as Senior Chief Fire Controlman Rick Crawford and Chief Gunner's Mate Larry Pousson constituted what Captain Fogarty called the "truth squad". If the school's instructors failed to mention something, or if what the instructors said wasn't quite the way things had been in the *New Jersey* during the Vietnam War period the veteran battleship men gave their future shipmates the correct information. In part, that was necessitated by the age of the equipment. In an era of digital computers and microchips, Crawford had to teach such things as vacuum tubes and mechanical computers that weren't covered in the normal Navy training programs.

For the men who would be working with the 16-inch guns, remembers Pousson, the turret crews were sent one at a time for four weeks of classroom training at Seal Beach, where there were no equipment mockups. "When we got back to the ship," he explains, "we started a training program to make sure what we learned in school was applied to the equipment and everybody got qualified." The reactivation schedule for one of the turrets had been speeded up so that it could serve as a hands-on training device for the crews of all three turrets. Men destined for the 5-inch/38 gun mounts were sent north to Seattle to practice on board an aging Naval Reserve Force destroyer equipped with such mounts.

In March 1982, the battleship came out of dry dock and was moored to a pier in the shipyard as work continued. The living barges were across the pier for the sake of convenience. Nearby was a sign which proclaimed that the area was "Battleship Country". As new men came into this country, they were introduced to Senior Chief Fire Controlman Al Gambetta and the I division. The division's purpose was to indoctrinate those just reporting for duty, and it would remain in operation after commissioning as well. Gambetta had developed a strong affection for the *New Jersey* when he served in her main battery plotting room during the Vietnam War. Now he was back again as the command master chief, the principal "sea daddy" for the enlisted men in the crew. When new people reported aboard, Gambetta and those working for him told the men about the ship and her policies and helped them solve their problems. New men also met their division officers, department heads, the exec, and the skipper. One thing that Captain Fogarty and Chief Gambetta made a particular point of was Admiral Hayward's "Pride and Professionalism" program. This meant wearing smart, squared-away uniforms, obeying the rules, and – above all – avoiding the use of drugs. When the men had been thus warned, Fogarty was stern and almost invariably unforgiving at captain's mast on the subject of drugs. Of the drug users delivered before him, he estimates that he threw more than 95 per cent of them out of the Navy.

As the year 1982 progressed, Captain Fogarty was a man pulled in many directions. He was making frequent speeches on behalf of the battleship in southern California and elsewhere in the country. He visited the state of New Jersey to meet Governor Thomas Kean and others. He went to Washington for a "charm school" gathering of commodore selectees, for he had already been chosen for promotion. He even attended a reunion in Dallas, Texas, of former crew members of the battleship *Tennessee*. When he was back in Long Beach, Fogarty had frequent conferences with shipyard officials. He recalls that the shipyard commander made a wise move in putting a widely respected supervisor in charge of the battleship project, because it ensured cooperation on the part of the union organization.

On 9 July, a "mast stepping" ceremony was held to mark the installation of the battleship's new tripod foremast. On 6 August, the men who were to be battleship sailors began moving aboard from the barges. The furnishing of the living compartments was substantially changed from the Vietnam period. For one thing, all the old racks and lockers had been moved out and replaced. Instead of the four-tier pipe frame bunks, there was now a new type known to Navymen as "coffin racks" because they were of much more substantial construction and had an arrangement whereby the mattress and frame lifted up like a lid to permit access to a horizontal locker underneath. The old square-front silver-colored lockers were gone, and in their place were standup vertical lockers less than a foot wide. The new racks were only three high, but they were still confining. Storekeeper Second Class Richard Wolpin had to squeeze to get his 73-inch frame into a 72-inch rack. One advantage that the new arrangement offered was greater privacy. Each bunk had its own reading light and a curtain which could be drawn.

The mess deck and galley area were renovated as well. In addition to the new equipment installed, a new philosophy went in as well – catering to a greater extent than before to individual tastes. The program, which was based on tests previously conducted in other Navy ships, was

run by Master Chief Mess Management Specialist Donald Smith, and it was a hit with *New Jersey* men. Given an allocation of $3.40 per man per day for food, Smith and his crew turned out meal after meal that had men saying the chow in the *New Jersey* was the best of their naval service. Part of the key to such success was variety. On the starboard side was a standard mess line with full-course meals. The port serving line was modeled on the fast-food establishments which had become a national phenomenon in the life span of the junior crew members. A new generation of Navymen had grown up on such fare and went for it eagerly. Among the selections available on the port side were hamburgers, cheeseburgers, hotdogs, sloppy joes, poor boy sandwiches, and french fries. The McDonald's chain was the obvious source for some of the menu items. The "Jersey burger" was patterned after the Big Mac and featured "secret Jersey sauce". For breakfast there were Jersey McMuffins. For the *New Jersey* man who wasn't tempted by either the fast food or the slow food, there was a salad bar. There were also special dinners, such as steak night, seafood night, and soul night. For the benefit of dieters in the crew, the calorie count of each item was listed on the serving line.

During the course of the time pierside, the *New Jersey*'s engineering plant was gradually brought back to life. On 6 May, for instance, boiler number seven was given a ceremonial lighting off by Captain Joseph Gildea, the shipyard commander. After that, the various other boilers were tested, as were the main engines, generators, reduction gears, pumps, and so forth. The underway watch organization was set up, and finally all seemed in readiness for the first sea trials, beginning on Saturday, 25 September. Not quite all, it turned out. With Captain Fogarty on the 08 level conning station and prepared to begin the ship's movement away from the pier, he learned that the ship's whistle wasn't working. He refused to go to sea until he had a whistle, and so departure was delayed until it was fixed.

For Lieutenant Commander Chris Johnson, under way for the first time as a ship's navigator, there was also an equipment malfunction to deal with. As the battleship headed away from the pier at the shipyard and out toward the harbor breakwater, Johnson's quartermasters were taking visual bearings with the gyrocompass peloruses on the bridge wings and calling them in to the chief quartermaster who was plotting the lines of bearing on a chart. All was going well, remembers Johnson, until "my port pelorus died." When the chief announced that the visual bearings were no longer producing position fixes, all eyes on the 08 level turned to Johnson. The shipyard's gyro man went below, and fifteen minutes later the gyro was working again. By that time, the ship was out of the harbor and headed to sea. The harbor pilot was experienced enough to handle the situation without incident, but it was another demonstration that sea trials could indeed be trying.

Right: The Vulcan/Phalanx close-in weapon system is test-fired on 20 October 1982, during the ship's sea trials. The white radome at top houses radar antennas. (Photo by PHC Terry Mitchell)

Below: The battleship is decked out in red, white, and blue for her recommissioning at Long Beach on 28 December 1982. (Photo by PH1 H. J. Gerwien)

Opposite page, top: As part of the recommissioning ceremony, Captain William Fogarty presents President Ronald Reagan a piece of teak deck planking which was replaced during reactivation. (Courtesy USS *New Jersey*)

Opposite page, bottom: Captain Michael Hicks, commanding officer of the Marine detachment, with his men on recommissioning day. (Photo by Ed Coffer)

The trials lasted several days, taking the battleship toward San Clemente Island near San Diego. A fairly high sea was running, and so a guided missile frigate was along to serve as lifeguard for the *New Jersey*, which did not yet have her boats on board. The battleship got nearly to full power, and the frigate, trying doggedly to keep up the pace, took green water over her bow, white water over her bridge, and lost her helo nets to the sea. Meanwhile, the *New Jersey* plowed steadily onward, throwing off waves with scarcely an effort. Men who had never been to sea in a battleship before came to the bridge and were awed by what they saw. Lieutenant Commander Johnson thought to himself, "I can see why Halsey could go into a typhoon [in December 1944] and not know it."

Once the first trials were ended, the battleship returned to the shipyard to fix some of the things which had gone wrong, then prepared for the second trials, beginning on 18 October. Two days later came an event long anticipated, the first firing of the 16-inch and 5-inch guns and the Vulcan/Phalanx system. Secretary of the Navy John Lehman, the ship's principal cheerleader, was on board, wearing a jacket which proclaimed, "The Battleship Is Back."

When the first 16-inch round went out, members of the crew who were topside began screaming and cheering for what was obviously a substantial mark of progress in the ship's return to service. Storekeeper Second Class Richard Wolpin was on the 05 level, not far from turret two. He was wearing protective "Mickey Mouse ears" headgear but still wasn't prepared for the concussion. He had a camera along to take pictures of the firings and found that there was nothing to it. He just held his finger on the shutter release button, and the explosive force of the guns going off made picture-taking essentially an involuntary reflex action.

In mid-November, the *New Jersey* went out and passed her third and final set of tests, the InSurv (Inspection and Survey) trials. The next major event was her fourth commissioning. Originally scheduled for 15 January 1983, the date was moved forward to 28 December 1982 in order to accommodate President Reagan's desire to participate during a year-end vacation trip to his California ranch. The schedule, which had been tight to begin with, became even tighter. Invitations were sent, the crew rehearsed, and security precautions gone over in great detail.

Bob Fulks, who had been a radarman in the *New Jersey*'s crew in 1968 and 1969, flew from Florida to California for the ceremony, then found that he couldn't get into the shipyard for a preview look on 27 December because the Secret Service had already buttoned up the place. On the day itself, Fulks and his wife showed up early and were glad they did because of the need to go through a security check which included passing through a metal detector and having agents conduct a thorough search through Mrs. Fulks's jammed purse. They made their way to

bleachers set up on Pier Echo, facing the starboard side of the ship.

After Reagan arrived by helicopter and inspected the *New Jersey*'s Marine detachment, he went aboard and spoke of the ship's role in his administration's rearmament program. In describing the *New Jersey*, Reagan said, "She's gray, she's had her face lifted, but she's still in the prime of life – the gallant lady *New Jersey*." At the conclusion of his fifteen-minute speech, the President, acting as Commander in Chief of the Armed Forces, said, "I hereby place the United States Ship *New Jersey* in commission. God bless and Godspeed." With that, the national anthem was played, and Senior Chief Don Davis, in his third tour of duty on board the ship, raised the American flag.

When Commander Richard McKenna, the executive officer, ordered the first watch set, Lieutenant Commander Johnson, as navigator, had the honor of being the first officer of the deck. Captain Fogarty instructed Johnson beforehand to count the individual rounds of the twenty-one-gun salute honoring President Reagan and to bring his salute down smartly after the twenty-first gun so Fogarty would know it was completed. Johnson never got that far. When the first gun was fired, he raised his right hand to the visor of his cap, and a gold button popped off the jacket of his blue uniform and rolled across the deck. He was so distracted that he lost track of the guns and didn't know when to lower his salute. Johnson wondered afterward what Captain Fogarty thought of a navigator who couldn't count to twenty-one.

During the early stages of the ceremony, the crew members were in ranks on the pier. Finally, they were called to man the ship. They hurried aboard and took up positions manning the rail on the main deck and up into the superstructure. The last man to go aboard, Gunner's Mate First Class Carl Farmer, was one of the shortest in the crew, because the ranks had been lined up by height. Along with the men running to their positions, a colorful array of signal flags was hoisted from bow to stern; the ship's deep-throated foghorn sounded; gun barrels and Tomahawk launchers rose to attention; the 5-inch mounts rotated; and the Vulcan/Phalanx mounts began spinning and bobbing. It was a spectacular show for the guests.

Once the formal ceremonies were over, Captain Fogarty conducted a tour of the ship for the President and found Reagan to be genuinely enthusiastic, taking an almost boyish pleasure in visiting the bridge, a turret, and other spaces. At the end of the tour, Fogarty and Reagan ended up in the captain's cabin. While dignitaries such as the Secretary of the Navy, Chief of Naval Operations, and the Commandant of the Marine Corps stood around waiting, Reagan exchanged pleasantries with Fogarty's mother. She recalled to him how she had listened to him when he was a radio announcer in Des Moines, Iowa, years earlier. He asked her if she remembered a certain speakeasy from that time, and indeed she did.

Above: The *New Jersey* fires her first Harpoon antiship missile on 23 March 1983 off Point Mugu, California. (Courtesy McDonnell Douglas)

Above center: The 82-foot Coast Guard patrol boat *Point Heyer* escorts the 887-foot *New Jersey* into San Francisco on 22 April 1983. (Photo by Paul J. Gardner, USCG; courtesy Robert Scheina)

Opposite page, top right: Senior Chief Gunner's Mate Don Davis, a member of the *New Jersey's* crew in the 1950s, 1960s, and 1980s, looks through a periscope inside turret one. (USN photo by Paul Soutar; courtesy *All Hands* magazine)

Opposite page, bottom: Block and tackle are used to pull a bore-cleaning brush through the barrel of a 16-inch gun. The circular port through which the picture was taken separates the individual gun room from the turret booth. (USN photo by Paul Soutar; courtesy *All Hands* magazine)

Once Reagan left, the huge crowd ashore was able to clamber aboard for refreshments. Putting some 10,000 people on board the ship soon made for a free-for-all. Despite the crowd, Gunner's Mate Farmer was delighted that his wife had been able to come out from Indiana to see that day's impressive ceremony. Until then, the battleship had been largely an abstraction to her, but here were her husband, the Navy's only battleship, and the President all together. Says Farmer, "That day of the ceremony helped make up for all the hard work."

The next major milestone was the structural firing of the 16-inch guns to see how newly installed equipment would stand up. The ship got under way on 7 March 1983 and was in the southern California operating area much of the month. When the big guns were trained around close to the superstructure and fired, Captain Fogarty was pleasantly surprised that there was no effect on new systems such as the Vulcan/Phalanx and the antennas for the SLQ-32 electronic warfare system that he had been concerned about. On the other hand, more mundane things were suffering. Chris Johnson says of the tests, "We told the captain we were destroying the bridge, and we were. I mean, speakers were blown apart. Things were just leaping off the bulkheads. And most of all, it was like you were getting punched." Lieutenant Commander Johnson was serving as officer of the deck, and he found that the junior officer who was conning the ship was affected to such a degree that his mental processes had a bit of difficulty making a connection. Johnson told him to bring the *New Jersey* around to head north, and the officer temporarily forgot the compass course, 000°, to go in that direction.

During the weapons tests in March, the *New Jersey* fired her 16-inch and 5-inch guns at a target sled. The Phalanx system was also put through its paces, splashing two drones. On 23 March, she became the first battleship to fire a Harpoon missile. It erupted from a canister launcher aft on the superstructure amid a blast of fire and smoke. Much of the crew had to be below decks for the missile firing, so Quartermaster John Trail was thrilled to have the opportunity to be topside and see what was going on. He was struck by the way the stubby wings unfolded after the missile left the canister and began the trajectory that would take it more than 40 miles to score a direct hit on an old LCU landing craft used as a target.

After spending the latter part of March in port at Long Beach, the *New Jersey's* crew got under way on 1 April for a two-week period of refresher training which included practice for the bridge and deck crews in going alongside other ships for underway replenishment. Captain Fogarty faced a situation which hadn't been encountered by previous conning officers of the *New Jersey*. The ship had matched up well with the low-freeboard, relatively short fleet oilers of yesteryear. On the other hand, when going alongside a new, long, high-sided replenishment oiler such as the USS *Wichita*, different hydrodynamic forces took effect. Rather than smoothly gliding along on parallel courses, there was sometimes a push-pull effect because of the way the underwater hull contours of the two large ships matched up. He found that there was a tendency for a venturi effect to build between ships and thus the need for special vigilance on the part of conning officers. He found as well that the position of the replenishment ship's hose rigs at a higher level than the *New Jersey's* imposed a greater likelihood of strain than with the older oilers.

Upon completion of the refresher training and a short stay in Long Beach, the battleship proceeded north to San

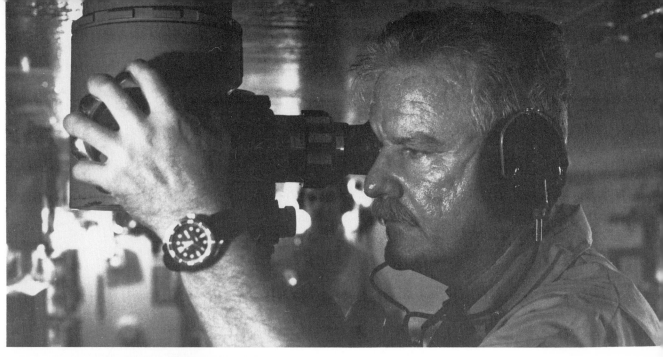

Francisco for a weekend visit which began on 22 April. Many of the crew members headed off to enjoy the club atmosphere in north San Francisco. Included among the many visitors to the ship were Mayor Dianne Feinstein and members of the local news media.

On the way out of San Francisco harbor, Lieutenant Commander Johnson had his gyrocompasses working this time, but he still felt uncomfortable with the quality of the visual fixes he and his quartermaster team were coming up with. So he asked the captain to slow down, and the ship proceeded out very carefully. It was then, says Johnson, that he came to the realization that his position plotting wasn't always going to work out so neatly as it did in textbooks, so he and his men would have to rely on radar, fathometer, navigator's eye, and other tricks of the trade. Still new as a navigator, he was finding out what many others had before him – that navigation is an art as well as a science. And he felt that Fogarty's caution was prudent and justified. The *New Jersey* and her captain were the focus of a great deal of attention by the public, the news media, and an often skeptical Congress. Anything untoward could set back the battleship program as a whole. Critics would be eager to seize on mishaps.

After San Francisco, the *New Jersey* returned to her home port for a few more days and then set out for San Clemente and her first shore bombardment requalification since the spring of 1969. It was time for the fire control organization to demonstrate its capability and to put into practice all those things which Senior Chief Crawford had been so patiently explaining to a new generation of fire controlmen. It was a test not only of the equipment but of following the procedures for . putting projectiles on specified targets and making the necessary corrections when supplied by spotters. The shore bombardment qualification also supplied further training and practice for the crews of the turrets. For Chief Gunner's Mate Larry Pousson, one of the workers in 1969, there was both the pleasure and the responsibility of being the top enlisted man in turret three.

Following the successful gunfire qualifications, the *New Jersey* joined up with other Third Fleet ships for ReadiEx 1-83, a mini-war game off the West Coast. Surveillance forces flew over trying to spot the *New Jersey* and her escorting destroyers for simulated launch of weapons. From time to time, ships such as the guided missile destroyer *Callaghan* and the guided missile frigate *John A. Moore* came alongside to starboard to take a drink from the battleship's newly installed refueling rig. The *Callaghan*, new to the fleet after having been intended originally for service in the Iranian Navy, was nearly forty years younger than the battleship, but both were front-line combatant ships of the U.S. fleet. Another reminder of the *New Jersey*'s longevity came in the form of a visit by helicopter from Commander Third Fleet, Vice Admiral William P. Lawrence. In speaking to the battleship's officers in the wardroom, he told them that this was the first time a Third Fleet commander had been on board the *New Jersey* since Admiral William F. Halsey left in early 1945.

Shortly after Lawrence's departure, the *New Jersey* set out to do something which was beyond the realm of possibility in Halsey's day. One of the arguments which

helped sell Congress on the reactivation of the battleship was the idea that she would be equipped with long-range missiles. Although the *New Jersey* was designed in the late 1930s to have an offensive role in ship-to-ship combat, she played that part only incidentally. For the most part, her years of active service were consumed in providing anti-aircraft protection for carriers, gunfire support for ground troops, and showing the flag. While all these roles were important, none had the glamour of wielding the big stick, going on offense. Long-range Tomahawk missiles enabled her to do that. The spring of 1983 was a time for testing.

On board for the test were a host of civilian technicians and Navy experts. The test was delayed several times in order to provide the *New Jersey* and the Tomahawk with the best chance. Even then, the conditions on Tuesday, 10 May, were not ideal; the day was sunny but windy. Crew members gathered with their cameras on the fantail to observe and photograph the test. In the early afternoon, the ship ran along parallel to San Nicholas Island, then turned to starboard to head out to sea. On the fantail, the crew had to scurry to and fro at times because the wind-whipped sea was producing waves so high that they leaped over the side of the ship and tossed showers of spray onto the deck. Up in the combat engagement center on the 02 deck in the superstructure, Lieutenant Commander Gene Bernard, the ship's missile systems officer, was watching consoles linked to the Tomahawk system and discussing the situation with visiting technicians. In

the amidships area of the superstructure, where a missile deck had been inserted after the removal of four 5-inch gun mounts between the stacks, one of the armored box launchers on the starboard side was elevated to firing position. The installation was designed so that the missile would go across the ship, and most of its fiery exhaust would be absorbed by a heavy metal blast shield.

At last, the waiting period was over. On the fantail, the author and hundreds of others watched as flame and smoke accompanied the exit of the missile body from the launcher. Then it hung in the air for just an instant. Was something wrong? No, the pause was the time for the Tomahawk's booster engine to kick on, and then the missile was on its way. It soared off into the bright blue sky, leaving a trail of smoke and picking up a convoy of escort planes to go inland with it. On the fantail, there was excited cheering. The missile grew ever smaller in the distance as it sped off to its target, some 500 miles away in Tonopah, Nevada. Eventually, the word came back to the ship. The Tomahawk test vehicle, which was not armed with a warhead, had scored a direct hit on its target. The New Jersey thus became the first surface warship to conduct a successful firing of the land-attack Tomahawk. (The Tomahawk also has an antiship version.)

After returning to port two days later, the New Jersey was in Long Beach for much of the next four weeks to prepare for her first deployment since commissioning. Again, the scheduling was brought about for political reasons – to demonstrate how quickly the ship could be ready for overseas duty. Her departure from Long Beach on 9 June was a time of triumph and expectation. True, the married members of the New Jersey's crew would be away from their families for three and a half months, but the overseas schedule – ten ports in seven countries – would provide plenty of interesting things to see and do. The idea of being feted in one port after another carried with it a sense of adventure; the enjoyment ahead would be a payback for the months of hard work and preparation that had brought the New Jersey to this point. At least that's the way it seemed at the time.

When the New Jersey arrived at Pearl Harbor on 17 June, the moment which made the deepest impression on the crew came while steaming past the Arizona memorial. A bugler played taps, and New Jersey men cast a wreath on the water near the memorial in honor of the battleship sailors entombed below. Lieutenant Commander Chris Johnson was especially moved, because he had a long association with the scene. Having spent part of his childhood in Hawaii as the son of a naval officer, he had observed the old Arizona seeping oil and remembered her from a time even before the striking white memorial was built over her hull. He felt that there was a kinship between battleship sailors of different generations. In his own case, that was literally true. His father, then an ensign, had been at Pearl Harbor as a member of the staff of Admiral

Husband Kimmel on the December morning in 1941 when the *Arizona* was sunk.

Liberty in Hawaii was as appealing as it had been for members of previous *New Jersey* crews, and the tie with the *Arizona* enhanced the experience. Quartermaster John Trail and two of his buddies from the navigation gang donned summer white uniforms with blue *New Jersey* patches on their right shoulders and headed for a tour of the *Arizona* memorial. While the three sat in the front row during a lecture, the guide said, "We have an extra-special treat here. We have three live battleship sailors from the *New Jersey*." With that, applause erupted from the entire crowd. On the boat run between the memorial and the landing ashore, the three men did little else besides pose for pictures. Tourists clamored to put their arms around the men and have photos taken with them. This indeed was an early payback, and it did much to reinforce the special feeling of serving in the ship. As it turned out, the day had an even happier ending. The *New Jersey* trio was picked up by a group of three women who evidently sensed the special allure of battleship men.

Later in the three-day stay, Trail and his friends went to Waikiki Beach for swimming and sunbathing. They saw a profusion of blue baseball caps with the *New Jersey*'s name and hull number stitched on in yellow. So sought after were the caps that people were offering $15 and $20 apiece for them. Trail and his friends discovered that the caps had barter value as well, using them on one occasion to get dates. Trail also found that his uniform was a means of getting free rides back to the naval base, because Honolulu people with cars were delighted to offer transportation in return for a guided tour of the ship. Trail had a never-ending supply of enthusiasm for the *New Jersey*, so for him, giving a guided tour wasn't just a price to be paid for a ride; it was something he enjoyed doing.

The *New Jersey* and her escort, the USS *Callaghan*, got under way on 20 June and headed westward toward the Philippines. Upon arrival in Manila on 3 July, the *New Jersey* had to anchor a mile and a half out in the roadstead because of the shallowness of water closer in. The U.S. Independence Day on 4 July was also Philippine-American Friendship Day, so Quartermaster Trail was somewhat surprised by what he learned when he pursued his interest in history during his time ashore. He went to an old fort and saw a display telling of the guerrilla war fought at the beginning of the century between U.S. forces and a Filipino insurrectionist named Emilio Aguinaldo. Besides the sightseeing, there were other pleasures to be had, including shopping for relatives back home, dancing with Filipino girls in bars, and a nighttime activity he describes as "hell-raising with the guys".

Back on board ship, there was a reception scheduled for the evening of 5 July, with Vice Admiral James R. Hogg, Commander of the U.S. Seventh Fleet, serving as host. Invited were some 200 of Manila's leaders, including those in the military and diplomatic services. The weather wasn't so hospitable as those in the battleship had hoped. Choppy water in Manila Bay, strong wind, and the possibility of rain almost forced cancellation of Admiral Hogg's program. As it was, the reception was delayed, attendance less than expected, and the whole thing moved from the 01 deck to the wardroom as a concession to the weather.

Once at sea again, from 6 until 11 July, the *New Jersey* joined other Seventh Fleet warships in an exercise known as "Battle Week 2-83". The ship steamed for a while in the battle group of the carrier *Midway*. One of the roles envisioned in the planning for battleships in the 1980s was that their missile batteries could add to carrier battle groups a punch which would reinforce that provided by the air wings. To demonstrate that capability, the *New Jersey* fired one of her Harpoon missiles on 9 July, scoring a direct hit on a target hulk.

Once the fleet exercise was concluded, the *New Jersey* pulled in on 12 July to the port that had been a paradise for her sailors during the Vietnam War – Subic Bay in the Philippines. Chief Gunner's Mate Larry Pousson was surprised by how civilized Olongapo city had become since his last visit there on board the battleship in 1969. He says, "I couldn't believe all the changes they had in '83 when I went back. Back then [1968–69], there were a lot of dirt streets and stuff like that, and now I went back – street lights, paved streets, sidewalks. It really had been cleaned up a lot." Alas, the rough weather which plagued the ship a week earlier at Manila was after her again, only it was worse this time. The crew had only one day of liberty ashore before an approaching typhoon forced their recall from liberty and the ship's hurried departure on the 13th. So urgent was the need to leave port in the face of the coming storm that some men were left behind and had to rejoin the ship later.

As it happened, the leave-taking from Subic was only a day earlier than planned, so the *New Jersey* did not return, but headed south toward the Equator and Singapore. The line-crossing ceremony this time was much the same as it had been for the previous crew in 1968; again, there was a "beauty show" beforehand with men in drag. But there was one significant difference. This time the ship was commanded by a pollywog, so Captain Fogarty had the dubious privilege of leading the parade of uninitiated. He was outfitted in khaki trousers, T-shirt, a loosely tied necktie, and the khaki cover from his scrambled-egg combination cap. In addition to getting his bottom paddled, the captain had to stick his face into a garbage-filled toilet bowl and blow bubbles.

Storekeeper Richard Wolpin, also a pollywog when 17 July began, considered the ceremony "degrading and fun at the same time". As he explains, "It degraded the person, but it was a Navy tradition, so I had to take it in stride." Initially, one of the officers in the supply depart-

ment wasn't going to permit Wolpin and other store-keepers to take part, telling them that they had too much work to do. Instead of feeling relieved, they considered themselves cheated because they did not want to be the only remaining pollywogs in a ship full of shellbacks. Through the intercession of their leading enlisted man, Senior Chief Storekeeper Robert Johnson, they appealed against the ruling and got it reversed. Wolpin was sore afterward but pleased to be so, especially after he had had a good shower.

One shellback who enjoyed himself during the initiation of more than 1,000 pollywogs was Quartermaster Third Class John Trail, the history buff. He wore a dress white jumper of the type which dated back to the pre-World War II era. The leader of the affair, playing the part of King Neptune, was Gunner's Mate First Class Curtis McAdams, a veteran of the old battleship *Nevada*. His not-so-regal crown proclaimed his feat of crossing the line in November 1943, nearly forty years before. While McAdams sat next to the pollywog princess from the beauty contest, the uninitiated came by to kiss his feet.

The next item on the schedule was a port visit in Singapore from 19 until 21 July. *New Jersey* men were struck by the cleanliness of the city, enforced through statutes against such things as spitting on sidewalks. Just as Chief Pousson had noticed changes in the past fifteen years at Subic Bay, he saw them also in Singapore. In place of people selling goods out of little shacks and roadside stands, he now saw highrises everywhere. But some things remained reassuringly the same: "All the vices were still there – the cars, the girls, the booze. Different faces, different names." In the financial district of Singapore, Storekeeper Second Class Richard Wolpin got the impression that he was seeing an Oriental version of New York's Wall Street. The uniform of the day for local males seemed to be a three-piece suit. The city was too ritzy for his tastes. Wolpin and three shipmates went out to dinner together and got hit with a check for a whopping $180, including $4.50 a throw for glasses of beer. He was just as happy that the ship's stay there was relatively short.

After a one-day transit, the *New Jersey* arrived in the resort community of Pattaya Beach, Thailand, which was probably the crew's favorite liberty port of the Western Pacific cruise. The beach gradient was a shallow one, so again the *New Jersey* had to anchor out, as she had done in Manila and Singapore, and have small boats haul men in on liberty. When they got to the beach, it was literally that. Since there were no piers, the boats ran right up onto the beach itself; men took off their shoes and socks and rolled up their trouser legs to wade ashore. Returning to the *New Jersey* after liberty was even more difficult, and some of the more unsteady among the men fell in the water in the process of trying to get aboard.

The men of the battleship were especially taken by the friendliness of Pattaya Beach residents, which resulted in part from the fact that visits there by Navy ships were a rare occurrence. As a consequence, local merchants welcomed the free-spending ways of the visitors. What's more, the people of Pattaya Beach hadn't experienced some of the less-than-pleasant aspects of sailors on liberty and so hadn't developed anti-Navy attitudes. Because the small town served as a resort for civilian foreign visitors also, it was set up to cater to the wishes of visiting sailors. Like Singapore, it was clean, and it featured a number of colorful attractions such as Hindu merchants peddling their wares, motorcycles available for rent, and low-priced tours to Bangkok.

Lieutenant Frank Brown was at Pattaya Beach with the cruiser *Sterett* at the same time that the *New Jersey* was there, and he also has recollections of the local friendliness. As the *Sterett* was coming in to anchor, she was approached by jet ski boats, which were essentially waterborne counterparts of snowmobiles. "About ten of these [boats] were circling the ship," he recalls, "and . . . these really sweet little things in bikinis were driving them. . . . Of course, these young kids were just about ready to dive over the side. . . . [The boats] kept going around the ship, and then one of these gals apparently spotted her boyfriend, who had been there a few months before, and off goes the top of the bikini. I swear, I thought the entire ship was going to go over the side."

In Thailand, as elsewhere during the course of the swing through foreign ports, Captain Fogarty was playing the public relations role at which he was so smooth. After thirty-seven reporters arrived aboard in helicopters, the skipper held a press conference to augment the tour of the ship supplied by Lieutenant-Commander Eric Willenbrock and his public affairs staff. Fogarty had been through so many presss interviews that the questions by now had considerable sameness to them, and his answers were down pat. In 1968, Captain Snyder had had to answer many questions about the possible threat posed by "Styx" missiles because they had been used to sink an Israeli destroyer the year before. Coincidentally, Fogarty was also asked about a missile threat because Exocet missiles fired by the Argentine Navy had sunk the British destroyer *Sheffield* in the 1982 Falklands War. Fogarty told a reporter from the *Bangkok Post* of the *New Jersey*'s heavy armor and said of the effect an Exocet would have: "It would be like a bee sting to me."

On 24 July, two days after her arrival in Thailand, the ship was ordered to cancel the remainder of her planned Western Pacific cruise, including visits scheduled for Hong Kong, Korea, Japan, and Guam. Instead, she was to steam to a position off the coast of Central America in order to reinforce the nation's naval presence there. The interest of the U.S. Government was especially piqued by an increasing number of Soviet and Communist bloc merchant ships steaming toward Nicaragua, presumably carrying vehicles and arms destined for the Sandinista regime there. The

aircraft carrier *Ranger* and her battle group had been on their way to the Western Pacific on 19 July when they were diverted to augment the naval forces on the Pacific side of Central America. Now the *New Jersey* would head there.

Once the *New Jersey* was at sea on 24 July, she steamed toward Subic Bay to begin resupplying for the long voyage to Central America. Fire Controlman Second Class Dan Clairmont was among the many listening when Captain Fogarty came on the general announcing system an hour or so out of port and told the crew where they were going. A lot of people were depressed, Clairmont says, because of the sudden change in plans. Those who had prudently saved their money to spend in Hong Kong, Korea, and Japan now wished they had spent it in the ports already visited. Along with the disappointment, though, Chris Johnson remembers the reaction of a number of officers who were used to the carrier escort duties they had known while serving in destroyers. He says their feeling was, "We're finally on a surface ship that counts. We, the surface Navy, finally have a ship that is really in the focus, that can go places and do things and isn't just escorting somebody else."

Lieutenant Frank Brown, who had been in Thailand during a temporary duty assignment in the *Sterett*, was transferred aboard the *New Jersey* by helo to ride part of the way to Subic after the cruiser was also diverted from her schedule. The Medical Service Corps officer had a chance to help out in the battleship's sick bay and was struck by the number of older men in the crew, certainly more than he was used to seeing in the average Navy ship. This came about from the recall to active duty of retired men and reservists. Gunner's Mate McAdams, for instance, the King Neptune of the Equator ceremony, was one of several who had been in the Navy in World War II. As a consequence of having a sprinkling of such veterans in the crew, Brown found himself seeing sick call visitors with other than the normal problems. Some came, for example, with complaints of lower back pains, while others were in sick bay to have their blood pressure checked to make sure their hypertension medicine was having the desired effect.

After two days in Subic Bay, the *New Jersey* left for Hawaii on 29 July. While at sea, she was joined by other ships destined for Pearl Harbor and thence Central America. They were the cruiser *Leahy*, guided missile destroyers *Robison* and *Buchanan*, destroyer *Ingersoll*, and frigate *Roark*. In essence, the *New Jersey* and those with her constituted a surface action group. This was a manifestation of yet another role envisioned for the reactivated battleships – to serve as centerpieces for surface combatant task groups which could operate in low-threat areas that didn't require the presence of an aircraft carrier battle group for self-defense.

While the *New Jersey* was in Pearl Harbor from 11 until 14 August, there was more Waikiki Beach sunbathing and swimming, and Fire Controlman Dan Clairmont had a joyous first wedding anniversary with his wife Gail. She and other wives of *New Jersey* men had caught super-saver flights from the West Coast for the ship's brief stay in Hawaii. All too soon, there were more goodbyes of the sort when the battleship left Long Beach in early June.

During the trip eastward from Hawaii, the *New Jersey* and the other five members of her task group conducted tactical exercises. On 17 and 18 August, the exercises also involved the USS *Ranger* and her battle group, which had completed duty off Central America. The commander of the battleship surface combatant task group was Rear Admiral Peter Hekman. By tradition, he should have been embarked in the *New Jersey* as the biggest ship, but the reactivation at Long Beach had wiped out her flag quarters and flag mess, so he was in the cruiser *Leahy* instead. The newer *Leahy* boasted more extensive command and control facilities than the *New Jersey* and also the Navy tactical data system (NTDS), something the battleship

probably won't receive until a yard overhaul in the late 1980s. During the 1981–82 reactivation, Admiral Halsey's old flag spaces were gutted to make room for Tomahawk missile control equipment and computers. Part of the former flag space on the 02 level was designated the combat engagement center and took over the functions previously performed by the combat information center down on the fourth deck. In the *New Jersey*'s most recent incarnation, the CIC is manned by a skeleton crew which serves as a backup for the people topside in the CEC.

The *New Jersey* and the five ships with her arrived off the west coast of Central America on 26 August. Their mission was officially indicated as training and surveillance. More to the point, the battleship and her consorts were providing naval presence, ready to exert themselves on behalf of U.S. national interests if the situation warranted. For the men on board the battleship, it was a time of watchful waiting and it certainly was a good deal less

Below: The replenishment oiler *Kansas City* refuels the *New Jersey* and the destroyer *Buchanan* on 12 August 1983. (U.S. Naval Institute Collection)

enjoyable than the port visit routine which had been so recently interrupted. During working days, recalls Gunner's Mate Carl Farmer, men cleaned their spaces and checked out machinery and equipment to make sure everything was operational if needed. To provide a change of pace, the ship held cookouts on the main deck from time to time, with various groups taking turns with the cooking. A number of crewmen had bought video cassette recorders in the Philippines, so small lounge areas and living compartments became sites for looking at tapes mailed from home; they supplemented the standard fare of programs available through the closed-circuit television.

The New Jersey and the destroyer Robison left the patrol station to make a port visit in Balboa, Panama, from 2 until 5 September. As usual, dignitaries came aboard, including a former New Jersey man, Vice Admiral Joseph Metcalf, who was now Commander Second Fleet. On 7 September, while back off the Central American coast, the New Jersey received a visit from U.S. Secretary of Defense Caspar Weinberger and the President of El Salvador, Alvaro Magana. The two men and their retinue were posted at various stations in the superstructure to witness a fire-power demonstration. In this case, it was an eight-gun broadside, which would have been nine except for the fact that the barrel liner was cracked and worn in the center gun of turret two so that it wasn't fired at any time during the deployment.

The New Jersey generally operated out of sight of land when off the coast, and it would have been tough to see the shore even if closer, because the weather was frequently overcast and rainy. Navigator Chris Johnson says, "I have never seen thundershowers erupt so quickly in my life as down there." Heavy rain was drenching the ship on 9 September when the New Jersey's SH-2 Sea Sprite helicopter brought aboard Captain Richard D. Milligan after a harrowing trip over from the frigate Roark, which had transported him out from Panama. Captain Fogarty met him on the fantail, and then the two ran for shelter in the after part of the superstructure. It was a wet welcome for the man who had been ordered in to relieve Captain Fogarty as commanding officer. The New Jersey was scheduled to return to Long Beach on 17 September and hold a change of command there on 1 October. Rather than wait for the ship to come in, Milligan thought it would be wise to go aboard and spend some time under way with Captain Fogarty before taking command. There was, however, to be no opportunity for a leisurely turnover period and ride back to Long Beach. On the very day of Captain Milligan's arrival, the New Jersey was ordered to leave the surface task group and steam south to a position off the Panama Canal. The day after that, she was ordered to anchor off Balboa, Panama, and prepare to go through the canal into the Atlantic Ocean.

Information as to plans for the ship leaked out to the crew in the form of rumors. When the ship got to Balboa, crew members were allowed to go ashore for a few hours to telephone their relatives and tell them that they would be going to an undisclosed location for an unknown period of time. Fire Controlman Second Class Dan Clairmont telephoned Santa Ana, California. He remembers, "I called my wife, and she was already in tears, because it had . . . been on the news that we were heading for Beirut, Lebanon. . . . I was really upset because we weren't told." Soon both Mr. and Mrs. Clairmont were crying at long-distance rates; the happy homecoming had been only seven days away, and now they had no idea when it would be.

The day of 12 September was spent going through the canal. Crew members who didn't have other duties were able to go topside and take pictures. John Trail and another quartermaster were trading off two-hour stints at the helm on the way through. When Trail was off duty, he could observe the sights but at the same time was supposed to maintain a sense of decorum. Thus, he was apprehensive when Captain Milligan came over and asked what he was doing when he was, in fact, using a pair of binoculars to check out a bikini-clad girl ashore. Milligan was so new on board that the crew didn't yet know how he would react to things. The concern was soon allayed when Milligan borrowed Trail's binoculars, took a look, said "She's not bad-looking," and walked away. This new guy was going to be all right, Trail decided.

For both Milligan and Fogarty, the change of plans forced some adjustments. With the likelihood that the New Jersey would be going into combat in the Middle East, Captain Fogarty had an understandable desire to stay. Milligan, who had commanded the cruiser Wainwright in the Mediterranean within the past year, was eager to command the battleship there. He thus felt a sense of satisfaction when ordered to relieve Fogarty forthwith and take the ship eastward. In a line that he has probably polished in after-dinner speeches, Milligan says of Fogarty, "When the ship was redirected, there was a little bit of reluctance, I think, in his mind to leave the ship. We're about the same size, so it would have been a hell of a fight to see who could throw who overboard."

On 13 September, the day after clearing the canal, the New Jersey was under way from Panama and soon chewing up the miles at 25 knots. The two captains went through an amiable but rushed turnover. Instead of having two or three weeks to finish fitness reports on the New Jersey's nearly seventy officers, Fogarty had more like two or three days. On 15 September, the ship slowed down briefly while north of Puerto Rico for a change of command ceremony on the forecastle. She was still moving along at such a clip that the relative wind made it difficult for crew members on deck to hear the words spoken by the principals. For Fogarty, it was a bittersweet leave-taking. As soon as he was relieved, he was frocked in the rank of commodore, and his one-star flag was broken at the top of the ship. On the other hand, the brief ceremony did not permit the sort of public acclaim that would have been his in Long Beach. More importantly, he was forced to withdraw prematurely from this ship which he loved so much that he got feelings of exhilaration when he thought about being in command of her. Sunglasses masked from most the moistness in the new commodore's eyes as he moved aft to the helicopter that would take him away.

Once the ceremony was over, the *New Jersey*'s speed climbed back up to 25 knots for the trip across the Atlantic. One result was that the customary vibration in the chief petty officers' quarters near the propellers became considerably worse than usual. Senior Chief Fire Controlman Rick Crawford remembers that the chiefs couldn't set their coffee cups down because the mess tables were shaking so much. They had to hold onto their plates while they ate. Chief Gunner's Mate Larry Pousson sometimes woke up at 2:00 or 3:00 in the morning and found twenty or thirty chiefs sitting up because they couldn't sleep. A number of them chose to bed down in their work spaces or elsewhere in the ship in order to get some relief.

When the *New Jersey* got off Rota, Spain, on 21 September, she slowed down for the first time since Puerto Rico so helos could ferry aboard mail, cargo, and new crew members who had initially reported to Long Beach. She soon went through the Strait of Gibraltar into the Mediterreanean. The speed run finally came to an end twelve days after it started. The battleship arrived off Lebanon, and Vice Admiral Edward Martin, Commander Sixth Fleet, came aboard. In a four-month period, from June to September, the battleship had been in all four of the U.S. Navy's numbered fleets – Third, Seventh, Second, and Sixth – and the commanders of all four had visited her.

The *New Jersey*'s mission off troubled Beirut would be to try to stabilize a situation which had gone from bad to worse. Initially, U.S. Marines had gone into Lebanon in the summer of 1982 as part of a multinational peacekeeping force designed to maintain order among the nation's warring factions; the situation was further snarled by the presence of Israelis, Syrians, and the Palestine Liberation Organization. The PLO had been evacuated successfully, but things blew up soon afterward when Palestinian refugees were massacred and President-elect Bashir Gemayel of Lebanon was assassinated. The Marines were transformed from peacekeepers to targets as they hunkered down in a compound at the Beirut International Airport. If tactical considerations had prevailed, they would have taken the high ground – the mountains overlooking the city. But this was a war of political rather than tactical maneuvering. The mountains were thus left to the Syrians, who regularly used the elevated vantage point to fire on the Marines. On 8 September, the day before the *New Jersey* was ordered to Panama, the frigate *Bowen* became the first American warship to provide shore bombardment in support of Lebanese military forces.

Given the steadily rising pressure in the area and the addition of naval gunfire to the explosive mixture, it is little wonder that the Joint Chiefs of Staff decided to order in the biggest and most powerful gunfire ship of all.

Within hours of the *New Jersey*'s arrival, a cease-fire was arranged ashore. It appeared that the battleship had achieved her purpose without firing a shot, the essence of gunboat diplomacy. In this instance, though, with the complex web of relationships and antagonisms, a cease-fire was as easily broken as it was established, and the situation soon degenerated to the status quo prior to the *New Jersey*'s arrival.

In lieu of orders for her to shoot, the *New Jersey*'s mission was again naval presence, and that was initially quite an anticlimax after the expectations which had developed during the furious steaming from Central America. From the ship's bridge, Captain Milligan could look toward the city of Beirut and see sunbathers on the beach, motorboat races, and – the most irritating of all – a merry-go-round which rotated steadily day and night as if it weren't in the middle of an urban battleground. That battleground was at its most bizarre during darkness. To Lieutenant Commander Chris Johnson, it seemed as if the Lebanese and others went to work during the daytime, then went home afterward, got out their guns, and started shooting. First came the small arms, then the machine guns, later the rocket launchers, and even tanks. Amidst this madness, it appeared at times as if the *New Jersey* would be called upon to join the fray. On a number of occasions recalls Gunner's Mate Larry Pousson, the orders did come through to man the turrets for possible firing missions. Men went to their stations, powder tanks were opened in the magazines, and powder bags sent up the hoists to the gun rooms. Projectiles were sent up to the turret cradles, ready to be rammed into gun breeches. The permission to fire didn't come, and the ammunition was sent back down and put away. Says Pousson: "This was really the frustrating part about it – the Marines getting pounded on, but you can't do anything about it."

The training of the *New Jersey*'s crew members had prepared them for this new existence in a military sense – they knew how to operate their equipment and fight the ship – but not a psychological one. One factor which helped enormously in their ability to cope was the presence of their new commanding officer. Captain Milligan quickly demonstrated that he had brought a seabag full of leadership qualities aboard with him. He was as much as possible, given the demands of the situation – a peripatetic skipper. He moved about the ship to talk to the men of the *New Jersey*, to learn of their concerns, and to do what he could to alleviate those concerns. A friendly, open man, he projected to the crew an air of warmth and sincerity. In his talks on the loudspeaker, the closed-circuit television, and in his visits to individuals, he communicated the idea that they were all in this together, and so he would share whatever information he could. When men went sunbathing on the battleship's decks, Milligan walked among them, leaning down to make new friends and to learn how things were going. When the situation did turn sour off Lebanon, the battleship's crew members had confidence that they were being led by a man they could depend upon.

The time off the coast of Beirut quickly settled into a stultifying routine. Men got up, went to their spaces, trained at their jobs, cleaned up, watched television, read, ate their meals, and cursed their collective fate. The early part of October was frustrating. Not only was the ship not able to go home, but she wasn't doing anything either – at least nothing overt. By her very presence, however, perhaps she was preventing something far worse from happening ashore. But then, in the early hours of Sunday, 23 October 1983, something far worse did happen ashore. The near-daily firing at the Marines' compound by rockets, artillery, and snipers had been bad enough, but now a suicidal terrorist drove a truck full of explosives into the compound and detonated it under the Marine barracks.

A shroud of fog blocked off the battleship's view of the beach. As the morning progressed, word began filtering to the crew that something had happened ashore – something bad. Then Captain Milligan came on the loudspeaker to report of the tragedy, and the ship went to general quarters. More than anything, the crew had a desire to retaliate for the hurt that had been done to so many of

their fellow Americans. But, as Captain Milligan knew well, it was not at all clear whom such retaliation could be aimed at, and the men were eventually released from their battle stations.

Quartermaster John Trail was in the battleship's armored conning tower that morning, and from time to time he looked at an electronic ticker back of the helmsman's station. It was bringing in the grim news, and with each report the number of deaths and injuries climbed higher and higher. Ultimately, the death toll mounted to 241 American servicemen, including the *New Jersey*'s Chief Electronics Technician Michael Gorchinski, who had gone ashore to help the Marines with their radars.

The battleship sent one of her doctors ashore, about three-fourths of her Marines for security duty, and a working party of Navy men to help in the efforts to rescue still-living men from the rubble of the building that had housed hundreds of healthy young Marines such a short time before. There was no hesitation in volunteering, says Milligan, despite the tenuous nature of the situation ashore. He says, "If they had taken 1,600, they probably could have gotten 1,600." The immediate reaction was a response to assist. Some of the *New Jersey*'s hospital corpsmen were involved ashore and some on board amphibious warfare ships. The wounded had not been brought to the battleship because she no longer had a surgeon as part of her crew.

In the wake of the terrorist bombing, the *New Jersey* continued to steam offshore; if anything, her men were even more alert than before, going to general quarters with alarming frequency because of the possibility that the ship herself would be the target of a terrorist operation.

Finally, there came a break from the pattern of steaming and waiting for the unknown. On 4 November, the *New Jersey* was permitted to travel to Alexandria, Egypt. She arrived there that morning and anchored outside the breakwater for a planned four-day port visit. Captain Milligan went ashore to make calls on local officials. Some men went on liberty, while others stayed on board in the duty section. Soon after the captain got back, the battleship received orders to get under way as soon as possible. The terrorists had struck again, this time blowing up a suicide truck at the Israeli military governor's headquarters in the village of Tyre and killing forty-six. The situation was too volatile for the *New Jersey* to stay away. The word went out to recall men from liberty. By midnight, the ship again was under way with all her men and boats on board. Then, as Milligan phrases it, he and the rest of the crew returned to "our home port off Beirut".

Back in Washington during that month of November, there were questions in the councils of government about what to do with the *New Jersey*. Navy officials advocated a return to Long Beach, because the deployment was nearing the six-month mark, and the crew was already well past the scheduled time for return. Members of the Marine Corps, whose compatriots had died in faraway Beirut and were continuing to be shot at, argued that there was a more compelling need than the welfare of the crew. The lives of the Marines were at stake, and so the *New Jersey* should stay. She was valuable as a deterrent and as a potential fire support ship. The Marine viewpoint prevailed, and the Joint Chiefs of Staff ordered the *New Jersey*'s stay off Lebanon extended indefinitely. Her sister ship *Iowa* was then in a shipyard in Pascagoula, Mississippi, undergoing reactivation. Money was soon approved to step up the pace and hasten her recommissioning. But even at the most optimistic, she wouldn't be able to replace the *New Jersey* until the late spring or early summer of 1984. It was now beyond question that the *New Jersey* would not be home for Christmas in 1983.

Almost immediately, a team of officers flew out from the Naval Military Personnel Command in Washington to confer with Captain Milligan about possible measures by which to provide relief for the men of the ship's crew. Back in World War II, those who sailed away in the *New Jersey* were in "for the duration". But that was a different era and a different kind of war. Now the deployment patterns and resulting expectations were different. Then, furthermore, the men in all ships faced such indefinite futures, not just those in one ship. In late 1983, the situation in the Navy's only battleship was clearly extraordinary and so extraordinary measures would be instituted. The most attractive proposal was to send members of the crew home on leave in relays. Reservists from the States would come out to take their places. New fathers could go home to see their babies for the first time. Crew members who had planned to get married could try to work out new arrangements after scheduled wedding dates had come and gone. Some men were already facing divorces, but perhaps there were some shaky marriages which could be saved if the husbands came home soon rather than half a year later.

Even before the leave program could be put into effect, there was more frustration. Part of the U.S. response to the shelling of the Marines ashore was to institute reconnaissance flights by photo-equipped F-14 fighter planes from the Task Force 60 aircraft carriers some 60–80 miles offshore. Under the rules of engagement then in effect, U.S. forces could fire only if fired upon, and the F-14s were being shot at as they flew their missions over Syrian-controlled areas of Lebanon. On 4 December, an air strike was launched against Syrian antiaircraft batteries from the carriers *Independence* and *John F. Kennedy*. Two U.S. planes were lost; one flier was killed and one taken prisoner. In the wake of the raid, there were questions as to why the operational commander, the Commander in Chief of the U.S. European Command, located in Germany, had not ordered battleship gunfire instead. The projectiles couldn't be shot down on their way to their targets, nor did they put Americans at risk of being captured. The principal argument against the use of the *New Jersey*'s

guns was the possibility that they might inflict injury on innocent civilians while in the process of shooting at legitimate military targets. This was yet another aspect of the Lebanese situation; there were no well-defined front lines dividing friend from foe.

When it came time for the first group of lucky *New Jersey* men to head home on leave, Captain Milligan set aside one block of seats for what he considered humanitarian cases, and the remainder of the 104 seats on the plane were distributed by lottery. The journey took twenty-eight hours. There would have been 104 men on board the Naval Reserve C-9 transport, but one of the men showed up for the flight obviously unprepared for a long journey, and so he was held back. During the remaining six flights in subsequent months, the 104 seats were filled every time. The crew members began with a helicopter ride to the tank landing ship *Manitowoc*, and she took them into Larnaca, Cyprus. From there, the plane hit a series of refueling stops – in Sigonella, Sicily; Lajes in the Azores; St. John's, Newfoundland; and Norfolk, Virginia.

While the happy *New Jersey* crew members were heading home, the first group of activated reservists arrived at the ship, having made the long, circuitous journey in the opposite direction. They had been flown from Cyprus to an amphibious assault ship and then rode the last lap in an LCM-8 landing craft. They climbed up the side of the *New Jersey*'s side by Jacob's ladder. Accompanying the approximately seventy-five reservists who would fill slots in the ship's organization – though not on a one-for-one basis – was Journalist Second Class Lance Johnson. He was on active duty at Naval Reserve headquarters in New Orleans and was sent along to provide public affairs coverage of the substitute crew members. Johnson recalls the considerable feeling of pleasure he experienced when he stepped aboard the deck of the battleship and was greeted by a *New Jersey* sailor who said, "Welcome aboard, shipmate."

The new men got into action almost immediately. They arrived on 13 December, and on the 14th the *New Jersey* was finally ordered to fire her big guns. The Syrians had continued to fire on U.S. reconnaissance planes, so the operational commander unleashed the *New Jersey*. Captain Milligan was even told specifically how many rounds the ship should fire – eleven. The number was limited mainly because the firing was intended as a signal. Milligan explains, "I think it was primarily an attempt to send a pretty strong message that, 'When we send the F-14 aircraft in for reconnaissance missions over Lebanon, we don't expect them to get shot at. This is going to be the price.'" A good deal of anger and frustration were dissipated that day, because crew members finally had the feeling that they were contributing.

Despite the happy mood, all was not well on board the battleship *New Jersey*. Though her projectiles had traveled some 16–18 miles beyond Beirut and scarred the landscape with craters as large as tennis courts, there was never any indication that they had hit the antiaircraft batteries or any information on how close they came. The Syrians sent back a signal of their own; they were contemptuous of the shooting. The lack of airborne observers frustrated members of the ship's fire control team. They were not able to benefit from normal practice in naval gunfire support, which calls for spotters to observe the fall of shot in relation to a target and then provide appropriate corrections to the fire controlmen on board ship.

In addition, there were problems with the 16-inch powder bags in the battleship's magazines. Variations in initial muzzle velocity – and thus variations in the distances projectiles would travel toward their targets – had become more apparent as the number of firings grew. Old powders, while all from the same grand lot, had aged differently during the many years they had been in storage since manufacture. Volatile chemicals in the powder had evaporated, causing each firing to produce a different and unknown initial velocity. The fire control team could measure this error as each round was fired by using a special doppler radar, known as a velocimeter, in a dome on top of each turret. The fire controlmen kept records of these after-the-fact readings, and they were helpful in predicting subsequent initial velocities. Range errors were reduced but not eliminated. The deteriorated powder was later replaced during rearming with bags which had come from storage on the East Coast and which proved to be more stable.

A major concern with firing of the 16-inch guns at Lebanon was that of collateral damage to civilians ashore. Captain Milligan says those on board the *New Jersey* "knew that the IV [initial velocity] problem only affected range dispersion. By adjusting the ship's position, a safe line of fire was developed, permitting mission accomplishment without undue danger of collateral damage."

In the meantime, even before the powder problem was solved, more solutions to the morale problem were at hand. The firing of 14 December had already done a great deal, as had the idea that more and more crewmen would be going home on leave as the R&R flights continued. Now came USO shows to entertain the crew. On 15 December, Las Vegas singer Wayne Newton visited and performed his routine for the crew on the fantail helo platform. That evening the *New Jersey* responded to a call for fire from ashore and shot forty rounds of 5-inch which silenced the guns firing on the Marines.

On 24 December, the ship was one stop on a tour of the area by Bob Hope. He had been on board the *New Jersey* on Christmas Day of 1968; here he was again, fifteen years later, almost to the day. With him were Brooke Shields, Cathy Lee Crosby, Ann Jillian, Julie Hayak (Miss USA), singer Vic Damone, and comedian George Kirby. More than 300 Marines from the Beirut compound were on board to help the crewmen enjoy the show. As usual, Hope

was funny, although some of his topical material went over the heads of men who had been out of touch with U.S. television for more than six months. Ann Jillian made probably the strongest impression on the men of the battleship because of the sense of genuineness and concern she brought. She was truly touched by the plight of the soldiers and Marines who were so far from home.

On Christmas Day itself, there were celebrations far different from the ones which would have been enjoyed back home and thus even more touching. Wives and children in the United States had made and sent videotapes in which they talked about events at home and expressed their love and concern for the *New Jersey* men who weren't there in person to celebrate. The tapes themselves were emotional, and they evoked emotional responses. Journalist Second Class Lance Johnson, though he had been on board less than two weeks, realized what the men were going through and the ways in which they were dealing with it. He was especially struck by a gathering of crew members in the mess deck on Christmas Day to sing carols. As the male voices joined in song, Johnson heard the sounds of Christmas in a way he had never before experienced.

The *New Jersey* pulled into hearby Haifa, Israel, on 29 December for a five-day port visit. Since the November stop in Alexandria, Egypt, had been aborted abruptly, this trip to Haifa marked the battleship's first full day in port in

111 days. Lance Johnson took a two-day trip to religious sites – Bethlehem, Jerusalem, and the Church of the Nativity. The guide in his tour bus was a man of perhaps seventy-five years. While pointing out the various historical landmarks, he also provided full particulars and capabilities on Israeli tanks and other pieces of military equipment which passed the bus.

Religion was more important in the life of Storekeeper Second Class Richard Wolpin, who is Jewish, than for many in the *New Jersey*'s crew during that period. He had got special leave when the ship was in Panama in September so that he could fly home to New Jersey and celebrate the holidays of Rosh Hanana and Yom Kippur with his parents. A trip to Israel thus meant much to him, especially since he was able to visit a friend from high school who was a student at the University of Haifa. For the New Year's holiday to begin 1984, Wolpin visited some relatives on his father's side, and accepted invitations as well from friendly Israeli citizens who asked him to come to their homes for dinner. He also went to Bethlehem and Jerusalem, and during the course of his travels was so attracted by the beauty of the Israeli female soldiers that he was sure it would take little effort for him to fall in love.

Before there could be an opportunity for that, however, the *New Jersey* weighed anchor on 3 January and returned to her station off the coast of Beirut. Soon the second group of reservists came in, and this time there were 104 *New Jersey* men ready to occupy the seats of the C-9

headed for the States. When the first group of crew members was getting back to the ship, the first contingent of reservists was leaving about the same time. Captain Milligan reflected on what a treat the whole experience had been for that initial group of reservists. His description of their time on board became a staple in the after-dinner routine he was called upon to deliver when the ship later returned home. In his tale, he recounted what the reservists had experienced: the 14 December main battery mission, the Wayne Newton show, the show with Bob Hope and the girls, the secondary battery mission, and the port visit to Haifa. Then came the punch line: "And we paid them, too."

Among the men who came to the *New Jersey* in January 1984 were some prospective crew members from the *Iowa*. The *New Jersey* people were glad to have them on board, not only to fill in for crew members on leave, but also because the training might speed the *Iowa*'s arrival to relieve the *New Jersey* off Beirut. Included in the *Iowa* group were three ensigns who had been undergoing training in Norfolk – John Donovan, Barry McDonough, and Greg Miller. One thing which impressed the newcomers was the great strain upon the officers of the *New Jersey*. They had been under pressure for months because of the operations off Beirut, and they faced the prospect of several more such months. It would be well to describe the ship's patrol routine for the winter of 1983–84 in some detail in order to appreciate the sources of that strain.

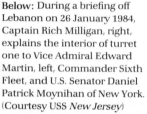
**Below:** During a briefing off Lebanon on 26 January 1984, Captain Rich Milligan, right, explains the interior of turret one to Vice Admiral Edward Martin, left, Commander Sixth Fleet, and U.S. Senator Daniel Patrick Moynihan of New York. (Courtesy USS *New Jersey*)

Above: Secretary of the Navy John Lehman speaks on the mess deck to Naval Reservists who relieved members of the *New Jersey*'s crew during the deployment off Lebanon. (Photo by JO2 Lance Johnson; courtesy Naval Reserve Association)

To be most effective in her presence role, the *New Jersey* had to operate in close to the beach and to remain ready to shoot at any time. That called for constant alertness. Generally, the battleship ran her patrol legs about two to three miles off the coast, and the destroyers with her picked patrol legs which were relatively close but out of her way. Even as she cruised back and forth, her fire controlmen down in the plotting room kept the Mark 13 radar constantly on a reference point ashore and had the computers set to provide solutions on short notice. One of the destroyers was the USS *Tattnall*, whose skipper was Commander Pete Deutermann. Since the battleship's old fire control system took longer to generate solutions than his modern Mark 86 type, the practice was that the *New Jersey* would settle on a course and stay on it for a while, and Deutermann would pick a course of his own to keep clear of the battleship. The *New Jersey*'s speed was generally in the five-to-ten knot range, and it was varied so that it would be more difficult for gunners ashore to obtain their own fire control solutions. The *Tattnall* generally steamed faster, because she was a more vulnerable target and because the more frequent U-turns necessitated by higher speed had less effect on her fire control setup. When the battleship ran her figure eight patterns, Ensign Donovan observed that at the end of each run parallel to the shore, the *New Jersey* habitually turned toward the

beach in coming around. Turret one was the ready turret, and the crews of the other turrets rotated through it. By turning as she did, the battleship could have the guns of turret one always ready to bear on potential targets.

The steaming routine was complicated for the *New Jersey*'s officers by the fact that the sea area off Beirut was highly congested. As part of the multinational peacekeeping force, she was operating with British, French, and Italian warships. Further, there were merchant ships of various nations, random patrols at times by Israeli vessels, and a Soviet *Kashin*-class destroyer. At night the latter went out to an area about 12 miles from the beach and shut down her engines to conserve fuel, because there were no ready sources of replenishment nearby.

The *New Jersey*'s SH-2 helicopter, which was assigned to the ship to provide over-the-horizon targeting information for her antiship missiles, had quite a different role off Lebanon. The *New Jersey* was in charge of managing the surface picture off Beirut, so, as Milligan recalls, the helo flew continuously on surveillance patrols to keep track of the many vessels of different nationalities which were in the area.

The whole purpose of the sea patrols by the ships, of course, was to protect the Marines in their vulnerable positions ashore. The destroyers were there to protect the Marines with their rapid call-for-fire response capability, and the battleship was there to augment the fire of the destroyers and to protect those destroyers as well. Captain Deutermann of the *Tattnall* says that such a role called for the *New Jersey* to be clearly visible from the shore: "The presence mission – it was important to be big and ugly out there, and the closer you got, the bigger and uglier you were." Under the rules of engagement, the offshore forces were authorized to supply only retaliatory fire. Deutermann is convinced that it was the presence of the *New Jersey* which kept the Syrian gunners on the beach from shooting at the destroyers. While the Syrians did fire on the F-14 reconnaissance planes, he surmises that they recognized that it would be an obvious step of escalation to shoot at the ships and could well bring 16-inch projectiles thundering down on their heads.

Because of the *New Jersey*'s proximity to the shore, the battleship's crew had to stay below decks to minimize their vulnerability. No more sunbathing and no more pleasant walks around the fantail. There was yet another reason for men to avoid going topside, and it was a factor which added greatly to the mental strain experienced by those running the ship. The bombing of the Marine compound on 23 October clearly demonstrated both a capability and willingness to take extreme measures to disrupt the multinational peacekeeping force in an effort to get it to leave. If the terrorists would strike on land, they might strike at sea as well, and they took pains to point this out in voice radio messages which called out the patrolling ships by name and threatened them. While random gunfire at the ships might bring unwelcome retaliation, a bold act of terrorism might drive them away entirely.

The threats to the ships ranged from the plausible to the outlandish. The Beirut International Airport, where the Marines were holed up, continued in operation throughout the period that the *New Jersey* was offshore. It was all too conceivable that terrorists could hijack one of the planes headed to or from the airport and crash it onto a ship. Intelligence messages bombarded the ships, warning of all manner of potential evils – hang gliders powered by lawn mower engines and possibly carrying men and satchel charges; speed boats filled with explosives; terrorist merchant ships, submarines, mines, rockets fired from trucks, and so forth. Even some of the really bizarre things seemed somehow possible, given the terrorists' willingness to kill themselves to achieve their aims. The situation was so fraught with possibilities that the *New Jersey* was required to be able to respond on very short notice. After the bombing of the Marine compound on 23 October, recalls Milligan, he never ventured far from the bridge because he had to be close to communications and ready to direct protective measures. He was thus inhibited in his ability to get out for the personal contact which had meant so much to him and the crew.

In this demanding atmosphere, a number of the *New Jersey*'s routines were adjusted. Down inside the ship, mealtimes turned out to be whenever men could get to the wardroom or mess decks. The food was served cafeteria style, and men just went in and filled up plates or trays when they felt the need. Ensign Donovan observed that there were few people watching movies in the wardroom, because most of the officers were either standing watches or sleeping in order to be ready for the next watch. Because a smaller proportion of the enlisted men had to stand watches than officers, there was more of a social life in the mess deck. Greg Miller says, "The morale was remarkably high, particularly among the enlisted personnel. They had a lot of activities going aboard the ship that were very enjoyable. Every night, in addition to the standard movies, they played games. They had bingo . . . certain nights of the week and other [nights they had] raffles. I felt like the chaplain [Commander Benny Hornsby] and a lot of the junior officers had key roles in keeping morale up."

Another thing which helped the morale of the crew was the outpouring of concern from the United States. Sometimes an entire grade school class wrote to the ship. Crew members could drop down to the post office and pick up handfuls of letters to read and answer. The Long Beach *Press-Telegram*, the newspaper in the ship's home port, sent to the *New Jersey* 1,500 copies of a special edition jammed with messages of support. For Valentine's Day, the ship received a giant heart, filled with 450 pounds of chocolates which were in 1,500 individual boxes for distribution to the crew members.

From time to time, the patrol routine was broken when the ship had to haul out from station and conduct an underway replenishment so that the hundreds of *New Jersey* men could keep eating and the engines could keep running. And the ammunition supply had to be taken care of, especially with the need to replace the deteriorated powder. On 26 January, for instance, the *New Jersey* had a long replenishment from the USS *Detroit*. The large, fast combat support ship sent the battleship forty-seven pallets of 16-inch powder. Each pallet contained six canisters, and each canister contained three bags – more than 800 bags in all.

Because of the obvious value of minimizing the time spent off station, such replenishments were a matter of necessity rather than convenience. Otherwise, the battleship was kept on a fairly short leash. Early in the new year, a reporter and photographer from *Life* magazine visited the ship. Their article, which appeared in the March 1984 issue, said of her "Having her close to shore is considered so important that when her skipper asks for permission to sail 50 miles out to sea to dump garbage, he is frequently turned down." The article also talked about the crew members' obvious desire to go home and their parody of Rolaids television commercials. When the men of the *New Jersey* were asked how they spelled relief, the answer was "I-O-W-A."

The situation for the peacekeeping force changed dramatically on 7 February 1984 when President Reagan announced in Washington that the United States was going to withdraw the bulk of the Marines from their position on shore and redeploy them to the ships of the amphibious force off the coast of Lebanon. A residual force would remain behind to protect the U.S. embassy and other American interests. As a consequence of the reduced force, there would be greater reliance in the future on air strikes and naval gunfire. Since the beginning of the new year, the *New Jersey* had had two call-for-fire missions with her 5-inch battery, shooting thirty-two rounds on 15 January and seven rounds on 7 February, the day of the President's announcement. Those paled into insignificance when compared with the events of 8 February.

Early on the afternoon of the eighth, the *New Jersey* was authorized to shoot at Druze and Syrian gun positions which were shelling Beirut. John Donovan recalls that Captain Milligan spoke to the crew on the general announcing system and said, "The *New Jersey* has a fire mission. Man your gunnery stations." The reaction in the ship was instantaneous. Says Donovan, "You could hear the crew cheering. They finally had something to do instead of just driving back and forth. You could hear them banging on the bulkheads and just running around."

Most of that day's targets were in mountains east of the town of Hammana, about 15 miles east of Beirut. They included artillery, antitank artillery, antiaircraft emplacements, and command bunkers. Because the day was a cloudy one with low overcast, and because some of the sites were antiaircraft batteries, aerial spotting was not feasible. Instead, the ship counted on volume of fire to

**Right:** Seaman Thomas Martin buffs the deck in a crew living compartment. The privacy curtains and "coffin racks" are a far cry from accommodations in *New Jersey* enlisted living spaces in years past. (Photo by JO2 Lance Johnson)

**Below:** CH-46 helicopters shuttle back and forth as the USS *Sylvania* replenishes the *New Jersey* during operations off Lebanon. (U.S. Naval Institute Collection)

blanket the targets. At long ranges, the 16-inch projectiles have patterns of dispersion. So, explains Milligan, "If you want to really get on target, you might have to move that dispersion pattern around a little bit." As a result of the firing of a number of missions that day and the expenditure of a total of 288 rounds, the *New Jersey* achieved what she set out to – the silencing of the gun batteries ashore.

Throughout much of the long day, which called for the ship to move from place to place between missions, Captain Milligan was in the combat engagement center on the 02 level. With him were the ship's weapons officer and a tactical action officer. Although Milligan was clearly in overall charge of the operation, he ran it by the principal of negation – interfering only if something needed to be corrected. His role was that of overseer and decision-maker. As Milligan explains, "I had awfully capable people, and if everything was going exactly the way it should go, then, of course, I wasn't going to step into anything. But, of course, I took all the reports. I knew exactly what was going on." Even so, observed Ensign John Donovan, the captain did a lot of pacing back and forth that day. There was an understandable desire to do something, and the system meant that subordinates were, in nearly all cases, doing things before they got to the captain's level.

With the commanding officer in the combat engagement center and viewing the situation by electronic means, the executive officer, Captain Richard McKenna, was on the bridge as the skipper's alter ego. McKenna had a supervisory function which included keeping an eye on the gun target line as safety observer and monitoring the ship-handling functions, as a captain did in days of old. As always, though, the exec had to keep up with paperwork, so he had a little table next to the captain's chair and handled administrative chores there. When he heard the salvo alarm for each projectile he ducked down to avoid the blast but kept his hands on the table so that his papers wouldn't be blown away. Once a round was gone, he stood up again and resumed writing.

**Below:** The *New Jersey* fires a broadside at Lebanon as part of her 288-round bombardment on 8 February 1984. (Courtesy USS *New Jersey*)

Ensign Greg Miller came to the conclusion that the officers and men of the *New Jersey* spent that day doing something which was at the same time satisfying and very demanding. Handling nearly 300 heavy projectiles and six times as many powder bags was exhausting physically, so there was a special concern to observe all the proper safety procedures in the turrets, the magazines, projectile decks, and so forth. Otherwise, tiredness could lead to carelessness or inattentiveness, and problems could result. The bombardment was carried off without a hitch. Remembers Miller, "It was an incredible strain on the crew, particularly the officers. The turret officers [and] the plotting room officers . . . were basically going in port-and-starboard shifts. But yet, we were so excited it really didn't matter. The adrenaline was really pumping."

Late in the afternoon, the firing was still in progress. Fire Controlman Dan Clairmont was off duty for a while in the port-and-starboard routine in the plotting room, and he had taken his life jacket to his bunk in case the massive bombardment provoked retaliation. As he lay in his rack, an urgent message came through the general announcing system, delivered in a shaking, frightened voice, "Now man all Harpoon stations." On the bridge, the junior officer of the deck looked at Ensign John Donovan and said, "My God, we're actually at war."

Ensign Barry McDonough saw a chief petty officer running down a passageway with the engagement keys for the Harpoon missile console in the combat engagement center. All sorts of thoughts went through McDonough's mind, including the notion that the Soviets might have decided to retaliate on behalf of the Syrians. McDonough's general quarters station was in the wardroom, which was to be set up as a battle dressing station. Even though general quarters hadn't been set, McDonough concluded it soon would be, so he went running forward to the wardroom, frantically whipped open the door from the starboard passageway, and ran right into the senior officers' table, where dinner was in

**Below:** Bow view of the firing on 8 February. (Courtesy USS *New Jersey*)

progress. The executive officer, Captain McKenna, looked up calmly from his meal in response to McDonough's dramatic entrance, and the ensign realized things weren't so bad as he thought. So, he says, "I figured I'd sit down and eat dinner."

Ensign John Donovan had come down from the bridge and begun eating also. Then another frantic message came through over the loudspeaker, because Commander Task Force 60 had ordered all Navy ships in the eastern Mediterranean to go to general quarters immediately. The general alarm went through its strident bong-bong-bong, and the man passing the word called the crew to battle stations. Donovan says of the word-passer: "He was terrified – you could tell. Everyone just looked at each other for a split second and said, 'Oh my God, this is it.'" Donovan decided that if he were going to war, he didn't know when he would next get to eat, so he determined to finish his lasagna. He was sufficiently unnerved that it took him five tries to get the last bite into his mouth, because it fell off the fork on the first four attempts. Even as he was finishing his meal, he observed that the mess specialists on duty weren't bothering to clear the wardroom tables in customary fashion. Instead, they just bundled up the tablecloths, plates, glasses, silverware, lasagna, and all – and tossed the whole pile into a corner. Before Donovan left the wardroom, two battle dressing stations had been set up.

Down in the mess deck, the menu that evening also had an Italian flavor. Storekeeper Second Class Richard Wolpin was in charge of a mess line, clicking off the numbers to show how many men were eating the spaghetti dinner. Then came the word over the loudspeaker. He remembers, "Everybody froze for a split second, then everybody scattered like ants when you pour water on them." Some people sent their trays clattering to the deck as they departed, leaving piles of spaghetti in their wake.

The threat did not materialize and the ship's crew relaxed from general quarters, although the firing of the big guns went on until the final 16-inch mission was finished at about 11:00 that night. In explaining the manning of the antiship missile battery that day, Milligan offers, "We did, in fact, man the Harpoon stations, based on a potential threat, and I'll say no more. And then I would also tell you that we were prepared the next morning for any potential retaliation against us."

The men of the *New Jersey* never did find out exactly what they had accomplished by their heavy gunfire on 8 February. Greg Miller recalls, "There was a big question mark over everyone's head on February the ninth. We wanted to know what had been done. Outwardly, what we observed was that everything quieted up in Beirut. . . . There was no small arms fire for maybe the entire week after that, that I was aware of." According to the "mess decks intelligence", the ship had taken out several Syrian gun emplacements, some rocket launchers, and a Syrian command post. The latter suggestion was heightened by a rumor that the *New Jersey*'s fire had killed a Syrian general and his staff. As of yet, neither the Defense Department nor the Navy has released an unclassified report on the results and effectiveness of the heavy shelling that day. The concussions from the many salvoes did produce internal damage in the ship, including bursting a water pipe in the captain's sea cabin. Milligan discovered that his bunk was soaked when he was about to lie down and rest in the early morning hours of 9 Feburary.

As it happened, there was no retaliation for the big day of shooting, and so the *New Jersey* resumed her pattern of patrolling off the beach, ready to respond if necessary. On 21 February, the Marines began their redeployment from the airport compound to the Sixth Fleet amphibious warfare ships offshore. On the 26th, the redeployment of the 22nd Marine Amphibious Unit was completed, and only a small force of Marines remained behind. Also on 26 February, the *New Jersey* fired thirteen rounds of 16-inch after U.S. reconnaissance planes were again fired upon by hostile forces ashore.

Throughout the early months of the new year, the R&R flights back to the States were continuing – amounting to seven eventually for a total of 727 men who managed to get home. The crew as a whole got a break on 2 March when the ship pulled in and anchored at Haifa, Israel, for a seven-day port visit. This was the first chance the crew had for liberty since last leaving Haifa on 3 January. After the second visit, the ship once again returned to her patrol station off Beirut. Though the bulk of the Marines had gone, the ship's presence was still considered necessary. On 21 March came still another USO show in the form of the Dallas Cowboy cheerleaders. They were a welcome sight for *New Jersey*'s crew members who got to see women so seldom.

On 2 April, Captain Milligan spoke to the crew on the closed-circuit television system to tell them that as far as he knew, the mission was going to continue until the ship was relieved by the *Iowa*. About an hour and a half later, he was called to the combat engagement center where he received a radio message directing the ship to leave Beirut right away. Three days later, the *New Jersey* was in Naples, Italy, and the six-month ordeal off the coast of Lebanon was over. With the Marine force having gone and the United States reluctantly concluding that its presence in the multinational force was not keeping peace after all, it would no longer be necessary to wait for the arrival of the *Iowa*. She wouldn't be coming.

The *New Jersey* stayed in the Italian city until 11 April and then went to the picturesque port of Villefranche, France, for a visit from 12 until 15 April. Back in the 1950s, when France was still in the NATO military setup, ships of the Sixth Fleet regularly called at Villefranche, and the fleet flagship was home-ported there. In the early 1960s, however, under President Charles de Gaulle, France pulled

its military forces out of NATO, and the Sixth Fleet moved its locus to Italy. In early 1984, France, Italy, and the United States had all been partners in the effort off Beirut, so it was a nice touch for those Mediterranean nations to put out the welcome mat on the way home.

After all the time off Lebanon without liberty, the situation had reversed itself. Now there were port visits back to back, and so the deployment was ending as it had begun, with stops in foreign ports. For Storekeeper Second Class Richard Wolpin, Villefranche was a delight. The French Government had requested that the battleship's crew members wear civilian clothes ashore, and so they went from place to place as American tourists. While in Monaco, Wolpin visited the ritzy section of Monte Carlo and concluded that the prices there were even worse than the ones he'd been put off by in Singapore. At Nice he saw lawn bowling and a beach set aside for nude sunbathing. And in Villefranche itself, he was invited home for dinner by a French man and his wife who came originally from Michigan.

On 15 April, the *New Jersey* was again under way, heading this time for the Strait of Gibraltar, which she passed through two days later. On 27 April, she went through the Panama Canal after a transatlantic crossing which wasn't so rapid as the one in September but still faster than normal for a peacetime passage. The *New Jersey* got back to her home port on 5 May with the crew in dress whites and paraded at every available space topside.

It was fifteen years to the day from the time of the *New Jersey*'s return to Long Beach from the Vietnam War. In both cases, the return had been delayed, but this time it was far, far longer. The ship was surrounded by small boats, and streams of water spouted skyward from fireboats.

Some 5,000 people were waiting to welcome the returning battleship that bright May day. Fire Controlman Dan Clairmont's eyes were filled with tears of happiness; he was also so eager to be ashore that it was hard to maintain the discipline that kept him standing at his spot on deck. On land, Clairmont's wife Gail and his father Ray, an ex-Navy man, held the two ends of a 5-foot-long hand-painted sign which welcomed their man in red, white, and blue. As tugboats moved the mighty grey warship in toward the pier, Gail Clairmont spotted her returning husband and began jumping up and down with excitement, screaming, "There he is."

For long minutes, which seemed even longer to those both on ship and on shore while the giant dreadnought was being moored to the pier, people on both sides waited anxiously for the brows to be put into place. At last – at long last – the waiting was over. The two groups swarmed toward each other and joined in hundreds of happy embraces. The USS *New Jersey* was home from her fourth war.

# CHAPTER VIII
# THE BATTLESHIP BATTLE GROUP
## May 1984 – May 1986

**Left:** A floating crane taken over from the Germans after World War II is used to move a new gun barrel into position in August 1984 at Long Beach. This marks the first replacement of a 16-inch gun in the *New Jersey* since her overhaul in the autumn of 1954. (Courtesy USS *New Jersey*)

As soon as she got back to Long Beach in early May 1984, the *New Jersey* was transformed from a combat-ready warship to a barracks vessel for those few who had to be on board at a given time. The next year would be spent in reversing the process and preparing her to assume her operational duties once again. The year after that would be devoted to getting her ready for a challenging new role as the centerpiece of the Navy's first battleship battle group.

The shipyard period in 1981–82 had not been a full overhaul. It was a modernization superimposed on a reactivation, and if there were items of shipyard work that were nice to have but not essential, they were deferred for the post-shakedown availability period scheduled for the autumn of 1983. If something worked at reactivation time, shipyard attention went to other things. Pieces of equipment that were supposed to hold up for a three-month deployment to the Western Pacific had instead been subjected to nearly eleven months of use, day in and day out, while at sea. Wear and tear had taken their toll on both men and equipment. Remedies were at hand for both.

For the ship herself, the Long Beach Naval Shipyard set to work fixing the many things which needed attention. For the crew, there had to be a duty section on board each day, but the rest of the men got liberty shortly after quarters each morning for the first month. During the second month back home, men were working only half days as they spent time with their families or otherwise enjoyed the pleasures of being ashore. Signalman Third Class Dave Hammond enjoyed resuming activities, such as going downtown to a movie or taking a long walk, that are normally taken for granted but just weren't possible during the long months at sea. "It was kind of strange being on land again after being out of circulation for so long," he remembers. He had the new experience of being able to look from the land to the sea, instead of the other way around. Men who had been out of touch with the popular culture began catching up on such things as current events, movies, and music they had missed during their absence.

Quartermaster John Trail got involved with the crew of the replica sailing ship used for the remake of the movie "Mutiny on the *Bounty*" and went out at times for rides with the crew. Disneyland was a popular attraction for *New Jersey* men and their families. Crew members could bring in their ticket stubs for recreational events – except for movies – and be reimbursed from the ship's welfare and recreation fund. The money had accumulated from the profits generated in the ship's store during the long deployment, so it was their own money they were using for their outings in Southern California. The Olympic Games were held in Los Angeles during that summer of 1984, and they drew the attention of crew members, sometimes in person and often on television. Lieutenant Eric Massa of the *New Jersey* established a most successful program for inter-ship athletics, setting up teams in such things as softball and bowling. Men formed a scuba-diving club, and there was even a rodeo club whose members rode brahma bulls while wearing wide-brimmed western hats with the ship's name on the front. Some men from the ship went on a busmen's holiday, visiting the *Missouri*, then at the outset of her reactivation period at Long Beach. They found it fascinating to compare the interior of the other ship – which appeared to have been sealed in a time capsule in the mid-1950s – with that of their own considerably more modernized vessel.

Symbolic of the *New Jersey*'s status that summer as a non-combatant was the offloading of ammunition at Seal Beach, California, from 4 to 7 June in preparation for her shipyard period. She returned to the Long Beach Naval Station on the seventh, but this stay was brief. On 9 June, just over a month after her return to home port, the battleship got under way for a leisurely seven-hour family day cruise toward Santa Catalina Island and back. Fire Control-man Dan Clairmont especially enjoyed the opportunity to bring his wife and other relatives aboard. After months of having him gone, they could now see the spaces in which he lived and worked instead of having to try to imagine what they were like. He and others had a chance to demonstrate their technical proficiency with the ship's gear. All told, there were 2,266 family members and guests on board that day as the ship ran through a series of pre-overhaul trials of her equipment. The guests enjoyed an open-air meal on the fantail. One visitor, John Whitmeyer, described the repast by saying, "We were fed mountains of barbecue chicken, hamburgers, hot dogs, and all that goes with a picnic. One's appetite improves at sea." Whitmeyer, a Navy veteran from World War II, served in the old battleship *New York* in 1943. The trip forty-one years later rekindled fond memories as the former quartermaster

Below: The new barrel is inserted into the center of turret two. (Courtesy USS *New Jersey*)

spent time around the bridge and went on a tour which included the turrets, gun mounts, plotting rooms, and engineering spaces. The *New Jersey*, with her ammunition offloaded, was escorted by the guided missile cruiser *Fox* during the day.

One sour note followed a few weeks later when the *Los Angeles Times* published a letter to the editor from Sandra Wilson of El Monte, California. She complained about the ship's excursion, saying it seemed "to be a waste of valuable energy and tax dollars for just a pleasure cruise for the crew's relatives". The newspaper was soon inundated with rejoinders defending the cruise, citing the hardships the families had put up with during the deployment just past. Another argument was that the dollars spent for the cruise would pay dividends in terms of morale; by keeping crew members content and building a sense of solidarity with their families, they would be retained in the Navy and would not have to be replaced by new men who would cost money to train.

On 15 June, the *New Jersey* shifted to pier one at the Long Beach Naval Shipyard and began her availability period. One example of the work which had been deferred during the reactivation was the replacement of the center 16-inch barrel of turret two. In the 1981–82 shipyard period, excessive wear was discovered in the barrel's liner, and so it was not to be used during the short summer deployment in 1983. Eventually, of course, there was a much longer delay before it could be used again. In August 1984, the barrel was replaced by one which had been in

storage for many years. The old barrel was taken out by a large floating crane known as Titan II, taken over from Germany after World War II. The replacement was a big, difficult job, involving wrenches which weighed more than fifty pounds and other tools which were more than 200 pounds. Robert Weston, a technical adviser from the naval ordnance station in Louisville, Kentucky, was quoted in *Surface Warfare* magazine concerning the complexity of the undertaking: "We're talking about a barrel 68' long weighing 239,156 lb. You can't work fast with something like that." It was the *New Jersey*'s first 16-inch barrel replacement since 1954.

Elsewhere in the ship, habitability was being improved in areas which hadn't received the full treatment during the reactivation. In the heads new deck coverings were put down and new partitions and privacy screens installed. The ancient interior communication system got a substantial upgrading. Chief Interior Communications Electrician Arturo Mota explains that the 1MC, the ship-wide general announcing system, was of an outmoded tube type which overheated during prolonged use. It had to be unkeyed briefly every forty-five to sixty seconds so it could cool. This caused problems during long messages or when the boatswain's mate of the watch piped the long call to chow. With a new system installed during the yard period, the troubles were a thing of the past. Mota was also involved in the modernization of the ship's telephone system. The old switchboard, down near the after main battery plotting room, had had to be manned in port by enlisted men serving as operators. Thanks to a new digital, computer-controlled system, the phones can now be programmed automatically to hook up to outside lines when in port and thus no longer need human operators.

Equipment was also installed and improved in the engineering spaces, including upgrades to the lube oil service pumps in the engine rooms. In October, the ship passed her light-off exam and was certified in early November to light off her propulsion plant once again. Then it was out to the Southern California operating area on 14–15 November for two days of sea trials to certify work done in the shipyard. Captain Rich Genet, the executive officer, was accustomed to post-overhaul sea details which represent collective confusion as a ship prepares for sea after a long time away. He was pleasantly surprised by how smoothly the *New Jersey*'s crew got her out of port and headed for sea. The yard period ended officially on 21 November when the battleship moved from the shipyard to the Long Beach Naval Station.

The move faciliated access for the members of crewmen's families as they came aboard the following day, 22 November, to celebrate Thanksgiving. It was a welcome contrast to the setting of 1983 when the holiday fell during the battleship's ceaseless patrolling off Lebanon. For the 1984 version Ensign Jim French, the *New Jersey*'s food service officer, had his staff of fifty cooks working for hours to prepare the feast to be served to 800 people. The first group of cooks started preparations at 6:00 p.m. on Wednesday, the day of the move to the naval station. At midnight, another crew set to work baking dinner rolls and pies. The turkey roasters put the birds in the ovens at 2:00 a.m. on Thanksgiving day, twelve hours before the meal was served. The dinner consisted of forty-four roasted turkeys, ten steamship rounds of beef, 300 pounds of baked ham, 400 pounds of mashed poatoes, forty gallons of gravy, and 300 pies – apple, cherry, and pumpkin – for dessert.

All too soon, it was back to sea again, on 3 December. First there was a partial reloading of ammunition at Seal Beach and then a trip to the operating area offshore to conduct further engineering trials and to test fire the 16-inch guns, 5-inch, and the Vulcan/Phalanx close-in weapon system. Included was the first firing of the center gun of turret two since 1969. In mid-January of 1985, the ship passed her inspection and survey (InSurv) trials and demonstrated that her material condition was satisfactory for fleet service.

Along with the rebuilding of the ship in a material sense, there also had to be a rebuilding in crew readiness. With the coming of the new year of 1985, there had been much turnover in the crew during the nearly eight months since the return to Long Beach. In December 1984, there had been an exodus of men who had served two years on board since the ship went into commission in late 1982. During the long in-port period, experienced petty officers such as Fire Controlman Dan Clairmont were passing on to new men the things they had learned. Clairmont, who had learned much under the tutelage of Senior Chief Rick Crawford in 1983, was now a senior man himself. He considered it an obligation to pass on his knowledge of the New Jersey's fire control systems as a legacy to those who would serve in the ship following his departure for civilian life.

There was, however, only so much that could be done with the ship in port, and the lectures and lessons by people such as Clairmont had to be applied during a period of refresher training which would exercise the crew as a whole. Refresher training was advanced two months for the ship, recalls Captain Genet, then the exec, and it was also shortened from six weeks to three because of the possibility that the New Jersey would be called for an out-of-area contingency operation. The situation which might have called back the New Jersey in a fashion similar to that of 1983 did not eventuate in 1985.

On 4 February, the New Jersey left Long Beach and steamed south for San Diego and exercises conducted by the fleet traning group based there. The training, interrupted by weekends in port, went on for much of the month. There was so much talent in the wardroom and among senior petty officers that the ship was able to overcome the large-scale crew member replacement it had experienced, including more than 50 per cent of the chief petty officers, since May 1984. Captain Genet remembers, "We had the same sort of minor traumas that any ship going through refresher training has, but it was largely a cakewalk." He was also struck by the crew's great pride in their ship. For instance, if the rubber fender of a tugboat made a black smudge mark on the battleship's hull, the boatswain's mates scrubbed and repainted the area right away. They wanted her appearance to befit her status.

One thing which provided some respite for the crew in between the training periods was the opportunity to use two new shipboard gymnasiums. The forward area had a piece of equipment known as a universal gym and was primarily for weight-lifting and strength development. The after gym was created in the area which had previously served as the brig but was no longer used in that role. It was set up for aerobic training with equipment such as stationary bicycles and rowing machines.

After the refresher training wrapped up on 28 February, the ship anchored off the Seal Beach Naval Weapons Station that evening and completed the loading of ammunition on 1 March. She arrived at Long Beach that day and soon began a twenty-day period in port for upkeep. During one of the battleship's returns to home port, Captain Rich Milligan saw evidence that confirmed the value of the sewage collection, holding, and transfer systems installed in the New Jersey and the rest of the Navy's ships. As the ship approached her assigned pier, there was a sea otter catching fish in the New Jersey's berth. "I don't think you would have seen that fifteen years ago," says Milligan. "I think that's a good indication of what that program's done for us, ecology-wise."

One highlight of the in-port period was a day of running sponsored by the New Jersey and two local businesses on Sunday, 10 March. Signalman Dave Hammond observed that the ship was making a conscious effort to provide the crew with recreational activities other than drinking. In addition to the shipboard gyms and plan of the day notes on various liberty activities ashore, there were athletic events such as the 10 March races. Included were a one-mile run and a 6.2-miler. Officially, the latter was 10 kilometers, but 6.2 miles had more of a ring to it because of the similarity to the New Jersey's hull number. The event was also opened to the first 1,000 members of the public who were willing to pay an entry fee of $9.00. Along with the chance to run, the civilians got a New Jersey T-shirt, refreshments, and a visit to the ship herself at the conclusion of the race.

Despite the best of efforts to channel men into non-alcoholic recreation, there continued to be those who followed the more traditional pursuits. Two establishments frequented by New Jersey men were the Fireside Inn and the Fleet Inn. To stimulate business, the bartenders wore BB-62 baseball caps and had photos of the battleship and other vessels on the walls.

In late March, the ship was under way once more as part of the long, long process of preparing her for her next overseas deployment; included was more and more training. In mid-April, she requalified her main and secondary battery guns at the shore bombardment range on San Clemente Island. Then it was back to port for another engineering test beginning on 6 May, the Operational Propulsion Plant Examination. The notorious OPPE became the bane of many a warship's existence when introduced in the 1970s because it set higher standards for conventional steam propulsion plants than many ships were used to maintaining. For years, the Navy's nuclear-powered ships had been forced to meet high standards, and now the standards were upgraded for the other ships as well. The *New Jersey* failed her first attempt at the OPPE. The test was terminated as incomplete on 9 May and later passed when conducted from 26 to 28 June.

Executive Officer Genet offers an explanation for the first test: "Perhaps we were a little bit too overconfident and perhaps also there were problems which surfaced in the bringing up of 1945 systems to 1985 standards which were not trivial in their resolution." Part of the difficulty was in the documentation of training done on the old systems. Also, for instance, the OPPE standards on such things as steam leaks and water leaks are much more stringent than when the *New Jersey*'s equipment was manufactured. It wasn't that the ship was unsafe, because she had been steaming for years. But her men had to do even better, and they were greatly assisted toward that goal by the work of Lieutenant Commander Jeff Quinn. Even though he was the *New Jersey*'s assistant weapons officer, he had previously been in a ship's engineering department and assisted the battleship's engineers in raising their operating documentation and procedures to the standards of the 1980s.

The ship was in and out of port the next several months, including a visit to San Diego in early June. On 9 June she was named winner of the Spokane Trophy. It had been donated by the citizens of that Washington city in 1908 and was presented for years thereafter to the Navy ship with the best gun turret marksmanship. After being in limbo since the beginning of World War II, the trophy was reinstated in 1985 to honor excellence in surface ship combat systems readiness.

On 10 June, the *New Jersey* embarked twenty-four members of the ship's assigned Naval Reserve unit from Trenton, New Jersey, so they could undergo their annual two weeks of active duty for training. On 16 June, the battleship took aboard fifteen first class midshipmen and fifteen third class for four weeks of summer training. The total of thirty was far below the hundreds who used to come aboard in the 1950s.

On 28 June, after passing the retest on her propulsion plant, the *New Jersey* arrived at Long Beach for a brief stay before leaving for the Central Pacific on 10 July in company

with the cruisers *Jouett*, *Halsey*, and *England*; the destroyers *Chandler*, *O'Brien*, and *Ingersoll*; and the frigate *Reasoner*. The battleship arrived in Pearl Harbor on 18 July and rendered honors to the *Arizona*, as she had during her visit in 1983. The effect on the *New Jersey*'s crew was much the same. Photographer's Mate Third Class Barry Orell observed that, "The atmosphere got almost churchlike. It was almost like a cold chill when you passed, then a festive occasion again." The festive occasions in Hawaii included the many liberty attractions usually available and highlighted this time by a luau for the crew. A pig underwent a long, slow cooking in the ground, and the crew also feasted on chicken, poi, and salmon. Following a local custom, Hawaiian girls lined up to greet a line of *New Jersey* men with kisses, something which Petty Officer Orell found to be a most agreeable practice. Some men found their way to the bars of Waikiki, and local citizens found their way to the ship for tours. Some were struck by the museum quality of the ship, including the many brass fittings such as voice tubes on the bridge.

Twenty-four more midshipmen came aboard at Pearl Harbor for training, and then the ship got under way on 22 July for an exercise in the Hawaiian operating area. Embarked for the day was actor Tom Selleck, who plays a former naval officer in the popular "Magnum P.I." television series. The ship was back to Pearl on 29 August and then again under way on 1 August for a voyage to San

Francisco. On 3 August, the *New Jersey* fired a nine-gun broadside with the main battery. Because of the previous problems with the center gun in turret two, this was the first time she fired a nine-gun salvo since recommissioning. Photographer's Mate Orell was assigned to take pictures and remembered afterward, "There was just such a massive ball of flame." Following the firing, he recalls, "The smell of gun powder just permeated the ship." He had seen other effects earlier in the photo lab, just forward of turret three. One day the firing of the 16-inch guns knocked out a fuse and turned out all the lights in the lab. The next day, the concussion from turret three turned all the lights back on.

The ship arrived at San Francisco on 8 August to enjoy a visit to the port and to participate in a celebration commemorating the fortieth anniversary of VJ Day, the victory over Japan. Because of modern sensitivities, however, the occasion was billed as the "Fortieth Anniversary of Peace in the Pacific". Mayor Dianne Feinstein of San Francisco made the men of the *New Jersey* feel especially welcome. The city had just won the Navy's competition to serve as home port for the *Missouri,* and the mayor was eager to extend hospitality. Chief Journalist Lon Cabot recalls that some crew members were invited into the homes of local residents. And there was a dance held for the men of the *New Jersey.* For the occasional crew member who had too much to drink, the San Francisco police joined the hospitable spirit. The police gave such men "courtesy rides" back to the ship rather than taking them to a police station and writing up an official report.

The ship was also hospitable; more than 21,000 visitors came aboard on 10 and 11 August. Tables were set up on deck to sell *New Jersey* souvenirs, including baseball caps, T-shirts, and so forth. One petty officer from the battleship recalls that the blue and gold embroidered caps were as good as legal tender ashore. He explains, "You could take a ballcap out in town and give it to a bartender and drink all night."

The ship was under way for some five hours on 13 August, steaming a circuit around San Francisco Bay to practice for the next day's official celebration. The crew was manning the rail topside at parade rest. The long period of standing, combined with brisk, chilly winds, dampened the men's ardor for the event. The next day the period of standing was shorter and more pleasant as the crew went through the real thing, joining other ships in making a circuit past the anchored aircraft carrier *Enterprise* with Vice President George Bush embarked. The *New Jersey* and *Enterprise* exchanged gun salutes as the battleship passed. Forty years earlier, the *New Jersey* and an earlier USS *Enterprise* were part of the victorious fleet at the end of World War II.

The ship left for Long Beach on 15 August with more than seventy male relatives of crew members on board for a three-day "tiger cruise". It was an extended version of the

Opposite page, top: On 3 August 1985, the *New Jersey* fires a nine-gun broadside for the first time since recommissioning. (PH2 Rich Sforza)

Opposite page, bottom: The San Francisco waterfront provides the backdrop on 14 August 1985 as the *New Jersey* fires a gun salute while steaming past the anchored carrier *Enterprise*. The occasion is the 40th anniversary of VJ Day. (AP/Wide World)

Top right: The crew mans the rail at San Francisco on 14 August. (Photo by Giorgio Arra; courtesy Norman Polmar)

Bottom right: This stern view of the ship at San Francisco shows the extent to which non-skid deck covering has been laid over the teak deck to enlarge the area for helicopter operations. (Photo by Giorgio Arra; courtesy Norman Polmar)

dependents' day cruise held off Southern California in June 1984.

On 7 September, during the course of a long in-port period at Long Beach, the battleship underwent a change of command. Captain Milligan had taken over on 15 September 1983, during the hurried transit toward the Mediterranean. Now he was relieved by Captain Lew Glenn in a much more traditional form in port with the customary pomp, circumstance, and visitors. On this occasion, Milligan received the acclaim due him for the long, arduous service off Lebanon and was frocked in the rank of commodore, for he had been chosen for flag rank by the previous year's selection board. In concluding a tour of nearly two years, Captain Rich Milligan was leaving as the officer with the longest tenure in command of the *New Jersey*. His two nearest predecessors in terms of length of service were Captain Carl Holden, skipper from May 1943 to January 1945, and Captain John Atkeson, from September 1953 to March 1955.

The new man – tall, thin, polished Lew Glenn – reported from a tour as executive assistant to the Deputy Chief of Naval Operations (Surface Warfare) in Washington. The easygoing, friendly new skipper brought a background combining postgraduate education, staff duty, and service in surface combatants. During the Vietnam War, he was flag lieutenant for Vice Admiral Elmo Zumwalt when the future Chief of Naval Operations was Commander U.S. Naval Forces Vietnam. The men of the *New Jersey* were to be concerned not so much with Glenn's background as with the qualities of leadership he brought to the battleship, and they liked what they saw – and heard.

During the latter part of his tour in command, Captain Milligan was no longer so accessible as he had been in the months soon after reporting aboard. Part of his isolation was inevitable because of the demands of staying in close reach of communication circuits while off Lebanon. Later, like many in the crew, he was doubtless tired after the month-in, month-out strains of watchful waiting near Beirut. Glenn, fresh from a desk job ashore, brought the zest of a man eager to get to sea after the confines of Pentagon duty. The early Glenn much resembled the early Milligan – frequently walking around the ship, striking up conversations with the sailors, eating in the various messes, and making himself accessible to anyone who wanted to speak personally with the commanding officer. His approach was fueled by an infectious enthusiasm and a desire to share his feeling for the ship with those serving in her. The closed-circuit television station has been a sometime medium for this approach, but far more frequent is Glenn's use of the general announcing system. *New Jersey* men have grown accustomed to being informed by him on an almost daily basis and even more frequently when the ship is at sea and operating. As one of the battleship's chief petty officers puts it, "The actual word is coming down to the deckplates to let us know what is going on."

Captain Glenn notes that many, many of the current crew members have the same sort of enthusiasm and desire to serve their ship well. As one example, he cites a master chief boilertender who found that rebricking the *New Jersey*'s eight boilers would be quite a costly task. Instead, the master chief organized the ship's force to do the job over the next several months, one boiler at a time. In some instances, it had been many years since the last rebricking. The old bricks that came out were covered with a heavy black slag, up to three-quarters of an inch thick, from the time when the ship still burned black oil. The new bricks, without the slag layer, provide more efficient burning, and, thanks to the lighter distillate fuel now used in the boilers, there shouldn't be a future problem with buildup of the tar-like residue. The crew saved hundreds of thousands of dollars by doing the job themselves.

In late October 1985, the *New Jersey* got under way for training off Southern California, including naval gunfire support qualification on the 30th and 31st at San Clemente Island. On 3 and 4 November, she took on more ammunition at Seal Beach, and then participated in a fleet readiness exercise. The workout provided a test of the usefulness of the missile-armed battleship in a combat environment. Part of the time was spent with a nuclear-powered aircraft carrier working up to prepare for a deployment to the Western Pacific. On one occasion the carrier and the battleship were separated by several hundred miles, recalls Captain Glenn, when the carrier's planes located some surface targets. Using targeting information provided by the aircraft, the *New Jersey* simulated firing at them with her missiles. The exercise ended with the battleship making a high-speed run at night and coming in for a simulated main battery shore bombardment mission at first light the next morning, as if

supporting an amphibious assault. After that, the *New Jersey* returned to her home port on 22 November.

She was back at sea again on 3 December and was soon trailed by a Soviet intelligence collection vessel. The *New Jersey* steamed south during the night with her electronic equipment turned off in order to be difficult to detect. Not long after midnight, the battleship turned north, having evaded the Soviet, and didn't turn on her electronc gear until shortly before her Tomahawk firing mission that day. In May 1983, the battleship fired a land-attack version of the missile. This time, she tried the antiship type. Chief Journalist Lon Cabot was on the fantail to photograph the firing and observed an almost circus-like atmosphere – "raw excitement," he says.

As had the Tomahawk in 1983, this one hesitated momentarily after leaving the launcher until the booster caught hold, then roared away. This time, however, there was a lower trajectory than for the much longer range of

**Left:** Aerial view amidships, showing eight armored box launchers for Tomahawk missiles and quadruple canister launchers for Harpoon. (Photo by Giorgio Arra; courtesy Norman Polmar)

**Right:** Captain Lew Glenn and his ship's officers sit for a formal portrait on the *New Jersey*'s forecastle on 2 October 1985. (Courtesy USS *New Jersey*)

the land-attack version, which went several hundred miles. As the missile flew away, trailing a plume of white smoke, Cabot remembers, "It was as much a spectator event in the middle of the ocean as if there had been a lot of civilians on board." The missile scored a direct hit on its target, making the first battleship test of an antiship Tomahawk a successful one. The *New Jersey* returned to Long Beach the following day and closed out the year with a leave period for the crew and a visit by Santa Claus for the children of crew members.

The Long Beach routine was interrupted for a while in mid-January 1986 as the ship again enjoyed the delights of San Francisco and once more opened up for general visiting. From mid-February to early March, the *New Jersey* was involved in yet another new role during her latest incarnation – preparation for deployment at the heart of a battleship battle group. Since World War II, the striking power of the U.S. Navy has been built around aircraft carriers. Combined with the escorts of their battle groups, they have conducted hundreds of overseas deployments on behalf of national interests. Because of the carriers' strenuous operating schedules, Navy planners have sought ways to provide relief for their crews. The tentative solution – for peacetime, at least – is to build some of the battle groups around battleships and have them substitute for carriers in the deployment rotation. During her at-sea period in early 1986, the *New Jersey* worked with the cruiser *Long Beach*, destroyers *Merrill* and *Fletcher*, frigates *Bronstein, Copeland, Stein*, and *Thach*, and the replenishment oiler *Wabash*.

Together the ships worked out tactics and procedures to be used during a deployment to the Western Pacific, beginning in mid-May. Captain Glenn explains that since the *New Jersey, Long Beach*, and *Merrill* all are equipped with Tomahawk missiles, the ships were able to demonstrate the concept of distributed offense – that several ships firing together could send missiles toward a target from different points on the compass. The various duties of a battle group were parcelled out to the major combatants, with the *New Jersey* running the surface warfare picture, the *Long Beach* handling antiair warfare, and the *Merrill* in charge on antisubmarine warfare. With all the combatants in the battle group equipped with Harpoon missiles, the ships were able to demonstrate a distributed capability in that area as well. The finale to the workup came with simultaneous firing of Harpoons from an aircraft, submarine, and surface ship. Glenn says, "We were able to accomplish this mission with three hits within minutes of each other, and . . . when they went to search for the target, there was nothing but debris."

As the *New Jersey* was returning to Long Beach following the workup, she encountered a long-lost sister. The *Missouri*, not yet in commission, was out on sea trials. It was the first time since 1954 that the two ships had operated within sight of each other. Signalman Second

Class Dave Hammond of the *New Jersey* exchanged a number of visual signals with the younger ship and welcomed her back. Photographer's Mate Barry Orell and his shipmates had a new experience in being able to observe another battleship's silhouette on the horizon. They were struck by the *Missouri*'s long, low profile and the rake of her bow. Now they knew what their own ship looked like to others.

With her return to home port on 8 March, the at-sea preparations were complete. Now it remained for the last items of upkeep and maintenance to be attended to during the two remaining months before deployment. Crew members got to spend more time with their families and to get their affairs in order for the months of absence ahead. Families were briefed on the people or agencies to contact in the event of emergencies. Several hundred *New Jersey* men and their guests gathered on the deck of the battleship for a striking Easter sunrise service. Captain Glenn, seeking a way for the ship to contribute to the community, offered a candlelight dinner for four in his cabin as an auction prize to raise money for the local symphony. Such is the ship's popularity that she drew a winning bid of $2,000. The crew, as before seeking non-alcoholic means of entertainment, formed a cast and rehearsed the patriotic play "1776", which was presented at the base theater of the Long Beach Naval Station at the beginning of May.

In preparation for her first-ever battle group deployment, the *New Jersey* added a surgeon to her crew. Since there would not be a carrier along to provide support for the small boys, the escorts would look to the battleship, as their predecessors had so often in times past, to keep the group self-sufficient. The deployment offered the prospect of tactical exercises, port visits, demonstrations of the newly constituted battle group's combatant capabilities, and – possibly – the *New Jersey*'s first venture into the Indian Ocean. When designed in the late 1930s, the ship was envisioned as part of the staunch backbone of the nation's defense. As her deployment began on 13 May 1986, just before the forty-third anniversary of her first commissioning, the USS *New Jersey* was again at the forefront of her country's naval might.

Right: Crew members on the *New Jersey*'s forecastle watch as the newly reactivated *Missouri*, background, undergoes sea trials off the coast of Southern California in March 1986. (Photo by PH2 Rick Sforza; courtesy USS *New Jersey*)

# APPENDIX 1
# COMMANDING OFFICERS OF *NEW JERSEY*

**Vice Admiral Carl Frederick Holden, U.S. Navy (Retired)**
**Commanding Officer, 23 May 1943–26 January 1945**
Born 25 May 1895 in Bangor, Maine. Entered U.S. Naval Academy in 1913 from Maine; graduated in March 1917. USS *Burrows* (DD-29), 1917–18. USS *Lansdale* (DD-101), 1918–19. USS *Mason* (DD-191), 1920–21. USS *Mahan* (DD-102), 1921–22. Postgraduate education in electrical communication engineering, Naval Postgraduate School, Annapolis, Maryland, and Harvard University, Cambridge, Massachusetts, 1922–24. Staff, Commander Destroyer Force Scouting Fleet, 1924–27. Member, U.S. Mission to Brazil, 1927–31. USS *Arizona* (BB-39), 1931–32. Staff, Commander Battleships Battle Force, 1932. Commanding Officer, USS *Tarbell* (DD-142), 1932–34. Staff, Commandant 14th Naval District, Pearl Harbor, Hawaii, 1934–36. USS *Idaho* (BB-42), 1936–37. Commanding Officer, USS *Ramapo* (AO-12), 1937–38. Communication Division, Office of the Chief of Naval Operations, Washington, D.C., 1938–40. Executive Officer, USS *Pennsylvania* (BB-38), 1940–41. Staff, Commander in Chief U.S. Fleet, Washington, D.C., 1942. Director of Naval Communications, Navy Department, Washington, D.C., 1942–43. Commanding Officer, USS *New Jersey* (BB-62), 1943–45. Commander Cruiser Division 18, 1945. Commander Training Command Atlantic Fleet, 1945–48. Commander Naval Base, New York, New York, 1948–51. Commander U.S. Naval Forces Germany, 1951–52. Retired from active duty 30 June 1952 and promoted to the rank of vice admiral on the basis of combat awards. Died 18 May 1953, St. Albans, New York.

**Admiral Edmund Tyler Wooldridge, U.S. Navy (Retired)**
**Commanding Officer, 26 January 1945–17 November 1945**
Born 5 January 1897 in Lawrenceburg, Kentucky. Entered U.S. Naval Academy in 1916 from Kentucky; graduated in June 1919 with the class of 1920. USS *Delaware* (BB-28), 1919–21. Naval Communications, Navy Department, Washington, D.C., 1921–22. USS *Delaware* (BB-28), 1922. USS *Galveston* (PG-31), 1922–23. USS *Chewink* (AM-39), Submarine Base, New London, Connecticut, 1923–24. USS *S-36* (SS-141), 1924–27. USS *Chaumont* (AP-5), 1927. Instructor U.S. Naval Academy, Annapolis, Maryland, 1927–29. Commanding Officer, USS *S-15* (SS-120), 1929–30. USS *Trenton* (CL-11), 1930–32. Naval Ammunition Depot, Hingham, Massachusetts, 1932–34. Staff, Commander Battleship Division Three, 1934–36. Commanding Officer, USS *Tattnall* (DD-125), 1936–37. Instructor U.S. Naval Academy, Annapolis, Maryland, 1937–39. Executive Officer, USS *Dobbin* (AD-3), 1939–41. Chief of Staff, Commander Task Force 24, 1941–43. Bureau of Naval Personnel, Navy Department, Washington, D.C., 1943–44. Commanding Officer, USS *New Jersey* (BB-62), 1945. Commander Cruiser Division 17, 1945–46. Commander Cruiser Division 13, 1946–47. Office of the Chief of Naval Operations, Washington, D.C., 1947–49. Commander Destroyer Force Atlantic Fleet, 1949–50. Deputy

Director for Politico-Military Affairs Joint Chiefs of Staff, Washington, D.C., 1950–53. Commander Battleship-Cruiser Force Atlantic Fleet, 1953–54. Commander Second Fleet/Striking Fleet Atlantic, 1954–55. Commandant, National War College, Washington, D.C., 1955–58. Placed on retired list 1 August 1958 and promoted to the rank of admiral on the basis of combat awards. Recalled to active duty as member of Ad Hoc Committee for Study and Revision of Officer Personnel Act, 1960–61. Released from active duty, 1 May 1961. Died 15 December 1968, Annapolis, Maryland.

**Rear Admiral Edward Mathew Thompson, U.S. Navy (Retired)**
**Commanding Officer, 17 November 1945–5 August 1946**
Born 15 February 1898 in Orestes, Indiana. Entered U.S. Naval Academy in 1917 from Kansas; graduated in June 1920 with the class of 1921A. USS *Arkansas* (BB-33), 1920–21. USS *Arizona* (BB-39), 1921–23. USS *Kennedy* (DD-306), 1923–26. Postgraduate education in mechanical engineering at Naval Postgraduate School, Annapolis, Maryland, and Columbia University, New York, New York, 1926–28. Staff, Commander Destroyer Squadron 14, 1928–29. USS *Barry* (DD-248), 1930. Staff, Commander Destroyer Squadron 14/Destroyer Squadron Three, 1930–31. New York Navy Yard, New York, New York, 1931–33. USS *Augusta* (CA-31), 1933–36. Bureau of Engineering, Navy Department, Washington, D.C., 1936–38. Commanding Officer, USS *Maury* (DD-401), 1938–40. Executive Officer, USS *Vestal* (AR-4), 1940–41. Office of the Chief Naval Operations, Office of the Secretary of the Navy, Navy Department, Washington, D.C., 1941–42. Executive Officer, USS *Massachusetts* (BB-59), 1942–43. Commander Destroyer Squadron 25, 1943–44. Officer in charge, Pacific Fleet Schools and Radar Center, Pearl Harbor, Hawaii, 1944–45. Staff, Commander Fifth Fleet, 1945. Commanding Officer, USS *New Jersey* (BB-62), 1945–46. Student, National War College, Washington, D.C., 1946–47. Chief of Staff, Commander Naval Forces Mediterranean/Commander Sixth Task Fleet, 1947–49. Office of the Chief of Naval Operations, Washington, D.C., 1949–50. Retired from active duty 1 July 1950 and promoted to the rank of rear admiral on the basis of combat awards. Died 24 January 1985, Bethesda, Maryland.

**Rear Admiral Leon Joseph Huffman, U.S. Navy (Retired)**
**Commanding Officer, 5 August 1946–23 May 1947**
Born 21 July 1898 in Tiffin, Ohio. Entered U.S. Naval Academy in 1918 from Ohio; graduated in June 1922. USS *Pennsylvania* (BB-38) 1922–25. Submarine School, New London, Connecticut, 1925. USS *S-11* (SS-116), 1925–29. Postgraduate education in general line course, Naval Postgraduate School, Annapolis, Maryland, 1929–30. Bureau of Navigation, Navy Department, Washington, D.C., 1930–31. Executive Officer, Commanding Officer, USS *S-46* (SS-157), 1931–34. Division of Fleet Training, Navy Department, Washington, D.C., 1934–36. Prospective Commanding Officer/Commanding

Captain Carl F. Holden.

Captain E. Tyler Wooldridge.

Captain Edward M. Thompson.

Captain Leon J. Huffman.

Captain George L. Menocal.

Commander J. Wilson Leverton, Jr.

Officer, USS *Pickerel* (SS-177), 1936–39. Bureau of Construction and Repair/Bureau of Ships, Navy Department, Washington, D.C., 1939–40. Office of U.S. Naval Attaché, London, England, 1940–41. Fleet Maintenance Division, Office of the Chief of Naval Operations, Washington, D.C., 1941. USS *Saratoga* (CV-3), 1941–42. Commander Submarine Division 42, 1942–43. Commander Submarine Division 43, 1943. Staff, Commander Submarines Atlantic Fleet, 1943–44. Commander Submarine Squadron 26, 1944–45. Staff, Commander in Chief Atlantic Fleet, 1945–46. Commanding Officer, USS *New Jersey* (BB-62), 1946–47. General Board, Navy Department, Washington, D.C., 1947–48. Chief of Staff, Commander Amphibious Force Pacific Fleet, 1948–50. Office of the Chief of Naval Operations, Washington, D.C., 1950–52. Commander Amphibious Group Four, 1952–53. Chief of Staff, Supreme Allied Commander Atlantic, 1953–55. Commander Submarine Force Pacific Fleet, 1955–56. Senior Member, Board of Inspection and Survey, Pacific Coast Section, 1956–57. Retired from active duty, 1 July 1957. Died 22 June 1974, Coronado, California.

**Rear Admiral George Lawrence Menocal, U.S. Navy (Retired)**
**Commanding Officer, 23 May 1947–14 February 1948**
Born 2 April 1899 in Key West, Florida. Entered U.S. Naval Academy in 1917 from North Carolina; graduated in June 1922. USS *Mississippi* (BB-41), 1922–25. Submarine School, New London, Connecticut, 1925. USS *S-9* (SS 114), 1925–29. Postgraduate education in general line school, Naval Postgraduate School, Annapolis, Maryland, 1929–30. American Electoral Mission, Nicaragua, 1930. Commanding Officer, USS *S-26* (SS-131), 1931–34. Student, Naval War College, Newport, Rhode Island, 1934–35. Staff, Commandant of the Sixth Naval District, Charleston, South Carolina, 1935–36. USS *Louisville* (CA-28), 1936–39. NROTC Unit, University of Washington, Seattle, Washington, 1939–40. Commanding Officer, USS *Charles F. Hughes* (DD-428), 1940–42. Commander Destroyer Division 14, 1942–43. Commander Destroyer Squadron Seven, 1943. Administrative Commander, Destroyer Squadron 27/Boston Representative, Commander Destroyers Atlantic Fleet, 1943–44. Staff, Commander First Naval District, Boston, Massachusetts, 1945–46. Head, Department of Foreign Languages, U.S. Naval Academy, Annapolis, Maryland, 1946–47. Commanding Officer, USS *New Jersey* (BB-62), 1947–48. Retired from active duty 1 March 1948 and promoted to the rank of rear admiral on the basis of combat awards. Died 2 January 1982, Fort Worth, Texas.

**Rear Admiral Joseph Wilson Leverton, Jr., U.S. Navy (Retired)**
**Commanding Officer, 14 February 1948–30 June 1948**
Born 26 January 1909 in Baltimore, Maryland. Entered U.S. Naval Academy in 1927 from Maryland; graduated in June 1931. USS *Augusta* (CA-31), 1931–36. USS *Tucker* (DD-374), 1936–38. Postgraduate education in the general line school, Naval Postgraduate School, Annapolis, Maryland, 1938–39. Bureau of Navigation, Navy Department, Washington, D.C., 1939–40. Commanding Officer, USS *Wasmuth* (DMS-15), 1940–43. Staff, Commander North Pacific Force, 1943. Staff, Commander Seventh Fleet, 1943–44. Staff, Commander Seventh Amphibious Force, 1944. Bureau of Ordance, Navy Department, Washington, D.C., 1944–47. Executive Officer, USS *New Jersey* (BB-62), 1947–48. Commanding Officer, USS *New Jersey* (BB-62), 1948. Student, Naval War College, Newport, Rhode Island, 1948–49. Staff, Industrial College of the Armed Forces, Washington, D.C., 1949–51. Commanding Officer, USS *Fremont* (APA-44), 1951–52. Head, Policy and Continental Defense Section;

Captain David M. Tyree.

Captain Francis D. McCorkle.

Captain Charles L. Melson.

Captain John C. Atkeson.

Captain Edward J. O'Donnell.

Captain Charles B. Brooks, Jr.

Delegate, Inter-American Defense Board and Assistant Head, Western Hemisphere Plans Section, Office of the Chief of Naval Operations, Washington, D.C., 1952–55. Commanding Officer, USS *Truckee* (AO-47), 1955–56. Commander Destroyer Squadron 2, 1956–57. Office of the Chief of Naval Operations, Washington, D.C., 1957–59. Commander Destroyer Flotilla One, 1959–60. Strategic Plans Division, Office of the Chief of Naval Operations, Washington, D.C., 1960–62. Staff, Commander in Chief Atlantic Fleet, 1962–64. Retired from active duty 1 January 1965. Admiral Leverton now lives in Whispering Pines, North Carolina.

**Rear Admiral David Merrill Tyree, U.S. Navy (Retired)**
**Commanding Officer, 21 November 1950–17 November 1951**
Born 23 January 1904 in Washington, D.C. Entered U.S. Naval Academy in 1921 from Kentucky; graduated in June 1925. USS *West Virginia* (BB-48), 1925–29. USS *Henshaw* (DD-278), 1929–30, USS *Wasmuth* (DD-338), 1930–32. Postgraduate education in ordnance, Naval Postgraduate School, Annapolis, Maryland, and University of Michigan, Ann Arbor, Michigan, 1932–34. Naval Gun Factory, Washington, D.C., 1934–35. USS *Indianapolis* (CA-35), 1935–36. Staff, Commander Base Force, 1936–38. Officer-in-Charge, Naval Magazine, Bellevue, D.C., 1938–40. USS *Salt Lake City* (CA-25), 1940–42. Staff, Commander Carrier Division One, 1942. Staff, Commander Task Force 17, 1942. Staff, Commander Amphibious Force South Pacific, 1942–43. Staff, Commander Third Amphibious Force, 1943–44. Bureau of Ordnance, Navy Department, Washington, D.C./Member, Chemical Warfare Committee, 1944–46. Chief of Staff, Commander Cruiser Division Three,1946–47. Commanding Officer, USS *Renville* (APA-227), 1947–48. Staff, National War College, Washington, D.C., 1948–50. Commanding Officer, USS *New Jersey* (BB-62), 1950–51. Director, Material Control Division, Office of the Deputy Chief of Naval Operations (Logistics), Washington, D.C., 1951–52. Assistant Chief of Naval Operations (Material), Washington, D.C., 1952–54. Commander Cruiser Division One, 1954–56. Superintendent, Naval Gun Factory, Washington, D.C., 1956–58. Commander Task Group 7.3/Deputy for the Navy, Joint Task Force Seven, 1958. Office of the Chief of Naval Operations, Washington, D.C., 1958. Commander Naval Support Force, Antarctica, 1959–63. Retired from active duty 1 August 1963. Died 25 August 1984, Portsmouth, Virginia.

**Rear Admiral Francis Douglas McCorkle, U.S. Navy (Retired)**
**Commanding Officer, 17 November 1951–20 October 1952**
Born 24 February 1903 in Greene County, Tennessee. Entered U.S. Naval Academy from Tennessee in 1922; graduated in June 1926. USS *New Mexico* (BB-40), 1926–30. USS *Preble* (DD-345), 1930–32. Instructor, U.S. Naval Academy, Annapolis, Maryland, 1932–34. USS *Portland* (CA-33), 1935–39. Bureau of Navigation, Navy Department, Washington, D.C., 1939–41. Commanding Officer, USS *Simpson* (DD-221), 1941–42. Commanding Officer, USS *Tillman* (DD-641), 1942–43. Staff, Commander Destroyers Atlantic Fleet, 1943–45. Commander Destroyer Squadron Five, 1945. Professor of Naval Science, NROTC Unit, Brown University, Providence, Rhode Island, 1945–48. Chief of Staff, Commander Destroyers Atlantic Fleet, 1948–50. Head, Department of Seamanship and Navigation, U.S. Naval Academy, Annapolis, Maryland, 1950–51. Commanding Officer, USS *New Jersey* (BB-62), 1951–52. Bureau of Naval Personnel, Washington, D.C., 1952–53. Director, Fleet Operations Division, Office of the Chief of Naval Operations, Washington, D.C., 1953–55. Commander Cruiser Division Three, 1955–56. Director of Personnel Policy, Office of the Assistant Secretary of Defense

Manpower, Personnel, and Reserve), Washington, D.C., 1956. Commander Naval Base, Key West, Florida, 1957–59. President of the Board of Inspection and Survey, Washington, D.C., 1959–60. Retired from active duty 1 December 1960. Admiral McCorkle now lives in Falmouth, Massachusetts.

**Vice Admiral Charles Leroy Melson, U.S. Navy (Retired)**
**Commanding Officer, 20 October 1952–24 October 1953**
Born 25 May 1904 in Richmond, Virginia. Entered U.S. Naval Academy in 1923 from Virginia; graduated in June 1927. USS *Trenton* (CL-11), 1927–29. USS *Penguin* (AM-33), 1929. USS *Napa* (AT-32), 1929. USS *McCormick* (DD-223), 1929–31. USS *Pittsburgh* (CA-4),1931. USS *Du Pont* (DD-152), 1931–32. Naval Operating Base, Norfolk, Virginia, 1932. USS *Dickerson* (DD-157), 1932–33. USS *Northampton* (CA-26), 1933–34. Postgraduate education in naval engineering, Naval Postgraduate School, Annapolis, Maryland, 1934–36. USS *Pennsylvania* (BB-38), 1936–37. USS *Patterson* (DD-392), 1937–40. Division of Fleet Training, Office of the Chief of Naval Operations, Washington, D.C., 1940–41. Staff, Commander in Chief U.S. Fleet, Washington, D.C., 1941–42. Commanding Officer, USS *Champlin* (DD-601), 1942–44. Commander Destroyer Division 32, 1944. Staff, Commander Destroyers Atlantic Fleet, 1944–45. Chief of Staff, Commander Battleship Division Five, 1945. Staff, Commander Atlantic Reserve Fleet, 1945–47. Student/Staff, Naval War College, Newport, Rhode Island, 1947–49. Commander Destroyer Squadron 20, 1949–50. Administrative Aide to Superintendent, U.S. Naval Academy, Annapolis, Maryland, 1950–52. Commanding Officer, USS *New Jersey* (BB-62), 1952–53. Chief of Staff, Commander Battleship-Cruiser Force Atlantic Fleet, 1953–55. Staff, Commander in Chief Atlantic Fleet, 1955–57. Commander Cruiser Division Four, 1957–58. Superintendent, U.S. Naval Academy, Annapolis, Maryland, 1958–60. Commander First Fleet, 1960–62. Commander U.S. Taiwan Defense Command, Taipei, Taiwan, 1962–64. President, Naval War College, Newport, Rhode Island, 1964–66. Retired from active duty 25 January 1966. Died 14 September 1981, Fort Lauderdale, Florida.

**Rear Admiral John Conner Atkeson, U.S. Navy (Retired)**
**Commanding Officer, 24 October 1953–18 March 1955**
Born 11 September 1905 in Columbia, Alabama. Entered U.S. Naval Academy in 1923 from Alabama; graduated in June 1927. USS *Arkansas* (BB-33), 1927–28. USS *Denver* (C-14), 1928–31. USS *Wyoming* (AG-17), 1931–33. USS *Leary* (DD-158), 1933–34. Postgraduate education in general line school, Naval Postgraduate School, Annapolis, Maryland, 1934–35. Instructor, U.S. Naval Academy, Annapolis, Maryland, 1935–36. Executive Officer, USS *Barry* (DD-248), 1936–39. Student, Naval War College, Newport, Rhode Island, 1939. Executive Officer, USS *Gilmer* (DD-233), 1939–40. Naval Training Station, Norfolk, Virginia, 1940–41. Commanding Officer, USS *Leary* (DD-158), 1941–42. Commanding Officer, USS *Bailey* (DD-492), 1942–43. Commanding Officer, USS *Healy* (DD-672), 1943–45. Commander Destroyer Division 20, 1945–46. Senior Member, Sub-board of Inspection and Survey, Norfolk, Virginia, 1946–48. Chief of Staff, Commander Destroyer Flotilla Two, 1948–49. Commander Destroyer Squadron 16, 1949–50. Senior Naval Member, Staff of Joint Munitions Allocations Commission, Washington, D.C., 1950–51. Material Control Division, Office of the Chief of Naval Operations, Washington, D.C., 1951–53. Commanding Officer, USS *New Jersey* (BB-62), 1953–55. Director, Undersea Warfare Division, Office of the Chief of Naval

Operations, Washington, D.C., 1955–56. Assigned to Fifth Naval District, Norfolk, Virginia, 1956–57. Retired from active duty 1 July 1957 and promoted to the rank of rear admiral on the basis of combat awards. Admiral Atkeson now lives in Norfolk, Virginia.

**Rear Admiral Edward Joseph O'Donnell, U.S. Navy (Retired)**
**Commanding Officer, 18 March 1955–31 May 1956**
Born 13 April 1907 in Boston, Massachusetts. Entered U.S. Naval Academy in 1925 from Massachusetts; graduated in June 1929. Instruction, Ford Instrument Company, Long Island City, New York, 1929. USS *Florida* (BB-30), 1929–30. Electoral mission to Nicaragua,1930. USS *John D. Ford* (DD-228), 1931–33. USS *Houston* (CA-30), 1933. USS *San Francisco* (CA-38), 1934–36. Postgraduate education in ordnance engineering, Naval Postgraduate School, Annapolis, Maryland, 1936–39. USS *Lexington* (CV-2), 1939–42. USS *Birmingham* (CL-62), 1942–44. Bureau of Ordnance, Navy Department, Washington, D.C., 1944–45. Staff, Commander Administrative Command, Amphibious Force Pacific Fleet, 1945–46. Commander Destroyer Division 32, 1946–47. Bureau of Ordnance, Navy Department, Washington, D.C., 1947–50. Staff, Commander Naval Forces Germany, 1950–52. Commanding Officer, USS *George Clymer* (APA-27), 1952–53. Naval Gun Factory, Washington, D.C., 1953–55. Commanding Officer, USS *New Jersey* (BB-62), 1955–56. Director, Administrative Division, Bureau of Ordnance, Navy Department, Washington, D.C., 1956–57. Commander Destroyer Flotilla Six, 1957–58. Director, Far East Region, Office of the Assistant Secretary of Defense (International Security Affairs), Washington, D.C., 1958–60. Commander Naval Base, Guantanamo Bay, Cuba, 1960–62. Senior Navy Member, Military Studies and Liaison Division, Weapons Systems Evaluation Group, Office of the Secretary of Defense, Washington, D.C., 1963–65. Superintendent, Naval Postgraduate School, Monterey, California, 1965–67. Retired from active duty 1 October 1967. Admiral O'Donnell now lives in Monterey, California.

**Rear Admiral Charles Ballance Brooks, Jr., U.S. Navy (Retired)**
**Commanding Officer, 31 May 1956–21 August 1957**
Born 4 May 1910 in Memphis, Tennessee. Entered U.S. Naval Academy in 1927 from Tennessee; graduated in June 1931. USS *New York* (BB-34), 1931–36. USS *Worden* (DD-352), 1936–37. Postgraduate education in communications at the Naval Postgraduate School, Annapolis, Maryland, 1937–39. Staff, Commander Cruiser Division Five, 1939–41. USS *Northampton* (CA-26)/Staff, Commander Cruisers Scouting Force, 1941–42. Staff, Commander Task Force 11, 1942–43. Staff, Commander Carrier Division One, 1943–44. Instructor, Naval Postgraduate School, Annapolis, Maryland, 1944–45. Staff, Commander Third Fleet, 1945. Executive Officer, USS *Indiana* (BB-58), 1945–46. Executive Officer, USS *Iowa* (BB-61), 1946–47. Commanding Officer, USS *Shelton* (DD-790), 1947–48. Officer detail, Bureau of Naval Personnel, Washington, D.C., 1948–51. Commanding Officer, USS *Randall* (APA-224), 1951–52. Staff, Commander Amphibious Group Four, 1952–53. Secretary of the Academic Board, U.S. Naval Academy, Annapolis, Maryland, 1953–56. Commanding Officer, USS *New Jersey* (BB-62), 1956–57. Chief-of-Staff, Commander Second Fleet, 1957–58. Joint Staff, Joint Chiefs-of-Staff, Washington, D.C., 1958–59. Deputy Standing Group Representative to North Atlantic Council, NATO, 1959–61. Commander Cruiser Division Two, 1961–62. Placed on retired list 1 November 1962. Recalled to active duty as Director of Naval Warfare Analyses, Office of the Chief of Naval Operations,

Captain J. Edward Snyder, Jr.

Captain Robert C. Peniston.

Captain William M. Fogarty.

and Deputy Scientific Officer, Center for Naval Analyses, Naval War College, Newport, Rhode Island. Released from active duty 1 November 1963. Died 25 July 1969, Portsmouth, Virginia.

**Rear Admiral Joseph Edward Snyder, Jr., U.S. Navy (Retired)**
**Commanding Officer, 6 April 1968–27 August 1969**
Born 23 October 1924 in Grand Forks, North Dakota. Entered U.S. Naval Academy in 1941 from North Dakota; graduated in June 1944 with the class of 1945. Naval Air Station, Jacksonville, Florida, 1944. USS *Pennsylvania* (BB-38), 1944–46. USS *Toledo* (CA-133), 1946–47. USS *Macon* (CA-132), 1947–48. Navy Special Weapons Unit, Los Alamos, New Mexico, 1948–49. Staff, Los Alamos Scientific Laboratory, 1949–51. USS *Holder* (DDE-819), 1951–52. Postgraduate education in ordnance (guided missiles), Naval Postgraduate School, Monterey, California, 1952–53. Postgraduate education in nuclear physics, Massachusetts Institute of Technology, Cambridge, Massachusetts, 1953–55. USS *Everett F. Larson* (DDR-830), 1955–56. USS *Heermann* (DD-532), 1956–57. Commanding Officer, USS *Calcaterra* (DER-390), 1957–58. Naval Weapons Representative, Lockheed Aircraft Corporation, Burbank, California, 1958–60. Student, Naval War College, Newport, Rhode Island, 1960–61. Commanding Officer, USS *Brownson* (DD-868), 1961–63. Special assistant to the Assistant Secretary of the Navy (Research and Development), Washington, D.C., 1963–67. Commanding Officer, USS *New Jersey* (BB-62), 1968–69. Chief of Staff, Commander Cruiser-Destroyer Force Atlantic Fleet, 1969–71. Commander Training Command Atlantic Fleet, 1971–72. Oceanographer of the Navy, 1972–79. Placed on retired list 1 July 1975 and continued on active duty in retired status until 1 June 1979. Admiral Snyder lives in McLean, Virginia.

**Captain Robert C Peniston, U.S. Navy (Retired)**
**Commanding Officer, 27 August 1969–17 December 1969**
Born 25 October 1922 at Chillicothe, Missouri. Entered U.S. Naval Academy in 1943 from Kansas; graduated in June 1946 with the class of 1947. USS *New Jersey* (BB-62), 1946–47. Recruit Training Command, Great Lakes, Illinois, 1947–48. Combat Information Center School, Glenview, Illinois, 1949. USS *Putnam* (DD-757), 1949–50. USS *Cone* (DD-866), 1950–51. USS *Williamsburg* (AGC-369), 1951–52. USS *Willis A. Lee* (DL-4), 1953–55. Bureau of Naval Personnel, Washington, D.C., 1955–57. Postgraduate education in personnel administration, Stanford University, 1957–58. USS *Nicholas* (DDE-449), 1958–59. Commanding Officer, USS *Savage* (DER-386), 1959–61. Naval War College, Newport, Rhode Island, 1961–62. Aide to President of War College, 1962–64. Commanding Officer, USS *Tattnall* (DDG-19), 1964–66. Bureau of Naval Personnel, 1966–69. Commanding Officer, USS *New Jersey* (BB-62), 1969. Commanding Officer, USS *Albany* (CG-10), 1970–71. Staff, Commander in Chief U.S. Atlantic Command/U.S. Atlantic Fleet, 1971–74. Staff, Chief of Naval Education and Training, Pensacola, Florida, 1974–76. Retired from active duty 1 June 1976. Captain Peniston is now Director of the Lee Chapel, Washington and Lee University, Lexington, Virginia.

**Rear Admiral William Miley Fogarty, U.S. Navy**
**Commanding Officer, 28 December 1982–15 September 1983**
Born 24 May 1936 in Des Moines, Iowa. Commissioned through NROTC unit upon graduation in 1958 from Iowa State University of Science and Technology, Ames, Iowa. USS *Gunston Hall* (LSD-5), 1958–60. USS *Outagamie County* (LST-1073), 1961–63. USS *Lofberg*

(DD-759), 1963–64. Staff, Commander Cruiser-Destroyer Force Pacific Fleet, 1964–66. Executive Officer, USS *Rowan* (DD-782), 1967–68. Commanding Officer, USS *Hooper* (DE-1026), 1967–68. Student, German Command and Staff College, Hamburg, Federal Republic of Germany, 1969–70. USS *Wasp* (CVS-18), 1971–72. Commanding Officer, USS *Jesse L. Brown* (DE-1089), 1973–74. Student, National War College, Washington, D.C., 1974–75. Postgraduate education, master's degree, in international affairs, George Washington University, Washington, D.C., 1975–75. Strategy, Plans and Policy Division, Office of the Chief of Naval Operations, Washington, D.C., 1975–76. Military assistant to the Special Assistant to the Secretary of Defense and Deputy Secretary of Defense, Washington, D.C., 1976–77. Executive assistant to the Deputy Under Secretary of the Navy, Washington, D.C., 1977–78. Commander Destroyer Squadron 26, 1979–80. Commander Destroyer Squadron Ten, 1980–81. Prospective Commanding Officer, *New Jersey* (BB-62), 1981–82. Commanding Officer, USS *New Jersey* (BB-62), 1982–83. Director, Force Level Plans and Warfare Appraisal Division, Office of the Chief of Naval Operations, Washington, D.C., 1983–86. Commander Amphibious Group Two, 1986–Present.

**Rear Admiral Richard David Milligan, U.S. Navy**
**Commanding Officer, 15 September 1983–7 September 1985**
Born 6 September 1936 at East Orange, New Jersey. Entered U.S. Naval Academy in 1955 from New Jersey; graduated in June 1959. USS *Ault* (DD-698), 1959–62. Aide to the Commandant, Sixth Naval District, Charleston, South Carolina, 1962–64. Commanding Officer, USS *Somersworth* (EPCER-849), 1964–65. Executive Officer, USS *Joseph K. Taussig* (DE-1030), 1965–67. Postgraduate education in management, master's degree, Naval Postgraduate School, Monterey, California, 1967–68. General Planning and Programming Division, Office of the Chief of Naval Operations, Washington, D.C., 1969–71. Commanding Officer, USS *McMorris* (DE-1036),

1971–73. Commanding Officer, USS *Whiple* (FF-1062), 1973–75. Student, Industrial College of the Armed Forces, Washington, D.C., 1975–76. Financial Resources Division, Bureau of Naval Personnel, Washington, D.C., 1976–77. Office of the Comptroller of the Navy, Washington, D.C., 1977–81. Commanding Officer, USS *Wainwright* (CG-28), 1982–83. Commanding Officer, USS *New Jersey* (BB-62), 1983–85. Comptroller, Naval Air Systems Command, Washington, D.C., 1985–Present.

**Captain Walter Lewis Glenn, Jr., U.S. Navy**
**Commanding Officer, 7 September 1985–Present**
Born 7 September 1940 in Anderson, South Carolina. Entered U.S. Naval Academy in 1958 from South Carolina; graduated in June 1962. USS *Vesole* (DDR-878), 1962–63. USS *Richard E. Byrd* (DDG-23), 1963–65. Postgraduate education in physics, master's degree, Naval Postgraduate School, Monterey, California, 1965–68. Aide to Commander Naval Forces Vietnam, Saigon, South Vietnam, 1968–69. USS *Tattnall* (DDG-19), 1969–70. Strategy, Plans and Policy Division, Office of the Chief of Naval Operations, Washington, D.C., 1970–71. Executive assistant to the Oceanographer of the Navy, Washington, D.C., 1971. Executive assistant to the Navy Deputy, National Atmospheric and Oceanic Administration, Department of Commerce, Washington, D.C., 1972. USS *Vreeland* (FF-1068), 1972–75. Bureau of Naval Personnel, Washington, D.C., 1975–76. Project manager for Manpower, Training and Personnel Study, 1977–78. Commanding Officer, USS *Mahan* (DDG-42), 1978–81. Administrative assistant/aide to the Chief of Naval Operations, Washington, D.C., 1981–82. Student, advanced management program, Harvard University Graduate School of Business, Cambridge, Massachusetts, 1982. Student, Industrial College of the Armed Forces, Washington, D.C., 1983. Executive assistant to the Deputy Chief of Naval Operations (Surface Warfare), Washington, D.C., 1983–85. Commanding Officer, USS *New Jersey* (BB-62), 1985–Present.

Right: Captain Richard D. Milligan.

Far right: Captain W. Lewis Glenn, Jr.

# APPENDIX 2
# DESIGN OF *NEW JERSEY*

The influences which went into the design of *New Jersey* and her *Iowa*-class sisters were many and competing. Perhaps foremost among these influences were the international naval limitation treaties of the 1920s and 1930s. Because battleships were still considered preeminent in a nation's defense and war-making ability during that era, the numbers and characteristics of battleships received particular emphasis in the treaties. The *New Jersey* would, in all likelihood, have been a bigger ship if her designers had not been operating under treaty restraints.

No new U.S. battleships were constructed between the early 1920s and the late 1930s. Ships of the *North Carolina* and *South Dakota* classes, which began construction between 1937 and 1940, were limited to a standard displacement of 35,000 tons each. For a time, it appeared that the *North Carolina* class would be outitted with 14-inch guns to comply with the London naval treaty of 1936, which was signed by the United States, Great Britain, and France – Japan having previously withdrawn from the conference leading to the agreement.

The possibility that Japan might defect had been provided for in the treaty. Japan had signed the 1922 Washington naval treaty which included a moratorium on battleship construction. With the moratorium coming to an end in the late thirties, the nations in the 1936 treaty agreed to abide by new limits – 35,000 tons and 14-inch guns – as long as all the signers of the 1922 treaty did so. If any nations did not agree, and this obviously meant Japan, the other countries were free to build battleships up to 45,000 tons and to arm them with 16-inch guns.

Japan remained silent about its intentions, but an article in a November 1937 issue of a Rome newspaper, *Giornale di'Italia*, discussed plans for construction of Japanese 46,000-ton battleships armed with 16-inch guns. (In fact, the *Yamato* class turned out to be 59,100 tons with 18.1-inch guns, but the United States did not learn of those dimensions until well after the *Yamato* and her sister *Musashi* were complete.) The U.S. Navy was in a quandary in establishing general specifications for its new battleships. On the one hand, it wanted to have the most capable warships it could; on the other, it did not want to set off a new shipbuilding race which could lead to larger and larger ships. If such a race did come to pass, the United States would be forced to keep up, and that might mean battleships too large to pass through the Panama Canal.

Continuing reports from abroad indicated that Japan had begun building three large battleships at about the beginning of April 1937. Since Japan could not provide assurances that it was living up to the 1936 treaty, the United States, Great Britain, and France agreed in June 1938 to a protocol modifying the treaty. New U.S. battleships could therefore be built with 16-inch guns, and the tonnage limitation per ship was raised from 35,000 to 45,000.

A congressional act of 17 May 1938 authorized the three battleships which eventually became *Iowa, New Jersey*, and *Missouri*. The act authorized a total of 105,000 tons (three 35,000 tonners) but included terms which permitted larger ships if the President determined ". . . that the interests of national defense so require, in which event the authorized composition of the United States Navy is hereby increased by one hundred thirty-five thousand tons." The latter figure, of course, provided for three 45,000-ton ships.

The Navy's Bureau of Construction and Repair, which was then responsible for preliminary design of new ships, had already been preparing studies leading to a 45,000-ton class. Dr Norman Friedman's excellent history of the design of U.S. battleships contains specifications for a number of options that were considered for the new class. Included were such variations as 18-inch guns or ships with four triple turrets of 16-inch guns. Also considered were fast and slow options. The latter was appropriate because the U.S. Navy had traditionally built battleships which emphasized firepower and armor protection rather than speed. Several of the proposed designs had standard displacements which exceeded 50,000 tons, but their beam dimensions would still permit them to squeeze through the 110-foot-wide locks of the Panama Canal.

Within the U.S. Navy of the day, an influential organization in the matter of determining ship characteristics was the General Board. The board comprised senior officers who were to see that new ships fulfilled the nation's strategic objectives and were well suited to oppose enemy warships. In March 1938, when preliminary agreement was obtained to invoke the escalator clause in the 1936 treaty, the General Board opted for a fast battleship. It would contain the same general armament scheme as the preceding *South Dakota* class – nine 16-inch guns and twenty 5-inch – but would have a speed of 33 knots. The speed was seen as necessary to catch and defeat fast Japanese cruisers operating as surface raiders. The new battleships would be given considerable range as well, to permit them to operate in the vast distances of the Pacific Ocean. The 33-knot speed would enable the new class to operate along with aircraft carriers, although conventional wisdom of the time envisaged that aircraft carriers would support the battleships rather than the other way around. Battleships were still deemed the Navy's primary offensive weapons.

In 1938, the Bureau of Construction and Repair continued to examine design characteristics for the new class. In June the General Board approved a design with a turret barbette size – 37 feet 3 inches in diameter – which would keep the ship within the 45,000-ton limit. As Dr Friedman puts it, "The treaty had been stretched by 10,000 tons, but it was not to be broken." Alas, one bureau did not know what another was doing. While Construction and Repair was proceeding with its plan to accommodate a turret with new lightweight 16-inch/50caliber guns, the Navy's Bureau of Ordnance was proceeding to design turrets for heavier 16-inch/50 guns which had been built in the 1920s for the original *South Dakota* class (BB-49 to BB-54). Construction of these six ships was cancelled under provisions of the 1922 Washington naval treaty, but dozens of the guns had already been manufactured by the time the treaty was concluded. The Bureau of Ordnance designed a turret to accommodate the old guns, and the barbette for such a turret was to be 39 feet in diameter. The barbette is a long vertical cylinder of armor steel which houses projectiles and machinery and serves as a base for the rotating turret on top. Something was obviously amiss if the Bureau of Ordnance was planning for a 39-foot barbette and the ship designers had left space for one measuring only 37 feet 3 inches.

The matter came to a head five months after the ship's design had supposedly been settled in June 1938. Dr E. Ray Lewis, who has devoted much study to U.S. battleship armament, has written, "The shambles confronting the Navy's planners as of early 1938 appears never to have been reported formally to the Secretary of the Navy; but, understandably, the meeting of the General Board, which was convened on 17 November to find a way out of this near catastrophic situation, was stormy." Because so much effort had already gone into designing a ship to fit within the 45,000-ton limit, and because the 45,000-ton ceiling was still considered inviolable, it was the turret which would have to change. In December 1938, the General Board recommended to the Secretary of the Navy a design which included the 37-foot 3-inch barbette and the corresponding turret with lightweight 16-inch guns rather than the leftovers from the never built *South Dakota* class. Thus, by the end of 1938 the general makeup of the *Iowa* class was essentially settled.

Dr Friedman contends that the *Iowa*-class ships ". . . were not much more than 33-knot versions of the 27-knot, 35,000 tonners that had preceded them. The *Iowa*s showed no advance at all in [armor] protection over the *South Dakota*s. The principal armament was a more powerful 16-inch gun, 5 calibers longer. Ten thousand tons was a very great price to pay for 6 knots." On the other hand, he points out that speed advantage made the class well suited for fast carrier task force operations and is a key to the longevity that the *New Jersey* and her sisters have enjoyed.

With hindsight, it is possible to observe several ironies in regard to the design of the *New Jersey*. For example, many of the characteristics – especially the type of guns and thus the size of barbette and overall tonnage of the ship – were dictated by the intent to adhere strictly to the 45,000-ton limit on standard displacement. Yet this limitation had already been shattered by the construction of the Japanese ships before the first piece of metal was put in place on the *Iowa* class. The 45,000-ton ceiling was a moot point already when the *Iowa*s were being built; they were beefed-up during construction in wartime, for by then even the modified treaty limitations had been rendered completely meaningless.

Much consideration was given to armor protection, including that incorporated in the massive conning tower from which the ship would be steered in battle. In February 1939, Rear Admiral Robert L. Ghormley, the director of war plans, argued for the building of an enclosed bridge forward of the conning tower, saying, "It is considered that the handling of the ship in formation in crowded waters is a matter of sufficient importance to warrant this change." The viewing slits through the conning tower armor provided extremely poor visibility and thus made it a difficult place from which to operate the ship. In January 1941, the Bureau of Ships argued for the elimination of the conning tower entirely through a desire to save weight and a belief that the risk of an enemy projectile hitting the conning station was slight. By then, however, there was a new director of war plans, Captain Richmond Kelly Turner. He argued in favor of retention of the conning tower, and it stayed in the design. Furthermore, Admiral Ghormley's call for a separate bridge was not heeded. The cramped, inconvenient conning tower was built into the *Iowa* class and has been a hindrance ever since. The irony is that *New Jersey* and her sisters never once fought the sort of gun duel with enemy ships for which an armored conning tower would have been beneficial. In the end, though, one should point out that ships have to be designed before battles take place – not with the benefit of hindsight.

Despite the drawbacks imposed by the 1936 treaty and an understandable inability to foresee just what shape the future would take, those who designed the *Iowa* class did their work well. The fact that the ships are in service nearly fifty years after those General Board deliberations of 1938 speaks well for the work of the designers. Along with their speed, their armor protection, and their firepower, the *Iowa*, *New Jersey*, *Missouri*, and *Wisconsin* have another characteristic as well. They look exactly the way warships should look. They are awesome and formidable, but they are also elegant and majestic. This appearance of both power and beauty has no doubt been a reason for the great appeal that these ships have long had for thousands of Navy men.

# APPENDIX 3
# USS *NEW JERSEY* SHIP'S DATA

## General Dimensions

Length overall: 887 feet, 6⅝ inches

Length at designed waterline: 859 feet, 10¼ inches

Extension beyond forward perpendicular: 20 feet, 0 inches (i.e. bow overhang)

Extension beyond aft perpendicular: 7 feet, 3 inches (stern overhang)

Beam to outside of plating, frames 121 to 129: 108 feet, 1⅜ inches

Freeboard at bow to design waterline: 35 feet, 8½ inches

Freeboard at stern to design waterline: 22 feet, 7⁷⁄₁₆ inches

Depth of inner bottom: 3 feet, 0¹⁄₁₆ inches

Frame spacing: 4 feet, 0 inches

Number of frames: 215

Displacement, standard, designed: 45,000 tons

Displacement to design waterline: 54,889 tons

Design waterline: 34 feet, 9¼ inches above the keel, which corresponds to designed normal load and draft

Draft at full-load displacement: 38 feet, 0 inches

Distance between turrets one and two (axis to axis): 72 feet, 0 inches

Distance between turrets two and three (axis to axis): 346 feet, 0 inches

## Engineering Plant

Boilers: Eight Babcock & Wilcox express type; designed working steam pressure; 634 pounds per square inch

Turbines: Four Westinghouse

Propellers: all four manufactured by Philadelphia Navy Yard
   Righthand inboard: five blades, 53,000 shaft horsepower
   Righthand outboard: four blades, 53,000 shaft horsepower
   Lefthand inboard: five blades, 53,000 shaft horsepower
   Lefthand outboard: four blades, 53,000 shaft horsepower

Total Shaft Horsepower: 212,000

Designed endurance: 15,000 nautical miles at 15 knots

Designed speed: 33 knots

## Armament

Nine 16-inch/50 caliber guns in three triple turrets; maximum elevation of 45° and maximum depression of 2°; limit of train fo[r] the six forward guns to positive stops is 210° relative to port and 150° relative to starboard; the after guns have a limit of train of 330° relative to port and 030° relative to starboard. The turret barbettes contain the following decks, top to bottom: shelf plate, turret pan, electric deck, upper shell handling platform, lower shell handling platform, and powder loading

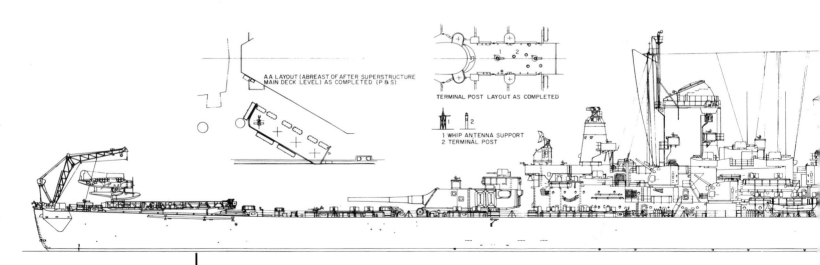

## OUTBOARD PROFILE AS COMPLETED, JULY 1943
DRAWN BY ALAN B. CHESLEY, 1984.

SCALE 0 5 10 15 20 30 40 50 FEET

A A LAYOUT (ABREAST OF AFTER SUPERSTRUCTURE MAIN DECK LEVEL) AS COMPLETED (P & S)

TERMINAL POST LAYOUT AS COMPLETED

1 WHIP ANTENNA SUPPORT
2 TERMINAL POST

platform. Turret two has one additional projectile platform. Projectile stowage: turret one, 405; turret two, 475; turret three, 385.

Twenty 5-inch/38 caliber dual-purpose guns in ten twin mounts. The guns of the secondary battery have a maximum elevation of 85° and a maximum depression of 15°. Four of the ten mounts, containing eight of the original twenty guns, were removed during the 1981–82 modernization to make room for a missile deck.

Sixty-four 40-mm. antiaircraft guns in sixteen quadruple mounts. The number was increased to eighty guns in twenty mounts during the ship's yard period in the autumn of 1943. Subsequently, some mounts were removed and reinstalled; the ship still had all twenty mounts at the time of decommissioning in 1957. All were removed during the 1967–68 modernization.

Forty-nine 20-mm. antiaircraft guns. This number was increased during World War II to fifty-seven – forty-one single mounts and eight twin mounts. All but a few of the 20-mm. mounts were removed during the 1947–48 inactivation. All the remaining 20-mm. mounts were removed during the yard period in 1952.

### Armor
Citadel from 03 to 05 level: top, 7.25 inches; bottom, 4 inches; sides, 17.3 inches

Tube from second deck to 03 level: 16 inches all the way around

Turrets: front, 17 inches over 2.5-inch special treatment steel; sides, 9.5 inches, rear, 12 inches; top, 7.25 inches

Barbettes down to second deck: 11.6 inches forward and aft; 17.3 inches on sides

Second deck plating, frames 50–166: 4.75-inch class B armor

Third deck plating, frames 166–189: 5.6-inch class B armor

Third deck plating, frames 189–203: 6.2-inch class B armor

Frame 203 bulkhead between third deck and first platform: 11.3-inch class A armor

Frame 166 bulkhead between second and third decks: 11.3-inch class A armor

Frame 50 bulkhead between second deck and hold: tapered from 11.3 inches to 8.5 inches, class A armor

Upper side belt between second and third decks, frames 50–166: 12.1-inch class A armor

Side belt steering gear armor between third deck and second platform deck, frames 189–203: 13.5-inch class A armor

Lower side belt between third deck and hold: frames 166–189, tapered from 13.5 inches to 5.625 inches at frame 166; tapered from 13.5 inches to 7.125 inches at frame 189, class B armor

Lower side belt between third deck and hold, frames 50–166: tapered from 12.1 inches to 1.62 inches, class B armor

### Rudders
There are two rudders located with the centers of their stocks 8 feet, 6 inches off the centerline of the ship at frame 201½. The area of each rudder is 340 square feet. The outside positive stops for each rudder limit the angle to 36.5°, port and starboard, from the zero helm position.

### Aircraft Crane
The crane was manufactured by C. H. Wheeler Manufacturing Company. It had a rated capacity of 9,300 pounds and an outreach of 41 feet, 6 inches. (The crane was removed from the ship during the 1981–82 modernization to facilitate helicopter operations on the fantail.)

### Anchors
Each anchor is the stockless bower type, weighing 30,000 pounds; each chain is 187 fathoms long, including the outboard swivel shot.

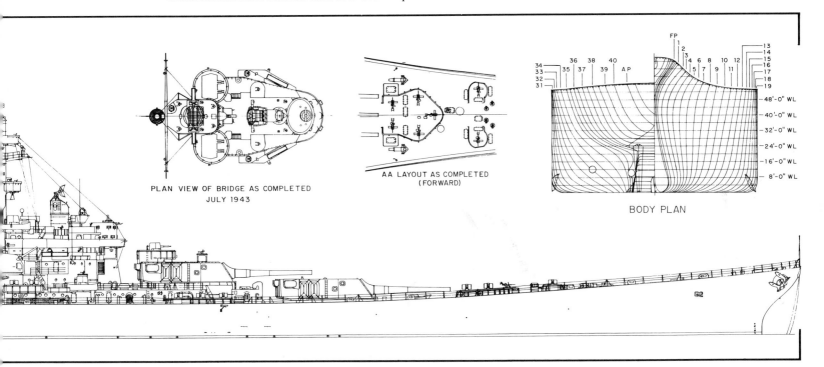

PLAN VIEW OF BRIDGE AS COMPLETED
JULY 1943

AA LAYOUT AS COMPLETED
(FORWARD)

BODY PLAN

**Embarked Aircraft**
1943–45: Three Vought OS2U Kingfisher floatplanes
1945–47: Two Curtiss SC-1 Seahawk floatplanes
1951–53: One Sikorsky HO3S-1 helicopter
1983–present: One Kaman SH-2 Seasprite helicopter

**Search Radar Antennas**
May 1943–May 1945: SK air search on foremast; SG surface search on mainmast and also on front of forward fire control tower

June 1945–February 1952: SK-2 air search and SG surface search on foremast
June 1945–August 1954: SP height-finder on mainmast
April 1952–present: SPS-10 surface search on foremast
April 1952–December 1969: SPS-6 air search on foremast
December 1954–inactivation in 1957: SPS-8A height-finder on mainmast
Summer 1982–present: SPS-49 air search on foremast

**OUTBOARD PROFILE AS OUTFITTED IN JULY 1945**
**OVERHEAD ARRANGEMENT, 1945**
DRAWN BY ALAN B. CHESLEY, 1984.

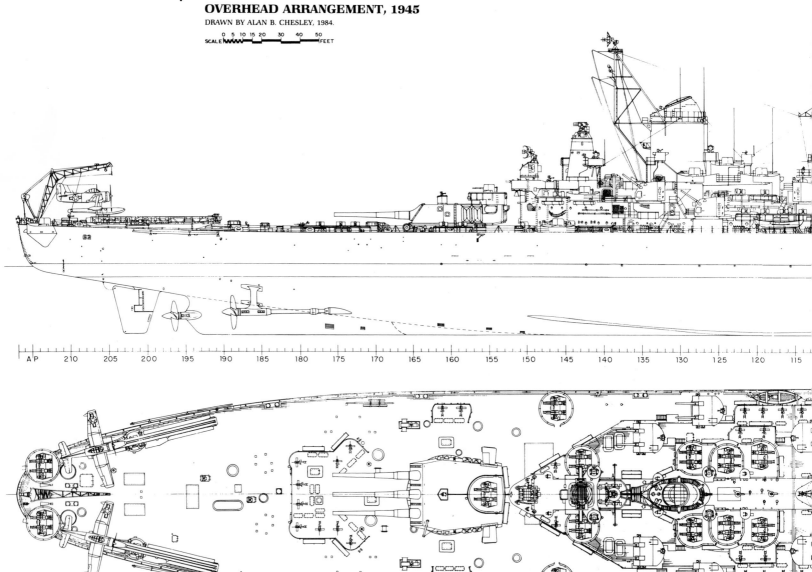

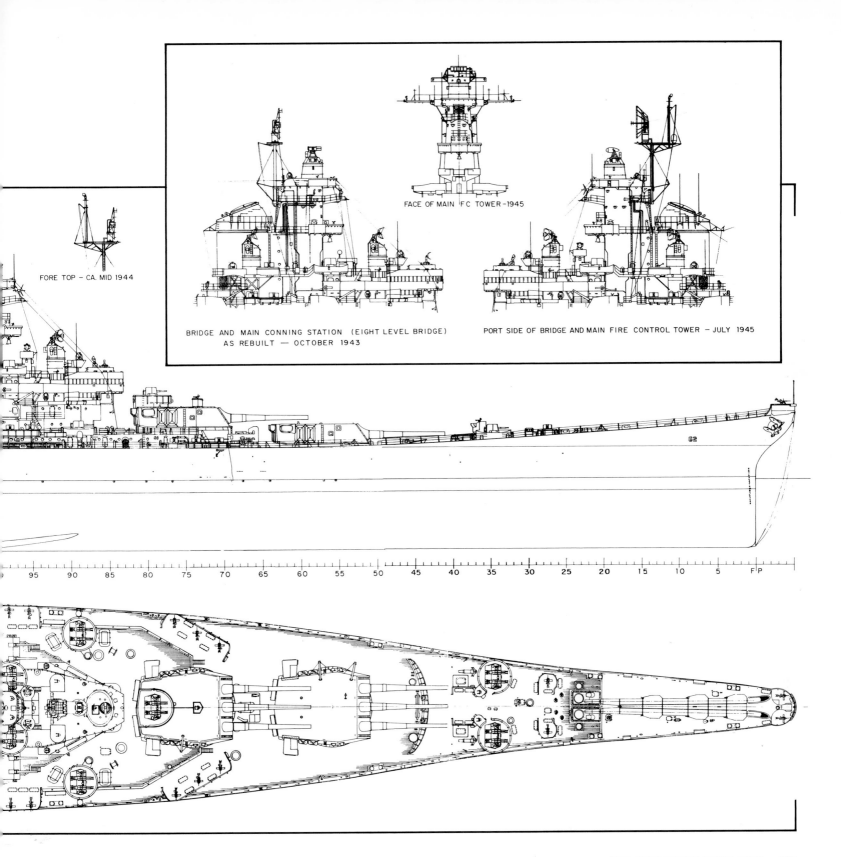

FORE TOP – CA. MID 1944

FACE OF MAIN FC TOWER –1945

BRIDGE AND MAIN CONNING STATION (EIGHT LEVEL BRIDGE)
AS REBUILT — OCTOBER 1943

PORT SIDE OF BRIDGE AND MAIN FIRE CONTROL TOWER – JULY 1945

95  90  85  80  75  70  65  60  55  50  45  40  35  30  25  20  15  10  5  F P

# SUPERSTRUCTURE DECKS AND PLATFORMS, 1945

DRAWN BY ALAN B. CHESLEY, 1984.

SCALE 0 5 10 15 20 30 40 50 FEET

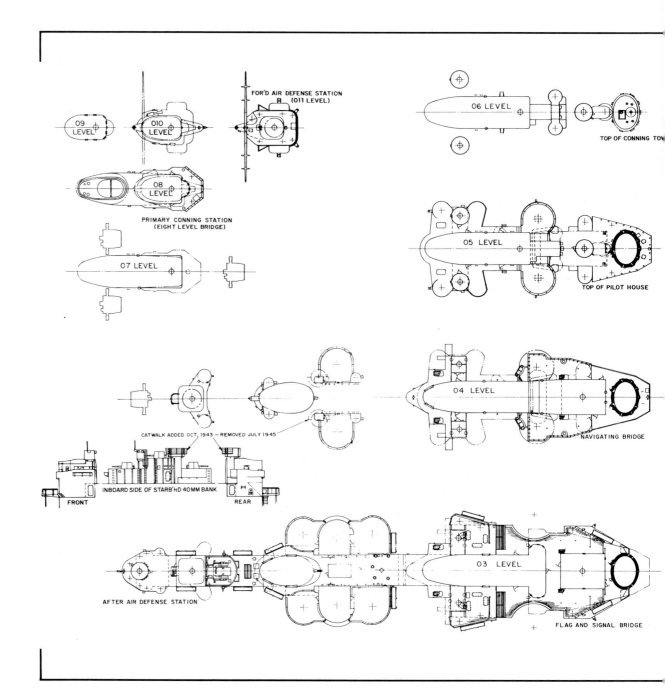

09 LEVEL

010 LEVEL

FOR'D AIR DEFENSE STATION (011 LEVEL)

06 LEVEL

TOP OF CONNING TOW

08 LEVEL

PRIMARY CONNING STATION (EIGHT LEVEL BRIDGE)

07 LEVEL

05 LEVEL

TOP OF PILOT HOUSE

04 LEVEL

CATWALK ADDED OCT. 1943 – REMOVED JULY 1945

NAVIGATING BRIDGE

FRONT

INBOARD SIDE OF STARB'RD 40MM BANK

REAR

AFTER AIR DEFENSE STATION

03 LEVEL

FLAG AND SIGNAL BRIDGE

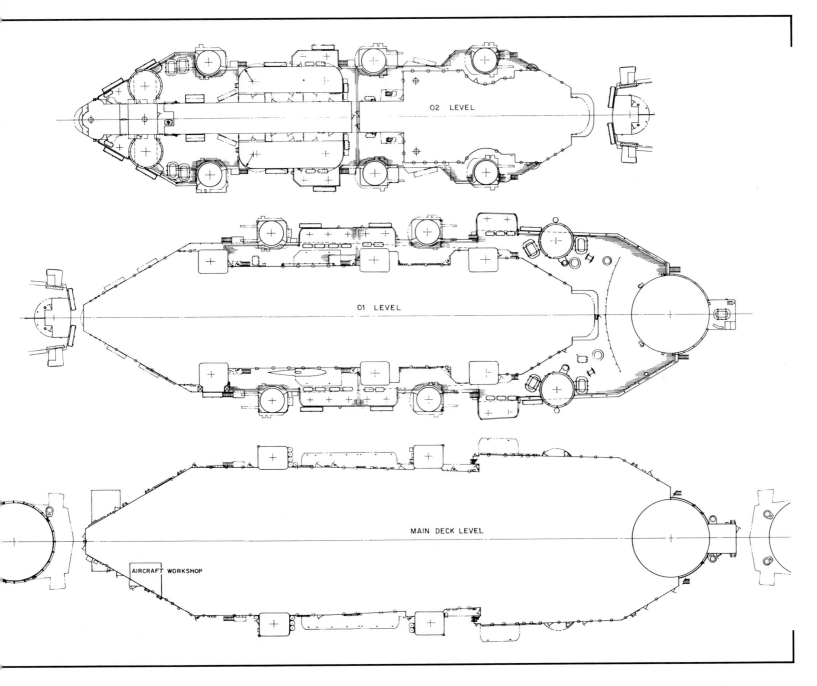

O2 LEVEL

O1 LEVEL

MAIN DECK LEVEL

AIRCRAFT WORKSHOP

## OUTBOARD PROFILE AS SHE APPEARED IN 1953
## (DEPLOYMENT OFF KOREA)

DRAWN BY ALAN B. CHESLEY, 1984.

SCALE 0 5 10 15 20 30 40 50 FEET

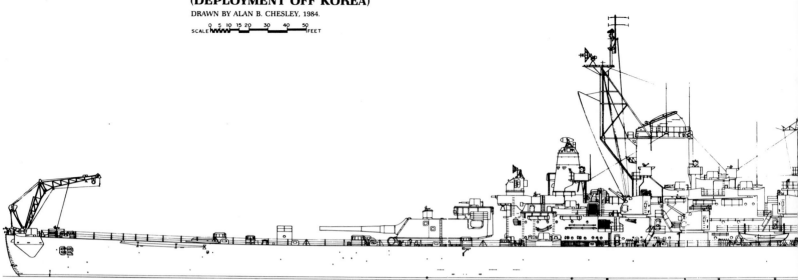

## INBOARD PROFILE, 1969

DRAWN BY ALAN B. CHESLEY, 1984.

SCALE 0 5 10 15 20 30 40 50 FEET

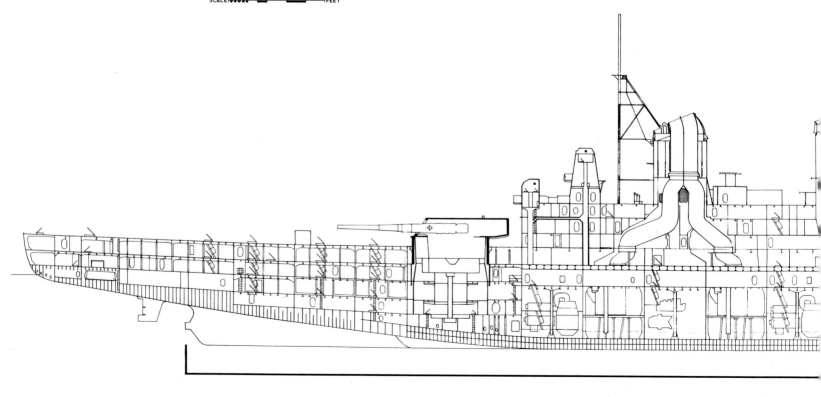

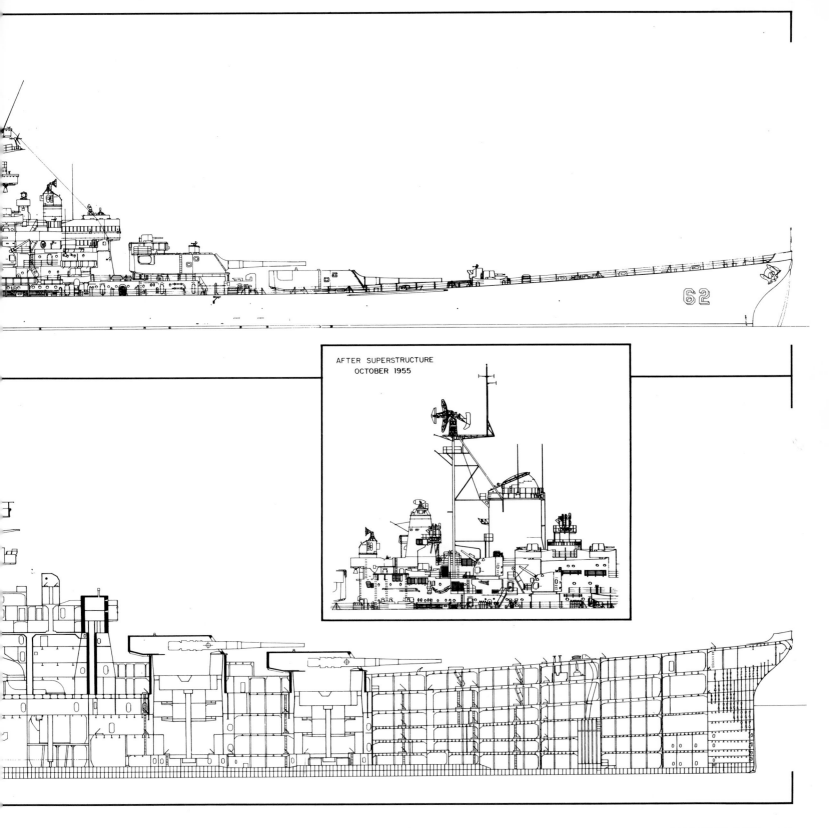

AFTER SUPERSTRUCTURE
OCTOBER 1955

62

**OUTBOARD PROFILE AS SHE APPEARED DURING
HER VIETNAM DEPLOYMENT, 1968–69
OVERHEAD ARRANGEMENT, 1969**

DRAWN BY ALAN B. CHESLEY, 1984.

SCALE 0 5 10 15 20 30 40 50 FEET

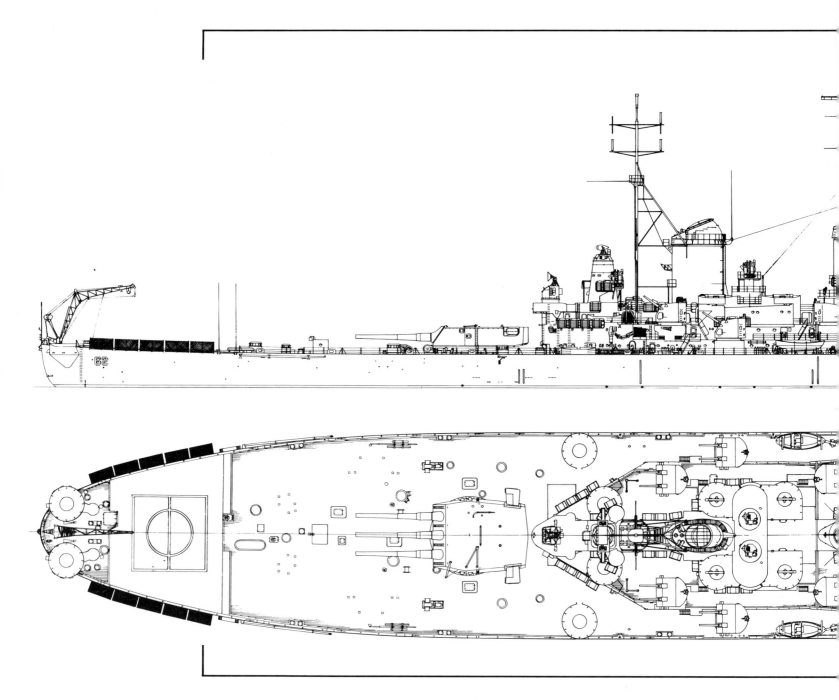

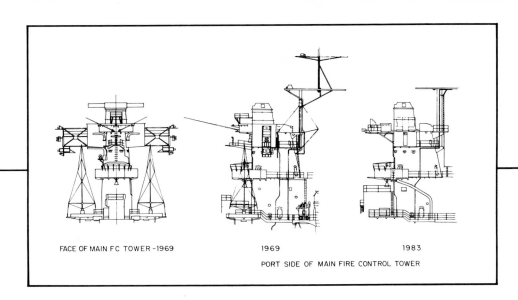

FACE OF MAIN F.C. TOWER -1969      1969      1983

PORT SIDE OF MAIN FIRE CONTROL TOWER

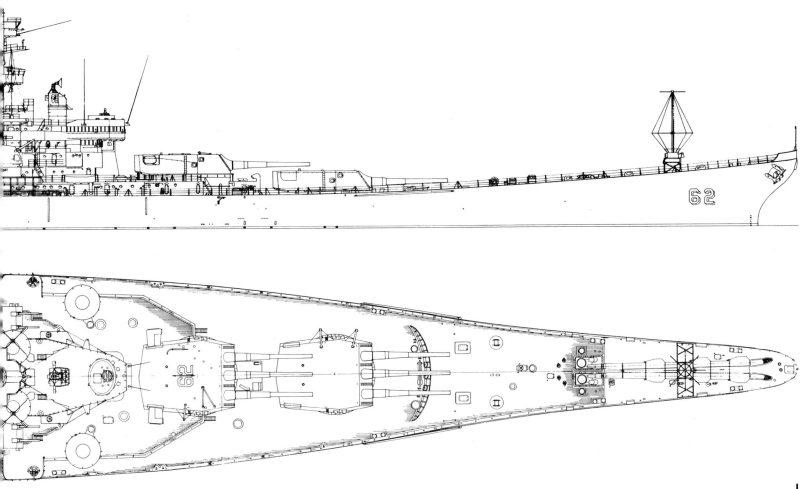

# APPENDIX 4
# CHANGES AND ADDITIONS DURING 1981–82
# MODERNIZATION

**OUTBOARD PROFILE AS OUTFITTED IN 1983**
**OVERHEAD ARRANGEMENT, 1983**

DRAWN BY ALAN B. CHESLEY, 1984.

SCALE 0 5 10 15 20 30 40 50 FEET

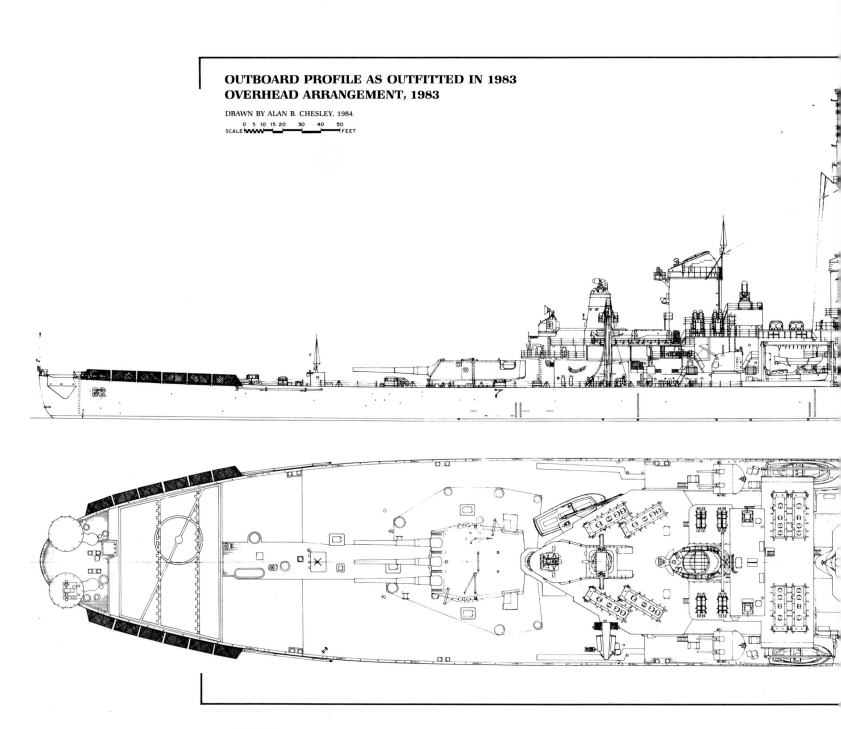

- Eight armored box launchers for a total of thirty-two Tomahawk cruise missiles; potential loads include a land-attack conventional version with a range of 700 nautical miles and an antiship version with a range of 250 nautical miles
- Four quadruple canister launchers for a total of sixteen Harpoon antiship missiles, each with a range of 60 nautical miles
- Four Vulcan/Phalanx close-in weapon systems for self-defense against aircraft and missiles
- Advanced communication systems
- SPS-49 air-search radar substituted for the less-capable SPS-6
- Aviation facilities, including an enlarged helicopter landing pad on the fantail, parking area, helicopter control booth on the after end of the superstructure, and helicopter glide slope indicator
- Conversion of the engineering plant to burn Navy distillate fuel in place of black oil

- A sewage collection, holding, and transfer system to comply with upgraded environmental requirements
- Improved habitability for the crew
- Removal of the stern crane to avoid interference with helicopter operations on the fantail
- Refueling rig on the starboard side to facilitate transfer of fuel to escorting ships
- SLQ-32 electronic countermeasure suite
- Satellite navigation and communication antennas
- Mark 36 super rapid-blooming offboard chaff (SRBOC) launchers
- New tripod foremast; removal of after mast
- Removal of four of the original ten 5-inch/38 twin mounts to make room for the installation of a missile deck between the smokestacks

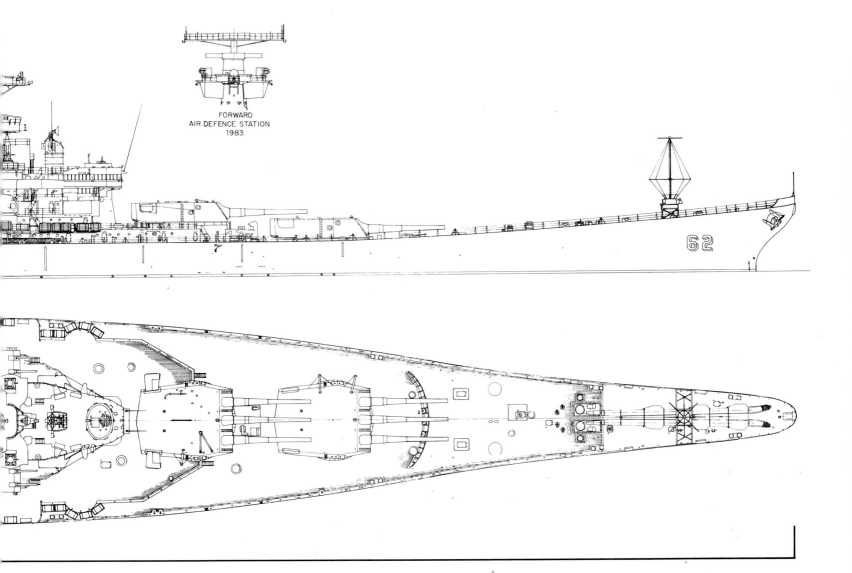

FORWARD
AIR DEFENCE STATION
1983

62

# SUPERSTRUCTURE DECKS AND PLATFORMS, 1983

**DRAWN BY ALAN B. CHESLEY, 1984.**

SCALE 0 5 10 15 20  30  40  50 FEET

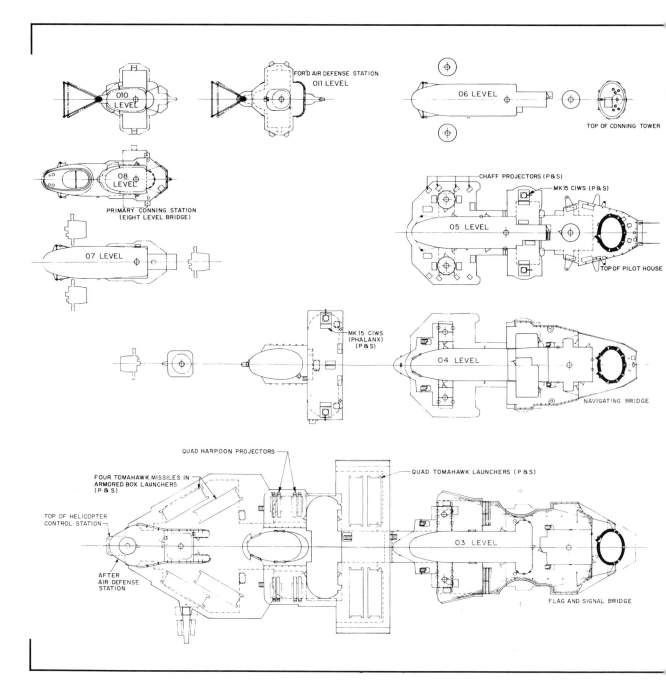

O10 LEVEL

FOR'D AIR DEFENSE STATION
O11 LEVEL

O6 LEVEL

TOP OF CONNING TOWER

O8 LEVEL

PRIMARY CONNING STATION
(EIGHT LEVEL BRIDGE)

O7 LEVEL

CHAFF PROJECTORS (P & S)

MK15 CIWS (P & S)

O5 LEVEL

TOP OF PILOT HOUSE

MK 15 CIWS
(PHALANX)
(P & S)

O4 LEVEL

NAVIGATING BRIDGE

QUAD HARPOON PROJECTORS

FOUR TOMAHAWK MISSILES IN
ARMORED BOX LAUNCHERS
(P & S)

QUAD TOMAHAWK LAUNCHERS (P & S)

TOP OF HELICOPTER
CONTROL STATION

O3 LEVEL

AFTER
AIR DEFENSE
STATION

FLAG AND SIGNAL BRIDGE

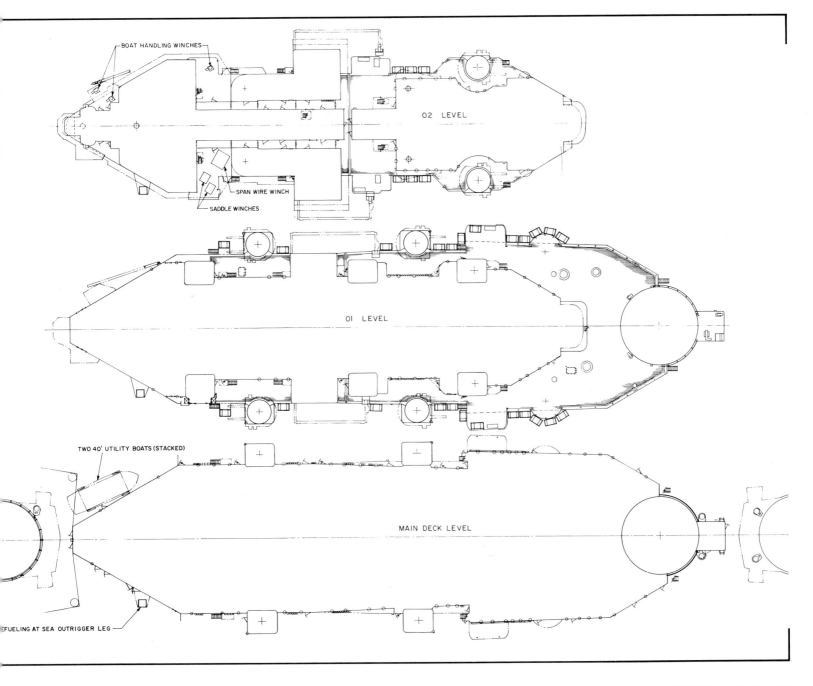

BOAT HANDLING WINCHES

O2 LEVEL

SPAN WIRE WINCH

SADDLE WINCHES

O1 LEVEL

TWO 40' UTILITY BOATS (STACKED)

MAIN DECK LEVEL

REFUELING AT SEA OUTRIGGER LEG

# SOURCES

Interviews with Author

Abhau, William C., Rear Admiral, USN(Ret.), at Annapolis, Maryland, 14 June 1983

Abrams, Richard, by telephone, 11 April 1984

Addison, Edward S., Captain, USN(Ret.), at Annapolis, Maryland, 29 June 1983

Albrecht, Carl J., Captain, USN, by telephone, 20 November 1985 and 1 December 1985

Alexander, Richard G., Captain, USN(Ret.), at Washington, D.C., 9 September 1970

Amend, Wayne A., by telephone, 5 October 1985

Anderson, Clyde B., Captain, USN(Ret.), at Virginia Beach, Virginia, 10 October 1983

Atkeson, John C., Rear Admiral, USN(Ret.), at Norfolk, Virginia, 27 February 1983

Bak, Michael, Jr., at Vienna, Virginia, 21 February 1984

Ballou, Joseph F., Commander, USN(Ret.), at Washington, D.C., 7 February 1986

Bartusch, Willard, by telephone, 1 August 1985

Begandy, Wayne, by telephone, 7 October 1985

Bitting, Frederick E., Commander, USN(Ret.), by telephone, 2 October 1985

Blanchette, Roland, by telephone, 6 September 1985

Bowler, Roland T. E., Jr., Commander, USN (Ret.), at Annapolis, Maryland, 29 August 1984

Brandt, King G., Commander, USNR(Ret.), by telephone, 11 February 1984

Brattin, Sherman, by telephone, 23 July 1985

Brega, Richard E., Captain, USN(Ret.), at Long Beach, California, 15 May 1983

Brooks, Clarence J., Jr., at Arlington, Virginia, 18 April 1983

Brown, Frank C., Lieutenant, MSC, USN, by telephone, 27 December 1985

Brown, Jacob, by telephone, 7 September 1985

Brown, Russell, by telephone, 27 June 1985

Cabot, Lon, Chief Journalist, USN, by telephone, 23 April 1986

Cantacuzene, Rodion, Captain, USN(Ret.), at Washington, D.C., 4 January 1983

Clairmont, Daniel R., by telephone, 15 August 1985

Crawford, R. A., Senior Chief Fire Controlman, USN(Ret.), on board the USS *Iowa* (BB-61) at Portsmouth, Virginia, 17 July 1985

Cruppenink, John, by telephone, 14 October 1985

Denby, John L., Commander, MC, USNR, by telephone, 27 November 1985

Deutermann, Peter T., Captain, USN, by telephone, 28 December 1985

Donovan, John, Lieutenant (junior grade), USN, on board the USS *Iowa* (BB-61) at Portsmouth, Virginia, 17 July 1985

Duffy, Daniel J., at Baltimore, Maryland, 26 October 1983

Dugan, William, by telephone, 2 August 1985

Duncan, Eugene G., at York, Pennsylvania, 1 November 1983

Dunning, Allan L., Captain, USN(Ret.), by telephone, 18 December 1983, and at Stonington, Connecticut, 19 September 1984

Edelstein, Julius C. C., at New York City, 2 July 1983

Elfelt, James S., Commander, USN, at Washington, D.C., 21 August 1970

Evans, John, by telephone, 6 October 1985

Fagan, Harry P., Jr., by telephone, 7 January 1984

Farmer, Carl V., Chief Gunner's Mate, USN, on board the USS *Iowa* (BB-61) at Portsmouth, Virginia, 19 July 1985

Faw, Roger A., at Accokeek, Maryland, 6 July 1985

Feigley, Thomas, by telephone, 29 November 1985

Fike, Irwin H., Captain, USN(Ret.), at Annapolis, Maryland, 30 April 1985

Flamboe, Edward E., Lieutenant, USN(Ret.), at Annapolis, Maryland, 19 November 1985

Fogarty, William M., Captain, USN, on board the USS *New Jersey* (BB-62), at sea, 10 May 1983

Frank, Allan, at Baltimore, Maryland, 19 June 1985

Fulks, Robert P., by telephone, 17 November 1985

Fuller, Philip J., at Reston, Virginia, 2 December 1983

Genet, Richard P., Captain, USN, at·Washington, D.C., 13 February 1986

Glenn, W. Lewis, Jr., Captain, USN, by telephone, 17 March 1986

Gray, Oscar E., Jr., Captain, USN(Ret.), at McLean, Virginia, 2 May 1985

Grimes, Roff, Jr., by telephone, 8 September 1985

Hamilton, Charles R., at Annapolis, Maryland, 19 June 1985

Hammond, David, Signalman Second Class, USN, by telephone, 25 April 1986

Harris, John R., Captain, USNR, by telephone, 21 November 1985

Harris, Noble C., at Annapolis, Maryland, 28 November 1983

Hartley, William, by telephone, 13 July 1985

Hayward, Eugene F., at Annapolis, Maryland, 29 February 1984

Heinl, Robert D., Jr., Colonel, USMC (Ret.), at Washington, D.C., 7 September 1970

Hill, George, Jr., at Chester, Maryland, 6 August 1985

Hunt, William J., by telephone, 25 July 1985

Huntington, Charles A., by telephone, 13 October 1985

Ivey, Louis A., Commander, MC, USNR, at Silver Spring, Maryland, 6 October 1983

Jacobus, Charles, Boatswain's Mate Second Class, USNR, at Moonachie, New Jersey, 30 July 1983

Johnson, Christopher H., Commander, USN, by telephone, 16 December 1985

Johnson, Lance K., Journalist Second Class, USNR, by telephone, 30 December 1985

Jung, Leonard J., Chief Musician, USN(Ret.), at Hyattsville, Maryland, 23 November 1983

Keithly, R. Myers, Captain, USN(Ret.), by telephone, 12 January 1984

Kelly, Donald V., by telephone, 30 July 1985

Kiehl, Elmer H., Captain, USN(Ret.), at Virginia Beach, Virginia, 10 October 1983

Kirk, Neville T., Captain, USNR(Ret.), at Annapolis, Maryland, 2 September 1984

Knoll, Robert G., by telephone, 1 August 1985

Kosmela, Walter T., Captain, USN(Ret.), at McLean, Virginia, 13 October 1983

Kubicki, Henry J., by telephone, 24 August 1984

Lavella, Andrew, Chief Personnelman, USN(Ret.), at Annapolis, Maryland, 13 August 1983

Leverton, J. Wilson, Jr., Rear Admiral, USN(Ret.), at Annapolis, Maryland, 1 June 1983

Lillis, Mark A., at Washington, D.C., 10 February 1984

Loughan, J. P., by telephone, 28 July 1985

Mamroth, Ellis, at Fraser, Pennsylvania, 4 December 1983

Mathias, Charles McC., at Washington, D.C., 18 February 1983

Maza, Rafael, by telephone, 7 July 1985

McCorkle, Francis D., Rear Admiral, USN (Ret.), at Providence, Rhode Island, 24 October 1982

McDonough, Barry, Lieutenant (junior grade), USN, on board the USS Iowa (BB-61), at Portsmouth, Virginia, 19 July 1985

McDowell, Mrs. Percival E., at Annapolis, Maryland, 26 December 1983

McDowell, Richard, by telephone, 5 October 1985

McElwain, Harry W., Captain, USN(Ret.), at Falls Church, Virginia, 13 October 1983

Mehling, Ben, by telephone, 1 October 1985

Meyer, Leo C., by telephone, 7 September 1985

Migrala, Walter M., Jr., Commander, USN, at Washington, D.C., 25 October 1983

Miller, Gregory H., Lieutenant (junior grade), USN, on board the USS Iowa (BB-61), at Portsmouth, Virginia, 16 July 1985

Milligan, Richard D. Commodore, USN, at Arlington, Virginia, 1 November 1985

Moore, Lewis, Chief Ship's Serviceman, USN(Ret.), by telephone, 22 November 1985

Moore, Robert L., Commander, USN(Ret.), by telephone, 26 August 1984

Moorer, Thomas H., Admiral, USN(Ret.), at Washington, D.C., 2 May 1985

Morse, Carl S., Lieutenant Commander, USN, at San Diego, California, 11 August 1973

Moto, Arturo, Chief Interior Communications Electrician, USN, by telephone, 23 April 1986

Mrozinski, Roman V., at Chevy Chase, Maryland, 20 June 1983

Mumford, Charles E., Lieutenant Commander, USN(Ret.), by telephone, 12 November 1985

Mumpower, Thomas S., Lieutenant, USN, on board the USS Iowa (BB-61), at Portsmouth, Virginia, 17 July 1985

O'Bryen, Dale, by telephone, 1 August 1985

O'Donnell, Edward J., Rear Admiral, USN(Ret.), at Monterey, California, 12 May 1983

Oliver, Frank, by telephone, 9 December 1983

Orell, Barry, Photographer's Mate Second Class, USN, by telephone, 24 April 1986

Parker, Edward N., Vice Admiral, USN(Ret.), by telephone, 7 October 1985

Parmelee, Robert M., by telephone, 31 July 1985

Peet, Raymond E., Vice Admiral, USN(Ret.), at Annapolis, Maryland, 17 May 1984

Peniston, Robert C, Captain, USN(Ret.), at Annapolis, Maryland, 12 November 1982

Poe, Donald T., Rear Admiral, USN(Ret.), by telephone, 10 August 1985

Pousson, Larry, Senior Chief Gunner's Mate, USN, on board the USS Iowa (BB-61), at Portsmouth, Virginia, 19 July 1985

Pratt, Richard R., Rear Admiral, USN(Ret.), at Chevy Chase, Maryland, 16 October 1983

Reed, Christopher, at East Douglas, Massachusetts, 20 September 1984

Reynolds, Harry O., Commander, USN(Ret.), at Yucaipa, California, 15 May 1983

Rice, Robert H., Vice Admiral, USN(Ret.), at Winter Park, Florida, 24 April 1984

Robie, William A., Captain, MC, USN(Ret.), by telephone, 1 August 1985

Rossie, John P., at Annapolis, Maryland, 2 May 1984

Rupp, David O., at York, Pennsylvania, 1 November 1983

Scarselletta, Albert, Senior Chief Storekeeper, USN(Ret.), by telephone, 23 November 1985

Shepherd, Lemuel C. III, Colonel, USMC(Ret.), at La Jolla, California, 14 May 1983

Smith, Arthur H., Chief Electrician's Mate, USN(Ret.), at Allentown, Pennsylvania, 29 October 1983

Snyder, J. Edward Jr., Rear Admiral USN (Ret.), at Newport, Rhode Island, 24 August 1970 and at McLean, Virginia, 26 November 1985

Sosnowski, William, by telephone, 20 November 1983

Soucek, Archie H., Captain, USN(Ret.), at Silver Spring, Maryland, 21 January 1983

Storm, Robert J., at Leesport, Pennsylvania, 29 October 1983

Strub, Henry, by telephone, 21 November 1985

Sullivan, John W., Captain, USN(Ret.), at Virginia Beach, Virginia, 10 October 1983

Swayze, Frank B., Captain, JAGC, USN, by telephone, 27 November 1985

Teller, George R., by telephone, 28 July 1985

Thompson, Edward M., Rear Admiral, USN(Ret.), at Alexandria, Virginia, 21 January 1983

Trail, John, Quartermaster Second Class, USN, by telephone, 10 November 1985

Trecartin, Allen, by telephone, 28 July 1985

Triola, Salvatore, by telephone, 6 October 1985

Tyree, David M., Rear Admiral, USN(Ret.), at Port Haywood, Virginia, 13 February 1983

Vaught, Roy L., Lieutenant, USN(Ret.), by telephone, 10 June 1984

Vining, Pierre G., Captain, USN(Ret.), by telephone, 9 October 1985

Walker, Edward K., Jr., Rear Admiral, SC, USN, at Arlington, Virginia, 8 August 1984

Walsh, John, by telephone, 5 October 1985

Watts, Charles R., Commander, USN(Ret.), at Arlington, Virginia, 28 February 1983

Westcott, Robert J., at Bridgeton, New Jersey, 16 June 1984

Wilhite, Drewery R., Captain, USN(Ret.), at Fort Sumner, Maryland, 1 February 1983

Winkelman, Val, Jr., by telephone, 10 August 1985

Wolpin, Richard B., Storekeeper First Class, USN, by telephone, 23 December 1985

## Letters to Author

Amend, Wayne A., 13 September 1985

Alexander, Richard G., Captain, USN (Ret.), 29 May 1986

Anderson, Clyde B., Captain, USN(Ret.), 2 October 1983

Bierley, John R., Captain, MC, USN(Ret.), 10 November 1983

Braybrook, William M., Captain, USN(Ret.), 28 January 1983

Cheyne, Scott, Lieutenant, USNR, 5 February 1974 and 22 February 1974 (tape recordings)

Coley, Charles C., Captain, USN(Ret.), 29 August 1985 (tape recording)

Conroy, Benjamin J., Jr., 20 August 1985 and 6 September 1985 (tape recordings)

Coyne, William D., Captain, USN(Ret.), 11 August 1983

Dale, Roland H., Captain, USN(Ret.), 21 August 1985

Dobie, E. W., Rear Admiral, USN(Ret.), 8 February 1984 and 23 February 1984

Douglas, Lee W., Lieutenant Commander, USNR(Ret.), 14 September 1983

Dudley, Clayton, R., Rear Admiral, USN(Ret.), 20 July 1985

Dunning, Allan L., Captain, USN(Ret.), 12 August 1985

Ekstrom, Clarence E., Vice Admiral, USN(Ret.), 10 June 1985

Forest, Joseph A., 8 February 1985

Fulks, Robert, P., 9 May 1983

Gill, Harold, 13 September 1985

Goode, Leonard T., 29 August 1985

Hastings, John S., 3 November 1985

Hayes, John J., Commander, USNR, 22 April 1984

Heselton, Leslie R., Captain, USN(Ret.), 9 August 1983 and 26 October 1983

Holste, Peter N., 1 November 1972 (tape recording)

Huff, Robert L., 16 April 1984

Keithly, R. Myers, Captain, USN(Ret.), 17 December 1983

Kiehl, Elmer H., Captain, USN(Ret.), 3 August 1983

Kierulff, Dudley J., Commander, SC, USN(Ret.), 22 January 1984

Kosmela, Walter T., Captain, USN(Ret.), 17 August 1983

Kretz, Walter T., Captain, SC, USN(Ret.), 4 September 1983 and 12 November 1983 (latter a tape recording)

Kuncevich, Sam, 17 April 1984

Leverton, J. Wilson, Jr., Rear Admiral, USN(Ret.), 7 March 1983

Lewis, John S., Commander, USNR, 17 November 1983

McCormick, John W., Captain, USN(Ret.), 4 June 1983 and 10 August 1985

Meilandt, Ralph L., Captain, SC, USN(Ret.), 19 August 1985

Moore, Robert L., Commander, USN(Ret.), 7 June 1983

Parsons, Joseph M., Commander, USN(Ret.), 21 November 1983 (tape recording) and 8 December 1983

Peniston, Robert C, Captain, USN(Ret.), 9 December 1982

Phelan, James F., Commander, USN(Ret.), 12 August 1985

Pinney, Frank L., Rear Admiral, USN(Ret.), 4 November 1977

Poe, Donald T., Rear Admiral, USN(Ret.), 8 August 1985 (tape recording)

Pratt, Richard R., Rear Admiral, USN(Ret.), 16 May 1983

Pringle, James F., Commander, USN(Ret.), 23 October 1983

Reed, Christopher, 21 February 1984

Rose, Rufus E., Vice Admiral, USN(Ret.), 11 August 1985

Rossie, John P., 13 August 1985

Sadler, Stuart T., Captain, USN(Ret.), 30 May 1983 (tape recording)

Scott, Arthur, 22 December 1985

Snyder, Philip W., Rear Admiral, USN(Ret.), 12 November 1983

Springe, Richard, 21 October 1985

Taylor, Roger C., Commander, USNR(Ret.), 10 November 1983

Terry, James H., Captain, USN(Ret.), 9 July 1985 and 22 July 1985

Tiernan, William H., 2 August 1985

Tyreee, David M., Rear Admiral, USN(Ret.), 21 February 1983

Vasey, Lloyd R., Rear Admiral, USN(Ret.), 21 August 1985

Wellborn, Charles, Jr., Vice Admiral, USN(Ret.), 16 December 1983

Winslow, Edward H., USN(Ret.), 10 November 1983

## Personal Letters

Brooks, Charles B., Jr., Captain, USN, to Captain John O. Miner, USN, 13 May 1957. Copy supplied by Mrs. Elizabeth Brunelli.

McGowan, Joseph A., Radarman Third Class, USNR, to Mrs. Ray McDonough, 4 February 1944. Copy supplied by Colonel Joseph A. McGowan, USAR.

Wooldridge, E. Tyler, Captain, USN, to Mrs. Marion Wooldridge, 11 August 1945; 12 August 1945; 15 August 1945; 29 August 1945. All letters supplied by Mrs. Wooldridge.

## Oral Histories

Atkeson, John C., Rear Admiral, USN(Ret.), East Carolina University Collection, Greenville, North Carolina

Bogan, Gerald F., Vice Admiral, USN(Ret.), U.S. Naval Institute Collection, Annapolis, Maryland

Duncan, Charles K., Admiral, USN(Ret.), U.S. Naval Institute Collection

Hustvedt, Olaf M., Vice Admiral, USN(Ret.), U.S. Naval Institute Collection

Kerr, Alex A., Captain, USN(Ret.), U.S. Naval Institute Collection

Melson, Charles L., Vice Admiral, USN(Ret.), U.S. Naval Institute Collection

Peet, Raymond E., Vice Admiral, USN(Ret.), U.S. Naval Institute Collection

## Official Letters

Director, War Plans Division, U.S. Navy, to Director, Fleet Maintenance Division, U.S. Navy, 10 February 1939. Held by Operational Archives Branch, Naval Historical Center, Washington, D.C.

Director, War Plans Division, U.S. Navy, to Chairman, General Board, U.S. Navy, 28 June 1939. Held by Operational Archives Branch.

Acting Secretary of the Navy to the Governor of New Jersey, 14 July 1939. Held by Ships Histories Section, Naval Historical Center.

Bureau of Ships, U.S. Navy, to Secretary of the Navy, 29 January 1941. Held by Operational Archives Branch.

Director, War Plans Division, U.S. Navy, to Director, Fleet Maintenance Division, U.S. Navy, 7 March 1941. Held by Operational Archives Branch.

Commanding Officer, USS *New Jersey* (BB-62) to Commander in Chief, U.S. Naval Forces, Eastern Atlantic and Mediterranean, Serial 073, 2 July 1955; Serial 1142, 25 July 1955; Serial 1509, 1 October 1956; Serial 1575, 19 October 1956. Held by Operational Archives Branch.

Commanding Officer, USS *New Jersey* (BB-62) to Commander Battleship-Cruiser Force, U.S. Atlantic Fleet, serial 1178, 28 July 1955. Held by Operational Archives Branch.

### Official Records

Action reports of the USS *New Jersey* (BB-62) for World War II: Serial 015 of 25 February 1944; Serial 034 of 21 March 1944; Serial 037 of 6 April 1944; Serial 049 of 6 May 1944; Serial 078 of 12 July 1944; Serial 0101 of 27 October 1944; Serial 0102 of 3 November 1944; Serial 0105 of 9 November 1944; Serial 0113 of 25 November 1944; Serial 0118 of 24 December 1944; Serial 011 of 25 January 1945; Serial 023 of 5 March 1945; Serial 037 of 31 March 1945; Serial 044 of 16 April 1945; Serial 0129 of 11 August 1945. Held by Operational Archives Branch, Naval Historical Center.

Action Reports of the USS *New Jersey* (BB-62) for the Korean War: Serial 081 of 10 August 1951; Serial 0110 of 11 October 1951; Serial 0111 of 11 October 1951; Serial 0112 of 11 October 1951; Serial 0115 of 22 October 1951; Serial 0116 of 22 October 1951; Serial 0117 of 22 October 1951; Serial 0118 of 22 October 1951; Serial 0126 of 14 November 1951; Serial 0127 of 17 November 1951; Serial 06 of 11 January 1952; Serial 090 of 16 April 1953; Serial 091 of 17 April 1953; Serial 099 of 25 April 1953; Serial 0102 of 3 May 1953; Serial 0104 of 4 May 1953; Serial 0108 of 8 May 1953; Serial 0109 of 9 May 1953; Serial 0117 of 7 June 1953; Serial 0119 of 15 June 1953; Serial 0128 of 6 July 1953; Serial 0131 of 14 July 1953; Serial 0132 of 14 July 1953; Serial 0151 of 28 July 1953; Serial 0152 of 28 July 1953; Serial 0163 of 11 August 1953. Held by Operational Archives Branch, Naval Historical Center.

Command Histories, USS *New Jersey* (BB-62), 1968, 1969, 1982, 1983, 1984, 1985. Held by Ships Histories Section, Naval Historical Center.

Deck Logs of the USS *New Jersey* (BB-62), May 1943–December 1945. Held by National Archives and Records Service, Washington, D.C.

Deck Logs of the USS *New Jersey* (BB-62), January 1946–June 1948, November 1950–August 1957. Held by Washington National Records Center, Suitland, Maryland.

Ship's name file of the USS *New Jersey* (BB-62). Held by Ships Histories Section, Naval Historical Center.

War Diaries of the USS *New Jersey* (BB-62), 1944–1945, 1950–1953. Held by Operational Archives Branch, Naval Historical Center.

### Speeches

Holden, Carl F., Captain, USN, remarks at the commissioning ceremony, 23 May 1943. Copy supplied by Mrs. Percival E. McDowell.

Leverton, J. Wilson, Jr., Rear Admiral, USN(Ret.), remarks at the decommissioning ceremony, 30 June 1948. Copy supplied by Rear Admiral Leverton.

Peniston, Robert C., Captain, USN, remarks at the decommissioning ceremony, 17 December 1969. Copy supplied by USS *New Jersey* public affairs officer.

### Books

Adams, Hans Christian, Colonel, USAF(Ret.), and Captain George F. Kosco, USN(Ret.). *Halsey's Typhoons*. New York: Crown Publishers, Inc., 1967.

Buell, Thomas B., Commander, USN(Ret.). *The Quiet Warrior: A Biography of Admiral Raymond A. Spruance*. Boston: Little, Brown and Company, 1974.

Calhoun, C. Raymond, Captain, USN(Ret.). *Typhoon: The Other Enemy*. Annapolis: Naval Institute Press, 1981.

Clark, Joseph J., Admiral, USN(Ret.), with Clark G. Reynolds. *Carrier Admiral*. New York: David McKay Company, Inc., 1967.

Cooper, Mickey. *The Big J: Matriarch of the Seas*. Bethlehem, Pennsylvania: privately published, 1982.

Dulin, Robert O., Jr., and William H. Garzke, Jr. *Battleships: United States Battleships in World War II*. Annapolis: Naval Institute Press, 1976 and subsequent editions.

Forrestal, E. P., Vice Admiral, USN(Ret.). *Admiral Raymond A. Spruance: A Study in Command*. Washington, D.C.: U.S. Government Printing Office, 1966.

Friedman, Norman. *Naval Radar*. Greenwich, England: Conway Maritime Press Ltd., 1981.

——. *U.S. Battleships: An Illustrated Design History*. Annapolis: Naval Institute Press, 1985.

Halsey, William F., Jr., Fleet Admiral, USN, and Lieutenant Commander Joseph Bryan III, USNR. *Admiral Halsey's Story*. New York: Whittlesey House, 1947.

Karig, Walter, Captain, USNR, Lieutenant Commander Russell L. Harris, USNR, and Lieutenant Commander Frank A. Manson, USN. *Battle Report: The End of an Empire*. New York: Rinehart and Company, Inc., 1948.

——. *Battle Report: Victory in the Pacific*. New York: Rinehart and Company, Inc., 1949.

Leifer, Neil. *Dreadnought Farewell*. Philadelphia: Kaye Publications, Inc., 1970.

——. *Dreadnought Returns*. Philadelphia: Baum Printing House, 1969.

Morison, Samuel Eliot. *Aleutians, Gilberts and Marshalls*, Volume VII of *History of United States Naval Operations in World War II*. Boston: Little, Brown and Company, 1951.

——. *New Guinea and the Marianas*, Volume VIII. Boston: Little, Brown and Company,1953.

——. *Leyte*, Volume XII. Boston: Little, Brown and Company, 1958.

——. *The Liberation of the Philippines: Luzon, Mindanao and the Visayas*, Volume XIII. Boston: Little, Brown and Company, 1959.

——. *Victory in the Pacific*, Volume XIV. Boston: Little, Brown and Company, 1960.

Potter, E. B. *Bull Halsey*. Annapolis: Naval Institute Press, 1985.

——. *Nimitz*. Annapolis: Naval Institute Press, 1976.

Reynolds, Clark G. *The Fast Carriers: The Forging of An Air navy.* New York: McGraw-Hill Book Company, 1968.

Sherman, Frederick C., Admiral, USN(Ret.). *Combat Command: The American Aircraft Carriers in the Pacific War.* New York: E. P. Dutton & Company, 1950.

Taylor, Theodore. *The Magnificent Mitscher.* W. W. Norton & Company, 1954.

Terzibaschitsch, Stefan. *Battleships of the U.S. Navy in World War II.* New York: Bonanza Books, 1977.

*New Jersey* Cruisebooks
*War Log* (1943–45)
*Salvo* (1950–51)
*A Half Year of History* (1953)
*U.S.S. New Jersey BB-62* (1955)
*Dreadnought 68–69*
*Dreadnought 83–84*

Pamphlets Published by the *New Jersey*
*The Log . . . of the U.S.S. New Jersey: 1943–1945*
*European Cruise 1947*
*Midshipman Cruise 1956*
Recommissioning Program, 6 April 1968
*Equator '68*
Familygram, various issues, 1968–69
Decommissioning Program, 17 December 1969
Recommissioning Program, 28 December 1982

Articles

Aston, William J., Midshipman, USN, and Midshipman Alexander G. B. Grosvenor, USN, "Midshipmen's Cruise," *National Geographic*, June 1948, pages 711–722.

Berger, Meyer, "U.S.S. New Jersey Being Reactivated," *The New York Times*, 27 September 1950, page 8.

"Big Flagship 'In Mothballs,' " *The New York Sun*, 22 May 1948, page 3.

Brewer, Ralph Wright, "The Reds are Firing Back at Us!" *Our Navy*, Mid-June 1952, pages 14–15.

Chantry, Allan J., Rear Admiral, USN, "Launching of U.S.S. 'New Jersey' and U.S.S. 'Wisconsin,' " *Transactions* of the Society of Naval Architects and Marine Engineers, 1944, pages 391–438.

Heinl, Robert D., Jr., Colonel, USMC (Ret.), "Welcome to the War," *US Naval Institute Proceedings*, March 1969, pages 58–62.

Hiatt, Fred, "U.S. Battleship to Stay in Mideast," *The Washington Post*, 29 November 1983, pages A1 and A11.

Jamieson, Robert D., "New Jersey Towed to LBSNY," *Deckplate*, November–December 1981, pages 16–23.

"Jersey's Own Ship Leaves for Cruise After Ceremonies Here," *Newark Evening News*, 24 May 1947, page 5.

Jones, Franklin P., "20,000 See Launching of Mightiest Warship," *Philadelphia Record*, 8 December 1942, page 4.

Kennett, Warren H., " 'Big J' Ready for Atom," *Newark Evening News*, 12 March 1951.

Lewis, Emanuel Raymond, "American Battleship Main Battery Armament: The Final Generation," *Warship International*, Number 4, 1976, pages 276–303.

Morse, Carl S., Lieutenant, USN, and Lieutenant (junior grade) Charles C. Bream, USN, "The Activation of the U.S.S. New Jersey (BB-62) at Philadelphia Naval Shipyard," *Naval Engineers Journal*, December 1968, pages 859–869

Pineda, R., "Battleship Gunners Tackle Turrets," *Surface Warfare*, November–December 1984, pages 22–24.

Ruch, Walter M., "Dreadnought Tops 26 Ship Launchings," *The New York Times*, 8 December 1942, pages 1, 20.

Schaefer, Crozier, "20,000 See Ship Floated," *Philadelphia Inquirer,* 8 December 1942, page 1.

Serig, Howard W., "The *Iowa* Class: Needed Once Again," *U.S. Naval Institute Proceedings*, May 1982, pages 134–149.

Starr, Mark, and Kim Willenson, "Right Ship in the Wrong Place?" *Newsweek*, 26 March 1984, page 41.

Stillwell, Paul, "The Battleship Battle, 1964–1967," *Marine Corps Gazette*, August 1981, pages 38–46.

"USS New Jersey: New Chapter for Battleships," *All Hands*, March 1983, pages 16–20.

Zeller, Bob, "When Smoke Cleared, 'Big Jay' Was in Service," *Long Beach Press-Telegram*, 29 December 1982, pages A1, A10.

Navy Newspapers

*Beacon* (published by Philadelphia Navy Yard), 7 December 1942. The entire issue is devoted to the launching of the *New Jersey*.

*Clean Sweep Down* (published on board the *New Jersey*), various issues, 1943.

*The Jerseyman* (published on board the *New Jersey*), various issues, 1944–45, 1952–56.

Unpublished Manuscripts

Soucek, Archie H., Lieutenant Commander, USN, 1945 personal diary. Copy supplied by Captain A. H. Soucek, USN(Ret.).

Stillwell, Paul, *USS New Jersey Public Affairs/Media Coverage During the Vietnam War* (master's degree thesis on file at the University of Missouri School of Journalism, Columbia, Missouri).

*United States Naval Administration in World War II: Commander in Chief Atlantic Fleet* (bound typescript on file at Navy Library, Naval Historical Center, Washington Navy Yard, Washington, D.C.).

# INDEX

Note: Numbers that are italicized indicate the pages on which photo captions pertaining to the given subject appear. The photo itself may or may not be on the same page. Numbers in Roman type apply to references in the text,